Quantitative Methods
for Business, Management and Finance

Louise Swift and Sally Piff

Second Edition

palgrave
macmillan

First published 1997 as
Mathematics and Statistics for Business, Management and Finance

First edition of *Quantitative Methods for Business, Management and Finance* 2001
Reprinted three times
Second edition 2005

Published by
PALGRAVE MACMILLAN
Houndmills, Basingstoke, Hampshire RG21 6XS and
175 Fifth Avenue, New York, N. Y. 10010
Companies and representatives throughout the world

PALGRAVE MACMILLAN is the global academic imprint of the Palgrave Macmillan division of St. Martin's Press, LLC and of Palgrave Macmillan Ltd. Macmillan® is a registered trademark in the United States, United Kingdom and other countries. Palgrave is a registered trademark in the European Union and other countries.

ISBN 13: 978–1–4039–3528–1
ISBN 10: 1–4039–3528–9

This book is printed on paper suitable for recycling and made from fully managed and sustained forest sources.

A catalogue record for this book is available from the British Library.

Library of Congress Cataloging-in-Publication Data
    Quantitative methods for business, management and finance / Louise Swift and Sally Piff.—2nd ed.
      p. cm.
    Includes bibliographical references and index.
    ISBN 1–4039–3528–9
    1. Industrial management—Statistical methods. 2. Commercial statistics. I. Piff, Sally, 1960– II. Title.
    HD30.215.S95 2005
    658'001'5195—dc22   2004065062

10 9 8 7 6 5 4 3 2 1
14 13 12 11 10 09 08 07 06 05

Printed and bound in China

To our families

Contents

Preface to the second edition ix
To the student ... please read this first xi
Choosing books for further work xv
Acknowledgements xix

EM ESSENTIAL MATHS

EM1 Numbers and symbols 2
1 Positive and negative numbers: adding and subtracting 4
2 Positive and negative numbers: multiplying and dividing 6
3 Combining addition, subtraction, multiplication and division 10
4 Using a calculator 14
5 Introducing letters and symbols 20
6 Working with symbols: adding, subtracting, multiplying, dividing 27

EM2 Simplifying expressions 33
1 Equivalent fractions and cancelling 34
2 Adding and subtracting fractions 40
3 Multiplying and dividing fractions 46
4 Putting it all together – and a note on percentages 54
5 Expanding brackets 57
6 Factorising 64
7 Powers 70
8 Powers of products and quotients 80
9 Fractional powers 85

EM3 Solving problems 93
1 How equations arise 94
2 Solutions to equations: recognising and guessing 97
3 A method for solving equations 101
4 Formulating and solving equations 108
5 Rearranging equations and substituting 111
6 Inequalities 123

EM4 Modelling using straight lines 133
1 Introducing straight lines 134
2 Interpretation of a and b 140
3 Linear equations for modelling 146
4 Pairs of linear equations 150

MM   MORE MATHS

MM1 Some special equations		**160**
1	Introducing logs	161
2	Solving equations when the unknown is a power	168
3	Quadratic equations	174
4	The expert equation solver	181

MM2 Modelling using curves		**188**
1	Functions	189
2	Quadratic curves	192
3	Some common functions	203
4	Variations on standard curves	208
5	When do these curves arise?	212
6	Curve sketching in general	217

MM3 Rates of change		**220**
1	The gradient of a curve	221
2	More differentiation	229
3	Interpreting derivatives	234
4	Maximising and minimising	242

DD   DESCRIBING DATA

DD1 Pictures of data		**256**
1	Frequencies and histograms	257
2	Stem and leaf diagrams	267
3	Pictures of one categorical variable: bar charts and pie charts	271
4	More graphs for numerical data	277
5	Categorical data that come in pairs	281
6	Lies, more lies and statistics?	286

DD2 Summarising data		**291**
1	The centre of a set of data	292
2	The spread of a set of data	298
3	Σ and a short-cut for variance	304
4	Quartiles	309
5	Technology to the rescue!	311
6	Constructing indices	314
7	Grouped data	318
8	Describing data: your toolkit	324

P   PROBABILITY

P1 Measuring uncertainty		**328**
1	Introduction to probability	329

2 Combining events: AND and OR 344
3 Conditional probability 352
4 Calculating joint or AND probabilities 360
5 More complicated probabilities – made simple! 368

P2   Numerical outcomes 375
1 Introducing random variables 376
2 Expectation: the long run average 384
3 The variance of a random variable 391
4 The binomial distribution 398
5 The Poisson distribution 415

P3   Continuous numerical outcomes 426
1 Probability density functions (pdfs) 427
2 The exponential distribution 440
3 Introducing the normal distribution 449
4 Calculating normal probabilities 460
5 The normal approximation to the binomial distribution 471

S STATISTICS

S1   Estimation 483
1 Samples 484
2 Estimating from a sample 490
3 How good is an estimator? 496
4 Interval estimates 505
5 Beware, variance unknown! 516

S2   Testing hypotheses 525
1 Introduction to testing 526
2 The structure of a test 533
3 Tests for the mean 539
4 Rejection regions: another approach to testing 555

S3   Correlation and regression 563
1 Data that come in pairs 564
2 Fitting a straight line to the data 574
3 The linear regression model 585
4 Extending the linear regression model: the multiple linear regression model 602

S4   Forecasting 611
1 Displaying time series 612
2 Introduction to forecasting 616
3 Coping with trend and seasonal effects 627
4 Forecasting series with a trend and seasonal effect 644

S5   Comparing two populations 648
1 The difference between two means 649
2 Difference between two means: small samples 657

3 Paired samples   663

S6   Categorical data   **672**
1 Proportions   674
2 More than two categories   680
3 Contingency tables   689
  Statistics formulae   699

BM   BUSINESS MODELLING

BM1   Linear programming models   **705**
1 A small linear programming problem   707
2 More complicated linear programming models   715

BM2   Planning projects   **725**
1 Drawing a project planning network   726
2 Scheduling activities   733

BM3   Models for inventory control   **742**
1 An inventory model   743
2 Making the model more realistic   749

BM4   Time and money   **757**
1 Calculating interest   758
2 Present values   767
3 Series of payments   775

BM5   Decision making   **789**
1 Introducing decision making   790
2 Payoff tables   793
3 Decision-making criteria   797
4 Decision trees   804

BM6   Controlling quality   **820**
1 Control charts for the mean   821
2 R-charts and p-charts   830

BM7   Simulating reality   **839**
1 Why simulate?   840
2 A simple simulation   841
3 Generating random inputs   847
4 Simulating from other probability distributions   853

Statistical tables   861

Index   874

Preface to the second edition

This book introduces Probability, Statistics and the main types of quantitative business model to the Business, Management or Finance student. It is intended for first year university and higher education courses in Quantitative Methods, but it will also be useful for MBA courses. It includes a detailed *Essential Maths* part (not just a revision chapter) which teaches the mathematical essentials from scratch in an approachable way and is suitable for self-tuition.

For *Probability*, *Describing Data*, *Statistics* and *Business Modelling* students are encouraged to make use of a spreadsheet or a statistical package, and as examples we give guidance in using Excel and SPSS where appropriate. The optional second part of the book, *More Maths*, provides some useful maths prerequisites for courses in subjects like Maths for Economics or Financial Mathematics.

The entire book is suitable for self-tuition. Throughout the text there are worked examples, usually labelled **Check this** to encourage the student to try them and to emphasise that quantitative skills are learnt by experience rather than by just reading. Each section of a chapter ends with a set of exercises which come with detailed solution guidelines (the **Work card**) and another set which lecturers can use as coursework (the **Assessment**).

This, the second edition, includes a new chapter on Decision Making and much revised chapters on Describing Data which place a greater emphasis on categorical data. It includes instructions on the use of SPSS statistical software. Several new features aim to help the reader find their way around. Each chapter now starts with a **Contexts** section, which comprises 'What is this chapter about?', 'Why is it useful?', 'Where does it fit in?', 'What do I need to know?' and 'Objectives'. Common pitfalls, hints and computer instructions are now clearly marked with symbols:

respectively. We also include advice on selecting books for further work and references for each chapter.

The much enhanced companion web site at www.palgrave.com/business/swift/ now includes realistic datasets for downloading extra exercises. It also has an Excel primer and an introduction to SPSS. In addition, lecturers can access an instructors' manual with solutions to all the assessment questions and a set of PowerPoint slides.

A plan showing the order in which the parts can be tackled is shown below. In all parts except Business Modelling the chapters are best approached sequentially, although Chapters S3 and S4 of Statistics can be omitted. Each Business Modelling chapter is largely self-contained and any could be omitted, although we feel it makes sense to do Chapter BM7, Simulating Reality, last. Some sections of Chapters BM6, Controlling Quality, and BM7, Simulating Reality, require some Statistics, but these are clearly marked in the text.

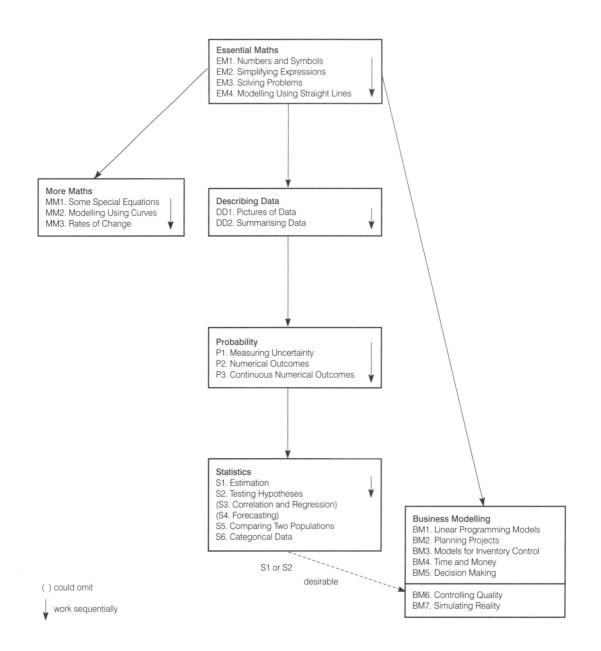

Essential Maths
EM1. Numbers and Symbols
EM2. Simplifying Expressions
EM3. Solving Problems
EM4. Modelling Using Straight Lines

More Maths
MM1. Some Special Equations
MM2. Modelling Using Curves
MM3. Rates of Change

Describing Data
DD1. Pictures of Data
DD2. Summarising Data

Probability
P1. Measuring Uncertainty
P2. Numerical Outcomes
P3. Continuous Numerical Outcomes

Statistics
S1. Estimation
S2. Testing Hypotheses
(S3. Correlation and Regression)
(S4. Forecasting)
S5. Comparing Two Populations
S6. Categorical Data

Business Modelling
BM1. Linear Programming Models
BM2. Planning Projects
BM3. Models for Inventory Control
BM4. Time and Money
BM5. Decision Making
BM6. Controlling Quality
BM7. Simulating Reality

S1 or S2

desirable

( ) could omit

work sequentially

To the student ... please read this first

A journey of a thousand miles begins with a single step

Chinese proverb

The information age

We live in the information age. At the touch of a keyboard all manner of information can be accessed by businesses, institutions and individuals. In business, information about the marketplace, company performance and customers is vital to maintaining competitive edge and high productivity. However, as more information accumulates the harder it is to stand back, see the 'shape' of it and use it for decision making. This means that today, more than ever, individuals working for just about any organisation need to be able to summarise information, draw sensible conclusions from it, and spot patterns, trends and relationships, which is what Quantitative Methods is all about.

But quantitative skills aren't just useful at work. As financial and consumer products become more complex and marketing material becomes more artful, it is increasingly necessary for individuals buying anything from a mobile phone to a mortgage to be able to interpret numerical information critically in order to avoid being duped.

Quantitative Methods – isn't it just Maths?
Quantitative Methods is about using information fully to make sensible decisions. As in Business generally, a logical mind will be your most valuable asset, but yes, some basic mathematical skills will also be necessary. However, we do realise that Maths was not everyone's favourite subject at school, so, in the first part of this book, we teach you everything you need, from the very beginning. We assume only that you can add, subtract, multiply and divide positive numbers and zero.

This book
Quantitative Methods for Business, Management and Finance has six parts: **Essential Maths (EM)**, **More Maths (MM)**, **Describing Data (DD)**, **Probability (P)**, **Statistics (S)** and **Business Modelling (BM)**.

In **Essential Maths** we assume only that you can add, subtract, multiply and divide positive numbers and zero and that you are familiar with numbers like 6.532 in which the fractional part is given using decimal places. Whilst **Essential Maths** is thorough and suitable for self-tuition, you can also use it with a teacher, for revision or reference or, if you are fairly confident mathematically, ignore it completely. As well as being preparation for the material that follows, **Essential Maths** and **Describing Data** together (see below) supply the hard-core quantitative skills that you will need in industry or commerce.

More Maths is not required for the rest of the book but gives students who didn't do Maths up to the age of 18 the additional Maths (non-linear functions and differentiation) they will need for courses like Maths for Economics or Financial Mathematics later in their degree.

Whilst today's managers and business people need the basic skills in **Essential Maths** they also need to be able to interpret and criticise graphical and numerical summaries of information and the next part, **Describing Data**, tells you how to do this.

Probability gives us ways of representing the uncertainty in the world around us, whilst probability models are an aid to decision making in their own right. Probability is also an essential tool for understanding the subject of Statistics, so this part of the book is a prerequisite for the next.

Statistics is about using partial (sample) information to make wider inferences about a complete set of data that is too big, too expensive, or even impossible to measure. It requires some knowledge of probability.

A whole range of business decision problems can be modelled using simple mathematical relationships and it is these models that we describe in the final part, **Business Modelling**.

How to use this book

When you study most arts or social science subjects you are usually expected to make use of several books and articles to complete a single item of work. On this course, however, you will probably have only one text (this one we hope) to support notes from your teacher or lecturer.

Having only one textbook may make the course sound more attractive in that it creates the illusion that less work is to be done, but the down-side is that you *cannot* read this sort of book as if it were a novel. In fact, it is highly unlikely that you will understand a new topic by just reading through. Even professional mathematicians and statisticians rarely understand a text or an article by simply reading it. So how should you *use* this book?

You need to get out some rough paper and a pen and, as each new step is presented, try to emulate it yourself. *Be sceptical*. Don't take anything on trust but scribble away until you can convince yourself, and don't expect to understand immediately! Most people are too easily discouraged when they don't grasp a concept immediately. You should realise that this is normal and that if you persevere things will suddenly 'click' and you will wonder why it was all so difficult before.

To encourage you to take time over each step, most of the worked examples in the text are marked **Check this**. We suggest that you work each one of these independently as you come across them and then compare your working with ours.

Whilst we admit that it may be possible to 'get by' by learning techniques and methods 'parrot' fashion, this is time-consuming and tedious and won't equip you to apply the work in your field. It is much better to *invest* some time to really *understand* what's going on. The payoff is that you will be much more versatile in the sort of problems you can solve in the future and won't need so much revision time for your exams.

To learn properly you must also try solving problems for yourself. Each section of a chapter ends with two sets of similar exercises, the **Work card** and the **Assessment**. The **Work card** is for you to work through yourself and full solutions are given, whereas your lecturer may set some of the **Assessments** as assessed coursework, so solutions are *not* provided.

Try to regard each problem as a puzzle. You *will* get stuck, and you *will* get answers completely wrong, but *do not despair*: this is part of the learning process. Be patient with yourself. If you are stuck on a particular problem, try a similar problem and see if you can do that. Sometimes it is possible to work backwards from the answer to see what you should have done. If you can't finish *any* questions of a particular type, go over the material in the text and the **Check this** examples once more and then try the problems again. Be careful not to waste hours (literally) on a single question. After a while make a note of it, to remind yourself to ask somebody later, and then move on.

Some of the topics in **Essential Maths** and **More Maths** may be revision for you, so to make best use of your time we have placed a **Test box** at the start of each section of a chapter. Each **Test box** contains a few 'diagnostic' questions and their answers. If you can do these easily and accurately then you could save time and pass directly onto the next section.

You will also come across the following symbols, at various points throughout the book, that indicate:

 useful hints for the task at hand

 common pitfalls to avoid

computer instructions.

Choosing books for further work

The market abounds with quantitative methods books, some better than others. Broadly speaking they vary in the following three main ways, so bear this in mind if you are selecting one:

1. **The content:** the content of a book may not always be apparent from its title. For instance, Quantitative Methods can mean just Maths, Maths and Statistics or even just the topics in the Business Modelling part of this book. (We have taken it to mean all three.) And whilst books which include Probability or Statistics in their titles have an obvious content, the topics we have included in the business modelling part of this book often come under the heading of Management Science or Operational (or Operations) Research. It is therefore a good idea to have a look at the contents pages of a book to check what it includes or excludes.
2. **The level of maths:** rather obviously, you want this to coincide with yours. For instance, our text starts from the very beginning and takes you through to differentiation, which is the start of the branch of Maths called Calculus. So read the preface of a book and have a look at the first couple of chapters to see if the Maths background assumed is right for you.
3. **The application area:** the application area will dictate the sort of examples that are used in the book but it will also affect the authors' choice of topics. Is it Business, Finance, Management, Accounting or some combination?

Some suggestions for further reading

Some texts that may be useful are listed, with brief descriptions, below. We will also, however, list the most suitable ones for each chapter at the chapter end. In alphabetical order of author:

Quantitative Methods for Business by David R. Anderson, Dennis J. Sweeney and Thomas A. Williams, 9th edn, Thomson South-Western.
A useful intermediate text as it expands on the Business Modelling part of our text. It assumes a basic mathematical knowledge, but does include the Probability you will need.

Statistics for Business and Economics by David R. Anderson, Dennis J. Sweeney and Thomas A. Williams, 8th edn, Thomson South-Western.
This provides more detail on the Describing Data, Probability and Statistics parts of our text and includes some more advanced topics; for instance, analysis of variance, experimental design and non-parametric methods. It assumes a basic knowledge of algebra.

Quantitative Methods for Accounting and Business Studies by Gordon Bancroft and George O'Sullivan, 3rd edn, McGraw-Hill.
This has a broadly similar content to our text but is intended for students taking professional accountancy examinations.

Quantitative Methods for Business and Economics by Glyn Burton, George Carrol and Stuart Wall, 2nd edn, Financial Times, Prentice-Hall.
A clear, alternative exposition of most of our topics, although it includes only Time and Money and Linear Programming from Business Modelling.

Introduction to Operations Research by Frederick S. Hillier and Gerald J. Lieberman, 7th edn, McGraw-Hill.
This is a major and longstanding detailed text on Operations Research and as such is useful for more advanced work on all the Business Modelling topics, except time and money and forecasting. It is aimed at Engineering and Maths students and so assumes 'high school' algebra; that is, at least the material in Essential Maths. It uses Excel.

Introduction to Management Science by Frederick S. Hillier and Mark S. Hillier, 2nd edn, McGraw-Hill.
An advanced treatment of the business modelling topics, including forecasting for business students with an emphasis on case studies.

Mathematics for Economics and Business by Ian Jacques, 4th edn, Pearson Education.
This is an excellent mathematical text which assumes little prior mathematical knowledge and goes beyond the material in our book. It is particularly geared towards Economics and includes partial differentiation, integration and matrices. It introduces some mathematical software, Maple as well as Excel.

Maths and Statistics for Business by M. Lawson, S. Hubbard and P. Pugh, Longman Scientific and Technical.
An approachable text which includes the same areas of Maths and Statistics as our text as well as some aspects of Linear Programming and Time and Money. Some mathematical background is assumed.

Statistics for Management and Economics by William Mendenhall, James R. Reinmuth and Robert J. Beaver, 7th edn, Duxbury Press.
This provides an excellent treatment of the Probability and Statistics topics and includes Quality Control and Decision Analysis from Business Modelling.

Applied Statistics and Probability for Engineers by Douglas C. Montgomery and George C. Runger, Wiley.
This is an excellent intermediate level Statistics text for non-mathematicians, although it does assume a basic level of maths.

Quantitative Approaches in Business Studies by Clare Morris, 6th edn, Prentice-Hall.
A well-written introduction to most of the topics we cover. It uses Excel.

Statistics for Business and Economics by Paul Newbold, William Carlson and Betty Thorne, 5th edn, Prentice-Hall.
A well-established text, renowned for being approachable and yet precise. It gives a more advanced and more mathematical treatment of the Probability and Statistics topics in our book in a similar, 'classical' order and uses both Excel and the statistical software Minitab.

Operations Research: Applications and Algorithms by Wayne L. Winston, 4th edn, Duxbury
   Press.
This intermediate to advanced text extends all the topics in Business Modelling (except
Time and Money) and provides the necessary additional Maths.

Acknowledgements

The authors would particularly like to thank Dennis Alden for his enthusiastic, conscientious and very versatile help with the preparation of this edition and Jan Janacek for the use (again) of his stats tables.

Excel is a registered trade mark of Microsoft Corporation.

SPSS is a registered trade mark of SPSS Inc.

Every effort has been made to trace copyright holders, but if any have been overlooked the publishers will be pleased to make the necessary arrangement at the first opportunity.

EM Essential Maths

If one thing is sure, the word 'Mathematics' always provokes some reaction. Some of you will have enjoyed Maths at school. Some of you will have taken it to A-level or the equivalent. Some of you always felt a dunce at it and some of you just hated it.

Some Quantitative Methods books go to great lengths to avoid Maths, using so many words to describe a formula that they either muddy the issue completely or leave the reader no wiser. Our philosophy is that a little Maths can go a long way and a few basic concepts are enough for most of the topics in this book. Without these basic ideas you will come across lots of things you don't understand in the rest of your degree and in the rest of your career and may cut yourself off from a wide range of future options. So, if you didn't get on with Maths at school give yourself a second chance and stop disadvantaging yourself and start afresh. There won't be any proofs, everything will be explained fully and we start at the very beginning.

As we said in 'To the student ...' in *Essential Maths* we assume only that you can add, subtract, divide and multiply positive numbers and zero and that you are familiar with numbers like 6.532, in which the fractional part is given using decimal places.

EM1
Numbers and symbols

The concept of number is the obvious distinction between beast and man. Thanks to number, the cry becomes song, noises acquire rhythm, the spring is transformed into a dance, force becomes dynamic, and outlines figures.

Joseph Marie de Maistre, French author

Contexts

What is this chapter about?
This chapter explains why numbers are important, both in society and in business. It reminds you about negative numbers and explains how to add, subtract, multiply and divide them and how to use brackets. It explains how to make rough estimates before using a calculator and how to round numbers. It goes on to describe how symbols can be used to represent general relationships between quantities and shows how symbols can be treated in a very similar way to numbers. It introduces the idea of a model and explains what a spreadsheet is.

Why is it useful?
Numbers are used everywhere to describe and measure, to allocate resources and to plan ahead. So the basic numeracy skills in this chapter are an essential skill of modern life. Most professional jobs these days require you to use a spreadsheet and a calculator and in Business, Management and Finance, you will frequently have to manipulate numbers and understand simple mathematical expressions which involve symbols, for instance to represent how budgets are allocated to different departments or calculate an interest payment. And any quantitative subject you study either in education or for professional examinations will require the work in this chapter.

Where does it fit in?
The first part of the chapter describes the basic operations of arithmetic, representing numbers and using a calculator, whereas the second part, using symbols instead of numbers, is really the very beginning of the subject of algebra. Your memories of school algebra might put you off but please bear with us – we show you that symbols can be used in exactly the same way as numbers and we start from the very beginning.

What do I need to know?
We assume only that you know how to add, subtract, multiply and divide positive numbers and zero and that you can cope with numbers like 5.123 in which the fractional part is given using decimal places. Most readers will have covered the work in this part of the book when they were younger. We realise that this may have been a long time ago and that not everyone got on with maths at school, so the explanations are thorough and completely self-contained.

Objectives

After your work on this chapter you should be able to:

- add, subtract, multiply and divide positive, negative and zero numbers;
- combine the operations above using brackets;
- make rough estimates before using a calculator;
- understand how to round to so many decimal places or significant figures and how to use scientific notation;
- use symbols to represent the relationships between quantities;
- understand the difference between constants and variables;
- evaluate an expression using particular values for the variables;
- understand the concept of a model;
- understand what a spreadsheet is;
- perform basic operations to simplify expressions containing symbols.

Imagine a world without numbers. Accurate measurement would be impossible. Physical phenomena like air temperature, medical diagnostics such as blood pressure or economic statistics like the inflation rate and unemployment figures would be impossible to quantify. We would be left saying vaguely that 'prices seem to have gone up', or 'tomorrow will be warmer', but further analysis and comparison would be impossible.

Our society allocates resources – raw materials, labour and property – almost entirely by ascribing monetary values to them. Without numbers your prospective career would not exist – no accounts, no economic models, no sales figures.

So we need numbers. They enable us to describe exactly how our world is now, to allocate resources and to plan into the future.

In management, you will have to represent quantities numerically, calculate them, analyse relationships between them and communicate your findings to clients and colleagues. This will often require you to use symbols to represent the quantities of interest. For instance, a general rule for calculating the amount received at the end of a year, on an investment of £A at an annual interest rate of r% is

$$A \times \left(1 + \frac{r}{100}\right)$$

(Don't worry if you don't understand this now – we will see how it is obtained later.)

In the first four sections of this chapter we will only use *numbers* but in the remaining sections we will use symbols as well. The ways of dealing with symbols are just the same as those for numbers – hardly surprising when you think that the symbols are standing in for numerical values anyway.

1 Positive and negative numbers: adding and subtracting

Here is the first diagnostic 'test box'. Take a minute to try it. If you can answer correctly, with no difficulty whatsoever, you could move directly on to Section 2.

Test box 1

Can you solve these?

  2 + (–5) =?   –3 – (–4) =?   3 – (–2) + (–5) =?

Solutions: –3, 1, 0.

Negative numbers

You are already familiar with numbers, and with decimal places. Numbers like 3, 1000, 10.24, and 3.1427 are all *positive* numbers; that is, they are *greater* than 0. For many applications (for example, temperatures in Celsius below freezing, profit and loss or credits and debits in a bank account) and as a tool for many mathematical skills it is useful to be able to talk about *negative* or *minus* numbers. These are numbers like –5, –7.74, –1000 or –1.0. We will often enclose them in brackets like (–5) or (–7.74) to show that the minus sign belongs to that number.

All these numbers, positive, negative and zero, can be represented on a line. Part of it is shown below. The dots at each end show that the line could continue forever in both directions.

```
... - + ---- + ---- + ---- + ---- + ---- + ---- + ---- + ---- + ---- + ---- + ---- + - ...
     –6   –5   –4   –3   –2   –1    0    1    2    3    4    5    6
```

Adding and subtracting negative numbers

We all know that 4 + 5 = 9, or 8 – 3 = 5, but it is less obvious how to add and subtract negative numbers.

Any sum can be represented by a traveller on a journey along the line above. He starts at one point on it and from there can go forwards (to the right) to higher numbers or backwards (to the left) to lower numbers. Adding and subtracting represent forward and backward progress respectively. For instance, for (–5) + 3, the traveller starts at –5 on the line and then moves 3 units forwards to arrive at –2, so (–5) + 3 = (–2). For (–4) – 1 she starts at –4 and moves one step backwards to (–5) so (–4) – 1 = (–5).

Check this

Use the line to convince yourself that $(-3) + 2 = (-1)$, that $(-3.7) + 1.7 = (-2)$ and that $(-1) - 3 = -4$.

When we need to add or subtract a *negative* number the direction must be reversed because the number is negative. For example, to calculate $3 + (-2)$, he starts at 3 on the line, would move forward for the addition but does the reverse because we are adding a negative number. So he moves 2 units backwards from 3 to arrive at 1 and we conclude that $3 + (-2) = 1$. In a similar way, to calculate $3 - (-2)$ he starts at 3, would move backwards for the subtraction but does the reverse because of the -2 and so moves 2 units forwards to 5.

Check this

Convince yourself that $(-3) + (-2) = (-5)$ and that $(-1) - (-2) = 1$.

Notice that as $3 + (-2)$ results in moving 2 units backwards it gives exactly the same result as $3 - 2$ and that as $3 - (-2)$ results in moving 2 units forwards it is the same as $3 + 2$. This is because 'forwards' and 'backwards' are the reverse of each other. For $3 - (-2)$ the effect is one of a double negative, the phrase 'I am *not not* going' or the opposite of an opposite.

So, plus a minus number is the same as minus a positive number (opposite signs), whereas minus a negative number is the same as plus a positive number (same signs) as shown below.

Adding and subtracting negative numbers

OPPOSITE SIGNS
    + (– number) or – (+ number) gives a –

SAME SIGNS
    – (– number) or + (+ number) gives a +

When evaluating sums it is usually easiest to rewrite them in terms of positive numbers only as we have done in the following examples.

Check these

$3 + (-5)$
$= 3 - 5 = -2$.

$1 - (-4)$
$= 1 + 4 = 5$.

$(-3) - 7 = -10$.

12.42 – (–3.1)
= 12.42 + 3.1 = 15.52.

When more than two numbers appear in a sum we work in the same way. For instance
3.2 – (–3) + (–2) – 1 = 3.2 + 3 – 2 – 1 = 3.2.

Check this

	–6.7	+	(–7)	–	(–0.1)	+	2.1		
=	–6.7	–	7	+	0.1	+	2.1	=	–11.5

2 Positive and negative numbers: multiplying and dividing

Test box 2

Can you do these?

(–3) × 2   (–4) × (–0.5)   –2 × 10   8 ÷ (–2)

–6 ÷ (–3)   –4 × 12 × (–2)

Solutions: (row-wise) –6, 2, –20, –4, 2, 96.

Multiplying negative numbers

Multiplication means 'times' so 2 × 3 is really 'two threes' or 3 + 3, 4 × 3 is 'four threes' 3 + 3 + 3 + 3 and so on. The order of multiplication does not matter so 2 × 3 is the same as 3 × 2 = 2 + 2 + 2, and 4 × 3 is the same as 3 × 4 = 4 + 4 + 4 and so on.

The number line in Section 1 can help us to work out how to multiply negative numbers.

The multiplication 2 × 3 is 3 + 3, so our traveller starts at 0 and travels forward 3, and then forward 3 again to reach 6. By similar reasoning 2 × (–3) = (–3) + (–3), so he starts at 0 and then travels *backwards* 3 steps and then backwards 3 steps again to reach –6, so we have that 2 × (–3) = –6. If the negative number comes first, we can reverse the order of multiplication. For instance, to calculate (–4) × 2 we regard this as 2 × (–4) and work out (–4) + (–4) = (–8).

The big problem comes when we want to multiply two negative numbers together, let's say (–5) × (–2). How can our traveller do backward steps of 2, *minus* 5 times? Or backward steps of 5, *minus* 2 times? Here we do need a leap of faith. The convention is that *a negative times a negative is a positive*. This rule was adopted because everything then falls into a pattern for later work.

The key results for multiplying positive and negative numbers are:

Multiplying numbers

of the **same** sign **gives a +**
of a **different** sign **gives a −**

that is,

+ × + = +
+ × − = −
− × + = −
− × − = +

Of course, to multiply more than two numbers together we just multiply the first two, then multiply the result by the third number and so on. A property of multiplication is that we will obtain the same result regardless of the order in which we multiply the numbers. For instance,

$$2 \times 3 \times 4 \times 5$$
$$= 6 \times 4 \times 5$$
$$= 24 \times 5 = 120$$

or we could have said

$$2 \times 3 \times 4 \times 5$$
$$= 2 \times 12 \times 5$$
$$= 2 \times 60 = 120$$

The result of multiplying two or more numbers together is called the *product* of those numbers. For instance 6 is the product of 2 and 3 and 100 is the product of 5 and 20.

Check this

What is the product of 6 and 30? Of 2 and −5 and 20?

Answers: 180 and −200.

Dividing negative numbers

The rules for division have to comply with those for multiplication. For example, because $4 \times 5 = 20$, 20 divided by 4 must be 5 and 20 divided by 5 must be 4. So the rules we have already met for multiplication using negative numbers dictate the rules for division. For instance, as $4 \times (-5) = -20$, we can deduce that $(-20) \div (-5) = 4$ and that $(-20) \div 4 = -5$.

Dividing numbers

of the **same** sign **gives a +**
of a **different** sign **gives a −**

that is,

$$+ \div + = +$$
$$+ \div - = -$$
$$- \div + = -$$
$$- \div - = +$$

Notice that the rules for the sign of a division using negative numbers are just the same as the rules for multiplication; that is, dividing numbers with *different* signs gives a negative result, whereas dividing those of the *same* sign gives a positive result.

Check these

$$10 \div (-5) = (-2)$$

$$-100 \div 20 = -5$$

$$-28 \div (-7) = 4.$$

Dividing by 0

It is *not* possible to divide by 0. How can a quantity be split into 0 parts?

Alternatives to the ÷ sign

You may remember that division can be written in several ways. The division $8 \div 2$ can also be written $\frac{8}{2}$ or 8/2 and the result is called the *quotient*. Writing a division in this way is particularly useful when a whole expression needs to be divided by another whole expression. For instance, the division of $80 - 20$ by $5 + 10$ can be written

$$\frac{80 - 20}{5 + 10}$$

Be especially careful about the exact length of the quotient line. For instance

$$1 + \frac{5 + 3}{2}$$

(which equals 5) is crucially different from

$$\frac{1 + 5 + 3}{2}$$

(which equals 4.5).

WORK CARD FOR 1 AND 2

1. Evaluate the following:
   a. $6 + (-3) - (-4)$
   b. $(-3) + (-7) - 11 - (-8)$
   c. $0 - (-3) - (-1) - (-4)$
   d. $-4 + 3 - (-2)$
   e. $-5 - (-2) + (-4)$

2. Evaluate the following:
   a. $6 \times (-3)$
   b. -4×5
   c. $(-8) \times (-8)$
   d. $6 \times (-1)$
   e. $(-5) \times (-10)$
   f. $(-60) \times (-2)$
   g. $(-2) \times (-60)$
   h. What is the product of 2 and 20?

3. Evaluate the following:
   a. $10 \div (-2)$
   b. $60 \div (-15)$
   c. $-12 \div 6$
   d. $-12 \div (-6)$
   e. $\dfrac{12}{6}$
   f. $\dfrac{12}{-6}$
   g. $\dfrac{-12}{6}$
   h. $\dfrac{-12}{-6}$

4. Evaluate the following:
   a. $(-4) \times (-3) \times (-5)$
   b. $(-4) \times 3 \times (-5)$
   c. $(-1) \times (-1) \times (-1) \times (-1) \times (-1) \times (-1)$
   d. $(-1) \times (-1) \times (-1) \times (-1) \times (-1) \times (-1) \times (-1)$
   e. $-1 \times -5 \times -10$
   f. $-1 \times -5 \times 10$

Solutions:

1. a. 7 b. –13 c. 8 d. 1 e. –7

2. a. –18 b. –20 c. 64 d. –6 e. 50 f. 120 g. 120 h. 40

3. a. –5 b. –4 c. –2 d. 2 e. 2 f. –2 g. –2 h. 2

4. a. –60 b. 60 c. 1 d. –1 e. –50 f. 50

ASSESSMENT FOR 1 AND 2

1. Calculate the following:
   a. $(-20) - (-10) - (-5)$
   b. $0 - 20 - (-10) + (-5)$
   c. $(-1) - (-1) - 1 + (-1)$

2. Evaluate:
   a. $10 \times (-5)$
   b. $(-2) \times 6$
   c. $(-5) \times (-10) \times (-3)$
   d. $\dfrac{-200}{10}$
   e. $\dfrac{200}{-10}$
   f. $-2 \times -2 \times -2 \times -2 \times -2$
   g. $-2 \times -2 \times -2 \times -2 \times -2 \times -2 \times -2$
   h. $\dfrac{-60}{-3}$
   i. $\dfrac{-40}{8}$
   j. $\dfrac{40}{-8}$
   k. $\dfrac{-40}{-8}$

3 Combining addition, subtraction, multiplication and division

Test box 3

$$4 \times 8 - 6 \div 2 \qquad 3 \times (50 - 10) \qquad \left(\frac{40 - 20}{10 - 5}\right) \times 3$$

$$((75 \div 25) + 2) \times 5$$

Solutions: 29, 120, 12, 25.

The order of operations

Calculate $3 - 2 \times 4$.

It may look simple enough, but there is a snag. There are two ways to proceed and they each give a different answer. You might have reasoned:

(i) subtract first to give $3 - 2 = 1$ and then calculate $1 \times 4 = 4$ so the answer is 4

or you might have said

(ii) multiply first, so $2 \times 4 = 8$, and $3 - 8 = -5$.

Which one did you do?

The answer depends on the order in which the calculations are performed – whether to subtract or multiply first – and so longer expressions may have many more than two alternative answers. This situation is unsatisfactory so we need some sort of rule which tells us in which order to perform the operations.

The accepted rule is to *multiply and divide first*, performing calculations from left to right and *then add and subtract*, also from left to right. So for the example above we should multiply first, so the second answer, $3 - 2 \times 4 = 3 - 8 = -5$, is correct.

Let's try $6 \times 2 \div 4 + 1$. The rule tells us to multiply and divide first, but there is both a multiplication and a division here, so we must work from left to right. The multiplication occurs before the division, so we multiply 6×2 first to give

$$12 \div 4 + 1,$$

then divide giving

$$3 + 1,$$

and finally do the addition,

$$= 4.$$

Check these

Remember to perform calculations from left to right if there is more than one multiplication/division or more than one addition/subtraction.

$$-2 + 7 \times 8 \div 2 \times 2$$
$$= -2 + \quad\quad 56 \quad\quad \div 2 \times 2$$
$$= -2 + \quad\quad\quad\quad 28 \quad\quad \times 2$$
$$= -2 + \quad\quad\quad\quad\quad\quad 56 = 54$$

$$50 - 32 \div 16 \times 2$$
$$= 50 - \quad\quad\quad 2 \times 2$$
$$= 50 - \quad\quad\quad\quad 4 \quad = 46$$

Introducing brackets

Suppose we need to multiply 2 + 3 by 4 − 2. We *cannot* write this as

$$2 + 3 \times 4 - 2$$

because applying the order of operations rule would give 2 + 12 − 2 = 12. To show that the numbers must be processed in a different order we use *brackets*.

When part of an expression must be evaluated first it must be enclosed in brackets. So the multiplication of 2 + 3 by 4 − 2 must be written (2 + 3) × (4 − 2). This indicates that we must first calculate 2 + 3, and then calculate 4 − 2, and finally multiply the results 5 × 2 = 10.

As evaluating the expressions in brackets takes priority over anything else, we can extend the rule for the order of operations to *brackets*, multiply and divide, add and subtract.

For example, to evaluate (9 − 2) × 10 − (2 × 3) we work out the brackets first to give

$$7 \times 10 - 6$$

then multiply to give

$$70 - 6$$

and finally subtract to obtain

$$= 64.$$

The order of operations in evaluating arithmetic expressions is

Brackets
Multiply and Divide (from left to right)
Add and Subtract (from left to right)

When multiplying by a bracket it is usual to omit the multiplication sign. So (2 + 3) × (4 − 2) is written (2 + 3)(4 − 2) and 2 × (4 + 7) is written 2(4 + 7).

Check these

	6	(4 − 6)	(4 + 2)	+	3	
=	6	×(−2)	×6	+	3	
=		(−12)	×6	+	3	
=			(−72)	+	3	= −69
	36	÷	(4 × 3)	−	5	
=	36	÷	12	−	5	
=			3	−	5	= −2

Quotients can be written using brackets, for instance,

$$\frac{80 - 20}{10 - 5}$$

can be written (80 − 20) ÷ (10 − 5) because everything *above* the line of a quotient is divided by everything *below* the line.

Sometimes more than one layer of brackets is necessary. Do not be put off by this. You will find that you have to work out the *inside* brackets first and then proceed outwards. For instance

$$(6(1 + 4)) ÷ 10 = (6 × 5) ÷ 10 = 30 ÷ 10 = 3.$$

Authors and lecturers are sometimes helpful and use different symbols for different 'layers' of brackets. For instance {[(2 + 3) + 5] × 7}. As you will not always encounter this we have often used only one symbol in our work.

Check this

	10	×	(2	+	(6 ÷ 3)	×	4)	
=	10	×	(2	+	2	×	4)	
=	10	×	(2	+		8)		
=	10	×			10			= 100

In practice, brackets are often used to clarify expressions when they are not strictly essential.

WORK CARD 3

1. Evaluate the following:

   a. (20 − 5) × (4 − 2)   **b.** 2 + (10 ÷ 5) × 3

   c. 2 × (10 ÷ 5) × 2   **d.** 2 × 10 ÷ (5 × 2)

   e. $\dfrac{10 + 20}{4 - 2}$ **f.** 2 × 2 × (27 ÷ 3) + (1 − 20)

   g. (4 × 2 × 2) + (5 × (−1))

WORK CARD 3 (CONTINUED)

2. Evaluate the following:

   a. $1 + 3 \times (4 + (8 \div 2))$

   b. $((50 \div 25) \times 8 \div (7 - 3)) \times 3$

   c. $12 - (4\,(8 \times (6 - 4)) - 5)$

   d. $\dfrac{18 \times (2 - 3 \times 4)}{(4 + 14)}$

   e. $\left(\dfrac{18 \div 3}{(4 \times 3) - 36}\right) \times 4$

   f. $(-10) \times \left(\left(\dfrac{100}{25} \times 2\right) + (60 \div 20)\right) + 1$

   g. $1 + \left(\dfrac{2 \times (2 + 4 \times 5)}{(2 \times 11) \div (22 \div 2)}\right)$

Solutions:

1. **a.** 30   **b.** 8   **c.** 8   **d.** 2   **e.** 15   **f.** 17   **g.** 11

2. **a.** 25   **b.** 12   **c.** −47   **d.** −10   **e.** −1   **f.** −109   **g.** 23

ASSESSMENT 3

1. Evaluate:

   a. $(40 \div 2) + (3 \times 4)$

   b. $-5 + (-3) \times 2 + 1$

   c. $6 \div (3 \times 2) + 4$

   d. $3 \times 3 \times (6 \div 2) + 3$

   e. $3 \times 3 \times 6 \div 2 + 3$

   f. $\dfrac{3 + 6}{5 - 2}$

   g. $\dfrac{10 - 2}{3 + 1} \div (-2)$

2. Evaluate:

   a. $(21 \div 7) + (50 \div (5 \times 2) + 1)$

   b. $\dfrac{77 \div 11}{108 \div (-3) \times 4}$

   c. $\left(\dfrac{40}{6 + 2}\left(3 + \dfrac{5 - (21 \div 7)}{6 - 4} \times \dfrac{48}{16}\right)\right) + 5$

   d. $\left(20\,000 / \left((1000 - (2 \times 5 \times 50)) \times \left(\dfrac{100}{50}\right)\right)\right) - 2$

   e. $\dfrac{30 + 3 \times 3}{10 + 3} + 5 \times \dfrac{10 + 100}{11}$

4 Using a calculator

Test box 4

1. Use a calculator to evaluate:

$$\frac{500}{1.2(20 + 34)}$$ to 6 decimal places.

2. Express the following to 3 decimal places:

   1.9755   10,002.9999   209.452   12.73   0.000123456

3. Express the numbers in question **2** to 3 significant figures.

4. Express the following in scientific notation:

   12,000,000   0.00001254

5. By estimating roughly, do you think that

   $$\frac{515 \times 6.1}{200} = 7.1$$

   is correct?

Solutions:

1. 7.716049 **2.** 1.976   10,003.000   209.452   12.730   0.000

3. 1.98   10,000   209   12.7   0.000123   **4.** 1.2×10^7 1.254×10^{-5}

5. Use rough estimates: $500 \times 6 = 3000$, divided by 200 gives 15, the answer doesn't look good.

Which sort of calculator?

You will need a fairly basic calculator with the usual +, −, ×, ÷ and also simple functions such as $\frac{1}{x}$, $\sqrt{x}$, x^2, log and ln (natural logarithm), 10^x, e^x, x^y. A memory would also be helpful.

The order of operations on a calculator

Like any other invaluable tool a calculator is only as good as its operator – the modern adage, 'garbage in garbage out' is extremely relevant here. The calculator will only produce the right answer if you supply the numbers and operations in the correct order – which may not be the order in which they are written.

Try to evaluate the following expressions using your calculator:

$$(20 + 30) \div 3$$

$$20 + (30 \div 3)$$

The answers you should have are 16.666666 and 30. To calculate the first expression you need to enter 20 + 30 on your calculator and then divide by 3. For the second one you need to evaluate the bracket 30 ÷ 3 first and *then* add 20. We should add that some calculators do provide bracket functions, which we suggest that you use with care.

Show your working

Think about the errors you make when you word-process, or type or write! These are usually apparent when you read through later. It is just as easy to press the wrong key on a calculator, but most machines won't display all your inputs. It is therefore a good idea to write out your intermediate workings and your train of thought for a problem and not just the final value the calculator gives you. By doing this mistakes are easier to spot, your work is easier to follow – for a colleague or for yourself later – and last but not least, if your answer is wrong but your method is right you will still get most of the available marks in an exam.

Rough estimates

Always keep in mind the *real* problem you are solving.

Be critical of the answer your calculator gives you. Look out for percentage decreases that are over 100, negative probabilities, or fractions when you expected whole numbers.

Other errors may be less obvious and so it is a good idea to perform a rough mental calculation to get an idea of the magnitude of the solution.

To illustrate this, consider the following scenarios – and their solutions. Which ones seem reasonable and which don't? *Don't* use a calculator.

> ### Check these
>
> 1. A university has 6782 students, about half of which can be expected to visit a campus catering outlet on any given term-time day. Lunches are £2–3 and coffee and a snack is about £1. The total takings for a day over all outlets is £6142. Does this seem reasonable?
>
> 2. At a bank there is a single queueing system and five cashiers. On average, during peak hours a customer arrives every 32 seconds. The situation is modelled mathematically (such models are called queueing models) to assess the effects of increasing or reducing the number of cashiers on duty. The final result from the model shows that on average 76% of customers would have to wait longer than five minutes if there were 4 cashiers, 56% if there were 5 cashiers and 66% if there were 6 cashiers.
>
> 3. I earn \$8.42 an hour and worked 96½ hours last month. My payslip for the month says \$585.19. Does this seem reasonable?
>
> 4. The interest I will earn on £6179 invested at a rate of 5% for the first £5000 and 7.2% on the remainder over a year is given by
>
> $$5000 \times \frac{5}{100} + 1179 \times \frac{7.2}{100}$$
>
> Using a calculator I obtain £334.88. Does this seem right?

Solutions:

1. Working in thousands, roughly 4000 students will visit an outlet, and if an equal number have coffee or lunch they will spend an average of about £1.75, making total revenue for the day about £7000. The result is about right.

2. The results are suspicious here as more cashiers should bring down the percentage of people who have to wait longer than 5 minutes, whereas here the figure for 6 cashiers is greater than for 5. Maybe the modelling procedure is inappropriate, or else a calculation is erroneous.

3. Approximately $8 for roughly 100 hours should give me $800, so something is wrong. In fact this wage is for 69.5 hours!

4. Yes, it seems reasonable. Say that the average rate of interest is about 6% and that the sum invested is about £6000. We would expect the interest to be about

$$6000 \times \frac{6}{100} = £360$$

Rounding: decimal places and significant figures

When you use a calculator or computer to perform a calculation the machine will only display a certain number of digits. The exact answer may need many more digits or even an infinite number of them. For instance, when we divide 5 by 17 our calculator shows 0.294117647.

Numbers can be rounded to a particular number of *decimal places* (*d.p.*) or a particular number of *significant figures* (*sig. fig.*).

The convention for rounding to a particular number of decimal places (d.p.) is that when the first digit to be *excluded* is between 5 and 9, we round up, and when it is between 0 and 4 we round down. So, for instance, 3.625 expressed to 2 decimal places rounds up to 3.63, and 3.624999 rounds down to 3.62. Remember to include 0s where appropriate. For instance, 3.634999 to 4 decimal places is 3.6350, and to 5 decimal places is 3.63500.

A second way of representing numbers approximately is to write them to a particular number of *significant figures* (sig. fig.). The left-most digit of a number is the most significant as it is the digit that represents the greatest value, the next from left-most is the second most significant and so on. So in the number 672.34 the '6' represents hundreds and is therefore the most significant figure, the '7' represents the number of tens and is the second most significant figure and so on.

To write a number to, say, 3 significant figures we use the three left-most digits, rounding the final one if necessary. As when rounding to so many decimal places, if the first *discarded* digit is 5 or more we round up and if it is between 0 and 4 we round down. For example, 6248.500052 to 3 sig. fig. is 6250, to 2 sig. fig. is 6200 and to 8 sig. fig. is 6248.5001.

> ## Check this
>
> What is 7,254,600 to 3 sig. fig., to 4 sig. fig?
> What is 0.00652445 to 3 sig. fig., to 5 sig. fig.?
>
> **Solutions:** 7,250,000, 7,255,000, 0.00652, 0.0065245.

Notice from the last example that any zeros after the decimal point but before the first non-zero digit do not count as 'significant'.

Most calculators display numbers to 8 or 10 significant figures.

In practice, the accuracy with which we need to record results depends on the application. You do not see newspaper headlines reporting that the inflation rate is

3.42534213%: it is usually given to just one decimal place; that is, 3.4%. A chemist analysing a substance may have measuring equipment that is only accurate to 0.001g so it is pointless to record the result to 6 decimal places. A statistical model that forecasts the percentage dividend payable by a company for the next 10 years to 32 decimal places is itself only an approximation, so it is meaningless to report the forecasts to more than perhaps 1 or 2 decimal places.

So, common sense must prevail when deciding how many decimal places or significant figures to give in the *answer* to a problem. However, it can be dangerous to round too much *during* your calculations. Consider the following example.

Past records show that 8892 2cm tacks were manufactured at a cost of £13.16. A management accountant needs to estimate the price at which the factory should sell a batch of 20,000 tacks and reasons as follows.

Cost of manufacturing 8892 tacks is £13.16.

$$\text{Cost per tack is } \frac{13.16}{8892} = £0.001 \text{ rounded to 3 d.p.}$$

A batch of 20,000 tacks therefore costs 20,000 × 0.001 = £20.

She concludes that if the factory sells a batch for £25 it will make a profit.

This is obviously an extreme example and we hope that you can see the source of error here. The accurate calculations are Cost per tack is

$$\frac{13.16}{8892}$$

so a batch of 20,000 tacks costs

$$20,000 \times \frac{13.16}{8892} = £29.60$$

so the factory would make a *loss* if it sold a batch for £25.

Computers and calculators perform all their calculations to a particular accuracy. When you write out calculations by hand you may round your intermediate values to a different number of decimal places and so your results may differ slightly from those of the machine.

Scientific notation

You may have noticed that when your calculator is faced with a very large or a very small number it resorts to another notation called *scientific notation*. For instance, calculate 123,456,789 × 1234 on your machine.

Our calculator display shows

The small raised 11 means 'multiplied by 10 to the power of 11'.

We will cover powers more thoroughly in Chapter EM2, but for now it is enough to know that 10 to the power of 11 is written 10^{11} and means 10 multiplied by itself 11 times, or

$$10 \times 10 \times 10 \times 10 \times 10 \times 10 \times 10 \times 10 \times 10 \times 10 \times 10.$$

So the number above can be written $1.523456776 \times 10^{11}$.

To multiply a number by 10 you may recall that we just move the decimal point one place to the right; for example, $1.523456776 \times 10 = 15.23456776$. So to multiply by 10, eleven times, we move the decimal point 11 places to the right. The number represented above is therefore 152345677600.0. Remember that this result is not likely to be exact as the calculator only displays a certain number of significant figures.

Very small numbers can be represented using negative powers of 10. Again, these are described in Chapter EM2. Multiplying by 10^{-5} is the same as dividing by 10^5 or 100,000. We can do this by moving the decimal point 5 places *to the left*. So if the diameter of an atomic particle is 0.000000000000000000014 mm it is much easier to write it as 1.4×10^{-20}, where multiplying a number by 10^{-20} equates to moving the decimal point 20 places to the left.

WORK CARD 4

1. Use a calculator to evaluate the following:

    $$\frac{24.15}{5(150+11)} \qquad \frac{42-20.04}{366 \times 24} \qquad \frac{120 \div 15}{85+35}$$

2. *Without* using a calculator, decide which of the following answers are most likely:

    a. $\dfrac{312.42 \times 7.54}{21} = 112.17366$ or 1.1217 or 0.01122

    b. 112 articles are purchased at £5.42 and a further 62 articles at £2.42. The total bill is £757.08, £1050.12 or £342.01?

    c. I purchase 300 euros at an exchange rate of 1.5 euro to £1. This costs me £200.00, £350.00 or £450.00?

    d. In a traffic census at an accident black spot, 938 cars are seen to pass in an hour. Of these, 300 are going at over 50 kilometres per hour (kph) and 638 are travelling more slowly. The average speed of these cars is calculated to be 36.4 kph, 51 kph or 16 kph?

3. Write the following to 3 decimal places:

    1.9755   10,002.9752   209.452   12.73   0.00012456

4. Express the numbers in question **3** to 3 significant figures.

5. Express the following in scientific notation

    12,000,000   0.00001254   9.999999999   999.999

6. Write the following numbers out in full

    2.678×10^6 4.1×10^{-9} 1×10^0

Solutions:

1. 0.03   0.0025   0.0$\dot{6}$ (remember the $\dot{6}$ means that the digit 6 repeats forever – it's called 6 *recurring*).

2. Use your calculator to check **a.**, **b.** and **c.** In **d.** the only reasonable answer is 36.4.

WORK CARD 4

3. 1.976   10,002.975   209.452   12.730   0.000

4. 1.98   10,000   209   12.7   0.000125

5. 1.2×10^7 1.254×10^{-5} 9.999999999×10^0 9.99999×10^2

6. 2,678,000   0.0000000041   1

ASSESSMENT 4

1. Evaluate the following using a calculator:

   $$\frac{312 \times 1.01}{42.7 - 21.5}$$ $432.2 - (543.2 - 10.17)/2.5$

2. Say which of the following results seem sensible and explain why. Do *not* use a calculator except to check your answer.

   a. A leisure aircraft is owned by a Flying Group. The Group estimate that maintenance costs are likely to be £1000 next year. The main running cost is fuel which currently costs £0.7 per litre, but will be £0.95 per litre next year. Last year the aircraft did 9000 km. Average fuel consumption is 2.9 km per litre. If the 10 members of the Group are to share costs equally, the Treasurer suggests that a suitable monthly cost per member which ensures that maintenance and fuel costs are covered is £32.90, £44.12 or £12.10.

   b. $\dfrac{111 + (20.5 \times 10.7)}{302}$ = 10.939, 1.0939 or 0.10939

   c. I give myself a budget of $100 a day for my 8-day holiday. At the start of my holiday I have £600 which I change into dollars at a rate of $1.57 = £1. During the holiday I do not exceed my budget. At the end of the holiday I calculate that I should have $40 or $142 or $10 left. (Ignore commission charges.)

3. Express the following to 4 decimal places

   13.66666   –3.156   200,000.00001   156.99999   55.12345

4. Express the numbers in question **3** to 2 significant figures.

5. Write the following in scientific notation

   3,000,051.0   0.0000009142   –102.01   4.14

6. Write the following numbers out in full

   3.42×10^8 1.004×10^{-6} 9.99×10^3

5 Introducing letters and symbols

Test box 5

The total cost of a holiday for four friends comprises the cost of four return flights at $\$f$ each and a charge of $70 per day for a rented cottage. Write down an expression for the cost of the holiday for each person, if they go for d days.

Evaluate $\dfrac{2st}{s+1}$ when $s = 2$ and $t = 6$.

Evaluate $3a + b$, when $a = 4$ and $b = 5$.

Simplify $\dfrac{a}{b} + 2 - 5a - 3\dfrac{a}{b} + a$

What is meant by 'modelling'? Have you ever used a spreadsheet?

Solutions:

$\dfrac{4f + 70d}{4}$ or $f + \dfrac{70d}{4}$,   8,   17, $-2\dfrac{a}{b} + 2 - 4a$

See the sub-sections on 'models' and 'using a spreadsheet' below.

Why use letters and symbols?

Suppose we have £200 and wish to purchase some euros. The exchange rate is £1 = 1.5 euros and for simplicity we will ignore any commission charge. Using a calculator we can work out that the £200 will buy $200 \times 1.5 = 300$ euros.

That's fine – but exchange rates fluctuate and not everyone wants to change exactly £200. It would be much more useful to develop a *general relationship* between the number of pounds, the exchange rate and the number of euros.

To obtain the figure of 300 euros we *multiplied* the number of pounds by the exchange rate so the relationship we seek is

$$\text{euros} = \text{pounds} \times \text{rate}$$

This relationship is valid for any number of pounds and any exchange rate. So to calculate, for instance, how many euros we would obtain when the exchange rate is 1.9 and we have £300 to spend we write out the relationship again:

$$\text{euros} = \text{pounds} \times \text{rate}$$

but *substitute* 300 instead of 'pounds' and 1.9 instead of 'rate' to give

$$\text{euros} = 300 \times 1.9$$

and so euros = 570. We would obtain 570 euros.

It is usual to use a single letter to represent each of the entities in a relationship. Letters like x and y are often used but sometimes we use 'meaningful' letters like e for euros, p for pounds and r for rate, in which case our relationship would be written

$$e = p \times r$$

However, it is common to omit the multiplication sign adjacent to symbols – just as we omit multiplication signs next to brackets – and so we could write this as

$$e = pr$$

A relationship like $e = pr$ is an *equation* (because it contains an = sign), or we could say that the *formula* for the number of euros, e, is pr.

Once we have an equation or formula it can be used in different ways to solve a variety of problems. For instance, suppose we know that we received 960 euros at the Bureau de Change in exchange for £800, but we can't remember what the exchange rate was. Substituting $e = 960$ and $p = 800$ into the equation above gives

$$960 = 800r$$

We now need to *solve* the equation for the unknown quantity r. We will see how to do this in Chapter EM3, but for now we will tell you that the solution is

$$r = \frac{960}{800} = 1.2$$

so the exchange rate was £1 = 1.2 euros.

This currency example is relatively uncomplicated but it has demonstrated that symbols are useful

(i)   to represent the general relationship between the quantities of interest; and so
(ii) to enable calculation of one quantity from the others.

Using symbols to represent relationships

We now concentrate on how to turn information on the quantities of interest into expressions involving symbols. There is no magic way of doing this but if you find it hard we suggest that you break the task into two steps as follows.

1. Read through the information you have been given, but as you come across each quantity, assign it a symbol. Make a written note of these.
2. Read through again, but as you read 'translate' each fact you are given into symbols.

We include some examples with commentary. Remember that multiplication signs are usually omitted next to symbols.

| Check these |

1. It costs £2000 (the fixed cost) to set up a production run in a factory, and then a further £5 (the variable cost per unit) for each item manufactured. Write down an expression for the total production cost.

Solution:
On a first reading we realise that we need a symbol for the number of items manufactured (say, n) and a symbol for the total production cost (say, C).

During a second read-through we make the following jottings, which culminate in the desired expression for total production cost.

Fixed cost		2000
n items at a cost of £5 per item $5 \times n$		$5n$
Total cost $C =$		$2000 + 5n$

2. A restaurant has two menus, a tourist menu at £8 and a gourmet menu at £15. Write down a formula for the cost of the food for a party in which t customers have the tourist menu and g customers choose the gourmet menu.

Solution:
The symbols t and g have already been chosen for us here, but we adopt C for the total cost. Reading through we would write down something like

Tourist menu £8	t customers	$8t$
Gourmet £15	g customers	$15g$
Total cost is $C =$		$8t + 15g$

3. I want to organise a group of friends to hire a boat on the river for the day. The basic hire cost is £60, but we must also pay for fuel which costs £5 an hour. Write down an expression for the cost per person, C. (This might be of interest to establish how many friends I need to ask to keep the cost per person down to a particular amount.)

Solution:
Suppose I ask $n - 1$ friends so there are n of us altogether, and hire a boat for h hours. The total cost will be $60 + 5h$, so the cost per person will be

$$C = \frac{60 + 5h}{n}$$

Constants and variables
In many applications some amounts will be fixed – like the cost of fuel in **3** or the price of the meal in **2**. These fixed amounts are called *constants*. They are usually numbers, although a symbol which represents a particular value, like $\pi = 3.14159$ (from the formula for the circumference of a circle, $2\pi r$, where r is the radius) is also a constant.

On the other hand, symbols that represent quantities that can change, such as the number of people n, or the number of hours, h in **3**, are called *variables*.

Evaluating expressions
Once you have an expression you will often need to calculate its value when the variables in it take particular values.

For instance, suppose the amount of tax payable on a salary of S at a tax rate of $t\%$ is given by

$$\frac{(S - 3000)t}{100}$$

If Paul earns a salary of £10,000 and the tax rate is 30% then he must pay

$$\frac{(10{,}000 - 3000) \times 30}{100} = £2100$$

All we have done is replace the symbols in the formula with the values we are interested in. This is called *substitution*.

Check this

The amount of interest I receive on an investment of £P at r% interest over one year *less* a management charge of £10 + 0.01P is

$$\frac{P(r-1)}{100} - 10$$

Calculate the amount of interest I would receive in the following cases

a. On an investment of £10,000 when the interest rate is 5%.

b. On an investment of £500 when the interest rate is 10%.

Solution:

a. $\dfrac{10{,}000 \times (5-1)}{100} - 10 = £390$

b. $\dfrac{500 \times (10-1)}{100} - 10 = £35$

Models

Much of the work you will do for your degree and beyond will require you to build financial, accounting and economic models. By a *model* we usually mean one or more equations which represent the real-life situation.

The advantage of a model is that it allows us to answer 'what if …' type questions, without changing the real system. We illustrate this with a simple model for a clothing manufacturer's business.

Suppose it costs $10,000 to design a particular item of ladies clothing, and the unit production cost is $15. We might model the profit as

Profit = price × number sold – (10,000 + 15 × number manufactured)

The model enables the manufacturer to calculate the profit for a variety of values of the unknown variables (price, number sold and number manufactured) so that he may choose the values for price and number manufactured that give the highest profit. (He is not likely to have any control on the number sold.)

A model does not pretend to be exact. It will often be based on (and only as good as) a series of assumptions that the modeller makes (and should state), but the hope is that the model is a reasonable approximation to the real situation.

A model may be as complex or as simple as we like. For instance, the model above makes the assumption that the number sold is unaffected by the price. It would probably be more realistic to assume that as the price increased the number of sales decreased. This could be built into the model by introducing another relationship, for instance

number sold = 1000 – (10 × price)

and the two relationships could be used together to find the best price and number to manufacture.

Using a spreadsheet

For those of you who are *not* familiar with spreadsheets, they are a type of computer software that comprises a grid of numerical quantities and the relationship between them. They have become a useful tool for building models in accountancy, business, finance and elsewhere.

The rows of a spreadsheet are numbered **1**, **2**, **3**, ..., etc. and columns are labelled **A**, **B**, **C**, ..., etc. so that each cell of the grid is uniquely identified by a letter and a number like **A1**, **B23** or **E2**.

Into a cell of a spreadsheet the user can either enter a number – in which case the cell always takes that value – or an expression giving the relationship between the current cell and the others. For instance, if I would like the total of cells **E12** and **E13** to appear in cell **E14** I would enter the expression

$$= E12 + E13$$

into cell **E14**. The exact format of this expression may differ depending on the spreadsheet package, but the principle is always the same.

Spreadsheets are programmed so that when a value in a cell is changed, all the values elsewhere in the spreadsheet, which are influenced by that cell's value, will be changed automatically. Thus, 'what if ...' questions can be answered by trial and error.

The spreadsheet screen can show two modes – one which shows the symbolic expressions in each cell and the other which gives the numerical values implied by these.

A simple spreadsheet which calculates student marks is shown below.

	A	B	C	D	E	F
1	student	c w 1 %	c w 2 %	overall c w	exam %	overall %
2	Catherine	58	66	= (B2+C2)/2	77	= 0.2*D2+0.8*E2
3	Sylvia	82	70	= (B3+C3)/2	45	= 0.2*D3+0.8*E3
4	Malcolm	55	45	= (B4+C4)/2	76	= 0.2*D4+0.8*E4
5	Dennis	78	70	= (B5+C5)/2	60	= 0.2*D5+0.8*E5
6	Veronica	90	82	= (B6+C6)/2	74	= 0.2*D6+0.8*E6
7	Gillian	60	62	= (B7+C7)/2	58	= 0.2*D7+0.8*E7
8						
9					average	= (F2+F3+F4+F5+F6+F7)/6

20% of the marks on a Maths course can be gained from coursework and 80% from the exam. The two pieces of coursework carry equal weight and are each marked out of 100. A spreadsheet which calculates and displays the overall coursework mark and the overall marks of each student, and calculates the class's average mark is shown above in formula mode. Notice that the expressions for the overall coursework marks require brackets.

The same spreadsheet in 'values' mode is shown below.

student	c w 1 %	c w 2 %	overall c w	exam %	overall %
Catherine	58	66	62	77	74
Sylvia	82	70	76	45	51.2
Malcolm	55	45	50	76	70.8
Dennis	78	70	74	60	62.8
Veronica	90	82	86	74	76.4
Gillian	60	62	61	58	58.6
				average	65.63

In this book we will make use of a spreadsheet program, Microsoft Excel, particularly for *Statistics* and *Business Modelling*.

WORK CARD 5

1. Write down expressions for the following. Start by naming the variables you need.
   a. The cost of an m metre length of a roll of carpet when the width of the roll of carpet is 4 m and the cost per square metre is £12.
   b. The cost of a group's meal at a pizzeria, when pizzas are £4 each and bottles of wine £7. No other food or drink is available.
   c. The amount a gardener earns in a week when he charges £5 per hour for manual work like weeding but £8 per hour for skilled gardening work.
   d. The net amount given or charged to me in one month by my bank when they give me 5% interest on my average balance over the month, but charge me 30p per debit transaction.
   e. The cost of petrol for a journey of L miles when my average fuel consumption is 30 miles per gallon and the cost of fuel is £p per litre. Assume there are 4.54 litres in a gallon.

2. Salaries in a computer consultancy firm are calculated according to the following formula.

   $$S = 8000 + 300(A - 20) + 1000Y$$

   where A is the age of the employee in years, and Y is the number of years of experience they have in computing.

   What will an employee's salary be if she
   a. Has just graduated at 21 with no work experience?
   b. Left school at 16 and has worked in computing for 4 years until today?
   c. Is now 60, but took up Computing work at the age of 52 for the first time?

3. A company has lent a sum of £P. It is to be repaid at r% interest in one year's time. The company calculates that the prevailing market interest rate is i%, so the present value to the company of the repayment is

WORK CARD 5 (CONTINUED)

$$V = \frac{P(1 + \frac{r}{100})}{1 + \frac{i}{100}}$$

Find the present value in each of the following cases:

a. The loan is £10,000 at 8% interest and the market interest rate is 10%.

b. The loan is £15,000 at 12% interest and the market interest rate is 10%.

c. The loan is £20,000 at 5% interest and the market interest rate is 5%.

Solutions:

1. a. $48m$ b. $4p + 7w$ c. $5m + 8s$ d. $0.05A - 0.3D$

   e. $\frac{L}{30} \times 4.54p$ (L is length of journey in miles)

2. a. 8300   b. 12,000   c. 28,000

3. a. £9818.18   b. £15,272.72   c. £20,000.

ASSESSMENT 5

1. Write down an expression for the floor area of a two-room flat when the first room has one and a half times the width and twice the breadth as the second. Start by naming the variables you are going to use.

2. I want to buy some Botswana pulas and the exchange rate is 8.25 BWP = £1 if I buy them abroad using a credit card or 8.5 BWP = £1 for a cash transaction at a Bureau de Change. The credit card company will charge me 2.3% commission on a credit card transaction whereas a Bureau de Change charges 2% commission plus a fee of £3.

   Write down an expression for the cost (including commission) of buying a particular number of Botswana pulas **(a)** by credit card and **(b)** from a Bureau de Change.

   (i) Evaluate each of these expressions for 700 BWP, 800 BWP and 1000 BWP respectively.

   (ii) Hazard a guess as to the number of pulas you would have to buy for the cost to be the same whether you use a credit card or cash. (To be continued later!)

3. A leisure aircraft is owned by the Broadland Flying Group which has 10 members. The costs of keeping the aircraft comprise maintenance costs (including insurance) and the running cost which is mainly fuel. Average fuel consumption is 9 miles per gallon.

   If the 10 members of the Group are to share costs equally, write down a formula to enable Gordon the treasurer to calculate the annual cost for each member if the aircraft travels n miles in a year, incurs maintenance costs of £M and fuel costs £3 a gallon.

4. Consider the model for the clothing manufacturer

Profit = price × number sold – (10,000 + 15 × number manufactured).

Set up a spreadsheet to investigate the profit, when the selling price is £18, for a range of values for the number sold and the number manufactured. Comment on your results. Adapt your spreadsheet to investigate how many items must be manufactured in order to break even (make a profit of 0) assuming that the number sold is the same as the number manufactured.

6 Working with symbols: adding, subtracting, multiplying, dividing

Test box 6

Simplify the following by collecting like terms:

$3pq + 2q + 2pq$

Write the following expressions more succinctly:

$3 \times (-2p) \times 2 \times p$ $2 \cdot 3 \cdot 5$

Solutions:

$5pq + 2q$

$-12p^2$ 30

To construct models and solve equations we need to know how to manipulate symbols. This need not be a problem if we remember that the symbols merely *stand in for the numbers* and so can be treated in exactly the same way. In this section we recall the work of Sections 1–3, but apply it particularly to expressions containing symbols.

Negative symbols

The rules for adding, subtracting, multiplying and dividing numbers apply equally well to symbols. We can summarise these rules as

Adding and subtracting

SAME SIGNS
   $-(-a)$ or $+(+a)$ gives $+a$

OPPOSITE SIGNS
   $+(-a)$ or $-(+a)$ gives $-a$

where a is any number, symbol or expression.

Multiplying and dividing

SAME SIGNS
multiplying $a \times b = ab$
$\quad\quad\quad\quad (-a)(-b) = ab$

dividing $\quad a \div b = \dfrac{a}{b}$

and $\quad\quad (-a) \div (-b) = \dfrac{-a}{-b} = \dfrac{a}{b}$

OPPOSITE SIGNS
multiplying $a \times (-b) = -ab$
$\quad\quad\quad\quad (-a) \times b = -ab$

dividing $\quad (-a) \div b = \dfrac{-a}{b} = -\dfrac{a}{b}$

$\quad\quad\quad\quad a \div (-b) = \dfrac{a}{-b} = -\dfrac{a}{b}$

Check these

$2 + (-a) = 2 - a$

$3 - (-a) = 3 + a$

$2 \times (-a) = -2a$

$(-3) \times (-a) = 3a$

$(-b) \times c = -bc$

$(-c) \times (-a) = ac$

$\dfrac{p}{-q} = -\dfrac{p}{q} \quad\quad \dfrac{a}{a} = 1 \quad\quad \dfrac{-x}{-x} = 1 \quad\quad \dfrac{-a}{a} = -1$

Addition and subtraction: collecting 'like terms'

Because $a + a + 2a$ means one 'a' plus one 'a' plus two 'a's the terms can be collected together and written as $4a$. We can do this because each term is the same apart from the number – called the *coefficient*, which it is multiplied by. It is just like saying that 'one banana plus another banana plus another two bananas gives four bananas'.

Even when we have more complicated terms we can collect them together *as long as they are the same*. For instance

$$2pq + pq - 5pq$$

simplifies to $-2pq$, or

$$\frac{s}{2r} + 4\frac{s}{2r}$$

is equivalent to

$$5\frac{s}{2r}$$

as each term is so many

$$\frac{s}{2r}s$$

Notice, however, that we *can't* collect together any terms in

$$3pq + p + q$$

as they are all multiples of different things – we can't add 3 bananas, an orange and a grapefruit!

Often just some of the terms in an expression can be collected together. For instance,

$$pq + 2p + 5pq$$

simplifies to $6pq + 2p$.

Check these

Where possible, simplify the following:

$5rs - 3rs + rs$

All the terms involve a number of rss, so the expression simplifies to $3rs$.

$9pq + 4q - 5pq - q$

The pq terms can be collected to give $9pq - 5pq = 4pq$, but the terms in q must be collected separately to give $4q - q = 3q$. So the expression simplifies to $4pq + 3q$.

$$3\frac{a}{2} - 2\frac{a}{2} + 5\frac{a}{2}$$

All the terms involve a number of $\frac{a}{2}$s, so the expression simplifies to $6\frac{a}{2}$.
We will see later that this can be simplified further to $3a$.

$2xz + 5zx - 3z$

You should spot here that xz is the same as zx (as the order in which we multiply doesn't effect the result), so we can collect together $2xz + 5zx$ to give $7xz$. The whole expression simplifies to $7xz - 3z$.

In the last example it would have been easier to spot that $2xz$ and $5zx$ could be collected together if the xz and zx terms had been written in the same way. It is therefore a good idea to write letters that are multiplied together in alphabetical order. This is one of the suggestions below.

Some conventions for multiplying

1. We have already said that there is no need to include a multiplication sign '×' next to a bracket or next to a symbol. As a consequence, whenever letters or brackets appear

adjacent to each other a multiplication sign is implied. For instance $2ab (c + d)$ means $2 \times a \times b \times (c + d)$.

2. We can't just drop the multiplication sign when multiplying two or more numbers as we wouldn't be able to tell when one number finished and the next one started. For example 357890 might mean 35×7890 or $3 \times 57 \times 890$ or many other possibilities. Instead we can shorten expressions by writing a slightly raised *dot* instead of the × sign. So $357 \times 8 \times 90$ could be written $357 \cdot 8 \cdot 90$.

3. When a number is multiplied by a letter it is conventional to write the number first so, for instance, we write $5n$ instead of $n5$.

4. When a mixture of numbers and symbols are multiplied together, it is more succinct to multiply the numbers together so, for instance, instead of $4 \times p \times q \times 2$ we would write $8pq$.

5. When several symbols are multiplied together it is usual to write them in alphabetical order. This means that 'like' terms can be spotted easily. So $cad \times 2$ would more usually be written $2acd$.

6. When a number or symbol is multiplied by itself we say it is 'squared', and we usually write the number with a 2 superscript. For instance, 3^2 is called 'three squared' and means 3×3. In a similar way $(ab)^2$ means $(ab) \times (ab)$.

Check this

Check that you understand what the following expressions mean

1. $3p(2 + a)$ $\qquad \dfrac{100}{rc} \qquad \dfrac{2 \cdot 3 \cdot 4}{ax} \qquad \dfrac{100\,pq}{3 \cdot 2 \cdot 1} \qquad \dfrac{a^2 b}{c^2}$

Write the following expressions more succinctly

2. $y \times z \times 2 \times a \qquad 3 \times b \times a \times 2 \qquad a \times 2b \times 5$

Solutions:

1. Writing out these expressions in long-hand using × for multiplication gives: $3 \times p \times (2 + a)$, $100 \div (r \times c)$, $(2 \times 3 \times 4) \div (a \times x)$, $(100 \times p \times q) \div (3 \times 2 \times 1)$, $(a \times a \times b) \div (c \times c)$

2. $2ayz$, $6ab$; remember that this is $a \times 2 \times b \times 5$, giving $10ab$.

Can I do this?

There are many more techniques for working with symbols and some will be considered in Chapter EM2. However, if you are in doubt as to whether two expressions are equivalent you can always evaluate both of them for some arbitrarily chosen numbers and see if the results are the same.

For instance, suppose you are unsure whether $p \times q$ is the same as $q \times p$. (We have picked an easy one to start with – we have already said that this is true.) If, for example, $p = 2$ and $q = 1$, then $p \times q = 2 \times 1 = 2$ and $q \times p = 1 \times 2 = 2$, so the expressions are equal for these values. Now try $p = -5$ and $q = 2$, putting a negative number to the test, and we have $p \times q = -5 \times 2 = -10$ and $q \times p = 2 \times -5 = -10$ which again are equal.

Be warned, however, that 'trying out' values like this does not constitute proof that the expressions are equal – you may just have been lucky and by chance selected values that worked. If the two expressions are *not* equal for the values you have chosen, then this does, however, prove that they are *not* equivalent expressions.

For instance, is it true that

$$\frac{m+n}{n}$$

is the same as *m*? Try some values for *m* and *n* to see whether this is true or not before you read on.

Check this

Is $\dfrac{m+n}{n}$ the same as *m*?

Solution:
We'll choose *m* = 100, *n* = 5 first. When we evaluate the two expressions we obtain

$$\frac{m+n}{n} = \frac{105}{5} = 21$$

whereas *m* = 100. No, this does *not* work. We don't need to try any more values for *m* and *n* as we only need to find one counter-example to show that the two expressions are not equal.

WORK CARD 6

1. Simplify, by collecting like terms where possible
   a. $b + b + b + a + a$
   b. $p + q + 2pq - q + 3qp$
   c. $2p + 2q + p + pqr - 2pqr$
   d. $2\dfrac{x}{y} + x - 2x + 3\dfrac{x}{y}$

2. Write the following expressions more succinctly
   a. $2 \times n \times 3 \times m$ b. $pq \times rs \times 3$
   c. $a \cdot 2 \cdot 10 \cdot zb$ d. $(z \times y) \times (2 \times w)$

3. You dimly recollect from your school career that it is valid to 'cancel down' and that

   $\dfrac{2a}{2b}$ is the same as $\dfrac{a}{b}$.

   Try out some numbers to see if this seems to be the case or not.

4. Is it true that

   $$\frac{1 + 2a}{2b} = \frac{1 + a}{b} ?$$

Solutions:

1. **a.** $3b + 2a$ **b.** $p + 5pq$ **c.** $3p + 2q - pqr$ **d.** $5\dfrac{x}{y} - x$

2. **a.** $6mn$ **b.** $3pqrs$ **c.** $20abz$ **d.** $2wyz$

3. Try for instance $a = 5$ and $b = 10$, $2a = 10$ and $2b = 20$, so

$$\frac{2a}{2b} = \frac{10}{20} = 0.5 = \frac{a}{b}$$

so it works. Now try one or more negative numbers, say $a = -1$ and $b = 3$; then

$$\frac{2a}{2b} = \frac{-2}{6} = -\frac{1}{3} \quad \text{and} \quad \frac{a}{b} = \frac{-1}{3} = -\frac{1}{3}$$

so again it works. In fact it is true and we cover it in the next section!

4. No it is not true. Try for instance $a = 1$, $b = 2$; then

$$\frac{1 + 2a}{2b} = \frac{3}{4} \quad \text{whereas} \quad \frac{1 + a}{b} = \frac{2}{2} = 1$$

which is clearly different.

1. Simplify by collecting like terms:

   a. $3x - 2xy + 3y + 3xy$

   b. $p - 2q - 2q^2 + q^2 - 3p^2$

   c. $3 \cdot \dfrac{a}{2b} + a - 2\dfrac{a}{2b} + 3a$

2. Write down the following expressions more succinctly:

   a. $\dfrac{f \times b \times 2 \cdot 3}{2 \times e \times d}$ **b.** $(c \times b) \times (a \times d) \times 3$

3. Investigate whether $a(b + d)$ is the same as $ab + d$.

EM2
Simplifying expressions

Kindly enter them in your notebook.
And, in order to refer to them conveniently,
let's call them A, B and Z.

(The tortoise in Lewis Carroll, 'What the tortoise said to Achilles')

Contexts

What is this chapter about?
In this chapter we see how to simplify expressions containing numbers and symbols. This involves adding and subtracting fractions, expanding brackets, factorising and powers.

Why is it useful?
This chapter extends the 'toolkit' introduced in the last chapter (EM1 Numbers and symbols) to enable you to cope with most mathematical expressions and to learn techniques like solving equations and drawing curves. Powers, in particular, are useful to model quantities in finance and economics and for calculating the value of money over time.

Where does it fit in?
This chapter continues the basics of algebra introduced in the last chapter. You will need the techniques in this chapter for the remainder of this book and for just about any quantitative subject you study.

What do I need to know?
You will only need the material in EM1.

Objectives

After your work on this chapter you should be able to:

- cancel down fractions to their simplest terms;
- cancel down fractions expressed in symbols;
- add and subtract, multiply and divide fractions;
- expand or multiply out brackets in an expression;
- factorise expressions;
- understand positive and negative powers;
- multiply and divide powers of the same number, calculate the power of a power;
- write down powers of products and quotients;
- understand and manipulate fractional powers.

In this chapter we see how expressions can be simplified. This will be useful for solving equations in the next chapter.

1 Equivalent fractions and cancelling

Test box 1

Which of the following fractions are equivalent to each other?

$$\frac{1}{3} \quad \frac{6}{9} \quad \frac{8}{20} \quad \frac{16}{28} \quad \frac{4}{6} \quad \frac{10}{25} \quad \frac{8}{14} \quad \frac{8}{12} \quad \frac{18}{54}$$

Solution: the first and ninth are equal to $\frac{1}{3}$, the second, fifth and eighth are all $\frac{2}{3}$, the third and sixth are both $\frac{2}{5}$, and the fourth and seventh are both $\frac{4}{7}$.

Express the following fractions in their simplest or lowest terms:

$$\frac{56}{64}, \quad \frac{48}{108}, \quad \frac{7}{11}, \quad \frac{42}{147}, \quad \frac{196}{154}$$

Solutions:

$$\frac{7}{8}, \quad \frac{4}{9}, \quad \frac{7}{11}, \quad \frac{2}{7}, \quad \frac{14}{11}$$

Simplify the following:

$$\frac{2p}{4q}, \quad \frac{3abc}{bc}, \quad \frac{6xy}{9xz}$$

Solutions:

$$\frac{p}{2q}, \qquad 3a, \qquad \frac{2y}{3z}$$

Fractions

From your schooldays you will probably recall that a fraction is one number 'over' another number, like $\frac{5}{3}$ or $\frac{2}{5}$. The number on the 'top' of the fraction is called the *numerator* and the number on the 'bottom' is the *denominator*.

There are *two* main ways of regarding fractions. Both can be useful at different times.

Fractions as a number of equal parts

The denominator (bottom) of a fraction shows the number of equally sized parts which a unit has been divided into, and the numerator (top) shows the number of these parts which are in the fraction. For instance, the fraction three-quarters $\frac{3}{4}$ means three of the parts obtained when a unit is divided into four as shown below.

one quarter	one quarter	one quarter	one quarter

three quarters	one quarter

A way of remembering the terminology 'numerator' is to remember that the numerator is the *number* of equally sized parts in the fraction.

In the same way $\frac{5}{8}$ is five of the parts obtained when a unit is divided into eight equal parts or $5 \times \frac{1}{8}$.

1/8	1/8	1/8	1/8	1/8	1/8	1/8	1/8

1/8	five eighths	1/8	1/8

Fractions as quotients

The second way of looking at fractions is as one number dividing another; $\frac{1}{2}$ is just 1 divided by 2, $1 \div 2$; and $\frac{3}{4}$ is 3 divided by 4, $3 \div 4$, as the diagram below shows:

Equivalent fractions

Some fractions are equivalent to each other.

For instance, $\frac{3}{4}$ is equivalent to $\frac{6}{8}$ because 3 divided by 4 is the same as 6 divided by 8, as shown below.

We could also show that both these are equivalent to $\frac{9}{12}$ or $\frac{18}{24}$ and so on.

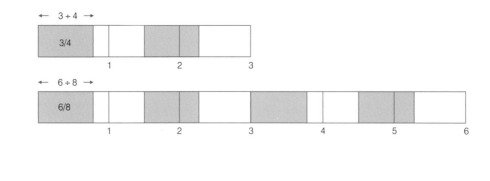

Check this

Convince yourself that $\frac{4}{14}$, $\frac{6}{21}$ and $\frac{2}{7}$ are all equivalent.

Can you see that to find an equivalent fraction all you need to do is multiply or divide *both* the numerator and denominator (top and bottom) by the same number?

For instance, if we take $\frac{10}{24}$ and divide both the numerator and denominator by 2 we get an equivalent fraction:

$$\frac{10 \div 2}{24 \div 2} = \frac{5}{12}$$

This is like saying that if we have 10 bottles of wine between 24 people at a party, we could split the bottles and the people into two similar groups and each person would still have the same amount to drink.

To obtain another fraction which is equivalent to $\frac{10}{24}$ we could multiply both the top and bottom by, for example, 3 to obtain

$$\frac{10 \times 3}{24 \times 3} = \frac{30}{72}$$

So

$$\frac{10}{24}, \frac{5}{12} \text{ and } \frac{30}{72}$$

are all equivalent to each other.

Check these

Express $\frac{3}{5}$ as $\frac{?}{10}$:

As we need to multiply the 5 by 2 to get a denominator of 10 an equivalent fraction is

$$\frac{3 \times 2}{5 \times 2} = \frac{6}{10}$$

Write $\frac{24}{36}$ equivalently in terms of sixths:

$$\frac{24}{36} = \frac{24 \div 6}{36 \div 6} = \frac{4}{6}$$

Write $\frac{2}{3}$ as $\frac{?}{39}$:

$$\frac{2}{3} = \frac{2 \times 13}{3 \times 13} = \frac{26}{39}$$

Expressing fractions in their simplest terms

Talking about 'seventy twoths' or 'thirty ninths' is unwieldly and in practice it is best to express fractions in terms of the lowest denominator possible. This is why we don't talk in terms of 'two quarters', or 'six eighths' but 'half' and 'three quarters'. We say that such fractions are in their *'lowest terms'* or *'simplest terms'*.

When a fraction is not already in its lowest terms it can be converted, in several stages if necessary. At each stage we find an equivalent fraction with a smaller denominator. This process, popularly called 'cancelling', is best explained by example.

To express the fraction $\frac{84}{162}$ in its lowest terms, we might first spot that both 84 and 162 are divisible by 2, so

$$\frac{84}{162} = \frac{84 \div 2}{162 \div 2} = \frac{42}{81}$$

This is still not in its lowest terms as both numerator and denominator can be divided by 3, so we continue:

$$= \frac{42 \div 3}{81 \div 3} = \frac{14}{27}$$

As no number divides both 14 and 27 the fraction is now in its lowest terms. Equivalently we could have noticed at the start that 84 and 162 both divide by 6, but it is often easier to work in stages.

Another example is:

> ### Check this
>
> $$\frac{63}{252} = \frac{63 \div 3}{252 \div 3} = \frac{21}{84} = \frac{21 \div 7}{84 \div 7} = \frac{3}{12} = \frac{1}{4}$$

When working by hand people usually cross out the numerator and denominator at each stage and write the new numerator and denominator adjacent, like this,

$$\frac{\cancel{42}}{\cancel{54}} = \frac{\cancel{21}}{\cancel{27}} = \frac{7}{9}$$

$$\text{i.e. } \frac{42}{54} = \frac{21}{27} = \frac{7}{9}$$

> ### Check these
>
> Express $\frac{126}{56}$ in the simplest terms possible:
>
> $$\frac{126}{56} = \frac{63}{28} = \frac{9}{4}$$

Cancel down $\frac{24}{54}$ to its lowest terms.

$$\frac{24}{54} = \frac{8}{18} = \frac{4}{9}$$

Express $\frac{21}{61}$ in its lowest terms.

This is a trick question as it is already in its lowest terms because no number divides both 21 and 61 to simplify the fraction.

Factors

The 'number' you have been using which divides both the numerator and the denominator of the fraction exactly is called a *common factor* of the two numbers. In general, a *factor* of a number is another number which divides the original number an exact number of times. For instance, 9 is a factor of 72 and 17 is a factor of 51, or we say that 36 has factors 2, 3, 4, 6, 9, 12, and 18. A more technical way of defining the lowest or simplest terms of a fraction is therefore to say that in its lowest terms, the numerator and denominator do *not* have a common factor.

The key facts in this section are:

> A fraction is $\dfrac{\text{numerator}}{\text{denominator}}$
>
> **To obtain an equivalent fraction**, multiply or divide both the numerator and the denominator by the same number
>
> **To express a fraction in its lowest or simplest terms**, cancel by dividing both numerator and denominator by a common factor until no further cancelling is possible

Fractions with symbols

But why bother with cancelling? Why can't we just divide two numbers using a calculator? The answer is that we can – although cancelling can often avoid some tedium – but the technique of cancelling also enables us to simplify fractions that contain symbols.

In a similar way to cancelling numerical fractions, provided we divide or multiply both the numerator and the denominator by the same constant, variable or expression we will get an equivalent fraction.

For instance, $\frac{25L}{20}$ can be cancelled as both the numerator and denominator divide by 5. We obtain

$$\frac{25L \div 5}{20 \div 5} = \frac{5L}{4}$$

In $\frac{ab}{a}$ both the numerator and denominator are multiples of a, so we can divide both of them by a to give

$$\frac{ab \div a}{a \div a} = \frac{b}{1} = b$$

Check these

Cancel $\frac{3x}{6y}$ as much as possible. As both $3x$ and $6y$ can be divided by 3 we obtain $\frac{x}{2y}$.

Simplify $\frac{2b}{b}$. We can divide both numerator and denominator by b to give $\frac{2}{1} = 2$. We might write this as

$$\frac{2\cancel{b}}{\cancel{b}} = \frac{2}{1} = 2$$

Simplify $\frac{mn}{n}$

Both the numerator and the denominator are multiples of n, so dividing each by n gives

$$\frac{mn \div n}{n \div n} = \frac{m}{1} = m$$

Again, we could write our calculations as

$$\frac{m\cancel{n}}{\cancel{n}} = m$$

Write down the equivalent fraction to $\frac{b}{2}$ that has a denominator of $4b$. To obtain a denominator of $4b$, the 2 must be multiplied by $2b$ (*check* $2 \times 2b = 4b$) so we must treat the numerator in exactly the same way to give

$$\frac{b}{2} = \frac{b \times 2b}{2 \times 2b} = \frac{2b^2}{4b}. \quad \text{(Recall } b^2 \text{ is shorthand for } b \times b.\text{)}$$

Simplify

$$\frac{abc}{2a}$$

Both numerator and denominator can be divided by a to give $\frac{bc}{2}$.

WORK CARD 1

1. Express the following as so many thirty-sixths:

    a. $\frac{5}{2}$ b. $\frac{4}{9}$ c. $\frac{18}{72}$ d. $\frac{5}{18}$ e. $\frac{4}{144}$

2. Express the following with a denominator of 80:

    a. $\frac{2}{10}$ b. $\frac{3}{8}$ c. $\frac{4}{160}$ d. $\frac{4}{5}$ e. $\frac{13}{16}$

3. Cancel the following fractions to their simplest terms:

    a. $\frac{15}{48}$ b. $\frac{1320}{44}$ c. $\frac{294}{700}$ d. $\frac{780}{104}$ e. $\frac{1392}{54}$ f. $\frac{120}{168}$

4. Simplify a. $\frac{3m}{9n}$ b. $\frac{pqr}{pr}$ c. $\frac{60q}{12qr}$

5. Six friends club together to buy c CDs at £12 each. Write down an expression to represent how much each will spend. Simplify the expression as much as possible.

Solutions:

1. a. $\dfrac{90}{36}$ b. $\dfrac{16}{36}$ c. $\dfrac{9}{36}$ d. $\dfrac{10}{36}$ e. $\dfrac{1}{36}$

2. a. $\dfrac{16}{80}$ b. $\dfrac{30}{80}$ c. $\dfrac{2}{80}$ d. $\dfrac{64}{80}$ e. $\dfrac{65}{80}$

3. a. $\dfrac{5}{16}$ b. 30 c. $\dfrac{21}{50}$ d. $\dfrac{15}{2}$ e. $\dfrac{232}{9}$ f. $\dfrac{5}{7}$

4. a. $\dfrac{m}{3n}$ b. q c. $\dfrac{5}{r}$

5. $\dfrac{12c}{6} = 2c$

ASSESSMENT 1

1. Express the following in twenty-fourths:

   a. $\dfrac{5}{12}$ b. $\dfrac{8}{48}$ c. $\dfrac{6}{36}$ d. $\dfrac{-5}{8}$ e. $\dfrac{15}{120}$

2. Write the following with a denominator of 32:

   a. $\dfrac{1}{4}$ b. $\dfrac{7}{16}$ c. $\dfrac{12}{128}$ d. $\dfrac{6}{24}$

3. Cancel the following to their simplest terms:

   a. $\dfrac{13}{39}$ b. $\dfrac{-25}{40}$ c. $\dfrac{42}{96}$ d. $\dfrac{78}{273}$ e. $\dfrac{243}{849}$

4. Simplify the following:

   a. $\dfrac{120p}{pq}$ b. $\dfrac{2h}{4j}$ c. $\dfrac{3ab}{6bc}$ d. $\dfrac{mn}{2n}$ e. $\dfrac{2(1+r)}{4}$

---

2 Adding and subtracting fractions

Test box 2

Evaluate the following without using a calculator

$$\frac{2}{3} - \frac{1}{4}, \qquad \frac{5}{12} + \frac{1}{8}, \qquad \frac{1}{10} + \frac{3}{16} - \frac{3}{80}$$

Evaluate:

$$\frac{3}{2} - \frac{9}{14} + \frac{3}{63}$$

without any denominator being greater than 100 at any stage.

Solutions:

$$\frac{5}{12}, \qquad \frac{13}{24}, \qquad \frac{1}{4}, \qquad \frac{19}{21}$$

Simplify:

$$\frac{2}{3a} + \frac{3}{2a}$$

Solution:

$$\frac{13}{6a}$$

When two fractions have the same denominator, adding or subtracting is easy because we are adding (or subtracting) like parts. For instance, $\frac{1}{4} + \frac{5}{4}$ adds *one* quarter to *five* quarters and so must give *six* quarters. In the same way, $\frac{6}{5} - \frac{4}{5}$ is *six* fifths minus *four* fifths and so is *two fifths*, $\frac{2}{5}$.

It is less straightforward to calculate say, $\frac{1}{2} + \frac{2}{5}$. Here we are adding halves to fifths so we are not adding like to like. What we need to do is to find equivalent fractions for one or more of the terms in the sum, so that both terms have the same denominator.

For example, consider the sum $\frac{1}{2} + \frac{2}{5}$. We need to find equivalent fractions for $\frac{1}{2}$ and $\frac{2}{5}$ that both have the same denominator. Both $\frac{1}{2}$ and $\frac{2}{5}$ can be expressed in tenths, $\frac{1}{2}$ is equivalent to

$$\frac{1 \times 5}{2 \times 5} = \frac{5}{10}$$

and $\frac{2}{5}$ is equivalent to

$$\frac{2 \times 2}{5 \times 2} = \frac{4}{10}$$

so the sum becomes

$$\frac{1}{2} + \frac{2}{5} = \frac{1 \times 5}{2 \times 5} + \frac{2 \times 2}{5 \times 2}$$

At this stage, both fractions in the sum are equivalent to the original ones, as both top and bottom of the first term have been multiplied by 5 and both top and bottom of the second term multiplied by 2. The denominator of both fractions is now 10 and the sum becomes

$$\frac{5}{10} + \frac{4}{10} = \frac{9}{10}$$

Check this

Evaluate:

$$\frac{3}{8} - \frac{1}{6}$$

Both fractions can be expressed equivalently with a denominator of 24, so we obtain

$$\frac{3 \times 3}{8 \times 3} - \frac{1 \times 4}{6 \times 4} = \frac{9}{24} - \frac{4}{24} = \frac{5}{24}$$

Here the *common denominator* is 24, but we could have used 48 (or 72 or anything that divides both 8 and 6). However, 24 is the easiest to use as it is the *lowest* common denominator. If you can't spot a common denominator of two fractions the product of the two denominators will always work.

Check these

Evaluate

$$\frac{7}{4} + \frac{3}{10}$$

The lowest common denominator is 20 so the sum becomes

$$\frac{7 \times 5}{4 \times 5} + \frac{3 \times 2}{10 \times 2} = \frac{35}{20} + \frac{6}{20} = \frac{41}{20}$$

We could equally well have used the product of the denominators 4×10 as the common denominator. This would have given

$$\frac{70}{40} + \frac{12}{40} = \frac{82}{40}$$

which we would then have cancelled to give $\frac{41}{20}$.

Evaluate:

$$\frac{9}{5} + \frac{11}{15}$$

The lowest common denominator is 15 so there is no need to change the second term. Our working is

$$\frac{9}{5} + \frac{11}{15} = \frac{9 \times 3}{5 \times 3} + \frac{11}{15} = \frac{27}{15} + \frac{11}{15} = \frac{38}{15}$$

Evaluate:

$$\frac{6}{20} + \frac{21}{5}$$

A common denominator is 20 and the answer is

$$\frac{90}{20} = \frac{9}{2}$$

Adding and subtracting *more than two fractions* is no different. You can either take the terms in pairs, or else look for a common denominator of *all* the terms. For instance, consider a sum involving three fractions:

$$\frac{7}{6} - \frac{2}{3} + \frac{3}{8}$$

The lowest common denominator for all three terms is 24; that is, the sum is equivalent to

$$\frac{28}{24} - \frac{16}{24} + \frac{9}{24} = \frac{21}{24} = \frac{7}{8}$$

When a common denominator for all three terms is difficult to spot it may be easier to take the terms in pairs. For the last example, summing the first two terms first gives

$$\frac{7}{6} - \frac{2}{3} + \frac{3}{8} = \frac{7}{6} - \frac{4}{6} + \frac{3}{8} = \frac{3}{6} + \frac{3}{8} = \frac{1}{2} + \frac{3}{8} = \frac{4}{8} + \frac{3}{8} = \frac{7}{8}$$

Check this

Evaluate $\dfrac{7}{168} - \dfrac{2}{3} - \dfrac{2}{7}$

$$= \frac{7}{168} - \frac{112}{168} - \frac{2}{7} = \frac{-105}{168} - \frac{2}{7} = -\frac{35}{56} - \frac{2}{7}$$

$$= -\frac{35}{56} - \frac{16}{56} = \frac{-51}{56}$$

We can also add and subtract fractions that include symbols. The method is exactly the same – convert each fraction into an equivalent fraction so that all the denominators are the same.

Let's try

$$\frac{2}{y} + \frac{3}{2y}$$

Both fractions have an equivalent fraction with $2y$ as the denominator; that is, $2y$ can be used as a common denominator. The sum becomes

$$\frac{2 \times 2}{y \times 2} + \frac{3}{2y} = \frac{4}{2y} + \frac{3}{2y} = \frac{7}{2y}$$

Check these

$$\frac{y}{2x} + \frac{y}{x}$$

Both terms can be represented with a common denominator of $2x$ to give

$$\frac{y}{2x} + \frac{2y}{2x} = \frac{3y}{2x}$$

$$\frac{a}{5b} + \frac{a}{2b}$$

A common denominator is 10b. Both terms need rewriting to give

$$\frac{2a}{10b} + \frac{5a}{10b} = \frac{7a}{10b}$$

$$\frac{5pq}{rs} + \frac{2p}{s}$$

A common denominator is rs, so the sum becomes

$$\frac{5pq}{rs} + \frac{2pr}{rs} = \frac{5pq + 2pr}{rs}$$

Notice that the terms in the numerator, 5pq and 2pr, cannot be collected together as they are not multiples of the same thing.

Bottles of wine cost $\$w$ at an off-licence. A friend goes in and buys 4 bottles between 5 of us for a party on Friday night, and another friend goes in and buys 3 bottles between 4 of us for another party on Saturday night. If I pay my share, write down and simplify an expression for the amount I will spend on wine this weekend.

I spend $\$\frac{4w}{5}$ for Friday night and $\$\frac{3w}{4}$ for Saturday, so the total is

$$\$\frac{4w}{5} + \$\frac{3w}{4}$$

which can be put over a common denominator of 20 to give

$$\$\frac{16w}{20} + \frac{15w}{20} = \$\frac{31w}{20}$$

WORK CARD 2

1. Calculate the following, expressing your result as a single fraction:

   a. $\frac{1}{2} + \frac{3}{8}$ **b.** $\frac{3}{5} - \frac{2}{7}$ **c.** $\frac{6}{32} + \frac{3}{8}$ **d.** $2 + \frac{5}{7}$

2. What is the lowest common denominator if two fractions have denominators of

   a. 6 and 9?

   b. 50 and 20?

   c. 32 and 48?

   d. 6 and 77?

   e. 8, 12 and 18?

   f. 4a and 6b?

3. Evaluate:

   a. $\dfrac{3}{128} + \dfrac{5}{96}$ b. $\dfrac{5}{6} - \dfrac{8}{27}$

4. Evaluate:

   a. $\dfrac{3}{42} - \dfrac{3}{56} + \dfrac{1}{7}$ b. $-\dfrac{1}{2} + \dfrac{2}{196} - \dfrac{3}{42}$

5. Simplify:

   a. $\dfrac{n}{3} + \dfrac{n}{6}$ b. $\dfrac{5}{y} - \dfrac{2}{3y}$ c. $\dfrac{2}{3m} + \dfrac{n}{2m}$ d. $\dfrac{b}{3b} - \dfrac{c}{ab}$

Solutions:

1. a. $\dfrac{7}{8}$ b. $\dfrac{11}{35}$ c. $\dfrac{18}{32} = \dfrac{9}{16}$ d. 2 is $\dfrac{2}{1}$, so a common denominator of $\dfrac{2}{1} + \dfrac{5}{7}$ is 7

   so the sum becomes $\dfrac{14}{7} + \dfrac{5}{7} = \dfrac{19}{7}$

2. a. 18 b. 100 c. 96 d. 462 e. 72 f. $12ab$

3. a. $\dfrac{29}{384}$ b. $\dfrac{29}{54}$

4. a. $\dfrac{9}{56}$ b. $\dfrac{-55}{98}$

5. a. $\dfrac{3n}{6}$ which cancels to $\dfrac{n}{2}$ b. $\dfrac{13}{3y}$ c. $\dfrac{4+3n}{6m}$ d. $\dfrac{ab-3c}{3ab}$

1. Calculate a. $\dfrac{1}{4} + \dfrac{3}{5}$ b. $\dfrac{5}{72} - \dfrac{7}{12}$

2. If two fractions have the following denominators, what is their lowest common denominator?

   a. 6 and 11

   b. 15 and 7

   c. 16 and 24

   d. 28 and 49

   e. 14 and 329

3. Calculate

   a. $\dfrac{6}{32} + \dfrac{5}{48}$ b. $\dfrac{3}{14} - \dfrac{5}{329}$ c. $\dfrac{6}{32} + \dfrac{7}{48} - \dfrac{5}{6}$

4. Calculate:

a. $\dfrac{2}{3} + \dfrac{5}{12} - \dfrac{1}{6}$ b. $\dfrac{2}{7} + \dfrac{6}{77} - \dfrac{3}{11}$ c. $\dfrac{7}{15} + \dfrac{1}{5} - \dfrac{1}{4}$

5. Simplify:

a. $\dfrac{x}{2} + \dfrac{x}{5}$ b. $\dfrac{7}{3x} - \dfrac{2}{6x}$ c. $\dfrac{a}{2n} + \dfrac{2a}{3n}$ d. $\dfrac{5}{3p} - \dfrac{2}{4p}$

3 Multiplying and dividing fractions

Test box 3

Calculate the following:

$$4 \times \dfrac{2}{7}, \quad \dfrac{2}{3} \times \dfrac{4}{5}, \quad \dfrac{a}{3} \times \dfrac{b}{3c}, \quad \dfrac{2}{7} \times \dfrac{1}{10} \times \dfrac{5}{2}, \quad \dfrac{6}{25} \div \dfrac{5}{8}, \quad \dfrac{4p}{r} \div \dfrac{2s}{r}, \quad \dfrac{\frac{4}{77}}{\frac{2}{11}}$$

Solutions:

$$\dfrac{8}{7}, \quad \dfrac{8}{15}, \quad \dfrac{ab}{9c}, \quad \dfrac{1}{14}, \quad \dfrac{48}{125}, \quad \dfrac{2p}{s}, \quad \dfrac{2}{7}$$

Solve the following without using a calculator, cancelling where possible to make the calculations easier:

$$\dfrac{352}{18} \times \dfrac{6}{22}, \quad \dfrac{100}{34} \times \dfrac{170}{7} \times \dfrac{49}{5}, \quad \dfrac{8rp}{3q} \times \dfrac{9}{2r}, \quad \dfrac{108}{39} \div \dfrac{18}{33}, \quad \dfrac{xy}{2z} \div \dfrac{6x}{3z}$$

Solutions:

$$\dfrac{16}{3}, \quad 700, \quad \dfrac{12p}{q}, \quad \dfrac{66}{13}, \quad \dfrac{y}{4}$$

Multiplying fractions

Consider $3 \times \frac{2}{7}$. Remember that the fraction $\frac{2}{7}$ represents *two* parts of size one seventh. Three times $\frac{2}{7}$ will therefore be *six* parts of size one seventh, and so

$$3 \times \dfrac{2}{7} = \dfrac{6}{7}$$

That is, to multiply a fraction by 3 we merely multiply the numerator by 3.

In general, to multiply a fraction by a number we multiply the numerator by the number.

$$5 \times \frac{2}{3} = \frac{10}{3} \quad \text{and} \quad -2 \times \frac{4}{9} = \frac{-8}{9}$$

This multiplication works for symbols as well. For instance,

$$a \times \frac{3}{2} = \frac{3a}{2} \quad \text{and} \quad ab\frac{c}{3} = \frac{abc}{3}$$

To multiply *two* fractions together we multiply the denominators together, and multiply the numerators together. So, for instance,

$$\frac{2}{3} \times \frac{3}{5} = \frac{2 \times 3}{3 \times 5} = \frac{6}{15}$$

A general way of expressing this rule for multiplying fractions is

$$\frac{a}{b} \times \frac{c}{d} = \frac{ac}{bd}$$

where *a*, *b*, *c* and *d* can be any numbers or symbols.

If you want to see why this works read on; otherwise, rejoin us at the next **Check these**.

Consider a square metre of carpet. We can divide it into thirds or fifths as shown below and represent $\frac{2}{3}$ or $\frac{3}{5}$ of the square metre by a shaded area:

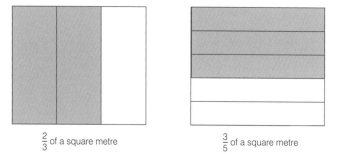

$\frac{2}{3}$ of a square metre $\frac{3}{5}$ of a square metre

To multiply $3 \times \frac{3}{5}$ we need to take three times the area $\frac{3}{5}$. So, to multiply $\frac{2}{3} \times \frac{3}{5}$ we need to take $\frac{2}{3}$ times the area $\frac{3}{5}$. Another way of saying this is $\frac{2}{3}$ *of* $\frac{3}{5}$. In fact, *of* is just another way of saying 'times' or 'multiplied by' for fractions. To represent $\frac{2}{3}$ of $\frac{3}{5}$ superimpose the two diagrams above to get a square divided into $3 \times 5 = 15$ small rectangles each of area $\frac{1}{15}$, as shown below:

$\frac{2}{3}$ of the original area of $\frac{3}{5}$ (or equivalently $\frac{3}{5}$ of the area of $\frac{2}{3}$) is represented by the dark shaded area. It is made up of six of the small rectangles and so measures $\frac{6}{15}$ of a square metre.

Notice that the denominator of our answer, 15, comes from the total number of small rectangles, which, as one square was divided into 3 and the other into 5, was the product of the denominators of the two fractions to be multiplied. Also, the numerator of the answer, 6, is the number of small rectangles in the overlap and is therefore the product of the numerators of the fractions.

Check these

$$\frac{5}{9} \times \frac{2}{4} = \frac{10}{36} = \frac{5}{18}$$

$$\frac{-3}{2} \times \frac{5}{7} = \frac{-15}{14}$$

Try the following multiplications, which involve symbols.

Check these

$$\frac{2}{y} \times \frac{z}{3} = \frac{2z}{3y}$$

$$\frac{10}{p} \times \frac{s}{r} = \frac{10s}{pr}$$

$$\frac{pq}{r} \times \frac{r}{2s} = \frac{pqr}{2rs}$$

Cancelling fractions

Some multiplications are equivalent to each other. For instance

$$\frac{5}{9} \times \frac{2}{4} \quad \text{is the same as} \quad \frac{2}{9} \times \frac{5}{4}$$

because they are

$$\frac{5 \times 2}{9 \times 4} \quad \text{and} \quad \frac{2 \times 5}{9 \times 4}$$

respectively and 2×5 is the same as 5×2. In the same way,

$$\frac{2}{3} \times \frac{7}{4} \quad \text{is the same as} \quad \frac{2}{4} \times \frac{7}{3}$$

In general, when fractions are multiplied the answer is the same as long as the numbers multiplied together 'on the top' are the same, and the numbers multiplied together 'on the bottom' are the same. That is

$$\frac{2}{9} \times \frac{5}{3} \quad \text{is the same as} \quad \frac{5}{9} \times \frac{2}{3}$$

as they both have a 5 and a 2 in the numerators and a 9 and a 3 in the denominators.

A consequence of this is that we can 'cancel' any component in a denominator of a multiplication with any component in a numerator. For example, when calculating

$$\frac{3}{5} \times \frac{11}{9}$$

we can cancel the 3 with the 9 to give

$$\frac{3^{1}}{5} \times \frac{11}{9_{3}} = \frac{1}{5} \times \frac{11}{3} = \frac{11}{15}$$

Check these

To calculate

$$\frac{8}{5} \times \frac{15}{7}$$

our working would be

$$\frac{8}{5_{1}} \times \frac{15^{3}}{7} = \frac{8 \times 3}{1 \times 7} = \frac{24}{7}$$

$$\frac{9}{10} \times \frac{25}{18} = \frac{9}{10_{2}} \times \frac{25^{5}}{18} = \frac{9^{1}}{10_{2}} \times \frac{25^{5}}{18_{2}} = \frac{1 \times 5}{2 \times 2} = \frac{5}{4}$$

Whilst this cancelling is useful when performing calculations by hand, our real reason for learning it is so that we can simplify expressions that contain symbols.

Check these

$$\frac{8}{p} \times \frac{r}{64} \quad \text{can be simplified to} \quad \frac{8^{1}}{p} \times \frac{r}{64_{8}} = \frac{r}{8p}$$

$$\frac{a}{bc} \times \frac{b}{ac}$$

First notice that the *a*s cancel, so we can cross them out as follows.

$$\frac{\cancel{a}}{bc} \times \frac{b}{\cancel{a}c} \quad \text{and rewrite as} \quad \frac{1}{bc} \times \frac{b}{c}$$

The *b*s in this expression can be cancelled, so we cross them out as in

$$\frac{1}{\cancel{b}c} \times \frac{\cancel{b}}{c} = \frac{1}{c} \times \frac{1}{c} = \frac{1}{c^{2}}$$

We could perform all our working at one go and write

$$\frac{a}{bc} \times \frac{b}{ac} = \frac{1}{c} \times \frac{1}{c} = \frac{1}{c^2}$$

Division of fractions

Consider $\frac{5}{7} \div 3$. Suppose we have 5 square metres of carpet, illustrated below. To obtain $\frac{5}{7}$ of a metre we would divide this into 7 equal pieces. We could then take any one of these $\frac{5}{7}$ m pieces and divide it into 3 as shown below.

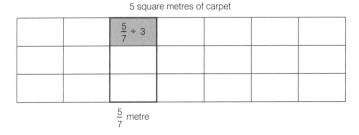

5 square metres of carpet

$\frac{5}{7} \div 3$

$\frac{5}{7}$ metre

The original 5 square metres has now been divided into $21 = 7 \times 3$ pieces, and so the area we require is $\frac{5}{21}$ square metres. To calculate $\frac{5}{7} \div 3$ we seem to have *multiplied* the denominator of $\frac{5}{7}$ by 3; that is

$$\frac{5}{7} \div 3 = \frac{5}{7 \times 3} = \frac{5}{21}$$

In general, to *divide* a fraction by a number we *multiply the denominator* by that number.

Check these

$$\frac{9}{2} \div 3 = \frac{9}{2 \times 3} = \frac{9}{6} = \frac{3}{2}$$

$$\frac{3}{4} \div 12 = \frac{3}{4 \times 12} = \frac{3}{48} = \frac{1}{16}$$

Now consider dividing by a fraction. Suppose we want $\frac{2}{3} \div \frac{1}{4}$. The rule is to turn the fraction upside-down and then multiply by it. For instance,

$$\frac{2}{3} \div \frac{3}{8} = \frac{2}{3} \times \frac{8}{3} = \frac{2 \times 8}{3 \times 3} = \frac{16}{9}$$

We can express this rule using symbols as

$$\frac{a}{b} \div \frac{c}{d} = \frac{a}{b} \times \frac{d}{c}$$

The fraction obtained by turning a fraction upside-down is called the *reciprocal* of the fraction. For instance $\frac{8}{3}$ is the reciprocal of $\frac{3}{8}$ and vice versa. Notice that two fractions that are the reciprocals of each other multiply to produce 1.

This rule also includes the case considered earlier of dividing a fraction by a whole number. For instance, for $\frac{5}{7} \div 3$, the reciprocal of 3 is $\frac{1}{3}$, so the answer is

$$\frac{5}{7} \times \frac{1}{3} = \frac{5 \times 1}{7 \times 3} = \frac{5}{21}$$

If you want to know why this rule works read on; otherwise, join us at the next **Check these**.

First consider $\frac{2}{3} \div \frac{1}{4}$. This is asking: how many quarters are there in two thirds? We reason as follows. In a unit there are 4 quarters, so in $\frac{2}{3}$ of a unit there are $\frac{2}{3} \times 4$ quarters. To *divide* by $\frac{1}{4}$ we seem to have *multiplied* by 4. Now consider $\frac{2}{3} \div \frac{3}{8}$ from above. This means how many $\frac{3}{8}$ths are there in $\frac{2}{3}$? By similar reasoning, there are 8 eighths in a unit, but these need grouping into sets of 3, so there are $\frac{8}{3}$ three eighths in a unit and $\frac{2}{3} \times \frac{8}{3}$ three eighths in two thirds. Instead of dividing by $\frac{3}{8}$ we have multiplied by $\frac{8}{3}$, so, as stated above, the rule for dividing by a fraction is to *multiply* by the *reciprocal* of the fraction.

Check these

Calculate $\dfrac{24}{35} \div \dfrac{2}{3} = \dfrac{24}{35} \times \dfrac{3}{2} = \dfrac{24^{12}}{35} \times \dfrac{3}{2_1} = \dfrac{36}{35}$

Try $\dfrac{18}{5} \div \dfrac{8}{7} = \dfrac{18}{5} \times \dfrac{7}{8} = \dfrac{18 \times 7}{5 \times 8} = \dfrac{18^9 \times 7}{5 \times 8_4} = \dfrac{63}{20}$

As ever, the same method applies when dividing by a fraction that contains symbols. Just turn the fraction upside-down and multiply.

Check these

$$\frac{2a}{3} \div \frac{4a}{9} = \frac{2a}{3} \times \frac{9}{4a}$$

Now, we perform the multiplication as usual, cancelling if it helps to simplify the expression. Continuing gives

$$\frac{2a}{3} \times \frac{9}{4_2 a} = \frac{9}{3 \times 2} = \frac{9}{6} = \frac{3}{2}$$

$$\frac{5}{p} \div \frac{10r}{pq} = \frac{5}{p} \times \frac{pq}{10r} = \frac{5q}{10r} = \frac{q}{2r}$$

We can summarise the work of this section using both words and symbols.

To multiply fractions: multiply both denominators together, and both numerators. So

$$\frac{a}{b} \times \frac{c}{d} = \frac{ac}{bd}$$

e.g.

$$\frac{2}{3} \times \frac{8}{9} = \frac{16}{27}$$

Cancel any component of the numerator with any component of the denominator to make the calculations easier, e.g.

$$\frac{2}{3} \times \frac{9}{8} = \frac{2^1}{3_1} \times \frac{9^3}{8_4} = \frac{3}{4}$$

or

$$\frac{2a}{p} \times \frac{p}{3a} = \frac{2}{3}$$

To divide fractions: multiply by the reciprocal. So,

$$\frac{a}{b} \div \frac{c}{d} = \frac{a}{b} \times \frac{d}{c} = \frac{ad}{bc}$$

e.g.

$$\frac{2}{3} \div \frac{9}{7} = \frac{2}{3} \times \frac{7}{9} = \frac{14}{27}$$

1. Multiply:

   a. $\dfrac{13}{3} \times \dfrac{2}{3}$　b. $\dfrac{5}{2} \times \dfrac{3}{7}$　c. $\dfrac{7}{9} \times \dfrac{2}{7}$　d. $\dfrac{3}{11} \times \dfrac{2}{11}$

2. Multiply the following using cancelling to simplify the calculations where possible:

   a. $\dfrac{13}{3} \times \dfrac{20}{39}$　b. $\dfrac{12}{5} \times \dfrac{25}{7}$　c. $\dfrac{6}{7} \times \dfrac{49}{4}$　d. $\dfrac{3}{5} \times \dfrac{15}{7} \times \dfrac{21}{-9}$　e. $\dfrac{100}{3} \times \dfrac{-18}{2} \times \dfrac{5}{3}$

3. Multiply the following, simplifying the resulting expression where possible:

   a. $\dfrac{p}{q} \times \dfrac{q}{r}$　b. $\dfrac{rst}{3} \times \dfrac{3}{5rt}$　c. $\dfrac{m}{np} \times \dfrac{p}{qr} \times \dfrac{q}{m}$　d. $ab\left(\dfrac{d}{2b}\right)$

4. Calculate the following:

   a. $\dfrac{2}{5} \div 3$　b. $\dfrac{3}{7} \div 2$　c. $\dfrac{3}{8} \div (-2)$

5. Evaluate:

   a. $\dfrac{3}{4} \div \dfrac{1}{8}$　b. $\dfrac{7}{9} \div \dfrac{2}{3}$　c. $\dfrac{-33}{2} \div \dfrac{11}{6}$　d. $\dfrac{5}{2} \times \dfrac{3}{10} \div \dfrac{20}{7}$

WORK CARD 3 (CONTINUED)

6. Simplify:

   a. $\dfrac{ab}{cd} \div b$ b. $\dfrac{f}{g} \div \dfrac{2h}{f}$ c. $m \times \dfrac{n}{m} \div 3n$

Solutions:

1. a. $\dfrac{26}{9}$ b. $\dfrac{15}{14}$ c. $\dfrac{14}{63} = \dfrac{2}{9}$ d. $\dfrac{6}{121}$

2. a. $\dfrac{20}{9}$ b. $\dfrac{60}{7}$ c. $\dfrac{21}{2}$ d. -3 e. -500

3. a. $\dfrac{p}{r}$ b. $\dfrac{s}{5}$ c. $\dfrac{1}{nr}$ d. $\dfrac{ad}{2}$

4. a. $\dfrac{2}{15}$ b. $\dfrac{3}{14}$ c. $\dfrac{3}{-16}$

5. a. 6 b. $\dfrac{7}{6}$ c. -9 d. $\dfrac{21}{80}$

6. a. $\dfrac{a}{cd}$ b. $\dfrac{f^2}{2gh}$ c. Work from left to right: $m \times \dfrac{n}{m} \div 3n = n \div 3n = n \times \dfrac{1}{3n} = \dfrac{1}{3}$

ASSESSMENT 3

1. Multiply a. $\dfrac{1}{2} \times \dfrac{1}{6}$ b. $\dfrac{9}{16} \times \dfrac{13}{2}$ c. $\dfrac{2}{3} \times \dfrac{5}{8}$

2. Calculate the following, cancelling where possible:

   a. $\dfrac{15}{7} \times \dfrac{2}{5}$ b. $\dfrac{7}{2} \times \dfrac{3}{49}$ c. $\dfrac{8}{9} \times \dfrac{3}{4}$ d. $\dfrac{5}{49} \times \dfrac{2}{50} \times \dfrac{7}{8}$ e. $\dfrac{-10}{9} \times \dfrac{3}{70} \times \dfrac{81}{6}$

3. Multiply the following, simplifying your answer where possible:

   a. $\dfrac{a}{2b} \times \dfrac{10}{3a}$ b. $3 \times \dfrac{m}{9}$ c. $\dfrac{5n}{8q} \times \dfrac{6q}{7n}$ d. $\dfrac{100q}{49np} \times \dfrac{70mn}{200qm}$

4. Evaluate:

   a. $\dfrac{3}{20} \div \dfrac{7}{40}$ b. $\dfrac{21}{5} \div \dfrac{7}{10}$ c. $\dfrac{8}{7} \div \dfrac{36}{2} \times \dfrac{8}{9}$ d. $\dfrac{7}{40} \times \dfrac{8}{9} \div \dfrac{6}{27}$

5. Simplify the following:

   a. $\dfrac{RP}{100} \div \dfrac{P}{400}$ b. $100 \times \dfrac{R}{350} \div \dfrac{R}{7}$ c. $ab \div \dfrac{b}{c}$

4 **Putting it all together – and a note on percentages**

Test box 4

Evaluate or simplify the following:

$$(2 + 10)\frac{5}{6} \div \frac{3}{15} \qquad (2ab + ab) \times \frac{c}{d} \div \frac{b}{d}$$

Calculate 7% of £350 without using a calculator.

If you are offered a discount of 15% on a restaurant meal priced at £25, how much will you actually pay?

Solutions: 50, $3ac$, £24.50, £21.25

You can now add, subtract, multiply and divide fractions. In the following examples we put these all together. Remember that the order in which we perform operations is

Brackets first
Multiply and divide (from left to right)
Add and subtract (from left to right).

Check these

Evaluate the following, simplifying where possible to save time:

$$\left(\frac{7}{8} - \frac{2}{3}\right) \times \frac{-1}{4} \div \frac{5}{6}$$

We calculate the brackets first, so

$$= \left(\frac{21}{24} - \frac{16}{24}\right) \times \frac{-1}{4} \div \frac{5}{6}$$

$$= \frac{5}{24} \times \frac{-1}{4} \div \frac{5}{6} = \frac{-5}{96} \div \frac{5}{6} = \frac{-\overset{-1}{5} \times \overset{}{6}}{\underset{16}{96} \times \overset{}{5}} = \frac{-1}{16}$$

$$8a \div \left(\frac{32}{a} \times 2a\right)$$

We must evaluate the bracket first. In

$$\frac{32}{a} \times 2a$$

the as cancel to give 64, so we have

$$8a \div 64 = \frac{8a}{64} = \frac{a}{8}$$

$$(3a + a) \times \frac{c}{2ab}$$

Evaluating the brackets first gives

$$4a \cdot \frac{c}{2ab} = \frac{2c}{b}$$

Percentages

Percentages are just hundredths so, for instance, five per cent of £80 is just $\frac{5}{100}$ of 80. Remembering that 'of' means the same as 'times' where fractions are concerned, this is $\frac{5}{100} \times 80$. We can calculate this easily by hand as it cancels nicely to

$$\frac{5}{100_{10}} \times 80^8 = \frac{5 \times 8}{10_2} = £4$$

Check these

Calculate 6% of £300.

$$\frac{6}{100} \times 300 = 6 \times 3 = £18$$

A clothes shop advertises that goods are on offer at 45% of the normal price. You have had your eye on a particular pair of jeans, full price £50, for some time. What do you expect to pay?

$$\frac{45}{100} \times 50 = \frac{45}{2} \times 1 = £22.50$$

When you buy a new CD player you receive a discount of 12.5% as you are a student. The list price is £240. What do you pay?

$$\frac{87.5}{100} \times 240 = \frac{87.5}{5} \times 12 = \frac{35}{2} \times 12 = 35 \times 6 = £210$$

To find out what percentage one number is of another we just divide the first number by the second to give a fraction and, to express it in hundredths, multiply by 100. In symbols,

$$a \text{ is } \frac{a}{b} \times 100 \text{ per cent of } b$$

Check this

What percentage is $25 of $400?

Solution:
The fraction is $\frac{25}{400}$, so the percentage required is $\frac{25}{400} \times 100$. This cancels nicely as

$$\frac{25}{400_4} \times 100 = \frac{25}{4} = 6.25\%$$

An accountant's salary increases from £24,000 to £25,440 in the annual pay round. What percentage increase is this?

The increase is £1440, so the fraction by which her salary increases is $\frac{1440}{24,000}$, which is

$$\frac{1440}{24,000} \times 100 = 6 \text{ per cent.}$$

WORK CARD 4

1. Simplify and evaluate the following:

    a. $\dfrac{5}{56} \div \left(\dfrac{3}{8} + \dfrac{3}{7}\right)$ b. $\dfrac{5}{13} \times \dfrac{2}{3} - \dfrac{13}{39}$ c. $\left(\dfrac{12}{25} \div \dfrac{7}{50}\right) \times \left(\dfrac{5}{12} - \dfrac{7}{16}\right)$

2. Simplify:

    a. $ab \times \dfrac{c}{d} \div \dfrac{b}{d}$ b. $\left(\dfrac{p}{q} + \dfrac{p}{2q}\right)\left(\dfrac{10}{6p}\right)$

3. Calculate **a.** 10% of 120; **b.** 36% of 850; **c.** 22.5% of 360 *by hand*.

4. A store buys a batch of sun loungers for £24 each. It marks them up (increases the price) by 12% for resale. What is the retail price? (Do not use a calculator.)

5. Last year a factory's labour costs were £325,000, whereas this year they have increased to £338,000. What percentage increase is this? (Do not use a calculator.)

Solutions:

1. **a.** $\dfrac{1}{9}$ **b.** $\dfrac{-1}{13}$ **c.** $\dfrac{-1}{14}$

2. **a.** ac **b.** $\dfrac{5}{2q}$

3. **a.** 12   **b.** 306   **c.** 81

4. £26.88

5. 4%

ASSESSMENT 4

1. Simplify and evaluate:

   a. $\dfrac{81}{27} \div 3$ b. $\dfrac{7}{3} + \dfrac{-4}{11} \div \dfrac{5}{44}$ c. $1 + \left(\dfrac{36}{45} \times \dfrac{5}{12}\right) \div \dfrac{2}{3}$ d. $\dfrac{4}{7} + \dfrac{6 \times 21}{2 \times 14}$

2. Simplify where possible:

   a. $\dfrac{5}{a}\left(\dfrac{a}{b}+\dfrac{2a}{3b}\right)$ b. $\left(\dfrac{1}{q}+\dfrac{1}{p}\right)\times pq$

3. As a student you receive a 24% discount on tickets to a concert. The full ticket price is £18. How much do you pay?

4. Employees of an electronics company receive a 15% discount on goods purchased. How much must they pay for a washing machine which retails at £420 and a dish-washer which normally costs £360?

5. A meal should have cost Federica £16 but she only pays £13.60 as she has a student discount card. What percentage discount has she received?

5 Expanding brackets

Test box 5

Evaluate the following by expanding the brackets:

   $12 \times (30 - 4)$ $(7000 + 35) \div 7$

Simplify the following:

   $\dfrac{pqr - 2pq}{pq}$ $w(x + y) - 2xw$

Expand the following:

   $(15 - a)(a + b)$ $\dfrac{b}{2}\left(2c - \dfrac{3}{b}\right)$

Solutions:

   $12 \times 30 - 12 \times 4 = 360 - 48 = 312$

   $\dfrac{7000}{7} + \dfrac{35}{7} = 1000 + 5 = 1005$

   $r - 2$, $yw - xw$, $15a + 15b - a^2 - ab$, $bc - \dfrac{3}{2}$

When we model real relationships using symbols we often obtain complicated expressions. It is often possible, however, to simplify these; for example, by cancelling. Another way that may help to simplify an expression is to *expand* or *multiply out the brackets*.

Why expand brackets?

Sometimes it is useful to be able to rewrite an expression that contains brackets, *without* the brackets. For example, consider the expression

$$2ab - 3(ab + 2)$$

We will learn shortly that an equivalent expression that does *not* have brackets is $2ab - 3ab - 6$. Now there are no brackets, the $2ab$ and the $3ab$ terms can be collected together, so the expression simplifies to $-ab - 6$.

As another example, let's take

$$\frac{1}{pq}(5pqr + 15pq)$$

If we retain the brackets this expression cannot be simplified further as the two terms inside the brackets cannot be collected together. However, the equivalent expression *without* the brackets is

$$\frac{1}{pq} \cdot 5pqr + \frac{1}{pq} \cdot 15pq$$

(remember that · means multiply). A glance at each term of this equation reveals that we can do a lot of cancelling. The first term becomes just $5r$ and the second is 15. So our original, complicated expression boils down to just $5r + 15$.

This technique of removing of the brackets is called *expanding* or *multiplying out* the brackets.

Expanding brackets: a(b + c)

It is easiest to describe the rules for expanding brackets using symbols. In the rule below, a, b, and c each represent any number, symbol or expression.

$$a(b + c) = ab + ac$$

We hope that you can see why the rule works. The bracket contains the sum of two things, $b + c$. The whole sum $(b + c)$ is then multiplied by a, so this is equivalent to b multiplied by a *as well as* c multiplied by a.

We can show this pictorially as follows. Consider the expression $3(2 + 4)$. The area of the strip below represents $2 + 4$:

2	4

$3(2 + 4)$ is therefore represented by the area of 3 such strips as shown below:

2	4
2	4
2	4

Notice that the '2' section has been repeated 3 times, as has the '4' section, so the area of the 3 strips is equivalent to $3 \times 2 + 3 \times 4$.

Note that $(b + c)a$ is just the same as $a(b + c)$ because the order in which we multiply doesn't matter.

We will now expand the brackets in some examples.

Check these

$2(p + q) = 2p + 2q$

$I(1 + R) = I + IR$

$2a(b + c) = 2ab + 2ac$

$-1(m + n) = -m - n$

$(1000 - 2) \times 40 = 40\,000 - 80 = 39\,920$. (Notice that this would give us a quick way of calculating 998×40 by hand.)

And now some examples in which expanding the brackets enables us to simplify an expression.

Check these

$x(y + z) - xy = xy + xz - xy = xz$

$\dfrac{f(g + h) - fh}{g} = \dfrac{fg + fh - fh}{g} = \dfrac{fg}{g} = f$

$2(r + s + t) - 2(r + s)$. Yes, the rule extends to brackets with more than 2 terms in the sum, so the expression becomes $2r + 2s + 2t - 2r - 2s = 2t$.

$\left(\dfrac{25}{8} + \dfrac{7}{64}\right) \times 8 = \dfrac{25 \times 8}{8} + \dfrac{7 \times 8}{64}$

and both terms cancel nicely to give

$25 + \dfrac{7}{8} = \dfrac{207}{8}$

A warning. Do not confuse $a(bc)$ with $a(b + c)$. In $a(bc)$, b and c are *multiplied* together, so the brackets are superfluous as the order in which we multiply doesn't matter; that is, $a(bc) = abc$.

There are two special cases of the expanding brackets rule that you will encounter a lot.

Consider $a + (b + c)$. This is the same as $a + 1(b + c)$, so the rule can be applied to $1(b + c)$ to give just $a + b + c$. This is hardly a surprise: something plus the sum of two other things is the sum of all three things. For example, verify that

$$10 + (5 + 2) = 10 + 5 + 2.$$

In the same way $a - (b + c)$ is exactly the same as $a + (-1)(b + c)$, which is $a - b - c$ when the brackets are expanded. That is, a minus the sum of b and c, is the same as a minus b, minus c. For example, verify that $100 - (50 + 30) = 100 - 50 - 30$.

Check these

Expand the brackets and simplify the following:

$a - (a + y)$

$a - (-a - y)$

Solutions: $-y$ and $2a + y$.

Expanding brackets: $(b + c)/a$

We can divide a sum in a bracket in a similar way. The rule is that

$$(b + c) \div a = \frac{b}{a} + \frac{c}{a}$$

Notice that every term in the bracket must be divided by a. Alternatively we could write this as

$$\frac{b + c}{a} = \frac{b}{a} + \frac{c}{a}$$

This often enables us to cancel.

Check these

$$(p + 2pq) \div p = \frac{p}{p} + \frac{2pq}{p} = 1 + 2q$$

$$\frac{ab + ac}{a} = \frac{ab}{a} + \frac{ac}{a} = b + c$$

$$\frac{700 - 7}{7} = \frac{700}{7} - \frac{7}{7} = 100 - 1 = 99$$

Notice that here we have avoided the 'nastier' division $\frac{693}{7}$.

$$(20mn - 10m) \div 5m = \frac{20mn}{5m} - \frac{10m}{5m} = 4n - 2$$

Care must be taken not to confuse

$$\frac{b + c}{a} \quad \text{with} \quad \frac{bc}{a}$$

Also notice that

$$\frac{a + b}{a} = 1 + \frac{b}{a}$$

whereas

$$\frac{ab}{a} = b$$

Products of brackets: $(a + b)(c + d)$

We don't really need a new rule to do this: $(a + b)(c + d)$ means that each term in $(a + b)$ must be multiplied by $(c + d)$; that is,

$$(a + b)(c + d) = a(c + d) + b(c + d)$$

which in turn is

$$= ac + ad + bc + bd.$$

So

$$(a + b)(c + d) = ac + ad + bc + bd.$$

Notice that every term in the first bracket is multiplied by *every* term in the second and then these are added up. For example,

$$(x - 2)(y + 1) = xy + x - 2y - 2.$$

As each bracket has two terms there will be four terms when we multiply out, although it may be possible to collect some terms together at the end.

We can demonstrate that the rule works by using numbers. Consider $(6 + 2) \times (4 - 5)$. This expands to

$$6 \times 4 + 6 \times (-5) + 2 \times 4 + 2 \times (-5) = 24 - 30 + 8 - 10$$
$$= -8$$

This is the correct result because $6 + 2 = 8$ and $4 - 5 = -1$, which multiply together to give -8.

Check these

Calculate the following by expanding the brackets:

$(4 - 6) \times (10 - 2) = 40 - 8 - 60 + 12 = -16$

$(-5 + 2) \times (3 + 1) = -15 - 5 + 6 + 2 = -12$

$(-2 - 2) \times (-3 - 4) = 6 + 8 + 6 + 8 = 28$

$(100 + 4) \times (10 + 3) = 1000 + 300 + 40 + 12 = 1352.$

Notice that the last example multiplies 104 by 13. If you did this by long multiplication you would calculate

$$
\begin{array}{r}
104 \times \\
13 \\
\hline
1000 \\
300 \\
40 \\
12 \\
\hline
1352
\end{array}
$$

so each step of the multiplication corresponds exactly to a term in the expansion.

Check these

Multiply out the following:

$(z + 1)(z - 3) = z^2 - 3z + z - 3 = z^2 - 2z - 3$

$(2p - 1)(p + q) = 2p^2 + 2pq - p - q$

$(a + b)(a - b) = a^2 - ab + ab - b^2 = a^2 - b^2.$

This is often useful the other way round; that is, $a^2 - b^2 = (a + b)(a - b)$ when it is known as the 'difference between two squares'. For example, $17^2 - 15^2 = (17 + 15)(17 - 15) = 32 \times 2 = 64$.

We summarise the work of this section as follows:

Expanding brackets

$a(b + c) = ab + ac$

$(b + c) \div a$, or equivalently $\dfrac{b+c}{a} = \dfrac{b}{a} + \dfrac{c}{a}$

$(a + b)(c + d) = ac + ad + bc + bd$

i.e. multiply each term in the first bracket by each term in the second bracket and add all these.

WORK CARD 5

1. Evaluate by multiplying out the brackets:
   a. $3 \times (1000 - 3)$ b. $(120 + 1) \times 12$ c. $(300 - 11) \times 11$

2. Simplify where possible:
   a. $(p + q)r - qr$ b. $2q - 2(5p + 3q)$ c. $mn - (6 - mn)$ d. $\dfrac{5}{q}\left(\dfrac{2q}{5} - \dfrac{aq}{10}\right)$

3. Evaluate, by removing the brackets first:
   a. $5 - (6 + 2)$ b. $5 - (6 - 2)$ c. $(4 - 2) - (-5 + 2)$ d. $10 - (3 - 2 + 1)$

4. Simplify:
   a. $ab - (bc - ab)$ b. $pqr - (2 + pqr)$ c. $(ab - b) - (ab + b)$

5. Evaluate *without* explicitly evaluating the brackets:
   a. $(600 - 6) \div 6$ b. $\dfrac{770 + 77}{11}$ c. $120 \div (10 + 12)$

6. Simplify:
   a. $\dfrac{5a + 3b}{ab}$ b. $\dfrac{5a \times 3b}{ab}$ c. $\dfrac{3pq + 6pqr}{pq}$ d. $(rs - 2s + sq) \div s$

7. Calculate the following quickly by expressing one of the terms as an addition or subtraction. For example, in **a.** calculate $(2100 + 42) \div 21$.

   a. $2142 \div 21$ **b.** 72×9 **c.** $995 \div 5$

8. Evaluate by multiplying out the brackets:

   a. $(50 + 5) \times (2 - 3)$ **b.** $(200 + 1) \times (80 - 3)$ **c.** $(100 - 1) \times (10 - 7)$

9. Expand and simplify if possible:

   a. $(p + 2)(q + 3)$ **b.** $(m - 1)(m + 2)$ **c.** $(p - q)(p + q)$ **d.** $pq + (p - q)(p - q)$

Solutions:

1. **a.** $3000 - 9 = 2991$ **b.** $1440 + 12 = 1452$ **c.** $3300 - 121 = 3179$

2. **a.** pr **b.** $-4q - 10p$ **c.** $2mn - 6$ **d.** $2 - \dfrac{a}{2}$

3. **a.** $5 - 6 - 2 = -3$ **b.** $5 - 6 + 2 = 1$ **c.** $4 - 2 + 5 - 2 = 5$ **d.** $10 - 3 + 2 - 1 = 8$

4. **a.** $2ab - bc$ **b.** -2 **c.** $-2b$

5. **a.** $100 - 1 = 99$ **b.** $70 + 7 = 77$ **c.** This is a trick: you can't do this without evaluating the brackets explicitly.

6. **a.** $\dfrac{5}{b} + \dfrac{3}{a}$ **b.** $\dfrac{15ab}{ab} = 15$ **c.** $3 + 6r$ **d.** $r - 2 + q$

7. **a.** $(2100 + 42)/21$ **b.** $(70 + 2) \times 9$ **c.** $(1000 - 5)/5$

8. **a.** $100 - 150 + 10 - 15 = -55$
   b. $16,000 - 600 + 80 - 3 = 15,477$
   c. $1000 - 700 - 10 + 7 = 297$

9. **a.** $pq + 3p + 2q + 6$
   b. $m^2 + 2m - m - 2 = m^2 + m - 2$
   c. $p^2 - q^2$ (difference between two squares)
   d. $pq + p^2 - pq - pq + q^2 = p^2 - pq + q^2$.

1. Calculate these *without* explicitly evaluating the expression in brackets:

   a. $5 \times (2000 - 7)$ **b.** $(100 + 5) \times 8$ **c.** $(600 - 1) \times 9$ **d.** $(100 - 1) \times 11$

2. Simplify:

   a. $2(a + 3) - 2a$ **b.** $\dfrac{x}{2}\left(\dfrac{4}{y} - \dfrac{6}{x}\right)$ **c.** $y\left(3x - \dfrac{3x}{y}\right) - 3xy$

3. Evaluate *without* explicitly evaluating the expression in brackets:

   a. $917.2 - (917.2 - 89.3)$ **b.** $67 - (55 - (-54) - 67)$

4. Evaluate by expanding the brackets:

   a. $(700 + 14) \div 7$ **b.** $(1800 - 9) \div 9$ **c.** $320 \div (4 + 8)$ **d.** $(1700 + 85)/5$

5. Simplify:

a. $\dfrac{4a + 2b}{2}$ b. $\dfrac{ab - bc}{b}$ c. $\dfrac{ab \cdot bc}{b}$ d. $(xz - 2xy + 3wx) \div x$

6. Calculate quickly by expressing one component as an addition or subtraction:

a. 63×11 b. $7575 \div 15$ c. $2222/22$ d. 699×14

7. Evaluate by multiplying out the brackets:

a. $(100 - 2)(50 + 1)$ b. $(10 - 1)(60 + 1)$ c. $(2000 - 3)(10 + 7)$ d. $(1000 + 4) \times (50 + 7)$

8. Simplify:

a. $(a - 2)(a + 3)$ b. $(p + 1)(1 - q)$ c. $(p + q)^2 - (p - q)^2$

6 Factorising

Test box 6

Factorise $5ma + 15m$, $y^2 + 4y - 5$, $a^2 + c^2 + 2ac$

Solutions: $5m(a + 3)$, $(y + 5)(y - 1)$, $(a + c)^2$.

We have already seen that expanding the brackets may help to simplify an expression. Another way, which will be useful when we come to solving equations in Chapter EM3, is by *factorising*.

What is factorising?

Factorising is the opposite of expanding brackets. To expand an expression we take it and write down its equivalent *without* the brackets, whereas to factorise, we take an expression and we insert some brackets. At the moment this may seem a rather futile operation, but we will see that it often enables us to cancel terms.

To factorise, we take an expression – or part of it – and replace it with two or more expressions – the *factors*, which multiply together to give the original expression. We are replacing the original expression by a product. For example, $3x + 6$ factorises to $3(x + 2)$. You can check that a factorisation is correct by multiplying out the brackets again; that is, $3(x + 2) = 3x + (3 \times 2) = 3x + 6$. You should always get back to the original expression.

Check these

Decide which of the following factorisations, **a** or **b**, are correct:

$4 + 8y$ factorises to **a.** $4(1 + 2y)$ or **b.** $4(1 + y)$

$3xy + 2y$ factorises to **a.** $3y(x + 2)$ or **b.** $y(3x + 2)$

$pqr - p$ factorises to **a.** $p(qr - 1)$ or **b.** $pq(r - 1)$

$R^2 + R - 2$ factorises to **a.** $(R - 1)(R + 2)$ or **b.** $R(R + 1 - 2)$

$ab + b - 2a - 2$ factorises to **a.** $(a + 1)(b - 1)$ or **b.** $(a + 1)(b - 2)$

Solutions:
Multiply out the brackets for each **a.** and **b.** to see which gives the original expression. For instance, in the second example **a.** multiplies out to $3yx + 6y$ which is clearly *not* equal to $3xy + 2y$. The solutions are **a., b., a., a., b.**

Why factorise?
To demonstrate the benefits of factorising let's take the expression

$$\frac{pqr - p}{qr - 1}$$

At present, it looks rather complicated, so it would be nice to simplify it. The numerator should look familiar to you as we factorised it as $pqr - p = p(qr - 1)$ in the **Check these** above. When we replace $pqr - p$ in the original expression with the factorisation we obtain

$$\frac{p(qr - 1)}{qr - 1}$$

Now it is apparent that both the numerator and the denominator can be divided by $qr - 1$, so we can cancel to give

$$\frac{p}{1} = p$$

The original expression simplifies to just p.

How to factorise
The simplest sort of factorisation is one like $3xy + 6y$. Each term is a multiple of $3y$, and so $3y$ must be one of the factors and we can write

$$3xy + 6y = 3y(? + ?).$$

The first ? is such that ? times $3y$ must be $3xy$, so ? must be x whereas the second ? is such that ? times $3y$ is $6y$, so the ? must be 2. The factorisation is therefore

$$3xy + 6y = 3y(x + 2).$$

Notice that these steps are the reverse of those we do to expand or multiply out brackets, as shown below.

$$\text{EXPAND} \quad \downarrow \quad \left| \begin{array}{c} 3y(x + 2) \\ 3y \cdot x + 3y \cdot 2 \\ 3xy + 6y \end{array} \right| \quad \uparrow \quad \text{FACTORISE}$$

> ### Check these
>
> Factorise the following:
>
> $3x - 3$.
>
> Both terms are a multiple of 3, so we can take the 3 outside the brackets to give $3(x - 1)$. You can check that this is OK by multiplying out the brackets to get back where you started.
>
> $4pq + 2p$.
>
> $2p$ is a factor of both terms so we could write $2p \cdot 2q + 2p \cdot 1 = 2p(2q + 1)$
>
> $m^2 + m$.
>
> Both terms have been multiplied by m, so the factorisation is $m(m + 1)$
>
> $5P(1 - P) + 10(1 - P)$.
>
> Both terms are a multiple of $5(1 - P)$ so the factorisation has the form $5(1 - P)(? + ?)$. The first term is $5(1 - P) \times P$ and the second is $5(1 - P) \times 2$, so the factorisation becomes $5(1 - P)(P + 2)$.

More complicated factorisations really have to be guessed. Remember that you are looking for two or more expressions that multiply together to give the original.

A particularly useful sort of factorisation that will help us to solve equations in Chapter MM1 is of expressions containing x, x^2 and a constant; for example, $x^2 - x - 6$ or $3x^2 + 12x - 15$. These are known as *quadratic* expressions. Of course, these expressions can be in any symbol – it doesn't have to be x. Here are some examples: multiply out the factorisation to check you agree.

> ### Check these
>
> $x^2 - x - 6 = (x + 2)(x - 3)$
>
> $2x^2 + 11x + 5 = (2x + 1)(x + 5)$
>
> $3x^2 + 12x - 15 = 3(x - 1)(x + 5)$
>
> $p^2 - 2p - 8 = (p + 2)(p - 4)$

There is some pattern here which can give us clues when factorising quadratic expressions. First, notice that all the factors take the form of a number of xs (or ps) plus or minus a number. Secondly, the product of the number of xs in each of the factors times the constant (if any) at the front gives the coefficient of the original x^2 term. For instance, in the third example the product of 1 and 1 and 3 is 3, the number of x^2s in the original expression. Thirdly, the constant term in the original expression is the product of the constant terms in the factors. For instance, in the third example –15 is the product of 3, –1 and 5.

For instance, to factorise $x^2 + 4x - 5$ we reason that as the coefficient of x^2 is 1 the product of the number of xs in each factor and any constant factor must be 1, so the factors we seek must be of the form $(x + ?)$ and $(x + ?)$. Further, the product of the two constant terms in the factors must be -5, so these could be -5 and 1 or 5 and -1. If we try $(x - 5)(x + 1)$ we obtain $x^2 - 4x - 5$, which is not what we want, whereas if we try $(x + 5)(x - 1)$ we get back to the original expression and we have obtained the correct factorisation.

Now try factorising some quadratic expressions yourself. Remember that it will take some trial and error – and that you will speed up with experience. The answers are self-checking in that you can multiply out the factors to see if you get back to the original expression, so try not to look at the solutions unless you are totally stuck.

Check these

$x^2 + x - 6$

$p^2 - 7p + 10$

$2y^2 - 2y - 4$

$2x^2 - x - 1$

$2x^2 - 13x - 7$

$x^2 + (a + b)x + ab.$

Solutions:

$(x - 2)(x + 3)$; $(p - 5)(p - 2)$; $2(y + 1)(y - 2)$,

$(2x + 1)(x - 1)$; $(x - 7)(2x + 1)$; $(x + a)(x + b)$.

With practice you will gradually learn to recognise some more common expressions and their factors. We list a few below. Remember that any other letter, number or expression could be used instead of a or b in the following.

Some common factorisations

$a^2 + b^2 + 2ab = (a + b)^2$

$a^2 + b^2 - 2ab = (a - b)^2$

$a^2 - b^2 = (a + b)(a - b)$

Check these

Factorise the following:

$X^2 - Y^2$

$a^2 - 9$

$4x^2 - 9y^2$

$p^2 + q^2 + 2pq$

$2n^2 + 2m^2 + 4mn$

$x^2 + 4 + 4x.$

Solutions:

$(X - Y)(X + Y)$; $(a - 3)(a + 3)$; $(2x + 3y)(2x - 3y)$; $(p + q)^2$; $2(n + m)^2$; $(x + 2)^2$.

We finish this section with some expressions that can be simplified by factorising.

Check these

Simplify the following expressions:

$$\frac{ab + ac}{b + c}$$

The numerator factorises to $a(b + c)$ so the expression becomes

$$\frac{a(b + c)}{b + c}$$

The $b + c$ terms cancel to give just a.

$$\frac{p + q}{p^2 - q^2}$$

The denominator factorises to $(p + q)(p - q)$ to give

$$\frac{p + q}{(p + q)(p - q)} = \frac{1}{p - q}$$

$$\frac{2CI + IR}{IR} = \frac{I(2C + R)}{IR} = \frac{2C + R}{R}$$

$$\frac{(p - 2q)q + q^2}{p - q}$$

You will need to multiply out the existing bracket here before you can factorise the numerator. This gives

$$\frac{pq - 2q^2 + q^2}{p - q} = \frac{pq - q^2}{p - q}$$

Now factorise the numerator to give

$$\frac{q(p - q)}{p - q}$$

The $(p - q)$s cancel to give just q.

Of course, expressions don't always factorise and cancel so nicely and sometimes you *will* be left with something awkward. The trick is to spot when you can simplify and when you can't – not always easy!

1. Factorise the following:
   a. $PR + 2PRS$ **b.** $8m - 4mn + 4mp$ **c.** $x^2 + 2xy - 3x$
   d. $x(a + b) - 2(a + b)$ **e.** $12P(1 + P) + 8(1 + P)$
   f. $2abc - 4bcd$ **g.** $4(a - b) + x(a - b)$

2. Factorise the following:
   a. $y^2 + 6y - 7$ **b.** $z^2 - 4z - 5$ **c.** $x^2 + 5x + 6$
   d. $2x^2 + 10x + 12$ **e.** $3x^2 + 2x - 1$ **f.** $5x^2 - 3x - 2$
   g. $x^2 + 6x$ **h.** $x^2 + (a - b)x - ab$
   i. $9a^2 - b^2$ **j.** $x^2 + 4y^2 + 4xy$

3. Simplify the following, where possible:
   a. $\dfrac{a(b + c) - ab + c^2}{a + c}$ **b.** $\dfrac{(x - y)(x + y) + y^2}{x + xy}$ **c.** $\dfrac{I + R}{9I + 9R}$

   d. $\dfrac{I + R + 1}{9I + 9R}$ **e.** $\dfrac{p(p + 2) - q(p + 2)}{p - q}$ **f.** $\dfrac{(p + 2) + p}{p + 2}$

Solutions:

1. **a.** $PR(1 + 2S)$ **b.** $4m(2 - n + p)$ **c.** $x(x + 2y - 3)$ **d.** Here, both terms are multiples of $(a + b)$ so take $(a + b)$ out of the brackets to give $(x - 2)(a + b)$
   e. Again, each term has $4(1 + P)$ in common so take this out of the brackets to give $4(1 + P)(3P + 2)$ **f.** $2bc(a - 2d)$ **g.** $(4 + x)(a - b)$

2. **a.** $(y - 1)(y + 7)$ **b.** $(z + 1)(z - 5)$ **c.** $(x + 2)(x + 3)$
   d. $2(x + 2)(x + 3)$ **e.** $(3x - 1)(x + 1)$ **f.** $(x - 1)(5x + 2)$
   g. $x(x + 6)$ **h.** $(x + a)(x - b)$ **i.** $(3a + b)(3a - b)$ **j.** $(x + 2y)^2$

3. **a.** c **b.** $\dfrac{x}{1 + y}$ **c.** $\dfrac{1}{9}$ **d.** no simplification possible.

   e. $(p + 2)$ is common to both terms in the numerator, giving

   $$\frac{(p + 2)(p - q)}{(p - q)} = p + 2$$

   f. The $(p + 2)$s cannot be cancelled so no simplification is possible.

1. Factorise:

   a. $5mz + 15m$ b. $12pq - 6p$ c. $3q(q + 3) - 2(q + 3)$

   d. $6a - 3ab + 9ac$ e. $12pqr + (r - 1)pq$

2. Factorise:

   a. $z^2 + 4z + 3$ b. $y^2 + 4y - 5$ c. $2x^2 + x - 1$

   d. $4x^2 + 2x - 2$ e. $x^2 + 6x + 9$ f. $x^2 - 8x + 15$

   g. $a^2 + 1 + 2a$ h. $s^2 - p^2$ i. $(s + 1)^2 - (p + 1)^2$ j. $a^2 + 9 + 6a$

3. Simplify where possible:

   a. $\dfrac{zx + zy}{x + y}$ b. $\dfrac{(p - 1)R + (p - 1)S}{R + S}$ c. $\dfrac{y(x - w) + w(y + x)}{2(y + w)}$

   d. $\dfrac{x - y}{x^2 - y^2}$ e. $(s + 1)^2 - (s - 1)^2$

7 Powers

Test box 7

Calculate:

$$4^2 \times 4^{-3}, \qquad \frac{\left(\frac{3}{5}\right)^2 \times \left(\frac{3}{5}\right)^3}{\left(\frac{3}{5}\right)^4}, \qquad 6^3 \div 6^5$$

Simplify:

$$a^b a^c, \qquad (x + y)^5 (x + y)^3, \qquad \frac{x^2}{x^y}, \qquad (a^2)^n$$

Solutions:

$$\frac{1}{4}, \frac{3}{5}, \frac{1}{36}, \quad a^{b+c}, \quad (x + y)^8, \quad x^{2-y}, \quad a^{2n}$$

Powers provide a shorthand way of representing repeated multiplications or divisions. They are useful to model quantities in finance and economics and for calculations involving the value of money over time.

Introduction to powers

The expression 2^7 is called '2 to the power of 7' and means two multiplied by itself 7 times, that is

$$2 \times 2 \times 2 \times 2 \times 2 \times 2 \times 2 = 128.$$

In the same way 3^5 is called '3 to the power of 5' and means 3 multiplied by itself five times or

$$3 \times 3 \times 3 \times 3 \times 3 = 243.$$

The power notations 2^7 and 3^5 merely give a shorthand way of writing out such expressions, which is especially useful for large indices. Imagine writing 17^{64} out in full! The superscripts like 7, 5 and 64 are called the power or *index*.

You will probably remember that a number to the power of two is said to be 'squared' or to the power of 3 is 'cubed', so 5^2 is five squared and 2^3 is two cubed.

The powers of 10 are easy to calculate: $10^2 = 100$, $10^3 = 1000$, $10^4 = 10,000$ and so on, and we have already seen (Chapter EM1, Section 4) that very large or small numbers can be expressed in scientific notation; that is, as a number between 1 and 9.9999 ... multiplied by a power of 10.

Arithmetic on powers of numbers has its own particular pattern. To use this fully it will sometimes be useful to talk about numbers like '3 to the power of 1' or 3^1 and '5 to the power of 1' or 5^1 although we know they are merely 3 and 5 themselves. Less obviously, 3^0, 2^0 or indeed any number to the power of 0 is taken to be 1. We will explain the reason for this later.

Negative numbers and fractions can be raised to a power in just the same way. For instance $(-1)^4 = (-1) \times (-1) \times (-1) \times (-1) = 1$ and $(-3)^3 = (-3) \times (-3) \times (-3) = -27$. Notice that even numbered powers of a negative number are positive and odd powers of a negative number are negative. As an example of the power of a fraction consider

$$\left(\frac{1}{2}\right)^5 = \left(\frac{1}{2}\right) \times \left(\frac{1}{2}\right) \times \left(\frac{1}{2}\right) \times \left(\frac{1}{2}\right) \times \left(\frac{1}{2}\right) = \frac{1}{32}$$

Check these

Evaluate:

$3^3 = 3 \times 3 \times 3 = 27$

$(-4)^2 = (-4) \times (-4) = 16$

$\left(\frac{2}{3}\right)^2 = \frac{2}{3} \times \frac{2}{3} = \frac{2 \times 2}{3 \times 3} = \frac{4}{9}$

$(-2)^4 = (-2) \times (-2) \times (-2) \times (-2) = 16$

$(-1)^0 = 1$

$\left(-\frac{2}{5}\right)^3 = \left(-\frac{2}{5}\right) \times \left(-\frac{2}{5}\right) \times \left(-\frac{2}{5}\right) = -\frac{8}{125}$

The power notation can be used in the same way for numbers, symbols or expressions.

Check these

Write out the following in full:

$a^3 = a \times a \times a$

$$\left(\frac{p}{q}\right)^3 = \frac{p}{q} \times \frac{p}{q} \times \frac{p}{q}$$

$$(-b)^2 = (-b) \times (-b)$$

$$(1 + x)^4 = (1 + x)(1 + x)(1 + x)(1 + x)$$

$$ab^3 = a \times b \times b \times b$$

$$(a + b)^0 = 1, \text{ as any expression to the power of 0 is 1.}$$

Negative powers

A negative power is the reciprocal of (that is, 1 divided by) the corresponding positive power. For instance,

$$2^{-3} = \frac{1}{2^3}, \; 5^{-2} = \frac{1}{5^2} \text{ and } b^{-3} = \frac{1}{b^3}$$

Check these

Evaluate the following:

$$2^{-2} = \frac{1}{2^2} = \frac{1}{4}$$

$$3^{-4} = \frac{1}{3^4} = \frac{1}{81}$$

$$\left(\frac{2}{3}\right)^{-2} = \frac{1}{\left(\frac{2}{3}\right)^2} = \frac{1}{\frac{4}{9}} = \frac{9}{4}$$

Express the following using only positive powers:

$$p^{-4} = \frac{1}{p^4}$$

$$(1 + a)^{-2} = \frac{1}{(1 + a)^2}$$

$$(ab)^{-1} = \frac{1}{ab}$$

$$\frac{1}{b^{-3}} = \frac{1}{\frac{1}{b^3}} = 1 \div \frac{1}{b^3} = b^3$$

Multiplying powers

Consider $2^2 \times 2^3$. Written out in full it is $(2 \times 2) \times (2 \times 2 \times 2)$. As the order in which we multiply doesn't matter we can drop the brackets, and this is just $2 \times 2 \times 2 \times 2 \times 2 = 2^5$. So $2^2 \times 2^3 = 2^5$. Now try $3^4 \times 3^2 = 3 \times 3 \times 3 \times 3 \times 3 \times 3 = 3^6$. We can do the same thing using symbols. For example, $b^2 \times b^3$ is $(b \times b) \times (b \times b \times b) = b^5$. Can you see the pattern? To multiply powers of the same number we just *add* the powers.

But does this work for negative powers? Consider $2^4 \times 2^{-5}$. Writing this out in full gives

$$2 \times 2 \times 2 \times 2 \times \frac{1}{2 \times 2 \times 2 \times 2 \times 2}$$

We can cancel all but one of the 2s in the denominator to give

$$2^4 \times 2^{-5} = \frac{1}{2} = 2^{-1}$$

and yes, adding the powers still works.

We conclude that to multiply powers of *the same number* or symbol we simply *add* the indices. This rule can be written

$$b^m \times b^n = b^{m+n}$$

Warnings. Do *not* confuse this with $b^m + b^n$, which *cannot* be simplified. Also, $b^m \times c^n$ cannot be simplified (unless $b = c$) as we are not talking about powers of the *same* number.

Check these

Evaluate or simplify:

$3^2 \times 3^3 = 3^5 = 243$

$5^{-5} \times 5^7 = 5^2 = 25$

$a^2 a = a^3$

$(-1)^5 \times (-1)^2 = (-1)^7 = -1$

$5^m \cdot 5^n = 5^{m+n}$

$p^5 p^{-2} = p^3$

$(1 + r)^6 (1 + r)^{20} = (1 + r)^{26}$

$\left(\dfrac{2}{5}\right)^3 \times \left(\dfrac{2}{5}\right)^{-2} = \left(\dfrac{2}{5}\right)^1 = \dfrac{2}{5}$

$\left(-\dfrac{1}{4}\right)^3 \times \left(-\dfrac{1}{4}\right)^{-5} = \left(-\dfrac{1}{4}\right)^{-2} = 1 \div \dfrac{1}{16} = 16$

$4^2 \times 4^{-3} \times 4^4 = 4^3 = 64$

$2^3 \times 2^{-5} \times 3^2 \times 3^2 = 2^{-2} \times 3^4 = \dfrac{1}{4} \times 81 = \dfrac{81}{4}$

$4^2 \times 4^{-1} \times 5^2 \times 2^2 \times 5^{-3} = 4^1 \times 5^{-1} \times 2^2 = 4 \times \dfrac{1}{5} \times 4 = \dfrac{16}{5}$

$pq^2 p^2 q^2 = p^3 q^4$

As you have seen from the examples above, adding the indices to multiply works for three or more powers of the same number as well.

An application of powers

Calculations of loan repayments and investment interest rely heavily on the use of powers. Suppose an amount A is placed in a bank account and the bank pays interest at a rate of say 10 per cent per year. At the end of the first year the amount will accumulate to

$$A\left(1 + \frac{10}{100}\right)$$

If this is left in the account and the interest rate remains the same, this new amount will increase by 10% during the second year so that the account balance at the end of the second year will be

$$A\left(1 + \frac{10}{100}\right)\left(1 + \frac{10}{100}\right) = A\left(1 + \frac{10}{100}\right)^2$$

If this balance remains in the account for a third year, it will become

$$A\left(1 + \frac{10}{100}\right)^2\left(1 + \frac{10}{100}\right) = A\left(1 + \frac{10}{100}\right)^3$$

by the end of the third year. We hope that you can see the pattern emerging. At the end of year n there will be

$$A\left(1 + \frac{10}{100}\right)^n$$

in the account.

A general formula for the amount accumulated after n years at an interest rate of r per cent is therefore

$$A\left(1 + \frac{r}{100}\right)^n$$

We do some more financial mathematics in Chapter BM4.

Powers of a power

Can you evaluate $(2^2)^3$? Remember that the expression in brackets must be calculated first so this means $2^2 = 4$, all cubed i.e. $4^3 = 64$. Writing the expression out in longhand gives,

$$(2^2)^3 = (2 \times 2)^3 = (2 \times 2) \times (2 \times 2) \times (2 \times 2) = 2 \times 2 \times 2 \times 2 \times 2 \times 2 = 2^6.$$

As we have multiplied two 2s together to square, and repeated this three times to cube, altogether we have multiplied 2 by itself 2×3 times. So

$$(2^2)^3 = 2^{2\times3}.$$

This is true in general. To calculate the *power of a power* all you need to do is *multiply the indices*. This rule can be written

$$(b^m)^n = b^{mn}$$

Check these

Calculate the following by adding the indices and check the result by writing it out in longhand:

$(5^4)^3 = 5^{4\times3}$

Check $(5^4)^3 = (5 \times 5 \times 5 \times 5) \times (5 \times 5 \times 5 \times 5) \times (5 \times 5 \times 5 \times 5) = 5^{12}$.

$((-2)^7)^2 = (-2)^{14}$

Check $((-2)^7)^2 = ((-2) \times (-2) \times (-2) \times (-2) \times (-2) \times (-2) \times (-2))$
$\times ((-2) \times (-2) \times (-2) \times (-2) \times (-2) \times (-2) \times (-2)) = (-2)^{14}$.

Multiplying the indices of powers of powers also works for symbols, negative powers and fractional numbers.

Check these

$(3^{-2})^3 = 3^{-6} \left(\text{in longhand } \dfrac{1}{3\times3} \times \dfrac{1}{3\times3} \times \dfrac{1}{3\times3} = \dfrac{1}{3^6} \right)$

$\left(\left(\dfrac{2}{3} \right)^3 \right)^{-2} = \left(\dfrac{2}{3} \right)^{-6} \left(\text{in longhand } \dfrac{1}{(\frac{2}{3} \times \frac{2}{3} \times \frac{2}{3}) \times (\frac{2}{3} \times \frac{2}{3} \times \frac{2}{3})} = \dfrac{1}{(\frac{2}{3})^6} \right)$

$(a^2)^4 = a^8$ (in longhand $(a \times a)\,(a \times a)\,(a \times a)\,(a \times a)$)

$((-p)^2)^2 = (-p)^4 = p^4$ (in longhand $((-p) \times (-p))((-p) \times (-p)) = (-p)^4$).

Dividing powers

So how do we divide powers? Again, we can approach the problem by writing out the powers in longhand. Consider $\dfrac{2^3}{2^5}$. This is

$$\frac{2 \times 2 \times 2}{2 \times 2 \times 2 \times 2 \times 2} = \frac{1}{2 \times 2} = 2^{-2}$$

It is no coincidence that this is 2^{3-5} because the rule for dividing powers of the same number or symbol is to *subtract* the indices. That is,

$$\frac{b^m}{b^n} = b^{m-n}$$

Check these

Calculate the following by subtracting the indices and check the result by writing it out in longhand:

$2^3 \div 2^4 = 2^{-1}$ **check** $\dfrac{2 \times 2 \times 2}{2 \times 2 \times 2 \times 2} = \dfrac{1}{2}$

$$3^2 \div 3^7 = 3^{-5} \quad \text{check} \quad \frac{3 \times 3}{3 \times 3 \times 3 \times 3 \times 3 \times 3 \times 3}$$

$$= \frac{1}{3 \times 3 \times 3 \times 3 \times 3} = 3^{-5}$$

$$5^2 \div 5^{-3} = 5^{2-(-3)} = 5^5 \quad \text{check} \quad 5^2 \div \frac{1}{5 \times 5 \times 5}$$

$$= \frac{5 \times 5 \times 5 \times 5 \times 5}{1} = 5^5$$

Notice in this last example that the subtraction rule applies just as well to negative indices.

$$(-2)^3 \div (-2)^4 = (-2)^{-1} = \frac{1}{-2} = -\frac{1}{2}$$

Check $\dfrac{(-2) \times (-2) \times (-2)}{(-2) \times (-2) \times (-2) \times (-2)} = \dfrac{1}{-2} = -\dfrac{1}{2}$

$$\left(\frac{2}{5}\right)^2 \div \left(\frac{2}{5}\right)^4 = \left(\frac{2}{5}\right)^{-2} = 1 \div \left(\frac{2}{5}\right)^2 = 1 \div \frac{4}{25} = \frac{25}{4}$$

Check $\dfrac{\frac{2}{5} \times \frac{2}{5}}{\frac{2}{5} \times \frac{2}{5} \times \frac{2}{5} \times \frac{2}{5}} = \dfrac{1}{\frac{2}{5} \times \frac{2}{5}} = \dfrac{25}{4}$

$$\frac{b^5}{b^2} = b^{5-2} = b^3 \quad \text{check} \quad \frac{b \times b \times b \times b \times b}{b \times b} = b^3$$

Simplify:

$$\frac{a^{b+c}}{a^c} = a^{b+c-c} = a^b$$

$$\frac{(1 + \frac{1}{10})^n}{(1 + \frac{1}{10})^{n-1}} = \left(1 + \frac{1}{10}\right)^{n-(n-1)} = \left(1 + \frac{1}{10}\right)^1 = 1 + \frac{1}{10}$$

Incidentally, the division rule is the reason why we adopt the convention that anything to the power of 0 is 1. Consider $2^3 \div 2^3$. As this is a number divided by itself the answer must be 1. The division rule gives $2^{3-3} = 2^0$. So $2^0 = 1$. Also, as $b^{-m} = b^{0-m}$ which the rule says is

$$b^0 \div b^m = 1 \div b^m = \frac{1}{b^m}$$

we have

$$b^{-m} = \frac{1}{b^m}$$

our definition of negative powers.

 As for multiplication you must be careful only to subtract the indices of powers of the *same number*. For instance, $\frac{2^2}{3^4}$ or $\frac{b^2}{a^3}$ *cannot* be simplified as the components are 2 to the power of ... and 3 to the power of ..., or b to the power of ... and a to the power of ... respectively.

Check these

Simplify the following:

$$\frac{2^3 \times 5^2}{2^2 \times 5^3} = 2^1 \times 5^{-1}$$

$$\frac{a^3 b^2}{a^2 b^3} = a^{3-2} b^{2-3} = ab^{-1} = \frac{a}{b}$$

$$\frac{7^3 \times 2^2 \times 3^{-2}}{2^3 \times 7^4 \times 3^2} = 7^{-1} \times 2^{-1} \times 3^{-4}$$

Now you know how to multiply, divide and power, powers. However, there is no need to learn these rules by heart. They are all based on the basic rule for the multiplication of powers – adding the indices. If you forget them you can always write out the problem as a multiplication. For instance, if you've forgotten the rule for the division of powers and need to calculate $\frac{5^4}{5^{-3}}$, write it as

$$5^4 \div 5^{-3} = 5^4 \times \frac{1}{5^{-3}} = 5^4 \times 5^3 = 5^7$$

The key results for powers so far are:

Negative powers

$$b^{-m} = \frac{1}{b^m}$$

To multiply powers of the same number add the indices

$$b^m b^n = b^{m+n}$$

To calculate the power of a power multiply the indices

$$(b^m)^n = b^{mn}$$

To divide powers of the same number subtract the indices

$$b^m \div b^n = b^{m-n}$$

---

1. Evaluate:

   a. 4^3 **b.** $(-3)^3$ **c.** $\left(\dfrac{3}{4}\right)^3$ **d.** $\left(\dfrac{2}{3}\right)^2$ **e.** $\left(\dfrac{3}{4}\right)^0$ **f.** 5^{-2} **g.** $\left(\dfrac{2}{5}\right)^{-3}$ **h.** $\left(-\dfrac{2}{5}\right)^{-3}$

2. Calculate:

   a. $2^3 \times 2^4$ **b.** $3^{-2} \times 3^4$ **c.** $(-2)^2 \times (-2)^3$ **d.** $(-4)^{27} \times (-4)^{-25}$

   e. $\left(\dfrac{1}{2}\right)^2 \times \left(\dfrac{1}{2}\right)^3$ **f.** $\left(\dfrac{1}{3}\right)^3 \times \left(\dfrac{1}{3}\right)^{-2} \times \left(\dfrac{1}{3}\right)^2$

3. Simplify:

   a. $a^7 a^5$ **b.** $3^p 3^q 3^r$ **c.** $5^x \cdot 5^y$ **d.** $2^x + 2^y$

   e. $\left(1 + \dfrac{r}{100}\right)^n \left(1 + \dfrac{r}{100}\right)^m$ **f.** $2^p 2^3 + 2^q 2^2$

4. Simplify and evaluate where possible:

   a. $3^2 \times 2^4 \times 2^{-1} \times 3^{-2}$ **b.** $2^1 \times \left(\dfrac{1}{2}\right)^3 \times 3^2 \times \left(\dfrac{1}{2}\right)^{-1} \times 2^2 \times 3$

   c. $(-5)^3 \times 2^8 \times 2^{-6} \times \left(\dfrac{1}{5}\right)^2$ **d.** $p^3 q^2 p^2 q^3$ **e.** $\dfrac{1}{1+r}(1+r)^3$

5. Evaluate:

   a. $(2^2)^3$ **b.** $(4^{-2})^2$ **c.** $((-1)^2)^3$

6. Simplify:

   a. $(7^{14})^{-2}$ **b.** $\left(\left(\dfrac{3}{4}\right)^7\right)^{-2}$ **c.** $\left(\left(\dfrac{5}{8}\right)^{-3}\right)^{13}$ **d.** $\left(\left(\dfrac{1}{a}\right)^2\right)^3$ **e.** $(b^{-2})^{-3}$

7. Simplify and evaluate where possible:

   a. $5^6 \div 5^4$ **b.** $\dfrac{6^2}{6^4}$ **c.** $\dfrac{\left(\frac{2}{3}\right)^3}{\left(\frac{2}{3}\right)^5}$ **d.** $\dfrac{(-3)^7}{(-3)^6}$ **e.** $\dfrac{(1+r)^{n+2}}{(1+r)^n}$ **f.** $\dfrac{g^{x+a}}{g^a}$

8. Simplify and evaluate:

   a. $\dfrac{5^2 \times 2^4}{2^5 \times 5^3}$ **b.** $\dfrac{2^8 \times 3^7 \times 3^2 \times 2^{-2} \times (\frac{1}{3})^{11}}{2^5 \times (\frac{1}{3})}$ **c.** $\dfrac{x^2(1+y)^3}{(1+y)^2 x^4}$

Solutions:

1. **a.** 64 **b.** –27 **c.** $\dfrac{27}{64}$ **d.** $\dfrac{4}{9}$ **e.** 1 **f.** $\dfrac{1}{25}$ **g.** $\dfrac{125}{8}$ **h.** $-\dfrac{125}{8}$

2. **a.** 128 **b.** 9 **c.** –32 **d.** 16 **e.** $\dfrac{1}{32}$ **f.** $\dfrac{1}{27}$

3. **a.** a^{12} **b.** 3^{p+q+r} **c.** 5^{x+y} **d.** No further simplification possible.

WORK CARD 7 (CONTINUED)

e. $\left(1 + \dfrac{r}{100}\right)^{m+n}$ f. $2^{p+3} + 2^{q+2}$

4. a. 8   b. 54   c. –20   d. $p^5 q^5$ e. $(1 + r)^2$

5. a. 64   b. $\dfrac{1}{256}$ c. 1

6. a. 7^{-28} b. $\left(\dfrac{3}{4}\right)^{-14}$ c. $\left(\dfrac{5}{8}\right)^{-39}$ d. a^{-6} e. b^6

7. a. 25   b. $\dfrac{1}{36}$ c. $\dfrac{9}{4}$ d. –3   e. $(1 + r)^2$ f. g^x

8. a. $\dfrac{1}{10}$ b. $\dfrac{2}{3}$ c. $\dfrac{1+y}{x^2}$

ASSESSMENT 7

1. Evaluate the following:

a. 5^3 b. $(-2)^5$ c. $\left(\dfrac{2}{5}\right)^5$ d. $\left(\dfrac{3}{4}\right)^1$ e. $\left(\dfrac{3}{8}\right)^0$ f. 6^{-3} g. $\left(\dfrac{1}{5}\right)^{-2}$

h. $\left(\dfrac{-3}{5}\right)^2$ i. $\left(\dfrac{2}{7}\right)^{-2}$

2. Evaluate:

a. $3^2 \times 3^3$ b. $2^5 \times 2^{-3}$ c. $(-1)^2 \times (-1)^3$ d. $(33)^{10} \times (33)^{-9}$

e. $\dfrac{1}{3} \times \left(\dfrac{1}{3}\right)^4 \times \left(\dfrac{1}{3}\right)^{-2}$

3. Simplify a. $2^k 2^{k+1}$ b. $q^r q^{1-r}$ c. $\left(\dfrac{p}{q}\right)^2 \left(\dfrac{p}{q}\right)^3 \left(\dfrac{p}{q}\right)^{-4}$

4. Simplify and evaluate where possible:

a. $4^3 \times 4^2 \times 3^1 \times 4^{-4} \times 3^{-2}$ b. $5^2 \times \left(\dfrac{1}{2}\right)^4 \times \left(\dfrac{1}{5}\right)^3 \times \left(-\dfrac{1}{2}\right)^2$

c. $(1 + r)^m s^m (1 + r)^{m+n} \left(\dfrac{1}{s}\right)^{m-1}$

5. Evaluate:

a. $(3^2)^{-2}$ b. $(4^3)^{-1}$ c. $((-2)^3)^0$

6. Simplify:

a. $(3^{-3})^{-6}$ b. $\left(\left(\dfrac{7}{8}\right)^2\right)^{-6}$ c. $((m+n)^2)^{-1}$ d. $(5^a)^b$

e. $\left(\left(\dfrac{p}{q}\right)^2\right)^{-2}$ f. $((1+r)^2)^n$

7. Simplify and evaluate where possible:

a. $6^4 \div 4^4$ b. $\dfrac{7^5}{7^3}$ c. $\dfrac{\left(\frac{3}{4}\right)^2}{\left(\frac{3}{4}\right)^4}$ d. $\dfrac{(-2)^5}{(-2)^4}$ e. $\dfrac{k^7}{k^5}$ f. $\dfrac{(-k)^7}{(-k)^5}$ g. $\dfrac{(1+r)^m}{(1+r)^n}$

8. Evaluate:

a. $\dfrac{2^2 \times 3^2 \times 2^{-1}}{3^7 \times \left(\frac{1}{3}\right)^2 \times 2^{-2}}$ b. $\dfrac{2^3 \times 3^2 \times 5^3}{5^2 \times 2^5}$

8 Powers of products and quotients

Test box 8

Evaluate *quickly* $\dfrac{(3 \times 4)^6}{3^2 \times 4^6}$, $\dfrac{24^3}{96^3}$

Simplify $\dfrac{(rs)^3}{s^2}$ and $\dfrac{(5p)^a}{5^a}$

Use cancelling to simplify $\dfrac{52^3\left(\frac{1}{2}\right)^2}{2^5 \times 13^2}$

Solutions: 81, $\dfrac{1}{64}$, $r^3 s$, $\dfrac{5^a p^a}{5^a} = p^a$, $\dfrac{13}{2}$

Now we consider rules for the power of a product and the power of a quotient, which can enable complicated expressions to be simplified.

The power of a product

Consider $(2 \times 3)^3$. Remember that this means $2 \times 3 = 6$, all cubed, that is $6^3 = 216$. In longhand this is $(2 \times 3) \times (2 \times 3) \times (2 \times 3)$. However, the order in which we multiply is unimportant so we can dispense with the brackets and reorder to give the equivalent expression $2 \times 2 \times 2 \times 3 \times 3 \times 3 = 2^3 \times 3^3$. So we have

$$(2 \times 3)^3 = 2^3 \times 3^3.$$

This works for any power of a product. The general rule is

$$(a \times b)^n = a^n \times b^n.$$

Now try these:

Check these

Write the following without the brackets:

$(3 \times 4)^3 = 3^3 \times 4^3$

$(6 \times 2)^{-3} = 6^{-3} \times 2^{-3}$

$(4 \times 5)^{-2} = 4^{-2} \times 5^{-2}$

$(2 \times 3 \times 4)^2 = 2^2 \times 3^2 \times 4^2.$

Notice from the last example that the rule extends to any number of items in the product.

Now the same but using symbols:

Check these

$(3x)^2 = 3^2 x^2 = 9x^2$

$(2ab)^m = 2^m a^m b^m$

$((1 + r)P)^3 = (1 + r)^3 P^3.$

Writing out powers of products in this way often allows us to simplify expressions. For example

$$\frac{(2ab)^m}{(5ab)^{m-1}} = \frac{2^m a^m b^m}{5^{m-1} a^{m-1} b^{m-1}} \quad \text{which cancels to} \quad \frac{2^m ab}{5^{m-1}}$$

In a similar way it is sometimes advantageous to replace a number by a product so that we can cancel down more easily.

For instance, consider $\frac{24^4}{6^3}$. If we replace the 24 by the product 4×6, we obtain

$$\frac{(4 \times 6)^4}{6^3} = \frac{4^4 \times 6^4}{6^3}$$

which now cancels to give $4^4 \times 6$, which is much easier to evaluate than the original expression.

Check these

$$\frac{6^5}{2^6} = \frac{(2 \times 3)^5}{2^6} = \frac{2^5 \times 3^5}{2^6} = \frac{3^5}{2} = \frac{243}{2}$$

$$\frac{24^{-3}}{4^{-4} \times 3^2} = \frac{(4 \times 3 \times 2)^{-3}}{4^{-4} \times 3^2} = \frac{4^{-3} \times 3^{-3} \times 2^{-3}}{4^{-4} \times 3^2} = 4^1 \times 3^{-5} \times 2^{-3}$$

$$= 2^2 \times 3^{-5} \times 2^{-3} = 2^{-1} \times 3^{-5} = \frac{1}{2 \times 243}$$

The power of a quotient

Consider $(\frac{5}{2})^3$. This is

$$\left(\frac{5}{2}\right) \times \left(\frac{5}{2}\right) \times \left(\frac{5}{2}\right) = \frac{5 \times 5 \times 5}{2 \times 2 \times 2} = \frac{5^3}{2^3}$$

So

$$\left(\frac{5}{2}\right)^3 = \left(\frac{5^3}{2^3}\right)$$

Again, it appears that we can remove the brackets and write each component of a quotient to the appropriate power. The rule is

$$\left(\frac{a}{b}\right)^n = \frac{a^n}{b^n}$$

Check these

Rewrite these without the brackets and simplify where possible:

$$\left(\frac{2}{3}\right)^3 = \frac{2^3}{3^3}$$

$$\left(\frac{3}{10}\right)^{-2} = \frac{3^{-2}}{10^{-2}} = \frac{100}{9}$$

$$\left(\frac{x}{y}\right)^5 y^3 = \frac{x^5}{y^5} y^3 = \frac{x^5}{y^2}$$

$$\left(\frac{2p}{q}\right)^3 \frac{1}{p^3} = \frac{2^3 p^3}{q^3} \frac{1}{p^3} = \frac{2^3}{q^3}$$

When the numerator and denominator of a quotient are raised to the *same power* we can use the rule the other way round; that is,

$$\frac{a^n}{b^n} = \left(\frac{a}{b}\right)^n$$

For example, an expression like $\frac{99^3}{11^3}$ is the same as

$$\left(\frac{99}{11}\right)^3 = 9^3$$

and we have avoided having to work out 99^3!

Applying the rule in reverse to

$$\frac{(36p)^6}{(12p)^6}$$

we obtain

$$\left(\frac{36p}{12p}\right)^6 = 3^6$$

which is much simpler than the original expression.

| Check these |

Simplify the following:

$$\frac{84^5}{21^5} = \left(\frac{84}{21}\right)^5 = 4^5$$

$$\frac{76^2}{19^2} = \left(\frac{76}{19}\right)^2 = 4^2$$

$$\frac{(2xy)^4}{(4x)^4} = \left(\frac{2xy}{4x}\right)^4 = \left(\frac{y}{2}\right)^4$$

$$\frac{(6abc)^3}{(3bc)^3} = \left(\frac{6abc}{3bc}\right)^3 = (2a)^3 = 8a^3$$

We can now summarise the work of this section.

The power of a product

$$(a \times b)^n = a^n \times b^n \qquad \text{e.g. } (2 \times 3)^4 = 2^4 \times 3^4$$

The power of a quotient

$$\left(\frac{a}{n}\right)^n = \frac{a^n}{b^n} \qquad \text{e.g. } \left(\frac{2}{3}\right)^5 = \frac{2^5}{3^5}$$

Don't learn these rules by heart – but remember what they represent. For instance, think of

$$\left(\frac{a}{b}\right)^n \text{ as } \left(\frac{a}{b}\right) \times \left(\frac{a}{b}\right) \times \left(\frac{a}{b}\right) \dots n \text{ times} = \frac{a^n}{b^n}$$

We will finish this section by working through some examples which use all the work we have done so far on powers.

Check these

Evaluate the following. There will often be more than one way of doing the intermediate steps. We have shown one of the quickest ways in each case.

$$10^2 \times \left(\frac{1}{2}\right)^2 \times (-1)^2 = \left(10 \times \frac{1}{2} \times (-1)\right)^2 = (-5)^2 = 25$$

$$\frac{6^2 \times 3^{-2}}{36} \times \frac{3^2}{2^{-2}} = \frac{6^2 \times 3^{-2} \times 3^2}{36 \times 2^{-2}} = \frac{1 \times 3^0}{2^{-2}} = \frac{1}{2^{-2}} = 2^2$$

Simplify the following:

$$\left(\frac{pq}{r}\right)^2 r^3 = \frac{(pq)^2 r^3}{r^2} = (pq)^2 r \text{ or } p^2 q^2 r$$

$$\frac{(amn)^2}{ma} = \frac{a^2 m^2 n^2}{ma} = amn^2$$

$$\frac{(96a)^3}{(12ab)^3} = \left(\frac{96a}{12ab}\right)^3 = \left(\frac{8}{b}\right)^3$$

WORK CARD 8

Examples marked * are more difficult and could be omitted.

1. Evaluate quickly:

   a. $(2 \times 2 \times 10)^3$ b. $\dfrac{92^3}{23^3}$ c. $\dfrac{368^4}{4^8 \times 23^3}$ d. $\dfrac{2^5 \times (3 \times 5)^3}{5^3 \times 8^3}$

2. Simplify:

   a. $\dfrac{98^3}{7^3 \times 2^3}$ b. $\dfrac{36^2 \times 48}{6^3 \times 2^4 \times 3}$ *c. $\dfrac{(\frac{1}{5})^2 \times (\frac{7}{8})^4 \times (\frac{1}{8})^3}{49^3 \times (\frac{5}{64})^3}$

   *d. $250^3 \times \dfrac{(\frac{1}{5})^4 \times (-2)^5 \times 27}{2^4 \times 3^{-4}}$

WORK CARD 8 (CONTINUED)

3. Simplify:

a. $\dfrac{(3a)^b}{3^b}$ b. $\dfrac{(r(1+r))^4}{(1+r)^4}$ c. $\left(\dfrac{b}{a}\right)^4 a^3$ d. $\dfrac{9^n}{99^n}$ e. $\dfrac{(2a)^n}{(4a)^n}$

Solutions:

1. a. 64,000 b. $4^3 = 64$ c. 23 d. $\dfrac{27}{16}$

2. a. 7^3 b. 6 c. $\dfrac{1}{7^2 \times 8 \times 5^5}$ d. $-2^4 \times 3^7 \times 5^5$

3. a. a^b b. r^4 c. $\dfrac{b^4}{a}$ d. $\left(\dfrac{1}{11}\right)^n$ e. $\dfrac{1}{2^n}$

ASSESSMENT 8

Examples marked * are more difficult and could be omitted.

1. Simplify and evaluate:

a. $\dfrac{49^3}{7^2 \times 98^2}$ b. $\dfrac{85^3}{17^3}$ c. $\dfrac{72^2 \times 4}{3^2 \times 2^3 \times 4^2}$ d. $\dfrac{105^4 \times 5^{-3}}{49 \times 36 \times 5}$ *e. $\dfrac{(\frac{1}{5})^{-4} \times 128^3 \times 49}{64^3 \times (10^1 - 3 \times 10^0)^3}$

2. Express in terms of 2 and 3 to the power of ... only:

*a. $\dfrac{132^2 \times (\frac{1}{4})^{-4} \times 8^5}{121 \times 2^7 \times 64^2}$ *b. $\dfrac{384 \times (\frac{1}{8})^3}{(\frac{1}{64})^2 \times 9^{-3}}$

3. Simplify a. $\dfrac{(3x)^q}{x^q}$ b. $(pqr)^n \cdot p^{-n}$ c. $\left(\dfrac{b}{a}\right)^3 \dfrac{a}{b^4}$ d. $\dfrac{(11^2)^m}{11^m}$ e. $\dfrac{(2pq)^n}{(4p)^n}$

9 Fractional powers

Test box 9

Evaluate:

$\sqrt[4]{81}, \quad \sqrt[3]{-125}, \quad 64^{2/3}, \quad \dfrac{48^{3/4}}{3^{3/4}}, \quad \dfrac{6^{1/3} \times 2^{1/3} \times 2^{7/3} \times 27^{-4/3}}{3^{1/3} \times 4^{3/2}}$

Solutions: ± 3, -5, 16, 8, $\dfrac{1}{81}$

Simplify:

$$\frac{a^{1/2}}{\sqrt{2}}\left(\frac{a}{2}\right)^{3/2}$$

Solution:

$$\frac{a^2}{4}$$

Square roots and cube roots

As $2^2 = 4$, we say that the *square root* of 4 is 2. We write this as $\sqrt{4} = 2$. We can also say that the square root of 9 is 3, or $\sqrt{9} = 3$, or that the square root of 64, $\sqrt{64} = 8$.

As $(-2)^2 = 4$ we could also say that $\sqrt{4} = -2$ or that $\sqrt{9} = -3$. So each positive number has two square roots – one positive and one negative. In many applications the square root is a physical quantity that cannot be negative and so we can abandon the negative square root. However, when we need to consider both roots we can write $\sqrt{4} = \pm 2$ or $\sqrt{9} = \pm 3$ and so on.

We can also talk about the *cube root* of a number. As $2^3 = 8$, the cube root of 8 is 2. We write this $\sqrt[3]{8} = 2$. In a similar way $\sqrt[3]{64} = 4$, and $\sqrt[3]{27} = 3$. We can also talk about the cube root of negative numbers, for instance $\sqrt[3]{-8} = -2$ because $(-2)^3 = -8$.

Check these

Calculate the following square or cube roots:

$\sqrt{16} = 4$ and -4 also written ± 4

$\sqrt{1} = 1$ and -1 also written ± 1

$\sqrt[3]{125} = 5$

$\sqrt[3]{-27} = -3$

$\sqrt[3]{-1} = -1$

Can you calculate $\sqrt{-4}$? The answer is 'no'. A number multiplied by itself is always a positive number, so a negative number cannot have a square root. (In fact, in more advanced mathematics one can use numbers called 'imaginary' numbers which are defined as the roots of minus numbers, but these need not concern us.)

Roots and fractional powers

Imagine now that these square and cube roots could be expressed as a power. That is, that we could write $\sqrt{4}$ as '4 to the power of something' or 4^{power}, where the power stands for a number. However, we know that the square root of 4, multiplied by itself must equal 4, that is

$$4^{\text{power}} \times 4^{\text{power}} = 4^1$$

The left-hand side of this is $4^{\text{power} + \text{power}}$ and the right-hand side is 4^1, so we can deduce that power + power = 1, and power = $\frac{1}{2}$. So $4^{1/2} \times 4^{1/2} = 4^1$ and we conclude that $\sqrt{4}$ can also be written $4^{1/2}$. By similar reasoning the square root of any number can be written as that number to the power of $\frac{1}{2}$; for instance, $\sqrt{9}$ can be written $9^{1/2}$ and $\sqrt{16}$ can be written $16^{1/2}$.

Can you work out what is meant by $8^{1/3}$? This is a number such that $8^{1/3} \times 8^{1/3} \times 8^{1/3} = 8^1$, so $8^{1/3}$ is the cube root of 8, $\sqrt[3]{8}$. Any number to the power of 1/3 is the cube root.

This index notation and the idea of roots of numbers extend logically. For instance, $16^{1/4}$ is the number such that $16^{1/4} \times 16^{1/4} \times 16^{1/4} \times 16^{1/4} = 16^1$ (add the powers on the left-hand side), so we say that $16^{1/4}$ is the fourth root of 16, also written $\sqrt[4]{16}$, which is 2 or –2.

Check these

Evaluate $16^{1/2}$, $25^{1/2}$, $81^{1/2}$, $27^{1/3}$, $(-27)^{1/3}$, $(-125)^{1/3}$, $81^{1/4}$, $1^{1/4}$, $32^{1/5}$, $64^{1/6}$

Solutions:

±4, ±5, ±9, 3, –3, –5, ±3, ±1, 2, ±2

Powers of any fraction

Conveniently, all the rules for manipulating powers that we met in Sections 7 and 8 also apply to fractional powers. Using these rules it is possible to calculate numbers to the power of *any fraction*. For instance, $8^{2/3} = 8^{1/3} \times 8^{1/3} = 2 \times 2 = 4$ and $32^{3/5} = 32^{1/5} \times 32^{1/5} \times 32^{1/5} = 2 \times 2 \times 2 = 8$.

It is often easier to evaluate these fractional powers using 'powers of powers' from Section 7. (Remember that the power of a power is the product of the indices; that is, $(b^m)^n = b^{mn}$.) For instance, as

$$\frac{2}{3} = 2 \times \frac{1}{3} \text{ or } \frac{1}{3} \times 2$$

to evaluate $8^{2/3}$ we can write it as $(8^2)^{1/3}$ or as $(8^{1/3})^2$. The hope in doing this is that at least one of these expressions is easy to evaluate. In this case, both are easy because $(8^2)^{1/3} = 64^{1/3} = 4$ and $(8^{1/3})^2 = 2^2 = 4$. In the same way, $9^{3/2}$ can be written $(9^3)^{1/2}$ or $(9^{1/2})^3$ and the second of these is easiest to evaluate as $(9^{1/2})^3 = 3^3 = 27$.

In general,

$$b^{p/q} = (b^p)^{1/q} \text{ or equivalently } b^{p/q} = (b^{1/q})^p.$$

We can evaluate negative fractional powers in the same way. For instance,

$$100^{-3/2} = (100^{1/2})^{-3} = 10^{-3} = \frac{1}{1000}$$

Notice that we have adopted the convention of taking the positive root when there is any choice.

Check these

Evaluate $27^{2/3}$, $9^{-1/2}$, $16^{3/4}$, $125^{-2/3}$, $(-1)^{3/5}$, $(81)^{-3/4}$, $16^{3/2}$

Solutions:

$(27)^{2/3} = (27^{1/3})^2 = 3^2 = 9$, $9^{-1/2} = (9^{1/2})^{-1} = 3^{-1} = \dfrac{1}{3}$, $16^{3/4} = (16^{1/4})^3 = 2^3 = 8$,

$125^{-2/3} = (125^{1/3})^{-2} = 5^{-2} = \dfrac{1}{25}$, $((-1)^{1/5})^3 = (-1)^3 = -1$, $(81^{1/4})^{-3} = 3^{-3} = \dfrac{1}{27}$,

$(16^{1/2})^3 = 4^3 = 64$

Fractional powers

The qth root of b is written

$b^{1/q}$ or $\sqrt[q]{b}$

$b^{p/q} = (b^{1/q})^p = (b^p)^{1/q}$

Calculating powers on a calculator

When faced with a power calculation like 7.27^5 or $500^{1/3}$ you will need to use your calculator. Brands vary but if you key in

$$7.27 \; x^y \; 5$$

you should see 20,308.22911... displayed.

To calculate a number to the power of a fraction like $\frac{1}{2}$, $\frac{1}{3}$, $\frac{1}{4}$ and so on (say $500^{1/3}$), use the inverse or shift key first so that

$$500 \; \text{inv} \; x^y \; 3$$

should give 7.93700526.

Fractional powers can be given as decimals. For instance, $125^{1.21}$ means $125^{121/100}$. On a calculator we would enter $125^{1.21}$ as

$$125 \; x^y \; 1.21$$

which is 344.5570304.

An application of fractional powers

In economics the output of a production process Q is related to the number of units of capital, K, and the number of units of labour, L, in the production process. A frequently used model is

$$Q = cK^a L^b$$

where c is a constant and a and b are fractions.

For example,

$$Q = 1000K^{1/4}L^{1/2}.$$

So if $K = 16$ and $L = 25$, then $Q = 1000 \times 16^{1/4} \times 25^{1/2} = 1000 \times 2 \times 5 = 10,000$.

We can use the model to study the effect of changing the levels of capital and labour. For instance, what happens to the output of the production process when capital and labour both double?

If capital and labour are now $2K$ and $2L$ respectively the new output will be

$$Q = 1000(2K)^{1/4}(2L)^{1/2}$$
$$= 1000 \times 2^{1/4}K^{1/4}2^{1/2}L^{1/2}$$
$$= 1000 \times 2^{3/4}K^{1/4}L^{1/2}$$

This is the original output times a factor of $2^{3/4}$. As $2^{3/4}$ is smaller than 2, output has less than doubled for double the labour and capital, and we say that the model exhibits *decreasing returns to scale*.

Some final examples

We finish up with some more complicated examples that use all the techniques for powers. Notice that sometimes the numbers may not work out 'nicely' and that, even after simplification, you may be left with some fractional powers.

Check these

Evaluate or simplify:

$$\frac{2^3 \times 2^{2/3}}{2^{5/3}} = 2^{3+2/3-5/3} = 2^2 = 4$$

$$a^{2/q}a^{3/q} = a^{5/q}$$

$$(a^m)^{n/m} = a^{mn/m} = a^n$$

$$\frac{3^{-3} \times \sqrt[3]{27}}{3^5} = \frac{3^{-3} \times 3}{3^5} = 3^{-7}$$

$$5^{-3}\sqrt[3]{125} = 5^{-3} \times 5 = 5^{-2} = \frac{1}{25}$$

$$\sqrt[3]{b^2}b^{1/3} = b^{2/3}b^{1/3} = b$$

$$c^{-m/n}c^{(m+1)/n} = c^{(-m+m+1)/n} = c^{1/n}$$

$$\sqrt{3} \times \sqrt{27} \times \sqrt[3]{2} \times \sqrt[3]{4} = 3^{1/2} \times (3^3)^{1/2} \times 2^{1/3} \times (2^2)^{1/3}$$
$$= 3^{1/2+3/2} \times 2^{1/3+2/3} = 3^2 \times 2 = 18$$

Evaluate:

$$\left(\frac{9}{4}\right)^{1/2} = \frac{9^{1/2}}{4^{1/2}} = \frac{3}{2}$$

Simplify:

$$\frac{x^{1/4}}{(16x)^{1/4}} = \frac{x^{1/4}}{16^{1/4}x^{1/4}} = \frac{1}{2}$$

$$\sqrt{a^2b^2} = (a^2b^2)^{1/2} = a^{2/2}b^{2/2} = ab$$

$$\left(\frac{125}{64}\right)^{2/3} = \frac{(125^{1/3})^2}{(64^{1/3})^2} = \frac{5^2}{4^2} = \frac{25}{16}$$

$$(81 \times 4)^{1/2} = 81^{1/2} \times 4^{1/2} = 9 \times 2 = 18$$

$$\sqrt{81 \times 4} = \sqrt{81} \times \sqrt{4} = 9 \times 2 = 18$$

$$\left(\frac{8}{27}\right)^{-1/3} = \frac{27^{1/3}}{8^{1/3}} = \frac{3}{2}$$

$$\frac{48}{\sqrt{2} \times 54^{1/3}} = \frac{2^4 \times 3}{2^{1/2} \times 27^{1/3} \times 2^{1/3}} = \frac{2^4}{2^{5/6}} = 2^{19/6}$$

$$a^{1/2}(a^{1/2} + a^{-1/2}) = a + a^0 = a + 1$$

$$\frac{b^{3/2} + b^{1/2}}{b^{1/2}} = \frac{b^{3/2}}{b^{1/2}} + \frac{b^{1/2}}{b^{1/2}} = b + 1$$

$$4^{-3/2} \times \left(\sqrt{64} + \left(\frac{1}{2}\right)^{5/2}\right) = 4^{-3/2} \times \left((4^3)^{1/2} + \left(\frac{1}{2}\right)^{5/2}\right) = 4^0 + 2^{-3} \times 2^{-5/2}$$

$$= 1 + 2^{-11/2}$$

WORK CARD 9

1. Calculate **a.** $\sqrt{400}$ **b.** $\sqrt[3]{27}$ **c.** $\sqrt[3]{-64}$

2. Evaluate **a.** $36^{1/2}$ **b.** $125^{1/3}$ **c.** $(-8)^{1/3}$ **d.** $(16)^{1/4}$ **e.** $1^{1/5}$ **f.** $(-1)^{1/5}$
   g. $243^{1/5}$

3. Evaluate **a.** $16^{3/2}$ **b.** $8^{-1/3}$ **c.** $125^{2/3}$ **d.** $27^{4/3}$ **e.** $81^{3/4}$ **f.** $(-27)^{2/3}$

4. Simplify and evaluate:

   a. $\dfrac{3^{7/3} \times \sqrt[3]{3}}{3^{5/3}}$ **b.** $\dfrac{4^3 \times 4^{-2}}{4^{3/2}}$ **c.** $\sqrt[c]{5}5^{2/c}$ **d.** $\dfrac{p^l q^m r^n}{p^{1/2} q^{m/2} r^{n/2}}$

5. Simplify and evaluate:

   a. $\sqrt{8} \times \sqrt{2}$ **b.** $\sqrt{64 \times 49}$ **c.** $\left(\dfrac{25}{64}\right)^{1/2}$ **d.** $\dfrac{128^{3/2}}{32^{3/2}}$ **e.** $\dfrac{(-72)^{1/3}}{9^{1/3}}$

6. Simplify:

   a. $(8^{1/2} + 8^{1/6}) \times 8^{1/6}$ b. $\dfrac{(\sqrt[4]{81} \times 81^{3/2})}{9^{5/2}}$ c. $\dfrac{32^{1/2}}{4^{3/2} \times 8^{1/6}}$ d. $\dfrac{49^{5/8} \times 3^{1/2}}{63^{3/4}}$

   e. $(7^{p/q} \cdot 7)^q$ f. $(a^{1/x}a^{1/y})^{xy}$

7. Use a calculator to evaluate a. 6.93^3 b. $400^{1/4}$ c. $21^{0.75}$

8. The formula to calculate the accrued sum (original amount + interest) of an amount of A after one month when the annual percentage rate is r% is

$$A\left(1 + \frac{r}{100}\right)^{1/12}$$

If $A = £10,000$ calculate the amount accrued after one month when the interest rate is 12%. If the interest is allowed to accumulate, how much will have accrued by the end of the second month? After 3 months? After a year?

Solutions:

1. a. ±20   b. 3   c. −4

2. a. ±6   b. 5   c. −2   d. ±2   e. 1   f. (−1)   g. 3

3. a. 64   b. $\frac{1}{2}$ c. 25   d. 81   e. 27   f. 9

4. a. 3   b. $\frac{1}{2}$ c. $5^{3/c}$ d. $p^{l/2}q^{m/2}r^{n/2}$

5. a. 4   b. 56   c. $\frac{5}{8}$ d. 8   e. −2

6. a. 6   b. 9   c. $\frac{1}{2}$ d. $\dfrac{\sqrt{7}}{3}$ e. 7^{p+q} f. a^{x+y}

7. a. 332.812557   b. 4.472135955   c. 9.809897532

8. $£10,000(1.12)^{1/12} = £10,094.89$ $£10,000(1.12)^{2/12} = £10,190.68$, $£10,000(1.12)^{3/12} = £10,287.37$. After one year $£10,000(1.12)^{12/12} = £11,200$.

1. Calculate:

   a. $\sqrt{225}$ b. $\sqrt[3]{-125}$ c. $\sqrt[3]{-27}$ d. $(49)^{1/2}$ e. $(-125)^{1/3}$ f. $(-32)^{1/5}$
   g. $1^{1/4}$ h. $128^{1/7}$

2. Evaluate:

   a. $16^{-3/4}$ b. $125^{-2/3}$ c. $(-27)^{4/3}$ d. $81^{-3/4}$ e. $(-27)^{-2/3}$

3. Simplify and evaluate if possible:

   a. $\dfrac{16^{-1/2} \times 16^2}{4^{3/2}}$ b. $(9^{3/2} \times 9^{3/4}) \div (9^{1/2} \times 9^{3/4})$ c. $32^{1/5} + 32^{3/5} \times 32^{1/5}$

d. $(7^a)^b/a7^{1/b}$ e. $\dfrac{(9y)^{1/2q}}{(27q)^{1/3q}}$

4. Simplify and evaluate:

   a. $\sqrt[3]{32} \times \sqrt[3]{2}$ b. $\sqrt[3]{125 \times 64}$ c. $\left(\dfrac{128}{18}\right)^{1/2}$ d. $\dfrac{24^{2/3}}{32^{2/3}}$ e. $\dfrac{\sqrt[3]{a^2 + b^2 + 2ab}}{\sqrt[3]{a+b}}$

5. Simplify:

   a. $\dfrac{80^{1/2}}{2^{5/2} \times 5^{1/2}}$ b. $(16^{5/8} + 4^{3/4}) \times 16^{1/8}$ c. $\dfrac{54^{1/2}}{3^{3/2} \times 6^{3/2}}$ d. $\sqrt{64^2 9 25^p}$

6. Use a calculator to evaluate:

   a. 7.7^4 b. $300^{0.25}$ c. $300^{1/4}$ d. $21^{7/8}$

7. The output of a production process is modelled by $Q = 500K^{1/3}L^{3/4}$, where K is the number of capital units and L is the number of labour units. Investigate the effect of (i) doubling capital and labour (ii) tripling capital and labour. Does the model exhibit increasing or decreasing returns to scale? Explain why you reach this conclusion.

EM3
Solving problems

What is algebra exactly, is it those 3 cornered things?

J.M. Barrie, novelist and dramatist, *Quality Street II*

Contexts

What is this chapter about?
This chapter explains what equations are, how they arise and how to solve them. It also considers expressions that contain inequalities and how to rearrange them.

Why is it useful?
We will see later in this book that many business decision problems can be formulated as a mathematical model and then solved mathematically. This mathematical solution method, more often than not, amounts to solving one or more equations or inequalities.

Where does it fit in?
This chapter builds on the material in EM1 and EM2 to expand your basic Maths toolkit.

What do I need to know?
You will need to be fluent in the techniques in the preceding two chapters, EM1 and EM2.

Objectives

After your work on this chapter you should be able to:

● understand how equations arise;
● recognise and guess solutions to equations;
● solve equations where the unknown is to the power of 1;
● rearrange an equation and substitute an expression;
● formulate and rearrange inequalities.

How much should a company produce to maximise profit? For how many years must a sum be invested so that it accrues to a particular amount? What level of inventory should be maintained to minimise ordering and carrying costs?

To solve quantitative business problems like this, the first step is to express the problem using symbols. The resulting symbolic expression will usually contain an = sign and so is called an *equation*. Techniques for formulating and solving equations are therefore very important for problem solving.

1 How equations arise

Test box 1

Write down an equation that relates d, the distance travelled on a car journey, with the speed per hour s and the journey's duration in hours h. If demand for a product is $Q = 100 - 0.5P$ where P is the unit price and the supply is $Q = 80 + 0.2P$, write down an equation that holds at the equilibrium value of P; that is, when supply equals demand.

Solutions:
$d = sh$, $100 - 0.5P = 80 + 0.2P$. Make sure that you understand how these are derived.

A reminder

In Chapters EM1 and EM2 we saw how to express relationships using symbols. Check that you understand how the following equations have arisen – you have already met the first two.

Check these

1. If S is the number of US dollars that can be purchased with p pounds when the exchange rate is r dollars to the pound, then the relationship between these quantities is

$$S = pr$$

2. When a group of n friends hire a boat on the river at a basic cost of £60 plus a fuel cost of £5 per hour for h hours, an equation describing the relationship between the cost per person C, h and n is

$$C = \frac{60 + 5h}{n}$$

3. An equation that relates the number of litres of fuel f used on a car journey, the number of kilometres k that can be driven per litre, the duration of the journey h in hours and the speed s in kilometres per hour is

$$fk = hs$$

You may need to think about this. It can help to realise that the left-hand side of the equation is the total number of kilometres that can be driven using f litres of fuel, and the right-hand side is the total number of kilometres that can be driven at speed s in h hours. As both the right-hand side and the left-hand side relate to the same journey and both represent the total distance travelled, they must be equal.

Substituting values

The equations given above represent general relationships about the quantities of interest; that is, they apply in any situation. For instance, in the boat trip example the equation

$$C = \frac{60 + 5h}{n}$$

is valid for any cost per head C, any number of hours h and any number of people n.

In a particular situation some of the quantities in an equation may take particular values. For example, if the party decide to hire the boat for 6 hours, h will be 6. A new, more specialized equation, relating the quantities that are still unknown, is obtained by substituting $h = 6$ into the original equation and is

$$C = \frac{60 + (5 \times 6)}{n} \quad \text{which simplifies to } C = \frac{90}{n}$$

Check these

An equation relating the amount of tax T I must pay at a rate of r% of everything I earn above $5000 is

$$T = \frac{(S - 5000)r}{100}$$

where S is my salary.

Write down the corresponding equation in the following cases and simplify it where possible:

a. When the tax rate is 30%;

b. When I know that I have been charged $4000 tax;

c. When I know that I have been charged $4000 tax and that my salary is $21,000.

Solutions:

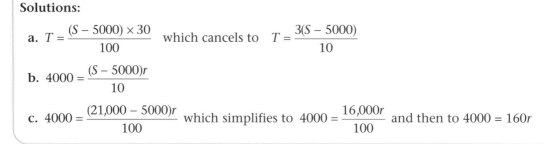

a. $T = \dfrac{(S - 5000) \times 30}{100}$ which cancels to $T = \dfrac{3(S - 5000)}{10}$

b. $4000 = \dfrac{(S - 5000)r}{10}$

c. $4000 = \dfrac{(21{,}000 - 5000)r}{100}$ which simplifies to $4000 = \dfrac{16{,}000r}{100}$ and then to $4000 = 160r$

1.   **a.** An investor invests $\$P$ for one year at an interest rate of $r\%$. Write down an equation relating I, the amount of interest he receives after one year, to r and P.

   b. A music enthusiast joins a recording club. There is an annual subscription of £S and then a price of £10 for each CD purchased. Write down an equation relating the amount he spends in a year, Y, to the number of CDs purchased during the year c.

   c. Continuing from **b**, CDs retail at £12 in the shops. Write down an equation relating X, the amount the music enthusiast saves in a year, to S and c. Simplify it if possible.

2.   **a.** It costs S to set up production in a factory and then there is a production cost of m per item. Write down an equation relating T, the total production cost, to x, the number of items produced.

   b. Write down the equation from **a** when the setup cost is £10,000 and m is 20 pence.

3.   Suppose the current exchange rate is r euros to £1 sterling:

   a. Write down an equation relating the amount of pounds p, the number of euros E and the rate r involved in an exchange transaction. (Disregard commission charges.)

   b. Suppose from **a** that the exchange rate is known to be 1.5 euros to £1. Write down the equation now.

   c. Suppose that I wish to obtain 5000 euros. Write down the equation now and simplify it if possible.

Solutions:

1.   **a.** $I = \dfrac{Pr}{100}$ **b.** $Y = S + 10c$ **c.** $X = 12c - (S + 10c) = 2c - S$.

2.   **a.** $T = S + mx$
   b. $T = 10{,}000 + 0.2x$ (be careful – the whole equation must be written using the same units, in this case pounds).

3.   **a.** $pr = E$ **b.** $1.5p = E$ **c.** $1.5P = 5000$.

ASSESSMENT 1

1. **a.** To convert fahrenheit to centigrade one must subtract 32 and then multiply by $\frac{5}{9}$. Write down an equation relating fahrenheit to centigrade.

   b. A library buys P paperback books at price p, and H hardback books at price h. Altogether they spend a total of T on the two types of book. Write down an equation relating P, p, H, and T.

   c. Refine the equation in **b** when hardbacks cost \$20 each and paperbacks cost \$10 each.

   d. The fare for a car and driver on a channel ferry crossing is F. Each additional passenger costs P. Write down an equation relating the cost per person C, to F and P when n people (including the driver) travel together in a car.

2. Demand for a product is modelled as $Q = 1000 - 0.5P$, where P is the price of a unit. Supply of the same product is modelled as $Q = 500 + P$. Write down an equation that is true at the equilibrium price.

3. I pay 25% tax on everything I earn above £3500 a year. Write down an equation relating my annual salary, S, to the amount of tax, T, I must pay. Now generalise this equation for a tax rate of $t\%$ and a threshold of £H.

2 Solutions to equations: recognising and guessing

Test box 2

Write down an equation to solve the following problem:

I have 10 coins in my purse and these are all 5p or 10p pieces. Altogether they are worth 65p. How many coins of each type do I have?

Which is the correct solution to the following equation: $y = -4$, -2 or 2?

$$\frac{2}{y+1} = 2 + \frac{8}{y}$$

Solutions: $5x + 10(10 - x) = 65$ where x is the number of 5p pieces or $5(10 - x) + 10x = 65$ where x is the number of 10p pieces. The correct solution is -2.

Equations to solve problems

Equations frequently arise in which only one quantity is unknown. Consider the following example, which is the sort of puzzle you may have seen in newspapers and magazines.

You are curious about your lecturer's age and she drops in conversation that her brother is four years younger than her and that the total of both their ages is 66. How old is your lecturer? (If you have the inclination, you could try to solve this puzzle by trial and error before you read on.)

To write down the problem in symbols, we do the usual thing; that is, read through and decide which symbols to use and then write down all the information given using these. The only symbol required here is the lecturer's age, which we'll call x. Then we have:

$$\text{Lecturer's age } \; x$$
$$\text{Brother's age } \; \underline{x - 4}$$
$$\text{Total age } \; x + (x - 4) = 66$$

and the problem boils down to the equation $2x - 4 = 66$. The lecturer's age is the value of x, for which this equation is true.

Check that you understand how the following were formulated.

| Check these |

1. An economics example:

The quantity demanded of a product Q depends on the price P at which the product is sold. As this *demand* usually falls as the price rises, a suitable model for this relationship might be $Q = 100 - 0.5P$. The producers of a good, however, can bring or supply more to the market if the price is higher, and so a suitable model for the *supply* might be $Q = 80 + 0.2P$.

For the market to be in equilibrium, the quantity demanded must be the same as the quantity supplied and the expressions for Q, given above, must be equivalent. So we can write

$100 - 0.5P = 80 + 0.2P$

This is the equilibrium equation which simplifies to $20 = 0.7P$. The value of P for which it is true is called the equilibrium price. This value is the *solution* of the equation.

2. Consider the following model to establish at what level of production a company breaks even; that is, its revenue is the same as its costs:

A company incurs £2000 in fixed costs (rent, lighting, administration) and then costs of £7 per unit manufactured. Each completed unit is sold for £17. How many units must the company produce to break even?

Let x be the number of units produced. The company's revenue will therefore be $17x$ and its total cost will be $2000 + 7x$. At break-even point, revenue must equal total cost and so

$17x = 2000 + 7x$

The solution of this equation is the break-even level of production.

Verifying solutions

When there is only one unknown quantity in an equation there is often only one value of the unknown quantity for which the equation is true. This value is called the *solution* of the equation and the process of finding it is called *solving the equation*.

For example, the equation

$$3x + 2 = 11$$

has one unknown quantity x, and $x = 3$ is the solution. We can confirm this by substituting $x = 3$ into it and verifying that $3 \cdot 3 + 2 = 11$.

Check these

Confirm that the following are correct:

The solution of $2(x + 1) = 20$ is $x = 9$

The solution of $\dfrac{y}{y - 1} = 2$ is $y = 2$

The solution of $4x + 5 = 10$ is $x = \frac{5}{4}$

The solution of the break-even example equation, $17x = 2000 + 7x$ is $x = 200$.

Guessing solutions

Try to solve the following equations by trial and error:

Check these

What is the solution of $2(x + 1) = 10$?

Find the solution of $\dfrac{20}{x} = 5$.

Find the solution of $\dfrac{y}{y - 2} = 3$

Returning to the problem of the lecturer's age, the equation was $2x - 4 = 66$; what is her age?

Solutions:

Try different values for the unknown x or y until you find one that works. The answers are $x = 4$, $x = 4$ and $y = 3$, $x = 35$.

We confess that we would like to have seen you struggle a bit to obtain some of the answers of the last **Check these**, to demonstrate that solving equations (and these are only simple ones) by *trial and error* is time-consuming and impractical. We consider a more systematic approach in the next section.

WORK CARD 2

1. Write down an equation to help solve each of the following problems, simplifying it where possible:
   a. My rectangular office is 1 metre longer than it is wide. If its perimeter is 10 metres, what are its dimensions?

WORK CARD 2 (CONTINUED)

b. I have 8 coins in my pocket. They are all 5p or 10p pieces. Their total value is 65p. How many of each type do I have?

c. Three years ago I was half my mother's present age. She is 29 years older than me. How old am I?

d. There are 52 more women students than men in the Accountancy department, making 308 students in all. How many women are there?

2. Which of the following are the correct solutions to the equation?

a. $5x - 2 = 8$. Is the solution $x = 2$, $x = 3$ or $x = 4$?

b. $12 = 4(x - 1)$. Is the solution $x = 3$, $x = 4$ or $x = 5$?

c. $\dfrac{3}{y - 1} = 3$. Is the solution $y = 1$, $y = 2$ or $y = 3$?

d. $2x + \dfrac{8}{x} = 10$. Is the solution $x = -4$, $x = 1$ or $x = 4$?

3. Use trial and error to find solutions to the equations you obtained in question 1. Don't dwell too long if you get stuck – we will learn a more systematic method of solution in Section 3.

Solutions:

1. **a.** $2x + 2(x + 1) = 10$ **b.** $5x + 10(8 - x) = 65$, where x is the number of 5p pieces or $5(8 - x) + 10x = 65$, where x is the number of 10p pieces.
c. $x - 3 = \frac{1}{2}(x + 29)$ **d.** $w - 52 + w = 308$.

2. **a.** 2 **b.** 4 **c.** 2 **d.** 4 and 1.

3. **a.** The width is 2 m. **b.** I have three 5p pieces and five 10p pieces. **c.** I am 35 **d.** There are 180 women.

ASSESSMENT 2

1. Write down equations for the following problems.

a. Paul and Louise go shopping. Paul spends twice as much as Louise, and they spend £90 in all. How much does each spend?

b. Find three consecutive whole numbers that total 48.

c. Colin's rectangular bedsit is twice as long as it is wide. Its total area is 50 square metres. How long is Colin's room?

d. I have just been Christmas shopping. I have spent £6 on each adult and twice as much on each child and bought presents for 13 people at a cost of £120 altogether. How many children have I bought for?

2. For each of the following equations, which solution is correct?

a. $7 + x = 8x$ $x = 0$, 1 or 2

b. $-40(x + 7) = 30x$ $x = -4$, 1 or 4

A2 (CONTINUED)

c. $\dfrac{5}{y} = \dfrac{2}{y-6}$ $y = 2, 5$ or 10

d. $\dfrac{x}{x+1} = 2$ $x = 2, 1$ or -2

3. Try to guess the solutions of the equations you formulated in question **1**.

3 A method for solving equations

Test box 3

Solve the equations $\dfrac{3}{r+1} = \dfrac{5}{r+2}$, $\dfrac{-1}{x-1} = 2 - \dfrac{x}{x-2}$

Solutions:
$r = 1/2$. In the second example it may appear that $x = 1$ is a solution, but at one stage in the working you need to multiply both sides of the equation by $x - 1$. You are not allowed to multiply by 0 so this is only OK if $x - 1$ is not equal to 0, which invalidates the solution $x = 1$, so there is no solution to this equation.

Many equations (those containing the unknown to the power of one) can be solved using the method in this section.

Equivalent equations

Consider the equation $3x = x + 2$. It says that, at its solution, $3x$ is the same as $x + 2$. Can you see that if we add an arbitrary number, say 1000 to each side of the equation, to give

$$3x + 1000 = x + 2 + 1000$$

the resulting equation will have the same solution? We could also subtract a number (say 500) from each side to give

$$3x - 500 = x + 2 - 500$$

or multiply by a number (say 2) to give

$$6x = 2x + 4$$

or divide by a number (for example 10), to give

$$\dfrac{3x}{10} = \dfrac{x+2}{10}$$

and the resulting equations would still have the same solution.

In general, provided we do *exactly the same to both sides* of an equation we will obtain an *equivalent equation*; that is, one that has the same solution. There is just one exception to this. You must *never* divide or multiply by 0, or an expression that might have a value of 0. We will explain why later.

> ## Check these
>
> Which of the equations in each group are equivalent?
>
> 1. **a.** $2x + 1 = 2$ **b.** $4x + 2 = 2$ **c.** $2x = 1$
>
> 2. **a.** $\dfrac{2}{x} = 8$ **b.** $\dfrac{1}{x} = 4$ **c.** $2 = 8x$
>
> 3. **a.** $5(x + 1) = 10(x + 2)$ **b.** $5x + 5 = 10x + 2$
>
>   **c.** $x + 1 = 2x + 4$ **d.** $x + 1 = 2(x + 2)$ **e.** $1 = x + 4$
>
> **Solutions:**
>
> 1. **a** and **c**
>
> 2. All of them
>
> 3. All except **b**

In the **Check these** above, equations **1c**, **2c** and **3e** respectively were 'simpler' than the others in that the solution of x was more apparent. For instance, in the first example, **1c**, $2x = 1$, the solution is $x = \frac{1}{2}$; in **2c**, $2 = 8x$, x must be $\frac{1}{4}$; and in **3e**, $1 = x + 4$, x must be -3.

This is the idea behind the method for solving equations. We find an equivalent equation that can be solved more easily than the original.

The solution method

We solve an equation in a series of steps. At each step we write down an equation which is equivalent to the previous one but that will be 'simpler' to solve. We continue until we obtain an equation like $x = 5$ or $x = 3$, in which the unknown quantity (x here) is 'isolated'; that is, it appears on one side of the equation only, on its own, so that the solution can be 'read off' immediately.

For example, to solve $3x = x + 2$ we subtract x from both sides to give

$$3x - x = x + 2 - x$$

which simplifies to

$$2x = 2.$$

Now we divide both sides by 2 to give

$$x = 1$$

and the solution is now easy to read off; merely $x = 1$.

We can check the solution is correct by substituting $x = 1$ back into the original equation.

Before you try solving some equations on your own, see if you can follow the reasoning in these examples. Remember the object is to isolate x so that it appears on one side of the equation only, on its own.

Check these

1. Solve $4x + 3 = 11$.

Whilst x only appears on the left-hand side it is not isolated because of the 3. To remove the 3 we need to subtract it from the left-hand side. However, we can only do this if we treat the right-hand side in the same way. Our first step is therefore to subtract 3 *from both sides* to give

$$4x + 3 - 3 = 11 - 3$$

which simplifies to

$$4x = 8.$$

Now we have $4x =$, whereas we would like $x =$, so we need to divide the left-hand side by 4. Again, we must treat both sides in the same way to give

$$x = \frac{8}{4}$$

We have isolated x, so the solution is $x = 2$.

2. Solve

$$\frac{5}{x} = 15$$

At present the unknown, x, is a denominator, whereas we are aiming at $x = \dots$. We must therefore multiply both sides of the equation by x to give

$$\frac{5}{x} x = 15x$$

which simplifies to

$$5 = 15x$$

The xs are now 'on top' and so less of a problem. All the xs appear on one side as required but there are 15 of them. To rectify this we need to divide the right-hand side by 15, which of course means that we must treat the other side of the equation in the same way. This gives

$$\frac{5}{15} = x$$

and, cancelling, we have the solution $x = \frac{1}{3}$.

3. Solve:

$$\frac{y}{y - 2} = 3$$

This is harder, as the unknown, y, appears in both the numerator and the denominator of the right-hand side. However, like the last example, it's best to get all the unknowns 'on the top', so we multiply by $y - 2$. This gives

$$y = 3(y - 2)$$

which already looks much more straightforward than the original equation. Remember, our goal is to get all the ys on the same side, and everything else to the other side. Here, we can't separate the y term on the right-hand side from the 2 as both are enclosed in the bracket. We therefore multiply out the bracket to give

$y = 3y - 6$

which looks more like the equations we have met before. To bring all the ys to one side we subtract $3y$ from both sides to give

$-2y = -6$

and then divide by -2 to give the solution

$y = 3$

 When solving equations the main difficulty is deciding which operation to do at each step. Whilst any operation is 'legal' (provided you do the same to both sides of the equation and don't multiply or divide by 0) an unhelpful choice of operation will make the equation even more complicated! If this happens go back a couple of steps and resume! It is better to learn how to solve equations by experience, but we offer the guidelines below. Try not to regard these as rules.

Guidelines for solving equations

At each step write down an equivalent equation, i.e. perform the same operation on both sides of the equation.

Do *not* multiply or divide by 0 or an expression with zero value.

Your aim is an equation like $x = \dots$ or $\dots = x$.

This goal will usually be achieved by accomplishing the following objectives in order:

1. Get x 'on top'
Do this by multiplying by any expressions containing x that are in the denominators of fractions.

2. Get x outside any brackets
Multiply out any brackets.

3. Get all the xs on one side
Collect together on one side of the equation all the terms involving x.

4. Get x alone on one side
Remove all other terms from that side of the equation.

Now try the following on your own. Remember that you can always check your solution by substituting it back into the original equation.

Check these

Solve the following:

1. $x + 12 = 3x + 6$

2. $5p + 7 = 2p + 3$

3. $\dfrac{5x}{7} = 20$

4. $s(s + 1) = s^2 + 6 - 2s$

5. $\dfrac{3}{r + 1} = \dfrac{5}{r + 2}$

Solutions:

1. $12 = 2x + 6$, $6 = 2x$, $3 = x$. The solution is $x = 3$.

2. $3p + 7 = 3$, $3p + 4 = 0$, $3p = -4$, $p = \dfrac{-4}{3}$

3. $5x = 140$, $x = \dfrac{140}{5} = 28$.

4. All the ss on the left-hand side are entangled so you need to multiply out the brackets first to give $s^2 + s = s^2 + 6 - 2s$, $s = 6 - 2s$, $3s = 6$, $s = 2$.

5. Multiplying by $r + 2$ gives

$$\frac{3(r + 2)}{r + 1} = 5$$

and then multiplying by $r + 1$ gives $3(r + 2) = 5(r + 1)$. However, these steps are only valid if neither $r + 2$ nor $r + 1$ are zero at the solution. We deal with this in the next sub-section, 'multiplying and dividing by 0'. Continuing gives $3r + 6 = 5r + 5$, $6 = 2r + 5$, $6 - 5 = 2r$, $r = \frac{1}{2}$.

It is quite possible that an equation does *not* have a solution. Consider the following example:

Check these

$$\frac{1}{3 - x} = \frac{1}{6 - x}$$

If we carry on as usual, we get rid of the xs in the denominator and multiply both sides by $3 - x$ to give

$$1 = \frac{3 - x}{6 - x}$$

and then multiply by $6 - x$ to give

$6 - x = 3 - x.$

Adding x to each side gives

$6 = 3$

This is plainly silly: we have a contradiction. We deduce from this (assuming we have not made any mistakes) that the original equation has *no* solution.

Multiplying and dividing by 0

Recall that you can perform any operation to both sides of an equation – *except* multiplying or dividing by 0.

Dividing by 0 is just not feasible. Try calculating anything divided by 0 on your calculator.

To see why multiplying by 0 creates problems, let's start off with a simple statement (which is also an equation) that has no solution.

$$3 = 4$$

If we multiply both sides by 0, we obtain

$$3 \times 0 = 4 \times 0$$
$$0 = 0$$

which *is* true. So multiplying both sides of an equation by zero does *not* give an equivalent equation. In the same way, if you multiply both sides by an expression that has a value of zero at the solution, your answer will be invalid, as shown in the following example:

Check these

Now try

$$\frac{2x}{x-2} = 1 + \frac{4}{x-2}$$

To remove the $x - 2$ in the denominators we multiply by $x - 2$. This gives

$2x = x - 2 + 4$

which is

$2x = x + 2$

Now we subtract x from each side to give

$x = 2$

This looks fine: the solution is $x = 2$ ... or is it? At the first step, we multiplied by $x - 2$. As the solution is $x = 2$, this equates to multiplying by zero – which is *not* allowed, so we conclude that $x = 2$ is *not* a valid solution. As no other solutions were found this means that the original equation does *not* have a solution.

What we should have done in the example above is to make a note, when multiplying by $x - 2$, that the step is only valid provided $x - 2$ is *not* 0, as shown below. Note the $\neq$, meaning 'is not equal to'.

$$\frac{2x}{x-2} = 1 + \frac{4}{x-2}$$

$2x = x - 2 + 4$ when $x - 2 \neq 0$; that is, $x \neq 2$.   ← *This is the note*

$2x = x + 2$

$x = 2$ but $x \neq 2$ from above, so there is no solution.

WORK CARD 3

1. Which of the following equations are equivalent? Show your working.

    a. $2x - 1 = 5$, $10x - 5 = 25$, $2x = 4$

    b. $\dfrac{2}{y} = 3$, $2 = 3y$, $2 = \dfrac{3}{y}$

    c. $\dfrac{x+1}{2} = 2x$, $x + \dfrac{1}{2} = 2x$, $4x = x + 1$, $3x = 1$

    d. $(x-1)(x+2) = 3$, $\dfrac{x-1}{3} = x + 2$, $\dfrac{x-1}{3} = \dfrac{1}{x+2}$

2. Solve the following equations:

    a. $2x + 3 = 9$ **b.** $\dfrac{7}{x} = 14$ **c.** $\dfrac{2x+3}{7} = 3$ **d.** $\dfrac{y}{2} = 2 + y$ **e.** $p(p-2) = p^2$

3. Solve the following equations:

    a. $\dfrac{5}{4}q = \dfrac{3}{2}q + 1$ **b.** $\dfrac{1}{z+1} = \dfrac{2}{z+2}$ **c.** $\dfrac{1}{w+1} = \dfrac{1}{w+2}$ **d.** $\dfrac{x}{2x-2} = 1 + \dfrac{1}{2x-2}$

Solutions:

1. The following equations are *different* **a.** 3rd   **b.** 3rd   **c.** 2nd   **d.** 2nd

2. **a.** 3   **b.** $\frac{1}{2}$ **c.** 9   **d.** −4   **e.** 0

3. **a.** −4   **b.** $z = 0$ **c.** No solution   **d.** $x = 1$, but you multiplied by $2x - 2$ to obtain this, so no solution.

ASSESSMENT 3

1. Which equations in each group are equivalent? Show your working.

    a. $2x + 1 = 5x + 3$, $1 = 3x + 3$, $2x = 5x + 2$

    b. $\dfrac{5}{z} = \dfrac{2}{z+1}$, $5(z+1) = 2$, $5(z+1) = 2z$

    c. $2x + 2 = 5(x-1)$, $2(x+2) = 5(x-1)$, $2x + 7 = 5x$

    d. $\dfrac{a}{x} = 2 + \dfrac{1}{a}$, $a = 2x + \dfrac{1}{a}$, $\dfrac{a^2}{x} = 2 + 1$

2. Solve the following equations where possible:

a. $5x + 9 = 49$ b. $\dfrac{8}{q} = 24$ c. $\dfrac{3y - 6}{3} = 10$ d. $r(r + 1) - r^2 = 2$

e. $(s - 1) = \dfrac{s^2}{s + 2}$ f. $\dfrac{7}{4}z = \dfrac{7}{6}(z - 1)$ g. $\dfrac{1}{p - 1} - \dfrac{1}{p - 2} = 0$

h. $\dfrac{2z}{z + 3} = 1 + \dfrac{2}{z + 3}$ i. $\dfrac{2z}{z + 3} = 1 - \dfrac{6}{z + 3}$

4 Formulating and solving equations

Test box 4

Solve the following problem using an equation:

   When my husband and I got married 8 years ago I was $\frac{9}{10}$ of his age. He is 3 years older than me. How old is my husband?

Solution:
If my husband's age is x, mine is $x - 3$, so

$$x - 3 - 8 = \frac{9}{10}(x - 8)$$

Solving this gives $x = 38$.

The good news is that there is no new work in this section. In Sections 1 and 2 we practised formulating equations and in Section 3 we learnt how to solve them. Now, we put these together and go from the original problem right through to the solution.

Check these

1. If the demand equation is $Q = 1000 - 2P$ and the supply equation is $Q = 500 + 3P$, where P is the unit price of a good, calculate the equilibrium price.

Solution:
At the equilibrium price $1000 - 2P = 500 + 3P$. To solve this, add $2P$ to each side to give $1000 = 500 + 5P$, and then subtract 500 from each side to give $500 = 5P$. Dividing by 5 gives $100 = P$, so the equilibrium price is $P = 100$.

2. I have 2 newspapers a week delivered for 5 weeks and then change to one newspaper a week for the next 6 weeks. At the end of 11 weeks my bill is £8. How much is one newspaper? (Assume that all newspapers are the same price.)

Solution:
Let x be the weekly cost of a newspaper. For 5 weeks the weekly cost will be $2x$ a week whereas for 6 weeks the cost will be x a week. The total cost is therefore $5 \cdot 2x + 6x$ or $16x$, which is equal to £8, giving the equation $16x = 8$.
 So the solution is $x = \frac{1}{2}$ and a single newspaper costs 50p.

3. A concert organiser anticipates selling 2000 tickets and that a quarter of these will be sold at the concessionary price of a 40% reduction. He needs to make $18,000 in ticket receipts. How much must a full price ticket be?

Solution:
Let p be the price of a full price ticket; 1500 people will buy one of these to yield receipts of $1500p$. The concessionary ticket will sell at $0.6p$ or $\frac{3p}{5}$, so the receipts from these will be

$$500 \times \frac{3p}{5} = 300p$$

Total receipts are therefore $1500p + 300p = 1800p$. These must be equivalent to $18,000 so we solve $1800p = 18,000$ to give $p = \$10$.

4. I can never remember the ages of my friend's two children. I recall that when the youngest was born the oldest was 2, and that a year ago the oldest was bragging that their ages added up to 14. How old are they now?

Solution:
Let x be the age of the oldest. The youngest is therefore $x - 2$ years old. Last year their ages must have been $x - 1$ and $x - 3$ respectively, giving the equation

$$x - 1 + x - 3 = 14$$

which simplifies to $2x - 4 = 14$. Solving this gives $x = 9$. The children are 9 and 7 years old.

5. An investment management company offers two charge structures. The annual charge is either 7% of the sum invested, or else it is £100 plus 2% of the sum invested. For what amount of investment is the annual charge the same under both structures?

Solution:
Let x be the sum invested. Under the first charge structure the annual charge is $\frac{7}{100}x$. Under the second the charge is

$$100 + \frac{2}{100}x$$

When these two charges are the same, x must be such that

$$\frac{7}{100}x = 100 + \frac{2}{100}x$$

This is the equation we have to solve. Note that it could also be written

$$\frac{7x}{100} = 100 + \frac{2x}{100}$$

To solve this we can multiply all through by 100 to give $7x = 100^2 + 2x$ and then subtract $2x$ from both sides to give $5x = 100^2$. We then divide by 5 to give

$$x = \frac{10,000}{5} = 2000$$

The charge structures are equal for an investment of £2000.

1. Find three consecutive whole numbers that total 33.

2. The demand for a good is given by $Q = 3000 - 3P$, where P is the price, whereas the supply is $Q = 2000 + 5P$. How many units of the good must be manufactured for supply to equal demand, and at what price?

3. I wish to buy some travellers' cheques. Bank 1 will sell them at 2% commission whereas Bank 2 charges a flat fee of $3 and then 1% commission. At what value of x will these charges be equal?

4. The formula for the amount of tax payable by an individual is

$$T = (S - 3000)\frac{t}{100}$$

where t is the tax rate (%) and S is their annual salary.
   If my annual tax statement says that £3000 tax has been deducted from my salary of £18,000, what is the current tax rate?

Solutions:

1. 10, 11, 12.

2. $P = 125$.

3. The equation is

$$\frac{2x}{100} = 3 + \frac{x}{100}$$

and the solution is $x = 300$.

4. 20%.

1. The standing charge for electricity is £15 per quarter. In addition to this customers are charged at £0.07 per kilowatt. My bill for a quarter is £50. How many kilowatts have I used? Use an equation to solve this problem.

2. I bought 3 packs of tiles and 5 pots of paint from a hardware store. I remember that tiles were $7 a pack and that the total bill was $76. How much was each pot of paint? Express the problem as an equation and solve it.

ASSESSMENT 4

3. An equation for the present value of a loan repayment due in a year's time is

$$V = \frac{P(1+r)}{1+i}$$

If $r = 0.08$ and $V = £9000$ for a loan of $P = £10,000$, what is i?

4. I want to buy some Botswana pulas and the exchange rate is BWP 8.25 = £1 if I buy them abroad using a credit card or BWP 8.5 = £1 for a cash transaction at a Bureau de Change. The credit card company will charge me 2.3% commission whereas the Bureau de Change charges 2% commission plus a fee of £3.

Write down an expression for the cost (including commission) of buying a particular number of Botswana pulas **a** by credit card, and **b** from a Bureau de Change.

(i) Evaluate each of these expressions for BWP700, BWP800 and BWP900 respectively;

(ii) Hazard a guess as to the number of Botswana pulas you would have to buy for the cost to be the same whether you used a credit card or cash;

(iii) Write down the equation that needs to be solved to calculate the number of pulas I would have to buy to make the cost the same whether I obtained the currency by credit card or from a Bureau de Change;

(iv) Solve this equation. Does the solution correspond to your guess in (ii)?

5 Rearranging equations and substituting

Test box 5

Express the following with y as the subject:

$$2x = \sqrt{3y - z} + 1$$

Express P in terms of I and r in the following:

$$I = \frac{P(r - 1)}{100} - 10$$

If

$$x = \frac{t}{\sqrt{1 + t^2}} \quad \text{and} \quad y = \frac{1}{\sqrt{1 + t^2}}$$

express $x^2 + y^2$ in terms of t.

Solutions:

$$y = \frac{(2x-1)^2 + z}{3}, \qquad P = \frac{100I + 1000}{r-1}, \qquad x^2 + y^2 \text{ simpifies to } 1.$$

Rearranging equations

Recall (from Chapter EM1, Section 5) that if the exchange rate is r euros to the pound and I have p pounds, the number of euros I can purchase is given by the equation

$$e = pr$$

As this equation is arranged as $e = ...$ it is easy to calculate the number of euros, e, when we know p and r. For instance, if $p = 100$ and $r = 1.5$ we would obtain $e = 100 \times 1.5 = 150$. We say that e is the *subject* of the equation and that this is a formula for e *in terms of* p and r.

In practice, we might need a formula for the number of pounds, p, in terms of e and r. That is, we might want the equivalent equation of form $p = ...$, so that p is the subject.

To obtain this we proceed as if we were solving the equation for p; that is, we perform a sequence of operations (except multiplying or dividing by zero) on both sides of the = sign until p is isolated on one side. The only difference is that now there are other symbols in the equation as well as p.

We start with

$$e = pr$$

The right-hand side contains p times r, so to isolate p we must divide both sides of the equation by r to give

$$\frac{e}{r} = p$$

This gives us the equation we require, although it is conventional to place the subject on the left-hand side of the equation; that is, to write

$$p = \frac{e}{r}$$

(Notice that this parallels the solution of an equation like $12 = 4p$ in which we would isolate p by dividing by 4.)

This process of changing the subject of an equation is called *rearranging* or *transposing* the equation.

| Check these |

1. Make x the subject of $y = 2x + 3$.

Solution:
We need to isolate x, so subtract 3 from both sides to give $y - 3 = 2x$, and then divide both sides by 2 to give

$$\frac{y-3}{2} = x$$

So

$$x = \frac{y - 3}{2}$$

2. Express y in terms of x when

$$x = \frac{3y - 5}{2}$$

Solution:
Multiply by 2 to give $2x = 3y - 5$, add 5 to each side to give $2x + 5 = 3y$ and finally divide by 3 to give

$$y = \frac{2x + 5}{3}$$

3. Make x the subject of $y = ax + b$.

Solution:
Do not be put off by all the symbols – this example is similar to the first. Subtract b from both sides to give $y - b = ax$, then divide by a to give

$$x = \frac{y - b}{a}$$

4. Transpose the following formula to make P the subject. $Pv = c + d$.

Solution:
Only one step is needed here. We merely need to divide both sides by v to give

$$P = \frac{c + d}{v}$$

5. $C = \dfrac{abd}{3}$. Make b the subject.

Solution:
First multiply by 3 to give $3C = abd$. Now b is multiplied by ad on the right-hand side so dividing by ad will isolate b to give

$$\frac{3C}{ad} = b \quad \text{or} \quad b = \frac{3C}{ad}$$

The final step in the following example is slightly harder.

Check this

Express x in terms of y when

$$y = \frac{x - 3}{x + 2}$$

Solution:
Multiply both sides by $x + 2$ to give $y(x + 2) = x - 3$. The xs can't be separated from the ys because of the bracket, so multiply it out to give $xy + 2y = x - 3$. We want all the x terms on one side, so subtracting x from both sides gives $xy - x + 2y = -3$ and then subtracting $2y$ gives $xy - x = -3 - 2y$.

  Now comes the hard bit. Remember, we want x on its own on one side. Notice that the left-hand side $xy - x$ can be written $x(y - 1)$; that is, it is a multiple of x. So we have $x(y - 1) = -3 - 2y$. We can now divide both sides by $y - 1$ to isolate x to obtain

$$x = \frac{-3 - 2y}{y - 1}$$

This is the required equation, although we would often write it as

$$x = \frac{3 + 2y}{1 - y}$$

(we have merely multiplied numerator and denominator by -1 so that there are fewer minus signs).

Like solving equations, there are no hard-and-fast rules for which operation to do when, but the guidelines below may help if you're struggling. Again, don't learn these by heart – it is better to gain experience by working through lots of examples.

Guidelines for rearranging equations

1. Remove square roots or other roots.
2. Get rid of fractions.
3. Multiply out brackets.
4. Factorise if necessary – to separate the desired subject.

Notice that **1** says that square and other roots should be removed first. Consider the following examples:

Check these

1. $\sqrt{x + 2y} = p$. Transform so that y is the subject.

Solution:
As suggested in the guidelines above, our first step to isolate y must be to get rid of the square root. We do this by squaring both sides of the equation. This is quite legal as we are still treating both sides in the same way. If we square the square root of something we get the 'something', so our equation becomes $x + 2y = p^2$.

The rest is straightforward:

$$2y = p^2 - x, \text{ so } y = \frac{p^2 - x}{2}$$

2. Now try expressing

$$a = \sqrt{\frac{b}{b + c}}$$

with b as the subject.

Solution:
Again, the square root is obscuring b so we square both sides to give

$$a^2 = \frac{b}{b + c}$$

Multiplying by $b + c$ gives $a^2(b + c) = b$, multiplying out the bracket gives $a^2b + a^2c = b$, which rearranges to $a^2b - b + a^2c = 0$ and then $a^2b - b = -a^2c$.

All the terms containing b are on the left-hand side but each is multiplied by something so we must factorise to give

$$b(a^2 - 1) = -a^2c \text{ and then } b = \frac{-a^2c}{(a^2 - 1)}$$

Notice that there is no benefit in squaring a square root unless it is alone on one side of the equation.

Check this

Express $\sqrt{\dfrac{f}{g}} + 2 = y$ with g as the subject.

Solution:
We must remove the square root, but it is *not* helpful to square both sides of the equation in its present form. Why? The left-hand side squared is

$$\left(\sqrt{\frac{f}{g}} + 2\right)\left(\sqrt{\frac{f}{g}} + 2\right) = \frac{f}{g} + 4\sqrt{\frac{f}{g}} + 4$$

so this does *not* remove the square root. To eliminate the square root sign we must isolate the square root on one side of the equation before we square both sides. Subtracting 2 from both sides to give

$$\sqrt{\frac{f}{g}} = y - 2 \text{ will do this.}$$

Now we can square both sides to give

$$\frac{f}{g} = (y - 2)^2$$

Further rearrangement gives

$$g = \frac{f}{(y-2)^2}$$

We transpose some useful everyday and financial equations below:

Check these

1. The amount of interest received I when a sum of P has been invested for one year at a rate of $r\%$ per annum is

$$I = \frac{rP}{100}$$

Express r in terms of I and P.

Solution:
Multiplying both sides by 100 gives $100I = rP$, so

$$\frac{100I}{P} = r \text{ or } r = \frac{100I}{P}$$

2. The formula relating degrees centigrade C to degrees fahrenheit F is

$$C = \frac{5}{9}(F - 32)$$

Express this with F as the subject.

Solution:
First multiply by 9 to give $9C = 5(F - 32)$, and then multiply out the bracket to obtain $9C = 5F - 160$. Now add 160 giving $9C + 160 = 5F$ and finally divide by 5. So

$$F = \frac{9C + 160}{5}$$

This is more usually written as

$$F = \frac{9}{5}C + 32$$

3. The amount I received on an investment of P at $r\%$ interest over one year less a management charge of $10 + 0.01P$ is

$$I = \frac{P}{100}(r - 1) - 10$$

Express P in terms of I and r.

Solution:
First add 10 to give

$$10 + I = \frac{P(r-1)}{100}$$

Now multiply by 100 to give $1000 + 100I = P(r-1)$ and then divide by $r-1$ to give

$$P = \frac{1000 + 100I}{r-1}$$

4. The formula for the area A of a circle is $A = \pi r^2$ where r is the circle's radius and π is the well-known constant. What is the radius in terms of the area?

Solution:
To isolate r we must first divide by π. This gives

$$\frac{A}{\pi} = r^2$$

We haven't dealt directly with a squared term before but the method is just the same as usual. Here, r^2 is on its own on one side of the equation and there are no other terms involving r, so we can take the square root of both sides of the equation to obtain

$$\sqrt{\frac{A}{\pi}} = r$$

The formula for the radius of a circle in terms of its area is therefore

$$r = \sqrt{\frac{A}{\pi}}$$

In general this formula is ambiguous as the square root could be positive or negative, but in this context it is all right as a radius *cannot* be negative.

Another example, which arises from management science, comes from the most widely used inventory control model. If you are interested in the background please read on, but otherwise you could hop to the next **Check this**.

Many organisations – shops, warehouses, hospital stores, etc. – hold stock or inventory so that they can satisfy demand immediately. Holding stock attracts two types of cost. Insurance, storage costs and interest paid on money tied up in inventory are collectively called *holding costs* whereas the cost of placing an order (administration, loading and transport) is known as the *ordering cost*. The policy for replenishing stock is often to place an order of a fixed size called the *fixed order quantity*, when stock reaches a certain level.

Many models have been suggested for inventory control. The simplest model for a single product assumes that demand occurs at a constant rate of d per unit time, the ordering cost is K, orders for a fixed order quantity q arrive immediately and that holding costs are h per unit per unit time.

After some working, which involves a branch of maths called calculus, the fixed order quantity q which gives the smallest total cost (holding cost + ordering cost) per unit time satisfies the equation

$$\frac{-Kd}{q^2} + \frac{h}{2} = 0$$

In practice, K, d and h are known and we are interested in how much to order so an expression is required for q in terms of K, d and h.

Check this

Rearrange the equation

$$\frac{-Kd}{q^2} + \frac{h}{2} = 0$$

with q as the subject.

Solution:
The desired subject, q, is currently in the denominator, so we start by multiplying all through by q^2. This gives

$$-Kd + \frac{hq^2}{2} = 0$$

Now add Kd to each side to give

$$\frac{hq^2}{2} = Kd$$

and multiply by 2 to give $hq^2 = 2Kd$. Isolating q^2 gives

$$q^2 = \frac{2Kd}{h}$$

Now, as for the radius of a circle problem above, we have a formula for the square of the subject. Taking square roots of both sides gives

$$q = \sqrt{\frac{2Kd}{h}}$$

Again, there is no ambiguity here as q is a quantity and so must be positive. The formula

$$\sqrt{\frac{2Kd}{h}}$$

is well-known and is called the *economic order quantity*. Inventory models are considered in more detail in *Business Modelling*, Chapter BM3.

Substituting expressions

We have often evaluated an expression by substituting values in place of the symbols. For instance, suppose the amount of tax I must pay on my salary S at tax rate t% is given by

$$T = \frac{(S - 3000)t}{100}$$

When my salary is £10,000 and the tax rate is 25% I must pay

$$T = \frac{(10,000 - 3000)25}{100} = £1750$$

Sometimes one or more of the variables in an expression can be expressed in terms of one or more other variables. It may then be useful to make some substitutions. This is best explained by example.

Suppose we are interested in the expression $x - y$ but we know that $x = t^2 + t$ and $y = t + 1$. We may, if we wish, express $x - y$ in terms of t by substituting $t^2 + t$ for x and $t + 1$ for y in $x - y$. This gives

$$t^2 + t - (t + 1)$$

which is

$$t^2 + t - t - 1$$

which simplifies further to

$$t^2 - 1$$

| Check these |

If $s = \sqrt{(1 - x^2)}$ and $t = \sqrt{(1 + x^2)}$ express

$$\frac{s^2 - 1}{s^2 - t^2}$$

in terms of x.

Solution:
Substituting $\sqrt{(1 - x^2)}$ for s and $\sqrt{(1 + x^2)}$ for t in

$$\frac{s^2 - 1}{s^2 - t^2}$$

gives

$$\frac{1 - x^2 - 1}{1 - x^2 - (1 + x^2)}$$

which simplifies to

$$\frac{-x^2}{-2x^2} = \frac{1}{2}$$

If $r + s = 1$, express $r^2 - s^2$ terms of r only.

Solution:
At first sight this seems trickier. We need to express the s in $r^2 - s^2$ in terms of r. The secret is to spot that the first equation can be rearranged to $s = 1 - r$, so substituting this in $r^2 - s^2$ gives $r^2 - (1 - r)^2$ which simplifies to $r^2 - (1 + r^2 - 2r) = 2r - 1$.

Try the following financial example:

> Check this
>
> In the UK, net salary N is gross salary G *less* a deduction for national insurance I and a deduction for tax T. So,
>
> $$N = G - I - T \qquad (1)$$
>
> However, I is one tenth of gross salary and tax is 25% of gross salary above £4000, and we also have
>
> $$I = \frac{G}{10} \qquad (2)$$
>
> and $T = \dfrac{G - 4000}{4}$ $\qquad (3)$
>
> Write down an equation expressing net salary in terms of gross salary only.
>
> **Solution:**
> We can obtain an equation for N in terms of G only by substituting expressions (2) and (3) for I and T in (1). This gives
>
> $$N = G - \frac{G}{10} - \frac{G - 4000}{4}$$
>
> This can be simplified by placing all terms on the right-hand side over a common denominator as follows.
>
> $$N = \frac{20G}{20} - \frac{2G}{20} - \frac{5(G - 4000)}{20}$$
> $$= \frac{20G - 2G - 5G + 20{,}000}{20} = \frac{13G + 20{,}000}{20}$$
>
> The new equation enables a solution for G or N to be found from a known value of the other. For instance, if I know that my net salary is £11,400 I must solve
>
> $$11{,}400 = \frac{13G + 20{,}000}{20}$$
>
> for G to find out my gross salary. (The solution is £16,000.)

1. **a.** Express $y = 5x - 2$ with x as the subject
   b. Write $f = VH$ with H as the subject
   c. Express $y = 2(x + 2)$ with x as the subject

2. Make x the subject of the following
   a. $y = \dfrac{2x + 1}{3}$ **b.** $y = \dfrac{1 - 5x}{2}$ **c.** $y = \dfrac{-2x - 1}{3x + 2}$

d. Make r the subject of $\dfrac{p}{q} = \dfrac{q}{r+s}$

e. Express x in terms of y, when $y = \dfrac{x-3}{x+2}$

3. a. The relationship between the number of kilometres travelled k and the equivalent number of miles m is $m = \frac{5}{8}k$. Rearrange this to give a formula for k in terms of m.

b. The diameter of a circle d is given by the formula $d = 2\pi r$ where r is the radius of the circle. Obtain a formula for the radius in terms of the diameter.

c. The relationship between the number of litres of fuel consumed on a journey f, average fuel consumption per kilometre in litres c, the duration of the journey in hours d, and the average speed in kilometres s, is given by

$$\frac{f}{c} = ds$$

Obtain a formula that will calculate average fuel consumption per kilometre in terms of duration, average speed and the number of litres consumed.

4. For any year the formula for the amount of tax payable by an individual is

$$T = (S - H)\frac{t}{100}$$

where t is the tax rate (%), H is the tax threshold and S is their annual salary. Rearrange this with H as the subject.

Peter has got his tax affairs in a muddle and is not sure that he has been charged at the correct threshold for the last few years. He knows that the tax rate is 25% throughout this time. Use your formula to calculate the tax thresholds at which Peter has been charged in the last two years when

a. Peter's annual tax statement for last year says that £3750 tax was deducted from his salary of £18,000;

b. The previous year's statement reports that Peter paid £3625 tax on his salary of £17,250.

5. a. If $p = \sqrt{(q^2 - 1)}$, express

$$\frac{p^2 + q^2}{p^2 - q^2}$$

in terms of q

b. If $y = c^2 + 1$, express $A = \sqrt{y + 2c}\sqrt{y - 2c}$ in terms of c and simplify if possible.

c. If $p + q = 1$, simplify

$$\sqrt{\frac{p^2 + q^2 + 2pq}{1 + p^2 - 2p}}$$

Solutions:

1. **a.** $x = \dfrac{y+2}{5}$ **b.** $H = \dfrac{f}{V}$ **c.** $\dfrac{y}{2} - 2$

2. **a.** $x = \dfrac{3y-1}{2}$ **b.** $x = \dfrac{1-2y}{5}$ **c.** $x = \dfrac{-1-2y}{3y+2}$ **d.** $r = \dfrac{q^2 - ps}{p}$ **e.** $x = \dfrac{2y+3}{1-y}$

3. **a.** $k = \dfrac{8}{5}m$ or $k = \dfrac{8m}{5}$ **b.** $r = \dfrac{d}{2\pi}$ **c.** $c = \dfrac{f}{ds}$

4. $H = S - \dfrac{100T}{t}$

    a. As $t = 25$, the formula becomes

    $H = S - \dfrac{100T}{25}$ or $H = S - 4T$

    So when $T = 3750$ and $S = 18{,}000$, $H = 18{,}000 - 15{,}000 = 3000$.

    b. When $T = 3625$ and $S = 17{,}250$, $H = 17{,}250 - 14{,}500 = 2750$.

5. **a.** $1 - 2q^2$ **b.** $\sqrt{c^2 + 1 + 2c}\sqrt{c^2 + 1 - 2c} = (c+1)(c-1)$ so $A = c^2 - 1$.   **c.** $\dfrac{1}{q}$

1. **a.** Express $5t - s = 3$ with s as the subject.

    b. Express $\dfrac{5}{y} + 3 = p$ with y as the subject.

    c. Express h in terms of W, a and r when $W = ar(r + h)$.

2. Express the following with x as the subject

    a. $y = \dfrac{2x-1}{2}$ **b.** $y = \dfrac{3+2x}{3}$ **c.** $y = \dfrac{x-3}{2x+1}$

3. Make q the subject of

    a. $\dfrac{p}{r} = \dfrac{r}{q+s}$ **b.** $pqr^2 = \dfrac{16}{pq}$ **c.** $\sqrt{\dfrac{3}{q}} + 1 = r$

4. **a.** Express the following in terms of P: $I = PrT$

    b. If $C = f + mx$, obtain a formula for x in terms of C, f and m.

    c. If the formula for the length of the hypotenuse of a triangle is $h = \sqrt{a^2 + b^2}$ where a and b are the lengths of the other two sides, write down a formula for the length of one of the sides, given the length of the hypotenuse and the length of the other side.

5. The present value V of an amount A that I will receive in 2 years' time, assuming a discount rate of $r\%$ is

$$V = \frac{A}{(1 + \frac{r}{100})^2}$$

Transpose this equation to make r the subject.

Use this equation to calculate r:

a. when the present value of an investment of $2000 is $1814.06;

b. when the present value of an investment of $10,000 is $8734.39.

6. a. If

$$x = \frac{t}{t+1}, \quad y = \frac{1}{t+1} \quad \text{and} \quad z = \frac{t-1}{t+1}$$

write $x^2 + y^2 - z^2$ in terms of t.

b. If $w = \sqrt{1 + x^2}$ and $v = \sqrt{1 - x^2}$, write

$$\frac{(w + v)^2 - 2wv}{(w - v)(w + v)}$$

in terms of x.

6 Inequalities

Test box 6

What do the signs $<$, $>$, $\leq$ and $\geq$ mean?

Rearrange $r > \dfrac{p}{-2}$ with p as the subject.

Rearrange $y + 3 < x < 2y - 2$ as an inequality for y.

Solutions:

Less than, greater than, less than or equal to, greater than or equal to.

$p > -2r$. Be careful about the direction of the sign here. When you multiply both sides of an inequality by a negative number, -2 here, you must reverse the direction of the sign.

$$\frac{x + 2}{2} < y < x - 3$$

We have seen that equations take the form

$$\text{expression} = \text{expression}.$$

Life, however, is not always so precise and we often have an *inequality*; that is, one expression is larger or smaller than another.

Some new signs

We need some signs to represent inequalities. These are:

> **Inequality signs**
>
> $>$ is greater than
>
> $\geq$ is greater than or equal to
>
> $<$ is less than
>
> $\leq$ is less than or equal to

So $a > b$ reads 'a is greater than b', $x \leq -2$ reads 'x is less than or equal to -2'. Notice that the narrow end of the sign always points to the smaller of the two expressions.

Check these

Which of the following are true? (Cover up the right-hand side of the page to work these.)

$5 > 2$	T
$2 > 2$	F
$2 \geq 2$	T
$3 \leq 3$	T
$3 > 3$	F
$3 > -1$	T
$-5 < -3$	T
$-5 \leq -3$	T
$-10 > -11$	T
$-1 < 1/2$	T
$x + 1 > x$	T
$2x > x$	F (not true when x is negative: try $x = -4$.)
$3 + 2x < 4 + 2x$	T

Applications of inequalities

Inequalities often arise as constraints on resources like money or raw materials. Check that you understand how the following inequalities arise:

Check these

1. University library expenditure on books and periodicals is apportioned according to the number of lecturers and students in each subject area. A budget of £L per year is allowed for each lecturer and a budget of £S per year for each student. This year the library has at most £165,000 to spend and there are 500 lecturers and 7000 students.

    Total expenditure is $500L + 7000S$ which must be less than or equal to £165,000 and so we have the inequality

    $$500L + 7000S \leq 165{,}000$$

2. A company has a budget of £10,000 this year for capital and labour expenditure. A unit of capital costs £100 whereas a unit of labour costs £50. The total cost of using K units of capital and L units of labour L is therefore $100K + 50L$. As total cost must be less than or equal to £10,000, K and L are subject to the constraint

    $$100K + 50L \leq 10{,}000$$

Inequalities are often useful to indicate that a variable or constant can only take a particular range of values. For instance, if a variable represents a physical quantity it cannot be negative and so we write $x \geq 0$.

Check this

In economics, consumption C and income Y are often modelled by $C = a + bY$. For a particular case, the constants a and b take particular values. However, notice that when Y increases by one unit, consumption increases by b units. However, only a proportion of an extra unit of income can be consumed and so to make sense our model must assume that b lies between 0 and 1 inclusive. This is written

$$b \geq 0 \quad \text{and} \quad b \leq 1$$

Two inequalities can often be combined into a single inequality. For instance, in the last example $b \geq 0$ and $b \leq 1$ can be written

$$0 \leq b \leq 1$$

Rearranging inequalities

It is useful to be able to rearrange inequalities. For instance, given an inequality like

$$\frac{2}{x} < 5$$

we may want to know what restrictions apply to x; that is, we may want the equivalent inequality in which x is the subject (i.e. x only appears on one side on its own). This is often called solving the inequality for x.

We know that we can rearrange an equation by performing any operation (except multiplying or dividing by zero) on both sides, but is this true for inequalities? To investigate this we will take a simple inequality and see how it is affected by various operations.

Check this

Take the inequality 3 > 2.
Try *adding* a number to both sides. Is the resulting inequality still true? Try several different numbers – is the inequality still true?
Now repeat the process, but *subtracting* a number from both sides.
Now multiply both sides of 3 > 2 by a number. Is the inequality still true? Try several different numbers. Try multiplying by a *negative number*.
Finally, try dividing both sides by a number. Again try several numbers, including at least one negative number. What do you conclude?

Your experiments should reflect the following.
Inequalities can be rearranged in just the same way as equations; that is, we can perform any operation (except multiplying or dividing by 0) on both sides except that

> *If we multiply or divide by a negative value, the direction of the inequality must be reversed*

'Reversing the direction of the inequality' means that > becomes <, < becomes >, ≥ becomes ≤ and ≤ becomes ≥.
We give some examples:

Check these

$5x + 2 \geq 3x - 1$. Solve this for x.

Solution:
Subtract $3x$ from both sides to give $2x + 2 \geq -1$. Now subtract 2 from both sides to obtain $2x \geq -3$ and then divide by 2 to obtain

$$x \geq \frac{-3}{2}$$

$2x < x - y$. Express this inequality with x as the subject.

Solution:
At present the xs occur on both sides. If we subtract x from each side we obtain $x < -y$.

$$\frac{2}{h} > 5$$

Write down an inequality for h. You may assume that $h > 0$.

Solution:
As h is positive we can multiply both sides by h to give $2 > 5h$. To isolate h, we divide by 5 and obtain

$$\frac{2}{5} > h$$

As for equations, it is conventional to write the subject of an inequality on the left-hand side, so this can be written

$$h < \frac{2}{5}$$

And now some trickier examples:

Check these

Rearrange

$$\frac{p}{-2} > 3$$

with p as the subject.

Solution:
Now we need to multiply both sides by –2, a negative value, so the direction of the inequality must be reversed. This gives $p < -6$.

Solve $100 - 2x \le 50$.

Solution:
Subtracting 100 from both sides gives $-2x \le -50$. Now we need to divide by –2 and so the direction of the inequality must be reversed to give $x \ge 25$.

When rearranging inequalities we must be careful if we multiply or divide by an expression which *could* take a negative value. The inequality must be reversed if the expression takes a negative value, but not if it takes a positive value, so we need to consider the two cases separately.

Check this

Rearrange

$$\frac{x}{a} < b$$

with x as the subject.

Solution:
To isolate x we need to multiply by a, but we do not know whether a is positive or negative. When a is positive, the inequality rearranges in the usual way to $x < ab$, but when a is negative we must change the direction of the sign to give $x > ab$. The whole solution should be written $x < ab$ when $a > 0$ and $x > ab$ when $a < 0$.

You will often see two inequalities combined, for instance

$$3 - x \le 1 \le 5 - x$$

To rearrange this you must split the inequality into its two parts, here $3 - x \le 1$ and $1 \le 5 - x$ and rearrange each of these in the normal way to have x as the subject.

Check this

If $3 - x \le 1 \le 5 - x$ write down an inequality for x.

Solution:
We must treat each side of the inequality separately; $3 - x \le 1$ rearranges to $2 \le x$ whereas $1 \le 5 - x$ becomes $4 \ge x$ so $x \le 4$. The two constraints on x are therefore $2 \le x$ and $x \le 4$. Note that both of these must hold simultaneously. We can write these more succinctly as $2 \le x \le 4$.

Always think about the meaning of an inequality – it may be impossible as in the second case in the following example:

Check these

Write

$$\frac{3}{x} > 2$$

with x as the subject.

Solution:
As we need to multiply by x and we don't know whether it is positive or negative we must consider the two cases separately. First, if $x > 0$ there is no problem as the inequality becomes

$$x < \frac{3}{2}$$

Second, if $x < 0$ we must reverse the direction, which gives

$$x > \frac{3}{2}$$

However, this is impossible when $x < 0$, so we can ignore this case. We conclude that the only range of values for x that satisfies the inequality is

$$0 < x < \frac{3}{2}$$

Formulate the following inequalities and solve them:

Check these

1. My company is willing to give me an office of at most 18 square metres. In our newly built premises all the rectangular offices have a width of 3 metres. Write down an inequality for the area of an office and rearrange this with the length of the office as the subject.

Solution:
Let the length of the office be x. The area is therefore $3x$ and so $3x \leq 18$. Rearranging this gives $x \leq 6$. The length can be at most 6 metres.

2. I offer the barman £10 for a round of 5 beers. I glance at the change he gives me and see that there is at least £1. Write this down as an inequality and rearrange it to establish an inequality for the price of a beer.

Solution:
If beer costs £x, my change is $10 - 5x$, so the inequality is $10 - 5x \geq 1$. Rearranging this gives

$$x \leq \frac{9}{5}$$

So a beer is at most £1.80.

3. Recall that distance d (km), speed s (kph) and time t (hours) for a journey are related by

$$d = st.$$

My car won't do more than 70 kph. Write down an inequality for the time taken on a journey of d km.

Solution:
As $s \leq 70$ and

$$s = \frac{d}{t}$$

we have

$$\frac{d}{t} \leq 70$$

This rearranges to

$$t \geq \frac{d}{70}$$

WORK CARD 6

1. Which of these are true?

  a. $5 \geq 3$ **b.** $6 < 6$ **c.** $0.999 < 1$ **d.** $\frac{3}{7} < 0.4$

  e. $-5 < -6$ **f.** $-\frac{1}{4} > -\frac{1}{5}$ **g.** $2 < 3$ **h.** $2 \times -4 < 3 \times -4$.

2. If $p > q$, are the following true or false? If they are false, write down a counter-example.

    a. $p - 1 > q - 1$ **b.** $2p > 2q$ **c.** $-2p > -2q$ **d.** $p - q > 0$

    e. $\dfrac{p}{3} > \dfrac{q}{3}$ **f.** $p^2 > q^2$ **g.** $p^3 > q^3$ **h.** $-p < -q$ **i.** $\dfrac{1}{p} > \dfrac{1}{q}$

3. Solve **a.** $2x - 3 \leq 5$ **b.** $3x > 5x + 2$ **c.** $5(x + 2) < 20$ **d.** $x - 1 \leq 2 \leq x + 2$

4. Rearrange the following with y as the subject:

    a. $2(y - 1) < 3$ **b.** $ay \geq -2$ where $a > 0$

    c. $ay \geq -2$ where $a < 0$ **d.** $y + m < 3 < y - 2m$

    e. $\dfrac{1}{y + 5} > 2$

5. A company has a maximum of £12,000 a month available for labour costs. Workers are paid £4 an hour and £6 an hour on overtime. If h is the number of man-hours worked on normal time and v is the number of man-hours of overtime worked, write down a constraint on h and v. Write down an inequality for the number of hours overtime available in all.

6. A company has a budget of £400 a day for labour costs and £200 for materials.

    A chair costs £50 in labour and £5 in materials to manufacture, whereas a bookcase costs £30 in labour and £10 in materials.

    The firm makes £6 profit on a chair and £5 on a bookcase.

    Write down an expression for the amount of profit and the two inequalities that must be satisfied by the number of chairs C produced daily and the number of bookcases B produced daily.

    This sort of model is called a linear programming model. Its objective is to establish how many of each product should be manufactured in order to maximise the profit, whilst keeping within the constraints on the amount of resources available.

Solutions:

T = true, F = false

1.   **a.** T   **b.** F   **c.** T   **d.** F   **e.** F   **f.** F   **g.** T   **h.** F.

2.   **a.** T   **b.** T   **c.** F for any p, q **d.** T   **e.** T   **f.** F (for instance for $p = -1$ $q = -2$)

    g. T   **h.** T   **i.** F for any p, q.

3.   **a.** $x \leq 4$ **b.** $x < -1$ **c.** $x < 2$ **d.** $0 \leq x \leq 3$

4.   **a.** $y < \dfrac{5}{2}$ **b.** $y \geq \dfrac{-2}{a}$ **c.** $y \leq -\dfrac{2}{a}$ **d.** $3 + 2m < y < 3 - m$

    e. When $y + 5 > 0$, the inequality rearranges to

$$y < \frac{-9}{2} \text{ so } -5 < y < \frac{-9}{2}$$

    but when $y + 5 < 0$ (so $y < -5$) it rearranges to

$$y > \frac{-9}{2}$$

so no values are possible. The only possibility is therefore

$$-5 < y < -\frac{9}{2}$$

5. The total labour cost is $4h + 6v$ and this must be at most £12,000 so the labour constraint is $4h + 6v \le 12{,}000$. Rearranging this with v as the subject gives

$$v \le \frac{12{,}000 - 4h}{6}$$

6. Profit $6C + 5B$. $50C + 30B \le 400$ labour constraint
   $5C + 10B \le 200$ material constraint.

---

1. Which of these are true?

   a. $7 < 8$ b. $7 \le 8$ c. $1.0001 \ge 1$ d. $-40 > -39$ e. $-\frac{5}{8} > -0.6$

   f. $2 \times -3 < 3 \times -3$ g. $\frac{-1}{5} < \frac{-1}{6}$

2. If $x \le y$, are the following true or false?

   a. $x + a \le y + a$ where a is a constant   b. $-2x \ge -2y$

   c. $x - y \le 0$ d. $\frac{1}{x} \le \frac{1}{y}$ e. $x^2 \le y^2$

3. Solve:

   a. $5x \ge 7x - 4$ b. $\frac{x}{5} + 2 < 3$

   Solve the following for z:

   c. $4(z - 10) > 2$ d. $3z + y < 7y - z$ e. $z - b < 2 < a + z$

4. Rearrange with z as the subject:

   a. $az < 1$ where $a > 0$ b. $az < 1$ where $a < 0$ c. $5z(1 + y) > 1$ where $y > 0$

   d. $\frac{5}{z - 2} < 7$

5. Sylvia wants to organise a group of friends (including herself) to get together and hold a party. A function room and disco cost £100 for the evening and a light buffet can be provided for £1 a head. Each friend will invite 30 guests. The friends and Sylvia will split costs equally but they do not want to pay more than £50 each. At least how many people must Sylvia ask to host the party with her?

6. There are 2 g of protein in 10 g of foodstuff *A* and 3 g of protein in 10 g of foodstuff *B*. In addition, there is 1 g of carbohydrate in 10 g of foodstuff *A* and 3 g in 10 g of foodstuff *B*.

   A man is placed on a diet consisting entirely of foodstuffs *A* and *B*. He must eat a minimum of 20 g of protein each day and 30 g of carbohydrate. Write down the inequalities imposed on the quantities of *A* and *B* that he must eat daily.

Further reading: see p. xv
Jacques is good on inequalities.

EM4
Modelling using straight lines

I admit that twice two makes four is an excellent thing but if we are to give everything its due, twice two makes five is an excellent thing too.

Feodor Dostoievski

Contexts

What is this chapter about?
This chapter explains how some equations, called linear equations, can be represented by a straight line on a graph and gives some examples of how such equations arise in business, management and finance.

Why is it useful?
Many real situations can be represented using linear equations; for instance, budget constraints or the relationship between production costs and the number of items produced. The techniques presented here are for two variables but the ideas extend to many variables. Further, one of the most widely used quantitative techniques for business, Linear Programming (see Chapter BM1), is based on linear equations.

Where does it fit in?
The material in this chapter is the very beginning of the branch of maths called linear algebra. It will be useful throughout the book but in particular, for Chapter BM1, Linear programming models.

What do I need to know?
You will need to understand the previous three chapters, EM1, EM2 and EM3.

Objectives

After your work on this chapter you should be able to:

- plot a straight line on a graph;
- calculate the slope or gradient of a line and the intercept with the y axis from the equation;
- model a situation, where appropriate, using a linear equation;
- recognise a linear equation in more than two variables and understand what a coefficient is;
- solve a pair of simultaneous equations in two variables.

The simplest equation that relates 2 or more variables is a *linear equation*. Many relationships in finance, economics and accountancy are naturally linear but linear equations are also often used as an approximation because they are easy to manipulate and interpret, and can be considered in groups.

In this chapter we mainly consider linear equations that contain only two variables. Such equations can be represented by a straight line on a graph, so we will also introduce graphs in this chapter.

1 Introducing straight lines

Test box 1

Which of the following can be represented by a straight line on a graph?

$y = 2x + 1$, $xy + 2 = y$, $5x + 4y = 20$.

Sketch the graph of the equation $5x + 4y = 20$.
Sketch the graph of $y = 0$.

Solutions:
The first and third only. The graph of $5x + 4y = 20$ goes through the points $(4,0)$ and $(0,5)$ and is a straight line. The graph of $y = 0$ is the x axis.

Co-ordinates and graphs
Consider the equation $y = 2x + 1$. For any value of x we can calculate the corresponding value of y. For instance, when $x = 1$, $y = 3$, when $x = 0$, $y = 1$ and when $x = -2$, $y = -3$. We say that y is a *function* of x.

All these *x,y* pairs can be represented by points on a graph. It is usual to position *x* along the horizontal axis of a graph and *y* on the vertical axis and list the *x,y* pairs, which are called *co-ordinates*, with *x* first. Figure 4.1 is a graph showing the points (1,3), (0,1) and (–2,–3). Notice that all three of these lie on a straight line.

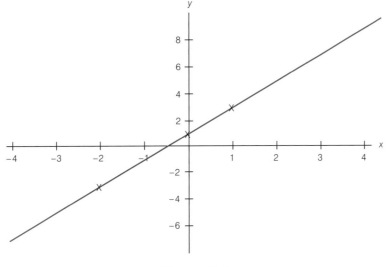

Figure 4.1

Now consider the equation $y = -3x + 2$. Again, we can calculate some (x,y) pairs.

Check this

Find three (x,y) pairs when $y = -3x + 2$.

Solution:
Take three values for *x* and for each calculate $y = -3x + 2$. For instance, when $x = 1$, $y = -3 + 2 = -1$, when $x = 0$, $y = 2$ and when $x = -5$, $y = 15 + 2 = 17$.

The following table shows some more *x*s and *y*s for $y = -3x + 2$:

x	–5	–4	–3	–2	–1	0	1	2	3	4	5
y	17	14	11	8	5	2	–1	–4	–7	–10	–13

Again, all these points lie on a straight line, as shown in Figure 4.2.

Linear equations
The points in Figures 4.1 and 4.2 lie on a straight line because any equation of the form

$$y = ax + b$$

where *a* and *b* are constants, gives points that lie on a straight line. Such equations are therefore called *linear equations*. Alternatively, we can say that *y* is a *linear function* of *x*.
  An equation of the form

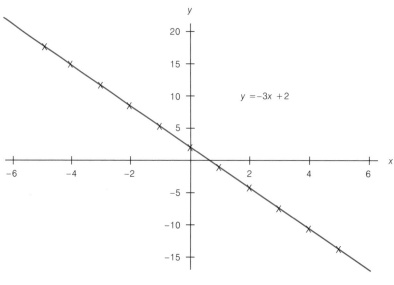

$y = -3x + 2$

Figure 4.2

$$cx + dy = e$$

where c, d, and e are constants is also linear as it can be rearranged into the form $y = ax + b$. For instance, $8x + 2y = 4$ rearranges to $8x - 4 = -2y$, and then to $-4x + 2 = y$, which has the form $y = ax + b$.

Notice that both forms of linear equation $y = ax + b$ and $cx + dy = e$ only contain multiples of x and y, and a constant. The numbers that multiply x or y (that is, a, c and d) are called the *coefficients* of x or y. If any other terms appear in the equation then it is *not* linear.

Check these

Which of the following are linear equations?

1. $2x + 1 = y$

2. $3y - 3 = x$

3. $xy - 5 = 1$

4. $x = 1$

5. $y = x^2 + 2$

6. $2x - 4y = 5$

7. $\pi y + 2x = 10$

8. $3\dfrac{x}{y} = 2$

Solutions:

1. Yes, clearly of form $y = ax + b$

2. Yes, rearranges to $y = \dfrac{x}{3} + 1$

3. No, x is multiplied by y here

4. Yes, this is a linear equation because it is $cx + dy = e$ where $c = 1$, $d = 0$ and $e = 1$

5. No, because the x is squared

6. Yes

7. Yes, π is just a number like any other

8. Yes, because it rearranges to $3x = 2y$

We have already met some linear equations. For instance, the demand equation $Q = 100 - 0.5P$ and supply equation $Q = 80 + 0.2P$ are both linear. Or if a firm incurs fixed costs (rent, administration, etc.) of £2000 per week and then a further cost of £7 per unit manufactured, the total cost of producing x units will be $C = 2000 + 7x$, which is also a linear equation.

Sketching straight lines

If you draw two dots on a piece of paper you will find that only one straight line can be drawn that goes through both of them. (Try this!) So, to draw the line representing a linear equation we only need to know two (x,y) points.

For instance, to sketch the graph of the equation $y = 3x + 3$, we pick two arbitrary values for x, say $x = 0$ and $x = 4$, calculate the corresponding y values, in this case $y = 3$ and $y = 15$, giving the points $(0,3)$ and $(4,15)$, and draw a straight line through these, as in Figure 4.3.

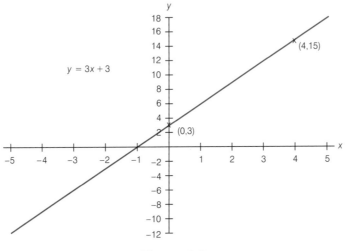

Figure 4.3

Check these

Sketch the following straight lines:

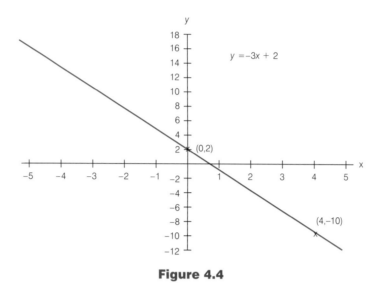

Figure 4.4

$y = -3x + 2$

Solution:
When $x = 0$ (this choice makes y easy to calculate), $y = 2$, and when $x = 4$, $y = -10$ so the points $(0,2)$ and $(4,-10)$ lie on the line. Joining these gives Figure 4.4.

$y = -5x + 3$

Solution:
When $x = 0$, $y = 3$ and when $x = -1$, $y = 8$ so the line passes through $(0,3)$ and $(-1,8)$.

$10 = 2x + 5y$

Solution:
The line goes through $(0,2)$ and $(5,0)$.

Some special straight lines

The straight line $x = 0$ joins all the points for which the x co-ordinate is zero. (The y co-ordinate can be anything.) So, in fact, $x = 0$ is the y axis. In the same way, the straight line $y = 0$ is the x axis.

The straight line $x = 4$ joins all points with x co-ordinate 4 (that is, points like $(4,0)$, $(4,1)$, $(4,20)$) and is therefore a vertical line passing through 4 on the x axis. In general, all the straight lines of the form $x = b$, where b is a number, will be vertical lines passing through the point $(b,0)$. In the same way all straight lines of the form $y = b$ are horizontal lines passing through the point $(0,b)$ on the y axis.

The lines $x = 4$, $x = -5$ and $y = 5$, $y = -6$ are shown in Figure 4.5.

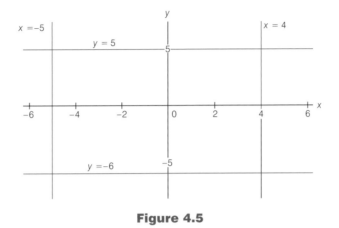

Figure 4.5

We summarise the work of this section as follows.

> **Linear equations and straight lines**
>
> Both the following forms are linear equations and can be represented by a straight line on a graph:
>
> $y = ax + b$
>
> $cx + dy = e$

WORK CARD 1

1. Plot the following groups of points. Do they lie on a straight line?
   a. (3,3) (4,4) (–1,–1)   b. (2,5) (1,2) (–1,–4)
   c. (0,0) (1,1) (3,9) (4,16)   d. (1,2) (2,4) (3,7)

2. Which of the following equations can be represented by a straight line on a graph (*a* and *b* are constants)?
   a. $2x + 1 = y$ b. $-y + x = 5$ c. $x^2 + 1 = y$ d. $ax - b = y$
   e. $\pi x + y = 7$ f. $x = 2$

3. Find two points on the following straight lines and hence sketch them:
   a. $y = 2x + 1$ b. $5x + 4y = 20$ c. $y = -3x + 2$
   d. $y = \dfrac{1}{2}x - 4$ e. $y = -1$

Solutions:

1. a. yes   b. yes   c. no – a curve   d. no

2. a. yes   b. yes   c. no   d. yes   e. yes   f. yes

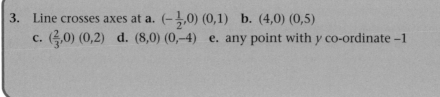

3.   Line crosses axes at **a.** $(-\frac{1}{2},0)$ $(0,1)$ **b.** $(4,0)$ $(0,5)$
     c. $(\frac{2}{3},0)$ $(0,2)$ **d.** $(8,0)$ $(0,-4)$ **e.** any point with y co-ordinate -1

ASSESSMENT 1

1. Sketch the following groups of points. Do they lie on a straight line?
   a. $(3,3)$ $(5,5)$ $(7,3)$ **b.** $(1,3)$ $(-2,-9)$ $(0,-1)$

2. Which of the following equations are linear?
   a. $3x - 1 = y$ **b.** $-y - x = 4$ **c.** $xy + 2 = y$ **d.** $x^3 - 1 = y$
   e. $\pi r x + b = y$, where r is a constant
   f. $\dfrac{2y}{x} + 1 = 0$ **g.** $y = -5$

3. Find two points on the following straight lines and hence sketch them:
   a. $2y = 3 + x$ **b.** $y = -5x + 2$ **c.** $40 = 2x + 5y$
   d. $ax + by = ab$ where both a and b are positive   **e.** $-x - 5 = 0$

2 Interpretation of *a* and *b*

Test box 2

Find the intercept with the y axis and the gradient of following straight lines:

   $y = 2x + 3,\quad y = -5x - 2$

Draw the lines $y = 2x + 1$, $y = x + 2$ and $y = x + 1$ on the same graph.

Solutions:
Intercept is 3 and slope is 2, intercept is –2 and slope is –5. For the graphs, see Figure 4.10 at the end of this section.

The intercept with the *y* axis

Consider the straight line $y = ax + b$. (Remember that the symbols a and b represent any number, so this is a general way of talking about a straight line like $y = 5x + 2$.) When the line crosses the y axis, $x = 0$, and so $y = 0 \cdot a + b = b$. We say that the straight line *intercepts* the y axis at $y = b$, as in Figure 4.6.

So the value of b in an equation of the form $y = ax + b$ immediately tells us where the line intercepts the y axis.

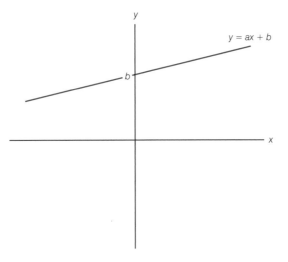

Figure 4.6

Check these

Say quickly where the following straight lines cross the y, Q or C axis:

$y = 2x + 10$

$y = 0.001 + 5x$

$Q = 100 - 0.5P$

$C = 2000 + 0.2x$

Solutions:
As all these are in $y = ax + b$ form reading off the constant term b in the equation gives the intercept with the y, Q or C axis; that is, 10, 0.001, 100, 2000.

The slope or gradient of a straight line

The *slope* or *gradient* of a straight line is the *increase in y* divided by the *increase in x* as you move from one point on the line to another.

For instance, two points on the straight line $y = 3x + 3$ are $(0,3)$ and $(4,15)$. From $(0,3)$ to $(4,15)$ y increases from 3 to 15 (that is, by $15 - 3 = 12$) and x increases from 0 to 4 (that is, by $4 - 0 = 4$), as shown in Figure 4.7.

The gradient of $y = 3x + 3$ is therefore $\frac{12}{4} = 3$.

In general, if two points on a straight line are (x_1, y_1) and (x_2, y_2), moving from y_1 to y_2 increases y by $y_2 - y_1$ and moving from x_1 to x_2 increases x by $x_2 - x_1$, so the gradient is

$$\text{gradient} = \frac{y_2 - y_1}{x_2 - x_1}$$

For example, the gradient of the straight line joining $(7,6)$ and $(3,5)$ is

$$\frac{5 - 6}{3 - 7} = \frac{-1}{-4} = \frac{1}{4}$$

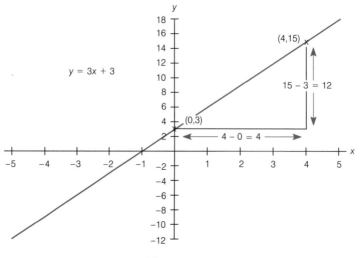

Figure 4.7

The Greek symbol delta, written Δ, is often used in maths and economics to denote a change, so if $\Delta x = x_2 - x_1$ and $\Delta y = y_2 - y_1$, as shown in Figure 4.8, the gradient is

$$\text{gradient} = \frac{\Delta y}{\Delta x}$$

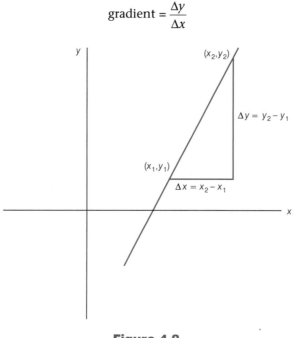

Figure 4.8

Check these

Find the gradient of the straight line joining the points (–1,3) and (2,9).

Solution:

The gradient $= \dfrac{y_2 - y_1}{x_2 - x_1} = \dfrac{9 - 3}{2 - (-1)} = \dfrac{6}{3} = 2$

Find the gradient of the straight line joining the points $(5,-2)$ and $(1,3)$.

Solution:

The gradient $= \dfrac{3 - (-2)}{1 - 5} = \dfrac{5}{-4} = -\dfrac{5}{4}$

Notice that the gradient in the last example is negative. A straight line has a positive gradient when an increase in x corresponds to an increase in y and a negative gradient when an increase in x corresponds to a *decrease* in y. A line with a positive gradient therefore slopes upwards from left to right, whereas one with a negative gradient slopes downwards from left to right. A straight line has a zero gradient if y does not increase at all. These are all shown in Figure 4.9.

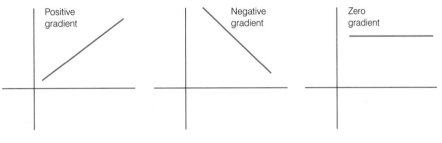

Figure 4.9

The gradient of a line from its equation

When the equation of a straight line is in the form $y = ax + b$, the gradient of the line is a. So, for instance, the straight line $y = -5x + 2$ has a gradient of -5.

We can prove this by noticing that two points on the line are $(0,b)$ and $(1, a + b)$. The gradient between these is

$$\frac{(a + b) - b}{1 - 0} = a$$

Check these

Find the gradients of the following straight lines:

$y = 2x + 3$

$y = -4x - 2$

$y = 2x$

$y = 2$

$2x + 3y = 6$

Solutions:

2, –4, 2, zero, rearrange this to $y = 2 - \frac{2}{3}x$ to give a gradient of $-\frac{2}{3}$.

Straight lines that have the same gradient but different intercepts with the y axis are parallel, so they never meet.

The relative positions of two or more straight lines can be sketched using their intercepts and gradients. For example, to sketch $y = x + 1$, $y = x + 2$ and $y = 2x + 1$ we would reason as follows: both $y = x + 1$ and $y = x + 2$ have the same gradient (1) so they are parallel and they intersect the y axis at 1 and 2 respectively; $y = 2x + 1$ is twice as steep as the others, and intersects the y axis at $y = 1$. The graphs are shown in Figure 4.10.

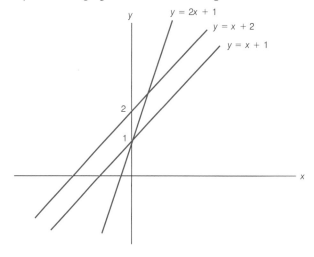

Figure 4.10

The key results in this section are:

In the equation of a straight line $y = ax + b$:

a is the **slope** or **gradient**

b is the **intercept** with the y axis

WORK CARD 2

1. Calculate the gradient of the line joining the following pairs of points:
   a. (–2,1) (4,3)   b. (–1,–1) (0,2)
   c. (0,0) (4,8)   d. (–1,–1) (–4,–7)

2. Calculate the intercept with the y axis and the gradient of the following straight lines:

WORK CARD 2 (CONTINUED)

a. $2x + 3y = 6$ b. $5x - 2y = -10$
c. $6x = -2y + 1$ d. $2x = 8y - 2$

3. Write down the intercept with the y axis and the gradient, and hence sketch the following straight lines:
   a. $y = 2x$ b. $y = 2x - 3$ c. $y = -2x$ d. $y = -2x + 3$

4. Sketch the following straight lines on the *same* graph, stating the gradient of each:

$y = 3x,$ $y = 2x,$ $y = x,$ $y = -x,$ $y = -2x$

Solutions:

1. a. $\frac{1}{3}$ b. 3   c. 2   d. 2

2. a. intercept 2, gradient $\frac{-2}{3}$ b. intercept 5, gradient $\frac{5}{2}$
    c. intercept $\frac{1}{2}$, gradient -3.   d. intercept $\frac{1}{4}$, gradient $\frac{1}{4}$

3. a. 0, gradient 2   b. -3, gradient 2   c. 0, gradient -2
    d. 3, gradient -2

4. All the lines pass through 0, their gradients are 3, 2, 1, -1, -2 respectively.

ASSESSMENT 2

1. Calculate the gradient of the line joining the following pairs of points and sketch the line:
   a. $(5,2)$ $(1,1)$ b. $(-1,-1)$ $(3,5)$ c. $(7,-1)$ $(6,-5)$ d. $(1,-2)$ $(-4,-7)$

2. Calculate the intercept with the y axis and the gradient of the following straight lines:
   a. $20y = -5x - 4$ b. $36x - 2 = 3y$ c. $4x = 4 - 4y$
   d. $ax - by = c$

3. Write down the intercept with the y axis and the gradient of the following straight lines, and hence sketch them:
   a. $y = 3x + 1$ b. $y = 3x - 3$ c. $y = 3x - 1$ d. $2y = 6x - 4$

4. Sketch the following straight lines:
   a. $y = 2x + \frac{2}{3}$ b. $y = -7x + 1$ c. $24x - 2y = 48$

3 Linear equations for modelling

Test box 3

A charity has at most £30,000 available to send some deprived children and adults by train to the seaside. The trip will cost £10 per adult and £6 per child.

Write down a linear equation relating x, the number of adults and y, the number of children, who can go assuming that the whole £30,000 is spent.

Sketch this equation on a graph and mark the feasible region of (x,y) points that represent the number of children and adults who can go on the outing if at most £30,000 is spent.

Solution:
$10x + 6y = 30,000$. On a graph this line joins the points (3000,0) and (0,5000). The area enclosed by this line and the x and y axes represents the feasible region.

Linear equations are often used in modelling because they are the simplest representation of the relationship between two or more variables. As with all models we do not always suppose that the linear equation is an *exact* representation of the real situation but we *do* hope that it provides a good approximation to it. Here are some examples.

Models for supply and demand

In economics it is usual to assume that as the price of a good P increases demand for it Q decreases. The simplest equation that can be used to represent this relationship has the form

$$Q = aP + b$$

where a and b are the constants. As Q must be smaller when P is larger, a is negative.

A particular demand equation might be

$$Q = 1000 - 5P$$

This is often given 'the other way round'; that is, by rearranging so that P is expressed in terms of Q, in this case $P = 200 - 0.2Q$.

In the same way the quantity that producers plan to bring to the market and the price are related by a supply equation. Again, a simple form might be the linear equation

$$Q = aP + b$$

As more of a good is usually produced when the price is high the slope, a, is usually positive.

Production costs

Production costs can be broadly split into two types: those that do not depend on the volume of goods manufactured (property, heating, lighting, etc.) known as fixed costs, and those that increase with the volume manufactured (unskilled labour, raw materials, etc.), known as variable costs.

When the variable cost is assumed to be the same for every unit manufactured the total production cost is a linear function of the quantity produced.

For instance, suppose it costs $2000 to rent, light and heat an industrial unit for a week and that each unit produced costs $10 in labour and raw materials. If Q units are produced in a week the total cost will be

$$C = 2000 + 10Q$$

Total cost is therefore a linear function of Q.

Notice that the slope of a graph of the total cost (10 in this example) is equal to the variable cost per unit, whereas the intercept with the vertical axis (2000) is the fixed cost.

Budget constraints

Suppose that a company has a budget of £2000 a week to spend on the manufacture of radios and televisions and that it costs £5 to make a radio and £40 to make a television. The number of radios manufactured in a week, x, and the number of televisions manufactured in a week, y, that spend the budget exactly are related by the equation

$$5x + 40y = 2000$$

This is a linear equation (in the $cx + dy = e$ form).

To sketch a graph of this equation we need not concern ourselves with negative values of x and y as the company cannot manufacture a negative number of items. The graph is shown in Figure 4.11.

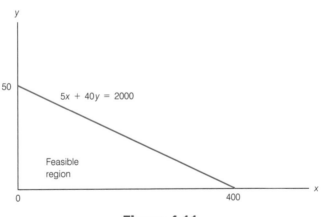

Figure 4.11

All the points below the line are such that $5x + 40y$ is less than 2000 and so are within budget, whereas all the points above the line result in overspending the budget. (Check this by picking any point above or below the line and calculating the expenditure $5x + 40y$.) The area below and on the line is therefore called the *feasible region* of the graph. Any point in the feasible region is within budget.

Linear equations with more variables

Now suppose that the company above makes radios, televisions, CD players and video recorders and that it costs £5 to make a radio, £40 to make a television, £20 to make a CD player and £30 to make a video recorder. They still have a budget of £2000 a week. The number of radios, x, televisions, y, CD players, z, and video recorders, w, that spend the budget exactly are related by the equation

$$5x + 40y + 20z + 30w = 2000$$

This equation has four variables (x,y,z,w) so we can't draw it on a graph (we would need four axes; that is, four dimensions). However, it is still a linear equation.

In general, a *linear equation* is one in which every term is a number multiplied by a variable and linear equations may include any number of variables. As usual, the numbers that multiply each variable (5, 40, 20 and 30 in the equation above) are called the *coefficients* of the variables.

Check these

Which of the following are linear equations in a, b, c, and d?

$10a + 3b + 10c - 5d = 0$

$10a + 3b^2 - 10c - 5d = 0$

$5ab + 10c - 5d = 10$

And which of the following are linear equations in x, y, and z?

$5x^2 + 3y + xz = 0$

$5x + \dfrac{2}{y} + z = 5$

Solutions:
Only the first one is linear. All the others have at least one term that is *not* a number multiplied by a variable.

Linear equations are a fundamental tool of quantitative modelling and you will almost certainly encounter them in courses you take in Finance, Economics and Accounting.

Curved graphs

A linear equation will not always be an adequate representation of the relationship between two variables and a curved graph may have to be used instead. In *More Maths*, Chapter MM2, we consider how to sketch curved graphs but for now, a rough way of doing it is to calculate some points on the curve and plot them on a graph as shown below.

Check this

Sketch the graph of $y = x^2 - x - 6$.

Solution:
The following table shows the values of y for each of the x values -4, -3, -2, -1, 0, 1, 2, 3, 4.

x	−4	−3	−2	−1	0	1	2	3	4
y	14	6	0	−4	−6	−6	−4	0	6

For instance, when $x = -2$, $y = (-2)^2 + 2 - 6 = 0$.

A graph showing these points is given in Figure 4.12.

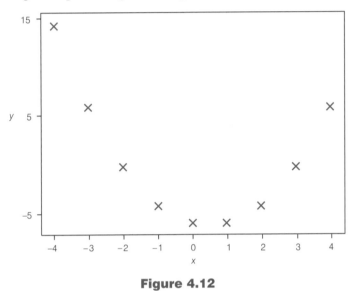

Figure 4.12

The function appears to have a curved U-shape, the base of the U lying somewhere between 0 and 1. We explain how to sketch such functions more accurately in *More Maths*, Chapter MM2, but in the meantime you might like to glance at *More Maths*, Chapter MM2, Figure 2.6, which is an exact plot of this function.

WORK CARD 3

1. Publishing costs for an accountancy textbook amount to £3000 and in addition it costs £3 per copy to print. The publishers receive £10 a copy from sales but must pay 10% of this to the author. Write down an expression for the publisher's total profit in terms of the number of copies printed. Assume that all copies are sold.

   Sketch a graph of this expression. How many copies must be sold to break even (make a profit of exactly zero)?

2. It costs a college £2000 a year for each Arts student and £3000 for each Science student. The total budget for students is £1,200,000. Write down the budget constraint for the number of Arts and the number of Science students. Sketch the feasible region on a graph.

Solutions:

1. $y = 6x - 3000$, when $y = 0$, $x = 500$, so 500 copies to break even.

2. $2x + 3y = 1200$. The feasible region is the area below the line.

1. A statistical model $y = 1000 + 11x$ is postulated to relate x, the amount a company spends on advertising in a month, to y, the average amount received in sales revenue the following month. Assuming the model is reasonable, answer the following questions:

   If no money is spent on advertising what will be the average sales figure the following month?

   If the company spends £500 on advertising what can they expect in sales revenue the following month (on average)?

   On average, how much will sales increase the following month for each £1 spent on advertising?

2. Demand for a product Q is known to be a linear function of its price P; that is, the relationship has the form $Q = aP + b$. When the price is £1 demand is 990, and for every extra unit increase in price demand decreases by 90.

   Write down the demand equation and sketch it.

4 Pairs of linear equations

Test box 4

Solve the following pair of linear equations:

$$3x + 5y = 13$$
$$-2x - 10y = -22$$

At what point (if any) does the following pair of straight lines intersect?

$$9y + 6x = 7$$
$$3y + 2x = 10$$

Solutions:
The solution is at (1,2). The second pair of lines are parallel and so they never meet.

One of the reasons why linear equations are so useful is that it is relatively easy to handle more than one of them at once, so that several simultaneously occurring relationships between the variables can be modelled. Not unnaturally, sets of equations considered together are called *simultaneous equations* so sets of linear equations, considered together, are called *simultaneous linear equations*.

The only chapter of this book that requires simultaneous linear equations is Linear programming models (*Business Modelling*, Chapter BM1). However, we have included them here, in *Essential Maths*, because they enable us to find the point where two lines on a graph meet, which is often useful. We will keep things relatively simple and consider just two equations with only two variables, although similar concepts apply to sets of more equations with more variables.

Pairs of linear equations and straight lines

Suppose that the demand for a good is modelled as

$$Q = -\tfrac{1}{2} P + 100$$

whereas the supply is $Q = 2P - 20$. The market is in equilibrium at the values of Q and P which make *both* these equations true; that is, at the *solution* to this pair of equations.

Both the equations are linear and so each can be represented by a straight line on a graph as shown in Figure 4.13.

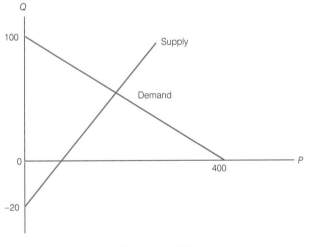

Figure 4.13

As the solution to the pair of equations is at the values of P and Q for which *both* equations hold, it must lie on *both* straight lines and so must be at the point where the two lines intersect.

We could try to calculate this point by plotting the graph exactly, but this would be tedious and not very precise. Instead, we will learn how to solve such pairs of linear equations exactly.

Solving pairs of linear equations

We will demonstrate the method for the example,

$$2x - y = -1 \tag{1}$$

$$14x + 3y = 43 \tag{2}$$

The equations are labelled (1) and (2) for convenience. Recall that we require the values of x and y for which both of these equations are true.

Remember (Chapter EM3, Section 3) that if we multiply or divide an equation all the way through we do *not* affect the solution, but we obtain an equivalent equation.

To solve these equations we multiply one of them by a number. This number is chosen so that either:

A: a term (other than the constant) appears in both equations

or

B: a term (other than the constant) is positive in one equation and negative in the other

For example, if we multiply equation (1) above by 7 we get

$$14x - 7y = -7 \tag{1'}$$

$$14x + 3y = 43 \tag{2'}$$

so that both equations contain the same term $14x$ (case **A**). *Alternatively*, we could have multiplied the original equation (1) by 3 to obtain

$$6x - 3y = -3 \tag{1''}$$

$$14x + 3y = 43 \tag{2''}$$

in which one equation contains $-3y$ and the other $3y$ (case **B**).

For case **A** (that is, if both equations contain an identical term), we *subtract* one equation from the other term by term as illustrated below. (1') minus (2') above gives

$$14x - \ 7y = -7 \tag{1'}$$

$$\underline{14x + \ 3y = 43} \tag{2'}$$
$$0x - 10y = -50$$

Notice that the $-10y$ arises from $-7y - (3y)$.

The resulting equation will only contain one variable and so will be easy to solve. Here, it is $-10y = -50$ which has solution $y = 5$.

Now we know that at the solution $y = 5$, all that remains is to find the corresponding value of x. To do this we substitute $y = 5$ into any of the equations used so far and solve for x. Taking equation (2) and substituting $y = 5$ gives

$$14x + 3y = 43$$
$$14x + 3 \cdot 5 = 43$$
$$14x + 15 = 43$$
$$14x = 28$$

and so $x = 2$.

The solution to the pair of original equations is therefore $x = 2$, $y = 5$ or the point (2,5). You can check this by substituting these values into both the original equations.

Alternatively if case **B** holds, we have

$$6x - 3y = -3 \tag{1''}$$

$$14x + 3y = 43 \tag{2''}$$

in which one equation contains a term $(-3y)$ which is the negative of a term in the other $(3y)$ we continue in a similar way to case **A** but now we *add* the two equations term by term. This gives

$$6x - 3y = -3$$
$$\underline{14x + 3y = 43}$$
$$20x + 0y = 40$$

Again, the resulting equation will only contain one variable and so will be easy to solve. For this example it is $20x = 40$, so $x = 2$. Finally we substitute $x = 2$ into any of the previous equations and solve for y. In this case, to obtain $y = 5$.

We summarise the method of solving a pair of linear equations as follows. Do not learn it by heart, but try to understand what you are doing at each stage.

1. Multiply both sides of one of the equations by a non-zero number. Choose this number so that either:

A the same term appears in both equations

$$e.g. \quad \begin{aligned} 5x + 2y &= 10 \\ x + 2y &= 2 \end{aligned}$$

OR

B a term appears in one equation and its negative in the other

$$e.g. \quad \begin{aligned} 5x - 2y &= 8 \\ 4x + 2y &= 10 \end{aligned}$$

2. If **A** holds *subtract* one equation from the other term by term to obtain a new equation that only contains one of the variables.

   If **B** holds *add* the two equations together term by term to obtain a new equation that only contains one of the variables.
3. Solve this new equation; it will only contain one variable.
4. Substitute your solution from **3** into any of the previous equations to solve for the other variable.

Check these

Solve the following pairs of linear equations:

$3x - y = 3$

$5x + 3y = 5$

Solution:
There is a $-y$ in the first equation and a $3y$ in the second so the most obvious action is to multiply the first equation by 3 so that it contains $-3y$ like the second equation. This gives $9x - 3y = 9$, $5x + 3y = 5$. Adding these two equations together term by term gives $14x + 0y = 14$, so $x = 1$. Substituting $x = 1$ back into the original equation, $3x - y = 3$, gives $3 - y = 3$, so $y = 0$. The solution is (1,0). Check this by substituting $x = 1$, $y = 0$ into the original equations.

$2x + 3y = 5$

$x + 2y = -6$

Solution:
Multiply the second equation by 2, so that both equations contain the term $2x$. The two equations are now $2x + 3y = 5$, $2x + 4y = -12$. Subtract the second equation from the first term by term to give $0x - y = 17$, so $y = -17$. Use any equation to calculate x when $y = -17$,

$2x + 3y = 5$ gives $2x - 51 = 5$, so $2x = 56$ and $x = 28$. The solution is $x = 28$, $y = -17$ or (28,–17).

$$y - 2x = 1$$
$$y - x = 2$$

Solution:
Here, both equations already contain an identical term y so we can subtract one equation from the other immediately. Taking the second from the first gives $0y - x = -1$, so $x = 1$. Substituting this into any equation, say $y - x = 2$, gives $y - 1 = 2$, so $y = 3$. The solution is (1,3).

When there isn't exactly one solution

All the above examples had exactly one solution (x,y) to the pair of linear equations because it was the point where the corresponding straight lines met. In most circumstances this will be the case. However, there are two other possibilities that you should be aware of.

Consider

$$3x - 4y = 12$$
$$-12x + 16y = 5$$

Solving this in the usual way we multiply the first equation by 4 to give

$$12x - 16y = 48$$
$$\underline{-12x + 16y = \quad 5} \quad \text{and add these to give}$$
$$0x + 0y = 53$$

As $0x + 0y$ is zero, this equation says that $0 = 53$, which is ridiculous. We have a contradiction. This tells us that there is *no solution* to the pair of equations.

To see what is happening here it is helpful to consider the slope and intercept of both lines; $3x - 4y = 12$ rearranges to $y = \frac{3}{4}x - 3$, and $-12x + 16y = 5$ rearranges to $y = \frac{3}{4}x + \frac{5}{16}$, so both lines have the same slope ($\frac{3}{4}$) but different intercepts with the y axis, so they must be parallel as shown in Figure 4.14. There is no solution to the equations because the lines never meet.

Now consider the equations

$$2x - 8y = 10$$
$$-x + 4y = -5$$

When we multiply the second equation by 2 we obtain

$$2x - 8y = 10$$
$$\underline{-2x + 8y = -10} \quad \text{and adding these gives}$$
$$0x + 0y = 0$$

The equation $0x + 0y = 0$ holds for any values of x and y, so this is telling us that both our original equations are equivalent; that is, both have the same line on a graph. Any point on this line is a solution to both equations so there are an infinite number of solutions to the pair of equations.

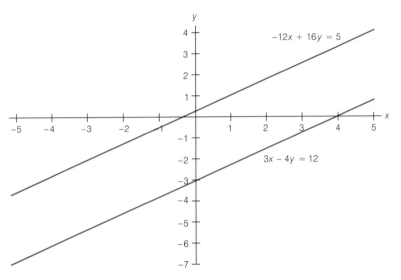

Figure 4.14

Check these

Find the solution (if any) to the following pairs of equations:

$$-7x + 2y = 7$$
$$-35x + 10y = 35$$

Solution:
Multiply the first equation by 5 to give $-35x + 10y = 35$. Both equations are the same now, so subtracting one from the other gives $0x + 0y = 0$. So both the original equations are equivalent. Any point on the line $-7x + 2y = 7$ is a solution.

$$3x - 12y = 7$$
$$-2x + 8y = 12$$

Solution:
Multiplying the second equation by $\frac{3}{2}$ gives $3x - 12y = 7$ and $-3x + 12y = 18$. Adding these gives $0x + 0y = 25$, which is impossible, so no solution exists. These two lines have the same gradient but a different intercept and so they are parallel.

$$2x - 5y = 7$$
$$6x + 6y = 14$$

Solution:
You could multiply the first equation by 3 to give $6x - 15y = 21$, and then subtract the second equation from the first to give $0x - 21y = -7$ so $y = -\frac{1}{3}$. Substituting this into the first equation gives $2x + \frac{5}{3} = 7$, so $2x = 7 - \frac{5}{3}$, and $x = \frac{8}{3}$.

A summary of the method for solving a pair of linear equations in two variables is given below. Sets of equations like this are often called simultaneous linear equations.

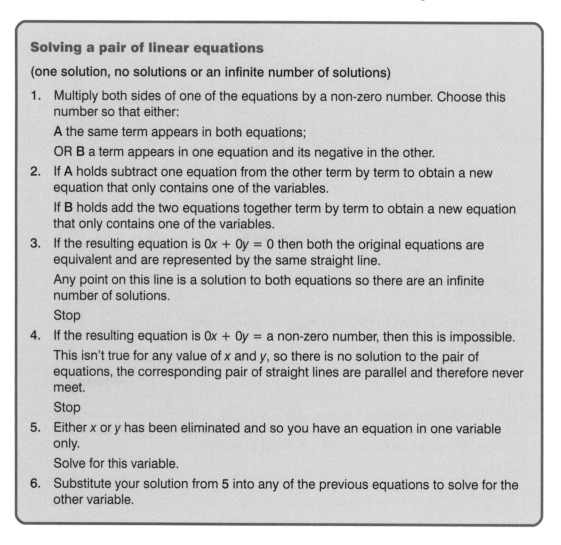

Solving a pair of linear equations

(one solution, no solutions or an infinite number of solutions)

1. Multiply both sides of one of the equations by a non-zero number. Choose this number so that either:

    A the same term appears in both equations;

    OR **B** a term appears in one equation and its negative in the other.

2. If **A** holds subtract one equation from the other term by term to obtain a new equation that only contains one of the variables.

    If **B** holds add the two equations together term by term to obtain a new equation that only contains one of the variables.

3. If the resulting equation is $0x + 0y = 0$ then both the original equations are equivalent and are represented by the same straight line.

    Any point on this line is a solution to both equations so there are an infinite number of solutions.

    Stop

4. If the resulting equation is $0x + 0y = $ a non-zero number, then this is impossible.

    This isn't true for any value of x and y, so there is no solution to the pair of equations, the corresponding pair of straight lines are parallel and therefore never meet.

    Stop

5. Either x or y has been eliminated and so you have an equation in one variable only.

    Solve for this variable.

6. Substitute your solution from **5** into any of the previous equations to solve for the other variable.

Finding market equilibrium

We return to the problem of the market equilibrium for the supply and demand equations discussed at the start of this section. The demand equation was

$$Q = -\frac{1}{2}P + 100$$

and the supply equation

$$Q = 2P - 20$$

A graph of the situation was shown in Figure 4.13 but we did not yet know how to calculate the point of intersection.

Employing the usual solution method we see that both equations already have a term Q so we can subtract one equation from the other immediately. Subtracting the second equation from the first gives

$$0 \cdot Q = -\frac{5}{2} P + 120$$

So

$$\frac{5}{2} P = 120 \quad \text{and} \quad P = \frac{240}{5} = 48$$

Substituting $P = 48$ into the first equation gives $Q = -\frac{1}{2} 48 + 100$, so $Q = 76$.
We conclude that the equilibrium price is 48 and equilibrium quantity is 76.

WORK CARD 4

1. Do the following pairs of straight lines intersect and if so where, or are they parallel or the same line?
    a. $y = 2x + 5$ $y = 3x + 1$
    b. $2y - 5x = 3$ $4y - 10x = 5$
    c. $2y + 3x = 6$ $y - x = 2$

2. Write down the solutions (if any) to the following pairs of equations:
    a. $y = 2x + 5$ $y = 3x + 1$
    b. $2y - 5x = 3$ $4y - 10x = 5$
    c. $2y + 3x = 6$ $y - x = 2$

3. Establish the nature of the solutions (if any) to the following pairs of linear equations:
    a. $6\pi x - \pi y = 3\pi$ $2x + y = 5$
    b. $ay - bx = 0$ $by + bx = \frac{1}{a} + \frac{1}{b}$

4. If the supply equation is $Q = -\frac{1}{2}P + 20$ and the demand equation is $Q = \frac{3}{2}P + 10$, determine the equilibrium price and quantity and sketch a graph to illustrate the situation.

Solutions:

1. a. $x = 4$, $y = 13$ b. parallel   c. $x = \frac{2}{5}$, $y = \frac{12}{5}$

2. Same as 1

3. a. $x = 1$, $y = 3$ b. $y = \frac{1}{ab}$, $x = \frac{1}{b^2}$

4. $P = 5$, $Q = 17.5$

ASSESSMENT 4

1. Sketch the following pairs of straight lines and find their point of intersection (if any):
   a. $3x - 2y = 6$ $9x - 6y = 18$
   b. $5y + x = 6$ $-10y - 2x = 9$
   c. $22x - 11y = 7$ $11y + 20x = 35$
   d. $3x - 2y = 3$ $x + 3y = 12$
2. Solve the following pairs of simultaneous equations:
   a. $ax - 2y = 2,$ $x + 3y = 3$
   b. $py + qx = 2,$ $qy - px = \dfrac{q^2 - p^2}{pq}$

Further reading: see p. xv

Jacques is useful here, particularly in an economics context.

MM More Maths

The material in *More Maths* is *not* required for the later parts of this book but it provides the additional mathematical techniques you will need if you want to take more advanced modules in subjects like Maths for Economics and Financial Mathematics. If you took Maths up to the age of 18 you will probably have covered most of the material before but be grateful of some revision, so we have placed a **Test box** at the start of each section of a chapter. Each **Test box** contains a few 'diagnostic' questions and their answers. If you can do these easily and accurately then you could save time and pass directly onto the next section.

MM1
Some special equations

Like so many ageing college people, Pnin had long ceased to notice the existence of students on the campus.

V. Nabokov, Russian born US novelist (*Pnin*, Chapter 3)

Contexts

What is this chapter about?
This chapter explains how to solve two special types of equation: (i) those where the unknown is a power, and (ii) those known as quadratic equations.

Why is it useful?
These types of equation arise frequently; for instance, in assessing the number of time periods required to repay a loan or to model the relationship between profit and the number of units produced by a company. However, the technique of rearranging the equation, described in EM3, is not sufficient to solve them and the methods in this chapter are required.

This chapter is also useful because, to solve the first type of equation, it introduces a device called the logarithm or log, which is widely used in financial, economic and statistical models.

Where does it fit in?
More Maths includes the mathematical techniques, additional to those in Essential Maths, that are the most useful for quantitative work.

What do I need to know?
You will need to be fluent in the material in Essential Maths, in particular the work on powers and factorising from Chapter EM2.

Objectives

After your work on this chapter you should be able to:

- understand what a log is and calculate logs on a calculator;
- write down an expression for the log of a product, quotient or power;
- solve equations when the unknown is a power by taking logs;
- recognise a quadratic equation;
- solve a quadratic equation by factorising or using a formula.

In Chapter EM3 you learnt the main technique for solving equations. You will, however, need a little extra help for some special types of equations. In this chapter we deal with **(i)** equations such as $2^{x+1} = 64$, in which the unknown is a power and **(ii)** equations of the form $ax^2 + bx + c = 0$, which are known as *quadratic* equations.

To solve equations in which the unknown is a power, we need a device called the *logarithm* or *log*, which we introduce in Section 1. Logs are also used widely in financial, economic and statistical models.

1 Introducing logs

Test box 1

Without using a calculator write down the values of

$\log_3 27$ $\qquad \log_{10} 1$ $\qquad \log_2 \left(\frac{1}{4}\right)$

Simplify: $\log_2(4p) - \log_2(8p)$ $\qquad \log_b b^3$

Use a calculator to evaluate $\log_{10} 150$ and $\log_e 150$.

Solutions:

$3, 0, -2, \log_2 \left(\dfrac{4p}{8p}\right) = \log_2 \left(\dfrac{1}{2}\right) = -1, 3, 2.176091$ and 5.010635 (to 6 d.p.)

Why do we need logs?

Consider the equation

$$2^x = 64.$$

You may be able to guess the solution, but suppose for now that you can't. How would you go about solving it?

Recall that in Chapter EM3 we solved equations by performing operations on both sides of the equation until we obtained $x = ...$ or $... = x$. The problem here is that x is a power and whether we add, subtract, multiply or divide the equation, x will still be a power. Try it and see!

Another equation that you cannot solve yet is

$$2^x = 4^{x+2}.$$

Again, the problem is that the xs are powers.

The same problem occurs when rearranging an equation such as $y = 10^x$ to have x as the subject.

The tool that you lack, which can remove a power index, is the *logarithm* or *log*. Those of you over a certain age will probably moan inwardly at this prospect because tables of logs were a tedious way of performing multiplication and division before calculators were commonplace. However, we are *not* going to use logs in this way at all. Here, we will use them as another operation that can be performed on both sides of an equation to solve or rearrange it.

First, we need to do a little groundwork. To understand you will need to be fluent in the work on powers from Chapter EM2.

Using logarithms

We know that

$$2^5 = 32.$$

An equivalent way of expressing the relationship between 2, 5 and 32 is

$$\log_2 32 = 5.$$

This reads as 'the log of 32 to base 2 is 5'.

As another example consider

$$3^4 = 81.$$

It can also be written

$$\log_3 81 = 4.$$

In general, the two statements

$$x = b^n \text{ and } \log_b x = n$$

are equivalent. Notice the relative positions of x, b and n. n is a power in the first statement but is not a power in the second. This is why logs are useful. They give us an equivalent way of writing an equation that gets rid of the power.

The number b, which is raised to a power in the first statement and is the log subscript in the second, is called the *base* of the log. By convention we only allow positive numbers as bases.

Check this

Use logs to write down equivalent statements to the following:

$2^4 = 16$

$3^2 = 9$

$10^3 = 1000$

$10^{0.5} = 3.162278$

Solutions:

$\log_2 16 = 4$, $\log_3 9 = 2$, $\log_{10} 1000 = 3$, $\log_{10} 3.162278 = 0.5$

Evaluating logs

We will often need to evaluate the log of a number; for instance, $\log_4 64$. This is like asking the question: if $\log_4 64 = n$, what is n? To answer this write down the equivalent statement to $\log_4 64 = n$; that is

$$4^n = 64$$

and then ask, what is n? As $4^3 = 64$, the answer is 3, so $\log_4 64 = 3$.

So the problem of determining $\log_4 64$ is one of answering the question, 'To what power must we raise 4 to get 64?'.

In general to evaluate $\log_b x$ we ask, 'To what power must we raise the base b to obtain x?'.

Check these

Check the following:

Evaluate $\log_{10} 100$.
Ask 'to what power must we raise 10 to get 100?' The answer is 2, as $10^2 = 100$.

Evaluate $\log_3 81$.
Ask 'to what power must we raise 3 to make 81?' The answer is 4, as $3^4 = 81$.

What is $\log_9 81$?
To what power must we raise 9 to make 81? The answer is 2.

Evaluate $\log_9 3$.
To what power must we raise 9 to make 3? 3 is the square root of 9 so the answer is $\frac{1}{2}$ or 0.5.

What is $\log_4 \frac{1}{16}$?
To what power must we raise 4 to get $\frac{1}{16}$? As $4^{-2} = \frac{1}{16}$ the answer is -2.

Check these

Write down:

$\log_7 49$

$\log_2 16$

$\log_2 \frac{1}{4}$

$\log_4 2$

Solutions: 2, 4, –2, $\frac{1}{2}$.

We can evaluate the log of any positive number, but the log of a negative number does *not exist*. (This is because the base *b* is always positive and so $x = b^n$ is always positive.)

There are three special logs that often crop up and so are worth remembering. They arise from the following statements containing powers:

$$b^0 = 1, b^1 = b \text{ and } b^n = b^n.$$

The equivalent 'log' statements are

$$\log_b 1 = 0, \log_b b = 1 \text{ and } \log_b b^n = n.$$

The first of these tells us that the log of 1 is always 0, whatever the base; the third says that the log to base *b* of any power of *b* is the power itself; and the second is the special case of this when the power is 1.

Check these

Write down:

$\log_3 3$

$\log_4 4^3$

$\log_a a$

$\log_c c^{20}$

$\log_{10} 1$

$\log_{99} 1$

Solutions: 1, 3, 1, 20, 0, 0.

Manipulating logs

Logs can be manipulated using their own set of rules. These rules hold for any base *provided the same base is used throughout the rule*, so we list them here without the *b* subscript.

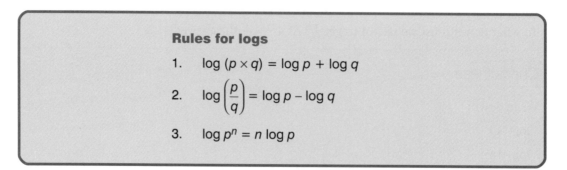

Rules for logs

1. $\log (p \times q) = \log p + \log q$

2. $\log \left(\dfrac{p}{q} \right) = \log p - \log q$

3. $\log p^n = n \log p$

Rules **1** and **2** tell you about the log of a product and a quotient. Rule **1** extends naturally, for instance, to

$$\log (pqr) = \log p + \log q + \log r$$

or

$$\log (pqrs) = \log p + \log q + \log r + \log s.$$

Rule **3** follows from rule **1** because

$$\log p^n = \log (p \times p \times p \times ... \times p) = \log p + \log p + \log p + ... + \log p = n \log p.$$

Check these

Check that the following are correct:

$\log_4 (16 \times 64) = \log_4 16 + \log_4 64$ (Rule **1**)

$\log_3 \dfrac{27}{243} = \log_3 27 - \log_3 243$ (Rule **2**)

$\log_5 25^6 = 6 \log_5 25$ (Rule **3**)

$\log_3 (27a) = \log_3 27 + \log_3 a$ (Rule **1**)

$\log_2 (8 + 4)$. Beware! This is *not* $\log_2 8 + \log_2 4$

Logs on a calculator

The logs evaluated so far have been 'nice' in that they involved well known relations like $2^4 = 16$ or $7^2 = 49$. When you need to evaluate a log which isn't 'nice' in this way you will have to use a calculator.

Most calculators have a **log** key. This will give the log *to the base 10* of the number displayed. For instance, to calculate $\log_{10} 200$, enter 200 and then press the **log** key to give 2.301029996.

You will probably also see a key called **ln**. This gives the log to the base of a special number, which, like π, has its own name and is called e. The number e has special properties that make it useful and which we shall consider later. For now it suffices to know that, to 6 decimal places, e = 2.718281. $\log_e x$ is often written ln x.

To check that you've found the **ln** key you could verify that $\log_e 200 = 5.298317367$.

The relationship between logs and powers

If you square a number, and then take the positive square root of the result you get back to the number you started with. For instance

$$+\sqrt{2^2} = 2.$$

Also, if you take the square root of a (positive) number, say $\sqrt{9}$, and then square it, $(\sqrt{9})^2 = 9$, you return to the original number. We say that squaring and taking the positive square root are the *inverse functions* of each other.

We have already met $\log_b b^n = n$. It tells us that if we raise b to a number (b^n), and then calculate $\log_b$ of the result we will return to the original number, n. It can also be shown that $b^{\log_b x} = x$ so if we take $\log_b$ of a number ($\log_b x$) and then calculate b to the power of the result we will return to the original number, x.

So the two operations, taking log to base b and calculating b to the power of are like squaring and square-rooting in that when done in succession (in either order) they return to the original number. They too are the inverse functions of each other.

We show this diagrammatically below.

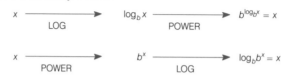

$$x \xrightarrow{\text{LOG}} \log_b x \xrightarrow{\text{POWER}} b^{\log_b x} = x$$

$$x \xrightarrow{\text{POWER}} b^x \xrightarrow{\text{LOG}} \log_b b^x = x$$

For example, take a number, say 6, and calculate 2^6, to give 64. Now calculate $\log_2 64$ and you will get 6 again. As another example, take a number, say 6, calculate $\log_{10} 6 = 0.77815125$ and then calculate $10^{0.77815125}$ which is 6 again. This will work for any base.

Check this

Choose any (positive) number. Use a calculator to calculate its log and now raise the base of the log to the power of the result. You should get your original number back. Try this for base 10 and base e and several numbers.

As there are quite a few of them, we summarise all the results for logs below.

Logs

$\log_b x$ is the log of x to base b

$\log_b x = n$ is an equivalent statement to $x = b^n$

e.g.

$\log_3 9 = 2$ is equivalent to $9 = 3^2$

To write down $\log_b x$ ask,

'To what power must I raise b to get x?'

e.g. to evaluate $\log_2 8$, ask,

'To what power must I raise 2 to get 8?'

Answer, 3

Special cases, worth noting, are

$\log_b 1 = 0$, $\log_b b = 1$, and $\log_b b^n = n$

On a calculator

log means $\log_{10}$

ln means $\log_e$ where e = 2.718281 ...

Manipulation rules

RULE 1 $\log_b (p \times q) = \log_b p + \log_b q$

RULE 2 $\log_b \left(\dfrac{p}{q}\right) = \log_b p - \log_b q$

RULE 3 $\log_b p^n = n \log_b p$

Logs and powers

$\log_b b^n = n$ $\qquad b^{\log_b x} = x$

so $\log_b$ and b^n are inverse functions

WORK CARD 1

1. Without using a calculator evaluate:

   a. $\log_5 125$ **b.** $\log_{10} 1000$ **c.** $\log_2 32$ **d.** $\log_4 4$

   e. $\log_2 \frac{1}{32}$ **f.** $\log_5 1$ **g.** $\log_2 \frac{1}{4}$ **h.** $\log_4 \frac{1}{4}$

   i. $\log_8 32$ **j.** $\log_9 27$

2. Without using a calculator calculate:

   a. $\log_4 (64 \times 64)$ **b.** $\log_3 (27 \times 81)$ **c.** $\log_3 \left(\dfrac{1}{27} \times \dfrac{1}{81}\right)$

   d. $\log_5 125 \div \log_5 25$ **e.** $\log_2 4 \times \log_2 8$ **f.** $\log_{10} 10^3$

   g. $\log_2 4^7$ **h.** $\log_2 \left(\dfrac{1}{32}\right)^8$ **i.** $\log_3 (27)^{-5}$ **j.** $\log_2 \sqrt{2}$

3. Calculate:

   a. $\log_5 5^9$ **b.** $\log_3 3^5$ **c.** $\log_2 2^8$ **d.** $3^{\log_3 4}$

4. Using a calculator evaluate:

   $\log_{10} 300 \qquad \log_e 300$

   Check your answers by raising to the appropriate power.

Solutions:

1. **a.** 3, **b.** 3, **c.** 5, **d.** 1, **e.** –5, **f.** 0, **g.** –2, **h.** –1, **i.** $\frac{5}{3}$ as $32 = (8^{1/3})^5$,
   j. $\frac{3}{2}$ as $27 = 9^{3/2}$

2. **a.** $3 + 3 = 6$, **b.** 7, **c.** –7, **d.** $\frac{3}{2}$, **e.** 6, **f.** 3, **g.** 14, **h.** –40, **i.** –15, **j.** $\frac{1}{2}$

3. **a.** 9 **b.** 5 **c.** 8 **d.** $3^{\log_3 4} = 4$ because $\log_3$ and 3 raised to a power are inverse functions of each other.

4. 2.4771 ... 5.70378 ... so $10^{2.4771...} = 300$ and $e^{5.70378...} = 300$.

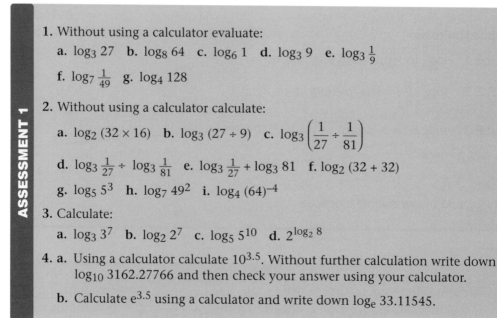

1. Without using a calculator evaluate:

    a. $\log_3 27$ **b.** $\log_8 64$ **c.** $\log_6 1$ **d.** $\log_3 9$ **e.** $\log_3 \frac{1}{9}$

    f. $\log_7 \frac{1}{49}$ **g.** $\log_4 128$

2. Without using a calculator calculate:

    a. $\log_2 (32 \times 16)$ **b.** $\log_3 (27 \div 9)$ **c.** $\log_3 \left(\frac{1}{27} \div \frac{1}{81} \right)$

    d. $\log_3 \frac{1}{27} \div \log_3 \frac{1}{81}$ **e.** $\log_3 \frac{1}{27} + \log_3 81$ **f.** $\log_2 (32 + 32)$

    g. $\log_5 5^3$ **h.** $\log_7 49^2$ **i.** $\log_4 (64)^{-4}$

3. Calculate:

    a. $\log_3 3^7$ **b.** $\log_2 2^7$ **c.** $\log_5 5^{10}$ **d.** $2^{\log_2 8}$

4. **a.** Using a calculator calculate $10^{3.5}$. Without further calculation write down $\log_{10} 3162.27766$ and then check your answer using your calculator.

    b. Calculate $e^{3.5}$ using a calculator and write down $\log_e 33.11545$.

2 Solving equations when the unknown is a power

Test box 2

Solve the equation $4^{x-1} = 8^{x+3}$.

Solution: You need to take logs of both sides. The solution is $x = -11$.

As we said earlier, logs are needed to solve equations in which the unknown is a power.

Taking logs
We return to the example

$$2^x = 64.$$

The usual rearrangement tools (adding, subtracting, dividing, multiplying) aren't enough to solve this because the unknown, x, will always remain a power, and so we can't get the equation into the form $x = \ldots$ or $\ldots = x$. The operation we need, which gets rid of the power, is 'taking logs'. By 'taking logs' we mean that instead of the equation

$$\text{LHS} = \text{RHS}$$

we write

$$\log (\text{LHS}) = \log (\text{RHS}).$$

So the log of the *whole* of the left-hand side of the original equation is equal to the log of the *whole* of the original right-hand side. As we have treated both sides in the same way we have an equivalent equation.

For example, taking logs of $2^x = 64$ gives

$$\log (2^x) = \log (64).$$

We can use any base to do this so there is no need to indicate one at this stage.

We can now apply Rule 3, $\log p^n = n \log p$, to the left-hand side of the equation, to bring x 'down to ground level' so that it is no longer a power.

Rule **3** says $\log (2^x) = x \log 2$ and so the equation becomes

$$x \log 2 = \log 64.$$

Now that x is no longer a power we can solve the equation in the usual way. Log 2 and log 64 are just numbers, so dividing each side by log 2 gives the solution

$$x = \frac{\log 64}{\log 2}.$$

All that remains is to evaluate the logs. We can use any base provided that we use the same one throughout, although sometimes a particular base may be easier. For instance, for this example base 2 is a good idea as $\log_2 64$ and $\log_2 2$ are both whole numbers. If no base seems obvious then we use a calculator and calculate the logs to base 10 or e.

To demonstrate this we will calculate

$$\frac{\log 64}{\log 2}$$

using both base 2 and base 10 below. Using base 2,

$$x = \frac{\log_2 64}{\log_2 2} = \frac{6}{1} = 6.$$

Using base 10 and a calculator

$$x = \frac{\log_{10} 64}{\log_{10} 2} = \frac{1.806180}{0.301030} = 6.$$

We conclude that the solution of $2^x = 64$ is $x = 6$.

Let's try some more examples.

Check these

Solve $3^x = 9^{x-2}$.

Solution:
Take logs to give $\log (3^x) = \log (9^{x-2})$. To bring x down to the same level as the rest of the equation we use Rule 3 and write $x \log 3$ instead of $\log (3^x)$ and $(x - 2) \log 9$ instead of $\log (9^{x-2})$. The equation becomes $x \log 3 = (x - 2) \log 9$. Remembering that log 3 and log 9 are just numbers, rearranging in the normal way gives $x \log 3 = x \log 9 - 2 \log 9$, $x(\log 3 - \log 9) = -2 \log 9$:

$$x = \frac{-2\log 9}{\log 3 - \log 9}.$$

Base 3 is easiest here as both 3 and 9 are powers of 3, and this gives

$$x = \frac{-2 \times 2}{1 - 2} = 4.$$

Check that $3^4 = 9^{4-2}$ to confirm the solution.

Solve $3^x = 10^{x+1}$.

Solution:
The unknown, x, is a power so we need to use logs. Taking logs gives $\log (3^x) = \log (10^{x+1})$. Using Rule **3**, we have $x \log 3 = (x + 1) \log 10$. Remember that $\log 3$ and $\log 10$ are just numbers so now we can rearrange the equation in the usual way. Multiplying out the bracket gives $x \log 3 = x \log 10 + \log 10$, and rearranging gives $x \log 3 - x \log 10 = \log 10$ and then $x (\log 3 - \log 10) = \log (10)$, so

$$x = \frac{\log 10}{\log 3 - \log 10}.$$

This is valid for any base. If we choose base 10 it will be easier to evaluate as $\log_{10} 10 = 1$, so

$$x = \frac{1}{\log_{10} 3 - 1}.$$

Using a calculator $\log_{10} 3 = 0.477121$, so $x = -1.912489$.

Remember that you can always check the solution to an equation by substituting it into the original equation. In the last example, substituting $x = -1.912489$ into the original equation gives $3^{-1.912489} = 10^{-0.912489}$.

Before taking logs we must isolate the term that contains the power.

Check this

Solve $5 + 2^{x+2} = 261$.

Solution:
As the unknown is a power we must take logs. However, if we take logs of both sides, we get $\log (5 + 2^{x+2})$ on the left-hand side, which can't be simplified, and won't enable x to be brought down to 'ground level'. We must therefore isolate the term that contains the power before taking logs. Here, we subtract 5 from both sides of the original equation to give $2^{x+2} = 256$ and *then* take logs to give $\log (2^{x+2}) = \log 256$. This is $(x + 2) \log 2 = \log 256$. Rearranging gives

$$x + 2 = \frac{\log 256}{\log 2}$$

and so

$$x = \frac{\log 256}{\log 2} - 2 = \frac{8}{1} - 2$$

using logs to base 2. The solution is $x = 6$. Again, we can check that $5 + 2^8 = 261$.

Rearranging equations

The same technique of 'taking logs' can be used to rearrange an equation when the desired subject is currently a power. For example, suppose $y = 10^q + 1$ and we want to express q (currently a power) in terms of y.

First of all we must isolate the term containing q to give

$$y - 1 = 10^q$$

We are now ready to take logs. This gives

$$\log (y - 1) = \log (10^q)$$

and using Rule **3**

$$\log (y - 1) = q \log 10.$$

The desired subject, q, is now at the same level as the rest of the equation, so we can rearrange as usual to give

$$q = \frac{\log(y - 1)}{\log 10}.$$

To isolate the new subject you may need to use any of the log rules we have given. Try this.

Check this

Express $x = 10a^{-y}$ with y as the subject.

Taking logs of both sides gives $\log x = \log (10a^{-y})$. $10a^{-y}$ is a product, so using Rule **1**, $\log (10a^{-y}) = \log 10 + \log (a^{-y})$. The equation becomes

$$\log x = \log 10 + \log (a^{-y})$$

and then $\log x = \log 10 - y \log a$ (using Rule **3**), which rearranges to

$$y = \frac{\log 10 - \log x}{\log a}.$$

We can also rearrange inequalities by taking logs.

Check this

Rearrange $3^x \geq 2$ with x as the subject.

As x is currently a power, we take logs of both sides to give $\log (3^x) \geq \log 2$. Using Rule **3** we have $x \log 3 \geq \log 2$ so x is now on the same level as the rest of the inequality. Dividing by $\log 3$ gives

$$x \geq \frac{\log 2}{\log 3}.$$

Recall that log 1 = 0 and so the log of any number between 0 and 1 is negative. If a log has a negative value, we must reverse the direction of the inequality sign when we divide or multiply by it, as in the following example.

Check this

Rearrange $(0.5)^x > a$ with x as the subject.

Taking logs gives $\log (0.5)^x > \log a$ and Rule **3** gives $x \log 0.5 > \log a$. As $\log 0.5$ is negative we must reverse the direction of the inequality when we divide by $\log 0.5$, so

$$x < \frac{\log a}{\log 0.5}$$

is the desired inequality.

An application

In Chapter EM2, Section 7, we showed that the formula for the sum accrued after n years when an amount, A, is invested at $r\%$ interest is

$$S = A\left(1 + \frac{r}{100}\right)^n.$$

In some circumstances we may want to know for how many years we must invest to accrue a particular sum. That is, we would like an expression for n in terms of S, A and r.

As the required subject, n, is currently a power we will need to take logs. Taking logs of both sides of the equation gives

$$\log S = \log\left(A\left(1 + \frac{r}{100}\right)^n\right)$$

(Notice that the brackets are vital here to ensure that we are taking the log of the whole of the right-hand side.) We now have the log of a product on the right-hand side so using Rule **1** gives

$$\log S = \log A + \log\left(\left(1 + \frac{r}{100}\right)^n\right)$$

and using Rule **3**,

$$\log S = \log A + n \log\left(1 + \frac{r}{100}\right).$$

Now n has been brought down to 'ground level' and we can rearrange as usual to give

$$\log S - \log A = n \log\left(1 + \frac{r}{100}\right)$$

and so

$$n = \frac{\log S - \log A}{\log(1 + \frac{r}{100})}.$$

This new equation, with n as the subject, can be used to solve problems like the one that follows.

If I have £1000 to invest and the interest rate is 5% per year, how many years will it take me to accumulate £2000?

To calculate this we just substitute $S = 2000$, $A = 1000$ and $r = 5$ into the equation we have just obtained to give

$$n = \frac{\log 2000 - \log 1000}{\log(1 + \frac{5}{100})}.$$

We can use any base to evaluate this. Using base e gives

$$n = \frac{7.600902 - 6.907755}{0.04879016} = 14.21 \text{ years}.$$

As n must be a whole number of years, I would have to wait 15 years – a long time!

WORK CARD 2

1. Solve the following using logs:
    a. $3^a = 81$ b. $2^x = 4^{x+2}$ c. $5^{x+2} = 125^{2-x}$
    d. $\left(\frac{1}{2}\right)^{3x} = 4^{-x-1}$ e. $\frac{1}{3^n} = 12^{n+2}$

2. Express the following with x as the subject:
    a. $s = P(1 + r)^x$ b. $z = 3 \times 4^{-x}$ c. $(2 + z) \cdot 2^x = 4$
    d. $z = e^{x^2/2}$ e. $10 = a^x b^y c^z$ f. $a^x > 500$ where $a > 0$

3. When interest is payable continuously at rate x, an investment of £P accumulates to $S = Pe^{tx}$ after t years.
    Express t in terms of the other variables. For how long must I invest £5000 at rate $x = 0.05$ to accumulate about £6920?

Solutions:

1. a. 4   b. –4   c. 1   d. 2   e. –1.3868528

2. a. $x = \dfrac{\log(s/p)}{\log(1 + r)}$ b. $x = \dfrac{\log 3 - \log z}{\log 4}$ c. $x = 2 - \log_2 (z + 2)$

    d. $x = \sqrt{2 \log_e z}$ e. $x = \dfrac{\log 10 - y \log b - z \log c}{\log a}$

    f. $x > \dfrac{\log 500}{\log a}$ if $a > 1$, $x < \dfrac{\log 500}{\log a}$ if $a < 1$

3. $t = \dfrac{\log_e S - \log_e P}{x}$ (About 6.5 years).

1. Solve using logs:

 a. $2^x = 8^{x-1}$ b. $3^y = 27^{y-2}$ c. $(\frac{1}{2})^{x+2} = 8^{-x}$ d. $3^{2x} = 2^{3x+1}$

2. Express the following with x as the subject:

 a. $y = 2 \times 5^x$ b. $4z - 3 = 3^x$ c. $2e^{x^2-1} = z$ d. $2(y + e^x) = 0$

 e. $V = \dfrac{P}{(1+r)^x}$ f. $10^{x+y} = 10^{100}$ g. $2^x < y < 2^{x+1}$

3. A model for the sales of a product, S, in terms of the amount spent on advertising, A, and the price of the product, p, is

 $$S = 1000\,(40 - pe^{-0.001A})$$

 Write down a formula that expresses advertising expenditure in terms of sales and price.

 If desired sales are \$20,000 and the price is \$40, how much should be spent on advertising?

3 Quadratic equations

Test box 3

Which of the following are quadratic equations?

 $y^2 - 2y = 3$ $x^3 + x^2 - 3 = 5$ $2^x + 5 - 1 = 0$

Use a formula to solve the following quadratic equations:

 $x^2 - 10x + 9 = 0$ $2x^2 - 3x + 2 = 0$

Solve the following equations by factorising:

 $x^2 - 3x - 10 = 0$ $2x^2 - x - 1 = 0$

Solutions:
Only the first equation is quadratic. $x = 9$ and $x = 1$. No solutions. $(x - 5)(x + 2)$ so $x = 5$ and $x = -2$. $(2x + 1)(x - 1)$ so $x = -\frac{1}{2}$ and $x = 1$.

What are quadratic equations?
The method of treating each side of an equation in the same way until a solution is obtained will not work for an equation like

$$x^2 - 3x + 2 = 0.$$

If you don't believe this – try it. The problem is that there are both an x^2 term and an x term in the equation. Such equations are called *quadratic equations* and their general form is

$$ax^2 + bx + c = 0$$

where a, b and c are constants; b and/or c can be zero but a must be non-zero, that is, there must always be a squared term. If there are any other terms in the equation then it is *not* a quadratic.

Check these

Which of the following are quadratic equations?

$5x^2 + 2x - 3 = 0$

$5x^2 + 2\sqrt{x} + 3 = 0$

$3x^2 - 2x + 3 = 3x$

$x^2 + x - x^3 + 5 = 0$

$P^2 - 2 = 5P$

Solutions:
The first, third and final equation are quadratic. The second contains a square root and the fourth contains x^3.

Recall that to solve an equation we want to know the value of x for which the equation is true. Quadratic equations may have no solution, or one or two solutions.

Check these

Are the following solutions to these quadratic equations correct?

$x^2 + 2x + 1 = 0$ $x = -1$

$2x^2 - 13x - 7 = 0$ $x = 7$ and $x = -\frac{1}{2}$

$P^2 - 3P + 4 = 0$ $P = 4$

$2Q^2 + Q - 6 = 2$ $Q = -2$ and $Q = \frac{3}{2}$

Solutions: Yes, Yes, No. This would be true if the right-hand side were 0, but it isn't so the solutions given are false.

How do quadratic equations arise?

$y = ax^2 + bx + c$ often represents the relationship between x and y more realistically than the simpler equation $y = ax + b$ and so it is frequently used in modelling. We will often be interested in the value of x for which $y = 0$, in which case we will need to solve $ax^2 + bx + c = 0$, a quadratic equation.

For instance, we will see later (Chapter MM2) that under certain assumptions about the demand and supply equations, and the costs incurred by a firm, the profit of a firm is related to the number of units produced by the firm, Q, as follows:

$$\text{profit} = aQ^2 + bQ + c$$

where a, b and c are constants.

So, to calculate the quantity that the firm must produce to break even (make zero profit) we need to solve the quadratic equation

$$aQ^2 + bQ + c = 0.$$

Quadratic equations often arise unexpectedly, as in the following example.

Check this

An investor purchases some shares for £7000. When the price per share increases by £1.50 she sells all but 1000 of the shares for £5000. How many shares did she buy originally?

Suppose she originally bought x shares. The price of these must have been $\frac{7000}{x}$ each. She sells $x - 1000$ shares for

$$\frac{7000}{x} + 1.5$$

and we know she obtains £5000 so

$$(x - 1000)\left(\frac{7000}{x} + 1.5\right) = 5000.$$

When we multiply this out we obtain

$$7000 + 1.5x - \frac{7{,}000{,}000}{x} - 1500 = 5000$$

which simplifies to

$$500 + 1.5x - \frac{7{,}000{,}000}{x} = 0.$$

Multiplying throughout by x (which is valid provided that x is not zero) we obtain

$$1.5x^2 + 500x - 7{,}000{,}000 = 0$$

which is a quadratic equation.

We will see in Section 4 that the solutions to this equation are $x = 2000$ and $x = -2333.\dot{3}$. The negative solution makes no sense for the number of shares purchased, so the investor bought 2000 shares originally.

Solving quadratic equations: using a formula

There is a formula to obtain the values of x that are solutions to a quadratic equation. It is a formula that many people remember because it was drummed into them at school, even if they don't remember what it is used for. The formula for the solution of $ax^2 + bx + c = 0$ is

$$x = \frac{-b \pm \sqrt{b^2 - 4ac}}{2a}$$

It gives possibly two solutions, one from taking the positive square root of $b^2 - 4ac$ and one from taking the negative square root.

Check this

For example, for $x^2 - 3x + 2 = 0$, $a = 1$, $b = -3$ and $c = 2$, so the formula gives

$$x = \frac{-(-3) \pm \sqrt{(-3)^2 - (4 \times 1 \times 2)}}{2 \times 1} = \frac{3 \pm \sqrt{1}}{2}$$

which is

$$\frac{3 - 1}{2} = 1 \quad \text{or} \quad \frac{3 + 1}{2} = 2.$$

So the solutions are $x = 1$ and $x = 2$. You can substitute each of these back into the original equation to check them.

In the above example the expression in the square root, $b^2 - 4ac$, took a value of 1, which is positive, so its square roots +1 and –1 could be found. However, when $b^2 - 4ac$ is negative no square root exists and *there is no solution* to the quadratic equation.

Check this

Solve $x^2 + 3x + 3 = 0$.

Solution:
The formula gives

$$x = \frac{-3 \pm \sqrt{3^2 - (4 \times 1 \times 3)}}{2 \times 1} = \frac{-3 \pm \sqrt{-3}}{2}.$$

As $\sqrt{-3}$ does not exist there is no solution to this equation.

In some areas of mathematics there is a concept of the square root of a negative number and so what is called an 'imaginary' solution to a quadratic equation can be found. Some texts would therefore say that there is no 'real' solution to the previous equation.

In the following example $b^2 - 4ac = 0$ and so the formula gives only one solution.

Check this

Solve $x^2 - 6x + 9 = 0$.

Solution:
Using the formula

$$x = \frac{6 \pm \sqrt{6^2 - (4 \times 1 \times 9)}}{2 \times 1} = \frac{6 \pm \sqrt{0}}{2}.$$

As the square root of 0 is 0, the solutions are

$$\frac{6+0}{2} \quad \text{and} \quad \frac{6-0}{2}$$

so only one solution, $x = 3$, exists.

Now some general practice at solving quadratics.

Check these

Solve $3x^2 + 8x + 4 = 0$.

Solution:
Using the formula

$$x = \frac{-8 \pm \sqrt{8^2 - (4 \times 3 \times 4)}}{2 \times 3} = \frac{-8 \pm \sqrt{16}}{6}$$

so $x = -2$ or $-\frac{2}{3}$.

Solve $3x^2 + 6x + 3 = 0$.

Solution:

$$x = \frac{-6 \pm \sqrt{6^2 - (4 \times 3 \times 3)}}{2 \times 3} = \frac{-6 \pm \sqrt{0}}{6}$$

so there is only one solution $x = -1$.

Solve $3x^2 + 5x + 3 = 0$.

Solution:

$$\frac{-5 \pm \sqrt{5^2 - (4 \times 3 \times 3)}}{2 \times 3} = \frac{-5 \pm \sqrt{-11}}{6}$$

No solution exists because $\sqrt{-11}$ does not exist.

Quadratic equations do not always have 'nice' solutions.

Check this

Solve $x^2 - 12x + 6 = 0$.

Solution:

$$x = \frac{12 \pm \sqrt{12^2 - (4 \times 1 \times 6)}}{2 \times 1} = \frac{12 \pm \sqrt{120}}{2} = 11.4772 \text{ or } 0.5228 \text{ to 4.d.p.}$$

Solving quadratics: factorising

The formula above always works, but if a quadratic factorises easily there is a quicker method. (If you need some revision on factorising look again at Chapter EM2, Section 6.)

We will explain by solving $x^2 - 3x + 2 = 0$ again. The left-hand side of this factorises to $(x - 1)(x - 2)$ (multiply out the brackets to check this) so the equation is

$$(x - 1)(x - 2) = 0.$$

For two numbers to multiply together to make zero, one or both of the numbers must be equal to zero. So, for the two brackets $(x - 1)$ and $(x - 2)$ to multiply together to make zero, one or both of the brackets must equal zero. This means that the solution(s) to the quadratic occur when $x - 1 = 0$ or when $x - 2 = 0$. When $x - 1 = 0$, $x = 1$ and when $x - 2 = 0$, $x = 2$ so the solutions are $x = 1$ and $x = 2$.

We have solved the quadratic equation by factorising and equating each factor to zero.

Check these

Solve the following equations by factorising:

$x^2 - x - 6 = 0$

$x^2 + 4x + 3 = 0$

$x^2 - 5x + 6 = 0$

$4x^2 - 6x + 2 = 0$

$x^2 - 2x = 0$

Solutions:

The first example factorises to $(x - 3)(x + 2)$ so the solutions are 3 and –2.

$(x + 1)(x + 3)$ so $x = -1$ or -3

$(x - 3)(x - 2)$ so $x = 2$ and 3

This is more difficult to factorise and it is a matter of trial and error to obtain $(2x - 1)(2x - 2)$, so the solutions are $2x - 1 = 0$, giving $x = \frac{1}{2}$, and $2x - 2 = 0$, giving $x = 1$.

Don't be put off because there is no constant term here: it actually makes the factorisation easier: $x(x - 2)$ so $x = 0$ or 2.

WORK CARD 3

1. Which of these are quadratic equations?
   a. $5x^2 - 4x - 2 = 0$ b. $4x^3 - 2x + 1 = 0$
   c. $2x^2 - \log x + 1 = 0$ d. $3x^2 = 5x - 4$

2. Find the solutions, if any, to the following equations:
   a. $x^2 + 5x - 6 = 0$ b. $3x^2 - 9x + 6 = 0$ c. $4x^2 - 4x + 1 = 0$
   d. $2z^2 - 10z + 1 = 0$ e. $z^2 - 7z + 1 = 0$ f. $8p^2 + 8p + 1 = 0$
   g. $x^2 - 2x + 2 = 0$

3. Factorise to solve:
   a. $x^2 - 3x + 2 = 0$ b. $x^2 + 4x + 4 = 0$ c. $x^2 - 5x = 0$
   d. $x^2 - 3ax + 2a^2 = 0$ e. $(x - 4)^2 = 4$ f. $x^2 - b^2 = 0$
   g. $2x^2 + 3x = 2$ h. $x^2 - 64 = 0$

4. The revenue received by a firm is assumed to be $Q(12 - 0.1Q)$ and the firm's costs are $90 + 2Q$, where Q is the quantity produced and sold. Calculate the value or values of Q at which the firm breaks even.

Solutions:

1. a. yes b. no, as there is a term x^3 c. no, as the equation contains $\log x$
   d. yes, as it rearranges to $ax^2 + bx + c = 0$

2. a. 1 and –6 b. $x = 1$ or 2 c. $\frac{1}{2}$ d. $5 \pm \dfrac{\sqrt{23}}{2}$
   e. $\dfrac{7}{2} \pm \dfrac{\sqrt{45}}{2}$ f. $\dfrac{1}{2} \pm \dfrac{\sqrt{2}}{4}$ g. no solution

3. a. $x = 1$ or 2 b. $x = -2, -2$ c. $x = 0$ or 5 d. $x = a$ and $2a$
   e. $x = 6$ or 2 f. $x = \pm b$ g. $x = \frac{1}{2}$ or –2 h. $x = \pm 8$

4. Solve $0.1Q^2 - 10Q + 90 = 0$ to give $Q = 10$ or 90.

ASSESSMENT 3

1. Solve the following quadratic equations where possible:
   a. $x^2 - 5x + 4 = 0$ b. $x^2 + 2x - 3 = 0$
   c. $x^2 + 3x = 0$ d. $2x^2 + 9x + 7 = 0$
   e. $2x^2 + 3x + 7 = 0$ f. $8x^2 + 8x + 2 = 0$

2. Solve the following quadratic equations by factorising:
   a. $x^2 + 2x - 35 = 0$ b. $x^2 + 2x - 8 = 0$ c. $x(x + 1) = 2$
   d. $2x^2 - 2x - 4 = 0$ e. $4x^2 + 3x - 1 = 0$

3. Solve the following equations where possible:
   a. $y^2 + 4y + 2 = 0$ b. $5x - x^2 + 1 = 0$ c. $27p^2 + 12p + 1 = 0$
   d. $5y + 2y^2 = -1$ e. $y^2 - 3y + 9 = 0$ f. $4x^2 + 25 - 20x = 0$

4. Each lorry working for a haulage firm drives between 30,000 and 45,000 miles a year. The company fits a statistical model to relate the miles travelled by each of its lorries last year to the revenue earned by each. They obtain the relationship

$$R = -0.05m^2 + 6m - 100$$

where R is the revenue (in £1000) and m is miles (in thousands).

a. How much revenue would you expect a lorry doing 40,000 miles in a year to earn?

b. To cover costs a lorry must earn revenue of at least £35,000 a year. How many miles a year must a lorry drive to earn revenue of £35,000?

c. Comment on the validity of the model when $m \leq 30$ or $m \geq 45$.

4 The expert equation solver

No, this isn't some wonderful new computer system. It's you! You should now be able to solve and rearrange most of the equations that you are likely to meet.

You have learnt to:

● Rearrange an equation by adding, subtracting, multiplying and dividing provided that you treat both sides of the equation in the same way (Chapter EM3, Section 3).
● Take logs when the unknown is a power (Section 2 of this chapter).
● Use the quadratic solution method when the equation is of the form $ax^2 + bx + c = 0$ (Section 3 of this chapter).

It is important to be able to recognise which technique to use, and when. To this end, in this section we provide a brief review of equation solving and present a variety of equations in a 'random' order to give you plenty of practice.

A review of solving equations

At any step you can write down an equivalent equation by performing the same operation on both sides of the equation, but you must *not* multiply or divide by 0 or an expression with zero value.

Your aim is an equation like $x = ...$ or $... = x$, although this may not always be possible.

Inequalities can be treated in exactly the same way except that you must reverse the direction of the inequality sign when you multiply or divide by a number or a variable that is negative. If there are two inequalities in the expression, then you must treat each one separately when rearranging. For instance, for $2c < y < 3b$, rearrange $2c < y$ and $y < 3b$ separately.

Check these

1. Solve $\dfrac{5x + 10}{2} = 4$

2. Rearrange the following with c as the subject:

$$3d^{1/2} = \frac{2 + a^2}{5c^2}$$

3. Write the following with x as the subject:

$$\frac{5}{x} \le 2$$

4. Rearrange $z + b > z - a > 2b$ with b as the subject.

Solutions:

1. $x = -\frac{2}{5}$

2. The object is to isolate c. Multiply by $5c^2$ to give $15d^{1/2}c^2 = 2 + a^2$, then divide by $15d^{1/2}$ to give

$$c^2 = \frac{2 + a^2}{15d^{1/2}}$$

Now, we can take the square root of both sides so that

$$c = \sqrt{\frac{2 + a^2}{15d^{1/2}}}$$

There are two solutions here as the square root can be positive or negative. The choice will depend on the context.

3. We must treat the two cases, $x < 0$ and $x > 0$, separately ($x = 0$ does not make sense as we cannot divide by 0). When $x < 0$, we need to reverse the inequality when multiplying by x, which gives $5 \le 2x$. We then divide by 2 to give $\frac{5}{2} \le x$ which is impossible when x is negative so we can ignore this solution. When $x > 0$ we obtain $x \le \frac{5}{2}$. The solution is therefore that $0 < x \le \frac{5}{2}$.

4. There are two inequalities here so we must consider each separately. $z + b > z - a$ becomes $b > -a$ and $z - a > 2b$ is equivalent to

$$\frac{z - a}{2} > b$$

so the solution is that $b > -a$ and

$$b < \frac{z - a}{2}$$

must hold. This is written more succinctly as

$$-a < b < \frac{z - a}{2}.$$

When the unknown or the desired subject of an equality is a power, taking logs may help.

Check this

Solve $12 \cdot 4^x = 3^{x+1}$

Solution:
Taking logs gives $\log 12 + x \log 4 = (x + 1) \log 3$ and rearranging gives $x (\log 4 - \log 3) = \log 3 - \log 12$ or equivalently $x \log \frac{4}{3} = \log \frac{1}{4}$ so using logs to base 10,

$$x = \frac{\log_{10} \frac{1}{4}}{\log_{10} \frac{4}{3}} = \frac{-0.602060}{0.124939} = -4.81883$$

Rearrange $a^p = 10y$ with p as the subject.

Solution:
Taking logs gives $\log (a^p) = \log (10y)$ so $p \log a = \log (10y)$ and

$$p = \frac{\log(10y)}{\log a}.$$

If, maybe after some rearrangement, the equation has the form

$$ax^2 + bx + c = 0$$

where a, b and c are constants then it is a quadratic equation. Using the formula

$$x = \frac{-b \pm \sqrt{b^2 - 4ac}}{2a}$$

will provide the solution(s) (if any). Sometimes the solutions can be obtained by factorising and setting each of the factors equal to zero.

Check this

Solve $2F^2 - 5F + 10 = 0$.

Solution:
Using the formula gives

$$F = \frac{5 \pm \sqrt{25 - (4 \times 2 \times 10)}}{4} = \frac{5 \pm \sqrt{-55}}{4}$$

so there are no solutions to this equation.

Solve $F^2 - 3F + 2 = 0$.

Solution:

$$F = \frac{3 \pm \sqrt{9 - (4 \times 1 \times 2)}}{2} = \frac{3 \pm \sqrt{1}}{2}$$

so $F = 1$ or 2. Alternatively you might notice that this equation factorises to $(F - 1)(F - 2) = 0$ and so the solutions could be obtained from $F - 1 = 0$ and $F - 2 = 0$.

Now a mixture of different types of equation to solve.

Check these

1. Solve $x^2 - 5x + 6 = 0$.

2. Rearrange

$$\frac{8z - 4y}{2} = 8$$

with y as the subject.

3. Solve $3^m = 9^{m-2}$ for m.

4. Rearrange

$$y = 1000\left(1 + \frac{i}{100}\right)^n$$

with n as the subject.

5. Rearrange $2 = \sqrt{a + x}$ with x as the subject.

6. Express $2y \leq y + 3 \leq 11 + 3y$ with y as the subject.

Solutions:

1. A quadratic, which factorises to $(x - 2)(x - 3)$, so the solutions are $x = 2$ and $x = 3$.

2. $y = 2z - 4$.

3. Take logs; the solution is $m = 4$.

4. $n = \dfrac{\log y - \log 1000}{\log(1 + \frac{i}{100})}$

5. Square both sides. $x = 4 - a$.

6. Take each inequality separately. $2y \leq y + 3$ gives $y \leq 3$ and $y + 3 \leq 11 + 3y$ gives $-4 \leq y$, so the full solution is $-4 \leq y \leq 3$.

WORK CARD 4

1. Solve $\dfrac{2}{s} = \dfrac{3}{s + 2}$.

2. Rearrange $S = 1000e^{nx/100}$ with n as the subject.

3. Rearrange:

$$5c = \frac{10a - 2}{3}$$

with a as the subject.

4. Solve $10z^2 - 5z = -1$.

5. If net income is gross income less national insurance and tax, that is

$$N = G - I - T$$

find an expression for G in terms of N when tax is 30% of gross salary above £3500 and national insurance is 10% of gross salary.

   If I receive a net salary of £10,650 under these conditions, what is my gross salary?

6. For values of P such that $0 < P < 4$ the demand function for a good can be modelled by $Q = P^2 - 8P + 26$. The supply function is $Q = 5 + 2P$ for these values of P. Calculate the equilibrium values of P and Q.

7. Discount jeans can be purchased from a wholesaler in lots of 50 or less for $18 a pair. The price of every pair in the lot decreases by 1.5 cents for each pair purchased above 50, up to 400 pairs. Mac buys a lot for $4464. How many pairs of jeans has he bought?

8. At the beginning of the academic year a student has £400 left from summer vacation work. Driving lessons cost £20 each and CDs cost £10. Write down an inequality for the number of driving lessons, d, and the number of CDs, c, that she can purchase. Rearrange this with c as the subject.

   She finds out that to learn to drive she will need 15 lessons. At most how many CDs can she buy now?

9. When interest is paid by monthly instalments, at a nominal rate of i%, the actual rate of interest (the annual percentage rate) is

$$r = \left(1 + \frac{i}{12}\right)^{12} - 1.$$

Express the nominal rate as a function of r.

10. The population of a city (in thousands) at the end of the tth year after 1970 is modelled as $200e^{0.05t}$. Using this model, during which year will the population of the city first exceed 1 million?

Solutions:

1. $s = 4$

2. $n = \dfrac{100}{x} \log_e\left(\dfrac{S}{1000}\right)$

3. $a = \dfrac{15c + 2}{10}$

4. No solution.

5. $G = \dfrac{N - 1050}{0.6}$, £16,000

6. Solving the quadratic gives $P = 3$ and 7, but we have been told that $0 < P < 4$ so only $P = 3$ is valid here. The corresponding Q is 11.

7. Price is $18 - 0.015(x - 50)$ where x is the number in the lot. So $x(18 - 0.015(x - 50)) = 4464$. Solving this quadratic gives 320 or 930. As he must have bought less than 400 pairs, he must have bought 320.

8. $20d + 10c \le 400$ which rearranges to $c \le 40 - 2d$. When $d = 15$, $c \le 10$.

9. $I = 12((1+r)^{1/12} - 1)$.

10. Solving $200e^{0.05t} = 1000$ gives

$$t = \frac{\log_e 5}{0.05} = 32.1887$$

so the population will exceed 1 million during 2003.

1. Solve $\dfrac{3}{5+r} = \dfrac{2}{r-1}$.

2. Solve $4^{2x} = 8^{x+1/6}$.

3. Rearrange

$$5y + 3 = \frac{8 + z}{z}$$

with z as the subject.

4. Solve $4^{-x} = 2^{x-9}$.

5. Solve $2x^2 + 9x - 5 = 0$.

6. The side of a square with the equivalent area to a circle of radius r is $s = \sqrt{\pi r^2}$. Write down a formula for the radius of the circle in terms of the side of the square.
    A carpet company makes circular rugs in two sizes, radius 1 metre and radius 2 metres. It wishes to start making square rugs in two sizes which have the same areas as the circular rugs. Calculate the dimensions the square rugs must have.

7. Revenue from a product is $R = xP$ where P is the unit price and x is the number sold. Price is related to the number sold by the demand function

$$P = 10 - \frac{x}{100}.$$

The total production cost is $C = 300 + 6x$.

Write down an expression for revenue in terms of x.

At what value of x is revenue equal to cost?

8. A nursery takes children under 5 at a cost of £15 per half-day, whereas a childminder will look after over-fives after school for £3 an hour.

   Sally has two sons and can earn £5 an hour for two to five hours during an afternoon. Andrew is 7 and will be at school for 2 hours of this time, but Christopher is 4 and will need care for the whole afternoon.

   Write down an inequality for the number of hours, x, Sally can work if her childcare costs are not to exceed her earnings.

   Rearrange the inequality with x as the subject. Should she accept a job for 4 hours?

9. The value of good quality wine is modelled as $V(1.01)^t$ where V is its value when it is placed into storage and t is the the number of years it is stored. It costs an estimated £1 to put aside and then retrieve a bottle of wine.

   Write down an inequality that holds when the appreciation in value exceeds the cost of put-aside. Rearrange this inequality so that t is the subject. For how many years (at least) should a bottle of wine, initially worth £10, be put aside?

10. Wheeler buys a batch of microwaves from a warehouse for a total of £11,250. The price is £50 each if 200 or fewer are purchased, but the unit price of every microwave in the batch decreases by 10p for each microwave purchased above 200, up to 400. How many microwaves did Wheeler buy?

Further reading: see p. xv
Jacques is useful.

MM2
Modelling using curves

The theory of space and time is a cultural artefact made possible by the invention of graph paper.

Jaques Vallee, *Co. Evolution Quarterly*, Winter 1977/8

Contexts

What is this chapter about?
This chapter explains how to sketch the graphs of a variety of curves and gives examples of how these curves arise in business, management and finance.

Why is it useful?
In business, finance and economics it is often unduly simplistic to model the relationships between variables using straight lines as we did in EM4, and more complicated models, which have a 'curved' graph, must be used.

Where does it fit in?
This chapter expands the work on linear models in EM4 by allowing more complicated relationships between the variables.

What do I need to know?
You will need to be familiar with all the material in Essential Maths and also Chapter MM1.

Objectives

After your work on this chapter you should:

- understand the idea of a function;
- be able to sketch a quadratic function;
- be able to use a break-even analysis to calculate the level of production that will maximise profit;
- be familiar with the shapes of x^n, a^n, $1/x$, $\log x$ and their variants;
- be able to attempt a sketch of any function.

In *Essential Maths*, Chapter EM4, we modelled the relationships between variables using linear equations. However, in finance, economics and business this is often unrealistic and more complicated models, which have a curved graph, are required.

In this chapter we introduce some useful non-linear functions and see how to draw their graphs.

1 Functions

Test box 1

What is a function?

If $f(x) = 2 \log_{10} x + 3$, what is $f(10)$? What is meant by $f(r)$?

Solutions:
Read the first sentence of this section to find out what a function is. $f(10) = 5$, and $f(r) = 2 \log_{10} r + 3$.

A rule that performs mathematical operations on one or more variables to produce a unique value is called a *function*.

For instance, $2x + 3$ is a function of x, $5y^2 - 3x$ is a function of x and y, and PQR is a function of P, Q and R.

Further, if $y = 2x + 3$, we say that y is a function of x, or if

$$S = A\left(1 + \frac{i}{100}\right)^n$$

we say that S is a function of A, i and n, and so on.

Check this

Which variable is a function of which variable(s) in the following?

$C = 100 + 0.01Q$

$T = x^2 - yz + z^2$

$r = +\sqrt{x^2 + y^2}$

Solutions:
C is a function of Q. T is a function of x, y and z. r is a function of x and y.

It is often convenient to give a function a name, for instance f or g, and then indicate the variable or expression to which it should be applied in brackets afterwards. For instance, if we define the function, f, as

$$f(x) = x^2 + 1,$$

$f(2)$ means $2^2 + 1$, $f(y)$ means $y^2 + 1$ and $f(z - 1)$ means $(z - 1)^2 + 1$ and so on. Or, if

$$g(y) = \frac{y}{y - 2}, \quad g(x) = \frac{x}{x - 2} \quad \text{and} \quad g(3) = \frac{3}{3 - 2} = 3$$

Check these

If $f(x) = x^2 + 1$ and $g(x) = x^2 - 1$, what is $h(x) = f(x) + g(x)$? What is $h(3)$?

Solution:
$h(x) = x^2 + 1 + x^2 - 1 = 2x^2$. As $h(x) = 2x^2$, $h(3) = 2 \times 9 = 18$

If

$$f(x) = \frac{x - 1}{x + 1}$$

what are $f(2)$, $f(0)$ and $f(z)$? What is $f(-1)$?

Solution:

$$f(2) = \frac{2 - 1}{2 + 1} = \frac{1}{3}, \quad f(0) = \frac{-1}{1} = -1, \quad f(z) = \frac{z - 1}{z + 1}, \quad f(-1) = \frac{-1 - 1}{-1 + 1} = \frac{-2}{0}$$

which cannot be evaluated. We say that the function

$$f(x) = \frac{x - 1}{x + 1}$$

is *not defined* at $x = -1$.

In the remainder of *More Maths* we will only concern ourselves with functions of one variable.

Graphs of functions of one variable

Functions of one variable can be represented on a graph. It is usual to plot the value of the function, say $f(x)$, on the vertical axis and the variable, x, on the horizontal axis. As we saw in Chapter EM4, functions of the form $f(x) = ax + b$, where a and b are constants, give a straight line and so they are called *linear functions*. We will now consider functions which are represented by a curved graph.

WORK CARD 1

1. If $f(x) = 2x\,(x - 1)$, what is meant by $f(z)$? What is meant by $f(2)$?

2. If $f(x) = +\sqrt{x^2 - 9}$ write down and evaluate the following if possible:
    a. $f(a)$ **b.** $f(5)$ **c.** $f(3)$ **d.** $f(2)$

3. Evaluate the function

    $$f(x) = \frac{x}{1 + x}$$

    where possible for $x = -3, -2, -1, 0, 1, 2$ and 3.

4. For what values of x is the function

    $$f(x) = \frac{1}{(x + 1)(x - 1)}$$

    not defined?

Solutions:

1. $f(z) = 2z\,(z - 1)$, $f(2) = 2 \cdot 2(2 - 1) = 4$

2. **a.** $+\sqrt{a^2 - 9}$ **b.** 4   **c.** 0   **d.** not defined because the square root of a negative number does not exist.

3. $\frac{3}{2}$, 2, not defined, 0, $\frac{1}{2}, \frac{2}{3}, \frac{3}{4}$

4. $+1$ and -1 as these are the values that give a 0 denominator.

ASSESSMENT 1

1. If $f(x) = 3x^2 + 2$ what is meant by $f(y)$? What is meant by $f(2)$?

2. Evaluate the following functions (where possible) at $x = 1$, $x = 0$ and $x = -1$:
    a. $x^2 + 3$ **b.** 10^{1+x} **c.** $\dfrac{1}{x^2 + 1}$ **d.** $\log_{10} x$ **e.** $+\sqrt{x + 1}$

3. List the values at which the function

    $$f(x) = \frac{1}{x^2 + 9}$$

    is not defined.

2 Quadratic curves

Test box 2

Which of the following are quadratic functions?

$y = 2x - 3$ $f(x) = 2x^2 - 3x + 2$ $y = xy + 2$ $y = 4x^2 - 3x + 2$

Sketch a graph of $y = 4x^2 + 2x - 2$.

Solutions:
The second and fourth equations are quadratic. The curve is a U-shape. It crosses the y axis at –2 and the x axis at $\frac{1}{2}$ and –1. The minimum is at $x = -\frac{1}{4}$.

A *quadratic function* has the form $y = ax^2 + bx + c$ (compare quadratic equations in Chapter MM1, Section 3) where a, b and c are constants. For example, $y = 2x^2 - 3x + 2$ is a quadratic function. Quadratic functions often present the most straightforward way of modelling a relationship that has a curved graph.

How do quadratic functions arise?

Quadratic functions often arise as a result of the assumptions of a model. For instance, in the final part of this section we will show why, in economics, revenue and profit are often modelled as quadratic functions and sketch their curves.

A quadratic function can be used to model a relationship when a linear function seems too much of an approximation.

For example, the graph in Figure 2.1 shows the turnover of a company and the amount it spends on advertising (both in £1000s), for 11 typical months.

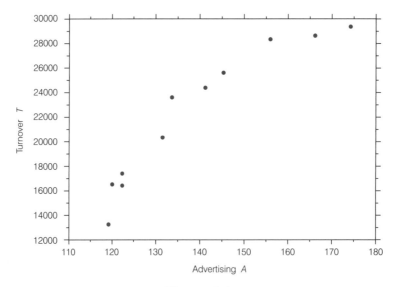

Figure 2.1

The company wishes to investigate the relationship between monthly advertising expenditure, A, and monthly turnover, T. The simplest model would be to express T as a linear function of A, that is

$$T = cA + d$$

where c and d are constants. However, if this model were appropriate the points on the graph would lie roughly on a straight line, whereas they seem to lie on a curve. This suggests that a quadratic model,

$$T = cA^2 + dA + e$$

where c, d, and e are constants, would probably be more suitable. In practice, the values of c, d and e would be estimated from the data and the suitability of the model assessed using the statistical methods described in *Correlation and Regression*, Chapter S3.

The simplest quadratic curves

The simplest quadratic curve is $y = x^2$. A table of values for $y = x^2$ is given below.

x	-5	-3	-1	0	1	3	5
$y = x^2$	25	9	1	0	1	9	25

Drawing these points on a graph as shown in Figure 2.2 gives some idea of the shape of the curve.

We can see that the points form a U-shape, with the base at (0,0). A completed graph of $y = x^2$ is shown in Figure 2.3.

Notice that positive and negative values of x give the same value of x^2 so the left-hand side of the U is a mirror-image of the right-hand side. We say that the curve is *symmetric* about the y axis. Also, as x^2 is never negative, the curve never goes below the x axis.

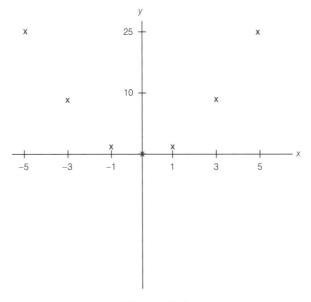

Figure 2.2

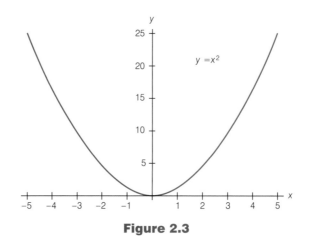

Figure 2.3

Another simple quadratic function is $y = -x^2$. As $-x^2$ has the opposite sign to x^2 the graph of $y = -x^2$ is a reflection of $y = x^2$ in the x axis. The curve therefore has an inverted U-shape with the maximum at (0,0) as shown in Figure 2.4.

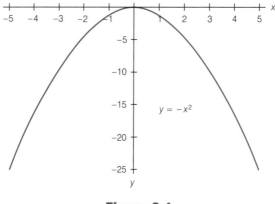

Figure 2.4

When a constant is added to a function its curve moves up or down. For instance, the graph of $y = x^2 + 1$, has exactly the same shape as the graph of $y = x^2$ but each y-value is one unit higher, so the curve is one unit higher as shown in Figure 2.5.

In the same way, the graph $y = x^2 - 5$ is just the graph $y = x^2$ moved down 5 units.

The curve $y = ax^2 + bx + c$

All quadratic functions have a U-shape or inverted U-shape. For instance, the graph of $y = x^2 - x - 6$ is shown in Figure 2.6.

To sketch a graph such as this we could calculate a table of values for x and y and then plot these points, but this would be tedious and the part of the graph where the U turns might not be included. It is more useful to sketch a quadratic function by answering the following questions.

We illustrate using the function $y = x^2 - 3x + 2$.

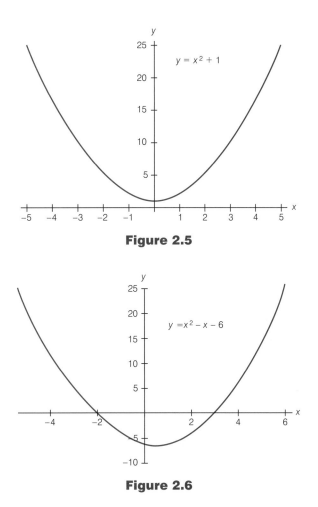

Figure 2.5

Figure 2.6

1. What is the coefficient of x^2?

   If it is positive the function has a U-shape. Otherwise it has an inverted U-shape.

   For example, $y = x^2 - 3x + 2$ has a U-shape because the x^2 is multiplied by 1, which is positive.

2. Where does the curve cross the y axis?

   When the curve crosses the y axis, $x = 0$ and so we can calculate the intercept with the y axis by substituting $x = 0$ into the equation.

   For example, the curve $y = x^2 - 3x + 2$ crosses the y axis at $y = 2$.

3. Where does the curve cross the x axis?

   This is more difficult to calculate. When the curve crosses the x axis, $y = 0$, so solving $ax^2 + bx + c = 0$ gives the x values of the crossing points. For instance, $y = x^2 - 3x + 2$ crosses the x axis at the solutions of $x^2 - 3x + 2 = 0$.

   Equations of the form $ax^2 + bx + c = 0$ are quadratic equations and we saw how to solve these in Chapter MM1 (Section 3). Remember, we may be able to spot factors, or we may have to use the formula

$$x = \frac{-b \pm \sqrt{b^2 - 4ac}}{2a}$$

When there are two solutions for x there are two points where the curve crosses the x axis. When there are no solutions there are no crossing points and so the whole curve lies above the x axis or the whole curve lies below it. (One solution means that the U or inverted U turns at a point on the x axis.)

For our example, the equation $x^2 - 3x + 2 = 0$ factorises to $(x - 2)(x - 1) = 0$, so the curve crosses the x axis at $x = 1$ and $x = 2$, i.e. at the points $(1,0)$ and $(2,0)$.

Once calculated, all these axis crossing points can be placed on a graph. As we know that the curve is a U- or inverted U-shape and that it does not cross the axes at any other points, we can attempt to join these up as shown in Figure 2.7, although we still do not know where the curve turns.

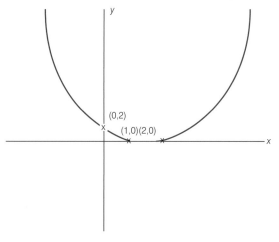

Figure 2.7

4. Where does the U or inverted U turn?

For now we ask you to believe the following (we will see why it is true in Chapter MM3).

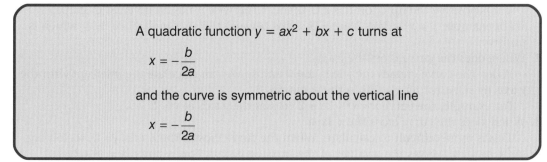

A quadratic function $y = ax^2 + bx + c$ turns at

$$x = -\frac{b}{2a}$$

and the curve is symmetric about the vertical line

$$x = -\frac{b}{2a}$$

So for $y = x^2 - 3x + 2$ the base of the U lies at

$$x = -\frac{-3}{2} = \frac{3}{2}$$

and the curve is symmetric about $x = \frac{3}{2}$. When $x = \frac{3}{2}$,

$$y = \frac{9}{4} - \frac{9}{2} + 2 = -\frac{1}{4}$$

so the turning point is

$$\left(\frac{3}{2}, -\frac{1}{4}\right)$$

5. Are any other points needed?

It is usually useful to calculate one or two further points as well. For instance, for $y = x^2 - 3x + 2$ we might calculate that when $x = 4$, $y = 6$ and when $x = -2$, $y = 12$.

Now we can use all the information gleaned from questions **1–5** to produce a sketch. A graph of $y = x^2 - 3x + 2$ is shown in Figure 2.8.

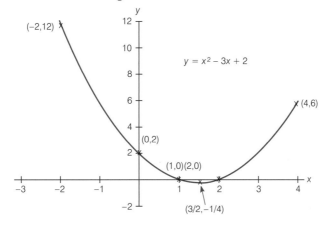

Figure 2.8

Check these

Sketch the following quadratic functions:

$$y = -x^2 + 2x + 3$$

Solution:
The graph must be an inverted U as the coefficient of x^2 is negative. When $x = 0$, $y = 3$ so the curve crosses the y axis at (0,3). It crosses the x axis at the solutions (if any) of $x^2 + 2x + 3 = 0$. Solving this (it factorises to $-(x - 3)(x + 1)$) gives $x = 3$ and $x = -1$. The turning point is at

$$x = -\frac{b}{2a} = \frac{-2}{-2} = 1, \ y = 4$$

and the curve is symmetric about $x = 1$. The resulting graph is shown in Figure 2.9.

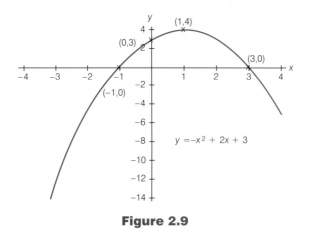

Figure 2.9

Sketch $y = 4x^2 + 2x - 2$

Solution:
The curve is a U-shape. It crosses the y axis at -2 and the x axis at $x = \frac{1}{2}$ and $x = -1$. The curve turns at $x = -\frac{1}{4}$ so it is symmetric about $x = -\frac{1}{4}$.

Sketch $y = x^2 + x + 1$

Solution:
The curve has a U-shape. When $x = 0$, $y = 1$ so it crosses the y axis at $(0,1)$. Using

$$x = \frac{-b \pm \sqrt{b^2 - 4ac}}{2a}$$

we see that there are no solutions to $x^2 + x + 1 = 0$, so the curve never crosses the x axis. The turning point is at $x = -\frac{1}{2}$, $y = \frac{3}{4}$. As we haven't found any x intercepts it is a good idea to find a few more points to gain an idea of the shape of the curve. We found $(-3,7)$ and $(3,13)$. The curve is shown in Figure 2.10.

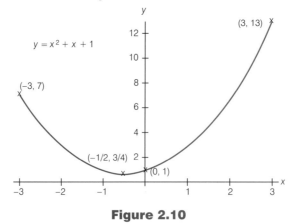

Figure 2.10

We summarise points **1–5** below.

Sketching quadratic functions y = ax² + bx + c

1. If *a* is positive the curve is a U-shape
   If *a* is negative the curve is an inverted U-shape
2. The curve crosses the *y* axis when *x* = 0, i.e. at *y* = *c*
3. It crosses the *x* axis when *y* = 0, at the solutions of $ax^2 + bx + c = 0$.
   If there are no solutions then the curve lies completely above or below the *x* axis
4. The curve turns at

$$x = -\frac{b}{2a}$$

   and is symmetric about the vertical line

$$x = -\frac{b}{2a}$$

5. Find and plot some further points if necessary

Application to break-even analysis

Quadratic functions arise in many situations. For example, in economics total revenue is often modelled as a quadratic function of the number of units sold due to the following reasoning.

Assume a linear demand function; for instance

$$P = 10 - 0.001Q$$

where *P* is price and *Q* is the quantity demanded.

The revenue received from the sale of *Q* units at unit price *P* is $R = QP$. So $R = Q(10 - 0.001Q)$ or $R = 10Q - 0.001Q^2$.

Notice that this is a quadratic function and that the curve will have an inverted U-shape. Also, when *Q* = 0, revenue is 0 as might be expected. The curve is shown in Figure 2.11.

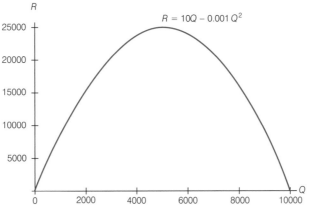

Figure 2.11

In general, any linear demand function will produce a quadratic revenue function.

A manufacturer is usually interested in the level of production that will maximise profit. We have already said that the total cost of production can be modelled as

$$C = \text{fixed cost} + Q(\text{variable unit cost})$$

where Q is the quantity produced.

Suppose

$$C = 4000 + 5Q.$$

When the number of items sold is the same as the quantity produced (that is, all items are sold) we can draw both the revenue, R, and total cost, C, functions on the same graph, as shown in Figure 2.12.

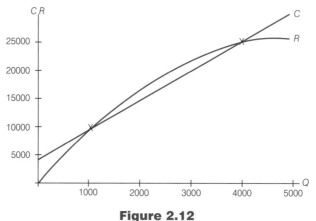

Figure 2.12

The manufacturer's profit is revenue less total cost, that is, $R - C$, which is represented on the graph by the vertical distance between the R curve and the C line. Profit is zero at the two points where the revenue curve and the cost line intersect, so the value of Q at these two points gives the level of production at which the firm breaks even. In between these values of Q revenue is greater than cost and the firm makes a profit.

The maximum profit is obtained at the value of Q where the vertical distance between the lines is the largest. We can calculate this value of Q by writing down an equation for profit as follows.

As profit $= R - C$, we can write

$$\text{profit} = 10Q - 0.001Q^2 - (4000 + 5Q)$$

which simplifies to

$$\text{profit} = -0.001Q^2 + 5Q - 4000.$$

As this is a quadratic function we know how to sketch it. It crosses the profit axis at profit $= -4000$, and the Q axis at $Q = 1000$ and $Q = 4000$. Further, it is an inverted U-shape and turns at

$$Q = \frac{-5}{2(-0.001)} = 2500$$

The curve is shown in Figure 2.13.

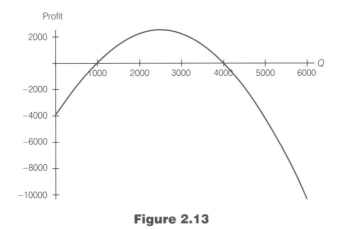

Figure 2.13

The maximum profit occurs at the turning point $Q = 2500$ and is therefore

$$\text{profit} = -0.001(2500^2) + 5(2500) - 4000 = 2250$$

1. Which of the following are (i) linear functions, (ii) quadratic functions, (iii) neither?
    a. $y = 2x - 1$　b. $y = 3x^2 + 2x - 1$　c. $y = x^{1/2} - x^2 + 2$
    d. $y = 2e^x - x^2 + 3$　e. $y = x - x^2 e^b$ where b is a constant
    f. $y = \dfrac{x^2}{x + 1}$　g. $y = e^a x + b$ where a and b are constants
    h. $g = 2h^2 - 2h + 2$

2. Sketch the following quadratic functions:
    a. $y = x^2 + 2x - 3$　b. $f = p^2 - 2$　c. $y = -x^2 - 1$
    d. $y = 2(x - 7)(x + 1)$　e. $y = 2x^2 + 5x - 3$
    f. $y = x^2 + 7 - 6x$　g. $P = 3Q - 2Q^2 + 1$

3. A firm incurs a fixed production cost of 1280 and a variable cost of 80 per unit of output. Its demand function is

    $$P = 100 - \frac{Q}{20}$$

    where P is the unit price and Q is the number of units of demand.
    (i)　Write down an equation for the total cost of production.
    (ii)　Revenue is $R = PQ$. Express revenue as a function of Q.
    (iii)　Express profit = revenue – total cost as a function of Q.
    (iv)　Sketch the graph of profit as a function of Q.
    (v)　How many units should be produced in order to maximise profit?

Solutions:

1. **a.** Linear **b.** quadratic **c.** neither as it contains $x^{1/2}$ **d.** neither **e.** quadratic as e^b is a constant **f.** neither **g.** linear as e^a is a constant **h.** quadratic.

2. **a.** Crosses y axis at $y = -3$, and x axis at $x = -3$ and $x = 1$, the minimum is at $(-1,-4)$ **b.** Crosses vertical f axis at $f = -2$, and p axis at $\sqrt{2}$ and $-\sqrt{2}$, the minimum is at $(0,-2)$ **c.** Crosses y axis at -1, but does not cross the x axis as equation $-x^2 - 1 = 0$ has no solutions; the maximum is at $(0,-1)$ **d.** The minimum is $(3,-32)$ and it crosses the y axis at -14, and the x axis at 7 and -1 (this is easy as the quadratic was given in factorised form) **e.** minimum at $(\frac{5}{4}, -\frac{49}{8})$, crosses y axis at -3 and x axis at -3 and $\frac{1}{2}$ **f.** Crosses the y axis at 7, $x^2 + 7 - 6x = 0$ has solutions $x = 3 \pm \sqrt{2}$ and the minimum is at $x = 3$ **g.** Crosses the vertical P axis at 1, $3Q - 2Q^2 + 1 = 0$ has solutions at

$$Q = \frac{3}{4} \pm \frac{\sqrt{17}}{4}$$

minimum is at

$$\frac{-b}{2a} = \frac{3}{4}$$

3. **(i)** $C = 1280 + 80Q$ **(ii)** $R = \left(100 - \dfrac{Q}{20}\right)Q$, so $R = 100Q - \dfrac{Q^2}{20}$

(iii) profit $= 100Q - \dfrac{Q^2}{20} - (1280 + 80Q) = \dfrac{-Q^2}{20} + 20Q - 1280$

(iv) The graph is an inverted-U and intersects the profit axis at -1280. Solving the quadratic

$$\frac{-Q^2}{20} + 20Q - 1280 = 0$$

gives $Q = 320$ and $Q = 80$ so the curve crosses the Q axis at 80 and 320. That is, the break-even point is at 80 or 320. The curve turns, so the profit is a maximum at $Q = 200$.

(v) Produce 200 units.

1. Are the following **(i)** linear functions **(ii)** quadratic functions or **(iii)** neither?

a. $y = x^2$ **b.** $y = 2\sqrt{x} + x^2$ **c.** $y = x^2 + \log a$ where a is a constant

d. $y = 2^{x+2} - 2x$ **e.** $y = +\sqrt{x} - x^2$

f. $p = e^z + z^2 + 1$ **g.** $y = \dfrac{1}{x+2}$ **h.** $y = \dfrac{1}{x^2 + 2 + 2x}$

ASSESSMENT 2 (CONTINUED)

2. Sketch the following:

a. $y = x^2 - 4x - 5$ b. $Q = 3P^2 + 1$ c. $y = 2x + x^2 - 1$
d. $y = 3(x - 1)(x - 3)$ e. $y = -(x - 1)(x - 3)$
f. $y = (x + 2)^2 - 1$ g. $y = 4x^2 + 3x + 1$

3. The demand for a product, Q, and its unit price, P, are related by

$$P = 30 - \frac{Q}{200}$$

Production costs the firm 1800 in fixed costs and 20 per unit in variable costs.

Assuming that all the units produced are sold, sketch a graph of profit against Q and calculate the level of production required to maximise profit.

3 Some common functions

Test box 3

Sketch the graphs of:

$$y = x^3, \quad f(x) = \log_{10}x, \quad P = \frac{1}{Q} \quad \text{and } y = e^x.$$

Now sketch the graphs of

$$y = 4x^3 \quad \text{and} \quad P = \frac{1}{Q} + 5$$

Solutions: See text.

In this section we consider some more functions that are useful in business, management and finance. We describe some applications in which they arise in Section 4.

$y = x^n$
We looked at the graph of $y = x^2$ at the start of Section 2. Now we look at functions like $y = x^3$, $y = x^4$, $y = x^5$ and so on.

We show a table of values for x^2, x^3, x^4, x^5 and x^6 below. Check that you agree with the table.

x	−3	−2	−1	0	1	2	3
$y = x^2$	9	4	1	0	1	4	9
$y = x^3$	−27	−8	−1	0	1	8	27
$y = x^4$	81	16	1	0	1	16	81
$y = x^5$	−243	−32	−1	0	1	32	243
$y = x^6$	729	64	1	0	1	64	729

First of all, let's look at the even powers of x (shaded). We already know that the graph of x^2 is a U-shape based at (0,0) and symmetric about the y axis.

All even powers of x, like $y = x^4$ or $y = x^6$, resemble $y = x^2$, in that they are U-shaped, symmetric about the y axis and have a base at (0,0). The table above confirms that the higher the power, the higher the y for a given x and so the steeper the rate of ascent of the sides of the U as shown in Figure 2.14.

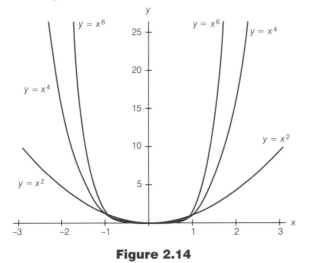

Figure 2.14

Odd powers of x behave in a similar way when x is positive, but when x is negative, y is negative so the left-hand side of the graph is not the left-hand side of the U in Figure 2.14 but is a mirror image of it where the mirror is the x axis. The graph in Figure 2.15 shows $y = x^3$, $y = x^5$ and, for comparison, $y = x^2$.

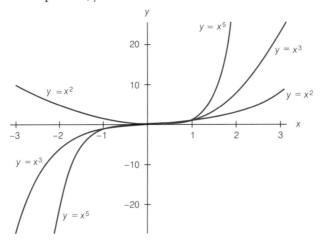

Figure 2.15

Notice that all curves of the form $y = x^n$ go through (0,0) and (1,1), although you should be wary of their behaviour relative to each other, between $x = 0$ and $x = 1$. For example, between 0 and 1, x^4 lies below x^2.

(If you don't believe this evaluate x^4 and x^2 at some values of x between 0 and 1. For instance, when $x = \frac{1}{2}$, $x^4 = \frac{1}{16}$ is smaller than $x^2 = \frac{1}{4}$.)

$y = a^x$

Consider the function $y = 2^x$. It exists for any value of x because we can have fractional or negative powers of 2.

When x is very large, 2^x will also be very large (think of 2^{50}, for instance) and when x is a very large negative number $2x$ will be positive and close to zero (think of $2^{-50} = \frac{1}{2^{50}}$). Further, when $x = 0$, $y = 1$. The graph of $y = 2^x$ is shown in Figure 2.16.

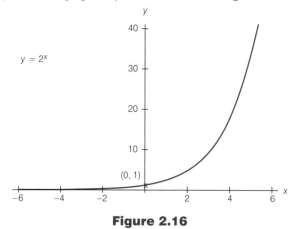

Figure 2.16

The graph of $y = 3^x$ also passes through $(0,1)$ and has similar properties to the graph of $y = 2^x$. However, 3^x is larger than 2^x when x is positive, (3^4 is larger than 2^4, for instance) and smaller when x is negative (for example, 3^{-1} is smaller than 2^{-1}), so the graph of 3^x ascends more rapidly than the graph of 2^x.

We will see later that the function $y = e^x$ is of particular interest. (Recall that e = 2.718282 (to 6 d.p.).) The graph of $y = e^x$ has similar features to those of $y = 2^x$ and $y = 3^x$ but lies in between them.

We show 2^x, 3^x and e^x on the same graph in Figure 2.17.

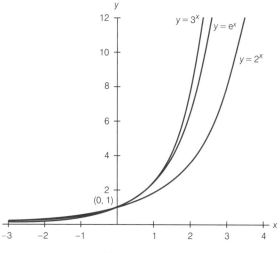

Figure 2.17

More generally, all graphs of the form $y = a^x$ where a is greater than 1 have a similar shape to those above. The higher the value of a, the steeper the curve.

$y = 1/x$

The graph of $y = \frac{1}{x}$ is shown in Figure 2.18.

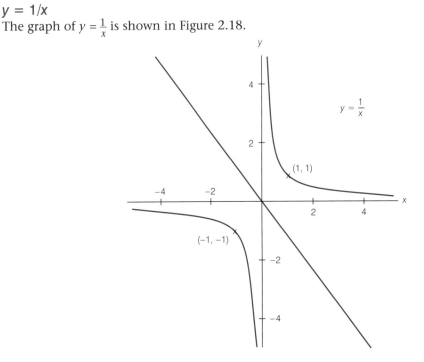

Figure 2.18

The positive section of the graph forms a sort of curved L-shape, and the negative section is a reflection of this in a diagonal line through (0,0) as shown. (This is the line $y = -x$.)

Notice that the graph never touches either axis, but gets closer and closer as x or y approaches 0. This is because larger positive values of x give smaller and smaller positive values of y (think of $\frac{1}{1}, \frac{1}{10}, \frac{1}{100}$ and so on), but never 0, whereas larger negative values of x give smaller and smaller negative values of y ($\frac{1}{-1}, \frac{1}{-10}, \frac{1}{-100}$ and so on), but never 0. Also, as x approaches 0, y gets very large and positive when x is positive (consider $\frac{1}{1}, \frac{1}{0.1}, \frac{1}{0.01}$ and so on), and large and negative when x is negative.

$y = \log x$

The log of a negative value does not exist and so we can only draw this function for positive values of x.

The exact shape of the curve depends on the base of the log but the general idea is always the same.

For any base, $\log 1 = 0$ and so all $\log x$ curves go through (1, 0). As x increases from $x = 1$, y increases (for example, think about $\log_{10} 10$, $\log_{10} 100$, $\log_{10} 1000$ and so on) and as x decreases from 1 to near 0, y becomes more and more negative (consider $\log_{10} 1 = 0$, $\log_{10} \frac{1}{10} = -1$, $\log_{10} \frac{1}{1000} = -3$).

When the base of the log is b, $\log b = 1$, so $y = \log_b x$ will pass through $(b,1)$.

We show the curves of $\log_2 x$, $\log_e x$ and $\log_{10} x$ in Figure 2.19. Notice that the larger the base, the slower the ascent of the curve.

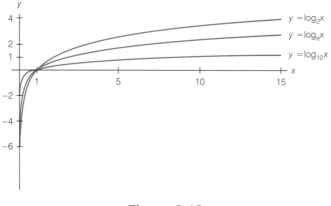

Figure 2.19

Sketch the following pairs of functions on the same graph. Try to puzzle out the shape of the curves rather than remember them.

1. $y = \log_3 x$ and $y = \log_4 x$

2. $y = x^5$ and $y = x^7$

3. $P = \dfrac{1}{Q}$ and $P = Q$

4. $y = e^x$ and $y = 2.5^x$

Solutions:

1. All log curves can be drawn for positive values of x only and pass through $(1,0)$. $\log_3 x$ passes through $(3,1)$ whereas $\log_4 x$ passes through $(4,1)$, so it is less steep. Both curves pass through $(1,0)$.

2. For x greater than 1, x^7 is steeper. When x is between 0 and 1, x^7 is below x^5 (for instance, when $x = \frac{1}{2}$, so $y = x^5 = \frac{1}{32}$, whereas $y = x^7 = \frac{1}{128}$). When x is negative the y values are the negative of those of the corresponding positive x so the left-hand side of the curve is a mirror image (in the x axis) of the left-hand side of the U. The curves meet at $(-1,-1)$, $(0,0)$ and $(1,1)$.

3. $P = \frac{1}{Q}$ is like $y = \frac{1}{x}$ but the axes are now P and Q. $P = Q$ is the straight line through $(0,0)$, $(1,1)$ and so on. The line and curve therefore meet at $(1,1)$ and $(-1,1)$. Each part of the curve is symmetric about the straight line.

4. $e = 2.718281$ and so $e > 2.5$ and the curve $y = e^x$ will lie above $y = 2.5^x$ when x is positive and below $y = 2.5^x$ when x is negative. The two curves both go through and meet at $(0,1)$. Both lie above the x axis as y is always positive.

WORK CARD 3

Sketch the following pairs of curves on the same graph:

1. $y = x^3$ and $y = x^2$

2. $y = \sqrt{x}$ and $y = x^{1/3}$

3. $y = x$ and $y = \log_e x$

4 **Variations on standard curves**

Test box 4

How is the curve $f(x) = 6 \log x$ related to the curve $f(x) = \log x$?

How is the curve $f(x) = 3^{x+2}$ related to the curve $f(x) = 3^x$?

Solution:
$f(x) = 6 \log x$ is 6 times as steep as $f(x) = \log x$, and so equivalent to expanding $f(x) = \log x$ vertically by a factor of 6. The curve is same as 3^x but shifted 2 units to the left.

In practice, the functions you need may not have the exact forms described in Section 3, but will be slight variants. For instance, you may need $y = 2^x + 5$ instead of $y = 2^x$ or $y = 6 \log x$ instead of $y = \log x$.

The variant will usually resemble the original curve but will be squeezed or elongated, vertically or horizontally and/or moved up or down or to the left or right.

We cannot consider every possible variation in this section but will illustrate how to work out the shape of these curves by example.

Check these

Sketch $y = 2^x + 5$.

Solution:
The y-values of this function will be 5 more than for $y = 2^x$, so the resulting curve will be exactly the same, but *5 units higher* (see Figure 2.20).

Sketch

$$y = \frac{1}{x} + 5$$

Solution:
This is a similar example. The curve will be the same as

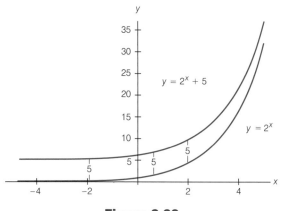

Figure 2.20

$$y = \frac{1}{x}$$

but 5 *units higher* (see Figure 2.21).

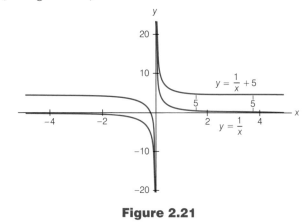

Figure 2.21

Check this

Sketch $y = 6 \log x$.

Solution:
This time each value of y will be 6 times the value of $y = \log x$, so the curve will be steeper as shown in Figure 2.22. Multiplying by 6 equates to *stretching the curve vertically* (assuming that the scales on the axes remain the same).

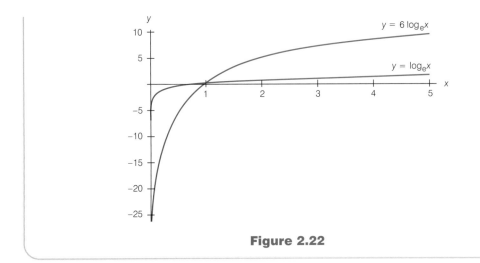

Figure 2.22

Check this

Sketch $y = 3^{x+2}$.

Solution:
The height of this curve at a particular value of x will be the same as the height of the standard curve $y = 3^x$ when x is 2 units more. For instance, $y = 3^{x+2}$ at $x = 1$ has the same height as $y = 3^x$ at $x = 3$. So the curve will be identical to $y = 3^x$ except that it will be 2 units to the left as shown in Figure 2.23.

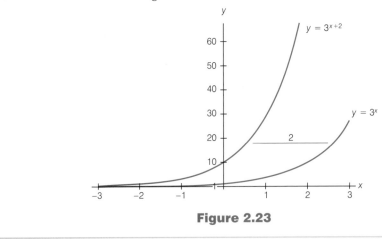

Figure 2.23

Check this

Sketch $y = (3x)^5$.

This is the same as $y = x^5$, but with $3x$ instead of x. So the value of $y = (3x)^5$ at $x = a$ is the same as the value of $y = x^5$ at $x = 3a$. For instance, when $x = 1$, $y = (3x)^5 = 3^5$, which is the same as $y = x^5$ when $x = 3$. This means that $y = (3x)^5$ is the same as the $y = x^5$ curve, but *squeezed horizontally* by a factor of 3. We show the two functions on the same graph in Figure 2.24.

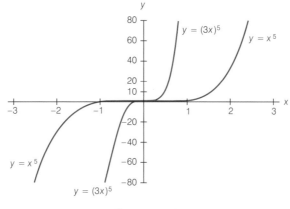

Figure 2.24

---

1. Sketch $y = 3x^2$ and $y = 3x^2 + 2$ on the same graph.

2. Sketch $y = x^4$, $y = x^4 - 1$ and $y = x^4 + 2$ on the same graph.

3. Sketch $y = 3^x$ and $y = -3^x$ on the same graph.

4. Sketch $y = \log_5 x$ and $y = \log_5 x + 2$, on the same graph.

5. Sketch the graphs of $y = x^2$, $y = (2x)^2$ and $y = (x + 1)^2$.

6. On the same graph, sketch $y = \log_{10} x$, $y = \log_{10}(x + 2)$ and $y = \log_{10}(x - 3)$.

7. Sketch the graph of $y = \dfrac{1}{x - 1}$.

Solution guidelines:

1. $y = 3x^2$ is the same U-shape as $y = x^2$ but with steeper sides. $y = 3x^2 + 2$ is the same curve 2 units higher so the base of the U will be at $(0,2)$.

2. $y = x^4$ is a U-shape, with the lowest point at $(0,0)$ like x^2, but much steeper and going through $(1,1)$, $(2,16)$ and so on. $y = x^4 - 1$ and $y = x^4 + 2$ will be the same shape but 1 unit lower and 2 units higher respectively with lowest points of $(0,-1)$ and $(0,2)$ respectively.

3. 3^x is also a U-shape, minimum $(0,0)$ shown in Figure 2.23. -3^x will be the negative of this and so will be a reflection of 3^x in the x axis.

4. $\log_5 x$ can only be calculated for positive values of x. It passes through the point $(1,0)$ and the point $(5,1)$. To the left of $(1,0)$, as x approaches 0, the curve slopes downwards very steeply, but never touches the y axis. $\log_5 x + 2$ is the same curve 2 units higher and so passes through $(1,2)$ and $(5,3)$.

WORK CARD 4

5. $y = x^2$ is well known.

    $y = (2x)^2$ is such that it has the same height as x^2 at half the value of x, so it is like $y = x^2$ but squeezed in to have half the width.

    $y = (x + 1)^2$ has the same value as $y = x^2$ does at a value of x 1 unit smaller, so it will be like $y = x^2$ but 1 unit to the left.

6. $\mathrm{Log}_{10}x$ has very large negative values for positive x close to 0, increases rapidly to pass $(1,0)$ and then continues to increase to $(10,1)$ and beyond. $\mathrm{Log}_{10}(x + 2)$ is the same shape but 2 units to the left, whereas $\log_{10}(x - 3)$ will have the same shape but 3 units to the right.

7. y cannot be evaluated when $x = 1$. The graph is like that of $\frac{1}{x}$ but attains the same y for an x 1 unit larger and so is 1 unit to the right. The right-hand side of the graph is an L-shaped curve passing through $(2,1)$ and the negative an inverted L curve passing through $(0,-1)$.

1. Sketch the functions $y = \log_e x$ and $y = \log_e x + 1$ on the same graph.

2. Sketch the curves $y = x^2$ and $y = x^2 - 2$ on the same graph.

3. Sketch the functions $y = x^3$ and $y = (2x)^3$ on the same graph.

4. Sketch the functions $y = 3x^2$ and $y = 6x^2$ on the same graph.

5. Sketch the function $Q = \dfrac{1}{P + 2}$

6. Sketch the functions $y = e^x$ and $y = e^{-x}$ on the same graph.

7. Sketch the functions $y = 1 + e^x$ and $y = e^{2x}$ on the same graph.

5 When do these curves arise?

Test box 5

Read this section anyway – it won't take long!

Some typical occurrences of the curves we have discussed in this chapter are described below.

Compound interest

The sum accrued from an investment of £1000 placed at an interest rate of $r\%$ for 5 years is

$$S = 1000\left(1 + \frac{r}{100}\right)^5.$$

(We will explain this in Chapter BM4.) A graph showing the relationship between S and r is shown in Figure 2.25; it has a slight curve.

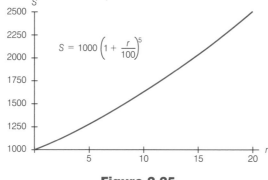

Figure 2.25

Continuous compounding

The sum accrued when £1000 is invested at a continuous rate of interest of 5% for n years is $S = 1000e^{0.05n}$. The graph of S as a function of n is shown in Figure 2.26.

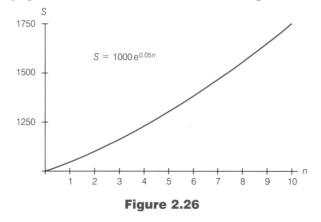

Figure 2.26

Production

We saw in Chapter EM4 that the total cost of production is often modelled as a fixed cost plus a cost per unit produced; that is, as a linear function of the quantity produced. For example, the total cost function might be $C = 100 + 2x$, where x units are produced.

However, the *average* cost per unit, AC, may also be of interest. To calculate this we divide the total cost, C, by the number of units produced, x, which for our example is

$$AC = \frac{100 + 2x}{x}$$

which can also be written

$$AC = \frac{100}{x} + 2$$

So the average cost curve resembles the $\frac{1}{x}$ curve, but the average cost has been multiplied by 100, and 2 has been added. As x is a physical quantity we need only consider non-negative values of x.

When x is small, AC will be very large. As x increases, AC decreases. When x is very large, $\frac{100}{x}$ will become very small and AC will gradually approach 2. The curve is shown in Figure 2.27.

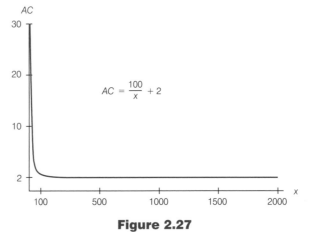

Figure 2.27

Inventory modelling

We briefly considered inventory control models in Chapter EM3, Section 5. In the simplest inventory control model it is assumed that items are ordered in batches of q, it costs K to order and take delivery of a batch and these items are sold (demanded) at a rate of d items per unit time.

As $\frac{d}{q}$ batches are required per unit time, the ordering cost per unit time is

$$T = \frac{d}{q} K$$

Usually d and K are known or assumed. For instance, if demand is 100 items per year and the ordering cost is 50

$$T = \frac{100}{q} \times 50 = \frac{5000}{q}$$

and the graph is as shown in Figure 2.28.

We consider inventory models more fully in Chapter BM3.

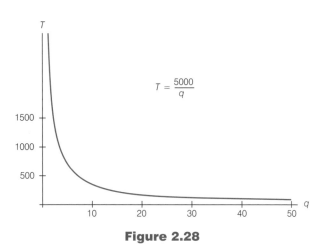

Figure 2.28

Sales

The sales of a company have increased gradually month by month. Sales S during month t are modelled as

$$S = 100 \log_{10} (9 + t)$$

The graph of this function is shown in Figure 2.29. Notice that sales increase at a slower rate as time goes on.

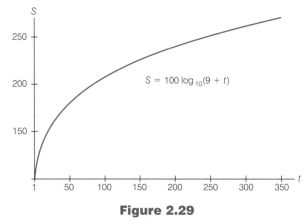

Figure 2.29

1. In a bulk purchase a company buys the first 20 copies of some software for £200 each and all additional copies for 100 each. Write down the average cost of one copy of the software as a function of the number of copies purchased, x, assuming that $x \geq 20$. Sketch the function.

2. On 1 January 2001, when the Introyou introduction agency was founded, they had 100 clients on their books. On 31 December 2002 (24 months later), they

have 153 clients. A sharp employee notices that a logarithmic model fits these two figures and suggests

$C = 100 \log (10 + t)$.

To which base did she intend the logarithm in this model to be? Sketch the growth of the client base for the first 24 months, and the model's predicted growth for the next 12 months.

Solutions:

1. The total cost is $4000 + 100(x - 20) = 100x + 2000$. The average cost is therefore

$$100 + \frac{2000}{x}$$

We are only concerned with positive values of x. The graph is the $\frac{1}{x}$ curve, stretched vertically by a factor of 2000 and then moved upwards by 100, although in this context the average cost is not valid for $x < 20$. Alternatively, it is perhaps easier to look at some values of x and say that when $x = 20$, $y = 200$ and as x increases the average cost reduces to 100, but never actually reaches 100.

2. Base 10 because $100 \log (10 + 0) = 100$ and $100 \log (10 + 24)$ is approximately 153.

1. If $100 is invested at a rate of 10% payable continuously the sum accrued after n years is $100e^{n/10}$. Sketch this function.

2. Ripoff restaurants can buy x frozen cheesecakes, where $x \leq 250$, from Gear Brothers Wholesale Catering at a price of $5 - 0.01x$ each. Sketch the total cost as a function of x.

   Customers choosing Ripoff's 'home-made' cheesecake pay £2 a slice, where there are 4 slices in each cheesecake. Sketch Ripoff's revenue from cheesecake sales on your graph and show their profit. Assume no wastage.

3. A fruit packaging company employs casual workers according to season. The staff canteen is given a budget of $200 a day to prepare a midday meal for all the employees. Sketch a graph of the budget per employee as a function of the number of employees.

6 Curve sketching in general

Test box 6

How would you go about sketching a function totally different to one of the standard forms we have given?

Solution: Read points **1–5** below for some quick revision.

In Section 3 we deduced the shapes of some standard curves from their equations. In the same way, the shape of any curve can usually be deduced by considering the following points. These are quite similar to the points we gave in Section 2 for sketching quadratic functions, except that now we have no prior knowledge of the shape of the curve.

Sketching a function
1. What happens to the curve for very large positive and very large negative values of x?
2. Where does the curve cross the y axis? That is, can the function be evaluated at $x = 0$, and if so, what is y? Otherwise what happens when x is close to 0?
3. Where does the curve cross the x axis? That is, is y ever 0, and if so, for what values of x? If not, for what values of x, if any, is y close to 0?
4. When you have studied Chapter MM3 you will be also be able to find if there are any values of x at which the curve turns.
5. Plot the points found above and calculate any more points necessary to show the shape of the curve.

An example
We illustrate this using the following 'nasty' function arising from learning curves.

Learning curves are often used in accountancy for cost estimation. They are used to model y, the overall average time it takes to produce a unit when x units are produced. A suitable model is

$$y = ax^b$$

where the constant, a, is the time it takes to produce the first unit. The other constant, b, is a measure of learning or progress. It is usually calculated by assuming that when output doubles, average time per unit becomes a proportion, r (called the rate of learning), of the original average time per unit. We will see in Chapter MM3 that b is related to r by

$$b = \frac{\log r}{\log 2}$$

so that when r is between 0 and 1, b will always be negative.

For instance, if the average time taken to produce a unit at a level of output is 80% of the average time when output is half this level, the rate of learning is $r = 0.8$ and $b = -0.3219$. Suppose also that $a = 1000$ so that the model is

$$y = 1000x^{-0.3219}$$

Sketching this curve presents a problem because, until now, we have only considered graphs of $y = x^n$ when n is a whole, positive number.

Following the points above, we reason as follows. As x represents the number of items produced we are only interested in positive values of x.

1. When x is large $x^{-0.3219}$ is roughly

$$\frac{1}{x^{1/3}}$$

and so will be 1 divided by a large number and therefore close to 0. As x becomes larger y gets closer to 0.

2. When $x = 0$, y cannot be evaluated as it requires division by 0. However, as x gets closer to 0, y becomes larger and larger.

3. There is no value of x at which $y = 0$.

4. It will help to calculate a few more points. For example, when $x = 2000$, $y = 86.58$ and when $x = 8000$, $y = 55.41$.

The learning curve is shown in Figure 2.30.

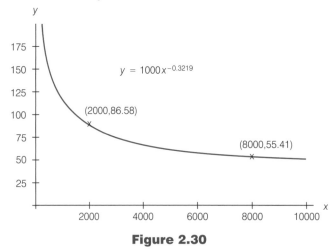

Figure 2.30

WORK CARD 6

1. Sketch the curve $y = 100 - e^{-x}$.

2. In queueing theory (a branch of Management Science) the probability that the time between successive customers arriving at a queue is less than x time units is

$$P = 1 - e^{-Ax}$$

where an average of A customers arrive per unit time.

Flyswift airlines wish to investigate patterns of passenger check-in behaviour at their desk at Tibenham International Airport. They observe that on average 1.2 passengers arrive every minute.

WORK CARD 6 (CONTINUED)

Sketch the probability that less than x minutes pass between successive arrivals, assuming that model above is appropriate.

Solutions:

1. When x is very large and positive e^{-x} will be close to 0 and so as x increases the function will get closer and closer to 100 from beneath. When x is a large negative value, e^{-x} will be very large and so $100 - e^{-x}$ will be large and negative. When $x = 0$, $y = 99$. When $y = 0$, $x = -\log_e 100$ which is approximately -4.6. The result is a curve ascending from left to right, starting with y large and negative, passing through $(-4.6, 0)$, $(0, 99)$ and getting closer and closer to $y = 100$ but never reaching it.

2. The probability that less than x minutes pass before the next customer arrives is $P = 1 - e^{-1.2x}$. As it is a time, x cannot take negative values. As x gets larger this approaches, but never reaches, exactly 1. When $x = 0$, $y = 0$ and no other value of x gives $y = 0$. The function therefore ascends from left to right. Some sample points are $(1, 0.6988)$ and $(5, 0.9975)$.

ASSESSMENT 6

1. The formula for the book value of an asset at the end of the nth year, when the fixed rate of annual depreciation charges is r, is

    $C(1 - r)^n$

    where C is the original cost of an asset. Draw a rough sketch of this function on the same graph **(i)** when $r = 0.1$ and **(ii)** when $r = 0.2$. Choose a sensible range of values for n.

2. Sketch the rough shape of the function $y = x^3 - 6x^2 + 11x - 6$ showing clearly where it crosses both axes. **Hint:** This factorises to $(x - 1)(x - 2)(x - 3)$ and when x is very large and positive or very large and negative the x^3 term 'dominates' in that it contributes most of the value of y.

MM3
Rates of change

Change is the lot of all.

Mary Tighe, Irish poet, 1772–1810

Contexts

What is this chapter about?
This chapter explains how the slope or gradient of a curve can be used to find out how one quantity changes when another related one does, and how this can help us sketch curves and find their highest and lowest points.

Why is it useful?
This chapter is useful because it is concerned with how one quantity changes when another one does. For instance, in a model of sales revenue and expenditure on advertising, we could establish how much extra sales revenue might result from a unit increase in advertising expenditure. However, the techniques in this chapter also enable us to find the values of one quantity which would result in the maximum or minimum of another related quantity – for instance, in Economics, the level of output that would produce the maximum profit.

   Also, more advanced courses in Quantitative Methods, Financial Mathematics or Mathematical Economics will require the material in this chapter.

Where does it fit in?
This chapter gently introduces the area of maths known as Calculus, which is concerned with rates of change. It introduces the technique known as differentiation, but we refer you to more advanced texts (see the references at the end of this chapter) if you need to do more, in particular if you need the technique called integration, which can be regarded as the 'reverse' of differentiation.

What do I need to know?
You will need to be familiar with all the preceding chapters of this book; that is, all Essential Maths, MM1 and MM2.

Objectives

After your work on this chapter you should:

- understand the idea of the gradient of a curve;
- be able to calculate the gradient of a curve at any point using a graph;
- understand what a derivative is and be familiar with the dy/dx notation.
- be able to calculate the derivative of x^n, $\log_e mx$, e^{mx};
- be able to differentiate sums, differences and multiples;
- be familiar with some applications of derivatives like 'marginal' functions, and elasticity;
- be able to use derivatives to find turning or stationary points and use second derivatives to classify these as local maxima or minima;
- be able to use the turning points to sketch curves.

In this chapter we will introduce the idea of the gradient of a curve to measure rates of change, describe the technique to find it, called *differentiation,* and show how it can be used to find the maximum or minimum of a function like profit, revenue or cost.

1 The gradient of a curve

Test box 1

How would you differentiate $y = x^4$?
What is the derivative of $f(x) = x^{-3}$?
What is the gradient of $f(x) = x^2$, when $x = 3$?

Solutions:

$$\frac{dy}{dx} = 4x^3, \quad f'(x) = -3x^{-4}, \quad f'(x) = 2x, \text{ so } f'(3) = 6$$

What is the gradient of a curve?

In Chapter EM4, Section 2, we said that the slope or gradient of a straight line is the increase or change in y divided by the corresponding increase or change in x between any two points on the line; that is

$$\text{gradient} = \frac{\Delta y}{\Delta x} = \frac{y_2 - y_1}{x_2 - x_1}$$

as shown in Figure 3.1.

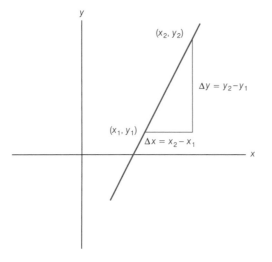

Figure 3.1

The gradient of a curve is less obvious to define. However, again, we would like it to represent the ratio of the change in y to the corresponding change in x.

Consider the curve on the graph in Figure 3.2 and two points, $P = (x_1, y_1)$ and $Q = (x_2, y_2)$ on the curve.

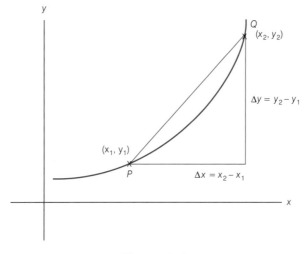

Figure 3.2

From P to Q, x increases by $x_2 - x_1$ and y increases by $y_2 - y_1$. The change in y divided by the corresponding change in x, is therefore

$$\frac{y_2 - y_1}{x_2 - x_1} = \frac{\Delta y}{\Delta x}.$$

Notice that this is the gradient of the straight line joining P and Q.

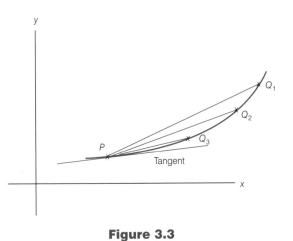

Figure 3.3

In the same way, the ratio of the change in y to the change in x between P and Q_1, on the graph in Figure 3.3, is the gradient of the straight line joining P and Q_1, the ratio of the change in y to the change in x between P and Q_2, is the gradient of the straight line between P and Q_2, and so on.

Figure 3.3 also shows a straight line, called the *tangent* to the curve at P, which just touches the curve at P but does not cross it. Notice that, as Q moves closer to P, the gradient of the straight line between P and Q becomes more and more like the gradient of the tangent. In fact, it can be shown mathematically that the ratio of the change in y to the change in x, between P and a point infinitesimally near to P, is the gradient of the tangent at P. This leads us to define the gradient of a curve at a point as follows.

> The gradient of a curve at a point is the gradient of the tangent to the curve at that point.

So the gradient of a curve at P is the gradient of the tangent at P, and is the change in y divided by the change in x, between P and a point infinitesimally near.

The gradient is different at different points on a curve. On the graph in Figure 3.4 the tangents at A, B and C have different gradients and so the curve has a different gradient at A, B and C, reflecting the fact that the curve is steeper at C, less steep at B and flatter still at A.

Calculating the gradient of a curve

The gradient of a curve at any point can be estimated by drawing an accurate graph, constructing a tangent and then calculating the gradient of the tangent. For example, the diagram in Figure 3.5 estimates that the gradient of the curve $y = x^2$ at $x = 2$ is about 4.

We could perform similar calculations to estimate the gradient of $y = x^2$ at any number of points. A table, showing the gradient of $y = x^2$ at a selection of values of x, is shown below.

x	−3	−2	−1	0	1	2	3
gradient	−6	−4	−2	0	2	4	6

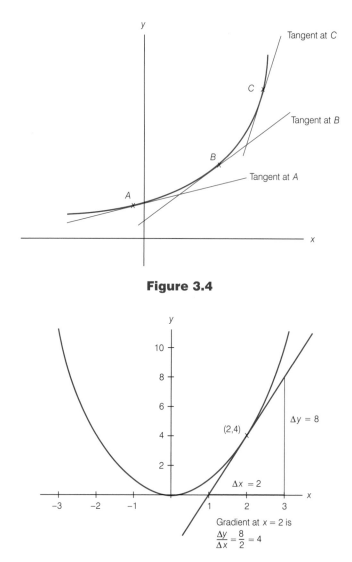

Figure 3.4

Figure 3.5

We have marked these gradients on the graph of $y = x^2$ in Figure 3.6.

Notice that the gradient of the left-hand side of the curve $y = x^2$ is negative. This is to be expected as the curve is sloping down from left to right at these points. The gradient at 0 is 0, because a tangent at this point, the base of the U, is horizontal.

You may also have spotted that at all these values of x, the gradient of the $y = x^2$ curve is twice the value of x. This is *not* just a coincidence. The gradient of $y = x^2$ is $2x$ for all values of x.

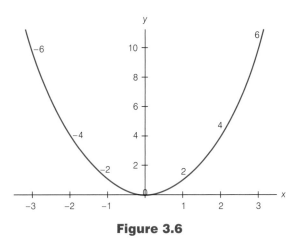

Figure 3.6

Check this

Use the graph in Figure 3.7 to estimate the gradient of $y = x^3$ at $x = 1.5$ and at $x = -1$. (Use a pencil, or tracing paper if this isn't your book!)

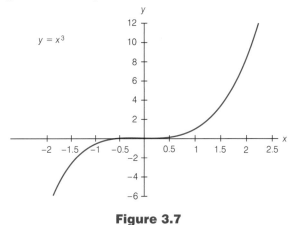

$y = x^3$

Figure 3.7

Solutions:
Draw a tangent at $x = 1.5$ and another at $x = -1$. Use $\frac{\Delta y}{\Delta x}$ to estimate the gradient of each tangent. The gradient at $x = 1.5$ should be 6.75 and at $x = -1$ should be 3. Your answers will only be approximate as the method is graphical.

In fact, the gradient of $y = x^3$ is $3x^2$ for any value of x.

Differentiation

We have told you that the gradient of $y = x^2$ is always $2x$ and that the gradient of $y = x^3$ is $3x^2$. These gradient functions are called *derivatives*. We say that $2x$ is the *derivative* of x^2, and that $3x^2$ is the derivative of x^3.

Because the derivative is the change in y divided by the change in x, between the point of interest and another infinitesimally near, it is often written

$$\frac{dy}{dx}$$

This is pronounced 'dee-y by dee-x'. Note that $\frac{dy}{dx}$ is one symbol: the two parts are *not* usually separated.

We are going to give you some rules for obtaining the derivative of a function. You will have to 'believe' these as the mathematics that derives them is beyond the scope of this book. We will start by considering the derivative of $y = x^n$.

The derivative of any function of the form $y = x^n$ is $\dfrac{dy}{dx} = nx^{n-1}$

Notice that the power in the derivative is one less than in the original function. For example, the derivative of $y = x^5$ is

$$\frac{dy}{dx} = 5x^4$$

This derivative rule applies when n takes any value – it can even be fractional or negative. For instance, when

$$y = \frac{1}{x^2}$$

this is $y = x^{-2}$ and so

$$\frac{dy}{dx} = -2x^{-3}$$

Now we can answer questions about the gradients of curves without drawing them.

Check these

What is the derivative of $y = x^3$?

If $y = x^3$, calculate $\dfrac{dy}{dx}$.

Calculate the gradient of the curve $y = x^4$ at $x = 3$.

What is the gradient of the curve $y = \dfrac{1}{x}$ at $x = 2$?

Solutions:
The first two are both

$$\frac{dy}{dx} = 3x^2$$

$$\frac{dy}{dx} = 4x^3$$

so when $x = 3$ the gradient is $(4 \times 27) = 108$.

$y = x^{-1}$ so $\dfrac{dy}{dx} = -x^{-2}$ and when $x = 2$, $\dfrac{dy}{dx} = -\dfrac{1}{4}$.

This process of writing down the derivative of a function is called *differentiation*.

Check these

Differentiate $y = x^5$

Differentiate $y = x$

Differentiate $y = \dfrac{1}{x^2}$

Solutions:

$$\frac{dy}{dx} = 5x^4, \quad \frac{dy}{dx} = 1, \quad \frac{dy}{dx} = -2x^{-3} = \frac{-2}{x^3}$$

An alternative notation

So far, we have differentiated functions of the form $y = \ldots$ and written their derivatives as $\frac{dy}{dx}$. However, when the function is presented as $f(x)$, it is often convenient to write the derivative as $f'(x)$ (pronounced, 'f dash x'). For instance, when $f(x) = x^2$, the derivative is $f'(x) = 2x$. This notation has the advantage that it can indicate the value of x at which the derivative is to be evaluated. For example, when $f(x) = x^3$, $f'(x) = 3x^2$ so $f'(1) = 3 \cdot 1^2 = 3$, $f'(2) = 3 \cdot 2^2 = 12$ and so on.

So far, we have learnt the following about differentiation.

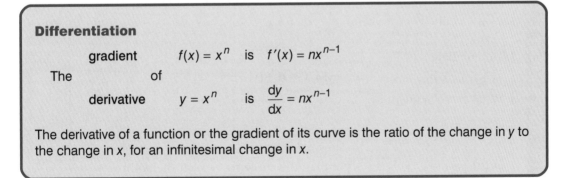

Differentiation

The $\quad$ gradient $\quad$ of $\quad$ $f(x) = x^n$ $\quad$ is $\quad$ $f'(x) = nx^{n-1}$

$\quad$ derivative $\quad$ $y = x^n$ $\quad$ is $\quad$ $\dfrac{dy}{dx} = nx^{n-1}$

The derivative of a function or the gradient of its curve is the ratio of the change in y to the change in x, for an infinitesimal change in x.

WORK CARD 1

1. Write down the derivatives of

   a. $y = x^5$ b. $y = x^4$ c. $y = \dfrac{1}{x}$ d. $y = x^{1/2}$ e. $y = x^{3/2}$

2. Differentiate

   a. $y = x^3$ b. $y = x^{-5}$ c. $f(x) = x^2$ d. $f(x) = x^b$

3. What is the gradient of

   $$f(x) = \dfrac{1}{x^2}$$

   at the point (1,1)? Is it steeper than the curve

   $$g(x) = \dfrac{1}{x}$$

   at the point (1,1)?

Solutions:

1. a. $\dfrac{dy}{dx} = 5x^4$ b. $\dfrac{dy}{dx} = 4x^3$ c. $\dfrac{dy}{dx} = -\dfrac{1}{x^2}$ d. $\dfrac{dy}{dx} = \dfrac{1}{2}x^{-1/2}$ e. $\dfrac{dy}{dx} = \dfrac{3}{2}x^{1/2}$

2. a. $\dfrac{dy}{dx} = 3x^2$ b. $\dfrac{dy}{dx} = -5x^{-6}$ c. $f'(x) = 2x$ d. $f'(x) = bx^{b-1}$

3. $f'(x) = -\dfrac{2}{x^3}$, so $f'(1) = -2$; $g'(x) = -\dfrac{1}{x^2}$ so $g'(1) = -1$, so both curves have a negative gradient but $f(x)$ is steeper.

ASSESSMENT 1

1. Write down the derivatives of

   a. $y = x^7$ b. $y = x^{-4}$ c. $y = \dfrac{1}{x^3}$ d. $y = x^{5/2}$ e. $y = x^{-1/2}$

2. Differentiate

   a. $y = x^{-3}$ b. $y = x^{-7/2}$ c. $f(x) = x^9$ d. $f(x) = x^a$

3. What is the gradient of

   $$f(x) = \dfrac{1}{x^3}$$

   at the point (1,1)? Is it steeper than the curve $g(x) = x^3$ at the point (1,1)?

2 **More differentiation**

Test box 2

Differentiate $\log_e 3x + 5e^{2x}$

Solution:

$$\frac{1}{x} + 10e^{2x}$$

In this section we give rules for differentiating log and e^x and for differentiating sums and multiples of functions.

Differentiating $\log_e x$ and e^x

Just as we had the rule that the derivative of $y = x^n$ is

$$\frac{dy}{dx} = nx^{n-1}$$

there are some rules for differentiating $y = \log_e x$ and $y = e^x$.

> The derivative of $y = \log_e mx$, where m is any constant, is $\dfrac{dy}{dx} = \dfrac{1}{x}$

For instance, when $y = \log_e 3x$,

$$\frac{dy}{dx} = \frac{1}{x}$$

We can only talk about logs of positive values, so for the log to make sense, mx must be greater than zero. The derivative of logs to other bases is more difficult, which is partly why base e is widely used.

> The derivative of $y = e^{mx}$ is $\dfrac{dy}{dx} = me^{mx}$

For example, if $y = e^{-2x}$

$$\frac{dy}{dx} = -2e^{-2x}$$

Notice that the derivative of e^x is e^x. This is one of the special properties of e that make it useful – the gradient function is the same as the original function! Try the following problems.

Check these

Differentiate $y = \log_e 2x$.

What is the derivative of $y = e^{3x}$?

What is the derivative of $f(x) = e^{-3x}$?

Differentiate $y = \log_e \dfrac{x}{3}$.

What is the gradient of the curve $f(x) = \log_e 3x$ at $x = 9$?

Solutions:

$\dfrac{dy}{dx} = \dfrac{1}{x}$, $\quad \dfrac{dy}{dx} = 3e^{3x}$, $\quad f'(x) = -3e^{-3x}$, $\quad \dfrac{dy}{dx} = \dfrac{1}{x}$ $(m = \tfrac{1}{3}$ here$)$, $\quad f'(x) = \dfrac{1}{x}$ so $f'(9) = \dfrac{1}{9}$

Differentiation of sums and differences

Consider a function such as

$$f(x) = x^5 + \log_e x$$

The problem with it is that it is the sum of two terms. Alternatively, it can be regarded as the sum of two functions, $g(x) = x^5$ and $h(x) = \log_e x$.

To differentiate the sum or the difference of two (or more) terms you merely differentiate each one separately and then sum or difference the derivatives.

For example, to differentiate

$$f(x) = x^5 + \log_e x$$

we know that the derivative of x^5 is $5x^4$, and that the derivative of $\log_e x$ is $\dfrac{1}{x}$ so

$$f'(x) = 5x + \dfrac{1}{x}$$

In the same way, if $y = e^{3x} - x^2$ the derivative is

$$\dfrac{dy}{dx} = 3e^{3x} - 2x$$

Check these

Differentiate $f(x) = 2x + x^3$.

Find the derivative of $y = x^2 - \dfrac{1}{x}$.

When $f(x) = e^x + x$, what is $f'(2)$?

Differentiate $y = \log_e 3x + x^5$.

Solutions:

$f'(x) = 2 + 3x^2$, $\quad \dfrac{dy}{dx} = 2x + \dfrac{1}{x^2}$, $\quad f'(x) = e^x + 1$, so $f'(2) = e^2 + 1$, $\quad \dfrac{dy}{dx} = \dfrac{1}{x} + 5x^4$

Derivatives of multiples

You will often have to differentiate functions like $y = 4x^3$, $y = 3\log_e 4x$ or $f(x) = 7e^{2x}$ which are x^n, $\log_e mx$ or e^{mx} multiplied by a constant. This does not present a problem – all you have to do is differentiate as usual, but keep the constant at the front. For instance, when

$$y = 4x^3$$

$$\frac{dy}{dx} = 4 \cdot 3x^2$$

which simplifies to

$$\frac{dy}{dx} = 12x^2$$

Notice that the derivative of $y = mx^n$ is

$$\frac{dy}{dx} = mnx^{n-1}$$

so the number at the front of the derivative is the product of the coefficient, m, and the power of x, n, in the original function.

Check these

Differentiate $f(x) = 6x^2$.

Solution: $f'(x) = 6 \cdot 2x^1 = 12x$.

Write down the derivative of $y = 3x^4$.

Solution: $\dfrac{dy}{dx} = 3 \cdot 4x^3 = 12x^3$

Differentiate $y = \dfrac{2}{x}$.

Solution: $y = 2x^{-1}$ so $\dfrac{dy}{dx} = 2 \cdot -1x^{-2} = \dfrac{-2}{x^2}$

Write down the derivative of $y = 5$.

Solution: $y = 5x^0$ so the derivative is $\dfrac{dy}{dx} = 5 \cdot 0x^{-1} = 0$

Notice in the last example that the derivative of $y = 5$, is 0. In fact, the derivative of $y = $ constant is always zero. This is hardly surprising because the graph of $y = $ constant is a horizontal straight line, so its gradient is zero.

Check these

Differentiate:

$f(x) = 3 \log_e 4x$

$y = 3e^x$

$y = 3e^{-x}$

$f(x) = 12x^3$

$f(x) = 2 \log_e 3x$

Solutions:

$f'(x) = 3\dfrac{1}{x} = \dfrac{3}{x}, \quad \dfrac{dy}{dx} = 3e^x, \quad \dfrac{dy}{dx} = -3e^{-x}, \quad f'(x) = 36x^2, \quad f'(x) = \dfrac{2}{x}$

Frequently, functions contain more than one term *and* terms multiplied by constants – try the following.

Check these

Differentiate:

$y = 5x + 3x^2$

$f(x) = 2 \log_e 2x - \log_e 3x$

$f(x) = e^{5x} + 5x^3 - \log_e x$

$y = 12 + e^{-x}$

Solutions:

$\dfrac{dy}{dx} = 5 + 6x, \quad f'(x) = \dfrac{2}{x} - \dfrac{1}{x} = \dfrac{1}{x}, \quad f'(x) = 5e^{5x} + 15x^2 - \dfrac{1}{x}, \quad \dfrac{dy}{dx} = 0 - e^{-x} = -e^{-x}$

Here are all the rules for differentiation that we have met so far.

Differentiation

$f(x)$ or y	$f'(x)$ or $\dfrac{dy}{dx}$
x^n	nx^{n-1}
$\log_e mx$	$\dfrac{1}{x}$
e^{mx}	me^{mx}

where n and m are constants

To differentiate a sum or difference

$$f(x) = g(x) \pm h(x) \qquad f'(x) = g'(x) \pm h'(x)$$

To differentiate a constant multiple

$$f(x) = cg(x) \qquad f'(x) = cg'(x)$$

where c is a constant

Most people do not find differentiation difficult once they have had some practice. We have therefore deliberately omitted any applications of differentiation at this stage so as not to detract from the techniques required.

WORK CARD 2

1. Write down the derivatives of:
   a. $f(x) = \log_e 3x$ b. $y = \log_e \dfrac{x}{2}$ c. $y = e^{3x}$ d. $y = e^{-5x}$

   e. $f(x) = e^{-x/2}$

2. Differentiate the following:
   a. $y = x^3 - x^2$ b. $f(x) = 3x^2 - 10x$ c. $g(x) = \log_e 2x - x^3$
   d. $y = 2e^x - 5x$

3. Differentiate:
   a. $f(x) = (x - 1)x^2$ b. $y = \log_e x^2$ c. $y = 2x^2 - 4x + 6x^4$

4. What is the gradient of the curve $y = x^3 - 2e^{-3x}$ at $x = 0$?

5. When $f(x) = 6 \log_e x - x^4$ what is $f'(x)$? Evaluate $f'(1)$, and $f'(-1)$.

Solutions:

1. a. $f'(x) = \dfrac{1}{x}$

   b. $\dfrac{dy}{dx} = \dfrac{1}{x}$ ($\dfrac{x}{2}$ is just $\dfrac{1}{2}$ times x and so is a multiple of x).

   c. $\dfrac{dy}{dx} = 3e^{3x}$

   d. $\dfrac{dy}{dx} = -5e^{-5x}$

   e. $f'(x) = \dfrac{-1}{2}e^{-x/2}$ (again $\dfrac{-x}{2}$ is just $\dfrac{-1}{2}$ times x and so a multiple of x).

2. a. $\dfrac{dy}{dx} = 3x^2 - 2x$ b. $f'(x) = 6x - 10$ c. $g'(x) = \dfrac{1}{x} - 3x^2$ d. $\dfrac{dy}{dx} = 2e^x - 5$

3. a. You need to multiply this out first to give $f(x) = x^3 - x^2$, so $f'(x) = 3x^2 - 2x$.

b. You can't differentiate this as it stands, but remember that $\log_e x^2 = \log_e x + \log_e x$ and so

$$\frac{dy}{dx} = \frac{1}{x} + \frac{1}{x} = \frac{2}{x}$$

c. $\dfrac{dy}{dx} = 4x - 4 + 24x^3$

4. $\dfrac{dy}{dx} = 3x^2 + 6e^{-3x}$, so at $x = 0$, $\dfrac{dy}{dx} = 6e^0 = 6$

5. $f'(x) = \dfrac{6}{x} - 4x^3$, so $f'(1) = 6 - 4 = 2$ and $f'(-1) = -6 + 4 = -2$

1. Differentiate:
   a. $y = e^{-2x}$ b. $f(x) = \log_e(-4x)$ c. $f(x) = e^{x/3}$ d. $f(x) = e^{5x}$

2. Write down the derivatives of:
   a. $y = x^4 - x^7$ b. $y = x^{-3} + x^{-2}$ c. $f(x) = x^2 + \log_e 3x$ d. $f(x) = e^{-2x} - 2x$

3. Differentiate:
   a. $y = 2\log_e 3x$ b. $f(x) = 3e^{2x}$ c. $y = 3x^2$ d. $y = 5x^2 - 3\log_e 7x$

4. What are the gradients of the following curves at $x = 1$?
   a. $y = x$ b. $y = x^2$ c. $y = \log_e x$ d. $y = e^x$

   Plot these functions on the same graph. Are the respective gradients what you would expect?

3 Interpreting derivatives

Test box 3

What is meant by the marginal revenue function?

If revenue R and demand Q are related by

$$R = 10Q - 0.001Q^2$$

what is the marginal revenue when $Q = 3000$?

Solution:
Marginal revenue is the ratio of the change in revenue to the change in demand when demand changes by a small amount. The marginal revenue function is

$$\frac{dR}{dQ} = 10 - 0.002Q$$

so when $Q = 3000$, the marginal revenue is 4.

Recall from Section 1 that the derivative of $y = f(x)$ at a particular point is the ratio of the change in y to the change in x between the point and a point infinitesimally near. Another way of saying this is that derivatives measure the instantaneous *rate of change* in y compared to x.

Of course, the variables concerned aren't always called x and y and sometimes we have to use other symbols. For instance, when

$$R = 20Q^2 + 2Q$$
$$\frac{dR}{dQ} = 40Q + 2$$

We say that the derivative of R *with respect to Q* is $40Q + 2$.

Differentiation is particularly useful in economics and finance. We give some examples of applications below.

Marginal revenue

In Chapter MM2, Section 2, we saw that as revenue is $R = QP$, where P is price and Q is the quantity sold and the demand function expresses P as a function of Q; if, for instance, $P = 10 - 0.001Q$, we can express revenue R as a function of Q; in this case,

$$R = QP = Q(10 - 0.001Q) = 10Q - 0.001Q^2$$

In general we can write $R = f(Q)$.

The gradient, $\frac{dR}{dQ}$, of this curve is called the *marginal revenue function*. It is the ratio of the change in R to the change in Q between a point (Q,R) and another infinitesimally near; that is, when Q changes only minutely.

When $R = 10Q - 0.001Q^2$, the marginal revenue is

$$\frac{dR}{dQ} = 10 - 0.002Q$$

So, a minute change in Q will result in a change in R that is $(10 - 0.002Q)$ times as large. For instance, when $Q = 2000$,

$$\frac{dR}{dQ} = 10 - 0.002 \cdot 2000 = 6$$

and the marginal revenue is 6. A minute change in Q will result in a change in R that is 6 times as large.

The graph in Figure 3.8 shows the revenue function $R = 10Q - 0.001Q^2$. The marginal revenue, $\frac{dR}{dQ}$, at any value of Q is the gradient of the curve at this point. We have shown the gradient at $Q = 2000$.

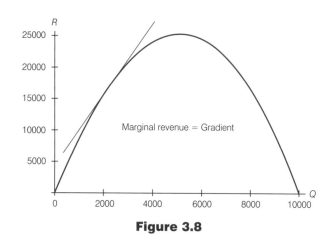

Figure 3.8

Other 'marginal' functions

Many other 'marginal' functions are used in economics and elsewhere and the idea is much the same.

For instance, suppose that output Q is assumed to be a function of labour hours L so $Q = f(L)$. The *marginal product of labour* is given by $\frac{dQ}{dL}$. It is the ratio of the change in Q to the change in L when L changes minutely.

For example, if

$$Q = 100L^{3/2}$$

the marginal product of labour function is

$$\frac{dQ}{dL} = \frac{3}{2}100L^{1/2} = 150L^{1/2}$$

So, a small change in labour from L hours results in $150L^{1/2}$ times that change in output. For example, when labour changes from $L = 4$, Q will change by 300 times as much.

Another 'marginal' function is *marginal cost*. We have already seen that total production cost C is a function of the quantity produced Q. The marginal cost is $\frac{dC}{dQ}$. For instance, when

$$C = 450 + 0.1Q^2$$

the marginal cost is

$$\frac{dC}{dQ} = 0.2Q$$

So when Q changes a small amount, the firm's total production cost changes by $0.2Q$ times that amount. For example, when $Q = 3$,

$$\frac{dC}{dQ} = 0.6$$

total cost changes by 0.6 times the small change in Q.

Check this

Suppose $Q = 40L^{4/5}$ where L is the number of labour hours (in thousands). What is the marginal product of labour when $L = 2$?

Solution:
The marginal product of labour is

$$\frac{dQ}{dL} = 40 \cdot \frac{4}{5} L^{-1/5} = 32L^{-1/5}$$

So when $L = 2$,

$$\frac{dQ}{dL} = 32 \cdot 2^{-1/5} = 27.86$$

A firm's fixed costs are £2000 a week and their variable costs are estimated at £10 per unit of output. Write down the total cost function. What is the marginal cost function? Evaluate the marginal cost when output is 50 and when output is 100.

Solution:
The total cost function is linear, $C = 2000 + 10Q$. The marginal cost function is

$$\frac{dC}{dQ} = 10$$

so the marginal cost for any value of Q is 10. This is not a surprise, as we already know that the additional cost of each unit of output is 10, the variable cost per unit.

Elasticity of demand

The *price elasticity of demand* is an economic measure of the sensitivity of the demand for a good to a small change in its price. It is defined as

$$E = -\frac{\text{Percentage change in demand}}{\text{Percentage change in price}}$$

A typical demand function is shown in Figure 3.9. When price *increases* from P_1 to P_2, the quantity demanded *decreases* from Q_1 to Q_2.

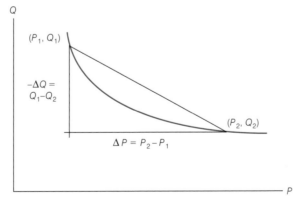

Figure 3.9

The percentage change in price is therefore

$$\frac{P_2 - P_1}{P_1} \times 100$$

which, if we write ΔP instead of $P_2 - P_1$, is

$$\frac{\Delta P}{P_1} \times 100$$

The corresponding percentage change in demand is

$$\frac{Q_2 - Q_1}{Q_1} \times 100 = \frac{\Delta Q}{Q_1} \times 100$$

which will be negative.

The price elasticity of demand when the price changes from P_1 to P_2 is therefore

$$E = -\frac{\frac{\Delta Q}{Q_1} \times 100}{\frac{\Delta P}{P_1} \times 100}$$

The 100s cancel so this simplifies to

$$E = -\frac{\frac{\Delta Q}{Q_1}}{\frac{\Delta P}{P_1}} = -\frac{\Delta Q}{Q_1}\frac{P_1}{\Delta P} = -\frac{\Delta Q}{\Delta P}\frac{P_1}{Q_1}$$

So

$$E = -\frac{\Delta Q}{\Delta P}\frac{P_1}{Q_1}$$

But this elasticity tells us the *average* effect on demand when price changes from P_1 to P_2. We would like an expression for the elasticity at a particular price, say at P_1.

To obtain this we use the formula for elasticity given above but for a point (P_2, Q_2) which is infinitesimally close to (P_1, Q_1). Recall that when the two points are extremely close, the ratio of the change in Q to the change in P, $\frac{\Delta Q}{\Delta P}$, is the derivative $\frac{dQ}{dP}$. The elasticity at P_1 is therefore

$$E = -\frac{dQ}{dP}\frac{P_1}{Q_1}$$

In general, at any price and demand (P, Q), the price elasticity of demand is defined as

$$E = -\frac{dQ}{dP}\frac{P}{Q}$$

As demand functions usually slope downwards $\frac{dQ}{dP}$ will be negative, so elasticity will be positive.

For instance, suppose the demand function is

$$Q = 100 - P^2$$

then

$$\frac{dQ}{dP} = -2P$$

and so

$$E = -(-2P)\frac{P}{Q} = \frac{2P^2}{Q}$$

For example, when price is $P = 4$, the price elasticity of demand is

$$E = \frac{2 \times 16}{100 - 16} = \frac{32}{84}$$

When price increases by a small percentage, demand will decrease by $\frac{32}{84}$ times this percentage.

When the percentage change in demand is greater than the percentage change in price, E will be greater than 1, and we say that demand is *elastic* as it is relatively sensitive to changes in price. When E is less than 1, the percentage change in demand is less than the percentage change in price and demand is said to be *inelastic*.

Check this

Suppose the demand function is $Q = -P^2 + 5P + 50$. What is the price elasticity of demand when $P = 5$? Is demand elastic or inelastic?

Solution:

$$\frac{dQ}{dP} = -2P + 5$$

so

$$E = -\frac{dQ}{dP}\frac{P}{Q} = -\frac{(-2P + 5)P}{Q}$$

When $P = 5$, this is

$$\frac{-(-10 + 5)5}{-25 + 25 + 50} = 0.5$$

As the percentage change in demand is only half the percentage change in price the demand is inelastic.

A useful dodge

Demand functions are often given with P as a function of Q, that is $P = f(Q)$, so that it is straightforward to find dP/dQ, but more difficult to obtain dQ/dP which is required to calculate the elasticity. (We would have to rearrange $P = f(Q)$ with Q as the subject before differentiating.) It is therefore useful to know that

$$\frac{dQ}{dP} = \frac{1}{\frac{dP}{dQ}}$$

That is, to find dQ/dP, differentiate the function $P = f(Q)$ in the usual way, and then find the reciprocal of dP/dQ.

Check these

Suppose the demand function is

$$P = \frac{5}{2Q}$$

What is the price elasticity of demand when $Q = 2$?

Solution:

$$E = -\frac{dQ}{dP}\frac{P}{Q}$$

P is given as a function of Q so it's easier to calculate

$$\frac{dP}{dQ} = -\frac{5}{2}Q^{-2} = -\frac{5}{2Q^2}$$

so

$$\frac{dQ}{dP} = -\frac{2Q^2}{5} \quad \text{and} \quad E = \frac{2PQ^2}{5Q} = \frac{2PQ}{5}$$

When $Q = 2$, $P = \frac{5}{4}$ and so

$$E = \frac{2 \cdot \frac{5}{4} \cdot 2}{5} = 1$$

WORK CARD 3

1. Write down the derivative of $Q = 120L^{3/4}$.

2. Differentiate $R = 50Q^2 - 2Q + 5$ with respect to Q.

3. If the revenue R and demand Q are related by $R = Q(50 - 2Q)$ find the marginal revenue function. What is the marginal revenue when $Q = 10$?

4. Suppose that output Q is $Q = 80L^{1/2}$, where L is the number of labour hours. Write down an expression for the marginal product of labour. What is the marginal product of labour when $L = 10{,}000$?

5. Find the marginal revenue function when the demand function is $P = 10 - 0.1Q$.

6. What is the price elasticity of demand when the demand function is $Q = 200 - P^2 - 6P$? Is demand elastic or inelastic when $P = 5$?

7. Calculate the price elasticity of demand when $P = 4$ if the demand function is $P = 10 - \sqrt{Q}$.

WORK CARD 3 (CONTINUED)

Solutions:

1. $\dfrac{dQ}{dL} = 90L^{-1/4}$

2. $\dfrac{dR}{dQ} = 100Q - 2$

3. $\dfrac{dR}{dQ} = 50 - 4Q$ so when $Q = 10$, marginal revenue is 10.

4. $\dfrac{dQ}{dL} = 40L^{-1/2}$. When $L = 10{,}000$ this is $40 \cdot \dfrac{1}{100} = 0.4$.

5. $R = PQ = (10 - 0.1Q)Q = 10Q - 0.1Q^2$. So $\dfrac{dR}{dQ} = 10 - 0.2Q$.

6. $\dfrac{dQ}{dP} = -2P - 6$

   so $E = (2P + 6) \cdot \dfrac{P}{200 - P^2 - 6P} = \dfrac{2P^2 + 6P}{200 - P^2 - 6P}$

   At $P = 5$,

   $$E = \dfrac{50 + 30}{145}$$

   which is < 1 so demand is inelastic. Demand is relatively insensitive to price changes.

7. P is given as a function of Q so it is easiest to calculate $\frac{dP}{dQ}$ here:

   $$\dfrac{dP}{dQ} = -\dfrac{1}{2}Q^{-1/2} \text{ so } \dfrac{dQ}{dP} = -2Q^{1/2}$$

   $$E = (2Q^{1/2}) \cdot \dfrac{10 - \sqrt{Q}}{Q}$$

   which simplifies to

   $$E = \dfrac{20\sqrt{Q} - 2Q}{Q}$$

   We need to evaluate this at $P = 4$. When $P = 4$, Q is the solution of $4 = 10 - \sqrt{Q}$, so $Q = 36$.

   $$E = \dfrac{20 \cdot 6 - 72}{36} = \dfrac{48}{36}$$

   This is greater than 1 so demand is elastic.

1. Differentiate $Q = 90L^{1/2}$ with respect to L.

2. What is the derivative of $R = 33Q - 4Q^2$ with respect to Q?

3. Suppose output Q is a function of the number of labour hours only and is $Q = 5L + 2L^2$. Write down an expression for the marginal product of labour. What is the marginal product of labour when $L = 500$?

4. Find the marginal revenue function when the demand function is

$$P = 8 - \frac{Q^2}{30}$$

What is the marginal revenue when $Q = 5$?

5. Given the demand function $Q = 500(10 - P)$ find the elasticity of demand when:
   a. $P = 2$ b. $P = 5$ c. $P = 6$

6. Given the demand function $P = 12 - Q^{1/3}$ calculate the price elasticities of demand when $P = 2$ and when $P = 8$.

4 Maximising and minimising

Test box 4

Calculate the turning (= stationary) points of $f(x) = 12x^3 - 4x + 5$ and classify them.

Solution:
$f'(x) = 36x^2 - 4$ and so the turning points lie at the solutions of $36x^2 - 4 = 0$, so $x = -\frac{1}{3}$ and $\frac{1}{3}$. The second derivative is $f''(x) = 72x$, so $f''(-\frac{1}{3}) = -24$ and $x = -\frac{1}{3}$ is a local maximum and $f''(\frac{1}{3}) = 24$, so $x = \frac{1}{3}$ is a local minimum.

Differentiation has wider uses than just calculating rates of change. We will now see that it can be used to calculate the points at which curves turn and so help to find the maximum and minimum values of functions.

Finding turning points

Consider the curve in Figure 3.10. It has three *turning points* or *stationary points*. Two of these are local *minima* and one is a local *maximum*.

A local maximum (or minimum) is just a turning point that is higher (or lower) than all the nearby points. Such points may or may not be the maximum or minimum points of the whole curve. In this example the left-hand local minimum is also the overall or *global* minimum.

Notice, as shown in Figure 3.11, that the gradient of the curve at a turning point is always zero.

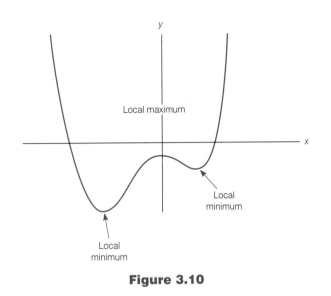

Figure 3.10

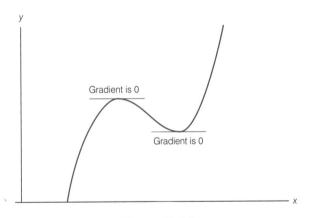

Figure 3.11

This suggests the following method of finding the stationary points directly from the equation of the function:

(i) Differentiate
(ii) Equate the derivative to 0
(iii) Solve for x

For example, suppose we want the turning points of the curve

$$y = 2x^3 - 9x^2 + 12x.$$

We differentiate to obtain

$$\frac{dy}{dx} = 6x^2 - 18x + 12$$

and equate this derivative to zero to give

$$6x^2 - 18x + 12 = 0$$

Solving this equation for x (divide all through by 6 to give $x^2 - 3x + 2 = 0$, which factorises to $(x - 1)(x - 2) = 0$), gives $x = 1$ and $x = 2$, so the stationary points are at $x = 1$ and $x = 2$. Substituting these values of x into $y = 2x^3 - 9x^2 + 12x$ gives the corresponding ys so the curve turns at (1,5) and (2,4).

(Incidentally this is how we knew, for Chapter MM2, Section 2, that the turning point of the quadratic function $y = ax^2 + bx + c$, is at

$$x = -\frac{b}{2a}$$

As a, b and c are just constants, differentiating $y = ax^2 + bx + c$ gives

$$\frac{dy}{dx} = 2ax + b$$

and equating this to zero and solving gives $2ax + b = 0$, $2ax = -b$, and so $x = -\frac{b}{2a}$.)

Check these

Find the stationary points of $y = x^3 - 3x^2$.

Solution:
First differentiate to give

$$\frac{dy}{dx} = 3x^2 - 6x$$

Now set the derivative equal to zero to give $3x^2 - 6x = 0$, and solve. The equation is $3x(x - 2) = 0$, so $x = 0$ or $x = 2$. The turning points are at $x = 0$ ($y = 0$) and $x = 2$ ($y = -4$).

Find the turning points of $f(x) = 3x^2 + 5x^3$.

Solution:
Differentiating gives $f'(x) = 6x + 15x^2$. Equating this to zero gives $6x + 15x^2 = 0$ which factorises to $3x (2 + 5x) = 0$, so the solutions are $x = 0$ and $x = \frac{-2}{5}$. When $x = 0$, $f(x) = 0$ and when $x = \frac{-2}{5}$, $f(x) = \frac{4}{25}$, so the stationary points are at $(0,0)$ and $(\frac{-2}{5}, \frac{4}{25})$.

Find the turning points of $f(x) = x^4 + x^3$.

Solution:
$f'(x) = 4x^3 + 3x^2 = 0$, which factorises to $x^2(4x + 3) = 0$ so the turning points are at $x = 0$ and $x = -\frac{3}{4}$.

Find the stationary points of $y = 2x^3 + 6x$.

Solution:

$$\frac{dy}{dx} = 6x^2 + 6$$

so the turning points are at $6x^2 + 6 = 0$. Dividing all through by 6 gives $x^2 + 1 = 0$ and then we rearrange to $x^2 = -1$! There are no solutions to this so the curve does not have any stationary points.

Second derivatives

It will be useful to know whether each stationary point is a local maximum or a local minimum. The method requires that we calculate something called the *second derivative*.

The second derivative of a function is denoted

$$\frac{d^2y}{dx^2}$$

and is obtained by differentiating the derivative of a function.

For example, when

$$y = 3x^3 - 5x^2,$$

the derivative is

$$\frac{dy}{dx} = 9x^2 - 10x$$

and the second derivative is

$$\frac{d^2y}{dx^2} = 18x - 10$$

We can evaluate the second derivative at any value of x. For instance, the second derivative of $y = 3x^3 - 5x^2$ at $x = 2$ is $(18 \times 2) - 10 = 26$.

The second derivative indicates the rate of change of the derivative function. When it is positive the derivative is increasing as x increases and when it is negative the derivative is decreasing as x increases.

We have already seen that the derivative of $f(x)$ can be written $f'(x)$. The notation extends naturally and you will often see the second derivative function written as $f''(x)$ ('f double-dash x').

Check this

Find the second derivative function of $y = 12x^2 - x^4$.

Solution:

$$\frac{dy}{dx} = 24x - 4x^3, \quad \frac{d^2y}{dx^2} = 24 - 12x^2$$

Evaluate the second derivative of $f(x) = 4x^3 - \log_e x$ at $x = 2$.

Solution:

$$f'(x) = 12x^2 - \frac{1}{x}$$

Differentiating again gives

$$f''(x) = 24x + \frac{1}{x^2}$$

so

$$f''(2) = 48 + \frac{1}{4} = 48.25$$

Maximum or minimum?

To find out whether a stationary point is a local maximum or a local minimum we do the following. We will explain why it works later. We will suppose the turning point we have found is at $x = a$.

1. Find the second derivative function $f''(x)$.
2. Evaluate the second derivative at the turning point; that is, evaluate $f''(a)$.
3. If $f''(a)$ is negative, the point is a local maximum and if it is positive, the point is a local minimum.

We demonstrate this for the function

$$f(x) = 2x^3 - 9x^2 + 12x$$

We have already found that the stationary points lie at $x = 1$ and $x = 2$. The derivative is

$$f'(x) = 6x^2 - 18x + 12$$

Differentiating again gives

$$f''(x) = 12x - 18$$

At $x = 1$ the second derivative is $f''(1) = -6$, which is negative and so the turning point at $x = 1$ is a local maximum, whereas $f''(2) = 6$, which is positive, so the stationary point at $x = 2$ is a local minimum.

We explain why this method works in the next paragraph – if you would rather not get involved in such details (although it may help you to remember the method) rejoin us at **Check this**.

The curve in Figure 3.12 has a local minimum and a local maximum. The gradient just before the local maximum is positive, at the local maximum it is 0 and just after the local

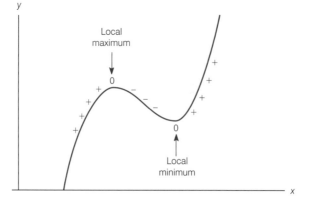

Figure 3.12

maximum it is negative. So around the local maximum the gradient is decreasing. Recall that when the gradient of a curve is decreasing the second derivative of the function is negative. We can therefore inspect the second derivative of a function at a stationary point and, if it is negative, we know we have a local maximum.

In a similar way, before a local minimum the gradient is negative, at a local minimum it is zero and after a local minimum it is positive, so around a local minimum the gradient of a curve is increasing and the second derivative is positive.

Check this

We have already found that the turning points of $y = x^3 - 3x^2$ are at (0,0) and (2,–4) and that

$$\frac{dy}{dx} = 3x^2 - 6x$$

but are they local maxima or local minima?

Solution:
The second derivative is

$$\frac{d^2y}{dx^2} = 6x - 6$$

At $x = 0$,

$$\frac{d^2y}{dx^2} = -6$$

which is negative, so we have a local maximum. At $x = 2$,

$$\frac{d^2y}{dx^2} = 6$$

which is positive, so the point is a local minimum.

Check this

Calculate the turning points of $f(x) = 12x^3 - 4x + 5$ and classify them.

Solution:
$f'(x) = 36x^2 - 4$ and so the stationary points lie at the solutions of $36x^2 - 4 = 0$, so $x = -\frac{1}{3}$ and $\frac{1}{3}$. The second derivative is $f''(x) = 72x$, so $f''(-\frac{1}{3}) = -24$ and $x = -\frac{1}{3}$ is a local maximum and $f''(\frac{1}{3}) = 24$, so $x = \frac{1}{3}$ is a local minimum.

Using stationary points to sketch curves

In Chapter MM2 we learnt how to use the equation of a function to sketch its curve. Knowledge of the turning points and their nature (maximum or minimum) can give further clues to the shape of a curve.

For example, to sketch $y = x^3 - 3x^2$ using the curve sketching skills from Chapter MM2 we would reason as follows. When x is large and positive, y is very large and when x is large and negative, y is negative and large. Also, when $y = 0$, $x = 0$ or 3, so the curve crosses the x axis at $x = 0$ and $x = 3$.

In addition, two **Check this** sections ago we found out that there is a local maximum at $(0,0)$ and a local minimum at $(2,-4)$.

All this information can be marked on a graph as in Figure 3.13.

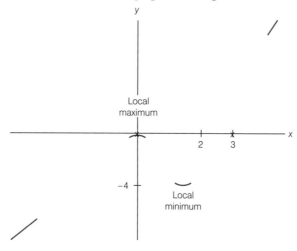

Figure 3.13

As the curve does not cross the axes or turn in any other places we have enough information to join up the pieces as shown in Figure 3.14.

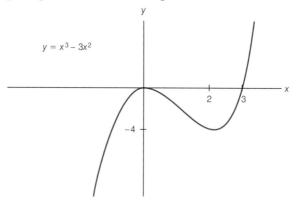

Figure 3.14

Inflexion points

We have not yet considered what it means when the second derivative is neither positive or negative – that is, when

$$\frac{d^2y}{dx^2} = 0$$

When the second derivative, d^2y/dx^2, is exactly equal to zero it is not clear which sort of stationary point we have. It may be a local maximum or a local minimum but it could be of a third (and final) type of stationary point called a *point of inflexion*. This is a sort of 'kink' in the curve at which the gradient is 0, but the curve does *not* change direction. A curve with an inflexion point is shown in Figure 3.15.

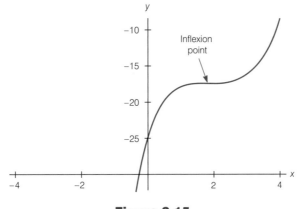

Figure 3.15

You won't often have to find inflexion points for applications but they can be useful for sketching curves.

When, at a stationary point, the second derivative is 0 the best way to classify the point is to look at the sign of the derivative just before and just after the point. As shown in Figure 3.16, if the point is a local maximum, the gradient, dy/dx, will be positive just to the left of the point and negative just to the right of it whereas if the point is a local minimum the gradient will be negative just to the left of it and positive just to the right. If, however, it is an inflexion point the curve will not change direction and the derivative will have the same sign (positive or negative) at either side of the point.

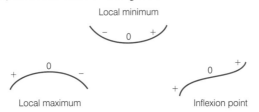

Figure 3.16 Signs of the derivative near stationary points.

| Check this |

The curve $y = x^3$ has a stationary point at $x = 0$. What sort of stationary point is this?

Solution:

$$\frac{dy}{dx} = 3x^2$$

so

$$\frac{d^2y}{dx^2} = 6x$$

which is 0 at the stationary point and so doesn't tell us whether $x = 0$ is a local maximum, local minimum or a point of inflexion. To find out we must look at the sign of dy/dx just to the left of $x = 0$ (say at $x = -0.1$) and just to the right of it (say at $x = 0.1$). As

$$\frac{dy}{dx} = 3x^2$$

it is positive at both $x = -0.1$ and at $x = 0.1$, so the curve does not change direction at $x = 0$ and there is an inflexion point.

Turning or stationary points

To find the turning or stationary points of a function

		y	$f(x)$
(i)	Differentiate	$\dfrac{dy}{dx}$	$f'(x)$
(ii)	Equate the derivative to 0	$\dfrac{dy}{dx} = 0$	$f'(x) = 0$
(iii)	Solve for x		

To classify the stationary or turning point at $x = a$

(i)	Find the second derivative	$\dfrac{d^2y}{dx^2}$	$f''(x)$
(ii)	Evaluate the second derivative at $x = a$	$\dfrac{d^2y}{dx^2}$ at $x = a$	$f''(a)$

If it is **Positive** – the point is a local **Minimum**
If it is **Negative** – the point is a local **Maximum**
If it is zero – examine $f'(x)$ to the left and right of a to establish whether the point is a local maximum, local minimum or an **Inflexion** point

---

Profit maximisation

The techniques we have covered in this section are important for locating the overall (global) maximum/minimum of a function, as these frequently occur at local maxima or minima. It is usually best to draw a rough sketch of the function to establish its shape before deciding where the global maximum or minimum are.

In the following example we are interested in finding the demand quantity Q that gives the maximum profit.

Suppose the demand function is

$$P = 36 - \frac{Q^2}{3}$$

and the total cost function is

$$C = 2Q^2 + 4Q$$

The revenue function is therefore

$$R = PQ = \left(36 - \frac{Q^2}{3}\right)Q = 36Q - \frac{Q^3}{3}$$

so profit, which we will call π ('pi'), is

$$\pi = R - C$$

$$= 36Q - \frac{Q^3}{3} - (2Q^2 + 4Q)$$

$$= 32Q - \frac{Q^3}{3} - 2Q^2$$

To find the value of Q that maximises the profit we differentiate π with respect to Q and set the derivative equal to 0 to give

$$\frac{d\pi}{dQ} = 32 - Q^2 - 4Q = 0$$

Solving this gives $Q = 4$ and $Q = -8$. The profit curve therefore has two turning points. As Q is a quantity we are not interested in the turning point at -8, so we need only consider the turning point at $Q = 4$.

Differentiating $\frac{d\pi}{dQ}$ again gives

$$\frac{d^2\pi}{dQ^2} = -2Q - 4$$

When $Q = 4$ this is negative so the turning point at $Q = 4$ is a local maximum.

To investigate whether the local maximum at $Q = 4$ is also the global maximum we need to sketch the shape of the curve (for positive values of Q). We reason as follows.

When Q is very large $Q^3/3$ and $2Q^2$ will be much larger than $32Q$, so

$$\pi = 32Q - \frac{Q^3}{3} - 2Q^2$$

will be large and negative. Also, when $Q = 0$, $\pi = 0$. These pieces of information and the local maximum at $Q = 4$ are marked on the sketch in Figure 3.17.

Bearing in mind that these pieces of curve must join up and that the only other turning point is when $Q = -8$, so the curve doesn't change direction anywhere else, we see that the local maximum at $Q = 4$ must also be the global maximum. A graph of the profit function is shown in Figure 3.18.

We conclude that profit is maximised at $Q = 4$.

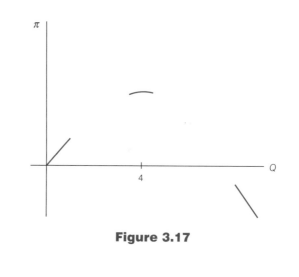

Figure 3.17

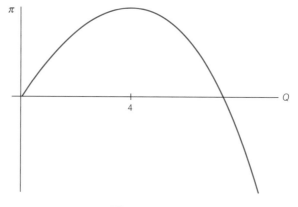

Figure 3.18

1. Find any local maxima and minima of $f(x) = 3x^2 + 3x - 5$.

2. Find and classify the turning points of

$$y = \frac{x^3}{3} + 2x^2 - 5x + 2$$

3. Find the stationary points of $f(x) = -x^3 + 15x^2 - 75x - 4$ and say whether they are local maxima, local minima or points of inflexion.

4. If $R = 33Q - 4Q^2$ and the total cost function is $C = Q^3 - 9Q^2 + 36Q + 6$, find the output Q that maximises profit.

5. The revenue earned by a charter coach on a weekend excursion is $R = 120x - x^2$, where x is the number of seats taken in the 50-seater bus. Find the maximum revenue and the number of passengers that produce it.

WORK CARD 4 (CONTINUED)

Solutions:

1. $f'(x) = 6x + 3$ so there is a stationary point when $6x + 3 = 0$; that is, when $x = -0.5$. $f''(x) = 6$ which is positive so this will be a local minimum.

2. There are turning points at $x = 1$ and $x = -5$. The second derivative function is $2x + 4$, so there is a local minimum at $x = 1$ and a local maximum at $x = -5$.

3. $f'(x) = -3x^2 + 30x - 75$ so at the stationary points $-x^2 + 10x - 25 = 0$. This factorises to $-(x - 5)^2$ so the only turning point is at $x = -5$. $f''(x) = -2x + 10$, so $f''(5) = 0$ and this could be a local maximum, local minimum or a point of inflexion. To find out which we investigate the sign of the derivative immediately before and after $x = 5$. $f'(4.5) = -0.75$ and $f'(5.5) = -0.75$, so the function has a negative slope both before and after the turning point and $x = 5$ is a point of inflexion.

4. Profit is $\pi = R - C = 33Q - 4Q^2 - (Q^3 - 9Q^2 + 36Q + 6) = -Q^3 + 5Q^2 - 3Q - 6$. So

$$\frac{d\pi}{dQ} = -3Q^2 + 10Q - 3 = 0$$

The solutions are at $Q = 3$ and $Q = \frac{1}{3}$.

$$\frac{d^2\pi}{dQ^2} = -6Q + 10$$

so at $Q = 3$ there is a local maximum and at $Q = \frac{1}{3}$ a local minimum. Profit will be large and negative for large values of Q, and there are no other turning points so we conclude that $Q = 3$ is also the global maximum.

5. There is a local maximum at $x = 60$. However, the bus cannot take more than 50 passengers. There are no other stationary points so the curve ascends to 60 and then decreases. The maximum revenue is therefore attained when the bus is full, i.e. $x = 50$.

ASSESSMENT 4

1. Find the stationary points of $y = 3x^3 - 6x^2 - 5x$. Classify each of them as local maxima, local minima or points of inflexion.

2. Use differentiation to find the maximum or minimum point of $f(z) = 5z^2 - 10z + 7$. Use differentiation again to find out whether it is a maximum or a minimum. Does this confirm what you know about the shape of quadratic functions?

3. Find and classify the stationary points of $y = 5x^3 - 4x^2 + x - 4$.

4. Find the turning points of

$$y = \log_e x - \frac{x^2}{2}$$

Are these maxima or minima or points of inflexion?

ASSESSMENT 4 (CONTINUED)

5. Find any local maxima or minima of $f(x) = x + e^{-x}$.

6. A firm's output is $Q = 120L^2 - 2L^4$, where L is the number of labour hours in thousands. How many labour hours maximise output?
   Write down an expression for the marginal product of labour $\frac{dQ}{dL}$ and find the value of L that maximises the marginal product of labour.

7. A company makes \$6 profit on each pair of gloves it manufactures. The number of thousand pairs of ladies' gloves x it can make in a week and the number of thousand men's gloves y are related by $x^2 + y = 5$.
   How many pairs of ladies' and men's gloves respectively should they manufacture in order to maximise profit? **Hint:** $y = 5 - x^2$.

Further reading: see p. xv

Jacques is particularly good here. It covers the material in our chapter, with economic applications, then continues far beyond to cover the main elements of calculus.

DD Describing data

Why describe data?

Nowadays, computer storage is cheap and more information is available than ever before. The idea of storing a lot of information is, presumably, to increase our knowledge of the market, our product, our staff and our competitors and hence enable us to make the most prudent business decisions. This should bring more precision and less waste but in practice there is often so much information that it is extremely hard to 'see the wood for the trees' and make sense of it. Information on its own is not enough, we also need the expertise to interpret it.

This is why, today more than ever, people in business (and many other fields) need to be able to understand and interpret visual and numerical summaries of data and be able to produce them themselves if necessary.

Using a computer

Although a computer can display and summarise data for you at the click of a mouse, it also makes it very easy to apply techniques that are not suitable, or sensible, and that produce silly results. To understand and interpret computer output and realise when something is wrong you still need to have an idea how to do the calculations yourself. The **WORK CARDS** and **ASSESSMENTS** therefore include smaller examples to do on a calculator as well as ones that are best tackled on a computer.

Your lecturer will usually tell you which software is available for your course. Some well-known and widely used statistical packages are SPSS and MINITAB. Alternatively, many of the functions we use are now available in Microsoft® Excel and other spreadsheets. We have therefore included guidance in the use of SPSS and Excel and typical output is shown at appropriate points in the text. An introduction to SPSS and Excel primer can be found on the companion web site.

DD1
Pictures of data

It is a capital mistake to theorize before one has data.

Sir Arthur Conan Doyle

Contexts

What is this chapter about?

This chapter explains how to display numerical information and how to interpret critically pictures of data that you see elsewhere. It explains how the spreadsheet Excel and the statistical software SPSS can be used to draw graphs of data.

Why is it useful?

Graphs appear everywhere: in adverts, marketing material, financial literature, research papers and web sites. Businesses and organisations use graphs in reports and presentations to communicate and influence decisions. Because it only takes seconds to draw a graph on a computer, 'bad' graphs – those which misrepresent the data, either intentionally or accidentally – are rife. In fact, 'bad' graphs are often produced deliberately to sell a product or influence the reader. So, whilst you will almost certainly have to prepare and interpret graphs at work, it is also important to have a critical awareness of them as an individual so that you can form your own opinions and make your own decisions.

Where does it fit in?

The subject of Statistics splits into Descriptive Statistics, which is about describing and summarising a set of data, and Inferential Statistics, which uses a sample from a larger set of data to make inferences about the larger set. This part of the book, Describing Data, introduces the main ideas of Descriptive Statistics. In particular, this chapter talks about representing data using pictures and the next chapter (DD2) explains how data can be summarised using numbers.

What do I need to know?

Although you could probably cope with this chapter without a full understanding of Essential Maths, it is desirable and you will need it for the next chapter and subsequent work.

Objectives

After your work on this chapter you should be able to:

● understand the difference between numerical and categorical data;
● calculate frequencies and relative frequencies;
● construct a stem and leaf diagram or histogram of a numerical variable;
● draw a scatter plot of two numerical variables;
● draw a bar chart or pie chart of a categorical variable;
● construct a contingency table or cross-tabulation of two categorical variables including row, column or total percentages;
● be sceptical about published graphs – do they represent the data fairly?

The following numbers show the percentage return on an ordinary share for 23 consecutive months:

| −0.2 | −2.1 | 1.0 | 0.1 | −0.5 | 2.4 | −2.3 | 1.5 | 1.2 | −0.6 | 2.4 | −1.2 | 1.7 |
| −1.3 | −1.2 | 0.9 | 0.5 | 0.1 | −0.1 | 0.3 | −0.4 | 0.5 | 0.9 | | | |

If you were an investor or a financial journalist it would be useful to be able to make some general statements about the returns on this share – in other words to *describe* the returns in some way.

How would you describe these figures? As there are only two lines of numbers it is perhaps easy to see that the largest is 2.4 and the smallest is −2.3, but this doesn't give any idea of how the numbers are spread out or *distributed* between this maximum and minimum.

The *distribution* of a set of data can be described in two general ways. We can draw pictures of the data (graphical methods), but also we can calculate quantities that summarise the distribution (numerical methods).

We consider graphical methods in this chapter and numerical methods in Chapter DD2.

We will start by considering data that are numerical or *quantitative*; that is, they record a measurement, such as the percentage return on an ordinary share above.

1 Frequencies and histograms

Frequencies and relative frequencies

To 'draw a picture' of a set of numerical data we must first split an interval enclosing the smallest and largest values into several non-overlapping classes of equal width. For the ordinary share return data the classes could be:

–3 to less than –2
–2 to less than –1
–1 to less than 0
 0 to less than 1
 1 to less than 2
 2 to less than 3

We can then go through the data and count up how many values lie in each class. These counts are called *frequencies*. For the returns data we obtain the following frequencies:

Class	Working	Frequency
–3 to under –2	11	2
–2 to under –1	111	3
–1 to under 0	1111	4
0 to under 1	~~++++~~ 111	8
1 to under 2	1111	4
2 to under 4	11	2
	Total:	23

The proportion of the data that falls in a class is called the *relative frequency* of that class. We calculate the relative frequencies by dividing the frequencies by the total number of items of data.

The frequencies and relative frequencies of the ordinary share returns data are shown below.

Class	Working	Frequency	Relative Frequency
–3 to under –2	11	2	$\frac{2}{23}$
–2 to under –1	111	3	$\frac{3}{23}$
–1 to under 0	1111	4	$\frac{4}{23}$
0 to under 1	~~++++~~ 111	8	$\frac{8}{23}$
1 to under 2	1111	4	$\frac{4}{23}$
2 to under 3	11	2	$\frac{2}{23}$
	Total:	23	1

Notice that the relative frequencies total 1.

Histograms
Either the frequencies or the relative frequencies can be shown pictorially in a *histogram*. Figure 1.1 shows a histogram of the frequencies of the returns data.

Now that we have a pictorial representation it is immediately apparent that the distribution of the returns lies between –3 and +3, and its histogram has an inverted U-shape.

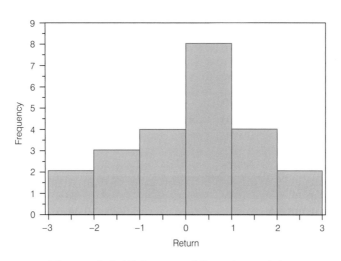

Figure 1.1 Histogram of the returns data.

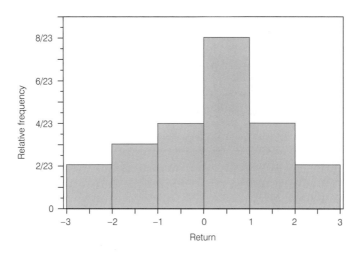

Figure 1.2 Relative frequency histogram of the returns data.

A histogram of the relative frequencies has exactly the same shape as a histogram of the frequencies. The only difference is in the labelling of the vertical axis. Figure 1.2 shows the relative frequency histogram of the returns data. Notice that only the vertical scale differs from Figure 1.1.

You should be aware that technically it is the *area* of each column of a histogram that represents the frequency or relative frequency and *not* the height of the column. Usually, the class widths are all equal, so both the height and the area of the columns represent the frequencies.

Check this

The following data gives the time in days it takes a manufacturing firm to supply price quotes to Internet customers. Work out the frequencies and relative frequencies, draw a histogram and *then* check whether you agree with what we've done. Try classes of 0 to under 2.5, 2.5 to under 5 and so on.

2.36	5.73	6.60	10.05	5.13	1.88	2.52	2.00	4.69
1.91	6.75	3.92	3.46	2.64	3.63	3.44	9.49	4.90
7.45	20.23	3.91	1.70	16.29	5.52	1.44		

Solution:

Class	Frequency	Relative frequency
0 to under 2.5	6	6/25 = 0.24
2.5 to under 5	9	9/25 = 0.36
5 to under 7.5	6	6/25 = 0.24
7.5 to under 10	1	1/25 = 0.04
10 to under 12.5	1	1/25 = 0.04
12.5 to under 15	0	0
15 to under 17.5	1	1/25 = 0.04
17.5 to under 20	0	0
20 to under 22.5	1	1/25 = 0.04
	25	1.0

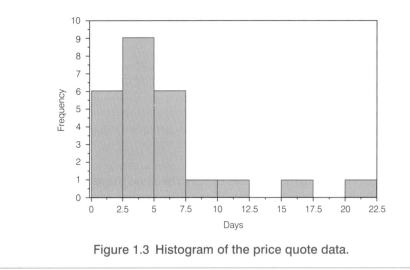

Figure 1.3 Histogram of the price quote data.

From the histogram in Figure 1.3 we can see that it is most common for price quotes to take only a few days but occasionally some may take much longer. As a result, the histogram of the price quotes does *not* have a peak in the centre but is peaked on one side. We say that the distribution is *skewed*. When the peak is on the right we say that the distribution is *skewed to the left* and when the peak is on the left, as here, the distribution is *skewed to the right*. When there is no obvious skew the distribution is roughly *symmetric*.

Choosing class widths

The data below shows the average salaries ($) of faculty in institutions of higher education in the USA for the 1982–3 academic year for the public and private sector and for each of the 50 states and the District of Columbia. * denotes that the value was not available.

State	Public	Private	State	Public	Private	State	Public	Private
1	23477	18476	18	24972	19651	35	25277	18266
2	41378	23067	19	24946	24332	36	27812	24340
3	30027	23529	20	23490	23924	37	27146	23500
4	22993	20247	21	27424	27349	38	25059	23635
5	31998	31218	22	27937	30598	39	27641	27238
6	26198	26092	23	28737	22923	40	26851	29509
7	29269	30129	24	28135	24262	41	24195	18971
8	27599	17383	25	*	17241	42	22272	18082
9	28459	28626	26	24675	23745	43	24384	23267
10	25290	23620	27	25979	19052	44	27257	25568
11	25966	19815	28	24224	21651	45	27280	19006
12	28576	18297	29	29121	*	46	25375	22547
13	24182	20475	30	23345	25831	47	25638	22105
14	26637	27898	31	29851	29760	48	26852	24016
15	25672	24868	32	27105	17784	49	22307	18916
16	26334	21960	33	30074	28741	50	27547	23889
17	25473	17532	34	24528	20110	51	29129	*

The frequencies and relative frequencies of the *public* sector faculty salaries data produced by some computer software are shown in Figure 1.4a. We used a different computer package from the earlier histograms – and this software uses 'count' instead of 'frequency' and 'per cent' instead of 'relative frequency'.

X_1: public

Bar:	From: (≥)	To: (<)	Count:	Per cent:	
1	22000	24000	6	11.764706%	
2	24000	26000	17	33.333333%	← Mode
3	26000	28000	15	29.411765%	
4	28000	30000	8	15.686275%	
5	30000	32000	3	5.882353%	
6	32000	34000	0	0%	
7	34000	36000	0	0%	
8	36000	38000	0	0%	
9	38000	40000	0	0%	
10	40000	42000	1	1.960784%	

Figure 1.4a Frequencies of public sector faculty salaries.

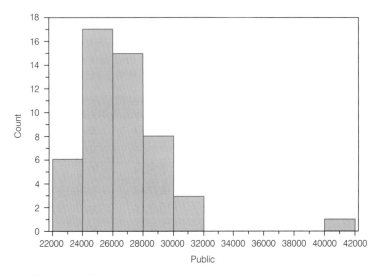

Figure 1.4b   Histogram of public sector faculty salaries.

A histogram of the frequencies is shown in Figure 1.4b. The distribution appears to be skewed to the right. The class width used for the public sector faculty salaries data in Figures 1.4a and 1.4b is 2000. A histogram of the same data in which the class width is only 1000 is shown in Figure 1.5.

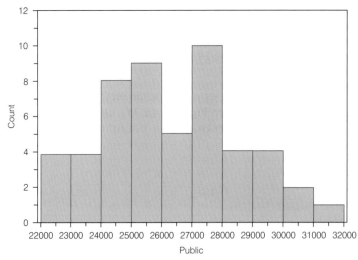

Figure 1.5   Histogram of the public sector faculty salaries data with class width 1000.

The histograms in Figures 1.4b and 1.5 are both useful in that they show the distribution of the data clearly. However, if a histogram has too many classes because the class width is too small we can lose sight of the overall shape of the distribution. For instance, the histogram in Figure 1.6a, of the ordinary share returns data with a class width of only 0.25, looks rather odd as lots of classes have very low frequencies.

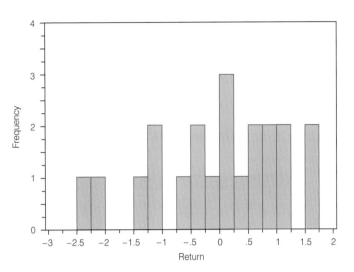

Figure 1.6a Silly histogram: too many classes for this number of data.

At the other extreme, if the class width is too large, a histogram can have too few classes. A histogram of the returns data with a class width of 2 so that there are only 3 classes is shown in Figure 1.6b. The shape of the distribution is lost because all the data is lumped together.

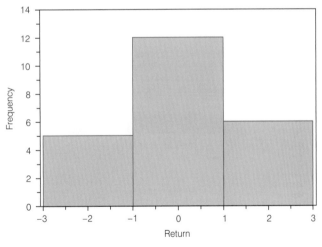

Figure 1.6b Silly histogram: too few classes for this number of data.

As a rule, when constructing histograms we suggest selecting the class width so that there are *between 5 and 20 classes*, although more classes would be acceptable for larger data sets.

Using a computer

We suggest at this point you re-read the part of the Introduction to *Describing Data,* which we called 'Using a computer' (p. 255). In most statistical programs, the user must first enter the data into the computer as a grid of values, often called the worksheet. Each column of the worksheet has a label (for instance SPSS's columns are var00001, var00002 ... etc.) , although users can change the labels to meaningful names if they wish.

Most statistical software draws histograms, although the terminology may vary slightly. The data is usually entered into a column of the worksheet and a simple command or two produces a histogram.

The SPSS command is

Graphs > Histogram

as shown in the screenshot below.

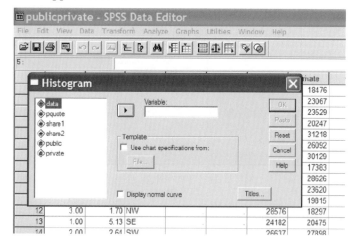

A dialog box will then appear as follows.

At a minimum the user must enter the column name or number containing the data into the Variable box. This can be done by highlighting that column in the list of all available columns e.g. **data** on the diagram above, and clicking the arrow in the centre of the box.

Most software will choose a default class width for you using a set of rules that will usually, but not always, give a useful histogram. However, if you wish to override this choice and make a number of detailed specifications about the graph you should use the SPSS command

Graphs > Interactive > Histogram

To generate frequencies and a histogram in Excel you will have to enter the data in one range of cells. Excel will choose the class widths for you but if you want to specify them yourself you must enter the boundaries of each class in ascending order in another range of cells (Excel calls these *bins*). The command

Tools > Data Analysis

gives you a list of statistical commands. If the command is not on the menu then you need to activate it beforehand by choosing **Tools > Add-Ins** and ticking **Analysis ToolPak**. When you select **Histogram** you will be shown a dialog box. Enter the range of cells where the data are and, if you want, the range of cells where the *bins* are. Excel will give the frequencies. To produce a histogram as well, tick **Chart Output**.

WORK CARD 1

1. A doctor's surgery studies the length of time patients arriving with a request for emergency service have to wait before treatment. The following data (waiting times in minutes) were collected for all emergencies over a typical one-month period.

    2, 5, 10, 12, 4, 4, 5, 17, 11, 8, 9, 8, 12, 21, 6, 8, 7, 13, 18, 3

    Tabulate the frequencies and relative frequencies and then display these data in a suitable manner. What comment can you make about the distribution?

2. The data below shows the ages of a sample of managers from Urban Child Care Centres in the United States:

42	30	26	36	32	32	34	26	57	50
30	55	58	30	37	58	50	64	30	52
53	49	40	33	30	43	47	46	49	32
50	61	40	31	32	30	31	40	40	60
52	74	28	37	23	29	35	43	25	54

    Type the data into a computer package (saving the file for future work) and obtain a histogram. Is the distribution of the data skewed or not? Have a 'play' with the software by producing a series of histograms with different class widths for this data. Look at the histograms with a critical eye to see which ones give a meaningful picture of the shape of the distribution and which don't.

Solution hints:

1. A class width of 3–5 gives a reasonable histogram. For a class width of 5 the classes could be: under 5, 5–9 inclusive, 10–14 inclusive, 15–19 inclusive, 20–24 inclusive. The data has more lower values than higher values and so is skewed.

2. The distribution is skewed to the right. As the class width increases there will be fewer and fewer classes until all the data is lumped together and the histogram doesn't tell you very much at all. A very small class width will mean that many classes have only 0, 1 or 2 values and again, the shape of the data is lost.

1. How much do executives of some of the largest corporations get paid? Business Week (1 May 1989) reported executive compensation for 1988, including salary and bonus. The data reported in thousands of dollars for 25 chairpersons and chief executive officers are as follows:

Boeing	846	Delta Airlines	457
Whirlpool	563	Chrysler	1466
Bank of Boston	1200	Coca-Cola	2164
Sherwin-Williams	746	DuPont	1611
Bristol-Myers	824	Motorola	824
General Mills	1310	Marriott	1007
Sara Lee	1367	Honeywell	575
Eastman Kodak	1252	Exxon	1354
Apple Computers	2479	Scott Paper	1238
Bausch & Lomb	927	CBS	1253
K Mart	925	AT&T	1284
Goodyear	1279	Philip Morris	1660
Teledyne	860		

Display these data in a suitable manner.

2. A financial analyst is interested in the amount of resources spent by computer hardware and software companies on research and development (R&D). She samples 30 such firms and calculates the percentage of total revenue they spent on R&D in the previous year. The results are given below.

Percentage of revenues spent on research and development

Company	(%)	Company	(%)	Company	(%)
1	6.0	11	7.9	21	8.0
2	10.4	12	6.8	22	7.7
3	10.5	13	7.4	23	7.4
4	9.0	14	9.5	24	6.5
5	7.3	15	8.1	25	9.5
6	6.6	16	13.5	26	8.2
7	6.9	17	9.9	27	6.9
8	8.2	18	6.9	28	7.2
9	7.1	19	11.1	29	8.2
10	8.1	20	8.2	30	6.7

Summarise these data using a computer by producing:

a. the frequencies

b. the relative frequencies (if possible)

c. a histogram.

Use the histogram to deduce the proportion of companies that spend 9% or more on R&D.

2 Stem and leaf diagrams

The *stem and leaf diagram* is a quick and useful way of displaying numerical data. It has the advantage, over a histogram, of retaining every value.

Suppose we had the (very small) data set 42, 59, 35, 25, 32. Each number contains so many 'tens' and so many 'units'. For instance, 59 comprises 5 'tens' and 9 'units'. We say that the *stem* of the number is the 5 and the *leaf* is the 9. On a stem and leaf diagram each row contains the numbers with a particular stem. A stem and leaf diagram of this data set is

```
2 |  5
3 |  5   2
4 |  2
5 |  9
↑     ↑
stem  leaf
```

Here, the stem unit is 10 and the leaf unit is 1. The choice of stem and leaf units depends on the magnitude of the data. For the returns data:

0.2	–2.1	1.0	0.1	–0.5	2.4	–2.3	1.5	1.2	–0.6	2.4	–1.2	1.7
–1.3	–1.2	0.9	0.5	0.1	–0.1	0.3	–0.4	0.5	0.9			

it is natural to choose a stem unit of 1 and a leaf unit of 0.1. A stem and leaf diagram for the returns data is given below.

```
–2 | 1   3
–1 | 2   3   2
–0 | 5   6   1   4
 0 | 2   1   9   5   1   3   5   9
 1 | 0   5   2   7
 2 | 4   4
```

Notice that by giving an equal amount of space to each leaf value, we have produced a histogram. However, a stem and leaf diagram gives more information than a histogram because the leaf tells us where, within each class, the data lies. It will also be useful when we need to place the data in ascending (or descending) order in Chapter DD2, Section 1, to calculate something called the median.

> ### Check this
>
> The data below show the percentage US unemployment rates for 39 consecutive years. Construct a stem and leaf diagram of the data.
>
> | 3.3 | 3.0 | 2.9 | 5.6 | 4.4 | 4.1 | 4.3 | 6.8 | 5.5 | 5.5 |
> |-----|-----|-----|-----|-----|-----|-----|-----|-----|-----|
> | 6.7 | 5.6 | 5.6 | 5.2 | 4.5 | 3.8 | 3.9 | 3.6 | 3.5 | 4.9 |
> | 5.9 | 5.6 | 4.9 | 5.6 | 8.5 | 7.7 | 7.0 | 6.0 | 5.8 | 7.1 |
> | 7.5 | 9.5 | 9.5 | 7.4 | 7.1 | 6.9 | 6.1 | 5.4 | 5.2 | |
>
> **Solution:** Taking a stem unit of 1 and a leaf unit of 0.1 gives

```
2 | 9
3 | 3  0  8  9  6  5
4 | 4  1  3  5  9  9
5 | 6  5  5  6  6  2  9  6  6  8  4  2
6 | 8  7  0  9  1
7 | 7  0  1  5  4  1
8 | 5
9 | 5  5
```

Choosing stem and leaf units

A stem and leaf diagram does not always record the data precisely. For instance, if the data were 102.1, 97.3, 76.7 ... the corresponding entries in a stem and leaf diagram with stem unit 10 and leaf unit 1 would be

```
  ⋮ |
  7 |  7
  8 |
  9 |  7
 10 |  2
  ⋮ |
  ↑      ↑
stem    leaf unit is 1
unit is 10
```

As the leaf unit is 1 and the data was given to 1 decimal place, the diagram records the data rounded to the nearest whole number.

Sometimes, when the natural choice of stem and leaf units is made, the resulting diagram is not very useful. For example, a stem and leaf diagram of the price quote data taking a stem unit of 10 and a leaf unit of 1 is

```
0 | 2 6 7 5 2 3 2 5 2 7 4 3 3 4 3 9 5 7 4 2 6 1
1 | 1 6
2 | 0
```

which conveys very little information about the distribution of the data as there are too few classes. (Alternatively, if we chose a stem unit of 1 and a leaf unit of 0.1 we would need 20 classes, which would be too many for only 25 data items.)

To overcome problems like this we can allow more than one row for each stem unit. For instance, for the price quote data we could allow two rows for each stem. The first row would contain data with leaf values 0–4 and the second row data with leaf values 5–9 as we show below.

```
0 | 2 2 3 2 2 4 3 3 4 3 4 2 1
0 | 6 7 5 5 7 9 5 7 6
1 | 1
1 | 6
2 | 0
```

Whilst this is an improvement and shows us that there are more data at the lower end of the stem = 0 class than at the upper, there are still only 5 classes. We could enlarge the number of classes further by allowing 5 rows of the stem and leaf diagram for each stem value. The first row would contain leaf values 0 and 1, the second, 2 and 3, third, 4 and 5 and so on.

Using software

When using software, unless you specify otherwise, the number of rows for each stem value will be chosen for you. For instance, SPSS's

Analyze > Descriptive Statistics > Explore...

command automatically assigns 1 row to each stem value for the price quote data and produces the following result:

The shape of the distribution is now much clearer. It is skewed to the right with a peak at about 3.

You should be aware that SPSS (and some other software) does not round data to the nearest leaf value – it truncates any extra digits. For instance, the lowest four numbers in the price quote data were 1.44, 1.70, 1.88 and 1.91. If we rounded them to one decimal place we would obtain 1.4, 1.7, 1.9, 1.9, but SPSS truncates them to 1.4, 1.7, 1.8, 1.9 and they are all shown in the first row of the stem and leaf diagram above.

SPSS's stem and leaf output for the public school faculty salaries from Section 1 is shown below. Notice that the stem width is 1000.

1. Draw a stem and leaf diagram for the age of child care managers data in question 2 of **Work card 1**, which we repeat below.

42	30	26	36	32	32	34	26	57	50
30	55	58	30	37	58	50	64	30	52
53	49	40	33	30	43	47	46	49	32
50	61	40	31	32	30	31	40	40	60
52	74	28	37	23	29	35	43	25	54

2. Draw a stem and leaf diagram for the doctor's surgery waiting time data in question 1 of **Work card 1**, which are repeated below. Make sure that you choose a suitable leaf unit.

   2, 5, 10, 12, 4, 4, 5, 17, 11, 8, 9, 8, 12, 21, 6, 8, 7, 13, 18, 3

3. Cash takings (in £s) at a coffee shop for a typical month of 24 working days are given below:

732.82	814.30	652.10	512.40	732.21	710.01
660.12	732.20	659.10	302.10	242.40	459.67
555.30	620.31	446.20	770.40	900.21	505.82
550.89	661.36	500.21	600.20	810.12	312.87

   Draw a stem and leaf diagram of the data.

4. Enter the data from questions 1, 2 and 3 into a computer and draw a stem and leaf diagram for each set of data. Does the software's choices of leaf unit agree with yours? If not, how does your diagram compare with the computer's? Maybe both are reasonable?

Solution guidelines

1. The management data suggests a leaf unit of 1, and a stem and leaf diagram with one row per stem unit gives 6 classes.

2. For the doctor's surgery data a leaf unit of 1 is sensible. However, you will need to use two rows to a stem unit otherwise there will only be three classes.

3. Here, some precision is lost as the obvious stem unit is 100. One row to each stem unit gives 8 classes which is reasonable for a sample size of 24. The distribution peaks at the stem value of 6 and is more or less symmetric.

1. Choosing a suitable leaf unit draw a stem and leaf diagram by hand for the executive salary data in **Assessment 1**, question 1. Keep your work as it will help you to order the data for later work. The data are

846	457	563	1466	
1200	2164	746	1611	
824	824	1310	1007	
1367	575	1252	1354	
2479	1238	927	1253	
925	1284	1279	1660	860

2. The following data shows the total subscriptions (in £1000) received by a trade union by direct debit from its members' bank accounts over a 15-month period. Draw a suitable stem and leaf diagram.

77.063	77.112	77.100	77.127	77.101
77.112	77.121	77.105	77.102	77.101
77.102	77.130	77.109	77.091	77.103

3. Use a computer to produce a stem and leaf diagram of the R&D data of **Assessment 1**, question 2, repeated below.

6.0	10.4	10.5	9.0	7.3
6.6	6.9	8.2	7.1	8.1
7.9	6.8	7.4	9.5	8.1
13.5	9.9	6.9	11.1	8.2
8.0	7.7	7.4	6.5	9.5
8.2	6.9	7.2	8.2	6.7

3 Pictures of one categorical variable: bar charts and pie charts

Bar charts

The data we have used so far have been numerical or *quantitative* so to draw a histogram or stem and leaf diagram we had to split the data into classes. Sometimes, however, the data are not numerical, but they record an attribute or a quality, and so are in classes or *categories* already. We call such data *qualitative* or *categorical* data.

Some examples of categorical data are:

● The nationalities of students in your maths class: Australian, Malaysian, Canadian, British
● The types of car driven by staff at your university: Ford, Chevrolet, Buick
● Answers to the following question in a survey:

Do you think that fuel for private motoring should be taxed more heavily than at present?

Yes
No
Don't know

● Preferred alcoholic beverage of a bar's customers: wine, beer, gin, vodka.

Like quantitative data the number of data items in each class are called the frequencies and the proportion of data items in each class are the relative frequencies. Consider the following example.

An oil company wants to open a new service station to serve the resident population of a city. There are four possible sites which lie in the NW, NE, SW and SE quarters of the city respectively. In an initial survey the company stop 30 motorists in the city centre and ask them which site they would be most likely to use.

The results of the survey are:

Customer	Quarter	Customer	Quarter
1	NW	16	NW
2	NE	17	NE
3	SE	18	NW
4	NW	19	SE
5	NW	20	SW
6	SW	21	NW
7	NE	22	SW
8	NE	23	SE
9	NW	24	SW
10	SW	25	NW
11	SW	26	SW
12	NW	27	SE
13	SE	28	SE
14	SW	29	NW
15	NW	30	NE

The frequencies and relative frequencies are:

Quarter	Frequency	Relative frequency
NE	5	0.167
NW	11	0.367
SE	6	0.200
SW	8	0.267
	30	1.000

Categorical data can also be reported as percentages as shown below.

Quarter	Frequency	Percentage
NE	5	16.7
NW	11	36.7
SE	6	20.0
SW	8	26.7
Total	30	100

It is important when reporting percentages or relative frequencies that you always include the number of data items they are based on. Reading that 43% of students admit to copying coursework may shock if the percentage is based on a large research study of 12 000 students but carries much less weight if it is based on a small sample of only 7 students.

A *bar chart* is merely a graph with a bar for each category. In Figure 1.7 the height of each bar shows the percentage of the data items in each category but the same picture could equally well represent the frequencies or relative frequencies if the vertical axis was labelled appropriately.

SPSS is particularly good at dealing with categorical data.

Bar charts can be produced in SPSS using

Graphs > Bar

Usually a whole number is assigned to each category name e.g. 1 = NE, 2 = NW, 3 = SE and 4 = SW. (This is done in the variable view window in the column headed 'Values'.) Once the variable has been set up in this way, the data can be input (in the data view window) as a number (e.g. 1, 2, 3 or 4) rather than a category name (e.g. NE, NW, SE or SW).

In order to produce the graph in Figure 1.7 you will need to define 'Simple chart where Data in Chart Are Summaries for groups of cases' and specify that bars represent % of cases in the subdialog box.

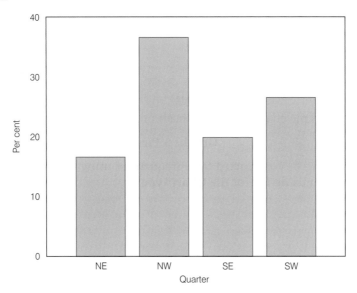

Figure 1.7

A great variety of options are available. For instance, the frequencies or percentage of more than one set of data can be shown side by side or stacked one on top of the other on the same graph. Further specifications can be made if the graph is produced using

Graphs > Interactive > Bar

In Excel the **Chart** command on the **Insert** menu enables many types of graph to be drawn. Select **Column** from **Chart type** to draw a bar chart.

You will need to have the categories in one column and the frequencies in another.

Pie charts

Another way of presenting categorical data that you are bound to have seen in newspapers and company brochures is the *pie chart*. The idea is simple. The whole of the data set is represented by a circle – the pie – which is divided into slices. The size of each slice reflects the number of data items in the corresponding category.

A pie chart of the service station data is shown in Figure 1.8.

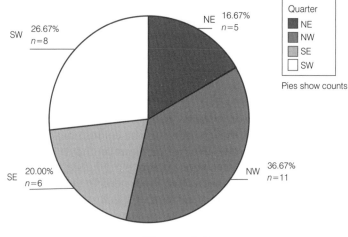

Figure 1.8

This was produced in SPSS by

Graphs > Interactive > Pie > Simple

although a less detailed pie chart could have been produced using

Graphs > Pie

In Excel pie charts can be constructed from frequencies using the chart menu as described above for bar charts but using **Pie** for the **Chart type**.

WORK CARD 3

1. What sort of cars are most often purchased by women? Assume that the data shown below were collected from a sample of 50 women who made a recent purchase of one of the top five selling automobiles.

Honda Accord	Ford Taurus	Honda Accord	Honda Accord
Ford Escort	Ford Taurus	Honda Accord	Ford Escort
Honda Accord	Ford Taurus	Honda Accord	Honda Accord
Ford Escort	Chevrolet Cavalier	Hyundai Excel	Chevrolet Cavalier
Ford Taurus	Ford Escort	Chevrolet Cavalier	Ford Escort
Hyundai Excel	Hyundai Excel	Ford Escort	Chevrolet Cavalier
Ford Escort	Honda Accord	Chevrolet Cavalier	Hyundai Excel
Ford Escort	Honda Accord	Chevrolet Cavalier	Ford Escort
Ford Escort	Ford Taurus	Honda Accord	Ford Taurus
Hyundai Excel	Chevrolet Cavalier	Ford Escort	Chevrolet Cavalier
Chevrolet Cavalier	Hyundai Excel	Ford Escort	Hyundai Excel
Ford Escort	Hyundai Excel	Ford Taurus	Ford Escort
Honda Accord	Ford Taurus		

Display this data in an appropriate way.

Solution:

1. Use a bar chart as the data is qualitative. The frequencies are Ford Escort 14, Ford Taurus 8, Chevrolet Cavalier 9, Honda Accord 11, Hyundai Excel 8.

ASSESSMENT 3

1. The following question was asked in a survey.

How often do you buy goods that conserve the environment; for instance, recycled paper?

All the time
Sometimes
Only when they are no more expensive
Rarely
Never

The following answers to the question were received from a sample of 40 respondents.

All the time
Only when they are no more expensive
Sometimes
Only when they are no more expensive
Only when they are no more expensive

Sometimes
Sometimes
Only when they are no more expensive
Rarely
All the time
Sometimes
Sometimes
Rarely
Rarely
Sometimes
Only when they are no more expensive
Only when they are no more expensive
Rarely
Never
Sometimes
Rarely
Rarely
All the time
Sometimes
Never
Only when they are no more expensive
Rarely
Rarely
All the time
All the time
Sometimes
Never
All the time
Sometimes
Only when they are no more expensive
Only when they are no more expensive
Sometimes
Rarely
Never
Never

Display the results in a suitable manner.

2. Conduct your own survey to investigate the proportion of people who are the eldest, second from eldest, third from eldest, etc. in a family. Ask a sample of 20 or more students what their position in the family is and display the results in a sensible manner. What conclusions do you draw?

4 **More graphs for numerical data**

Numerical data that occur in pairs: scatter plots

The following data gives the percentage returns on 2 ordinary shares for 9 consecutive months.

Month	Share 1	Share 2
1	1.4	1.3
2	1.2	1.4
3	2.2	1.4
4	1.5	1.4
5	1.0	1.5
6	1.2	1.2
7	1.8	1.5
8	2.5	1.5
9	2.0	1.5

Notice that the data come in pairs – a pair for each month (1.4,1.3), (1.2,1.4) and so on.

The most effective way of presenting paired data like this is to plot the pairs as co-ordinates on a graph. This is called a *scatter* plot. A scatter plot of the share return data is given in Figure 1.9.

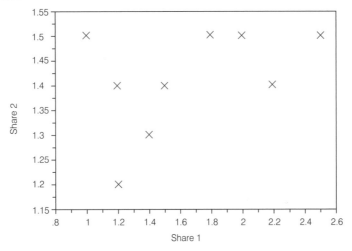

Figure 1.9 Scatter plot of the returns of Share 1 and Share 2.

This shows us that when the first share's return is large the second share's return tends to be large as well, so we can say that the returns on the two shares appear to be *correlated*. 'Correlated' here means more or less the same as it does in common use except that, as we will see in Chapter S3, in Statistics it is defined a little more precisely.

Scatter plots can be obtained in SPSS by placing the pairs in two columns and using

Graphs > Scatter ...

As usual further specifications are possible.

Scatter plots can be produced in Excel using **Insert > Chart** and selecting **Chart type XY (Scatter)**.

Sequential data: time series plots

Open any newspaper and there is likely to be a graph showing how some economic or social factor has changed in the last few months or years. The graph usually has time (months or years) on the horizontal axis and the values of interest on the vertical axis as shown in Figure 1.10 for some company sales data.

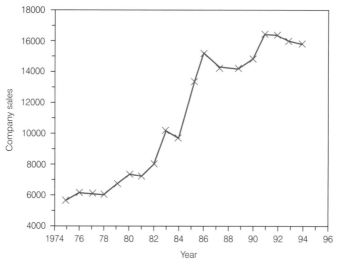

Figure 1.10 Company sales, 1974–94.

Such data is usually recorded at equal intervals of time – daily, weekly, monthly, etc. and so is called a *time series*. The crucial thing about time series data is that the sequence of it must be preserved. We consider time series in more detail in Chapter S4. A display like Figure 1.10 is usually called a *time series plot*.

A time series plot of a column of data can be obtained in SPSS using

Graphs > Sequence ...

In Excel, time series plots can be constructed using the chart menu, as described above for histograms, and selecting **Line** for **Chart type**.

1. Is there a relationship between the amount a corporation spends on advertising and its sales volume? The data below shows data for 10 randomly selected months. Use software to produce a graph that begins to investigate this. The data are given below.

WORK CARD 4 (CONTINUED)

Month	Advertising expenditure ($10,000)	Sales volume ($10,000)
1	1.2	101
2	0.8	92
3	1.0	110
4	1.3	120
5	0.7	90
6	0.8	82
7	1.0	93
8	0.6	75
9	0.9	91
10	1.1	105
11	0.7	85

2. The data given below is quarterly primary fuel consumption in the UK from 1965–85. Use statistical software to obtain a time series plot of the data. What does it tell you about fuel consumption?

| Year | Quarter | | | |
	1	2	3	4
1965	874	679	616	816
1966	866	700	603	814
1967	843	719	594	819
1968	906	703	634	844
1969	952	745	635	871
1970	981	759	674	900
1971	957	760	649	891
1972	915	780	683	949
1973	995	809	705	970
1974	881	781	706	954
1975	932	752	630	883
1976	959	752	654	933
1977	980	796	691	917
1978	983	979	690	920
1979	1076	830	713	938
1980	1001	759	969	871
1981	919	720	633	900
1982	927	704	630	857

WORK CARD 4 (CONTINUED)

	Quarter			
Year	1	2	3	4
1983	912	725	635	847
1984	938	692	925	946
1985	974	746	670	874

Solution:

1. Yes, a scatter plot shows that as advertising expenditure increases so does sales volume.

2. A time series plot (see Chapter S4, Figure 4.3) shows that the data are clearly seasonal – more energy is consumed in the winter quarter and less in the summer.

ASSESSMENT 4

1. Obtain a time series plot of the following values of the Dow Jones Index for 78 consecutive days (row-wise) and comment.

110.94	110.69	110.43	110.56
110.75	110.84	110.46	110.56
110.46	110.05	109.60	109.31
109.31	109.25	109.02	108.54
108.77	109.02	109.44	109.38
109.53	109.89	110.56	110.56
110.72	111.23	111.48	111.58
111.90	112.19	112.06	111.96
111.68	111.36	111.42	112.00
112.22	112.70	113.15	114.36
114.65	115.06	115.86	116.40
116.44	116.88	118.07	118.51
119.28	119.79	119.70	119.28
119.66	120.14	120.97	121.13
121.55	121.96	122.26	123.79
124.11	124.14	123.37	123.02
122.86	123.02	123.11	123.05
123.05	122.83	123.18	122.67
122.73	122.86	122.67	122.09
122.00	121.23		

5 Categorical data that come in pairs

Contingency tables

Sometimes we are given categorical data that come in pairs. For example, the data below shows some data from a survey of 310 graduates six months after leaving education. For each graduate we have two pieces of categorical data: (a) whether the graduate was male or female (gender); and (b) whether he or she is in a permanent job, temporary job or unemployed (employment status).

Graduate no.	Gender	Employment status
1	MALE	UNEMP
2	MALE	TEMP
3	FEMALE	TEMP
4	FEMALE	PERM
5	FEMALE	TEMP
6	MALE	PERM
7	MALE	PERM
⋮	⋮	⋮

As gender can take two different values and employment status three, only six possible pairs of values are possible and we can summarise the data with a list of the frequencies of each pair. The frequencies for all the graduates are given below.

Gender	Employment status	Frequency
MALE	PERM	170
MALE	TEMP	28
MALE	UNEMP	20
FEMALE	PERM	57
FEMALE	TEMP	27
FEMALE	UNEMP	8

Whilst this list summarises the data completely it does not make it easy to draw conclusions about the relationship between gender and employment status or even each one individually. It is therefore more usual to display the frequencies in a *contingency table* or *cross tabulation* as shown below.

		Employment Status		
		Permanent	Temporary	Unemployed
Gender	Male	170	28	20
	Female	57	27	8

Notice that each row corresponds to a category of gender and each column to a category of employment status and the numbers in the cells of the table are the frequencies of the corresponding combination of gender and employment status. For example, of the 310 graduates, 170 are male and in permanent employment whereas 27 are female and in temporary employment.

It is usual to include row and column totals as follows.

	Permanent	Temporary	Unemployed	Total
Male	170	28	20	218
Female	57	27	8	92
Total	227	55	28	310

Notice that the row totals give the frequencies of each category of gender and the column totals the frequencies of each category of employment status.

The frequencies alone, however, don't tell us a great deal and we are usually more interested in the *proportions* or *percentages* of the data that have various qualities or attributes.

Reporting percentages

Three different types of percentage can be calculated depending on our reasons for looking at the data.

The table from the survey of graduates is repeated below but now each cell contains the percentage of *all* 310 graduates that fall in that cell. For instance, the percentage in the Female–Temporary cell is $100 \times 27/ 310 = 8.7\%$. The percentages are usually enclosed in brackets to distinguish them from the frequencies.

	Permanent	Temporary	Unemployed	Total
Male	170 (54.8%)	28 (9.0%)	20 (6.5%)	218 (70.3%)
Female	57 (18.4%)	27 (8.7%)	8 (2.6%)	92 (29.7%)
Total	227 (73.2%)	55 (17.7%)	28 (9.0%)	310 (100.0%)

We can now easily see, for instance, that over half the graduates are male and in permanent work (54.8%) or that only 2.6% are female and unemployed. Notice that the percentages in the cells add up to 100%. Also, the percentages associated with the row totals give the proportions of male and female graduates and the percentages associated with the column totals are those for each type of employment.

Now suppose we want to compare males with females. This amounts to comparing *rows* of the table and we need *row percentages*. A row percentage is the percentage of the items *in the row* that are in that cell, so to calculate row percentages we divide the frequency in each cell by the corresponding *row* total. For example, the row percentage in the Female–Unemployed cell is $100 \times 8/92 = 8.7\%$. It means that 8.7% of females are unemployed.

Check this

Without 'cheating' by looking below, use the frequencies from the table above to calculate the row percentage of the Male–Unemployed cell.

Solution:
20 graduates are in the Male–Unemployed cell out of a total of 218 male workers so the percentage required is $100 \times 20/218 = 9.2\%$.
   The complete table of row percentages is shown below.

Row percentages

	Permanent	Temporary	Unemployed	Total
Male	170 (78.0%)	28 (12.8%)	20 (9.2%)	218 (100.0%)
Female	57 (62.0%)	27 (29.3%)	8 (8.7%)	92 (100.0%)
Total	227 (73.2%)	55 (17.7%)	28 (9.0%)	310 (100.0%)

It is now clear that the percentage unemployed is similar for males and females (9.2% compared to 8.7%), but that a much greater proportion of females than males are in temporary work (29.3% compared to 12.8%). Notice that the percentages in each row add up to 100%.

We can compare categories of employment status in an analogous way using *column percentages*. Column percentages are calculated by dividing the frequency in each cell by the *column* total as shown below. Notice that the percentages in each *column* add up to 100%.

Column percentages

	Permanent	Temporary	Unemployed	Total
Male	170 (74.9%)	28 (50.9%)	20 (71.4%)	218 (70.3%)
Female	57 (25.1%)	27 (49.1%)	8 (28.6%)	92 (29.7%)
Total	227 (100.0%)	55 (100.0%)	28 (100.0%)	310 (100.0%)

From the column percentages it is now evident, for instance, that whereas about three-quarters (74.9%) of the permanent workers are male only just over half the temporary workers (50.9%) are male.
   It is quite usual to report only percentages in the cells of a table and omit the frequencies, particularly when space is limited. This is quite acceptable provided that you always include the number of items, usually denoted n, which the percentages are based on. For example, the graduate data might be presented in a research report as follows.

Employment status of graduates six months after graduation %

	n	Permanent	Temporary	Unemployed
Male	218	78.0	12.8	9.2
Female	92	62.0	29.2	8.7
Total	310	73.2	17.7	9.1

On a computer each category will usually have to be entered as a number as described in Section 3, Bar charts and pie charts. Data from the first seven graduates are shown below. The first column or *variable* merely identifies the graduate, the second is their employment status six months after graduation (0 = Permanent job, 1 = Temporary job, 2 = Unemployed) and the third is their gender (0 = Male, 1 = Female).

ID	Employment status	Gender
1	2	0
2	1	0
3	1	1
4	0	1
5	1	1
6	0	0
7	0	0
⋮	⋮	⋮

To compile a table using SPSS select

Analyze > Descriptive Statistics > Crosstabs

Enter the name of the variable you want in the rows and the variable you want in the columns. To obtain percentages as well tick row or column or total percentages under Cells... as required. (SPSS does allow you to have more than one of these, but the resulting table can look rather confused.)

WORK CARD 5

1. An insurance company commissions some market research to investigate whether unskilled, skilled or manual workers are equally likely to have taken out medical insurance. A summary of the data collected from a random sample of 150 workers is shown below.

Type of worker	Medical insurance?	Frequency
Unskilled	No	45
Skilled	No	47
Professional	No	23
Unskilled	Yes	5
Skilled	Yes	13
Professional	Yes	17

Construct a contingency table for these data showing percentages that help to assess whether the different worker groups are equally likely to have taken out medical insurance. Comment on your results.

Solution:

1. As we want to compare worker types we will put worker type in the rows and then calculate row percentages.

	No insurance	Insurance	Total
Unskilled	45 (90.0%)	5 (10.0%)	50 (100.0%)
Skilled	47 (78.3%)	13 (21.7%)	60 (100.0%)
Professional	23 (57.5%)	17 (42.5%)	40 (100.0%)
Total	115 (76.7%)	35 (23.3%)	150

This table makes it clear that 10% of unskilled workers have insurance, rising to 21.7% of skilled workers and 42.5% of professional workers. As workers must have or not have insurance we could display the data as follows.

Percentage of workers with insurance

Unskilled ($n = 50$)   10.0

Skilled ($n = 60$)   21.7

Professional ($n = 40$)   42.5

1. All students registered at a university are eligible to become members of the university sports centre, as are members of university staff and their families. Members use a swipe card to enter the complex, which includes a swimming pool and a gym. A computer system has information on whether members are students, staff or other, and records the number of visits the member makes. It does not, however, have details of the member's age or record which facilities the member uses.

The sports centre's management are interested in patterns of usage for marketing purposes and to report to funding bodies. A questionnaire is sent to a random sample of every 10th member and 304 replies are received. In addition, the number of times the member has visited in the last 3 months is extracted from the computer system.

The file *sportscentre* on the web site contains the status (staff, student or other), gender and age (less than 22, 22–29, 30–49 or 50 and over) of each respondent, the number of visits in the last 3 months, whether they used the pool during that period, and whether they used the gym.

Construct one or more tables to investigate each of the following issues. Comment briefly on your results.

(i) Are males and females equally likely to use the pool?

(ii) Are staff, students and 'other' equally likely to use the pool?

(iii) Is the age distribution of those who have used the pool similar to that of those who haven't?

Use a table to investigate whether the distribution of the number of visits is similar for staff, students and 'other'. Hint: you will have to divide the number of visits into classes.

2. What sort of display would be most suitable for the following data?

(i) The amount of taxation paid by a light engineering company and its annual profit for 20 consecutive years.

(ii) The types of premises occupied by all the small businesses in a town – office, factory, warehouse, etc.

(iii) The salary of a trainee accountant in his/her first year of training at 30 major accountancy firms.

(iv) The number of trainee accountants enrolling for professional examinations each year since 1960.

(v) The number of years of experience and the current salary of a random sample of economists working for a New York bank.

6 Lies, more lies and statistics?

Politicians and journalists are very good at presenting data in a way that is misleading. Whilst this is sometimes deliberate as an attempt to support their views, it can also happen accidentally through ignorance.

As a member of the general public, and certainly as someone who is contemplating a career in business, it is surely a good idea to be sufficiently discerning so that you can spot when you are being duped. So, be critical of data and its presentation – wherever it appears.

To show what can be done by unthinking or unscrupulous writers, have a look at some contrasting displays of the same data.

Check this

Figure 1.11 shows a graph given to sales representatives of a frozen food company at a sales meeting, whereas Figure 1.12 shows a graph published for shareholders in the company's annual report. *Both are based on the same sales figures!* Comment on the differences between the graphs. What message is being relayed to **(i)** the company's reps and **(ii)** the company's shareholders?

Solution:
The second graph (Figure 1.12) shows sales figures over a much longer period – the horizontal axis has a wider range than the first graph (Figure 1.11). So Figure 1.11 highlights the recent very small decline in sales to the sales reps – presumably to frighten them into working harder, whereas Figure 1.12 shows the shareholders a meteoric growth in sales.

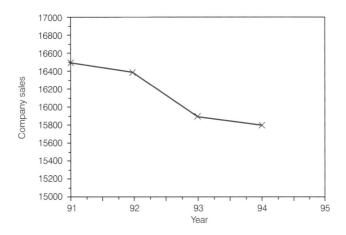

Figure 1.11 Company sales plot shown to sales representatives.

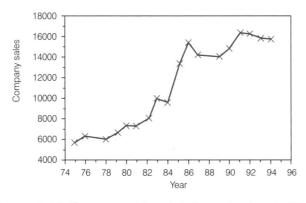

Figure 1.12 Company sales plot shown to shareholders.

Check this

Figures 1.13 and 1.14 both show recent changes in the average salary of a lecturer in Great Britain. The first appears in the government literature and the second in the lecturers' union newsletter. Explain why each publication has chosen that particular graph.

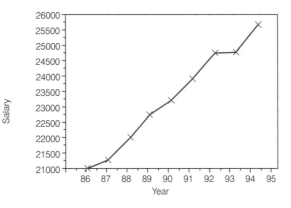

Figure 1.13 Government publication of rise in lecturers' average salaries.

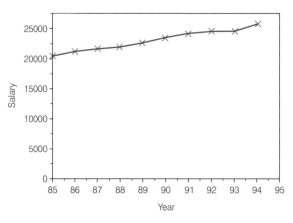

Figure 1.14 Lecturers' union publication of rise in lecturers' average salaries.

Solution:
Figure 1.13 shows a dramatic increase in average salary because the vertical axis only covers the range £21,000 upwards and the relatively small increases in salary have been 'stretched' so that they look large. For the union publication in Figure 1.14 the opposite effect has been achieved by including all salaries from 0 upwards so that the salary increases look small. The government has published the first graph to give the impression that lecturers' salaries have increased vastly, whereas the union showed the second graph to show that salaries have barely increased at all.

Check this

Consider the scatter plots in Figures 1.15 and 1.16 of the returns on two ordinary shares considered in Section 4 and comment on their differences. Compare the plots with Figure 1.9.

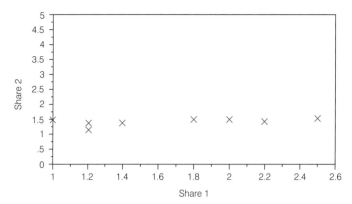

Figure 1.15 Another scatter plot of the returns on Share 1 and Share 2.

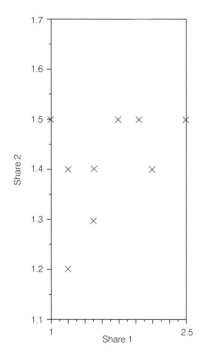

Figure 1.16 Yet another scatter plot of the returns on Share 1 and Share 2.

Solution:
According to Figure 1.15, as the return on Share 1 increases the return on Share 2 remains much the same and there does not appear to be a relationship between the returns of the two shares. In Figure 1.16, however, the vertical axis has smaller range and has been elongated and the horizontal axis shortened to show that when Share 1's return is larger the return on Share 2 tends to be larger as well.

Pictures of data: your toolkit

The **frequencies** of a set of data are the number of values in each class or category

The **relative frequencies** are the proportion of the values within each class

Displays for numerical data

A **histogram** displays the frequencies or relative frequencies in each class

A **stem and leaf diagram** retains information on all the values

A **scatter plot** shows the relationship between pairs of numerical variables

A **time series plot** shows data that occur at regular time intervals

Displays for categorical data

A **bar chart** shows the frequencies of categorical data

A **pie chart** shows the proportion of the data in each category

A **contingency table** or **cross-tabulation** shows the frequencies of two categorical variables. It may include row, column or total percentages.

Further reading: see p. xv

Anderson *et al.* (Statistics) and Mendenhall *et al.* both provide a more comprehensive, more mathematical approach.

Morris includes tips on how to design a table.

Newbold *et al.* is comprehensive and uses Excel.

DD2
Summarising data

Bloom, do me a favor. Move a few decimal points around. You can do it. You're an accountant. You're in a noble profession.

Zero Mostel pleading for some shady accounting from Gene Wilder
in Mel Brooks' *The Producers*

Contexts

What is this chapter about?
This chapter describes how a set of numerical data can be described using a few summary quantities. It explains how to use these quantities to construct a boxplot (a useful means of comparing two or more variables) and how to calculate index numbers.

Why is it useful?
Summary quantities like the mean and standard deviation appear widely in articles and reports as they enable us to make comparisons between different sets of data. In Inferential Statistics, when the data are a sample from a wider population, the summary quantities can be used as *estimates* of the corresponding population quantities.

Where does it fit in?
This chapter, with the last chapter (DD1), forms the basis of Descriptive Statistics, the part of the subject of Statistics that is concerned with describing a set of data. In the last chapter we used graphs to summarise the data but in this chapter we use numerical quantities.

What do I need to know?
You will need to be familiar with Essential Maths and the last chapter (DD1 Pictures of data).

Objectives

After studying this chapter you should be able to:

- calculate the mean, median and, where appropriate, the mode of a set of numerical data;
- understand the relative positions of the median and mean in a symmetric or skewed distribution;
- compute the range, variance, standard deviation and quartiles of a set of data;
- have some concept of the proportion of data that lies within so many standard deviations of the mean (Chebysheff);
- understand the use of the summation sign;
- obtain these quantities using a computer;
- construct some simple indices.

Consider the price quote data from the last chapter which we repeat below:

2.36	5.73	6.60	10.05	5.13	1.88	2.52	2.00	4.69
1.91	6.75	3.92	3.46	2.64	3.63	3.44	9.49	4.90
7.45	20.23	3.91	1.70	16.29	5.52	1.44		

We have already seen how to represent these data graphically – but how would you attempt to describe them *without* the aid of pictures – perhaps using a few summary numbers only? (If you haven't done stats before, take a few moments to consider how you would do this.)

In this chapter we will explain how to calculate some quantities that 'describe' a set of numerical data and consider how useful each of these is.

These quantities fall into two broad types. Some measure where the centre of the data is, and the others measure how spread out or dispersed it is. We will start by looking at ways of measuring the 'centre' of a set of data.

1 The centre of a set of data

Samples and populations

As the price quote data is for 25 quotes only it is a *sample* from the *population* of all price quotes given by the company in the past or present, under similar circumstances. *For the time being we will assume that all the sets of data we consider are samples.*

It will be convenient to say that the number of items in a sample is n and label the items in the sample x_1, x_2, x_3 and so on, so that the final item of data is x_n.

The average

Newspapers, magazines and everyday conversation often mention the 'average'. We hear that little Freddie is 'below average' at reading, the 'average' number of children in a family is 1.8 or that the 'average' gate figures at a series of international football matches are so many thousand. What is usually meant by 'average' is what is statistically known as the *mean*.

The mean of a set of values is their total divided by the number of items. For instance, the mean of 4, 8 and 9 is

$$\frac{4 + 8 + 9}{3} = 7$$

We usually employ the symbol $\bar{x}$ (pronounced, '*x* bar') to represent the mean of a sample. A general formula for the mean of a sample of *n* items is therefore

$$\bar{x} = \frac{x_1 + x_2 + x_3 + \ldots + x_n}{n}$$

The dots in the middle of the numerator just mean 'and so on'.

For instance, when there are 5 values in the sample, the formula for the mean is

$$\bar{x} = \frac{x_1 + x_2 + x_3 + x_4 + x_5}{5}$$

Check this

What is the mean of the price quote data?

Solution:
The mean of the price quote data is $\bar{x} = 5.5056$ (there are 25 items of data). It is easiest to use a calculator to do this. Many have special functions that total the data, and some will calculate the mean for you, but if you only need the mean it is just as easy to add up all the numbers and divide by the sample size.

Two other quantities are useful measures of the centre a set of data – the *median* and the *mode*.

The median

The word median is a bit like 'middle', and the *median* is just that – the middle item of the data when the data is placed in ascending (or descending) order.

Recall that there are *n* items of data in our sample. The median is therefore the $(n + 1)/2$th from smallest (or largest). For instance, if the data is

46 54 42 45 32

$n = 5$, so the median is the $(5 + 1)/2 = 3$rd from smallest or largest. Placing the data in ascending order gives 32 42 45 46 54, so the median is 45.

When the sample size, *n*, is an even number, $(n + 1)/2$ is not a whole number, so the median is taken as the average of the two middle values. For instance, if the sample is

46 54 42 45 32 57

$n = 6$, so the median is the $(6 + 1)/2 = 3.5$th from smallest item, which we take as the average of the 3rd and 4th from smallest values. Placing the data in order gives 32 42 45 46 54 57, so the median is 45.5.

Consider the following data:

$$32 \quad 42 \quad 45 \quad 46 \quad 54$$

The mean is 43.8 and the median is 45. Now suppose that instead of one of the values we had a very extreme value; for instance, suppose the final item was 5000 instead of 54. The data would now be

$$32 \quad 42 \quad 45 \quad 46 \quad 5000$$

The mean is now 1033, *but the median has not changed*: it is still 45.

In general, the median is *not* influenced by the presence of very large or very small numbers, so, when there are just a few extreme numbers that are not typical, it is often used in preference to the mean.

Check this

Calculate the median of the price quote data.

Solution:
There are 25 values so the median is the 13th from smallest (or largest) value. Placing 25 values in ascending order appears onerous but the stem and leaf diagram shown below (repeated from Chapter DD1) can help.

PQUOTE				
Frequency	Stem	and	Leaf	
4.00	1	.	4789	
4.00	2	.	0356	
5.00	3	.	44699	
2.00	4	.	69	
3.00	5	.	157	
2.00	6	.	67	
1.00	7	.	4	
.00	8	.		
1.00	9	.	4	
1.00	10	.	0	
2.00	Extremes		(>=16.3)	

Stem-and-Leaf Plot

Stem width: 1.00
Each leaf: 1 case(s)

The first class contains the four smallest values, the second class the four next smallest and so on. So the 13th from smallest must be the largest value in the third class, which is therefore the largest of the 2 values with stem 3 and leaf 9.

Returning to the original data we see that the 2 values with stem 3 and leaf 9 are 3.91 and 3.92. The largest of these, 3.92, is therefore the median.

The mode

Think of the French phrase, 'à la mode', which means 'in fashion' and you've got the idea. The *mode* is the 'most fashionable' number – the value that occurs most often in the data. For instance the mode of

42 33 42 47 42 47

is 42.

It is often meaningless to calculate the mode, as few or no values may be repeated. For instance, for the data

1 5 1 6 8 9 5 6 7

three values (1, 5 and 6) are repeated twice so there are three modes and none is very helpful as a measure of the centre of the data.

We can always, however, calculate the *modal class* of a histogram or frequency table; that is, the class with the highest frequency. For instance, the price quote data has no repeated values, so there isn't a mode; the modal class of the histogram in Figure 1.3 (Chapter DD1) is '2.5 to under 5'.

Mean, medians, modes and histograms

The histogram of a distribution with one peak might look like Figure 2.1, Figure 2.2 or Figure 2.3.

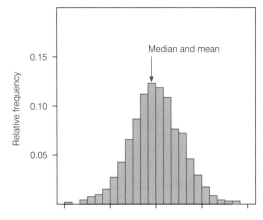

Figure 2.1 A (roughly) symmetric distribution.

Figure 2.1 shows a distribution that is roughly symmetric – the right-hand side of the histogram is almost a mirror image of the left-hand side. When the distribution is exactly symmetric every value to the left of the 'mirror' line is balanced by one to the right, so the mean and median will both be at the mirror line.

The distribution in Figure 2.2 is skewed. We say it is positively skewed or skewed to the right, as there are just a few high extreme values on the right. These extreme values raise the mean of the data but do not affect the median, so the mean will be greater than the median.

Figure 2.3 shows the opposite situation, when the data is skewed to the left and a few extremely low values pull the mean down so that it is less than the median.

In both Figures 2.2 and 2.3 the median lies between the mean and the mode.

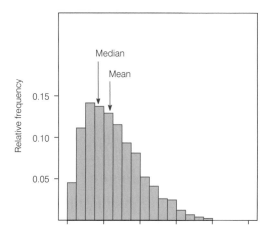

Figure 2.2 Distribution skewed to the right.

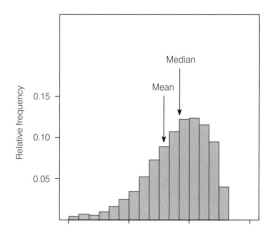

Figure 2.3 Distribution skewed to the left.

The relative values of the mode, median and mean can therefore tell us whether the distribution is skewed to the left or right. When the mean is greater than the median, the data is skewed to the right. When the mean is less than the median the data is skewed to the left. When the mean and the median are (approximately) equal, the distribution is (roughly) symmetric.

> Check this
>
> The mean of the price quote data is 5.5056 and the median is 3.92. Without looking at a graphical display what can you deduce about the symmetry or skewness of the distribution?
>
> **Solution:**
> As the mean is quite a bit larger than the median, a few very high values are pulling up the mean but not affecting the median. The distribution is therefore skewed to the right. (Confirm this by looking at Figure 2.3 again.)

WORK CARD 1

1. Calculate the mean of the doctor's waiting times data from Chapter DD1 **Work card 1** and reprinted below.

   2, 5, 10, 12, 4, 4, 5, 17, 11, 8, 9, 8, 12, 21, 6, 8, 7, 13, 18, 3

   Look at the histogram of the data which you drew for Chapter DD1's **Work card 1**, question 1. From the shape of the histogram would you expect the median to be more or less than the mean? Now calculate the median and see if you are right. Can you calculate a mode here and if so, what is it?

2. Calculate the mean and median of the executive salary data repeated below:

846	457	563	1466	
1200	2164	746	1611	
824	824	1310	1007	
1367	575	1252	1354	
2479	1238	927	1253	
9251	284	1279	1660	860

3. Calculate the mean and median of the R&D data:

6.0	10.4	10.5	9.0	7.3
6.6	6.9	8.2	7.1	8.1
7.9	6.8	7.4	9.5	8.1
13.5	9.9	6.9	11.1	8.2
8.0	7.7	7.4	6.5	9.5
8.2	6.9	7.2	8.2	6.7

   Are their relative positions what you would expect from a histogram of the data? (You may have drawn this already for **Assessment 1**, question 2, in Chapter DD1.) What is the modal class of the histogram?

Solution guidelines:

1. $\bar{x}$ = 9.15. The histogram was skewed to the right so we would expect the median to be smaller than the mean. There are 20 items of data so the median will lie between the 10th and 11th and is therefore 8. The mode here is 8 as it appears 3 times.

2. $\bar{x}$ = 1178.84 and the median is 1238.

3. $\bar{x}$ = 8.19 and the median is 7.95. As the mean is larger there are a few extremely large values and so the distribution is skewed to the right. This was expected from the histogram drawn for **Assessment 1**, question 2, in Chapter DD1. The modal class of a histogram with class widths of 1 starting at 6, is the '6 to under 7' class.

1. Calculate the mean, median and mode of the following set of data:

   8 9 10 11 4 6 7 7 8 9 11 7 7 3 0 10

2. Calculate the mean and median of the ages of the managers of Urban Child Care centres:

42	26	32	34	57	30	58	37
50	30	53	40	30	47	49	50
40	32	31	40	52	28	23	35
25	30	36	32	26	50	55	30
58	64	52	49	33	43	46	32
61	31	30	40	60	74	37	29
43	54						

   Would you expect the distribution of the data to be skewed to the left or right or symmetric?

3. In a survey of households conducted by the Traffic Department of a town council the following information on car ownership was collected:

Number of cars per household	Number of households
0	300
1	420
2	180
3	60
4	40

   Calculate the mean and median car ownership of these households. Can you calculate the mode and if so, what is it?

4. Comment on the following newspaper cuttings!

   ... concerted cries of rage from university teachers about low salaries – around £9000 a year at the bottom and £28,000 at the very top, with the great bulk stuck well below the median. (*The Sunday Times*, 23 April 1989)

   Low sex-drives are surprisingly common – at least one in 10 people has a lower-than-average libido. (*TV Quick*)

2 The spread of a set of data

The mean, median and mode each tell us something about the centre of the data, but they do not give any information of how the data is spread out. In this section we consider measures of the spread or dispersion of data.

Consider the following simple data sets:

$$
\begin{array}{ccccccc}
A & 0 & 48 & 49 & 51 & 52 & 100 \\
B & 47 & 48 & 49 & 51 & 52 & 53
\end{array}
$$

Both have a mean of 50 and a median of 50 (both are symmetric) yet they are very different. It is not enough to describe data by measuring where the centre of it lies: we must also consider how it is dispersed.

The simplest way of measuring the spread of some data is to calculate the range, but we shall see that this is *not* the most reliable way.

The range

As you might expect, the *range* is merely the difference between the largest and the smallest values of the data. For data A above the range is $100 - 0 = 100$ and for data B it is much smaller at $53 - 47 = 6$. However, compare data A with a new set of data, C, given below.

$$
\begin{array}{ccccccc}
A & 0 & 48 & 49 & 51 & 52 & 100 \\
C & 0 & 1 & 1 & 99 & 99 & 100
\end{array}
$$

Both A and C have a range of 100 and yet the values in A are much more central than those in C. The range of a set of data is therefore *not* a good measure of the spread because it uses only the smallest and largest values. We need a measure of spread which is calculated using *all* the data.

Variance

The most versatile measure of the spread of a set of data is the *variance*. It is one of the most crucial ideas of statistics and will pop up time and time again, so make sure that you understand this and the following section particularly thoroughly.

There is a short-cut way to calculate the variance but for now we will do things a longer way which makes the idea easier to understand.

To calculate the variance of a sample of data (the long way),

(1) Subtract the mean of the sample, $\bar{x}$, from each data item
(2) Square each of these
(3) Add up all the squares
(4) Divide by one less than the number of items of data, $n - 1$. (Those of you who have studied stats before may have divided by n and not $n - 1$. When the data is a sample it is better to divide by $n - 1$, although it won't make much difference when n is large.)

It is probably easiest to work in columns as shown below. For instance, to calculate the variance of data A (we already know that the mean is 50), we have

Data	(1) Data $- \bar{x}$	(2) (Data $- \bar{x}$)^2
0	−50	2500
48	−2	4
49	−1	1
51	1	1
52	2	4
100	50	2500
	(3) total	5010
	(4) $\div 5 =$	1002

The variance of data A is 1002.

The variance of a sample is usually symbolised by s^2. The square root of this is called the *standard deviation* and is written s.d. or s. So, as $s^2 = 1002$, the s.d. of data A is $s = \sqrt{1002} = 31.65$.

As the variance of a sample of data is based on the sum of the differences between each value and the mean, it is larger when the values are further from the mean and the data are more spread out and smaller when the values are closer to the mean. It is a good measure of spread because it can discern between samples like data A and data C (repeated below) which have the same range.

$$A \quad 0 \quad 48 \quad 49 \quad 51 \quad 52 \quad 100$$
$$C \quad 0 \quad 1 \quad 1 \quad 99 \quad 99 \quad 100$$

The variance of data C is $s^2 = 2920.8$ (you can confirm this) whereas we have already calculated that the variance of A is $s^2 = 1002$. Data C has a larger variance as it is much more spread out than data A.

Check this

Calculate the variance and standard deviation of data B (repeated below) by laying out your calculations in columns.

$$B \quad 47 \quad 48 \quad 49 \quad 51 \quad 52 \quad 53$$

Solution:

Data	(1) Data $- \bar{x}$	(2) (Data $- \bar{x})^2$
47	−3	9
48	−2	4
49	−1	1
51	1	1
52	2	4
53	3	9
		28

The sum of squared deviations of the data from their mean is 28, so $s^2 = \frac{28}{5} = 5.6$ and $s = 2.366$. As might be expected these are both much smaller than the variance and standard deviation respectively of data A and data C.

To give a feel for variance Figure 2.4 shows the histograms of three sets of data. Each data set has 400 values, is approximately symmetric and has a mean of 30. However, the variance of the first set of data is 9, of the second set is 25 and of the third set is 100 (standard deviations 3, 5 and 10 respectively).

Looking at the histograms we see that all the values in the first are very concentrated around 30, the data in the second are slightly more varied, whereas the final set of data spreads out even further.

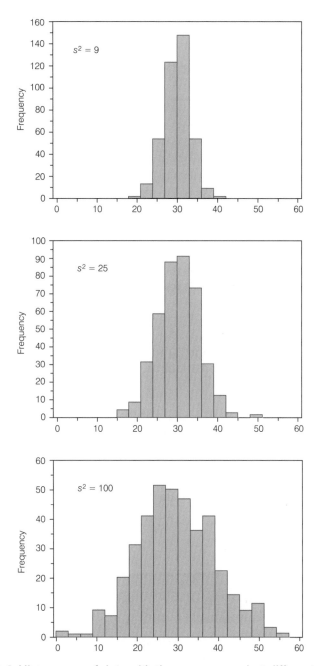

Figure 2.4 Histograms of data with the same mean but different variances.

How spread out is the data?

Suppose we read in a report that the mean of a sample of data is $\bar{x} = 50$ and that the sample variance is $s^2 = 25$, but we are not given the actual data. This tells us that the data are more 'spread out' than a set of data with a variance of, say, 9 and less dispersed than a set with variance 100. However, there is also a useful result (called Chebysheff's result, after a

Russian mathematician) which gives us some idea of the proportion of the data that lies within a particular distance of the mean.

Chebysheff's result applies to any constant, k, that is greater than or equal to 1. It says that:

a proportion of *at least*

$$1 - \frac{1}{k^2}$$

of the values in a sample lie within ks of the sample mean, $\bar{x}$, where s is the standard deviation.

To illustrate this, suppose we know that the mean of a sample of data is $\bar{x} = 20$ and that the variance is $s^2 = 25$. Chebysheff's result for $k = 2$ allows us to say that at least

$$1 - \frac{1}{2^2} = 0.75$$

of the values are between $20 - (2 \times 5)$ and $20 + (2 \times 5)$. That is, at least three-quarters of the items in the sample lie between 10 and 30. In the same way, Chebysheff's result for $k = 3$ tells us that at least

$$1 - \frac{1}{3^2} = 88.9\%$$

of the data lies between $20 - (3 \times 5)$ and $20 + (3 \times 5)$, so between 5 and 35 and the result for $k = 1.5$ says that

$$1 - \frac{1}{1.5^2} = 55.5\% \text{ of the data lies between 12.5 and 27.5}$$

WORK CARD 2

1. Use the method given in this section to calculate the variance of the following sample. Lay out your working in columns.

   | 45 | 42 | 38 | 45 | 50 |

2. In a survey 500 respondents had an average income of £18,300 with standard deviation £5010. Which of the following statements is true? Explain your answers.

   (i) At least 375 of the respondents have a salary between £8280 and £28,320.

   (ii) At most 125 of the respondents have a salary that is more than £28,320.

   (iii) Exactly 89% of respondents have a salary that lies between £3270 and £33,330.

WORK CARD 2 (CONTINUED)

Solutions:

1. The sample mean is $\bar{x} = 44$. So your working should be:

Data	Data − $\bar{x}$	(Data − $\bar{x}$)^2
45	1	1
42	−2	4
38	−6	36
45	1	1
50	6	36

$$78 \text{ so } s^2 = \frac{78}{4} = 19.5$$

2. **(i)** True, take $k = 2$. **(ii)** True from **(i)**. At most, 125 respondents have a salary that is less than £8100 or more than £28,320, so it follows that at most 125 can have a salary that is more than £28,320. **(iii)** False. It is true that *at least* 89% (approximately) of respondents have salaries between £3270 and £33,330.

ASSESSMENT 2

1. At a glance say which of these samples has the largest variance. Explain your answer.

   | A | 3 | 5 | 7 | 9 | 11 |
   | B | 3 | 7 | 7 | 7 | 11 |

   Confirm or contradict your answer by calculating the variance of each sample.

2. A friend wishes to invest some money in one of three ordinary shares. For each company the mean and standard deviation of the annual percentage returns over the last 10 years are given below.

Name	Mean (%)	Standard (%)
Peter Hugh Films	8	5
Beatrice Bakeries	5	2
Albert's Woodcraft	5	1

   On the basis of this information
   a. Which company would you advise against?
   b. If your friend is very well-off and is really making the investment for 'fun', which would you recommend?
   c. If your friend requires a relatively secure ordinary share investment, which of these companies would you recommend?

3. In its end of year report the Finance and Economics Faculty of a university publishes that 200 students obtained a degree that year. These had an average overall percentage mark of 59%, with a standard deviation of 10%.

On the basis of this information alone make a statement concerning

a. The number of students who obtained between 39% and 79%.

b. The number of students who obtained less than 39% or more than 79%.

c. The number of students who obtained more than 89%.

d. A range of marks which 50% of students attained.

3 Σ **and a short-cut for variance**

There is a quicker method of calculating the variance of a sample. To explain it we need to introduce a special symbol, Σ, called 'sigma', which means, 'the sum of'.

Introducing the summation sign Σ

In Section 1 we said that we would label a set of data $x_1, x_2, x_3, \ldots x_n$. This enables us to write down formulae for functions of the data. For instance, the sum of the first 2 items of the data is

$$x_1 + x_2$$

and the mean of a sample of n values is

$$\bar{x} = \frac{x_1 + x_2 + x_3 + \ldots + x_n}{n}$$

The numerator of this formula, $x_1 + x_2 + x_3 + \ldots + x_n$ is rather cumbersome to write out. It is much quicker to write it using the Greek symbol Σ. Σ (pronounced 'sigma') placed in front of an expression just means, 'the sum of' so 'the sum of the xs' is written

$$\Sigma x = x_1 + x_2 + \ldots + x_n$$

In a similar way, Σx^2 means the sum of the x^2s; that is,

$$\Sigma x^2 = x_1^2 + x_2^2 + x_3^2 + \ldots + x_n^2$$

The formula for the sample mean can therefore be written

$$\bar{x} = \frac{\Sigma x}{n}$$

When you encounter a new formula which includes a Σ and you can't immediately see what it means, try writing it out in full without the summation sign. For example, the expression $\Sigma 2(x + 1)$ means, 'the sum of all the $2(x + 1)$s' and writing it out term by term gives

$$2(x_1 + 1) + 2(x_2 + 1) + 2(x_3 + 1) + \ldots + 2(x_n + 1)$$

For a set of data

$$0, 48, 49, 51, 52, 100$$

this would be

$$
\begin{aligned}
&2(0+1) && +\,2(48+1) + 2(49+1) + 2(51+1) + 2(52+1) \\
&2 && +\,98 \quad\;\; +\,100 \quad\;\; +\,104 \quad\;\; +\,106 \\
&+2(100+1) = \\
&\quad 202 \quad\;\; =\,612
\end{aligned}
$$

Formulae for the variance

In Section 2 we calculated the variance of a sample, s^2, using a set of written instructions. Now we are going to write down the corresponding formula. The instructions, now shown with the parallel symbols, are

(1) subtract the mean from each data item: $x - \bar{x}$
(2) square each of these: $(x - \bar{x})^2$
(3) add up all the squares: $\Sigma(x - \bar{x})^2$
(4) divide by one less than the size of the data, $n - 1$. The corresponding formula for the sample variance is therefore

$$s^2 = \frac{\Sigma(x - \bar{x})^2}{n - 1}$$

Make sure that you understand why this formula means the same as the written instructions.

This way of calculating the variance is the most intuitive because it uses each of the deviations of the data from the mean, $x - \bar{x}$, in an obvious way. However, it is tedious to calculate, and, if the sample mean $\bar{x}$ has to be rounded because it has too many decimal places, will not be accurate.

An equivalent formula, which should be used instead as it is quicker and more accurate, is

$$s^2 = \frac{\Sigma x^2 - \frac{(\Sigma x)^2}{n}}{n - 1}$$

At first sight this may look nasty, but the only difficult bits are Σx and Σx^2 so we calculate these first.

For example, for data A,

$$0, 48, 49, 51, 52, 100$$

we have

$$\Sigma x = 0 + 48 + 49 + 51 + 52 + 100 = 300$$

and

$$\Sigma x^2 = 0^2 + 48^2 + 49^2 + 51^2 + 52^2 + 100^2 = 20{,}010$$

There are 6 items in the sample, so $n = 6$ and $n - 1 = 5$, so the sample variance is

$$s^2 = \frac{20{,}010 - \frac{300^2}{6}}{5} = \frac{20{,}010 - 15{,}000}{5} = 1002$$

which agrees with the previous calculations.

Be careful to distinguish between $(\Sigma x)^2$ and Σx^2. They are *not* the same. As any expression in brackets must be calculated first, $(\Sigma x)^2$ means sum the data first and then square the sum; that is, $(\Sigma x)^2 = (x_1 + x_2 + x_3 + \dots + x_n)^2$. Conversely, Σx^2 means square each data item first, and then total all of these:

$$\Sigma x^2 = x_1^2 + x_2^2 + x_3^2 + \dots + x_n^2$$

Check this

Use the new formula to calculate the sample variance of the following data:

5 7 8 9 12

Solution: $\Sigma x = 41$, $\Sigma x^2 = 363$.

So $s^2 = \dfrac{363 - \frac{41^2}{5}}{4} = 6.7$

So, the two very important formulae you need that calculate the mean and the variance of a sample are:

The **mean** of a sample is $\bar{x} = \dfrac{\Sigma x}{n}$

The **variance** of a sample is $s^2 = \dfrac{\Sigma x^2 - \frac{(\Sigma x)^2}{n}}{n-1}$

Variances on calculators and spreadsheets

Many scientific calculators include a function to calculate s^2, although it may often be labelled σ_{N-1}^2. It is fine to use this as a check on your calculations, **but** it is easy to enter the data wrongly and difficult to trace an error. We recommend that you use the formula given above and show your intermediate working, i.e. your figures for Σx and Σx^2. (Again your calculator may have a function for these.) That way, if you make an isolated arithmetic mistake you will still get most of the marks in an exam for using the correct method.

If you want to use a spreadsheet to calculate the variance you will need one column for the data, and another for the squares of the data. Summing these gives Σx and Σx^2 respectively which can be substituted into the variance formula.

WORK CARD 3

1. Practise the mechanics of calculating the variance of a set of data. For the data:

    3 7 9 5 7 9 11 5

    (i) Calculate Σx.

    (ii) Calculate Σx^2.

    (iii) Calculate the variance s^2.

2. **(i)** Compare the variances and ranges of the following samples and comment:

      A 9 9 9 9 10 11 11 11 11

      B 1 3 5 7 10 13 15 17 19

  (ii) Compare the variances and ranges of the following samples and comment:

      A 5 5 5 5 10 15 15 15 15

      B 1 10 10 10 10 10 10 10 19

3. Until now an office cleaning firm has used two different industrial vacuum cleaner companies to supply parts when its equipment breaks down. Now it wishes to take out a maintenance contract with just one of these companies and needs to select which one. The times (in days) it took for the appropriate part to be delivered after the last 20 breakdowns have been recorded and are given below. Of these, 8 were with company *A* and 12 with company *B*.

    Co. *A* 1 2 8 1 2 2 7 1

    Co. *B* 5 6 4 3 5 7 6 5 4 4 5 6

  (i)   Calculate the mean delivery time for each company.

  (ii) Calculate the standard deviation of the delivery times for each company.

  (iii) Calculate the range for each company.

  What advice would you give to the office cleaning firm on the basis of your results?

4. First-year Finance students at a university take a compulsory course in Economics and another in Statistics. It is hoped that both courses are at a similar level and produce a similar distribution of exam results. The following table shows a summary of the results for 100 students:

Subject	Σx	Σx^2
Economics	6200	425,400
Statistics	6500	525,600

  By calculating the mean and variance of each set of data comment on whether it is reasonable to assume that the distribution of the Economics exam results are similar to those of the Statistics exam.

Solutions:

1. **(i)** 56 **(ii)** 440 **(iii)** 6.8571

2. **(i)** The variance (1) and range (2) of *A* are both smaller than those of *B* (41 and 18).

  (ii) The variance of sample *A* at 25 is larger than that of *B* which is 20.25 whereas the range of *A* (10) is *smaller* than that of *B* (18).

3. **(i)** means are 3 and 5 for A and B respectively. **(ii)** S.d. for company A is 2.828 and for B is 1.128. **(iii)** The ranges are 7 and 4 respectively. Advice depends on the cleaning firm's objectives. A has a lower mean but fluctuates much more than company B. If, for instance, a daily cost was incurred for each day's wait – perhaps for rental of another machine – then the mean wait is of most importance and company A should be chosen. Alternatively, if the cleaning company was able to manage its equipment to cover for broken machines as long as the delivery time was known, then company B would be preferred as it shows much less variation in times.

4. For Economics $\bar{x} = 62$, $s^2 = 414.14$ whereas for Statistics $\bar{x} = 65$, $s^2 = 1041.41$. There is not much difference in the means of these distributions but the Statistics marks have a much larger variance. This is probably because marks for an essay subject like Economics marks tend to be less extreme than maths marks.

1. A company is concerned about the delivery time of invoices sent through the post. It conducts a survey by telephoning a random sample of 10 customers who were sent invoices the previous week. The following delivery times were reported (days):

    1 2 2 3 1 1 1 2 3 1

    The postal service maintains that business letters should take an average of 1.8 days with a standard deviation of 0.7 days. On the basis of the standard deviation and mean only do you think this sample supports this claim? (We will see later how to perform a more structured test of whether or not a sample comes from a population with particular properties.)

2. Quality control procedures in a Turkish Delight factory require that the variance of each sample of 10 bars of confectionery drawn throughout the working day is at most 8 g. Does this sample pass the test? The weights in grams are

    28 34 33 27 31 30 32 35 26 25

3. In a survey the starting salaries of a random sample of 100 recent graduates from the Accountancy department of a university are collected and a sample of 80 recent History of Art graduate leavers. Some summary statistics (in £thousand) follow:

Department	Σx	Σx^2
Accountancy	1502	23,240
History of Art	944	12,200

    Calculate the mean and variance of each sample and use these to compare the salaries of Accountancy and History of Art graduates.

4 **Quartiles**

We already know that the median of a set of data is the value such that half the data are smaller than it and half are larger. The *quartiles* are like the median but they establish the quarter and three-quarter points of the data instead of the half-way point. (Quartiles sound a bit like quarters don't they?)

Just as the median is the $0.5(n + 1)$th from smallest item of data, the *lower quartile* is the $0.25(n + 1)$th value and the *upper quartile* is the $0.75(n + 1)$th value when the data are arranged in ascending order.

For example, suppose the data is

$$1, 3, 4, 8, 6, 9, 3, 4, 1, 2, 5$$

which becomes

$$1, 1, 2, 3, 3, 4, 4, 5, 6, 8, 9$$

when placed in ascending order. There are $n = 11$ items, so the lower quartile is the $0.25(11 + 1) = 3$rd from smallest and the upper quartile is the $0.75(11 + 1) = 9$th from smallest. So the lower quartile is 2 and the upper quartile is 6 (and the median is 4).

Notice that one-quarter of the data are smaller (and three-quarters larger) than the lower quartile and three-quarters of the data are smaller (and one-quarter larger) than the upper quartile. The distance between the quartiles – which is called the *inter-quartile* range – therefore gives some idea of the spread of the data.

We conveniently chose a sample of size $n = 11$ above, so that $0.25(n + 1)$ and $0.75(n + 1)$ were whole numbers. When they are not whole numbers we must calculate an intermediate value – a process called *interpolation*.

For example, suppose that a new sample, placed in ascending order, is

$$1\ 3\ 4\ 6\ 8\ 9$$

$n = 6$ so the lower and upper quartiles are at the $0.25 \times 7 = 1.75$th position and the $0.75 \times 7 = 5.25$th position, respectively. We therefore take the lower quartile to be the number $\frac{3}{4}$ of the way between the first and second items of data, 1 and 3 (that is 2.5) and the upper quartile to be $\frac{1}{4}$ of the distance between the fifth and sixth items, 8 and 9 (that is 8.25). The median is in the $0.5 \times 7 = 3.5$th position and so is 5.

Check this

Calculate the quartiles and the inter-quartile range of the following data sets:

Data *D*   1 7 3 5 1 3 7 9 9
Data *E*   1 1 1 9 9 9 5 5 5

Solution:
$n = 9$ for both samples, so the quartiles lie at the 2.5th and 7.5th values when placed in ascending order. In order, the data sets are

Data *D*   1 1 3 3 5 7 7 9 9
Data *E*   1 1 1 5 5 5 9 9 9

For data D the lower quartile lies mid-way between the 2nd and 3rd values and so is 2, whereas the upper quartile is mid-way between the 7th and 8th, so is 8. For data E the lower quartile is mid-way between 1 and 1 and so is 1 and the upper quartile mid-way between 9 and 9 so is 9. So the quartiles of data D are 2 and 8 (inter-quartile range 6) and the quartiles of data E are 1 and 9 (inter-quartile range 8). The increased inter-quartile range in data E reflects the fact that the data is more spread out.

WORK CARD 4

1. Calculate the lower and upper quartiles of the samples of delivery times of both vacuum cleaner companies from **Work card 3**, question 3, and shown again below. For company B, what length of time is such that 75% of deliveries take longer?

    Co. A 1 2 8 1 2 2 7 1
    Co. B 5 6 4 3 5 7 6 5 4 4 5 6

2. Calculate the upper and lower quartiles and the median of the following data
    2 6 1.1 7 11.5 5 8.2 1 7.5 9.8 10.2 4

Solutions:

1. For company A $n = 8$ so the quartiles are the 2.25th and the 6.75th from smallest values which is a quarter of the distance between 1 and 1, so is 1, and three-quarters of the distance between 2 and 7, so is 5.75. In a similar way the quartiles for company B are 4 and 6. So 75% of company B's deliveries take longer than 4 days (the lower quartile).

2. $n + 1 = 13$ so you need the 3.25th and 9.75th from smallest values for the quartiles. The third from smallest is 2 and the 4th from smallest is 4 so one-quarter of the way between is 2.5. The 9th from smallest is 8.2 and the 10th from smallest is 9.8 so three-quarters of the way between is 9.4. The quartiles are 2.5 and 9.4. The median is 6.5.

ASSESSMENT 4

1. Calculate the lower and upper quartiles of the Turkish Delight data (Assessment 3, question 2). The data are:
    28 34 33 27 31 30 32 35 26 25

2. Calculate the lower and upper quartiles and median of the data displayed in the following stem and leaf diagram:

    1   0   1   3   4
    1   5   7   9   9
    2   2   2   3   4   4
    2   5   5   6   7   7   8   9
    3   0   0   1   1   1   2   4   4
    3   1   2   2   3   3   3
    4   0   1   1   2
    4   5   7

5 Technology to the rescue!

We have encouraged you to calculate statistics like the mean, variance and quartiles using a calculator, so that you get a 'feel' for these quantities. In practice, however, it is much quicker and easier to use statistical software or a spreadsheet.

Often, just one command produces a whole plethora of statistics about a sample. For instance SPSS's

Analyze > Descriptive Statistics > Descriptives…

produces the following output for the public and private sector faculty salaries data from Chapter DD1, Section 1. The data are in columns of the worksheet called 'public' and 'private'.

	N	Range	Minimum	Maximum	Mean		Std.	Variance	Skewness		Kurtosis	
	Statistic	Statistic	Statistic	Statistic	Statistic	Std. Error	Statistic	Statistic	Statistic	Std. Error	Statistic	Std. Error
PRIVATE	49	13977	17241	31218	23123.29	564.45	3951.174	1.6E+07	.318	.340	–.816	.668
PUBLIC	50	19106	22272	41378	26721.86	429.05	3033.812	9204017	2.307	.337	10.140	.662
Valid N (listwise)	48											

N is the number of data items. Range, Minimum, Maximum, Mean, Std. and Variance statistics are self-explanatory. Std. Error Mean will be explained in later chapters. Skewness and kurtosis are further measures of the shape of the data, but we do not consider them in this book.

We conclude from this output that public sector salaries are, on average, greater than those of the private sector. However, the standard deviation and variance of the private sector salaries are higher, indicating that private sector salaries are more spread out.

Analyze > Descriptive Statistics > Explore

gives some additional statistics, including the inter-quartile range.

In Excel the data analysis tool, **Descriptive Statistics**, produces all the statistics we have mentioned plus some others.

WORK CARD 5

1. A bank is concerned about its level of customer service and conducts a survey into the time that elapses from the moment a customer enters the bank to the moment they finish their transaction. The survey results (to the nearest minute) are as follows:

11	2	5	4	3	9	9	1	4	3	9	2	3
7	6	9	8	31	10	5	0	4	5	7	6	0
5	10	8	2	7	5	2	16	4	13	2	2	2
2	6	11	5	2	4	2	1	11	14	1		

   Enter the data into some statistical software and use this to display the data in an appropriate manner and calculate summary statistics such as the mean, median, quartiles and range. Comment on the shape of the distribution.

2. A bookstore samples its order record to examine the number of days between placing an order and receiving the goods. The results (in days) are shown below.

Surface transportation

18 20 24 23 28 32 24 39 18 29 25 27 19 24 21
19 24 27 33 37 15 20 26 21 17 26 25 23 25 35

Air freight

12 12 13 21 18 14 9 16 18 14 13 11 15 11 17
14 12 13 11 17 19 16 14 14 12 11 15 13 9 15

Use the numerical methods you have learnt to assess and comment on the differences between air and freight transportation. You will need to calculate the means, medians, variances, range, and quartiles. Use a computer!

Solution guidelines:

1. The histogram is clearly skewed to the right so just a few customers have to wait a very long time. Mean is 6, median 5, standard deviation 5.253. The range is 30 from 0 to 31 minutes and the quartiles are 2 and 9.

2. Surface ranges from 15 to 39 with mean 24.8, standard deviation 5.92 whereas air ranges from 9 to 21 with mean 13.967 and s.d. 2.883. The medians are 24 and 14 respectively. It is clearly quicker on average and more predictable (because the standard deviation is smaller) to transport by air.

1. It is crucial that an airline has a reputation for punctuality. The percentage of arriving flights that were punctual over a one-year period is calculated for 28 airports for two different airlines Hi-Fli and Icarus-line. By calculating suitable statistics and drawing appropriate displays of the data, comment on and compare the punctuality record of the two airlines.

Percentage of punctual flights					
Airport	Hi-Fli	Icarus	Airport	Hi-Fli	Icarus
1	53	76	15	81	78
2	85	87	16	79	84
3	95	78	17	93	84
4	82	77	18	69	85
5	73	79	19	98	79
6	78	81	20	79	83
7	43	80	21	91	78
8	77	81	22	69	82
9	71	77	23	85	82

| Percentage of punctual flights | | | | | |
Airport	Hi-Fli	Icarus	Airport	Hi-Fli	Icarus
10	84	77	24	91	84
11	88	78	25	80	81
12	78	80	26	98	81
13	84	82	27	88	89
14	78	85	28	72	83

2. The Wig and Pen public house in the City of London cooks both restaurant meals (a set three-course menu) and bar meals at lunch time. It is a small pub and the landlady feels that providing both bar and restaurant meals is too labour intensive. She feels that perhaps she should offer restaurant food only or alternatively close the restaurant and provide bar meals only.

To investigate the financial repercussions of this, a random sample of 40 bar-meal customers and 40 restaurant customers was taken. Their expenditure per head as summarised by some statistical software is shown below.

Write a couple of paragraphs describing the distributions of the expenditure of restaurant and bar customers and comparing them. What recommendations would you make to the landlady?

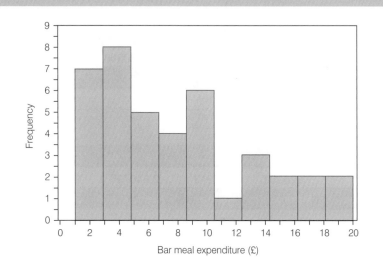

Figure 2.5 Wig and Pen: Bar meal expenditure.

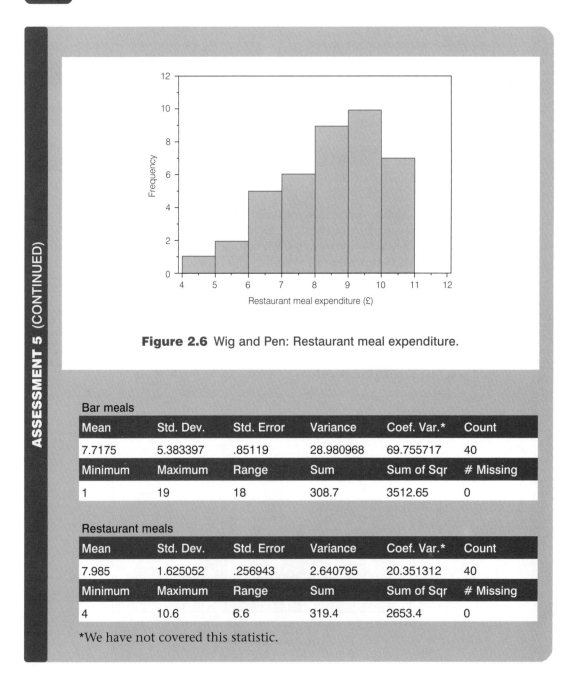

Figure 2.6 Wig and Pen: Restaurant meal expenditure.

Bar meals

Mean	Std. Dev.	Std. Error	Variance	Coef. Var.*	Count
7.7175	5.383397	.85119	28.980968	69.755717	40
Minimum	**Maximum**	**Range**	**Sum**	**Sum of Sqr**	**# Missing**
1	19	18	308.7	3512.65	0

Restaurant meals

Mean	Std. Dev.	Std. Error	Variance	Coef. Var.*	Count
7.985	1.625052	.256943	2.640795	20.351312	40
Minimum	**Maximum**	**Range**	**Sum**	**Sum of Sqr**	**# Missing**
4	10.6	6.6	319.4	2653.4	0

*We have not covered this statistic.

6 Constructing indices

Index numbers are a way of describing the changes that occur to a series of numbers over time. Each measurement is expressed as a percentage of a previous measurement, called a *base value*. We'll illustrate by example.

A property portfolio has the following valuations (£100,000s) at the end of each of five years.

1996   174
1997   197
1998   190
1999   200
2000   224

We will take the base period as 1996 although it does not have to be the first in the series. The index number of the base value is always 100. The index numbers for the other periods are:

$$\frac{\text{value}}{\text{base value}} \times 100$$

So, for instance, the index number for 1997 is

$$\frac{197}{174} \times 100 = 113.2$$

Check this

Calculate the index numbers for the other periods.

Solution:
These are

$$\frac{190}{174} \times 100 = 109.2, \quad \frac{200}{174} \times 100 = 114.9 \quad \text{and} \quad \frac{224}{174} \times 100 = 128.7$$

respectively.

A glance at the index over the five-year period (below) shows, for instance, that the 1998 valuation is 9.2% more than the 1996 valuation, the 1999 valuation is 14.9% more than the 1996 valuation and so on.

Year	Valuation	Index number
1996	174	100
1997	197	113.2
1998	190	109.2
1999	200	114.9
2000	224	128.7

Changes between periods other than the base period can be calculated using either the index numbers or the original data and, apart from rounding errors, both will give the same results. For instance, the percentage change in valuation between 1998 and 1999 as a percentage of the 1998 figure can be calculated using the original data:

$$\frac{200 - 190}{190} \times 100 = 5.3\% \quad \text{or the index numbers} \quad \frac{114.9 - 109.2}{109.2} \times 100 = 5.2\%$$

Aggregate indices

Sometimes we are not interested in the changes in a single measurement but in a combination of several measurements. For instance, a house price index is compiled from the prices of houses of many different types and sizes; a stock exchange index like the *Financial Times* All-Share or *Dow Jones* is compiled from a range of stock prices and so on. Such indices are called *aggregate indices*.

Suppose we wish to compile an index of food prices. One way to do this would be to collect the price of a representative sample of food items at each time period and calculate the sum of these. In this way the index would be

$$\frac{\text{Sum of prices today}}{\text{Sum of prices in base period}} \times 100$$

However, notice that this treats each price equally. Whilst in some circumstances this may be 'fair', if we want a general measure of food prices we should really give more importance to widely consumed items like bread than less frequently used items like mustard or soy sauce. What we need is a combined measure of price that *weights* each price by the *quantity* of that item consumed. By this, all we mean is that we will multiply each price by the corresponding quantity to obtain the total amount spent on each product and then add these up. In this way our index would be

$$\frac{\text{Total expenditure today}}{\text{Total expenditure in base period}} \times 100$$

However, this is still not satisfactory because, over time, the quantities may change. For instance, the population may be eating less red meat than it did a few years ago or more vegetables, or more junk food. Also, a change in price may attract or discourage purchasers. The above index reflects changes in the quantities consumed as well as the change in price, which is *not* what we want.

We would like a measure of the change in price *for the same quantities of goods*. However, this begs the question: Which quantities should we use? Two obvious possibilities are the quantities from the base period and the quantities for the current period and both of these are widely used.

The *base-weighted* or *Laspeyre* price index is the most commonly used. It is calculated using the quantities of goods from the base year; that is, it is

$$\frac{\text{Cost of base period quantities at today's prices}}{\text{Cost of base period quantities at base period prices}} \times 100$$

It has the advantage that the quantities remain the same every year (as the base year doesn't change) and so don't need to be recalculated each time. Its disadvantage, however, is that if there have been big changes in the way people spend their money the quantities will be out of date.

Alternatively, the *current-weighted* price index or *Paasche* index uses the latest quantities from the end of the current time period and so the index is

$$\frac{\text{Cost of current period quantities at today's prices}}{\text{Cost of current period quantities at base period prices}} \times 100$$

Although the quantities are up-to-date, they change every period and the denominator of the index has to be recalculated each time. Consequently, individual index numbers can only be compared with the base period and not with each other.

Let's try an example of both these types of index. Suppose we want to compile a price index for students at a particular university and that these students spend money on four categories: food and transport, entertainment, books, and rent. The quantities, q, of each category purchased in years 1, 2 and 3 (thousands of units) and their price in £s, p, are shown below.

	Year 1		Year 2		Year 3	
	p	q	p	q	p	q
Food and transport	30	300	32	250	35	260
Entertainment	25	200	27	200	28	200
Books	50	100	80	80	80	90
Rent	60	44	80	44	80	44

Suppose we wish to compare year 2 with year 1. The base-weighted index gives

$$\frac{32 \times 300 + 27 \times 200 + 80 \times 100 + 80 \times 44}{30 \times 300 + 25 \times 200 + 50 \times 100 + 60 \times 44} \times 100 = \frac{26,520}{21,640} \times 100 = 122.6$$

The current-weighted index gives

$$\frac{32 \times 250 + 27 \times 200 + 80 \times 80 + 80 \times 44}{30 \times 250 + 25 \times 200 + 50 \times 80 + 60 \times 44} \times 100 = \frac{23,320}{19,140} \times 100 = 121.8$$

The base-weighted index has a higher percentage increase mainly because the huge increase in book prices has more impact because more books were purchased in the base year. It is also interesting to note that the total expenditure in year 1 is £21,640 and in year 2 is £23,320, giving an increase in total expenditure of only 7.8% compared with 22.6% and 21.8% for the base-weighted and current-weighted indices. The larger percentage increases indicated by the indices are because although only a little more was spent in year 2, this bought smaller quantities of goods.

WORK CARD 6

1. Calculate the base-weighted index and current-weighted index of year 3 of the student price data (repeated below) taking year 2 as the base period. Comment on your results and compare them with an index of total expenditure for these periods.

	Year 1		Year 2		Year 3	
	p	q	p	q	p	q
Food and transport	30	300	32	250	35	260
Entertainment	25	200	27	200	28	200
Books	50	100	80	80	80	90
Rent	60	44	80	44	80	44

Solution:

The base-weighted index is

$$\frac{35 \times 250 + 28 \times 200 + 80 \times 80 + 80 \times 44}{32 \times 250 + 27 \times 200 + 80 \times 80 + 80 \times 44} \times 100 = \frac{24{,}270}{23{,}320} \times 100 = 104.1$$

The current-weighted index is

$$\frac{35 \times 260 + 28 \times 200 + 80 \times 90 + 80 \times 44}{32 \times 260 + 27 \times 200 + 80 \times 90 + 80 \times 44} \times 100 = \frac{25{,}420}{24{,}440} \times 100 = 104.0$$

The quantities do not differ greatly between years 2 and 3 and so there is not much difference between the indices. Notice, however, that total expenditure increases by 9% from year 2 to year 3.

1. Consider how you would attempt to construct an index of student rents (or wages from employment) in your area, taking a year ago as the base period. What information would you need, what sort of index would you construct and why, and what problems might you encounter? Illustrate your answer by asking some second-year students what they were paying (earning) a year ago and making guesses (list these) about the information you require.

2. Find out as much as you can about the construction of the retail price index (or the equivalent in your country).

7 Grouped data

Sometimes the analyst is not given the exact values of a set of numerical data or else the information is simply not available. For instance, how often have you filled in questionnaires with questions like this?

> Please tick your age
>
> 15–24
>
> 25–34
>
> 35–54
>
> 55–64
>
> 65 or over

Suppose a sample of 100 randomly chosen readers of a computer magazine answer this question and that the results are:

Age	Frequency
15–24	15
25–34	20
35–54	30
55–64	15
65 and over	20

Although age is a quantitative (numerical) variable, the age data produced by this question will only be available in classes.

Pictorial representation

As data like this is already in classes it is tempting to think that we can immediately draw a histogram. We must be careful, however, because we have always drawn histograms in which the classes had equal width. Here, most classes have a width of 10 years but the 35–54 age group is wider than the others and the 65 and over group is open-ended. Before we can draw a histogram we need to adjust the data so that all the class widths are the same.

As most of the classes are 10 years wide it seems sensible to adopt a class width of 10. We will therefore divide the 35–54 group into 35–44 and 45–54. Of the 30 respondents who lie in the 35–54 age group our best guess (in the absence of any further information) is that half of them are between 35–44 years old and half between 45–54, so we will give each of the new classes, 35–44 and 44–54, a frequency of 15.

The other class that needs adjustment is the 65 and over class. Here, we must decide on a reasonable upper age limit and then partition the 65 and over group into 10-year-wide classes. If we assume that the oldest reader is at most 84 years old, the oldest age group will have a class width of 20, and so we can apportion the 20 respondents aged 65 and over into two classes, 65–74 and 75–84, each with a frequency of 10. (Alternatively we could make a more elaborate – and realistic? – assumption that there are fewer older readers and split the over-65s so that more are in the younger group.)

Notice that these adjustments to the class frequencies are merely 'best guesses'.

After these adjustments the frequencies become

Age	Frequency
15–24	15
25–34	20
35–44	15
45–54	15
55–64	15
65–74	10
75–84	10

and the corresponding histogram is shown in Figure 2.7.

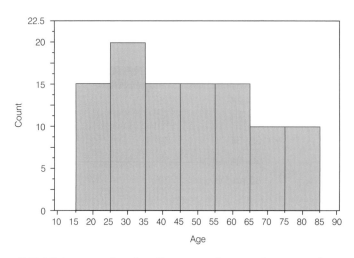

Figure 2.7 Histogram showing the ages of computer magazine readers.

This shows us that the number of readers is highest in the 25–34 age group, and is much the same at other ages, except for slightly less over 65. Notice that we would have drawn false conclusions (namely that there were more readers at all ages 35–54) if we had not adjusted the frequencies to classes of equal width.

Summary statistics

As we don't have the exact ages of our sample of 100 readers, it is not possible to calculate an *exact* mean, median, mode, variance or quartiles. However, by making a few assumptions, we *can* obtain good approximations!

The simplest assumption to make is that *all the values in each class are equal to the midpoint of each class*. For instance, we assume, for the computer magazine data, that the 15 readers in the 15–24 age group (i.e. aged between 15.0 and 24.99 years) are all aged 20; the 20 readers in the 25–34 age group are all aged 30 and so on as shown below.

Age	Frequency	Midpoint
15–24	15	20
25–34	20	30
35–54	30	45
55–64	15	60
65 and over	20	75 (assuming maximum age is 85)

We can then use the midpoints to calculate the (approximate) mean and variance in exactly the same way as usual as follows.

There are 100 items of data, x_1, x_2, x_3, ..., x_{100}. We are assuming that the first 15 are all 20, the next 20 are all 30, the next 30 are all 45 and so on. So

$$\Sigma x = (15 \times 20) + (20 \times 30) + (30 \times 45) + (15 \times 60) + (20 \times 75) = 4650$$

and

$$\Sigma x^2 = (15 \times 20^2) + (20 \times 30^2) + (30 \times 45^2) + (15 \times 60^2) + (20 \times 75^2) = 251{,}250$$

As $n = 100$ the usual formulae give

$$\bar{x} = \frac{\Sigma x}{n} = \frac{4650}{100} = 46.5$$

and

$$s^2 = \frac{\Sigma x^2 - \frac{(\Sigma x)^2}{n}}{n-1} = \frac{251{,}250 - \frac{4650^2}{100}}{99} = 353.7879, \text{ so } s = 18.81$$

So the approximate mean of the computer magazine reader data is 46.5 and the approximate variance is 353.7879.

Check this

The age distribution of a sample of 200 non-corporate customers of a computer company is given below. Calculate an approximate mean and variance and use these to compare the distribution with the age distribution of the computer magazine readers.

Age	Frequency
15–19	30
20–29	60
30–39	50
40–59	40
60 and over	20

Solution:

Age	Frequency	Midpoint
15–19	30	17.5
20–29	60	25
30–39	50	35
40–59	40	50
60 and over	20	70 (assuming maximum age is 80)

$$\Sigma x = (30 \times 17.5) + (60 \times 25) + (50 \times 35) + (40 \times 50) + (20 \times 70) = 7175$$

$$\Sigma x^2 = (30 \times 17.5^2) + (60 \times 25^2) + (50 \times 35^2) + (40 \times 50^2) + (20 \times 70^2) = 305{,}937.5$$

So

$$\bar{x} = \frac{7175}{200} = 35.875, \quad s^2 = \frac{305{,}937.5 - \frac{7175^2}{200}}{199} = 243.891$$

and $s = 15.62$.

> The mean age of the computer company's customers is over 10 years younger than that of the computer magazine readers and the standard deviation is lower so their ages are less varied.

Some books give special formulae for the mean and variance when quantitative data is given in classes but we think that our common sense approach does just as well. The special formulae achieve the same results but merely take advantage of the fact that, as the midpoint is used instead of every item of data in a class, there are a lot of repeated values.

1. A newspaper-commissioned survey on business expectations asks 70 randomly selected businesses to forecast the percentage growth in their turnover for the next year. The results are

0–under 2%	20
2–under 5%	30
5–under 10%	20

   Calculate an approximate average forecast of percentage growth in turnover and an approximate sample variance. State any assumptions you make about the data.

2. In a medium-sized city there are 86 houses for sale of a similar size. The frequency distribution of the asking prices is

Price ($)	Frequency
50,000–under 60,000	21
60,000–under 70,000	27
70,000–under 80,000	18
80,000–under 90,000	11
90,000–under 100,000	6
100,000–under 110,000	3

   Find an approximate mean house price. By making a different assumption about the distribution of house prices within each class, suggest an approximate median.

3. A college claims that the marks of all its examinations are scaled to have a mean of 50% and a standard deviation of 10%. The following results are published for the first-year Accountancy exam:

Less than 30%	40
30%–under 50%	60
50%–under 60%	40
60%–under 70%	30
Over 70%	30

Calculate an (approximate) average mark. State any assumptions you make about the exact distribution of the marks. What is the (approximate) standard deviation of the marks? Can you tell whether the college's claim is correct?

Solutions:

1. Assuming that the data in each class is at the midpoint, $\Sigma x = 275$ and $\Sigma x^2 = 1512.5$, so an approximate average is 3.93% and an approximate sample variance is 6.2629.

2. Approximate the mean by assuming that the data in each class is at the midpoint. It is easiest to work in thousands so

    $$\Sigma x = (21 \times 55) + (27 \times 65) + \ldots + (3 \times 105) = 6080$$

    and the approximate mean is

    $$\frac{6080}{86} = 70.69767, \text{ i.e. } \$70,698$$

    The median must lie between the 43rd and 44th value when placed in order. This will be between the 22nd and 23rd cheapest of the \$60–70,000 class. If we assume that the *prices occur at regular intervals throughout this class* then the median is

    $$\$60,000 + \frac{22.5}{27} \times \$10,000 = \$68,333$$

3. Your results will depend on the assumptions you make about the classes containing the lowest and highest marks. If we assume that the under 30% class is really 20–30% and that the over 70% class is 70–80% then

    $$\Sigma x = (25 \times 40) + (40 \times 60) + (55 \times 40) + (65 \times 30) + (75 \times 30) = 9800$$

    and an approximate mean is 49%. By similar assumption $\Sigma x^2 = 537,500$, so $s^2 = 287.94$ and the standard deviation is $s = 16.97$. As your mean is only an approximation the college's claim of 50% may be all right. The standard deviation looks much higher than 10% which is rather suspicious, but again yours is an approximation so this does not give you hard evidence. If this happened in 'real life' further investigation might be a good idea!

1. After a television appeal a charity is inundated with postal donations. These are going to take some weeks to process so to obtain a preliminary estimate of receipts they open a random sample of 100 letters and classify the amounts enclosed as follows.

Amount (£)	Number of letters
0–under 5	5
5–under 10	40

Amount (£)	Number of letters
10–under 30	30
30–under 50	15
50 or more	10

Estimate the average amount included in a letter. By weighing the post-bags they estimate that they have received 20,000 letters. Can you estimate their total receipts?

2. A machine on a poultry processing plant sorts chickens by size into 4 categories. Each day the totals in each category are used to estimate the average weight of processed birds. The totals for a particular day are:

small	0–less than 1000 g	150
medium	1000–less than 2000 g	170
large	2000–less than 3000 g	130
very large	3000 g or more	60

Calculate an estimate of the average weight and standard deviation of the weight on this particular day.

3. Are men more experienced drivers than women? Ask a sample of several male and several female students the following question. (Change the time intervals if necessary.)

How long have you been driving?
   less than 1 year
   1–under 2 years
   2–under 5 years
   more than 5 years

Use these frequencies to estimate for men and women separately (i) the mean length of driving experience and (ii) the standard deviation. What do you conclude? Can you conclude that this result holds for *all* men and *all* women? If not, why not?

8 Describing data: your toolkit

You now have a variety of tools at your diposal to help describe a set of data. Here is a checklist – your 'toolkit' – to remind you of the techniques available.

The **frequencies** of a set of data are the number of values in each class or category
The **relative frequencies** are the proportion of the values within each class

Displays for numerical data
A **histogram** displays the frequencies or relative frequencies in each class
A **stem and leaf diagram** retains information on all the values
A **scatter plot** shows the relationship between pairs of numerical variables
A **time series plot** shows data which occur at regular time intervals

Displays for categorical data
A **bar chart** shows the frequencies of categorical data
A **pie chart** shows the proportion of the data in each category
A **contingency table** or **cross-tabulation** shows the frequencies of two categorical
variables. It may include row, column or total percentages.

Summarising data

The **mean** of a sample is $\bar{x} = \dfrac{\Sigma x}{n}$

The **mode** is the data value with the highest frequency

The **modal class** is the class of data with the highest frequency

The **variance** of a sample is $s^2 = \dfrac{\Sigma x^2 - (\Sigma x)^2/n}{n-1}$

The **range** is the maximum minus the minimum of the data

When the data is placed in ascending order:

the **median** is the $\dfrac{n+1}{2}$th value

the **lower quartile** is the 0.25 $(n + 1)$th value

the **upper quartile** is the 0.75 $(n + 1)$th value

An **index number** is $\dfrac{\text{current value}}{\text{base value}} \times 100$

ASSESSMENT 8

The following exercises make use of a more complex data set and require you to use a range of techniques from *Describing Data*. The data can be found in the *vizafizz* file on the web site and the 'toolkit' at the end of this chapter provides a useful reminder of the techniques we have covered.

A drinks manufacturer has developed a low-alcohol bottled cocktail which it intends to launch onto the drinks market after a major advertising campaign. An advertising agency has produced two alternative TV advertisements and a market research company has been commissioned to ascertain what type of customer should be targeted and how effective the TV advertisements are likely to be. The market research company stopped people under 30 years at lunchtime in a busy shopping street of several major cities and asked if they would be willing to give up 10 minutes to answer a questionnaire in return for a voucher for a free drink at one of the local clubs. Those who agreed were randomly shown either one of the TV advertisements or a picture and description of the product. An interviewer then asked them questions from a questionnaire. A selection of these questions is shown below and the corresponding data are given in *vizafizz*.

1. Tick your age
   Under 21 ❏   21–24 years ❏   25 years or over ❏

2. Are you male? ❏   or female? ❏

3. (To be answered by interviewer.) Which TV advert did the respondent see?
   Type 1 ❏   Type 2 ❏   No TV advertisement ❏

4. How much do you estimate you spend on drinks in pubs, bars and clubs in a typical week? (Give figure to the nearest pound.) ....

5. If Vizafizz cost the same amount as competing bottled drinks, would you drink it?
   Yes ❏   No ❏

1. Briefly summarise the answers to each survey question using both graphical and numerical methods. Comment on your findings.

2. Use graphs and numerical summaries of the data to investigate whether:
   (i)   males and females differ in how much they spend on drink in a week
   (ii) weekly expenditure on drink differs for those who say they would drink Vizafizz and those who wouldn't.

Further reading: see p. xv

Morris contains similar material to our text but her formulae may be slightly different. She has a whole chapter on index numbers.

Mendenhall *et al.* provide more detail but assume slightly more maths.

Newbold *et al.* is comprehensive and uses Excel.

P Probability

It is *likely* to rain tomorrow.

I will *probably* have to have an operation.

There *might be* a general election next year.

Demand for new cars *may* decrease if the government imposes an extra 5% tax.

The *chances are* that Norwich City (football team) will win on Saturday.

The student bar will *probably* be empty tonight as exams start tomorrow.

The English language is particularly rich in expressions that convey uncertainty. We hear or say statements like these every day. In business, however, we need to be more precise as important decisions will be based on such uncertainties.

Probability gives us a precise way of measuring uncertainty. Using Probability we can develop models that convey how likely an outcome is, or how likely a variable is to take particular values.

As well as being useful in its own right, Probability is also an essential tool for understanding Statistics, so this part of the book is a prerequisite for the next.

P1
Measuring uncertainty

In all probability I'll lose my virility
And you your fertility and desirability
And this liability of total sterility
Will lead to hostility and a sense of futility.
So let's act with agility
While we have the facility
For we'll soon reach senility
And lose the ability

Tom Lehrer, 'When you are old and grey'

Contexts

What is this chapter about?
This chapter describes how to calculate the probabilities of particular events happening.

Why is it useful?
Businesses and organisations operate in a climate of uncertainty and this chapter describes a structured way of assessing the likelihood of chance events, which is invaluable for decision making. Also, in Statistics, probability is used to express how certain we are about the inferences made from a sample.

Where does it fit in?
The material in this chapter forms an introduction to the subject of Probability. Whilst Probability is a branch of mathematics in its own right, it is also an essential tool for inferential statistics, so this chapter is essential for the Statistics part of this book.

What do I need to know?
You will need the basic maths in Essential Maths.

Objectives

After your work on this chapter you should:

- be more precise in estimating a probability;
- be familiar with the terminology of outcomes and events;
- be able to use Venn diagrams to illustrate outcomes and events;
- understand what is meant by a complementary event;
- be able to calculate the probabilities of AND and OR events;
- understand the concept of mutually exclusive events;
- understand the ideas of conditional probability and independent events;
- be able to calculate conditional probabilities;
- be able to use a decision tree to calculate more complicated probabilities.

Why learn about probability? We live in an uncertain world. When we get up in the morning we cannot say exactly who we are going to meet, what the weather will be like or which events will be on the television news during the day.

In our everyday lives, we cope with this uncertainty by making hundreds of guesses, calculated risks and some gambles. We cross the road at a particular time because *the chances are* that no traffic will come haring round a corner and run us down. We don't take a coat with us for the weekend because it is *unlikely* to be cold. We allow a particular length of time to travel to an important interview because it will *probably* be enough.

All these decisions are made by assessing the relative *probability* of all the possible outcomes – even if we do this unconsciously and intuitively. Business decisions are made in a similar climate of uncertainty. A publisher must decide how large the print run of a new book should be to avoid unsold copies and yet ensure availability. A manufacturer must make spending decisions based on cash flow predictions. A stock market dealer decides to sell a particular share because a financial model tells her that the price is likely to fall.

The penalties for estimating chances inaccurately and hence making a 'wrong' decision vary from minor inconvenience, to loss of income to bankruptcy. So, in business, (and other fields) we endeavour to measure uncertainty using the science of probability. An understanding of probability is also an essential requirement for Statistics because the inferences made from a sample about a population are always uncertain.

We start, in this chapter, by learning how to evaluate and manipulate probabilities.

1 Introduction to probability

The language of probability

Rather than make vague statements containing 'likely', 'maybe' or 'probably' we need to be more precise, so the probability of a particular event is usually measured as a percentage or a fraction. For instance, the probability that a (fair) coin gives a head when tossed is 50% or 0.5 or the probability that a dice gives a 6 is $\frac{1}{6}$ or 16.6%.

A probability is always between 0 and 1 inclusive. If the probability of an event is 1, the event is a certainty and it will definitely occur, whereas if the probability of an event is 0, it cannot happen.

How is probability measured?

Probability can be measured in two (or maybe three) ways depending on the circumstances.

When outcomes are equally likely

Suppose I toss a fair coin. There are two possible outcomes, head or tail. As the coin is fair it is reasonable to assume that these are *equally likely*. The probability of tossing a head is therefore

$$P(Head) = \frac{\text{Number of outcomes that are } Head}{\text{Total number of outcomes}} = \frac{1}{2} = 0.5$$

In the same way, when I throw a fair dice there are 6 possible outcomes, 1, 2, 3, 4, 5 and 6, and it is reasonable to assume that these are all equally likely. The probability of throwing an even number is therefore

$$P(Even) = \frac{\text{Number of outcomes that are } Even}{\text{Total number of outcomes}} = \frac{3}{6} = 0.5$$

Suppose there is a state lottery in which a million tickets are issued and that there are 3 major prizes and 100 minor prizes. We assume that each ticket has an equal chance of winning. If I buy a ticket the probability that it will win a major prize is

$$P(Major\ Prize) = \frac{\text{Number of tickets that win a } Major\ Prize}{\text{Total number of tickets}} = \frac{3}{1,000,000}$$

The probability of winning a minor prize is

$$P(Minor\ Prize) = \frac{\text{Number of tickets that win a } Minor\ Prize}{\text{Total number of tickets}} = \frac{100}{1,000,000}$$

In general, *when all the outcomes are equally likely* the probability that a particular event occurs is

$$P(Event) = \frac{\text{The number of outcomes in that the } Event \text{ occurs}}{\text{Total number of possible outcomes}}$$

Notice that all of these examples rely entirely on the assumption that *each outcome is equally likely*. There are many situations, particularly manmade constructions like lottery tickets and dice, for which this is reasonable, but it is often not the case.

When outcomes are *not* equally likely

More often than not all the possible outcomes are *not* equally likely. Here are some examples.

Tomorrow has two possible outcomes for me – either I will get run over by a car, or else I will *not* get run over by a car. It is *not* reasonable (I hope) to assume that these are equally likely outcomes.

Tomorrow also has two possible outcomes for you. Either you will win a large sum of money, or you won't. Regrettably, these also are *not* equally likely.

In Britain there are 3 main political parties: Conservative, Labour and Liberal Democrat. At the next general election there are therefore 3 possible outcomes for the winning party. However, these are *not* equally likely.

Consider the last exam you took. Before you sat the exam there were two possible outcomes – you could pass or you could fail. Were these equally likely or not? If you did a lot of revision then maybe you had a very high probability, near 1, of passing, but if you did no work then your chances were perhaps very small, near 0. So, unless your chances of success happened to be exactly 0.5, the two outcomes were not equally likely.

When outcomes are *not* equally likely how do we measure probabilities?

The answer is that there is no absolutely accurate, theoretical way. In practice, we usually look at any data that is available from past repetitions of the same situation and use the proportion of times that the event of interest has happened. That is,

$$P(Event) = \frac{\text{The number of times in which the } Event \text{ of interest occurred}}{\text{Total number of times}}$$

For example, suppose we want to calculate the probability that an electronic chip produced by a machine is defective. If records show that out of 8000 electronic chips already produced by the machine only 80 were defective then an estimate of the probability of a defective chip is

$$P(Defective) = \frac{\text{Number of } Defective \text{ chips produced}}{\text{Total number of chips produced}} = \frac{80}{8000} = 0.01$$

Alternatively, suppose a sales representative made 1000 calls last year and 150 of these resulted in a sale. An estimate of the probability that an individual call results in a sale is therefore

$$P(Sale) = \frac{\text{Number of calls resulting in a } Sale}{\text{Total number of calls}} = \frac{150}{1000} = 0.15$$

Notice that a probability calculated this way is the same as the relative frequency of the event (see Chapter DD1, Section 1), so this is often called the *relative frequency approach* to probability. It can be proved mathematically that the relative frequency gradually approaches the true probability as the number of repetitions becomes larger.

Check this

Gill is told that she needs a particular knee operation and that she should need between 1 and 3 days in hospital. The health authority's records show the number of patients who have required 1, 2 or 3 days hospitalisation for the same operation is as follows.

1 day   700 patients
2 days   350 patients
3 days   150 patients

What is the probability that Gill will need 3 days in hospital?

Solution:
The probability that Gill will need 3 days in hospital is

$$P(3\ Days) = \frac{\text{Number of patients taking 3 } Days}{\text{Total number of patients}} = \frac{150}{1200} = 0.125$$

Subjective probability

The third way of assessing a probability has no theoretical grounding and is not even based on past data. It is purely subjective. It is the 'gut feeling' or guess. This is what we use when we peer out of the window before going out to decide whether to take an umbrella or not. We are using our past experience to tell us the chance of rain. In the same way a doctor relies on his clinical experience when he decides which treatment to give a patient – he has intuitively assessed the chances of improvement for each possible treatment.

Subjective probability is usually used only as a 'last resort'; that is, when the outcomes are not equally likely and no past data is available.

Check this

Which of the following probabilities can be calculated or estimated **(i)** from equally likely outcomes, **(ii)** from historic data or **(iii)** subjectively? Calculate the probabilities where possible.

1. The probability of obtaining a king when a card is chosen at random from a pack of cards.

2. The probability that the bus you catch to work is late this morning.

3. The probability that it will rain in London on a day in September.

4. The probability that a TV audience for an episode of a particular soap opera exceeds 20 million.

5. The probability that you will be able to find a job this summer vacation.

Solutions:

1. Each card is equally likely, so

$$P(King) = \frac{\text{Number of cards which are } Kings}{\text{Total number of cards}} = \frac{4}{52} = \frac{1}{13}$$

2. If you have records of the number of mornings the bus has and has not been late over a time period you could calculate

$$P(Late) = \frac{\text{Number of mornings bus was } Late}{\text{Total number of mornings}}.$$

Otherwise you would have to use a subjective guess.

3. Meteorological records could provide data on London rainfall in September:

$$P(Rain) = \frac{\text{Number of } Rainy \text{ days}}{\text{Total number of days}}$$

4. Past viewing figures could establish

$$P(\textit{Over 20 Million}) = \frac{\text{Number of episodes with } \textit{Over 20 Million } \text{viewers}}{\text{Total number of episodes}}$$

5. Even if you had records of the numbers of students in your area who had or didn't have jobs last year, employment conditions may have changed and maybe some students didn't try to get work. You will probably have to resort to subjective probability here.

Outcomes

So far we have used the word 'outcome' loosely. By 'outcome' we mean the result of a chance situation such that a list of all possible outcomes covers every possibility (it is exhaustive) and no outcome overlaps any of the others (we say the outcomes are mutually exclusive). In this way the chance situation will result in *exactly* one outcome and the sum of the probabilities of all possible outcomes will be 1.

For example, when I buy a ticket in the state lottery, a list of the possible outcomes and their probabilities might be

Outcome	Probability
Win major prize	$\dfrac{3}{1,000,000}$
Win minor prize	$\dfrac{100}{1,000,000}$
Do not win a prize	$\dfrac{999,897}{1,000,000}$
	1.0

Exactly one of these outcomes will happen when I buy a ticket.

Check this

Write down all the possible outcomes and their probabilities when a dice is thrown.

Solution:
The possible outcomes are 1, 2, 3, 4, 5 or 6, which each have a probability of $\frac{1}{6}$. Therefore we have

Outcome	Probability
1	1/6
2	1/6
3	1/6
4	1/6
5	1/6
6	1/6
	1.0

Events

Sometimes it is convenient to group a collection of outcomes together. We will call such a group of outcomes an *event*.

For instance, throwing an even number on a dice is the event that comprises the outcomes 2, 4, or 6 or winning the state lottery described above comprises two outcomes, 'win minor prize' and 'win major prize'.

We now state an important fact.

> The probability of an event is the sum of the probabilities of the outcomes that are included in that event.

For instance, the probability that a dice gives an even number is the probability of throwing a 2 plus the probability of throwing a 4 plus the probability of throwing a 6, that is

$$P(Even) = P(2) + P(4) + P(6) = \frac{1}{6} + \frac{1}{6} + \frac{1}{6} = \frac{1}{2}$$

In the same way, the probability of winning a prize in the state lottery is

$$P(Prize) = P(Minor\ Prize) + P(Major\ Prize)$$
$$= \frac{100}{1{,}000{,}000} + \frac{3}{1{,}000{,}000} = \frac{103}{1{,}000{,}000}$$

As another example, suppose that the career destination of an Accountancy graduate from a university has the following probabilities:

Destination	Probability
Accountancy	0.5
Insurance	0.05
Banking	0.05
Other finance	0.1
University teaching	0.05
Teaching	0.1
Other	0.15
	1.0

These 7 career destinations give all the possible outcomes for a particular graduate, so their probabilities total 1. The probability of the event, 'career destination is finance' (where finance includes accountancy, insurance, banking and other finance) is therefore

$$P(Finance) = P(Accountancy) + P(Insurance) + P(Banking) + P(Other\ finance)$$
$$= 0.5 + 0.05 + 0.05 + 0.1$$
$$= 0.7$$

Check these

Use the career destination probabilities above to calculate the probability of the following events:

(i) A graduate goes into some sort of teaching.

(ii) A graduate does not go into accountancy.

(iii) A graduate uses his/her degree (that is, goes to one of the first 6 destinations).

(iv) A graduate who uses his/her degree, goes into accountancy.

Solution:

(i) $P(Teach) = P(Teaching) + P(University\ Teaching) = 0.1 + 0.05 = 0.15.$

(ii) $P(Not\ Accountancy)$ is the sum of the probabilities of all the outcomes that are not accountancy; that is, $0.05 + 0.05 + 0.1 + 0.05 + 0.1 + 0.15 = 0.5$, although we will see later that it is quicker to calculate $P(Not\ Accountancy) = 1 - P(Accountancy) = 1 - 0.5.$

(iii) The sum of the first 6 probabilities, $P(Uses\ Degree) = 0.5 + 0.05 + 0.05 + 0.1 + 0.05 + 0.1 = 0.85.$

(iv) This is more difficult and we haven't really covered the material yet. At this stage it is probably best tackled by considering the proportions of graduates to whom it applies. We are only concerned with the 85% of graduates who use their degree. This 85% includes all those graduates, 50% of the whole, who enter accountancy. So the proportion of the 85% who enter accountancy is $\frac{50}{85}$.

Check this

Suppose you toss two fair coins. List all the possible outcomes and their probabilities. Use your list to calculate the probability of obtaining exactly one head.

Solution: The possible outcomes are

	First coin	Second coin
Outcome 1	*Head*	*Head*
Outcome 2	*Head*	*Tail*
Outcome 3	*Tail*	*Head*
Outcome 4	*Tail*	*Tail*

These four outcomes are all equally likely, so the probability of each outcome is $\frac{1}{4}$ and a list of the probabilities is:

	First coin	Second coin	Probability
Outcome 1	Head	Head	1/4
Outcome 2	Head	Tail	1/4
Outcome 3	Tail	Head	1/4
Outcome 4	Tail	Tail	1/4
			1

The probability of the event 'exactly one head' is therefore the sum of the probabilities of outcomes 2 and 3, which is

$$P(1\ Head) = P(Head\ Tail) + (Tail\ Head) = \frac{1}{4} + \frac{1}{4} = \frac{1}{2}$$

Check this

The number of male and female students on the following degree courses in the business school at a university are as follows. There are 1500 students altogether.

	Accountancy	Economics	Finance	Business Information Systems
Male	330	360	90	120
Female	120	390	60	30

Using this data, if you select a student at random

(i) What is the probability that they are doing an economics degree?

(ii) What is the probability that they are male?

(iii) What is the probability that they are female and doing economics or finance?

Solution:
Here we have 8 outcomes for the gender/course of a student. The associated probabilities can be obtained by dividing all the frequencies by 1500 to give

	Accountancy	Economics	Finance	Business Information Systems
Male	0.22	0.24	0.06	0.08
Female	0.08	0.26	0.04	0.02

The probabilities of the events requested in **(i)**, **(ii)** and **(iii)** can be found by summing the probabilities of the appropriate outcomes. For instance,

(i) $P(Economics) = P(Male\ and\ Economics) + P(Female\ and\ Economics)$

$$= 0.24 \qquad\qquad + 0.26$$
$$= 0.5$$

(ii) The event 'Male' comprises four outcomes ('Male and Accountancy', 'Male and Economics', etc.) so

$P(Male) = 0.22 + 0.24 + 0.06 + 0.08 = 0.6$

(iii) This comprises 2 outcomes, 'Female and Economics' and 'Female and Finance', so
$P(Female \; and \; Economics \; or \; Finance) = 0.26 + 0.04 = 0.3$.

Venn diagrams

A good way of showing outcomes and events is to draw a Venn diagram. On a Venn diagram each possible outcome is represented by a point. An event is represented by a loop or circle that encloses the group of outcomes that make up that event.

In Figure 1.1 each point represents a possible outcome for the business school in the last example and the loop is the event, 'Student is male'.

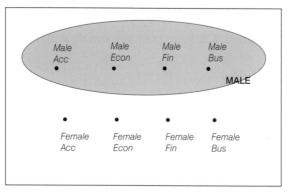

Figure 1.1 Venn diagram: one event.

More than one event can be shown on the same diagram. Figure 1.2 shows the event 'Student is male' and the event 'Student does finance'. Notice that the outcome(s) inside the overlap of the two loops are those that are in both events.

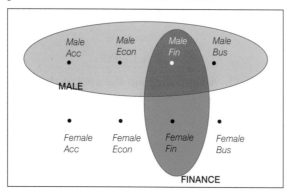

Figure 1.2 Venn diagram: two events.

When solving problems it is often useful to label the events, event A, event B and so on. For instance, when selecting a card from a pack of cards we might define the events

A: Select a royal card (King, Queen or Jack)
B: Select a spade

Figure 1.3 shows events *A* and *B*.

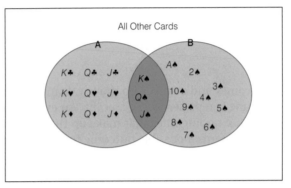

Figure 1.3 Venn diagram: events A and B.

Complementary events

The two events

I will be run over by a bus tomorrow and
I will *not* be run over by a bus tomorrow

have a special relationship in that one is the negation of the other. It is therefore easiest to call one of them event *A* and the other event *Not A*. So we have the *complementary* events

A: I will be run over by a bus tomorrow
Not A: I will *not* be run over by a bus tomorrow.

As one or other of a pair of complementary events must occur, their probabilities must total 1 so

$$P(A) + P(Not\ A) = 1$$

which rearranges to

$$P(Not\ A) = 1 - P(A).$$

When an event is illustrated in a Venn diagram the area of the diagram *outside* the event *A* loop represents the event *Not A* as shown in Figure 1.4.

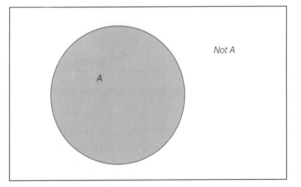

Figure 1.4 Event *not A*.

Sometimes it is easier to calculate *P(Not A)* instead of *P(A)* as in the following example.

Check this

When three coins are thrown, what is the probability of getting at least one head?

Solution:
The long way of solving this is to enumerate all the possible outcomes:

1st coin	2nd coin	3rd coin
Head	Head	Head
Head	Head	Tail
Head	Tail	Head
Head	Tail	Tail
Tail	Head	Head
Tail	Head	Tail
Tail	Tail	Head
Tail	Tail	Tail

and then count how many of the 8 outcomes have one or more heads.

It is much easier, however, to calculate the probability of the complementary event of getting no heads – because the only possible outcome is

Tail, Tail, Tail – so $P(\text{No heads}) = \dfrac{1}{8}$

and then calculate

$P(\text{At least one head}) = 1 - P(\text{No heads}) = 1 - \dfrac{1}{8} = \dfrac{7}{8}$

So we have:

Probability

When outcomes are **equally likely**:

$$P(\text{Event}) = \frac{\text{The number of outcomes in which the } \textit{Event} \text{ occurs}}{\text{Total number of outcomes}}$$

When outcomes are **not equally likely** we use the relative frequency of historic data:

$$P(\text{Event}) = \frac{\text{The number of times the } \textit{Event} \text{ occurs}}{\text{Total number of times}}$$

An **event** is a collection of outcomes and

P(*Event*) = the sum of the probabilities of the outcomes that are included
                in the event

Complementary events
For any event A

   P(*Not A*) = 1 – P(A)

1. **a.** Write down the probability of getting a heart when selecting a card from a pack of cards.

    b. What is the probability that a new-born baby is a boy?

    c. In the last 100 working days the FT index has risen for 6 days, remained the same for 20 days, and dropped for 74 days. At close of business today it is 2721. Using this data, what is the probability that it is greater than 2721 at close of business tomorrow?

    d. What is the probability that you will break your leg tomorrow?

2. A bank made 500 car loans last year. The amounts were as follows:

£	Number of loans
under 1000	27
1000–3999	99
4000–5999	298
6000+	76

    One of these is sampled at random by the bank. What is the probability that it is:

    a. Under £1000?
    b. Greater than or equal to £4000?

3. A couple plan to have 2 children. Assuming that a boy or a girl is equally likely at each birth:

    (i)   Write down a list of possible outcomes for the sexes of the children.
    (ii) Write down the probabilities for these outcomes.
    (iii) What is the probability that they will have two boys?

4. A market researcher conducted a shopping centre survey of customers to study two characteristics – the use of public transport to get to the centre and the time of arrival. The results are shown below.

Number of customers

	9 am–5 pm	5 pm–8 pm
Public	170	30
Not public	50	250

  (i) Write down the possible outcomes and the associated probabilities for an individual customer.

  (ii) What is the probability that a customer arrives by public transport?

  (iii) Show all the possible outcomes on a Venn diagram, and indicate
  A: uses public transport
  B: arrives after 5pm

5. Two dice are thrown. Write down all possible outcomes of the pair of dice and the corresponding probabilities.
  a. What is the probability that both dice show a 6?
  b. What is the probability that the total on the two dice is 4?

Solutions:

1. **a.** $\frac{13}{52} = \frac{1}{4}$ as each card is equally likely.
  b. There are two equally likely outcomes so the probability is a half. (Although some birth statistics may quote that fractionally more boys are born than girls.)
  c. $P(Rises) = \dfrac{\text{Number of days it rose}}{\text{Total number of days}} = \dfrac{6}{100}$

  assuming that conditions remain the same.
  d. Subjective probability required here unless you have access to orthopaedic records and even then your risk will vary depending on which sport you do etc. The main point is that the two possible outcomes, 'break leg' and 'don't break leg' are *not* equally likely, so the probability is *not* a half.

2. **a.** $\frac{27}{500}$ **b.** $\frac{374}{500}$

3. **(i)** The outcomes are

First child	Second child
Boy	Boy
Boy	Girl
Girl	Boy
Girl	Girl

WORK CARD 1 (CONTINUED)

(ii)   The probability of each of these is equal and so is $\frac{1}{4}$.

(iii)   Only the first outcome is two boys so the probability of two boys is $\frac{1}{4}$.

4.   (i)   The probabilities are

	9 am–5 pm	5 pm–8 pm
Public	0.34	0.06
Not public	0.1	0.5

(ii) $P(Public) = 0.34 + 0.06 = 0.4$

(iii)   There are 4 possible outcomes. The event A will be a loop enclosing the outcomes 'Public and 9 am–5 pm' and 'Public and 5 pm–8 pm' and event B, a loop enclosing 'Public and 5 pm–8 pm' and 'Not public and 5 pm–8 pm'.

5.   There are 36 possible outcomes, each is equally likely and so the probability of each is $\frac{1}{36}$. They are

1st dice	2nd dice
1	1
1	2
1	3
1	4
1	5
1	6
2	1
2	2
⋮	⋮
etc.	
6	6

a. $P(6,6) = \frac{1}{36}$ as only one outcome out of the 36 is in this event.

b. $P(Total = 4)$ is more difficult. There are 3 outcomes in this event, 1,3; 2,2; and 3,1 so the probability is $\frac{1}{36} + \frac{1}{36} + \frac{1}{36} = \frac{1}{12}$.

ASSESSMENT 1

1. a. A university has three residences for students. The first has 500 single study bedrooms, the second has 1000 and the third has 2000. When a student is allocated randomly to a residence, what is the probability that it is the second residence?
   b. What is the probability that I draw a two or a four when I pick a card at random from a pack of playing cards?
   c. Five men and 3 women are short-listed for a job. What is the probability that a man gets the job? What assumption do you need to make to calculate this probability?
   d. An air steward is training with a well-known UK airline. He knows that of the 200 trained stewards currently employed by the Company, 80 work on the London–Paris route, 50 on London–Amsterdam and the remainder on internal flights. What is the probability that, after training, the new steward's work will take him out of the UK?

2. The following table shows the number of recent graduate employees of a large computer company whose salaries lie within three salary bands.

	Under £15,000	£15,000 – £25,000	£25,000 – £30,000
Male	25	175	220
Female	40	200	120

A recent graduate employee is selected at random for a newspaper interview. Construct a table showing the probabilities of all possible salary/sex outcomes.
   a. Mark all possible outcomes on a Venn diagram.
   b. Indicate the following two events on the diagram:
   A: Earns £15,000 or more.
   B: Woman earns less than £25,000.

3. The table below lists percentage unemployment rates for the 15 Atlantic coast states of the United States for two consecutive years. One of the 15 states is to be selected and the direction and amount of change in its unemployment rate from the first to the second year is to be observed. Assume that each state has an equal probability of being selected.

State	Year 1	Year 2	State	Year 1	Year 2
Connecticut	3.3	3.8	New Jersey	5.0	4.0
Delaware	3.2	4.3	New York	6.3	4.9
Florida	5.3	5.7	North Carolina	5.3	4.5
Georgia	5.5	5.9	Pennsylvania	6.8	5.7
Maine	5.3	4.4	Rhode Island	4.4	3.8
Maryland	4.2	4.5	South Carolina	6.2	5.6
Massachusetts	3.8	3.2	Virginia	5.0	4.2
New Hampshire	2.8	2.5			

a. What is the probability that Pennsylvania will be selected? Florida? Virginia?

b. What is the probability of selecting a state that had no change in its unemployment rate?

c. What is the probability of selecting a state whose unemployment rate increased? Decreased?

d. What is the probability of selecting a state whose unemployment rate increased 1% or more? Decreased 1% or more?

4. The suit spades is separated from a pack of cards, so that there are just 13 cards. A card is now selected at random from these 13 cards. Draw a Venn diagram and show which areas of the diagram represent the following events:

A: Card is an even number.
B: Card is a 3 or a 5.
C: Card is not a royal (not a *K*, *Q* or *J*).

2 Combining events: AND and OR

Sometimes events can be combined to define a more complicated event. The two ways of doing this involve AND or OR.

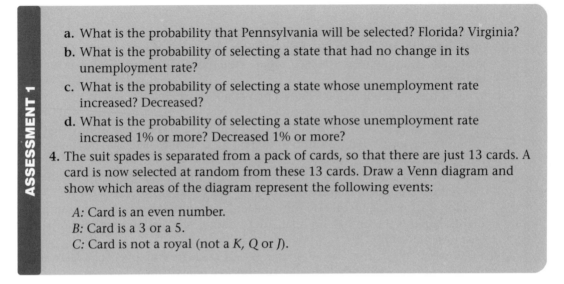

Figure 1.5 Event *A* AND *B*.

The event A AND B

Suppose we have two events *A* and *B*. It may be possible for both event *A* *and* event *B* to occur; that is, there may be one or more outcomes that are in both events. We define the event *A* AND *B* as

A AND *B*: Both *A* and *B* happen

For instance, suppose that when throwing a single dice the two events *A* and *B* are:

A: an even number is thrown
B: a 5 or a 6 is thrown

then the event *A* AND *B* will be throwing a 6.

The probabilities of 'AND' events like this are often called *joint* probabilities.

On a Venn diagram the event *A* AND *B* is represented by the overlap of the *A* event loop and the *B* event loop as shown in Figure 1.5. This is sometimes called the *intersection* of *A* and *B*.

Check this

To ratify the standard of an exam, after the papers have been marked an external examiner selects one candidate at random for interview. The events *A*, *B* and *C* are defined as follows:

A: Candidate gained 40% or more
B: Candidate gained less than 70%
C: Candidate is male

Describe each of the following events and shade the appropriate areas on a Venn diagram.

(i)   *A* AND *B*
(ii)   *B* AND *C*
(iii) *A* AND *Not C*

Solution:

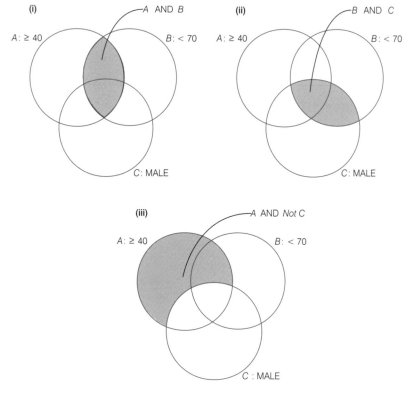

Figure 1.6 Events *A* AND *B*, *B* AND *C*, *A* AND *Not C*.

(i) *A* AND *B* is the event 'gained 40% or more and gained less than 70%'; that is, the candidate gained 40–69%

(ii) *B* AND *C* is the event, 'male candidate and gained less than 70%'

(iii) *A* AND *Not C* is 'female and gained 40% or more' as shown in Figure 1.6.

The event *A* OR *B*

The second way in which events can be combined is using OR. By the event *A* OR *B* we mean that event *A* happens *or* event *B* happens *or both*.

For example, suppose that on throwing a single dice the two events *A* and *B* are:

A: An odd number is thrown
B: A 5 or a 6 is thrown

then the event *A* OR *B* is throwing a 1, 3, 5 or 6.

On a Venn diagram *A* OR *B* is represented by the total area inside one or both of the *A* and *B* loops (see Figure 1.7).

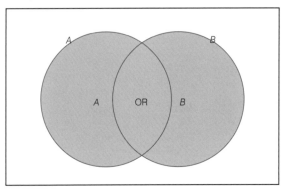

Figure 1.7 A Venn diagram showing the event *A* OR *B*.

Check this

A courier is selected by a travel firm for special duties. Define the events:

A: He/she speaks French
B: He/she speaks German
C: He/she speaks Italian.

Describe the events *A* OR *B* and *A* OR *C*.

Solution:
The event *A* OR *B* is the event, 'the courier speaks French or German or both' whereas *A* OR *C* is the event, 'the courier speaks French or Italian or both'.

Calculating the probabilities of AND and OR events from each other

As with any other event, the probabilities of A AND B and A OR B can be calculated by summing the probabilities of all the outcomes in the event.

However, when an A OR B or an A AND B probability is already known, the following relationship between $P(A$ AND $B)$ and $P(A$ OR $B)$ can save some time.

This relationship is

$$P(A \text{ OR } B) = P(A) + P(B) - P(A \text{ AND } B)$$

or equivalently, this rearranges to

$$P(A \text{ AND } B) = P(A) + P(B) - P(A \text{ OR } B).$$

(This is the same as the previous one but with A AND B and A OR B swapped.)

To see why this is true, look at the Venn diagram in Figure 1.7 again. Notice that the area representing A OR B can be formed by taking the area in A and appending the area in B. However, by doing this the area in the intersection will have been included twice so we must take the area in the intersection away. This is like saying that a list of all the outcomes in A OR B could be constructed by listing all the outcomes in A and all the outcomes in B and then deleting one set of the outcomes in A AND B as these will have been included twice.

As the probability of an event is the sum of the probabilities of the outcomes comprising that event we have the result given above,

$$P(A \text{ OR } B) = P(A) + P(B) - P(A \text{ AND } B).$$

Examples of the use of this relationship are given below.

Check these

When selecting a card at random from a pack, there is a probability of $\frac{3}{13}$ of obtaining a royal card (K, Q, J) and a probability of $\frac{1}{2}$ of obtaining a red card. The probability of obtaining a card that is red and royal is $\frac{6}{52} = \frac{3}{26}$. Use these to find out the probability of selecting a card that is red or royal.

Solution:
We start by defining events from the information given. We have

A: Royal
B: Red

and we know that $P(A) = \frac{3}{13}$, $P(B) = \frac{1}{2}$ and $P(A \text{ AND } B) = \frac{3}{26}$.

The probability we need is $P(A$ OR $B)$. Using the formula:

$$P(A \text{ OR } B) = P(A) + P(B) - P(A \text{ AND } B) = \frac{3}{13} + \frac{1}{2} - \frac{3}{26} = \frac{6 + 13 - 3}{26} = \frac{16}{26} = \frac{8}{13}$$

A chemical plant holds a ballot for all its employees to decide whether or not to accept a new pay deal. At the ballot, 80% of the employees voted and it is known that 60% of the employees are union members. The union ascertains that 90% of the employees are either union members or voted (or both). What is the probability that an employee selected at random is a union member who voted?

Solution:
We label the events as follows:

A: The employee voted
B: The employee is a union member

so A OR B is the event 'union member or voted' and A AND B is the event, 'union member and voted'.
   We have been given $P(A) = 0.8$, $P(B) = 0.6$ and $P(A\ OR\ B) = 0.9$ and need $P(A\ AND\ B)$. From the formula

$$P(A\ AND\ B) = P(A) + P(B) - P(A\ OR\ B)$$

we have $P(A\ AND\ B) = 0.8 + 0.6 - 0.9 = 0.5$.
   We conclude that there is a 50% probability that an employee selected at random is a union member who voted.

Mutually exclusive events

When two (or more) events *cannot* occur at the same time we say they are *mutually exclusive* (because they exclude each other!). Examples of mutually exclusive events are:

A: A person is over 60 years old
B: A person is under 18

because the same person cannot be over 60 and under 18.

C: A coin falls heads
D: A coin falls tails

because a coin cannot fall both heads and tails.
   The result of a particular football match for my home team can be:

E: Won
F: Drawn
G: Lost

These events are mutually exclusive – only one of them can happen.
   However, the events that an individual is:

H: Married
I : Single
J : Divorced

are *not* mutually exclusive because it is possible to be both single and divorced.
   When two events, A and B, are mutually exclusive there are no outcomes in A AND B and so $P(A\ AND\ B) = 0$. The two statements

1. A and B are mutually exclusive
2. $P(A\ AND\ B) = 0$

are therefore equivalent.
   So when A and B are mutually exclusive, the relationship

$$P(A\ OR\ B) = P(A) + P(B) - P(A\ AND\ B)$$

becomes

$$P(A\ OR\ B) = P(A) + P(B)$$

Check this

At a concert concessionary tickets are available to those who are under 18 and those who are over 60. It is known that 20% of tickets are sold to those under 18 and 30% to the over 60s. What is the probability that an individual chosen at random has a concessionary ticket?

Solution:
The two events A: individual is under 18 and B: individual is over 60 are mutually exclusive so $P(A\ \text{OR}\ B) = P(A) + P(B) = 0.2 + 0.3 = 0.5$.

When two events are mutually exclusive their two loops on a Venn diagram do *not* intersect, as shown in Figure 1.8.

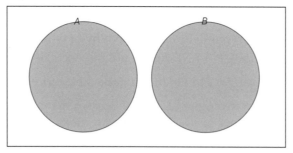

Figure 1.8 A and B are mutually exclusive events.

Combining events

$P(A\ \text{AND}\ B) = P(A) + P(B) - P(A\ \text{OR}\ B)$

or equivalently

$P(A\ \text{OR}\ B) = P(A) + P(B) - P(A\ \text{AND}\ B)$

The following two statements are equivalent:

A and B are **mutually exclusive**

$P(A\ \text{AND}\ B) = 0$

When A and B are mutually exclusive

$P(A\ \text{OR}\ B) = P(A) + P(B)$

WORK CARD 2

1. Recall the market research shopping centre survey to study the use of public transport to get to the centre and the time of arrival. The results are repeated below:

Number of customers

	9 am–5 pm	5 pm–8 pm
Public	170	30
Not public	50	250

Suppose event A is 'arrives between 9am and 5pm' and event B is, 'arrives by public transport'.

a. Describe in words what is meant by A OR B.

b. Describe in words what is meant by A AND B.

c. Are events A and B mutually exclusive? Why or why not?

d. Calculate $P(A)$, $P(B)$, $P(A$ AND $B)$ and use these to calculate $P(A$ OR $B)$.

Confirm your answer for $P(A$ OR $B)$ using the table of frequencies directly.

2. After completing an inventory of 3 warehouses, a manufacturer of golf club shafts described its stock of 12,246 shafts with the percentages given in the table.

Type of shaft

		Regular (%)	Hard (%)	Extra hard (%)
	1	19	8	3
Warehouse	2	14	8	2
	3	28	18	0

A shaft is selected at random.

Let A be the event that the shaft is regular, B be the event that it is extra hard and C be the event that the shaft is from warehouse 3.

Describe in words the characteristics of a golf club shaft portrayed by the following events and find the probability of each:

A AND C, A OR C, A AND B, A OR B

Are the events A and B mutually exclusive? Why or why not?

3. A newspaper report describing types of occupation of professional workers states that '24.6% of all workers are managerial, 55.2% of all workers are male, and 66.1% are male or managerial (or both)'. What percentage of professional workers are male and managerial?

4. Draw a Venn diagram to show the following events relating to a particular company:

A: Employs 5 or fewer people

B: Owns its own premises

C: Employs more than 30 people

Which pairs of events are mutually exclusive and which aren't? Explain your answers.

Solutions:

1. **a.** Customer arrives between 9am and 5pm or arrives by public transport or both.

   b. Customer arrives by public transport and between 9am and 5pm.

   c. These events are not mutually exclusive because both can happen at once – a customer may arrive by public transport and between 9am and 5pm. Alternatively, we could say that they are not mutually exclusive because $P(A$ AND $B)$ is not 0.

   d. $P(A) = \dfrac{220}{500}$, $P(B) = \dfrac{200}{500}$, $P(A$ AND $B) = \dfrac{170}{500}$

   so $P(A$ OR $B) = \dfrac{220}{500} + \dfrac{200}{500} - \dfrac{170}{500} = \dfrac{250}{500} = 0.5$

   Confirming this from the table gives

   $$\frac{170 + 30 + 50}{500} = \frac{250}{500} = 0.5$$

2. Regular and from warehouse 3, regular or from warehouse 3, regular and extra hard, regular or extra hard. $P(A$ AND $C) = 0.28$, $P(A$ OR $C) = 0.19 + 0.14 + 0.28 + 0.18 + 0.0 = 0.79$, $P(A$ AND $B) = 0$, $P(A$ OR $B) = 0.19 + 0.14 + 0.28 + 0.03 + 0.02 + 0 = 0.66$.
   A and B are mutually exclusive because $P(A$ AND $B) = 0$.

3. It makes no difference whether we work in probabilities or percentages.
   Here, we know $P(Managerial) = 0.246$, $P(Male) = 0.552$ and $P(Managerial$ OR $male) = 0.661$. Using the relation $P(A$ AND $B) = P(A) + P(B) - P(A$ OR $B)$ gives $P(Managerial$ AND $Male) = 0.246 + 0.552 - 0.661 = 0.137$.

4. Events A and C are mutually exclusive, but A and B, and B and C are not. So in the diagram, the A and C loops should be non-intersecting. The B loop should intersect both the A loop and the C loop.

WORK CARD 2 (CONTINUED)

ASSESSMENT 2

1. An energy agency mailed questionnaires on energy conservation to 1000 homeowners; 500 questionnaires were returned. One of the returned questionnaires is selected at random. Consider the following events:

   A: Home is built of brick
   B: Home is more than 30 years old
   C: Home is heated with oil

ASSESSMENT 2 (CONTINUED)

Denote each of the following as AND or OR events.

   a. Home is more than 30 years old and heated with oil.

   b. Home is heated with oil or is more than 30 years old.

   c. Home is constructed of brick and not heated with oil.

   d. Home is constructed of brick and heated with oil and more than 30 years old.

Are the events *A*, *B* and *C* mutually exclusive or not? Explain your answer.

2. In a particular city 20% of people subscribe to the morning newspaper, 30% to the evening newspaper and 10% subscribe to both.

   Determine the probability that an individual from this city subscribes to the morning newspaper or the evening newspaper or both. Are the events, 'subscribe to morning newspaper', and 'do not subscribe to morning newspaper' mutually exclusive or not? Say why or why not.

3. There are 50 workers on an assembly line. Of these, 5 produce work late, 6 assemble defective products and 2 both produce late work and assemble defective products.

   One worker is to be selected at random for a TV interview. What is the probability that this worker produces late work or assembles defective products or both?

4. Describe 3 events for a particular situation in which 2 of these events are mutually exclusive but the other one isn't. Explain why this is so. Draw a Venn diagram illustrating the 3 events. Be inventive!

3 Conditional probability

What are conditional probabilities?

Sometimes additional information may influence the probability of an event. Consider the following example.

Trish has applied for an internal post. She knows that 5 people, 3 women and 2 men, have been short-listed including herself and so, knowing nothing about the other candidates, she judges that her chance of success is

$$P(Success) = \frac{1}{5}$$

However, shortly before the management's decision is announced one of the managers lets slip that the successful applicant is a woman. As there are only 3 women under consideration Trish calculates that her probability of success is now $\frac{1}{3}$. The extra information – that the successful applicant is female – has changed the probability.

The probability of Trish's success in the light of the new information that a woman has been appointed is called the *conditional probability* of success *given* that a woman has been appointed. If we define the events *Success* and *Woman* in an obvious way we can write this probability

$$P(Success|Woman)$$

It reads the 'probability of *Success* given *Woman*'.

In general, when we have two events *A* and *B*, the probability $P(A \mid B)$ is the *conditional* probability of *A given B* and means the probability that *A* occurs *when we know* that *B* has occurred. The vertical line means, 'given' and the event to the right of it is the 'additional information'.

Another example

Suppose that in a game your opponent has thrown a dice but you have not seen the result. We define the events:

Event *A:* Throw is a 6
Event *B:* Throw is an even number

The probability of throwing a 6 is $P(A)$. Of the 6 possible outcomes, 1, 2, 3, 4, 5 and 6 that are all equally likely, only one is in event *A*, so

$$P(A) = \frac{1}{6}$$

Now, suppose your opponent tells you that they have thrown an even number. This extra information changes the probability that they have thrown a 6 because now there are only 3 possible outcomes, 2, 4, and 6. As only one of these outcomes is in event *A* the conditional probability of throwing a six given that the throw is even is

$$P(A \mid B) = \frac{1}{3}$$

Calculating conditional probabilities

In general, the formula for calculating the conditional probability of *A* given *B* is

$$P(A \mid B) = \frac{P(A \text{ AND } B)}{P(B)}$$

We will explain this using the relative frequency approach to probability, but similar reasoning applies when there are equally likely outcomes.

Recall that using the relative frequency approach, the probability of an event is the same as the proportion or relative frequency of times the event has occurred in the past. For instance, $P(A)$ is the proportion of times event *A* has occurred.

The conditional probability $P(A \mid B)$ is the probability of *A* occurring when we know that *B* has occurred and so it is the proportion of all the times that event *B* has occurred for which event *A* has also occurred. It is therefore the number of times that events *A* and *B* have both occurred divided by the number of times event *B* has occurred. This is the same as the proportion of all times that *A* AND *B* has occurred divided by the proportion of all times that event *B* has occurred which is

$$P(A \mid B) = \frac{P(A \text{ AND } B)}{P(B)}$$

as given above.

This is easiest to see using a Venn diagram such as the one in Figure 1.9 where each area represents the probability or relative frequency of the corresponding event so that $P(A)$ is represented by the event *A* loop and so on.

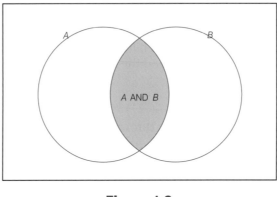

Figure 1.9

For the conditional probability $P(A \mid B)$ we *know* that B has happened and so we need only look at the B loop of the Venn diagram repeated in Figure 1.10. The conditional probability, $P(A \mid B)$, is the proportion of the event B loop that is in event A and so is the A AND B area divided by the B area.

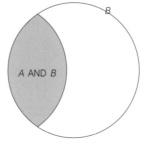

Figure 1.10

Check this

Seventy per cent of the households in a city take a morning paper whereas 20% of the households take both the *Evening News* and a morning paper.

What is the probability that a household that takes a morning paper takes the *Evening News*?

Solution:
You will see questions about conditional probability worded in many different ways. The trick is to read the information supplied to assess which event is given or known. Here we want the probability that a household takes the *Evening News* – *given* that they take the morning paper. It is the same as asking, 'what proportion of the households who take a morning paper, take the *Evening News*'.

To solve this we define:

A: Household takes *Evening News*
B: Household takes morning paper

We have been given $P(B) = 0.7$, $P(A \text{ AND } B) = 0.2$ and we require $P(A \mid B)$. From the formula this is

$$\frac{P(A \text{ AND } B)}{P(B)} = \frac{0.2}{0.7} = 0.2857$$

Be careful: it is easy to get the conditional probability $P(A \mid B)$ confused with $P(A \text{ AND } B)$. Remember that $P(A \text{ AND } B)$ is the proportion of *all* times in which A AND B occurs whereas $P(A \mid B)$ is the proportion of the times B occurs, in which A occurs. You need to recognise this difference in the following example:

Check this

A computer retailer conducts a survey of 200 computer purchasers and obtains the following results.

Age

	Less than 30	30–44	45 and over
Male	60	20	40
Female	40	30	10

A customer is selected at random.

a. What is the probability that the customer is male and aged 30–44?

b. If the selected customer is aged 30–44 what is the probability that they are male?

Solution:

a. The probability that a customer is male *and* aged 30–44 is the probability of the male and 30–44 cell in the table and is $\frac{20}{200} = 0.1$.

This is *not* a conditional probability. Question **b.**, however, asks for the probability that a customer is male, *given* that they are aged 30–44. This is the conditional probability:

$$P(Male \mid 30\text{–}44) = \frac{P(Male \text{ AND } 30\text{–}44)}{P(30\text{–}44)}$$

$P(Male \text{ AND } 30\text{–}44) = 0.1$ as calculated in **a.** and

$$P(30\text{–}44) = \frac{20 + 30}{200} = 0.25$$

from the table so $P(Male \mid 30\text{–}44) = \frac{0.1}{0.25} = 0.4$

Notice, in the last example, that calculating the conditional probability that a customer is male *given* that they are 30–44 is the same as taking only the 30–44 column of the table of frequencies and calculating the unconditional probability that a customer is male, which is $\frac{20}{20+30}$.

Independent events

For the computer purchasers' example above

$$P(Male) = \frac{60 + 20 + 40}{200} = 0.6$$

whereas we have just found that

$$P(Male \mid 30\text{--}44) = 0.4$$

The additional information that the selected customer is 30–44 changed the probability that the customer is male.

We say that the events *Male* and 30–44 are *dependent*. By this we mean that whether one of them happens or not influences the probability of the other.

In general, the following three statements are all equivalent to each other and so any one implies the others.

> $P(A \mid B)$ is different from $P(A)$
>
> $P(B \mid A)$ is different from $P(B)$
>
> A and B are *dependent*

In a similar way the following three statements are equivalent to each other and so any one implies the others.

> $P(A \mid B) = P(A)$
>
> $P(B \mid A) = P(B)$
>
> A and B are *independent*

The idea of dependence and independence is crucial in Statistics. In particular, many models require an assumption of independence. Even if you are having problems with probability definitions, try to remember that two events are independent when the occurrence/non-occurrence of one does *not* change the probability of the occurrence/non-occurrence of the other.

Check these

Do you think each of the following pairs of events are independent or dependent? Explain your answers.

a. An individual has a high IQ
An individual is accepted for a university place

b. A patient takes an abnormally long time to recover from an operation
 The patient is elderly

c. A student plays table-tennis
 A student is good at Maths

d. A student plays chess
 A student is good at Maths

e. An individual has a large outstanding credit card debt
 An individual is allowed to extend his bank overdraft

f. An individual eats out 3 or more times a week
 An individual earns more than the national average wage

Solutions:
For each pair of events ask yourself whether the occurrence or non-occurrence of one of these events affects the probability that the other one is true.

a. Rumour has it that you have to be intelligent to get to university! Someone with a high IQ is more likely to be accepted for a university place than someone with a low IQ, so the events are *dependent*.

b. An elderly patient is more likely to take longer to recover than a younger patient so again the events are *dependent*.

c. There is no reason why a student who plays table tennis should be good or bad at Maths. The two events are *independent*.

d. We conjecture that students who are good at Maths are more likely to play chess so these events are *dependent*.

e. An individual's financial position is likely to affect a bank's decision to extend his overdraft, so the two events are *dependent*.

f. One would expect that a more affluent person is more likely to eat out more than a poorer person, so the two events are *dependent*

Confusion: independent events vs mutually exclusive events

Many students confuse the idea of independent events with the idea of mutually exclusive events. Recall that two events are mutually exclusive if they *cannot* both happen. For instance, when a single dice is thrown the events A an even number is observed and B a 5 is observed are mutually exclusive. On the other hand, the events C an even number is observed and D the number is a 4 are *not* mutually exclusive. When two events are mutually exclusive the probability that they both happen is zero; that is, $P(A \text{ AND } B) = 0$.

Two events are independent when the occurrence or non-occurrence of one event does *not* affect the probability of the other event; that is, when two events A and B are independent, $P(A \mid B) = P(A)$ and $P(B \mid A) = P(B)$. For instance, when a card is selected at random from a pack of cards the event A card is a heart and the event B card is a 2 are independent, because the probability of a two is 1/13, whether A happens or not.

When A and B are mutually exclusive we know that if A occurs B cannot occur, so $P(B \mid A) = 0$ whereas $P(B)$ will be non-zero. Two mutually exclusive events are therefore *not* independent.

1. A company produces video tapes at two factories; 40% of all the tapes are produced by factory *A* and the remainder by factory *B*. Altogether 2% of the video tapes are produced by factory *A* and defective.

   What is the probability that a tape is defective given that it was manufactured by factory *A*?

2. A fast-food chain with 700 outlets describes the geographic location of its restaurants with the following table:

		Region			
		NE	SE	SW	NW
	Under 10,000	35	42	21	70
Population	10,000–100,000	70	105	84	35
	over 100,000	175	28	35	0

   A Health and Safety organisation select a restaurant at random for a hygiene inspection.

   a. What is the probability that a restaurant in the NE is chosen?

   b. It leaks out that the chosen restaurant is from a large city of population over 100,000. Now what is the probability it is in the NE?

   c. Are the events, 'restaurant is in the NE' and 'restaurant is in a city with a population of over 100,000' independent or not? Explain your answer. Show these two events on a Venn diagram.

3. Refer to the data from the table in question 2.

   One restaurant is rumoured to have won the prestigious 'Happy Eater' award.

   a. If all the restaurants have an equal chance of winning what is the probability the winner is from a small town of population less than 10,000?

   b. If rumour also says that the winner is in the SE of the country, what is the probability that the winner is from a small town of population less than 10,000?

   Are the events, 'restaurant is in small town' and 'restaurant is in SE' independent? Explain your answer.

4. Are the following pairs of events independent or not?

   a. A card is selected at random from a pack of cards
      It is a heart. It is a king

   b. The total of two dice is 10 or more
      One of the dice shows a 5

   c. A particular student:
      Speaks Cantonese
      Comes from Hong Kong

   d. The sky is cloudy
      It will rain today

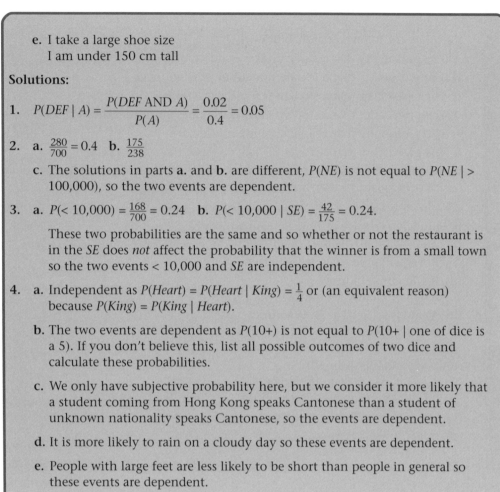

WORK CARD 3 (CONTINUED)

e. I take a large shoe size
I am under 150 cm tall

Solutions:

1. $P(DEF \mid A) = \dfrac{P(DEF \text{ AND } A)}{P(A)} = \dfrac{0.02}{0.4} = 0.05$

2. **a.** $\dfrac{280}{700} = 0.4$ **b.** $\dfrac{175}{238}$

   c. The solutions in parts **a.** and **b.** are different, $P(NE)$ is not equal to $P(NE \mid > 100{,}000)$, so the two events are dependent.

3. **a.** $P(< 10{,}000) = \dfrac{168}{700} = 0.24$ **b.** $P(< 10{,}000 \mid SE) = \dfrac{42}{175} = 0.24.$

   These two probabilities are the same and so whether or not the restaurant is in the *SE* does *not* affect the probability that the winner is from a small town so the two events < 10,000 and *SE* are independent.

4. **a.** Independent as $P(Heart) = P(Heart \mid King) = \frac{1}{4}$ or (an equivalent reason) because $P(King) = P(King \mid Heart)$.

   b. The two events are dependent as $P(10+)$ is not equal to $P(10+ \mid$ one of dice is a 5). If you don't believe this, list all possible outcomes of two dice and calculate these probabilities.

   c. We only have subjective probability here, but we consider it more likely that a student coming from Hong Kong speaks Cantonese than a student of unknown nationality speaks Cantonese, so the events are dependent.

   d. It is more likely to rain on a cloudy day so these events are dependent.

   e. People with large feet are less likely to be short than people in general so these events are dependent.

ASSESSMENT 3

1. A trade union knows that 15% of the employees in a shoe plant are both union members and are willing to strike. Altogether 35% of employees are union members. What is the probability that an employee who is a union member is willing to go out on strike?

2. Consider again the data from Section 1 giving the number of male and female students on various degree courses in the business school of a university and repeated below. There are 1500 students altogether.

	Accountancy	Economics	Finance	Business Information Systems
Male	330	360	90	120
Female	120	390	60	30

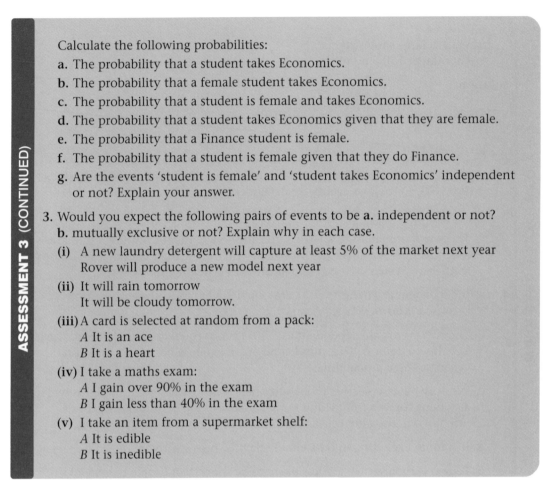

ASSESSMENT 3 (CONTINUED)

Calculate the following probabilities:

a. The probability that a student takes Economics.

b. The probability that a female student takes Economics.

c. The probability that a student is female and takes Economics.

d. The probability that a student takes Economics given that they are female.

e. The probability that a Finance student is female.

f. The probability that a student is female given that they do Finance.

g. Are the events 'student is female' and 'student takes Economics' independent or not? Explain your answer.

3. Would you expect the following pairs of events to be **a.** independent or not? **b.** mutually exclusive or not? Explain why in each case.

(i) A new laundry detergent will capture at least 5% of the market next year
Rover will produce a new model next year

(ii) It will rain tomorrow
It will be cloudy tomorrow.

(iii) A card is selected at random from a pack:
A It is an ace
B It is a heart

(iv) I take a maths exam:
A I gain over 90% in the exam
B I gain less than 40% in the exam

(v) I take an item from a supermarket shelf:
A It is edible
B It is inedible

4 Calculating joint or AND probabilities

Joint probabilities

Recall that the conditional probability of *A* given *B* is

$$P(A \mid B) = \frac{P(A \text{ AND } B)}{P(B)}$$

Multiplying both sides of this by $P(B)$ gives

$$P(A \text{ AND } B) = P(A \mid B)\, P(B)$$

This gives us a formula for the probability of the event *A* AND *B* in terms of $P(B)$ and $P(A \mid B)$. By similar reasoning we also have

$$P(A \text{ AND } B) = P(B \mid A)\, P(A)$$

These relationships are often useful when we know $P(A)$ and $P(B \mid A)$ or $P(B)$ and $P(A \mid B)$ and need to calculate $P(A \text{ AND } B)$.

Check these

I select two cards from a pack of cards. What is the probability that they are both aces?

Solution: We will define:

 A: First card is an ace
 B: Second card is an ace

We require P (A AND B). Notice that these events are *de*pendent because the probability that the second card is an ace depends on whether or not the first card is an ace. The formula is $P(A \text{ AND } B) = P(B \mid A) P(A)$.
 $P(A) = \frac{1}{13}$ (4 cards out of 52 are aces) and $P(B \mid A) = \frac{3}{51}$ (when the first card is an ace, only 3 out of the remaining 51 cards are aces), so

$$P(A \text{ AND } B) = \frac{3}{51} \cdot \frac{1}{13} = 0.004525$$

Forty per cent of the British population are under 20. Of these 60% regularly watch 'Neighbours'.
 If a British person is selected at random, what is the probability that he/she is under 20 and regularly watches 'Neighbours'?

Solution: Define the events:

 A: Under 20
 B: Regular 'Neighbours' viewer

We know that $P(A) = 0.4$ and that $P(B \mid A) = 0.6$ so

$$P(A \text{ AND } B) = P(B \mid A) P(A) = 0.6 \times 0.4 = 0.24$$

Joint probabilities for independent events

When two events, A and B, are *in*dependent we know that $P(A \mid B) = P(A)$ and $P(B \mid A) = P(B)$ so

$$P(A \text{ AND } B) = P(A \mid B) P(B) \text{ and } P(A \text{ AND } B) = P(B \mid A) P(A)$$

both become

$$P(A \text{ AND } B) = P(A) P(B)$$

That is, when two events are independent we need only multiply their respective probabilities to find their joint probability.

Check these

I toss a fair coin and then throw a dice. What is the probability that I obtain a head and a six?

Solution:
Define:

 A: Coin throws a head
 B: Dice gives a 6

We require $P(A$ AND $B)$. As the probabilities of the dice throw are not influenced by the result of the coin the events are independent and $P(A$ AND $B) = P(A) P(B)$.

As $P(A) = \dfrac{1}{2}$ and $P(B) = \dfrac{1}{6}$, $P(A$ AND $B) = \dfrac{1}{2} \cdot \dfrac{1}{6} = \dfrac{1}{12}$

Paul has a 10% chance of being stopped by customs on the way back from a European business trip and a 25% chance of being stopped on his return from a business trip to Saudi Arabia. He plans a trip to Milan (Italy) during one week and a trip to Jeddah (Saudi Arabia) the following week. What is the probability that customs stop him both times?

Solution:
We define:

  A: Stopped on return from Milan
  B: Stopped on return from Jeddah

Casting aside any suspicion aroused by his being a frequent traveller, we assume that these events are independent. We require $P(A$ AND $B) = P(A)P(B) = 0.1 \times 0.25 = 0.025$.

To enter Breaker's campus coffee bar I need to go through 2 consecutive double-sided doors. At each double door one side opens and the other doesn't, but I never remember which side works and so am equally likely to try either side first. What is the probability that I open both double-sided doors at the first attempt?

Solution:
We define:

  A: First attempt at first double-sided door is correct
  B: First attempt at second double-sided door is correct

I require $P(A$ AND $B)$. We assume that my success or otherwise in opening the first door does not affect the chances of opening the second door correctly so the two events are independent and $P(A$ AND $B) = P(A) P(B)$. At each door I am equally likely to try each side first, so $P(A) = \dfrac{1}{2}$, $P(B) = \dfrac{1}{2}$, and so

  $P(A$ AND $B) = \dfrac{1}{2} \cdot \dfrac{1}{2} = \dfrac{1}{4}$

This rule for calculating the AND probabilities of independent events extends to any number of events. For instance, when the events A, B, C and D are all independent

$$P(A \text{ AND } B \text{ AND } C \text{ AND } D) = P(A) P(B) P(C) P(D)$$

Check these

The probability that Jack goes out on a Friday night is 0.5, that he goes out on a Saturday night is 0.7 and that he goes out on a Sunday night is 0.2. Assuming that he is no more or less likely to go out on a particular night because he has been out or hasn't on another night, calculate the probability that he goes out on Friday, Saturday and Sunday in one weekend.

Solution:
The three events:

  A: Goes out on Friday
  B: Goes out on Saturday
  C: Goes out on Sunday

are independent, so the probability of all three happening is the product of all three probabilities; that is

  $P(A \text{ AND } B \text{ AND } C) = P(A)\,P(B)\,P(C)$

and the probability he goes out on all three nights is $0.5 \times 0.7 \times 0.2 = 0.07$.

The daily returns on a particular ordinary share on different days are assumed to be independent of each other. Suppose a particular share has a negative daily return with a probability of 0.4, a positive return with a probability of 0.5 and a zero return with a probability of 0.1. Calculate the following probabilities:

a. The return is positive for 3 consecutive days

b. The return is positive for 4 consecutive days and is negative on the fifth day

Solution:
Define the events:

  1+: Positive return on day 1
  2+: Positive return on day 2
  3+: Positive return on day 3

a. As the returns on different days are independent these events are independent, so

  $P(1+ \text{ AND } 2+ \text{ AND } 3+) = P(1+)\,P(2+)\,P(3+) = 0.5^3 = 0.125$

b. Now define:

  1+: Positive return on day 1
  2+: Positive return on day 2
  3+: Positive return on day 3
  4+: Positive return on day 4
  5–: Negative return on day 5

Again, as the returns on different days are independent these events are independent, so the required probability

  $P(1+ \text{ AND } 2+ \text{ AND } 3+ \text{ AND } 4+ \text{ AND } 5-) = P(1+)\,P(2+)\,P(3+)\,P(4+)\,P(5-) = 0.5^4\,0.4 = 0.025$

The corresponding result for the joint probability of a series of *dependent* events can be written

  $P(A \text{ AND } B \text{ AND } C \text{ AND } D) = P(A)\,P(B\,|\,A)\,P(C\,|\,B \text{ AND } A)\,P(D\,|\,A \text{ AND } B \text{ AND } C)$

Notice that this is a natural extension of $P(A \text{ AND } B) = P(B\,|\,A)\,P(A)$ and that each factor in this probability is the conditional probability of an event given that all the previous events have occurred.

Check this

An Accountancy degree course takes three years. Ninety-six per cent of first-year students pass the first year at the first attempt. Of those who pass the first year at the first attempt 89% pass the second year at the first attempt and of those who pass both the first and second year at the first attempt 97% pass the third year at the first attempt.
  What is the probability that a student passes all three years at the first attempt?

Solution:
If we define the events:

 A: Student passes first year at first attempt.
 B: Student passes second year at first attempt.
 C: Student passes third year at first attempt.

the information we have been given is $P(A) = 0.96$, $P(B \mid A) = 0.89$ and $P(C \mid A$ AND $B) = 0.97$.
  We require

  $P(A$ AND B AND $C) = P(A)\, P(B \mid A)\, P(C \mid B$ AND $A) = 0.96 \times 0.89 \times 0.97 = 0.8288$

We repeat the results from this and Section 3 below. You only need to learn those marked * as all the others can be deduced from these.

Conditional probabilities and independence

The conditional probability of event *A* given event *B* is

$$P(A \mid B) = \frac{P(A \text{ AND } B)}{P(B)} \ *$$

The conditional probability of event *B* given event *A* is

$$P(B \mid A) = \frac{P(A \text{ AND } B)}{P(A)}$$

Independence and dependence

The following three statements* are all equivalent to each other, so any one implies the others

 $P(A \mid B)$ is different from $P(A)$

 $P(B \mid A)$ is different from $P(B)$

 A and *B* are *dependent*

In a similar way the following three statements are equivalent to each other*, so any one implies the others.

$P(A \mid B) = P(A)$

$P(B \mid A) = P(B)$

A and *B* are *independent*

AND probabilities

$P(A \text{ AND } B) = P(A \mid B) P(B) = P(B \mid A) P(A)$

When the events *A* and *B* are *independent* this becomes

$P(A \text{ AND } B) = P(A) P(B)$

which extends to any number of events. For instance, when *A*, *B*, *C* and *D* are independent

$P(A \text{ AND } B \text{ AND } C \text{ AND } D) = P(A) P(B) P(C) P(D)$

and when *A*, *B*, *C* and *D* are *dependent*

$P(A \text{ AND } B \text{ AND } C \text{ AND } D) = P(A) P(B \mid A) P(C \mid B \text{ AND } A) P(D \mid A \text{ AND } B \text{ AND } C)*$

WORK CARD 4

1. Out of 20 films to be shown by the student union on Friday and Saturday nights this term there are 6 that Greg wants to see. If he does not go to a film there is a 30% chance he will go to the student union bar. If he goes to a film there is a 60% chance that he will go to the student union bar afterwards.

    What is the probability that on a particular Friday or Saturday night this term he goes to a film and then on to the bar?

2. When the weather is stormy the probability that the lifeboat service of a small coastal town is called out is 40%. When weather isn't stormy the probability is 10%. It is only stormy about 1 night in 20 throughout the year. What is the probability that it is stormy and the lifeboat service are called out on a particular night?

3. Two cards are drawn at random from a pack of playing cards. What is the probability that both are royal (*K Q J*) if
    (i) The first card is not replaced in the pack.
    (ii) The first card is replaced in the pack before the second is drawn.

4. Matthew has a children's game in which two faces of a six-sided dice are 1s, two are 2s and two are 3s. He throws the dice 5 times. What is the probability that he gets a 1 every time?

5. To make a journey I must take a taxi, a train and then a bus. If any one of these is late I will be late for an important meeting. I estimate that the probability that the taxi is late is 0.2, the probability that the train is late is 0.4 and the probability that the bus is late is 0.1. What is the probability that I am not late for the meeting? What assumption is necessary to calculate this probability?

6. An office purchases a new computer system. The manufacturer states that there is a 5% probability that the machine first breaks down in the first year. If it has not broken down during the first year there is a probability of 10% that it breaks down during the second year. If it doesn't break down during the first or second year there is a probability of 30% that it breaks down in the third year.

Calculate the probability that it doesn't break down during the first two years.

Calculate the probability that it doesn't break down during the first three years.

Now suppose that the computer system undergoes a massive service at the start of each year. The chances of breakdown in a particular year are now considered to be the same, 5% for every year. Now, what is the probability that the system doesn't break down for 3 years?

Solutions:

1. $P(Film \text{ AND } Bar) = P(Bar \mid Film) \, P(Film) = 0.6 \times 0.3 = 0.18$.

2. $P(Stormy \text{ AND } Lifeboat) = P(Lifeboat \mid Stormy) \, P(Stormy) = 0.4 \times 0.05 = 0.02$.

3. Define the events, A: first card is royal B: second card is royal. $P(A \text{ AND } B) = P(B \mid A)P(A)$. For **(i)** $P(A) = \frac{12}{52}$ and the card is not replaced, so $P(B \mid A) = \frac{11}{51}$ (11 cards out of 51 are now royal), so

$$P(A \text{ AND } B) = \frac{11}{51} \times \frac{12}{52} = 0.04977$$

(ii) Because the first card is replaced the outcome of the first card has no bearing on the probability of the second, so the events A and B are independent and

$$P(A \text{ AND } B) = P(A) \, P(B) = \frac{12}{52} \times \frac{12}{52} = 0.05325$$

4. The result of each dice throw is independent of the others so

$$P(\text{All are 1s}) = \frac{1}{3}\frac{1}{3}\frac{1}{3}\frac{1}{3}\frac{1}{3} = \left(\frac{1}{3}\right)^5 = \frac{1}{243}$$

5. $P(None\ Late)$

$= P(Taxi\ Not\ Late)P(Train\ Not\ Late)P(Bus\ Not\ Late)$
$= 0.8 \times 0.6 \times 0.9 = 0.432$

This assumes that the events that the taxi, bus and train are not late are independent of each other.

6. It is easiest to label the events:

   A: Does not break down in year 1
   B: Does not break down in year 2
   C: Does not break down in year 3

WORK CARD 4

We have been given $P(A) = 0.95$, $P(B \mid A) = 0.90$ and $P(C \mid A \text{ AND } B) = 0.7$. We require $P(A \text{ AND } B) = P(A) \, P(B \mid A) = 0.95 \times 0.90 = 0.855$.

$$P(A \text{ AND } B \text{ AND } C) = P(A) \, P(B \mid A) P(C \mid A \text{ AND } B) = 0.95 \times 0.9 \times 0.7 = 0.5985$$

When the system is serviced each year the probability of a breakdown remains the same and is not influenced by what has happened earlier so each year is independent of the others and $P(A \text{ AND } B \text{ AND } C) = P(A)P(B)P(C) = 0.95^3 = 0.8574$.

ASSESSMENT 4

1. When I walk to work I meet my colleague, Jan, about one day out of three. When I cycle to work I meet him about one day out of two. I walk to work when the weather is good which is about 60% of the time. On any one working day what is the probability that I walk to work and meet him?

2. Thirty per cent of the students in the school choir also play in the orchestra and 20% of the students in the school sing in the choir. What is the probability that a student in the school is in both the orchestra and the choir?

3. A light aircraft has two engines. It usually uses both engines although it can fly with only one. Each engine has a probability of 0.01 of breaking down during a particular 2-hour flight. What is the probability that both engines fail during a particular 2-hour flight? What assumption must you make to calculate this?

4. A football team has won 110 out of 200 matches in the last two years. Assuming that this is typical and that the results of each of a series of matches are independent, calculate the probability that the team wins all of a series of 5 matches.

   This is obviously an inadequate model for the football team. Firstly, the probability of a win will depend on the reputation of their opponents. Secondly, the team may be more or less likely to win, because they have won or lost the previous match so the match results are not independent. We will improve the model to take account of the second factor only.

   Suppose the team won 80 out of the 110 matches that followed a win and won 30 out of the 90 matches that followed a loss (or draw). Assuming that the last match played was a win, calculate the probability:

   a. That they win the next two matches.

   b. That they lose or draw both the next two matches.

   c. That they win the first and lose or draw the second.

5. A taxi company runs 4 taxis. Two are older and the probability that a particular one of these breaks down on a particular day is 0.1. The other two are newer and the probability that a particular one breaks down on a particular day is 0.05. On a particular day what is the probability that all 4 taxis break down? State any assumptions you make.

   What is the probability that the two newer taxis break down but the older ones continue to work?

5 **More complicated probabilities – made simple!**

Before you panic at this title and decide to skip this section we will say that although we will be working with more complex probabilities we are going to use a device called the *tree diagram* which uses a visual representation to avoid manipulating lots of symbols.

Constructing a tree diagram

Tree diagrams are best explained by illustration. Consider the following problem.

University lecturers in two departments are asked whether they prefer to read the *Financial Times* or another, non-financial, broadsheet newspaper; 20% of Maths lecturers preferred the *FT*, whereas 40% of those in the Accountancy department preferred the *FT*. It is known that there are twice as many Maths lecturers as Accountancy lecturers.

I see a lecturer in the shared Maths and Accountancy common-room but he/she is hidden behind a *Financial Times*. What is the probability that he/she is an Accountancy lecturer?

To solve this problem we define the events *FT*, *Not FT*, *Maths* and *ACC* in an obvious way. We want to find $P(ACC \mid FT)$.

A tree diagram showing the probabilities we have been given is shown in Figure 1.11.

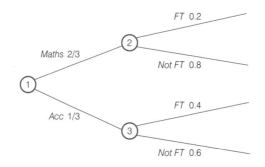

Figure 1.11 Tree diagram of *FT* readership.

Notice that each successive branching corresponds to another step which is used to generate possible outcomes. All lecturers start at node 1. At node 1 there are two possible outcomes – a lecturer is in Maths with probability 2/3 or Accountancy with probability 1/3. Each of these outcomes has a branch that is labelled with the appropriate probability.

At node 2, we know that the lecturer is a Maths lecturer but given this, there are two possible outcomes – either they prefer the *FT* or they do not. Each branch out of node 2 represents one of these outcomes and is labelled with the appropriate conditional probability given that the the lecturer is a Maths lecturer. The *FT* branch is labelled with the probability $P(FT \mid Maths) = 0.2$ and the *Not FT* branch with $P(Not\ FT \mid Maths) = 0.8$.

Node 3 and its branches are the same but for Accountancy lecturers.

Notice that the probabilities on each branch of the tree are the conditional probabilities *given* that all previous nodes have occurred.

Probabilities of terminal nodes

On the right-hand side of the tree we have a terminal node for every possible outcome. Here we have 4 terminal nodes representing the outcomes *Maths* AND *FT, Maths* AND *Not FT, Acc* AND *FT, Acc* AND *Not FT*.

Because all the probabilities on a tree diagram are conditional on the previous node, the probability of any node of the tree (including terminal nodes) occurring is the product of all the conditional probabilities leading up to that node. This is because of the final result of the last section

$$P(A \text{ AND } B \text{ AND } C \text{ AND } D) = P(A) \, P(B \mid A) \, P(C \mid B \text{ AND } A) \, P(D \mid A \text{ AND } B \text{ AND } C).$$

For example, the second terminal node from the top of our tree is the outcome *Maths* AND *Not FT* and its probability, found by multiplying the two probabilities leading to it, is $\frac{2}{3} \times 0.8 = 0.533\dot{3}$.

In Figure 1.12 we show the probabilities of all the terminal nodes. As all possible outcomes will have been generated by the tree and each outcome is mutually exclusive the probabilities of the terminal nodes add up to 1.

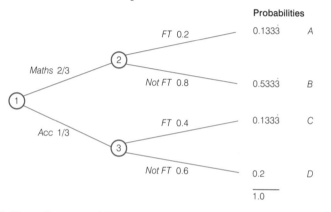

Figure 1.12 Tree diagram of *FT* readership showing terminal node probabilities.

Probabilities of events
Any event will be composed of one or more of these 'terminal node' outcomes. For instance, the event, 'lecturer prefers the *FT*' is composed of the two outcomes labelled *A* and *C* on Figure 1.12, and therefore

$$P(FT) = P(A) + P(C) = 0.133\dot{3} + 0.133\dot{3} = 0.266\dot{6}$$

Conditional probabilities
A conditional probability can be calculated by expressing it in terms of these 'terminal node' outcomes. To find $P(Acc \mid FT)$ as originally requested, recall from Section 3 that

$$P(Acc \mid FT) = \frac{P(Acc \text{ AND } FT)}{P(FT)}$$

The event in the numerator, *Acc* AND *FT*, is outcome *C* in the tree diagram (Figure 1.12), so $P(Acc \text{ AND } FT) = P(C) = 0.133\dot{3}$ and, as stated above, the event in the denominator, *FT*, comprises the two outcomes *A* and *C*, so $P(FT) = P(A) + P(C) = 0.266\dot{6}$. The conditional probability required is therefore

$$P(Acc \mid FT) = \frac{0.133\dot{3}}{0.266\dot{6}} = 0.5$$

We conclude that the probability that the lecturer hiding behind an *FT* in the common-room is an Accountancy lecturer is 0.5.

This was a 'two tier' example in that we had two separate classifications – Maths or Accountancy and then *FT* or *not FT*. However, the method works for more tiers and when more than two branches emanate from a node as illustrated in the next example.

Check this

A textile company uses 3 different service companies, Alpha, Beta and Gamma to repair machinery when it breaks down. When a piece of machinery breaks down there is a 20% chance that it is sent to Alpha and a 40% chance that it is sent to each of Beta and Gamma. A study of these companies' service times over the last two years has revealed the following.

The probability that broken machinery sent to Alpha is returned within a week is 0.5. The probability that broken machinery sent to Beta is returned within a week is 0.6 and the same probability for Gamma is 0.4.

Machinery returned within a week by Alpha or Beta has an 80% probability of being satisfactorily repaired, whereas machinery returned within a week by Gamma has a 90% probability of being satisfactorily repaired.

Machinery sent to Alpha or Beta, taking longer than a week, has a 90% probability of being satisfactorily repaired whereas machinery sent to Gamma and taking longer than a week is always satisfactorily repaired.

If a piece of machinery has taken over a week and is *not* satisfactorily repaired, what is the probability that it was sent to Alpha?

Solution:
The tree diagram using an obvious notation is given in Figure 1.13. It has 3 tiers – for the service company, the time taken and whether the repair is satisfactory or not.

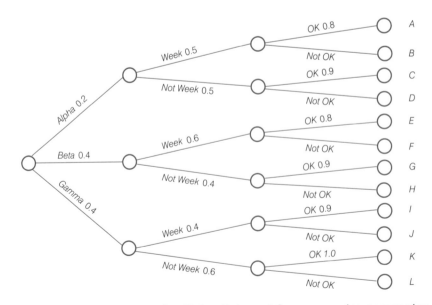

Figure 1.13 Tree diagram for Alpha, Beta and Gamma service companies.

From the tree there are 12 terminal node outcomes which we have labelled *A–L*. We require

$$P(Alpha \mid Not\ Week\ \text{AND}\ Not\ OK) = \frac{P(Alpha\ \text{AND}\ Not\ Week\ \text{AND}\ Not\ OK)}{P(Not\ Week\ \text{AND}\ Not\ OK)}$$

which is

$$\frac{P(D)}{P(D) + P(H) + P(L)}$$

as the event *Not Week* AND *Not OK* comprises the outcomes *D*, *H*, and *L* from the tree diagram in Figure 1.13. Multiplying the probabilities gives $P(D) = 0.2 \times 0.5 \times 0.1 = 0.01$, $P(H) = 0.4 \times 0.4 \times 0.1 = 0.016$ and $P(L) = 0.4 \times 0.6 \times 0 = 0$, so the desired probability is

$$\frac{0.01}{0.01 + 0.016 + 0} = 0.3846$$

We conclude that if a piece of machinery has taken over a week and has not been repaired satisfactorily there is a 38% chance that it was sent to Alpha.

WORK CARD 5

1. An electrical goods retail warehouse concludes from a customer survey that 40% of customers who seek advice from the sales staff buy an appliance and that 20% of those entering the warehouse who do not seek such advice buy an appliance. If 30% of all customers entering the warehouse seek advice, what is the probability that a customer entering the warehouse buys an appliance?

2. In a recent survey, working women were asked 'Do you think of your job as a career?' The percentage of 'yes' answers for each of several age groups is given below

Age	Percentage of women in this age group answering 'yes'
18–29	37
30–39	52
40–49	48
50+	43

Assume that a randomly selected woman is equally likely to be in any of these age categories.

(i) A woman is selected at random from the 18–29 age group. What is the probability that she thinks of her job as a career?

(ii) What is the probability that a woman selected at random from the population of working women of all ages over 18 thinks of her job as a career? (A tree diagram may help here.)

(iii) More difficult. Given that a woman thinks of her job as a career, what is the probability that she is aged 50+?

(iv) Suppose a sample of three women were taken from the population of working women. What is the probability that all three regard their job as a career?

(v) What is the probability that none of the three women sampled in (iv) regard their job as a career?

3. A market research firm has been asked to assess what proportion of a shop's customers has ever shoplifted. They stop a random sample of customers in the shop and adopt the following means of finding an answer to this delicate question.

    Each respondent was asked to toss a coin and hide the result from the interviewer. If the result was a head they were to answer question A, 'Is your age in years an odd number?' If the result was a tail they were to answer B, 'Have you ever shoplifted?': 27% of the respondents gave a 'yes' answer. Estimate the percentage of customers who have ever shoplifted.

    Hint: Use a tree diagram but mark the unknown probability with a p.

Solutions:

1. Draw a tree. The first branching is for 'seeks advice' or 'does not seek advice' and the second branching is for 'buys' or 'doesn't buy'. There are therefore 4 outcomes. The event 'buy' comprises two of these. Adding the probabilities gives 0.26.

2. (i) This is supplied to us already and is 0.37.

   (ii) The first branching of the tree diagram will be for age group and the second for whether or not she considers her work a career. There are then 8 outcomes and the probability of 4 of these gives the probability that she considers her work a career, 0.45.

   (iii) $P(50+ \mid Yes) = \dfrac{P(50+ \text{ AND } Yes)}{P(Yes)}$

   The event in the numerator is one of the terminal node outcomes and has probability 0.1075 and the denominator was calculated in (ii) and is 0.45.

   $$P(50+ \mid Yes) = \frac{0.1075}{0.45} = 0.2388$$

   (iv) From (ii) the probability that an individual woman considers her job as a career is 0.45. The probability that 3 women say 'yes' is 0.45^3.

   (v) The probability that none says 'yes' is 0.55^3.

3. A tree diagram can be constructed as usual except that it will have the unknown probability, p, for the conditional probability of a 'yes' given that a tail was tossed as shown in Figure 1.14.

    We have been told that the probability of a Yes answer is 0.27. This is the sum of the probabilities of the first and third outcomes and so $0.25 + 0.5p = 0.27$. Solving this for p gives $0.5p = 0.02$, so $p = 0.04$. We estimate that 4% of respondents have shoplifted.

WORK CARD 5 (CONTINUED)

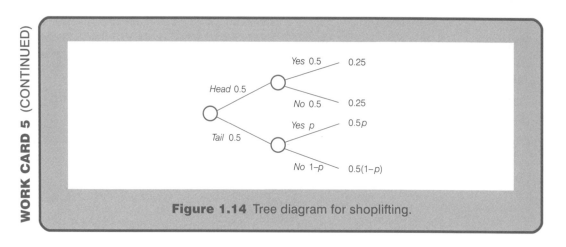

Figure 1.14 Tree diagram for shoplifting.

ASSESSMENT 5

1. A software company surveyed office managers to determine the probability that they would buy a new graphics package; 80% of the managers said they would buy the package. Of these, 40% were also interested in upgrading their computer hardware. Of those managers who were *not* interested in purchasing the graphics package only 10% were interested in upgrading their computer hardware.

   Denote event *B*, 'manager would buy package' and event *U*, 'manager would upgrade'.

   (i) Write down the percentage information supplied above in terms of probabilities and the events *B*, *Not B*, *U* and *Not U*.

   (ii) Using a tree diagram or otherwise calculate the probability that an office manager who is interested in upgrading is also interested in purchasing the new graphics package.

2. To ascertain the proportion of married people who have had extra-marital affairs the following survey procedure was used on 1000 married people.

   They were asked to think (but not say) which day of the week their most recent birthday fell on.

   If their last birthday was on a Monday, Tuesday or Wednesday they were to answer the question 'Have you ever had an extra-marital affair?'.

   If their last birthday was on Thursday, Friday, Saturday or Sunday they were to answer 'Is your age an even number?'.

   In the survey 330 people answered 'yes'. Can you estimate the proportion of people who have had extra-marital affairs?

Further reading: see p. xv

Anderson *et al.* (Statistics) and Mendenhall both contain more detail but assume more maths of the reader.

Newbold *et al.* is excellent but does take a more mathematical approach than most 'business' texts.

P2
Numerical outcomes

Woody Allen on bisexuality: It immediately doubles your chances for a date on Saturday night.

New York Times, December 1975 (Author – from your work on Chapter P1 – true or false?)

Contexts

What is this chapter about?
The uncertain event of interest is often a measurement that takes a numerical value – for instance, the number of items that will be sold or the number of defective items in a batch. In this chapter we consider some of the patterns which the probabilities of such outcomes can have, called probability distributions.

Why is it useful?
Being able to predict how likely various values are is a valuable aid to planning and decision making. In Inferential Statistics all estimates made from a sample are uncertain and so are expressed in terms of probabilities.

Where does it fit in?
The subject of Probability is largely concerned with the probabilities associated with random variables; that is, measurements that take different values according to chance. There are two types of random variable: discrete and continuous. In this chapter we consider discrete random variables, and in particular two patterns for the probabilities or probability distributions: the binomial distribution and the Poisson distribution. In the next chapter we consider continuous random variables.

What do I need to know?
You must be at ease with the last chapter, P1, and the maths required for it.

Objectives

After your work on this chapter you should:

- understand what a random variable is;
- know the difference between a continuous and a discrete random variable;
- understand what is meant by the probability distribution of a discrete random variable;
- be able to calculate the expected value and variance of a discrete random variable;
- understand the difference between the expected value of a random variable and a sample mean;
- understand the idea of the expected value of any function of a discrete random variable and be able to calculate it;
- have some idea of the (minimum) proportion of a distribution that will lie within so many standard deviations of the mean (Chebysheff);
- know when to use and be able to calculate binomial probabilities;
- know when to use and be able to calculate Poisson probabilities; including the Poisson approximation to the binomial distribution.

The outcomes of a chance situation are often numbers. For instance, the number observed when throwing a die, the price of a particular ordinary share at close of business today or the temperature in Rome at midday tomorrow.

When a variable can take different values according to chance it is called a *random variable*.

In this chapter we distinguish between two types of random variable: discrete and continuous, and then concentrate on some characteristics and particular types of discrete random variables. In Chapter P3 we discuss continuous random variables.

1 Introducing random variables

What is a random variable?
The possible outcomes of a chance situation are often numbers. Here are some examples.

- The number of boys in a family of four children chosen at random (0, 1, 2, 3 or 4).
- The maximum temperature in Paris on a particular day (–20 to +40 degrees centigrade).
- The percentage of respondents who vote Conservative in an opinion poll (between 0 and 100%).
- The mark given to a competitor by the judges in a gymnastics competition (between 5 and 6).
- The age of a student selected at random (17–90).
- The number of telephone calls received by a switchboard in an hour (0, 1, 2, 3, etc.).
- The time it takes an athlete to run 100m (10+ seconds?).

When all the possible outcomes of a random situation are numbers, the measurement concerned is called a *random variable* – because it takes different values according to chance. (Remember that a variable is a quantity that can take any one of a set of values.)

In contrast, the result of tossing a coin or the nationality of a student chosen from a class are *not* random variables because their outcomes are not numbers. We call such random quantities *categorical variables*.

Check this

Are the following random variables or not?

A   The colour of the next car to go past my flat.
B   The depth of the sea at a randomly chosen point.
C   The number of phone calls received by a switchboard in half an hour.
D   The party that wins the next election.
E   The number of attempts an individual needs to pass their driving test.
F   The brand of toothpaste a shopper buys.
G   Whether or not a person has a degree.
H   The price of a particular share at close of business tomorrow.
I   The number of students who pass an exam.
J   The proportion of students who pass an exam.
K   The time taken for an athlete to run 1500 metres.
L   Whether or not an employee earns more than £20,000.

Solution:
Only those with numerical outcomes are random variables; that is, all *except A, D, F, G,* and *L.*

Types of random variable
Random variables fall into two distinct types.

> A *continuous* random variable can take *any value* within a range whereas a *discrete* random variable can only take *some* values within a range as shown below.

DISCRETE

CONTINUOUS

The result of throwing a dice is a discrete random variable because it can only take *some* of the values between 1 and 6 inclusive. We can't have a dice throw of 5.2 or 3.5, for instance! Other examples of discrete random variables are:

● The number of cars arriving at a toll booth in a 5-minute period.
● The number of defective items in a batch.

- The number of people queuing at a supermarket checkout.
- The loser's score in a *game* of tennis (0, 15, 30, 40).

Some examples of continuous random variables are:

- The minimum temperature on a particular day.
- The percentage of sediment in a batch of a chemical (so the range is 0–100%).
- The amount of water used by a household in a day (which must be 0 or more).

In theory, the value of a continuous random variable can have any degree of precision, but in practice it can only be measured and recorded to a finite number of decimal places.

It is important to be able to distinguish between discrete and continuous random variables because they require different techniques.

There is sometimes a fine distinction between discrete and continuous random variables. For instance, when a discrete random variable can take many, many possible values – such as the number of babies born in the UK in a year or a student's weekly income in pence – it can be treated as a continuous random variable. We will consider this more in Chapter P3.

Check this

Are the following random variables continuous or discrete? Explain your answers.

B   The depth of the sea at a randomly chosen point.
C   The number of phone calls received by a switchboard in a minute.
E   The number of attempts an individual needs to pass their driving test.
H   The price of a particular share at close of business tomorrow.
I   The number of students who pass an exam.
J   The proportion of a large group of students who pass an exam.
K   The time taken for an athlete to run 1500 metres.
M   The number of heads when a coin is tossed 10 times in succession.

Solutions:
To establish whether a random variable is discrete or continuous ask yourself whether it can take *any value* within its range. For *B*, the depth of the sea can be any positive number and so it is a continuous random variable. *C* is discrete – it can only be 0, 1, 2, 3, . . . *E* is discrete – it must be 1, 2, 3, etc. *H* is continuous – it can take any positive value. *I* is discrete as we must have a whole number of students. If there are n students *J* is a proportion which is a multiple of $\frac{1}{n}$, so technically it is a discrete random variable. However, as the group is larger it can take any one of many adjacent values between 0 and 1 and so be treated as a continuous random variable. *K* is any time within the possible range and so is continuous. *M* can only be 0, 1, 2, 3, . . ., 10 heads and so is discrete.

In the rest of this chapter we consider discrete random variables only, although we will extend many of the ideas to continuous random variables in Chapter P3.

Probability distributions

It is usual to give a random variable a label, often X. The probability that X takes a particular value, say x, can then be written $P(x)$ or $P(X = x)$. For instance, the probability that X takes a value of 2 can be written $P(2)$ or $P(X = 2)$.

Notice that we use a capital letter for the random variable when it does not take a particular value and the corresponding lower-case letter for particular values that it may take.

The *probability distribution* of X, the number shown on a single die, is:

x	$P(x)$
1	1/6
2	1/6
3	1/6
4	1/6
5	1/6
6	1/6
	1

As you can see this is just a list of all the possible outcomes and their probabilities. We produced similar lists for our work on probability in Chapter P1. The only difference is that now the outcomes are all numerical.

> The probability distribution of a discrete random variable, X, is a list of all the possible values X can take and the associated probabilities.

As the probability distribution includes all the possible outcomes for X, and these outcomes are mutually exclusive (only one can occur at once) the sum of the probabilities in a probability distribution is always 1.

Check this

A coin is tossed twice. What is the probability distribution of X, the number of heads observed?

Solution:
0, 1 or 2 heads can be observed so the probability distribution is a list of the probabilities of 0, 1 and 2 heads. There are 4 equally likely outcomes and so each has a probability of 1/4.

1st toss	2nd toss
Head	Head
Head	Tail
Tail	Head
Tail	Tail

One of these outcomes gives 0 heads, 2 give 1 head and 1 gives 2 heads so the probability distribution of X, the number of heads, is

x	$P(x)$
0	1/4
1	1/2
2	1/4

Here are some more probability distributions. We will see in Sections 4 and 5 that the first of these is a *binomial* probability distribution and the second is a *Poisson* probability distribution.

X is the number of boys in a family of 4 children.

x	$P(x)$
0	1/16
1	1/4
2	3/8
3	1/4
4	1/16

X is the number of defectives in a batch of 50 items.

x	$P(x)$
0	0.6065
1	0.3033
2	0.0758
3	0.0126
4	0.0016
5	0.0002

Sometimes the probabilities, $P(x)$, can be given by a formula. For instance, the probability distribution

x	$P(x)$
1	0.1
2	0.2
3	0.3
4	0.4

could also be written $P(x) = \frac{x}{10}$ for $x = 1, 2, 3, 4$.

Probability distributions and distributions of data

In Chapter DD1, Section 1, we talked about the *distribution* of a set of data, meaning how the data was spread out. You may be wondering whether there's any connection between this use of the word distribution and its use in the expression probability *distribution*. The answer is that yes, there is.

Remember that a probability can be estimated using the proportion of times (relative frequency) that each outcome occurs in many past repetitions of the random situation (Chapter P1, Section 1) and that this approaches the true probability as the number of repetitions increases.

As a consequence, when a large amount of past data is available the distribution of the data approaches the probability distribution of the random variable. For instance, if I rolled a die several thousand times, I would expect to throw a 1, about 1/6th of the times, a 2, 1/6th of the times and so on.

When we had a sample of data we used the sample mean $\bar{x}$ and the sample variance s^2 (and other numerical measures) to help describe the centre and dispersion of the data respectively. We will see that we can use analogous measures of a probability distribution for the same purpose.

WORK CARD 1

1. Which of the following are random variables? Explain your answer.
   a. The number of bicycles a cycle shop sells each day.
   b. The most common destination of all the trains that depart late from a station on a particular day.
   c. The proportion of trains that depart late from a station on a particular day.
   d. The amount you spend on a round of drinks.
   e. The number of drinks you buy in a round of drinks.
   f. Today's weather.

2. Are the following random variables discrete or continuous?
   a. The number of questions answered correctly in a 20-question exam.
   b. The time taken to serve a customer at a bank.
   c. The price of gold at the end of each working day.
   d. The annual rate of return on an investment.
   e. The number of cars arriving at the Channel Tunnel every hour.

3. A survey about television ownership reports that 96% of households own at least 1 television set. Of these, 40% own 2 television sets, 25% own 3 sets, 5% own 4 sets and none owns 5 or more sets. Write down the probability distribution of the random variable, X, the number of television sets owned by a household.

4. The probability distribution of the number of cars owned by a household in the east of England is

x	P(x)
0	0.2
1	0.4
2	0.3
3	0.05
4	0.05

a. What is the probability that a randomly chosen household runs 2 or more cars?

b. If a randomly chosen household runs 2 or more cars what is the probability that they run exactly 2?

5. In a children's game the dice have two faces marked with a 1, two faces marked with a 2 and two faces with a 3. Write down the probability distribution for the total of the numbers shown on two such dice. **Hint:** Write down all the possible outcomes of the two dice and count up the number of these equally likely outcomes which gives a total of 2, 3, 4, 5, and 6.

6. In a game I throw two fair coins. If I throw two heads my opponent will give me £5, but after any other outcome I must pay him £2. What is the probability distribution of my gain or loss from one throw?

Solutions:

1. **b.** and **f.** (unless it is a numerical measure like rainfall or temperature) are not random variables as the possible outcomes are not numerical.

2. The first and last are discrete.

3.

x	P(x)
0	0.04
1	0.288
2	0.384
3	0.24
4	0.048
5	0

4. **a.** $P(2 \text{ or more}) = P(2) + P(3) + P(4) = 0.3 + 0.05 + 0.05 = 0.4$.

   b. We want the conditional probability of 2 cars given that they run 2 or more, i.e.

$$P(2 \,|\, 2 \text{ or more}) = \frac{P(2 \text{ AND } 2 \text{ or more})}{P(2 \text{ or more})} = \frac{P(2)}{P(2 \text{ or more})}$$

$$= \frac{0.3}{0.4} = 0.75$$

5. The possible outcomes are 1 1, 1 2, 1 3, 2 1, 2 2, 2 3, 3 1, 3 2, 3 3. These are all equally likely – so each has a probability of 1/9. One outcome has a total of 2, 2 outcomes a total of 3, 3 a total of 4, 2 a total of 5 and 1 a total of 6 so the probability distribution of the total, X, is

x	P(x)
2	1/9
3	2/9
4	3/9
5	2/9
6	1/9

6. The probability that I throw two heads is 1/4, so I will receive £5 with a probability of 1/4. In the same way I will pay £2 with a probability of 3/4, so the probability distribution of X, my gain/loss, is

x	P(x)
5	1/4
−2	3/4

1. Which of the following are random variables?
   a. Whether a product is defective or satisfactory.
   b. Whether a student passes or fails an exam.
   c. A student's exam mark.
   d. The average mark of the whole class in an exam.
   e. The proportion of male students in a class.
   f. A score of 1 when I throw a head on a coin and a score of 0 when I throw a tail.

2. Are the following discrete or continuous random variables?
   a. The number of viewers for a particular showing of a television soap.
   b. The number of printing errors in an edition of a newspaper.
   c. The average age of a class of students.
   d. The sample variance of the age of a class of students.
   e. The monthly UK rate of inflation when it is reported to only 1 decimal place.

3. Describe a random variable with each of the following properties:
   a. It is discrete and takes positive whole number (integer) values only.
   b. It is continuous and can take any value: positive, zero or negative.

ASSESSMENT 1 (CONTINUED)

c. It is discrete but can take some non-integer values.

d. It is continuous between 0 and 100 inclusive.

e. It is between 0 and 1 inclusive and continuous.

4. Students are given 3 chances to pass a professional examination. A student who has passed is selected at random. The probability distribution of X, the attempt at which this student passed, is given as

$$P(x) = \frac{0.4^{x-1}\,0.6}{0.936} \quad \text{for} \quad x = 1, 2 \text{ and } 3$$

Write out the probability distribution of X.

What *proportion* of the students who pass, pass at the third and final attempt?

5. Harold and Valerie have a son and a daughter who live in other towns. On a given night the probability that their son will phone is 0.2 and the probability that their daughter will phone is 0.3. What is the probability distribution of the number of calls they receive from their offspring on a particular night? (Use a tree diagram if it helps you.) You may assume that the events 'son calls' and 'daughter calls' are independent.

2 Expectation: the long run average

Just as we can describe a set of data using summary measures like the mean and variance, it is often useful to describe the characteristics of a random variable.

Introduction to expectation

Consider the following example, repeated from **Work card 1**.

In a game I throw two fair coins. If I throw two heads my opponent will give me £5, but if not, I must pay him £2. The probability distribution of X, the amount I gain, is

x	P(x)
5	1/4
−2	3/4

Before you read on, would you play such a game?

One way to judge whether this game offers a good deal for me would be to find out how much I would gain, on average, if we played the game a great number of times.

Suppose I play the game 10,000 times. As this is a large number of times I would expect to throw two heads and so receive £5 approximately $10,000 \times 1/4$ times. In the same way I would expect to pay £2 approximately $10,000 \times 3/4$ times. Over 10,000 games, I would expect to receive $£5 \times 10,000 \times 1/4$ but pay out $£2 \times 10,000 \times 3/4$ so my expected gain (which may be negative) over 10,000 games is

$$5 \times 10,000 \times 1/4 - 2 \times 10,000 \times 3/4$$

Dividing this by 10,000 gives my expected gain for a single game:

$$\frac{5 \times 10{,}000 \times 1/4 - 2 \times 10{,}000 \times 3/4}{10{,}000}$$

As both terms in the numerator divide by 10,000 we have

$$\text{expected gain} = 5 \times 1/4 - 2 \times 3/4$$

which is –1/4. On average, I will lose 25p on each game!

Notice that the expected gain is the sum of the amounts of each win or loss, x, multiplied by their respective probabilities of occurring, $P(x)$.

Expected values: in general

The *expected value, expectation,* or *mean* of a random variable, X, is usually written $E(X)$ or represented by the Greek symbol μ (pronounced, 'mu'). It is simply the long-run average value that X takes. That is, it is the average value X would take if the situation that produces it were repeated an infinite number of times.

The expected value of X can be calculated from the probability distribution of X by taking each possible value that X can take, multiplying it by its probability and then adding all the results up. That is, each possible value of X is 'weighted' by its probability, and then these are summed. The formula for expected value is therefore

$$E(X) = \Sigma x P(x)$$

(For those of you who have not met it before, the symbol Σ is the capital Greek letter 'sigma'. When placed in front of an expression it means 'the sum of'.) For example, in the coin-tossing game my gain, X, can take the value 5 with probability 1/4, or –2 with probability 3/4 so we calculate $5 \times 1/4$ and $-2 \times 3/4$ and then add these up to get an expected value of –1/4.

A sensible way of calculating the expected value is to work in columns as follows. Place each of the possible values of X, in column 1, and the corresponding $P(x)$s in column 2 (so columns 1 and 2 contain the probability distribution). Then multiply each item in column 1 by the corresponding item in column 2 and place the result, $xP(x)$, in a third column as shown below for the coin-tossing game.

x	$P(x)$	$xP(x)$
5	1/4	5/4
–2	3/4	–6/4
		$\mu = E(X) = -1/4$

The expected value of the random variable X is the sum of column 3, $\Sigma x P(x)$.

Check this

I am dealt one card from a standard pack. If it is a heart I must pay my opponent £1, but if it is the ace of spades, diamonds or clubs he will pay me £13. What is the expected value of my gain?

Solution:
The probability of a heart is $\frac{1}{4}$ and the probability of the ace of spades, diamonds or clubs is $\frac{3}{52}$ so the probability distribution of my gain is as given in the first two columns below. The third column contains the first column, x, multiplied by $P(x)$ from the second column.

x	$P(x)$	$xP(x)$
−1	1/4	−1/4
13	3/52	3/4
	$\mu = E(X) = 1/2$	

The total of the third column is 1/2, so $\mu = E(X) = 1/2$. I will win an average of 50p on each game. Well worth continuing!

Notice that the expected value of a random variable does *not* have to be one of the possible values it can take. In the example above the expected value was 50p, which cannot be won or lost in a single game.

Check this

What is the expected value of a random variable that has the following probability distribution?

x	$P(x)$
1	0.5
2	0.3
5	0.2

Solution:
Working in columns gives

x	$P(x)$	$xP(x)$
1	0.5	0.5
2	0.3	0.6
5	0.2	1.0
		2.1

so $\mu = E(X) = 2.1$. The long run average of this random variable is 2.1.

And now the sort of problem that might be useful in industry.

Check this

The number of defectives, X, in a batch of 50 items has the following probability distribution. (The reason for this distribution will be apparent when we study the Poisson distribution later on in this chapter.) What is the average number of defectives in a batch?

x	$P(x)$
0	0.6065
1	0.3033
2	0.0758
3	0.0126
4	0.0016
5	0.0002
6 or more	0.0000

The expected value is $\mu = E(X) = \Sigma xP(x)$. We can either construct a column for $xP(x)$ and then sum it or equivalently write

$$E(X) = (0 \times 0.6065) + (1 \times 0.3033) + (2 \times 0.0758)$$
$$= (3 \times 0.0126) + (4 \times 0.0016) + (5 \times 0.0002)$$
$$= 0.5001$$

On average there is about half a defective in a batch of 50 items.

Why is μ different from $\bar{x}$?

If you have covered the material in *Describing Data* you will recall that the average value of a *sample of data*,

$$\bar{x} = \frac{\Sigma x}{n}$$

is called the sample *mean*. Now, however, we have the *mean*, μ, of a random variable. There is often confusion between $\bar{x}$ and μ, so we will try to clear up any misunderstanding now.

$\bar{x} = \Sigma x/n$ is the average of a sample of *data*. The xs here are the values n in the sample. Each is equally important and is incorporated into $\bar{x}$ in the same way.

On the other hand, $\mu = E(X) = \Sigma xP(x)$ is the average value of a *random variable*, X. Each x in this formula is one of the possible outcomes for X. Some values of X are more likely than others so each x is multiplied by its probability $P(x)$.

The connection between $\bar{x}$ and μ is that if the situation that produces the random variable, X, is repeated a very large number of times, n, to give a set of data, $x_1, x_2, ..., x_n$ the mean of the data, $\bar{x} = \Sigma x/n$ approaches μ.

The expected value of X^2

We will need the expected value of X^2, $E(X^2)$, in the next section. It is the long run average value of the square of X. It is calculated in just the same way as $E(X)$ except that x^2 and not x is multiplied by the probabilities, $P(x)$, that is

$$E(X^2) = \Sigma x^2 P(x)$$

Consider the following example. A rug manufacturer produces square ornamental rugs. 50% of the rugs produced have sides of length 1 metre, 30% have sides of length 2 metres and the remainder have sides of length 5 metres.

The probability distribution of X, the length of the side of a rug chosen at random, is therefore

x	P(x)
1	0.5
2	0.3
5	0.2

So

$$E(X^2) = \Sigma x^2 P(x) = 1^2 \times 0.5 + 2^2 \times 0.3 + 5^2 \times 0.2 = 6.7$$

As the rugs are square, X^2 is the *area* of a rug chosen at random so, whereas $E(X)$ is the average length of the side of a rug, $E(X^2)$ is the average *area* of a rug.

We could have arranged the calculations for $E(X^2)$ in columns, as shown below.

x	P(x)	x²	x²P(x)
1	0.5	1	0.5
2	0.3	4	1.2
5	0.2	25	5.0
	$E(X^2) = \Sigma x^2 P(x) = 6.7$		

Check this

If X has the following probability distribution, what is the expected value of X^2?

x	P(x)
1	0.4
2	0.2
3	0.4

Solution:
We require $E(X^2) = \Sigma x^2 P(x) = 1^2 \times 0.4 + 2^2 \times 0.2 + 3^2 \times 0.4 = 4.8$. The expected value of X^2 is 4.8.

The expected value of any function of X

The expected value of any expression involving X is the long run average value of that expression and is evaluated in a way similar to the expected value of X^2. For instance, the expected value of $2X - 3$ is the long run average value of $2X - 3$ and is

$$E(2X - 3) = \Sigma(2x - 3)P(x)$$

It is calculated below for the random variable in the last example. Make sure you understand where all the figures have come from.

x	P(x)	2x – 3	(2x – 3)P(x)
1	0.4	–1	–0.4
2	0.2	1	0.2
3	0.4	3	1.2
	$E(2X - 3) = \Sigma(2x - 3)P(x) = 1.0$		

So, the average value of $2X - 3$ is 1.

The **mean** or **expected value** or **expectation** of a random variable, X, is

$$\mu = E(X) = \Sigma xP(x)$$

In particular,

$$E(X^2) = \Sigma x^2 P(x)$$

WORK CARD 2

1. In my junk mail I find a free lottery ticket. The accompanying literature says that I have a chance of 0.1 of winning £10 and a chance of 0.05 of winning £100. According to the literature what is the expected value of my win?

2. The probability distribution of the number of fire-engines, X, required by a town's fire service on a particular night is

Number	Probability of engines
0	0.1
1	0.4
2	0.3
3	0.1
4	0.1

Calculate the mean of X.

3. The probability distribution of the number of children per household in a suburban district is given below.

x	P(x)
0	0.18
1	0.39
2	0.24

x	P(x)
3	0.14
4	0.04
5	0.01

Calculate the mean number of children per household.

4. In a word game like Scrabble it is possible to form words with 3, 4 or 5 letters. The probability distribution of the length of the word formed in any one turn is

x	P(x)
3	0.5
4	0.3
5	0.2

As longer words are much more difficult to form, 9 points are awarded for a three-letter word, 16 points for a four-letter word and 25 points for a five-letter word; that is, the points awarded are the square of the word's length.
   Calculate the expected length of a word formed in any one turn and the expected number of points awarded in any one turn.

Solutions:

1. $\Sigma xP(x) = 10 \times 0.1 + 100 \times 0.05 = 1 + 5 = 6$. My expected win is £6.

2. $\mu = E(X) = \Sigma xP(x) = 1.7$.

3. $\mu = E(X) = \Sigma xP(x) = 1.5$.

4. $\mu = E(X) = \Sigma xP(x) = 3.7$ so the average word length is 3.7. The number of points awarded is the square of the word length and so the expected number of points awarded is $E(X^2) = \Sigma x^2 P(x) = 14.3$.

1. Consider this (oversimplified) model of an insurance company.
   A motor insurance company calculates that in a given year each policyholder will make a minor claim of $1000 with a probability of 0.1 and a major claim of $10,000 with a probability of 0.01. At what level should the company fix the annual premium in order to break even? (Ignore company expenses!)

2. A volunteer ambulance service handles up to 5 service calls in any one day. The following probability distribution for the number of service calls is assumed:

x	P(x)
0	0.10
1	0.15
2	0.30
3	0.20
4	0.15
5	0.10

Calculate the expected value of the number of service calls on a particular day.

3. I pay £5 to throw two dice. If I get a double 6 I will win £100, if I throw a single 6, I will win £10. What is the expected value of my gain?

4. On any one attempt a student has a 70% chance of passing her driving test. The probability of passing first time is therefore 0.7. In general, the probability that she passes at the xth attempt is

$P(x) = 0.7 \times 0.3^{x-1}$

Write down the probability distribution of the random variable, X, the number of test attempts. Use this probability distribution to calculate the mean number of attempts.

3 The variance of a random variable

The expected value, μ, of a random variable is a measure of the average value it will attain after many repetitions but it does not give any indication of how these values are spread out.

In Chapter DD1 we used the sample variance, s^2, to describe the spread of a set of data. Now we will define the variance of a random variable.

What is the variance of a random variable?

The Greek symbol σ^2 (pronounced 'sigma squared') is always used to denote the variance of a random variable. The variance of a random variable, X, is

$$\sigma^2 = E((X - \mu)^2)$$

where $\mu = E(X)$ as usual.

This may look a little awe-inspiring, so you will be pleased to know that we will *not* use this formula for calculations. However, this formula does help us understand what variance is.

The formula, given above, for variance is the expected value of $(X - \mu)^2$. $X - \mu$ is the amount by which X differs from its mean, $(X - \mu)^2$ is the square of this, so the variance, $\sigma^2 = E(X - \mu)^2$, is the average amount of the square of the deviation of X from its mean. A large variance therefore indicates that the random variable X tends to take values that are very spread out, and a small one that it tends to take values close to its mean. As each squared deviation is positive or zero the variance is always positive or zero.

We will use the fire-engine example from **Work card 2** as an illustration.

The number of fire-engines required on a given night has the following probability distribution, which we already know has a mean of $\mu = 1.7$.

Number of engines (x)	P(x)
0	0.1
1	0.4
2	0.3
3	0.1
4	0.1

As X can be 0, 1, 2, 3, or 4 the possible values for $X - \mu$ are −1.7, −0.7, 0.3, 1.3, and 2.3 and these occur with probabilities 0.1, 0.4, 0.3, 0.1 and 0.1 respectively. The squares of these, $(X - \mu)^2$, are 2.89, 0.49, 0.09, 1.69, and 5.29 and so these also occur with probabilities 0.1, 0.4, 0.3, 0.1 and 0.1 respectively. The expected value of $(X - \mu)^2$ is therefore

$$E((X - \mu)^2) = \Sigma(x - \mu)^2 P(x)$$
$$= (2.89 \times 0.1) + (0.49 \times 0.4) + (0.09 \times 0.3) + (1.69 \times 0.1) + (5.29 \times 0.1) = 1.21$$

So the variance of the number of fire-engines required is $\sigma^2 = 1.21$.

Calculating the variance of a random variable

An equivalent and quicker formula for the variance of a random variable, X, that it is best to use is

$$\sigma^2 = E(X^2) - \mu^2$$

We already know how to calculate $E(X^2)$ and μ. The variance of the number of fire-engines required on a given night is calculated again, using the formula below.

x	P(x)	xP(x)	x²	x²P(x)
0	0.1	0.0	0	0.0
1	0.4	0.4	1	0.4
2	0.3	0.6	4	1.2
3	0.1	0.3	9	0.9
4	0.1	0.4	16	1.6

$$\mu = E(X) = 1.7 \qquad E(X^2) = 4.1$$

So $\sigma^2 = E(X^2) - \mu^2 = 4.1 - 1.7^2 = 1.21$.

The *standard deviation* (s.d.) of a random variable is the square root of the variance and so it is symbolised by σ. For example, the standard deviation of the number of fire-engines is $\sigma = \sqrt{1.21} = 1.1$.

Check this

The random variables X and Y have the following probability distributions:

x	P(x)
1	0.01
2	0.98
3	0.01

y	P(y)
1	0.49
2	0.02
3	0.49

Calculate the variances and standard deviations of X and Y and use these to compare the two distributions. Is this what you would expect?

Solution:
To calculate the variance of X we need μ and $E(X^2)$.
   Recall that $\mu = E(X) = \Sigma xP(x)$ and $E(X^2) = \Sigma x^2P(x)$. We will use columns as shown below.

x	P(x)	xP(x)	x²	x²P(x)
1	0.01	0.01	1	0.01
2	0.98	1.96	4	3.92
3	0.01	0.03	9	0.09
		$\mu_x = E(X) = 2.0$		$E(X^2) = 4.02$

So $\sigma_x^2 = E(X^2) - \mu_x^2 = 4.02 - 2^2 = 0.02$. The variance of X is 0.02, so the standard deviation is 0.1414.
   To calculate the variance of Y we have:

y	P(y)	yP(y)	y²	y²P(y)
1	0.49	0.49	1	0.49
2	0.02	0.04	4	0.08
3	0.49	1.47	9	4.41
		$\mu_y = E(Y) = 2.0$		$E(Y^2) = 4.98$

So $\sigma_y^2 = E(Y^2) - \mu_y^2 = 4.98 - 2^2 = 0.98$.
   The variance of Y is much larger than that of X. This is because although X and Y have the same expected value Y is much more likely to take values of 1 or 3 and so the values it takes are more spread out.

Confusion: s^2 and σ^2

At this stage many students become confused because, if they have already covered the material in *Describing Data*, there seem to be two different kinds of variance! In *Describing Data*, Chapter DD2, we defined the variance of a sample of data as

$$s^2 = \frac{\Sigma x^2 - \frac{(\Sigma x)^2}{n}}{n-1}$$

whereas in this chapter we introduced the variance of a random variable

$$\sigma^2 = E(X^2) - \mu^2$$
$$= \Sigma x^2 P(x) - \mu^2$$

The situation parallels that of $\bar{x}$ and μ. s^2 is a measure of the spread of a *sample* of data, so the xs in the formula are the actual items in the sample. On the other hand, σ^2 is a measure of the spread of the *random variable* X and the xs in the expression are the possible values that X can take. These values are not equally likely and so each is weighted by $P(x)$ in the formula.

s^2 and σ^2 are related in that when the situation that produces a random variable is repeated many times, the s^2 calculated from the resulting data will approach σ^2 of the random variable.

But what does variance really mean?

To get more of a 'feel' for standard deviation and variance we state a result due to Chebysheff. (You may remember his result for a set of data from *Describing Data*, we now have the corresponding result for a random variable.)

It says that when k is any positive number greater than 1:

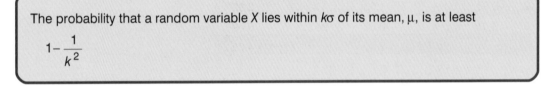

The probability that a random variable X lies within $k\sigma$ of its mean, μ, is at least

$$1 - \frac{1}{k^2}$$

So, for example, when $k = 2$, Chebysheff's result tells us that the probability that a random variable lies between $\mu - 2\sigma$ and $\mu + 2\sigma$ is at least $1 - \frac{1}{4} = 0.75$. Alternatively, when $k = 4$ the probability that a random variable lies between $\mu - 4\sigma$ and $\mu + 4\sigma$ is at least $1 - \frac{1}{16} = 0.9375$. So, if we were told, for instance, that a random variable had a mean of 100 and a standard deviation of 1.5, we would instantly know that at least 93.75% of the time it would take values between 94 and 106.

Check these

The weight of a chocolate bar has a mean of 50g and a standard deviation of 2g. The probability that a single bar weighs between 44g and 56g is at least 0.89. Is this statement true or false?

A random variable has a mean of 30 and a variance of 9. The probability that it lies between 25.5 and 34.5 is. . . . . (fill the gap).

The probability that the random variable above lies more than 12 away from the mean is 6.25%. True or false?

Solutions: True. In the second question the standard deviation is 3, so 25.5 and 34.5 are 1.5 standard deviations away from the mean, and $P(25.5 < X < 34.5)$ is at least $1 - \frac{1}{1.5^2} = 0.5555$. The final statement is true because the probability that this random variable lies within 12 of the mean is $1 - \frac{1}{4^2} = 0.9375$, so the probability that it lies more than 12 from the mean is 0.0625.

The **variance** of a random variable X is

$$\sigma^2 = E(X^2) - \mu^2$$
$$= \Sigma x^2 P(x) - \mu^2$$

The **standard deviation** of a random variable, X, is

$$\sigma = \sqrt{\sigma^2}$$

The probability that a random variable, X, lies within $k\sigma$ of its mean, μ, is at least

$$1 - \frac{1}{k^2}$$

WORK CARD 3

1. Calculate the mean, variance and standard deviation of the random variable, X, which has the following probability distribution:

x	P(x)
−1	0.1
0	0.2
1	0.4
2	0.3

2. The probability distribution of the number of children per household in a suburban district (you found the mean in **Work card 2**) is repeated below:

x	P(x)
0	0.18
1	0.39
2	0.24
3	0.14
4	0.04
5	0.01

    Calculate the variance and standard deviation of the number of children per household. (The mean is 1.5.)

WORK CARD 3 (CONTINUED)

3. In a word game like Scrabble it is possible to form words with 3, 4 or 5 letters. The probability distribution of the length of the word formed in any one turn is

x	P(x)
3	0.5
4	0.3
5	0.2

   In **Work card 2** you established that the mean of X is 3.7. Calculate the variance of the length of a word formed in any one turn.

4. You are told that the monthly percentage return on an ordinary share has a mean of 1 and a standard deviation of 0.5.
   Comment on the likelihood of a negative return.

Solutions:

1. It's easiest to use the column format as shown in the text. You need columns for $xP(x)$, x^2 and $x^2P(x)$. Summing the $xP(x)$ and $x^2P(x)$ columns gives $\Sigma xP(x) = 0.9$ and $\Sigma x^2P(x) = 1.7$ so $\sigma^2 = 1.7 - 0.9^2 = 0.89$. The standard deviation is therefore $\sqrt{0.89} = 0.9434$.

2. $\Sigma xP(x) = 1.5$, $\Sigma x^2P(x) = 3.5$ so $\sigma^2 = 3.5 - 1.5^2 = 1.25$ and $\sigma = 1.118$.

3. $\Sigma xP(x) = 3.7$, $\Sigma x^2P(x) = 14.3$ so $\sigma^2 = 14.3 - 3.7^2 = 0.61$.

4. For the return to be less than 0, it would have to be more than 2 standard deviations away from the mean. We know that the probability that a random variable takes a value within 2σ from its mean is at least $1 - \frac{1}{4} = 0.75$, so the probability that it takes a value more than 2σ from the mean is *at most* 0.25. This will include returns above 2, so the probability of a negative return is at most 0.25.

ASSESSMENT 3

1. We already know that the distribution of the number of heads obtained when two coins are tossed is

x	P(x)
0	1/4
1	1/2
2	1/4

   Calculate the mean and variance of the number of heads.

2. A volunteer ambulance service handles up to 5 service calls in any one day. The following probability distribution for the number of service calls is assumed:

ASSESSMENT 3 (CONTINUED)

x	P(x)
0	0.10
1	0.15
2	0.30
3	0.20
4	0.15
5	0.10

Calculate the variance and standard deviation of the number of service calls.

3. The number of complaints received each hour at the customer service desk of a large retail store, X, has the following distribution.

x	P(x)
0	0.10
1	0.18
2	0.35
3	0.22
4	0.15

Calculate the variance and standard deviation of the number of complaints received in an hour.

4. Two courier firms are competing for a contract to deliver in the City of London for an investment company. Both have provided figures, based on historic data, for the probability of delivery times of $\frac{1}{2}$, 1, $1\frac{1}{2}$ and 2 hours.

Firm A		Firm B	
x	P(x)	x	P(x)
0.5	0.6	0.5	0.1
1	0.1	1	0.7
1.5	0.10	1.5	0.15
2	0.2	2	0.05

Calculate the mean and variance of the delivery time for both courier firms. On the basis of these which firm would you employ and why?

5. If the mean weight of packets of digestive biscuits produced by a process is 250g, with a standard deviation of 2g, which of the following statements are true? Explain your reasoning.

   a. At least 96% of packets weigh between 240g and 260g.

   b. At most 11% of packets weigh less than 244g or more than 256g.

c. At most 11% of packets weigh between 246g and 254g.

d. At most 93.75% of packets weigh between 242g and 258g.

e. At least 90% of packets weigh between 242g and 258g.

4 The binomial distribution

Whilst we can, as stated earlier, estimate probabilities using historical data, this is often unnecessary as the nature of the random situation may suggest a well-known probability distribution. In this chapter we introduce you to two of the most useful probability distributions, the binomial distribution in this section and the Poisson distribution in Section 5.

Using a well-known probability distribution has the advantage that the mean, variance and other properties have been worked out for you already. The main problem, if any, is in deciding which distribution is appropriate for a particular random situation so we will pay particular attention to this. We start by learning to recognise situations for which the binomial probability distribution is appropriate.

Binomial situations

A *binomial situation* is a random situation that has the following form:

1. There are n identical 'trials'. The word 'trial' here just means 'happening' or 'repetition'.
2. Each 'trial' has two possible outcomes. We will generally call these success and failure, even if the outcome we have labelled 'success' is not particularly desirable.
3. At each trial the probability of a success is the same. We will call this p, so at each trial

$$P(success) = p$$

4. The result of each trial is independent of all the others. (That is, the success or failure of any trial does not affect the probabilities of the success or failure of the other trials.)

At the moment this may seem a bit abstract but we illustrate using the following example.

Eight students sit an exam and each student has a probability of 60% of passing. This is a binomial situation because:

1. There are $n = 8$ students and we know of no differences between them so these are the identical trials.
2. Each trial has two outcomes: pass or fail.
3. The probability that an individual student passes is $p = 0.6$.
4. We are left to assume that the probability that each student passes is *not* influenced by whether any other students pass or fail; that is, each student's result is independent of the others.

We describe some more binomial situations below.

Check this

Explain why the following are binomial situations and, if possible, say what n and p are for each. Remember that each of the four conditions above must hold.

1. I toss a coin twice.

Solution:
Each toss is a trial and has exactly two outcomes, head or tail. At each trial $P(head) = \frac{1}{2}$, so $p = 0.5$. There are two tosses and so the number of trials is $n = 2$. Whether one toss is a head or a tail does not affect the probability of a head or a tail on the other toss so the two tosses are independent.

2. 10 customers enter a store. Each customer either buys, or doesn't buy, something.

Solution:
There are 10 customers so $n = 10$. Each customer is a trial that has two possible outcomes: buys or doesn't buy. $P(buys)$ has not been given but is assumed to be the same for each trial, so this is p. For this to be a binomial situation we must also assume that the probability that each customer buys or doesn't buy is not influenced by whether the other customers buy or don't buy.

3. 50 similar items are produced by a machine and each is graded as defective or satisfactory.

Solution:
Here there are 50 trials, so $n = 50$. At each trial $p = P(defective)$ which we do not know. We must assume, for a binomial situation, that the probability that an item is defective or not is not influenced by the status of the other items.

The binomial random variable

In these binomial situations the random variable of interest, X, is the number of trials that are a success. For the 8 students taking the exam this is the number who pass. For the shop example it is the number of customers who buy, and for the machine example, above, it is the number of defective items produced.

As there are n trials in all, X can only take integer values from 0 to n inclusive.

We are going to present you with the formula for the probability of x successes, but you won't understand it yet as it contains a symbol you haven't met before.

The probability of x successes in a binomial experiment with n trials and a probability of success at each trial of p is

$$P(x) = {}^nC_x p^x (1 - p)^{n-x}$$

The symbol ${}^nC_x$ is the problem.

Combinations for binomial probabilities

${}^nC_x$ is pronounced 'n C x' or 'n choose x' and is called a *combination*. It represents *the number of ways in which x objects can be chosen from n objects.*

For instance, suppose we have three objects A, B and C and we need to select two of them. We can do this in three ways:

AB
AC
BC

(Order does not matter, *AB* is the same as *BA*.) So $^3C_2 = 3$.

Suppose 5 people are up for 2 jobs. If these are Albert, Beatrice, Catherine, Delia and Edna then the different ways in which two people can be chosen are

AB *AC* *AD* *AE*
BC *BD* *BE*
CD *CE*
DE

There are 10 of these, so $^5C_2 = 10$.

Notice that when 2 people out of 5 are selected, the remaining 3 people are *not* selected. So the number of ways of choosing 2 people out of 5 is the same as the number of ways of rejecting 3 people out of 5, so $^5C_2 = {}^5C_3$. In general, the number of ways of selecting *x* objects out of *n* is the same as the number of ways of selecting $n - x$ objects out of *n*; that is

$$^nC_x = {}^nC_{n-x}$$

Check this

A company currently produces 6 brands of washing liquid, Jiffy, Kleenee, Lemonfresh, Machineclean, Newear and Ochay. To reduce marketing costs they must stop production of 3 of them and continue with the remaining 3. In how many ways can this be done?

Solution:
Again a systematic list of all combinations of 3 liquids is required as follows.

JKL *JKM* *JKN* *JKO*
JLM *JLN* *JLO*
JMN *JMO*
JNO

KLM *KLN* *KLO*
KMN *KMO*
KNO

LMN *LMO*
LNO

MNO

Try to find some more if you want, but we are convinced that there are no more than these 20 combinations. We conclude that $^6C_3 = 20$.

In the last example it is becoming apparent that enumerating all the possible combinations like this is cumbersome when *n* is large. Suppose there are 15 local government councillors and 5 of them are required for a committee .... It would take a long time to list all the combinations and then count them. (In fact there are 3003 combinations!) Fortunately there is a formula for ^nC_x, the number of ways of choosing x objects from n. It is

$$^nC_x = \frac{n!}{x!(n-x)!}$$

Any number followed by a ! sign is called a *factorial* and means multiply together all the integers up to and including that number. For instance

$$5! \text{ means } 5 \times 4 \times 3 \times 2 \times 1$$

$$3! \text{ means } 3 \times 2 \times 1$$

$$10! \text{ means } 10 \times 9 \times 8 \times 7 \times 6 \times 5 \times 4 \times 3 \times 2 \times 1$$

and so on. We also define $0! = 1$ which has been adopted so that $^nC_n = 1$ (there is only one way of choosing n objects out of n).

Check this

A furniture delivery van only has time to make 5 out of the 8 calls that are scheduled today. How many ways can the driver choose the 5 calls he will make?

Solution: We require

$$^8C_5 = \frac{8!}{5!(8-5)!} = \frac{8!}{5!3!} = \frac{8 \times 7 \times 6 \times 5 \times 4 \times 3 \times 2 \times 1}{5 \times 4 \times 3 \times 2 \times 1 \times 3 \times 2 \times 1}$$

When evaluating a combination like this you will always find that some cancelling is possible. Here, we have $5 \times 4 \times 3 \times 2 \times 1$ in both numerator and denominator. which we can cancel to give

$$^8C_5 = \frac{8 \times 7 \times 6}{3 \times 2 \times 1} = 56$$

There are 56 ways of choosing 5 calls out of 8.

Check this

A team of 7 players must be chosen from a squad of 11 for a netball team. In how many ways can this be done?

Solution: We require

$$^{11}C_7 = \frac{11!}{7!4!} = \frac{11 \times 10 \times 9 \times 8 \times 7 \times 6 \times 5 \times 4 \times 3 \times 2 \times 1}{7 \times 6 \times 5 \times 4 \times 3 \times 2 \times 1 \times 4 \times 3 \times 2 \times 1}$$

$7 \times 6 \times 5 \times 4 \times 3 \times 2 \times 1$ is a factor of both the numerator and the denominator, so it cancels to give

$$^{11}C_7 = \frac{11 \times 10 \times 9 \times 8}{4 \times 3 \times 2 \times 1} = 330$$

Cancelling out becomes a necessity when large numbers are involved.

Check this

There are 30 checkouts at a supermarket, but on a Sunday afternoon only 10 cashiers are available to staff them. In how many ways can we choose which checkouts are staffed?

Solution:
We require

$$^{30}C_{10} = \frac{30!}{10!\,20!}$$

Try to evaluate 30! with a calculator. The answer is somewhere in the region of 2.65×10^{32} and we are dealing with extremely large numbers here which brings the risk of rounding error. As

$$\frac{30!}{20!} = 30 \times 29 \times 28 \times 27 \times 26 \times 25 \times 24 \times 23 \times 22 \times 21$$

$$^{30}C_{10} = \frac{30 \times 29 \times 28 \times 27 \times 26 \times 25 \times 24 \times 23 \times 22 \times 21}{10 \times 9 \times 8 \times 7 \times 6 \times 5 \times 4 \times 3 \times 2 \times 1}$$

and further cancelling gives:

$$= \frac{\cancel{30} \times 29 \times 28^7 \times 27^3 \times 26^{13} \times 25^5 \times 24^3 \times 23 \times 22^{11} \times 21}{10 \times 9 \times 8 \times 7 \times 6 \times 5 \times 4 \times 3 \times 2 \times 1}$$

$$= 30{,}045{,}015 \text{ ways}$$

Evaluating binomial probabilities

Now that we know about combinations we can evaluate the formula for binomial probabilities that we gave earlier. Recall that for a binomial situation with n trials, each with a probability of success p, the probability of x successes is

$$P(x) = {}^{n}C_x p^x (1 - p)^{n-x}$$

where

$$^{n}C_x = \frac{n!}{x!(n - x)!}$$

Try the following.

Check this

10 customers walk into a shop. The probability that an individual customer buys something is 0.3.

a. What is the probability that exactly 2 customers buy?

b. What is the probability that exactly 6 customers buy?

c. What is the probability that no customers buy?

Solution: For this example, $n = 10$ and $p = 0.3$.

a. Using the formula:

$$P(2) = {}^{10}C_2 0.3^2 0.7^{10-2} = \frac{10!}{2!8!} 0.3^2 0.7^8$$

$$= \frac{10 \times 9}{2 \times 1} 0.3^2 0.7^8$$

$$= 45 \times 0.3^2 \times 0.7^8 = 0.233474$$

There is a 23.3% chance that exactly 2 customers buy.

b.

$$P(6) = {}^{10}C_6 0.3^6 0.7^4 = \frac{10!}{6!4!} 0.3^6 0.7^4 = \frac{10 \times 9 \times 8 \times 7}{4 \times 3 \times 2 \times 1} 0.3^6 0.7^4$$

$$= 210 \ 0.3^6 0.7^4 = 0.036757$$

There is a 3.7% chance that exactly 6 customers will buy.

c. $P(0) = {}^{10}C_0 0.3^0 0.7^{10} = \frac{10!}{0!10!} 0.3^0 0.7^{10} = 1 \times 1 \times 0.7^{10} = 0.028248$

remembering that $0! = 1$.
There is a 2.8% chance that no customers buy.

Check this

45% of voters are known to be Conservative. What is the probability that out of a sample of 8 voters exactly 5 vote Conservative?

Solution: $P(5) = {}^8C_5 \ 0.45^5 \ 0.55^3$.
However,

$$\begin{aligned}
{}^8C_5 &= \frac{8!}{5!3!} = \frac{8 \times 7 \times 6 \times 5 \times 4 \times 3 \times 2 \times 1}{5 \times 4 \times 3 \times 2 \times 1 \times 3 \times 2 \times 1} \\
&= \frac{8 \times 7 \times 6}{3 \times 2 \times 1} = 56
\end{aligned}$$

so

$$P(5) = 56 \times 0.45^5 \times 0.55^3 = 0.171925$$

Why does the formula for a binomial probability work?

So far we have avoided discussion of why the binomial formula works. This may be difficult so we will start with a general explanation and then illustrate it with a specific case.

Consider a binomial situation with n identical trials, each of which results in a success with a probability of p or a failure with a probability of $1 - p$. One way of obtaining x successes is for all the successes to occur first, as shown below.

$$\underbrace{S, S, \ldots, S}_{x \text{ successes}} \quad \underbrace{F, F, \ldots, F}_{n-x \text{ failures}}$$

As each trial is independent (by assumption) the probability of this is found by multiplying the probability of a success, p, x times and the probability of a failure, $1 - p$, $n - x$ times to give

$$\underbrace{p \cdot p, \ldots, p}_{x \text{ times}} \quad \underbrace{(1 - p)(1 - p) \ldots (1 - p)}_{n-x \text{ times}} = p^x (1 - p)^{n-x}$$

However, the event, x successes, includes all the outcomes in which any group of x of the trials are successes, not just the outcome in which the first x trials are successes. For instance, it includes

$$\underbrace{S, S, \ldots, S}_{x-1 \text{ successes}} \quad \underbrace{F, F, \ldots, F}_{n-x \text{ failures}} \quad \underbrace{S}_{\text{one success}}$$

and

$$\underbrace{F, F, \ldots, F}_{n-x \text{ failures}} \quad \underbrace{S, S, \ldots, S}_{x \text{ successes}}$$

There are ^nC_x such outcomes because each outcome is a way of obtaining x successes from n trials and as each includes x successes and $n - x$ failures they each have a probability of $p^x(1 - p)^{n-x}$. The total probability of x successes is found by adding together ^nC_x of these probabilities and is therefore the binomial probability

$$P(x) = {}^nC_x p^x (1 - p)^{n-x}$$

More specifically, consider the binominal situation in which 3 customers enter a store and where the probability that each customer buys is $p = 0.3$. What is the probability, $P(2)$, that exactly 2 customers buy?

One way in which exactly 2 customers buy is

First customer	Second customer	Third customer
Buy	*Buy*	*Notbuy*

As this is a binomial situation, we can also assume that each customer's action is independent of the others, so the probability of this outcome is the product of the probabilities for each customer; that is (using an obvious notation),

$$P(Buy \; Buy \; Notbuy) = p \times p \times (1 - p) = 0.3 \times 0.3 \times 0.7 = 0.3^2 \, 0.7$$

Notice that this is p raised to the power of the number of customers who buy multiplied by $(1 - p)$ raised to the power of the number of customers who don't buy.

However, this is not the only outcome in which exactly 2 customers buy. In this outcome the 2 customers who buy are the first and second but they could be the first and third customers or the second and third. Each of these outcomes corresponds to a way of choosing the 2 buying customers out of the 3, so altogether there are $^3C_2 = 3$ of them. They are

First customer	Second customer	Third customer
Buy	*Buy*	*Notbuy*
Buy	*Notbuy*	*Buy*
Notbuy	*Buy*	*Buy*

Each outcome has two buys and one not buy and so has the same probability of $0.3^2\,0.7$.
   The probability that 2 customers buy is therefore the sum of the probabilities of all 3 outcomes

$$P(2) = 3 \times 0.3^2\,0.7$$

Notice that $3 = {}^3C_2$ is the number of ways in which 2 customers can be chosen out of 3, 0.3^2 is p to the power of the number of customers who buy and 0.7 is $1 - p$ to the power of the number of customers who don't buy.

Check this

Suppose 10% of people are left-handed. In a small office, 3 out of the 4 staff are left-handed. Calculate the probability of this happening *without* using the binomial formula directly.

Solution: This is a binomial situation with $n = 4$ and $p = 0.1$. We require $P(3)$. There are ${}^4C_3 = 4$ ways that 3 out of 4 people can be left-handed. These are

1st person	2nd person	3rd person	4th person
R	L	L	L
L	R	L	L
L	L	R	L
L	L	L	R

Each of these outcomes has a probability of $0.1^3\,0.9$ as it contains 3 right-handers and 1 left-hander (assuming that each person's handedness is independent) and $P(3)$ is the sum of the probabilities of each of these so $P(3) = {}^4C_3\,0.1^3\,0.9 = 0.0036$.

Cumulative binomial probabilities

So far we have calculated the probability of *exactly x* successes. It is more usual to require the probability that there are *a* successes *or fewer*. These are called *cumulative* binomial probabilities. For instance, we may be interested, for the sample of 8 voters, in the probability that two or fewer vote Conservative.
   To calculate cumulative probabilities we must add up all the component probabilities. For instance, the probability that X is 2 or less is

$$P(X \le 2) = P(X = 0) + P(X = 1) + P(X = 2)$$

or the probability that X is less than 5 is

$$P(X < 5) = P(X = 0) + P(X = 1) + P(X = 2) + P(X = 3) + P(X = 4)$$

Check this

45% of voters are known to be Conservative. What is the probability that out of a sample of 8 voters 2 or fewer vote Conservative?

Solution:

$$P(X \le 2) = P(0) \qquad\qquad +P(1) \qquad\qquad +P(2)$$
$$= {}^8C_0\, 0.45^0\, 0.55^8 + {}^8C_1\, 0.45^1\, 0.55^7 + {}^8C_2\, 0.45^2\, 0.55^6$$
$$= 0.00837339 \qquad +0.05480767 \qquad +0.15694923$$
$$= 0.22013029$$

Using tables

To calculate $P(X \le 2)$ in the last example we had to calculate 3 separate binomial probabilities and then add them up. Suppose, in another example, that you were asked for the probability that X was less or equal to, say, 9. You would need

$$P(X \le 9) = P(0) + P(1) + P(2) + P(3) + P(4) + P(5) + P(6) + P(7) + P(8) + P(9)$$

and you would have to calculate 10 different probabilities and then add them up. Tedious!

Help is at hand in the form of published tables of the cumulative probabilities $p(X \le a)$ of the binomial distribution such as the one in Table I at the end of this book (p. 862–866).

Several published sets of statistical tables are available. Although these take largely the same form, it is probably best to get to know your way around one particular set. (Which will be recommended by your lecturer.)

A table of binomial probabilities has a separate grid for each value of n (usually from 1 to 20 inclusive). Each column of a grid contains the cumulative probabilities $P(X \le 0)$, $P(X \le 1)$, $P(X \le 2)$ ... $P(X \le n)$ for a particular value of p. We show the structure of the grid for $n = 8$ below.

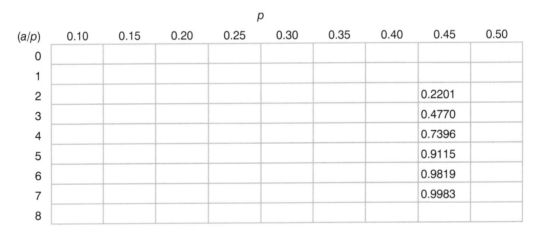

$n = 8$

p

(a/p)	0.10	0.15	0.20	0.25	0.30	0.35	0.40	0.45	0.50
0									
1									
2								0.2201	
3								0.4770	
4								0.7396	
5								0.9115	
6								0.9819	
7								0.9983	
8									

Use the grid above from the binomial tables to solve the following problems.

Check this

For the sample of 8 voters considered in the last example, in which the probability that an individual voter votes Conservative is 0.45, confirm that the probability that 2 or fewer voters vote Conservative is 0.2201.

Solution: On the grid for $n = 8$, look up the entry for $a = 2$ and $p = 0.45$.

Check this

What is the probability that 4 or more voters in the sample vote Conservative?

Solution:
We want $P(X \geq 4)$, but cumulative binomial tables give $P(X \leq a)$ so this is not available directly. However, we can use $P(X \geq 4) = 1 - P(X \leq 3) = 1 - 0.4770 = 0.5230$.

Check this

What is the probability that between 5 and 7 inclusive of the voters (that is, 5, 6 or 7) in the sample vote Conservative?

Solution:
Again, this cannot be found directly from a table of $P(X \leq a)$. However, the probability that X lies between 5 and 7 inclusive is the probability that X is 7 or less minus the probability that X is 4 or less; that is

$$P(5 \leq X \leq 7) = P(X \leq 7) - P(X \leq 4)$$
$$= 0.9983 - 0.7396 = 0.2587$$

Many tables do not give any probabilities for values of p that are greater than 0.5. This is because any problem in which $p > 0.5$ can be rephrased as a problem in which $p < 0.5$.

For example, suppose that 8 customers enter a shop, and that the probability that each *buys* is 0.55 (so we can't use tables). We would like to know the probability that 5 or fewer customers buy.

The trick we use is to rewrite the problem in terms of customers *not buying* because the probability that an individual customer *doesn't buy* is $1 - 0.55 = 0.45$, which we *can* look up in the table. Five or fewer customers *buying* is the same as 3 or more customers *not buying*, so the problem can be rephrased as the probability that 3 or more customers don't buy when the probability that an individual customer doesn't buy is 0.45; that is, $P(X \geq 3)$ when $p = 0.45$.

Using the table for $n = 8$ and $p = 0.45$ gives

$$P(X \geq 3) = 1 - P(X \leq 2) = 1 - 0.2201 = 0.7799$$

Try another example like this. You will need Table I or another table of binomial probabilities.

Check this

There is a 90% probability that each of 12 jury members casts a vote of not guilty. What is the probability that 7 or more members vote not guilty? Assume that each jury member's vote is independent of the others.

Solution:
$p = 0.9$ for the problem as presented and so we can't look up the probability directly in a table.

Seven or more voting *not guilty* is the same as 5 or less voting guilty. The probability that an individual votes guilty is 0.1, so we require $P(X \le 5)$ when $n = 12$ and $p = 0.1$. Using Table I (p. 864) gives 0.9995.

In these examples we used the fact that the probability of x successes in n trials when the probability of a success in a single trial is p is the same as the probability of $n - x$ successes in n trials when the probability of success in a single trial is $1 - p$.

Even more help: using a computer

Most statistical software can calculate **a.** the binomial probabilities $P(X = a)$ and **b.** the cumulative binomial probabilities $P(X \le a)$.

The SPSS command is

Transform > Compute

We use the **PDF.BINOM** function for **a** and the **CDF.BINOM** function for **b**.

We use SPSS in the following example.

Check this

25 coffee drinkers were asked which brand of coffee they drink at home. If Beanco have 25% of the market what is the probability that **a.** exactly 7 people out of the 25 surveyed drink Beanco and **b.** 7 or fewer out of the 25 surveyed drink the product?

Solution: Tables will not help us here as they usually stop at $n = 20$.

a. We require $P(X = 7)$ where $n = 25$ and $p = 0.25$.

Using SPSS's **Transform > Compute** tool, you will need to name a column for the result ('the target variable') and select the **PDF.BINOM** function. Enter 7, 25, 0.25 in the three spaces and the result 0.1654 will appear in the named column.

b. We require $P(X \le 7)$ when $n = 25$ and $p = 0.25$.

This time use the **CDF.BINOM** function in the same way. The result is 0.7265.

From these results the probability that *exactly* 7 people from a sample of 25 drink Beanco is 0.1654 but the probability that 7 or *fewer* out of a sample of 25 drink Beanco is 0.7265.

In Excel the BINOMDIST function will calculate binomial probabilities for you. The arguments are x, n, p and then TRUE for the cumulative probability of x successes or FALSE for the probability of x successes.

The mean and variance of a binomial random variable

In Sections 2 and 3 we saw how to calculate the expected value (mean) and variance of a random variable from its probability distribution. We can calculate the expected value (mean) and variance of a binomial random variable in exactly the same way.

The following table shows calculations for the expected value (mean) and variance of the number of boys in a family of 4 children, a binomial distribution with $n = 4$ and $p = 0.5$.

X is the number of boys in a family of 4 children.

x	P(x)	xP(x)	x²	x²P(x)
0	1/16	0	0	0
1	1/4	1/4	1	1/4
2	3/8	3/4	4	3/2
3	1/4	3/4	9	9/4
4	1/16	1/4	16	1
		$\mu = E(X) = 2$		$E(X^2) = 5$

So $\sigma^2 = 5 - 2^2 = 1$

This is practical for a small value of n such as this, but imagine doing it for, say, an $n = 20$ binomial distribution – there would be 21 probabilities and so 21 rows to work on. Fortunately, there is no need to do this because the mean and variance of a binomial random variable are directly related to n and p.

Using some maths it can be shown that:

> The expected value (mean or expectation) of a binomial random variable is $\mu = np$
>
> The variance of a binomial random variable is $\sigma^2 = np(1 - p)$

We will make more use of these results in Chapter P3.

Check this

40% of the patients who a dentist sees for a check-up need a subsequent appointment for dental treatment. Over the course of a week the dentist gives 100 check-ups. What are the mean and variance of the number of these patients who require a subsequent appointment?

Solution:
Assuming that the probability of a subsequent appointment is 0.4 for every patient (obviously only an approximation) we have a binomial situation, with $n = 100$ and $p = 0.4$. The binomial random variable is the number of patients who require another appointment. The mean of this random variable is $np = 100 \times 0.4 = 40$ and the variance is $np(1 - p) = 100 \times 0.4 \times 0.6 = 24$.

Pictures of the binomial probability distribution

Figure 2.1 shows the binomial probability distribution when $n = 7$ and $p = 0.1$. As p is less than 0.5, successes are *less* likely than failures, so the probabilities are higher for lower values of X and the distribution is skewed to the right.

In Figure 2.2 we show another binomial distribution with $n = 7$ but now $p = 0.7$ so successes are more likely than failures and the distribution is skewed to the left.

In Figure 2.3, $n = 7$ again, but now $p = 0.5$ so successes and failures are equally likely and the distribution is symmetric.

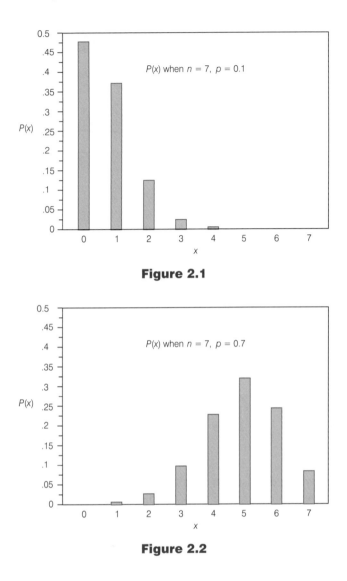

Figure 2.1

Figure 2.2

In general, a binomial distribution is symmetric when $p = 0.5$, skewed to the left when $p > 0.5$ and skewed to the right when $p < 0.5$, for any value of n.

It is interesting to see what happens to the plot of the probabilities when n is very large. Figure 2.4 shows the binomial distribution for $n = 200$ and $p = 0.15$. Notice that although the distribution has a mean of 30, so values of the random variable are at the lower end of the range 0 to 200, it looks symmetric and has a sort of 'bell'-shape. This is a feature of binomial distributions when n is large. Remember this bell-shape – it will occur again!

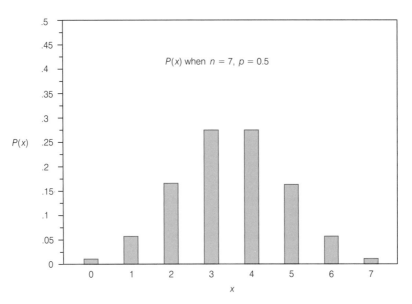

Figure 2.3

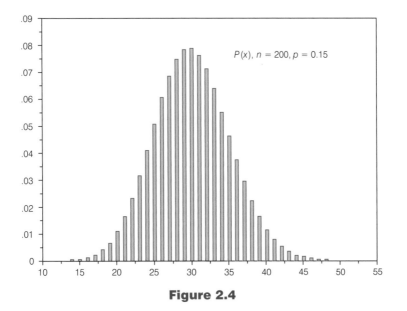

Figure 2.4

The binomial distribution

A binomial random variable, X, is the number of successes when

1. There are n identical 'trials'.
2. Each 'trial' has exactly two possible outcomes, success or failure.

3. At each trial

$P(success) = p$

4. The result of each trial is independent of all the others.

The probability of x successes is

$$P(x) = {}^nC_x p^x (1-p)^{n-x}$$

where

$${}^nC_x = \frac{n!}{x!(n-x)!} \text{ and } n! = n(n-1)(n-2) \dots 3 \cdot 2 \cdot 1 \text{ and so on.}$$

The expected value (mean) and variance of X are

$$\mu = np \qquad \sigma^2 = np(1-p)$$

WORK CARD 4

1. What assumptions are necessary for the following to be binomial situations? What is the binomial random variable in each case?

    a. The probability that exploratory digging by an oil company finds oil is 0.15. 10 such digs are scheduled this month scattered about the globe.

    b. A tennis player serves an ace with a fixed probability. During a match she serves 120 times.

    c. 10% of American truck drivers are women. 10 truck drivers are selected at random to be interviewed.

    d. A series of bets on red at roulette.

2. a. 12 members of a club have been nominated for 3 committee positions. In how many ways can they be chosen?

    b. In how many ways can you select 4 playing cards from a pack of 52?

    c. I have 9 shirts. Each day of the (5-day) week I choose one at random to wear. I wash them on Saturday. How many different combinations of shirts can I place in the washing machine?

    d. During a lecture I randomly pick 3 students out of 50 to answer questions. In how many ways can I do this?

    e. A firm is trying to encourage women to fill executive positions. For the latest batch of trainees it wishes to fill 7 vacancies with 5 women and 2 men. It interviews 7 women and 8 men making a total of 15 candidates for 7 vacancies. In how many ways can the vacancies be filled?

3. The probability of a type of TV set breaking down during its guarantee period of one year is 0.2. A guest house buys 3 such sets.

    a. Calculate the probability that exactly 2 sets break down during the guarantee period.

WORK CARD 4 (CONTINUED)

b. Calculate the probability that all 3 sets break down during the guarantee period.

c. Calculate the probability that 2 or more sets break down during the guarantee period.

4. Five fire alarms are installed in a house. In the event of a fire the probability of each one working properly is 0.95. In the event of a fire:

   a. What is the probability that all 5 will be activated?

   b. What is the probability that 3 or more will function?

   c. What is the probability that none will work?

5. The response rate of a questionnaire survey is typically about 25%. Assume that you have sent out 15 forms.

   a. What is the probability that none are returned?

   b. What is the probability that *exactly* 5 are returned?

   c. What is the probability that fewer than 10 are returned? (Use tables.)

   d. How many, on average, would you expect to be returned?

   e. Is the distribution of the number of returns skewed to the left or right?

   f. Calculate the variance of the distribution of the number of returned surveys.

6. 'Yum yum' bars are manufactured on a production line. When the line is functioning correctly the probability that any single bar is overweight is 0.01. Every day the Quality Control Inspector takes a sample of 100 bars from the production line, and rejects all that day's output if more than 2 bars are overweight. For what proportion of days will he reject all the output?

7. The probability that a share price rises from one day to the next is 0.4. A portfolio contains 80 different shares.

   What assumptions are necessary for the number of shares that have prices that rise on a particular day to be a binomial random variable? What is the mean and variance of the number of share prices that rise on a given day?

Solutions:

1. **a.** Assume that the outcome at each dig is independent of the others. The number of successful digs is the binomial random variable, $n = 10$ and $p = 0.15$.

   b. The binomial random variable is the number of aces served out of 120.

   c. Assume that the probability that any one of the truck drivers is a woman is 0.1 and that the sex of each truck driver is independent of the others. The binomial random variable is the number out of the 10 who are women.

   d. Each bet is independent of the others and has a fixed probability of a success so the number of successful bets out of a fixed number of bets is a binomial random variable.

2. **a.** $^{12}C_3 = 220$ **b.** $^{52}C_4 = 270{,}725$ **c.** $^9C_5 = 126$ **d.** $^{50}C_3 = 19{,}600$

   e. $^7C_5 \times {}^8C_2 = 21 \times 28 = 588$ because there are $^7C_5$ ways of selecting the women and for each of these ways there are $^8C_2$ ways of selecting the men.

WORK CARD 4 (CONTINUED)

3. **a.** $P(2) = 3 \cdot 0.2^2\, 0.8 = 0.096$ **b.** $P(3) = 0.2^3 = 0.008$ **c.** $P(2\ or\ more) = P(2) + P(3) = 0.104$

4. **a.** 0.7738   **b.** $P(3) + P(4) + P(5) = 0.9988$ **c.** 0.0000003

5. **a.** $0.75^{15} = 0.0134$ **b.** 0.1651   **c.** $P(X < 10) = P(X \le 9) = 0.9992$ **d.** $np = 3.75$
    e. to the right as $p < 0.5$ **f.** $np(1 - p) = 2.8125$

6. We want $P(X > 2) = 1 - P(X \le 2) = 1 - P(0) - P(1) - P(2)$
    $= 1 - 1\, 0.01^0\, 0.99^{100} - 100\, 0.01^1\, 0.99^{99} - 4950\, 0.01^2\, 0.99^{98}$
    $= 1 - 0.366032 - 0.369730 - 0.184865 = 0.079373$

7. This will be a binomial situation if whether or not any one share in the portfolio rises does not affect the probability that the other share prices rise; that is, the price rises of individual shares are independent. The mean will be $np = 32$ and the variance will be $np(1 - p) = 19.2$.

ASSESSMENT 4

1. Which of the following are binomial situations? Do you need to make any additional assumptions? If the situation is binomial, what is the binomial random variable?
    a. A football team playing a series of matches.
    b. The number of phone calls every hour received at a doctor's surgery.
    c. The airline with the worse punctuality record recorded that 60.3% of flights were late arriving; 10 flights are scheduled each day. (Consider all the circumstances associated with connecting flights.)
    d. An office worker aims to catch the 8.25 bus to work every morning. She misses the bus about 1 day out of 5. Consider the number of days in a week which she misses her bus for work.

2. In how many ways can I choose the following?
    a. I have 6 T-shirts and I arbitrarily choose 3 to take on holiday with me.
    b. I have a list of 10 people to call, but only have time to make 3 calls tonight.
    c. I have 8 friends and I can invite just 4 to a dinner party.
    d. I have 5 male friends and 3 female friends and I want to invite 2 men and 2 women to a dinner party.

3. At my university 22% of the students enrolled are 'mature'; that is, aged 21 or over.
    a. If I take a random sample of 5 students from the enrolment register what is the probability that exactly two students are mature?
    b. If I take a random sample of 7 students from the enrolment register what is the probability that exactly two students are mature?
    c. If I take a random sample of 7 students from the enrolment register what is the probability that 2 or fewer students are mature?

4. A coin is tossed 10 times and the number of heads recorded. Calculate the following.
   a. The probability that there are 8 heads.
   b. The probability that there are 4 heads.
   c. The probability that there are 1 or 2 heads.
   d. The probability that there are 0 heads.

5. A company has sold 15 extended warranties for washing machines. The probability that a particular washing machine breaks down during the period of the warranty is 0.1. The company will make a profit on the warranties if 5 or fewer machines break down – what is the probability of this occurring?

6. In America, 53% of households contribute to some religion, 24% to some health charity, and 15% donate to education. A fund-raiser conducts a survey of 30 American households. Use software to answer the following questions.
   a. What is the probability that fewer than half the surveyed households give to some religion?
   b. What is the probability that more than 10 give to a health charity?
   c. What is the probability that exactly 2 households give to education?
   d. What is the mean and variance of the random variable, X, the number of households out of the 30 who give to religion?

5 The Poisson distribution

The Poisson distribution (pronounced 'Pwassong' – the French word for fish, but named after a mathematician) is another probability distribution that occurs frequently. In particular, it is used in queueing theory to model the number of people who join a queue during a particular time interval. There are two broad sets of circumstances for which a Poisson distribution is appropriate:

(i)   to model the number of occurrences of a particular rare event in a time interval
(ii) as an approximation to the binomial distribution.

The number of occurrences of a particular rare event in a time interval
The Poisson distribution is often appropriate to model the number of times a particular event happens in a time interval. For instance,

● the number of road accidents on a particular street corner during a year,
● the number of phone calls received by a switchboard each minute,
● the number of people who join a queue during a 5-minute time interval.

We can represent the time period in question by a line and show the occurrence of each event as an X. For instance, the diagram below shows the times at which 7 people arrive at a queue during a 5-minute time interval.

There are two conditions for the number of occurrences of an event in a time interval to have a Poisson distribution:

(i) The event occurs an average of μ times during the time interval of interest. Events occur at the same average rate throughout the time period.

This means that the mean of a Poisson random variable is μ, and that the mean number of occurrences in, say, 0.1 of these time intervals is 0.1μ, in 1.2 of these time intervals is 1.2μ and so on.

(ii) Events happen independently and individually, so the number of events that occur in any time interval is independent of the number of events that occur in any other *non-overlapping* time interval.

For instance, the number of people who join a queue during the first minute of a 5-minute time period does not influence the probability distribution of the number of people who join the queue during the second minute of the 5-minute interval. Also, only one event can happen at a time. For instance, a Poisson distribution is not suitable for the number of individuals who join a queue if some of them arrive in twos and threes.

Check this

Which of the following random variables might have a Poisson probability distribution? Explain your answers and state any assumptions that are necessary.

a. The number of borrowers who join the queue at the issue desk of a library during a minute.

b. The number of times my car will not start in the morning during a year. It is more reliable in summer than in winter.

c. The number of people who arrive at a restaurant during a particular half-hour period. Most of them arrive in parties of 2, 3 and 4.

d. The number of people arriving at a supermarket check-out queue during a five-minute period at the supermarket's busiest time on a Friday evening.

Solutions:

a. This has a Poisson distribution if the average rate at which borrowers join the queue is the same for every minute-long period, they arrive individually and arrivals are independent; for instance, the presence of a long queue (indicating a lot of recent arrivals) does not deter new arrivals.

b. The average number of non-starts in any time period does not occur at the same rate throughout the year so a Poisson distribution is not suitable.

c. The number of people is not a Poisson random variable because arrivals are not independent as they may occur in groups. However, the number of groups to arrive in a period for which the mean rate is constant may be Poisson.

d. It is reasonable to assume that this has a Poisson distribution provided that the average rate of arrivals is constant (so, for instance, people do not join another queue when this one is long) and people arrive individually – that is, people do not shop together. If people do arrive in groups, but only have one trolley per group, the number of trolleys presented at the queue could be modelled as a Poisson random variable.

When a random variable X has a Poisson probability distribution the probability that it takes a value x is

$$P(x) = \frac{\mu^x e^{-\mu}}{x!}$$

where μ is the average number of occurrences of the event in the time interval of interest. If you haven't met e before, it is a 'special' number, a bit like π ('pi'), which pops up a lot in mathematics because it has particular properties. It is *approximately* 2.718282, but if you press the e button on your calculator you will see more decimal places. Also, recall that $x!$ means $x(x-1)(x-2)\ldots 3 \cdot 2 \cdot 1$.

So, for instance, when an event occurs an average of 5 times in a minute the probability that it occurs exactly once in a minute is

$$P(1) = \frac{5^1 e^{-2}}{1!} = 0.033690$$

Check this

The number of patients admitted to a regional hospital each day with a particular rare disease has a mean of 2.

On a particular day what is the probability that:

a. no patients are admitted

b. exactly one patient is admitted

c. exactly two patients are admitted

d. more than two patients are admitted.

Solution: As the mean is $\mu = 2$, we just use the formula

$$P(x) = \frac{2^x e^{-2}}{x!}$$

a. $P(0) = \dfrac{2^0 e^{-2}}{0!}$. Recall that $0! = 1$ so $P(0) = e^{-2} = 0.135335$

b. $P(1) = \dfrac{2^1 e^{-2}}{1!} = 2e^{-2} = 0.270671$

c. $P(2) = \dfrac{2^2 e^{-2}}{2!} = 2e^{-2} = 0.270671$

d. $P(X > 2) = 1 - P(0) - P(1) - P(2) = 0.323323$

In the above example the time interval of interest was 1 day, and the mean number of admissions, μ, was also given for 1 day. Any length of time can be taken as the time interval of interest provided that the mean, μ, applies to the same length of time.

Check this

The number of people arriving at a sports injury clinic during a *10-minute* interval is known to have a mean of 3.
　What is the probability that 2 or more people arrive during a *5-minute* interval?

Solution:
We are being asked about a 5-minute interval so we need the mean number of arrivals in 5 minutes. A mean of 3 people per 10-minute interval is equivalent to a mean of 1.5 people during a 5-minute interval, so $\mu = 1.5$.

$$P(X \geq 2) = 1 - P(0) - P(1) = 1 - \frac{1.5^0 e^{-1.5}}{0!} - \frac{1.5^1 e^{-1.5}}{1!} = 0.442175$$

The Poisson approximation to the binomial distribution

Recall that the conditions for a binomial situation are:

1. There are n identical 'trials'.
2. Each 'trial' has two possible outcomes: success or failure.
3. At each trial $P(success) = p$.
4. The result of each trial is independent of all the others.

The number of successes has a binomial probability distribution. However, suppose further that:

5. The chance of success, p, is very small and may be unknown.
6. The number of trials, n, is very large and again may be unknown.
7. The average number of successes, $\mu = np$, is known and is not large, say $\mu \leq 7$.

When conditions **5**, **6** and **7** hold as well as **1**, **2**, **3**, and **4**, the number of successes still has a binomial distribution but the Poisson distribution provides a very good approximation. This is useful because when n is large, binomial probabilities can be very tedious to calculate and they are not published in tables.

For instance, the following binomial random variables approximately have Poisson probabilities.

● The number of AIDS cases per 10,000 people (because the probability that an individual has AIDS is very small, there are 10,000 people, which is a large number and the average number of cases is less than or equal to 7).
● The number of aircraft from a particular large airline that crash in a particular year (because there are a large number of aircraft, the probability that an individual aircraft crashes is very small and the average number of crashes is less than or equal to 7).
● The number of students from a year group who fall ill during the year, and have to withdraw (because there are a large number of students, the probability that an individual student falls ill is very small and the average number of withdrawals for this reason is less than or equal to 7).

Notice that all these random variables are the number of occurrences of a rare event in a large population.

Check this

The Poisson distribution gives good approximate probabilities for the following binomial random variables. In each case explain why and state any additional assumptions which are required.

a. The number of defective items out of batch of 1000 when the probability that an individual item is defective is 0.005.

b. The number of prize-winning crisp packets purchased by a school when the crisp manufacturer includes a prize of a £10 note in 1 packet out of every 100, and the school purchases 200 packets.

c. The number of males aged 40 insured by a particular insurance company who die between their 40th and 41st birthdays. The probability that an individual male dies in his 41st year is 0.001.

Solution:

a. $n = 1000$ which is large and $p = 0.005$ so $\mu = np = 5$ which is less than or equal to 7, so the Poisson approximation is appropriate. We must also assume that the probability that each item is defective is unaffected by whether or not the other items are defective – that is, that each item is independent.

b. $n = 200$ and so is large, $p = 0.01$, so $\mu = 2$ which is less than or equal to 7 and a Poisson approximation is appropriate.

c. A Poisson approximation is appropriate provided that the number of policyholders, n is large, and that $\mu = np \le 7$, where $p = 0.001$.

When a binomial random variable, X, satisfies the above conditions (**1–7**) the probability that x successes occur is approximately the Poisson probability,

$$P(x) = \frac{\mu^x e^{-\mu}}{x!}$$

where μ is the mean of the binominal distribution, $\mu = np$.

Check this

The probability that a particular automobile part is defective is known to be 0.001. A total of 3000 parts are required in the assembly of a car.

a. Use the binomial probability distribution to calculate the probability that there are no defectives. Now calculate the approximate probability using the Poisson distribution.

b. Calculate the probability of exactly 5 defectives. Try using both the binomial distribution and the Poisson approximation to obtain your answer.

Solution:
The distribution of the number of defectives is binomial, with $n = 3000$ and $p = 0.001$, so the mean is $\mu = np = 3$. As n is large, and p is small so that $\mu \leq 7$ we can approximate by a Poisson distribution.

a. Using the binomial distribution, the probability of 0 defectives is
$$P(0) = {}^{3000}C_{3000}\, 0.001^0\, 0.999^{3000} = 0.999^{3000} = 0.0497124.$$
   Although n is large this was not a problem to calculate because any combination of form ${}^nC_n = 1$.
   Using the Poisson approximation, $\mu = 3$ and so

$$P(0) = \frac{3^0 e^{-3}}{0!} = 0.049787$$

Notice that the results are very similar.

b. We require $P(5)$. The binomial probability is $P(5) = {}^{3000}C_5\, 0.001^5\, 0.999^{2995}$.

$${}^{3000}C_5 = \frac{3000!}{5!\,2995!} = \frac{3000 \times 2999 \times 2998 \times 2997 \times 2996}{5 \times 4 \times 3 \times 2 \times 1} = 2.018257871 \times 10^{15}$$

(using a calculator). This is shown to only 10 significant figures and so is not likely to be accurate, which presents a problem in calculating the binomial probability.
   Using the Poisson approximation is much more straightforward and gives

$$P(5) = \frac{3^5 e^{-5}}{5!} = 0.013644$$

Check this

It is estimated that 1% of applications for a new type of bank account must be returned to the applicant because the form has been filled out incorrectly. A small branch receives 80 applications for the account each week.

a. Calculate the probability that no applications are returned to the applicant in a given week.

b. Calculate the probability that 3 or more applications are returned to the applicant in a given week.

Solution:
The number of applications returned is a binomial random variable for which n is large and p is small, and $\mu = 0.8 \leq 7$ so we can approximate the probabilities using a Poisson distribution.

a. We require $P(0) = \dfrac{e^{-0.8} 0.8^0}{0!} = 0.449329$

b. $P(X \geq 3) = 1 - P(0) - P(1) - P(2)$

$$P(1) = \frac{e^{-0.8}0.8^1}{1!} = 0.359463$$

$$P(2) = \frac{e^{-0.8}0.8^2}{2!} = 0.143785, \text{ so}$$

$$P(X \geq 3) = 1 - 0.449329 - 0.359463 - 0.143785 = 0.047423$$

Using a computer

Most statistical software will calculate Poisson probabilities for you. The SPSS command is

Transform > Compute

followed by using the **PDF.POISSON** function for the probability density function or **CDF.POISSON** for the cumulative distribution function as described in Section 4 for the binomial distribution.

In Excel the POISSON function will calculate Poisson probabilities. The arguments are x, the mean μ, and TRUE or FALSE depending on whether you want the cumulative probability of x, $P(X \leq x)$, or the probability of x, $P(X = x)$.

Use a computer to check the results obtained in the last **Check this**.

The mean and variance of the Poisson distribution

We already know that the mean or expected value of a Poisson random variable appears directly in the formula for its probabilities

$$P(x) = \frac{\mu^x e^{-\mu}}{x!}$$

and is μ. However, it can be shown that the variance of a Poisson random variable is also μ.

The Poisson distribution

$$P(x) = \frac{\mu^x e^{-\mu}}{x!}$$

The Poisson distribution is appropriate

(i) to model the number of times a rare event occurs in a time interval when:

- on average, the events occur μ times in the time interval and the event occurs at the same average rate throughout the time interval;
- events happen individually and independently.

(ii) as an approximation to the binomial distribution when

n is large

p is very small

$\mu = np$ is known and ≤ 7

1. Which of the following random variables might you model using a Poisson distribution? Explain your answers and state any assumptions that you need to make.

    a. The number of deep sea trawlers that run aground off the British coast during a particular year.

    b. The number of claims over £10 million made to an insurance company during the month of June.

    c. The number of job advertisements in my local paper each week that are for my type of work. (I have very specialist skills.)

    d. The number of power cuts that occur in a year in a rural area.

    e. The number of job advertisements in my local paper each week for bar work.

    f. The number of job advertisements on the notice board of my local Post Office that are for bar work. There are 12 on the board at any one time.

2. The number of letters Mary receives each day has a Poisson distribution with a mean of 2. What is the probability that on a particular day she receives

    a. no letters?

    b. 4 or more letters?

3. On average, a large airline loses half an aircraft a year through accident. What is the probability they lose:

    a. no aircraft in a given year?

    b. two or more?

4. A large hotel knows that, on average, 1% of its customers require a special diet for medical reasons. It is hosting a conference for 400 people.

    (i)   Which probability distribution would you suggest for calculating the *exact* probability that no customers at the conference will require a special diet? Calculate this probability.

    (ii) Which probability distribution do you suggest as an approximation to this and why? Calculate an approximate probability that no customers require a special diet.

    (iii) Compare your answers to (i) and (ii).

    (iv) From past records the hotel knows that 0.1% of its customers will require medical attention while staying in the hotel. Calculate the exact and approximate probability that no customers out of the 400 will require medical attention while attending the conference. Is the approximation better or worse than the approximation used in (ii)? Why?

5. A photographic manufacturer produces the same number of lenses (over 5000) each week. On average 3.5 of these are found to be defective. Calculate an approximate probability that:

    (i)   no defective lenses are produced in a week

    (ii) less than 3 defective lens are produced in a week

6. An average of 2.2 power cuts occur in a rural area in a year. What is the probability that a year passes with no power cuts? What is the probability that 2 or more power cuts occur in a year? What assumptions are necessary when making your calculations?

Solutions:

1. **a.** We assume that the probability that an individual trawler runs aground is small and that there are a large number of trawlers – so we can use a Poisson random variable.

   b. Provided there are a large number of policies and there is a very small probability that each makes such a large claim so that there are an average of 7 or fewer claims, we approximate using a Poisson distribution.

   c. Assuming the same number of advertisements appear each week and that only a small proportion are suitable for me a Poisson approximation is appropriate.

   d. Assume that the average number of power cuts in any period is proportionate to the length of the period, the number of power cuts may have a Poisson distribution.

   e. Assuming again that the same number of advertisments appear each week this is a binomial random variable. If we assume that a high proportion of the advertisements are for bar work, a Poisson approximation is not suitable.

   f. This is a binomial random variable, a Poisson approximation is not appropriate because there are only 12 trials.

2. $\mu = 2$, so

   a. $P(0) = \dfrac{2^0 e^{-2}}{0!} = 0.135335$

   b. $P(X > 4) = 1 - P(0) - P(1) - P(2) - P(3)$

   $$= 1 - \frac{2^0 e^{-2}}{0!} - \frac{2^1 e^{-2}}{1!} - \frac{2^2 e^{-2}}{2!} - \frac{2^3 e^{-2}}{3!}$$

   $$= 1 - 0.135335 - 0.270671 - 0.270671 - 0.180447 = 0.142876$$

3. $\mu = 0.5$.

   a. $P(0) = \dfrac{0.5^0 e^{-0.5}}{0!} = 0.606531$

   b. $P(X \leq 2) = 1 - P(0) - P(1)$

   $$= 1 - 0.606531 - \frac{0.5^1 e^{-0.5}}{1!} = 1 - 0.606531 - 0.303265 = 0.090204$$

4. **(i)** Binomial $n = 400$, $p = 0.01$ so $P(0) = 0.99^{400} = 0.017951$

   (ii) As n is large and p is small, and $\mu = 4 \leq 7$ we can use the Poisson approximation:

   $$P(0) = \frac{e^{-4} 4^0}{0!} = 0.018316$$

(iii) The answers are close – the approximation is 102% of the exact figure.

(iv) Now n is the same, but p is smaller so the approximation should be better. Using the binomial distribution $P(0) = 0.999^{400} = 0.670186$ and using the Poisson approximation

$$P(0) = \frac{e^{-0.4}0.4^0}{0!} = 0.670320$$

and now the approximation is 100.02% of the exact figure.

5. **(i)** $P(0) = \frac{3.5^0 e^{-3.5}}{0!} = 0.030197$

   (ii) $P(X < 3) = P(0) + P(1) + P(2) = 0.030197 + 0.105691 + 0.184959 = 0.320847$

6. $P(0) = \frac{e^{-2.2}2.2^0}{0!} = 0.110803.$

$P(2 \text{ or more}) = 1 - P(0) - P(1) = 1 - 0.110803 - 0.243767 = 0.645430$. We assume that the occurrence of power cuts in any time period is independent of the occurrence of power cuts in any non-overlapping time period and that the average number of power cuts in any time interval is proportional to the length of the time interval.

1. When the probability of each possible outcome is the same, a discrete random variable is said to have a *discrete uniform distribution*. For instance, the number shown on a die has a discrete uniform distribution because the probability of each number from 1 to 6 is $\frac{1}{6}$.

   Do the following random variables have a Poisson, binomial, discrete uniform or another probability distribution? State any assumptions that are necessary for your answers.

   a. The total observed on 2 dice.

   b. The number of cars passing a quiet junction in a minute.

   c. The number of wine glasses I break during a year.

   d. The number, out of 100 purchasers at a store, who want their purchase wrapped in a paper bag.

   e. The number of clues I can do on a crossword with 20 clues when the probability that I can do a particular crossword clue when I see it in isolation is 0.8.

   f. The date of the month of an individual's birthday.

   g. If Sunday is 7, Monday is 1, Tuesday is 2 and so on, the day of the week of an individual's next birthday.

   h. The number of students out of a seminar group of 10 who are tee-totallers.

   i. The number of tee-totallers out of a lecture group of 100 students.

2. On average, a bank makes 3 mistakes out of every 10,000 transactions. If 10,000 transactions are audited, what is the probability that more than 4 mistakes are found?

3. Stand or sit in a public place where you can count the number of people who pass. Decide on a short time interval in which, on average, only a few people will pass. For at least 20 of these time intervals count the number of *groups* of people who pass in each time interval. (For instance, sit and count the number of groups who join a coffee bar queue during 20, 15-second intervals.)

   You should now have a sample of 20 or more values.

   a. Use the sample to estimate the probability distribution of the number of groups who pass during a time interval.
   b. Suggest a well known probability distribution for the number of groups who pass during a time interval. Use the mean of the sample of data you have collected as an estimate of the mean of this theoretical distribution and then calculate the probabilities.
   c. How do the probabilities obtained in **b** compare with those from **a**?
   d. Why are your probabilities different to the theoretical probabilities?
   e. Do you think the well-known distribution is a good model for the number of people who pass in a time interval? If not, can you think of any reasons why it is not?
   f. Why didn't we ask you to count the total number of *individuals* arriving at the queue?

4. There are 20 students in a lecture group and the probability that an individual student is late is 0.01; 20 students attend the lecture. What is the probability that no students arrive late? (Assume that the students arrive individually and that the punctuality or otherwise of a student does not affect the probability that another student is late.)

   Suppose 200 students eventually arrive at the lecture. Use first the binomial and then the Poisson distributions to calculate the probability that none of these students were late. Comment on your results.

Further reading: see p. xv

Anderson *et al.* (Statistics) contains more detail.

Mendenhall *et al.*

Newbold *et al.* is excellent but does take a more mathematical approach than most 'business' texts.

P3
Continuous numerical outcomes

Our actions are only throws of the dice in the sightless night of chance

Franz Grillparzer, *Die Ahnfrau*

Contexts

What is this chapter about?
In this chapter we consider the probabilities associated with continuous random variables; that is, numerical outcomes that can take any value within a range – for instance, the height of a 20-year-old male, the duration of a call to a call centre, or the depth of the sea at a randomly chosen point.

Why is it useful?
As we said in the previous chapter, being able to predict how likely various values are is invaluable for planning and decision making. This chapter widens the repertoire of 'patterns' of probabilities or probability distributions. In particular, it includes some of the most commonly occurring distributions: the normal distribution, which is essential for inferential statistics, and the exponential distribution.

Where does it fit in?
Much of the subject of Probability is concerned with the probabilities associated with random variables; that is, measurements that take an uncertain numerical value. There are two types of random variable: discrete and continuous. The last chapter (P2) was concerned with discrete random variables and this chapter considers continuous random variables.

What do I need to know?
You must be at ease with the last two chapters (P1 and P2) and, of course, with the material in Essential Maths.

Objectives

After your work on this chapter you should be:

- able to use a probability density function (pdf) to represent the probabilities associated with a continuous random variable;
- able to calculate the probabilities associated with the uniform and exponential distributions;
- familiar with the normal distribution and the standard normal distribution and able to calculate their probabilities using tables or a computer;
- able to decide when it is appropriate to model a random variable using any of the above distributions;
- able to use the normal distribution as an approximation to the binomial, when appropriate.

After considering discrete random variables in Chapter P2 we now move on to continuous random variables – that is, random variables that can take *any* value within a range.

We start this chapter by introducing the *probability density function (pdf)* of a continuous random variable and showing how probabilities can be calculated from it. We then consider three special continuous distributions: the *uniform*, the *exponential* and the *normal*. The normal distribution is particularly important as it is perhaps the most widely used distribution and it plays a key role in Statistics.

1 Probability density functions (pdfs)

A continuous random variable is a random variable that can take *any value* within a range, for instance,

- the annual rate of inflation for the UK,
- the time it takes a runner to complete a marathon,
- the time it takes a particular Formula One racing driver to complete a lap at the Monaco Grand Prix,
- human body temperature when in good health,
- the time between phone calls received at a switchboard,
- the weight of a new-born baby,
- the amount of your electricity bill in the winter quarter.

Notice that continuous random variables are usually measurements as opposed to 'counts'. On the other hand, discrete random variables are those that can only take *a selection of values* within their range, for instance, the number of cars that pass a motorway check-point in a minute, or the number of students who pass an exam out of a class of 30.

The probability distribution of a continuous random variable

We already know that the probability distribution of a discrete random variable is a list of all its possible values and their probabilities. For example, a typical probability distribution for a discrete random variable, X, might be

x	P(x)
0	0.01
1	0.5
2	0.4
3	0.07
4	0.02

Before you read on, can you see why we can't represent the probabilities of a continuous random variable in the same way?

The reason is that a continuous random variable can take *any value* within its range and so a list of all the possible values would be infinitely long. For instance, the time it takes a runner to complete a marathon can be recorded to any number of decimal places and so, in theory, an infinite number of different times are possible. In practice of course, the time will only be recorded to the nearest tenth or hundredth of a second, and so there will be a very large number rather than an infinite number of possible times.

So we do not write down the probability distribution of a continuous random variable in the manner shown above because the number of probabilities required would be infinite or, at best, prohibitively large. Also, as the total of the probabilities in a probability distribution has to be 1, most of these probabilities would be extremely small.

To avoid this problem the probability structure associated with a continuous random variable is represented using a *probability density function* (*pdf*) (sometimes just called the probability distribution again). The graph in Figure 3.1 shows the pdf of a random variable, X. As you can see, it is just a curve that lies on or above the x axis of a graph.

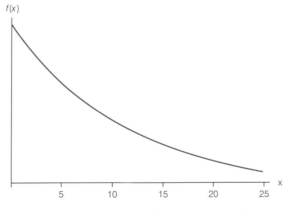

Figure 3.1 A probability density function.

The pdf is chosen so that the area underneath the curve between any two values on the x axis is the probability that X falls between these two values. For instance, area A in the graph in Figure 3.2 shows the probability that X lies between 10 and 15, $P(10 < X < 15)$ and area B shows the probability that X is less than 5; that is, $P(X < 5)$.

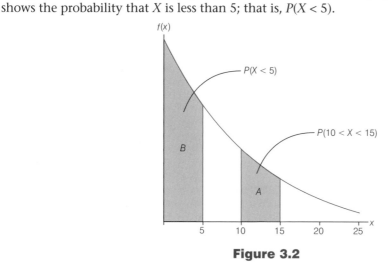

Figure 3.2

It follows that the total area under a pdf curve must be 1 because the probability that X takes a value that lies somewhere on the x axis is 1.

The pdf curve is usually given by a formula in x which we will refer to as $f(x)$. For instance, the pdf shown in Figures 3.1 and 3.2 is $f(x) = 0.1e^{-0.1x}$, where e is just the number 2.71828... as usual.

As another example, consider the following pdf. As before, the area under the whole curve is 1 but this time X can take both positive and negative values. Area C in Figure 3.3 is the probability that X lies between –1 and 1.5.

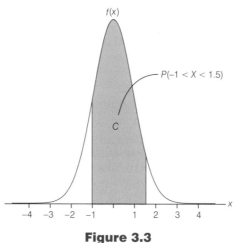

Figure 3.3

So the pdf of a random variable X is a curve, given by the formula $f(x)$, with the following properties:

(i)   it lies on or above the x axis,

(ii) the area under the whole curve is 1, and

(iii) the area under the curve between any two values a and b is $P(a < X < b)$.

Check this

Which of the sketches in Figure 3.4 could be pdfs?

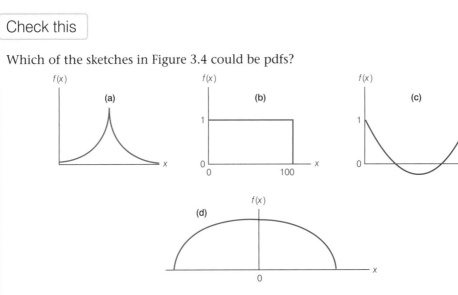

Figure 3.4

Solutions:
a. and **d.** could be pdfs, provided that the scale on the horizontal axis is such that the area underneath the curve is 1. The area under the curve in **b.** is 100 so this cannot be a pdf. The curve in **c.** goes below the x axis and so could not be a pdf.

As a continuous random variable can take an infinite number of possible values, the probability that it takes any individual one is 0. This means that for continuous random variables it doesn't matter whether we talk about, for instance, $P(X < 5)$ or $P(X \le 5)$, or about $P(-1 < X < 1.5)$ or $P(-1 \le X \le 5)$ because the end points of any interval contribute a zero probability.

Using pdfs for discrete random variables
When a discrete random variable has a huge number of possible values it is impractical to work with the (discrete) probability distribution.

For instance, suppose a large motor manufacturer sells between 10,000 to 12,000 cars inclusive a month. The discrete probability distribution of X, the number of cars sold in a month, contains 2001 probabilities, $P(X = 10,000)$, $P(X = 10,001)$, $P(X = 10,002)$ and so on up to $P(X = 12,000)$ and the probabilites which are usually of interest like $P(X > 10,500)$ or $P(X < 11,700)$ are usually the sum of many of these. This is cumbersome and we are not likely to be able to estimate all 2001 probabilities accurately. It is much easier to represent the probabilities approximately using a pdf (maybe like the one in Figure 3.5) and treat car sales as a continuous random variable. Any errors due to the fact that X is really discrete are usually small.

Pdfs and histograms
Suppose X is the duration of the working life of a type of electronic chip. The manufacturer takes a sample of 20 such chips and tests their lifetimes. A histogram of the lifetimes of these 20 chips is shown in Figure 3.6.

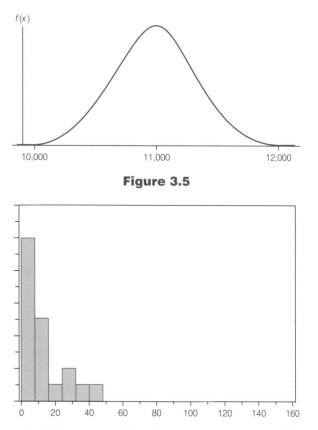

Figure 3.5

Figure 3.6 Histogram of the lifetimes of a sample of 20 chips.

The distribution is clearly skewed to the right. A larger sample, of 100 chips, gives the histogram in Figure 3.7.

This has a similar general shape to the histogram in Figure 3.6 but shows a little more detail because the class width can be narrower as there are more data. A sample of 2000 chips gives the histogram in Figure 3.8, which is even finer.

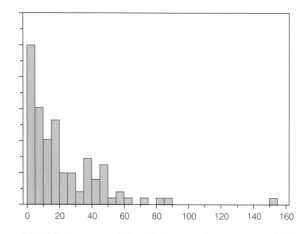

Figure 3.7 Histogram of the lifetimes of a sample of 100 chips.

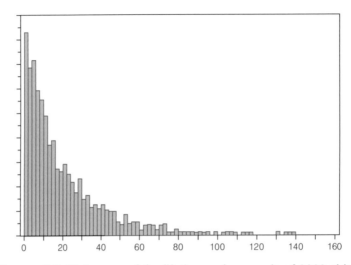

Figure 3.8 Histogram of the lifetimes of a sample of 2000 chips.

We could continue by taking larger and larger samples. As the size of the sample increased the class width could be reduced further and the corresponding histograms would gradually approach the shape of the pdf of the lifetime of a chip, which is shown in Figure 3.9.

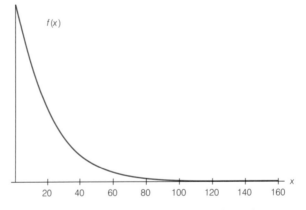

Figure 3.9 Pdf of the lifetime of a chip.

So the pdf can be regarded as the histogram of an infinite number of repetitions of the random variable. (We had a similar result for discrete random variables – that the relative frequencies of a large number of values of a discrete random variable approach the probabilities.)

Drawing pdfs

To get a feel for pdfs try sketching a rough pdf for the following random variables. Remember that you are really just drawing a histogram of lots of repetitions of the random variable.

Check this

Draw a rough graph of a plausible pdf for the following random variables.

a. The age of an undergraduate student selected at random from your university.

b. The number of minutes to the next bus, when you have just missed one.

c. The winning ticket in a lottery in which 10,000 tickets are numbered consecutively from 1 to 10,000.

d. The height of an adult man.

e. The height of an adult woman.

f. The height of an adult.

Solutions:
No exact answers are possible here – it depends what is assumed about the random variable of interest. We suggest the following sketches:

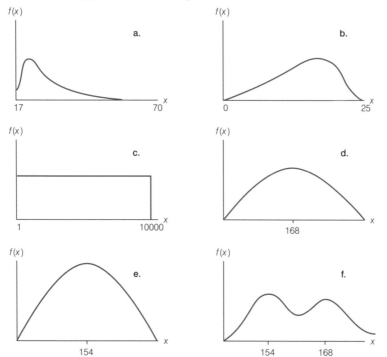

a. assumes that a student cannot be younger than 17, that the ages between about 18 and 22 are most common and that the higher the age above this, the less common it is.

b. We have assumed that until a due time of 20 minutes the bus becomes more likely to arrive and that one is certain to arrive within 25 minutes.

c. This is a discrete random variable but there are 10,000 possibilities so we can approximate the probability distribution using a pdf. Each ticket number is equally likely so the pdf has equal height throughout the range.

d. We have assumed that the most likely height of a man is about 168 cm and that the more a height deviates from this the less likely it is.

e. We have assumed that the most likely height of a woman is 154 cm and that the more a height deviates from this the less likely it is.

f. As half adults are men and half are women the resulting distribution will be a combination of those in **d.** and **e.** and a pdf with two modes (peaks) will result.

Calculating continuous probabilities: the uniform distribution

When all the possible values of a continuous random variable are equally likely to occur we say it has a *uniform* distribution. The uniform distribution is the simplest of a few well-known continuous distributions that occur often. Consider the following example.

An office fire-drill is scheduled for a particular day, and the fire alarm is equally likely to ring at any time between 9am and 5pm. The time the fire alarm starts, measured in minutes after 9am, is therefore a random variable, X, which is equally likely to take any value between 0 and 480. A sketch of the pdf of X, with a reminder that the total area under a pdf is 1, is shown in Figure 3.10.

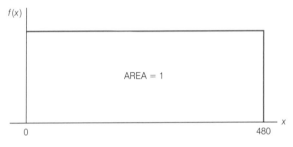

Figure 3.10

The pdf is the same height throughout the range of X and so the equation of this pdf has the form $f(x)$ = height. The area under the pdf, which must equal 1, is a rectangle with base 480, so 480 × height = 1, and it follows that that the height must be 1/480. So the pdf is $f(x)$ = 1/480 for any value of x between 0 and 480. We write this as

$$f(x) = \frac{1}{480} \text{ for } 0 \le x \le 480$$

Now we have found the pdf we can use it to calculate probabilities about X. For instance, the probability that the fire alarm sounds between 1pm and 2pm, $P(240 < X < 300)$, is the area under the pdf between 240 and 300, which is shown in Figure 3.11.

This area is a rectangle with base 60 (= 300 – 240) and height $\frac{1}{480}$, so $P(240 < X < 300) = \frac{1}{8}$. (Some readers may think that this probability was obvious from the start, but we have used this method because it applies to more complicated pdfs as well.)

In general, when a random variable is equally likely to take any value between a and b, (where $a < b$) we say it has a *uniform distribution over the interval from a to b* and because the area under the the pdf between a and b must be 1, as shown in Figure 3.12, its pdf is

$$f(x) = \frac{1}{b-a}$$

for $a \le x \le b$.

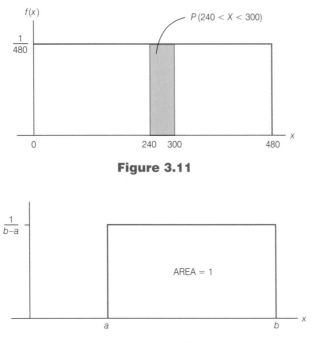

Figure 3.11

Figure 3.12

Check this

A local authority is responsible for a stretch of road 3km long, through a town. A gas main runs along the length of the road. The Gas Company has requested permission to dig up the road in one place but has neglected to tell the local authority exactly where.

a. Let X be the distance of the gas works from one end of the road. Sketch the pdf of X.

b. What is $f(x)$?

c. The stretch of road between the 1.5 and 2.75 kilometres from one end goes through the town centre and gas works there would cause severe disruption. What is the probability that this happens?

Figure 3.13

Solution:

a. Assuming that any point along the road from 0 to 3km from one end is equally likely we have a uniform distribution over the interval 0 to 3, as shown in Figure 3.13.

b. The base of the rectangle under this pdf is 3, so, as the area under the rectangle must be 1, the pdf is $f(x) = \frac{1}{3}$ for $0 \le x \le 3$.

c. $P(1.5 < X < 2.75)$ is the area of the rectangle under the pdf between 1.5 and 2.75. This has height 1/3 and base 1.25, so the probability is 0.4167.

Most pdfs are curves rather than straight lines, so we can't usually use geometry like this to calculate the areas corresponding to probabilities. For some pdfs there is a convenient formula for these areas and for others specially compiled tables of probabilities are available.

The expected value and variance of a continuous distribution

In Chapter P2 we introduced the concepts of the expected value (mean) and variance of a discrete random variable. These ideas extend to continuous random variables although the method of calculation for continuous random variables requires a mathematical method called integration which is not covered by this book. This doesn't matter, however, because there are formulae for the mean and variance of all the well-known distributions which we will give as we introduce each distribution.

For instance, the mean of a random variable that is uniformly distributed in the interval from a to b, and so has pdf

$$f(x) = \frac{1}{b-a}$$

is

$$\mu = \frac{a+b}{2}$$

and the variance is

$$\sigma^2 = \frac{(b-a)^2}{12}$$

(The mean may be obvious to you as the distribution is symmetric and $\frac{a+b}{2}$ is in the middle.) For example, for the fire alarm problem where X was equally likely to take any value between 0 and 480, $a = 0$ and $b = 480$, so the mean is

$$\mu = \frac{0 + 480}{2} = 240$$

and the variance is

$$\sigma^2 = \frac{(480 - 0)^2}{12} = 19{,}200$$

Check this

A train is equally likely to arrive at a station at any time between 6.10 pm and 6.40pm.

(i) What is the pdf of X, the number of minutes it arrives past 6pm?

(ii) Calculate the mean and variance of X.

Solution:

(i) X is equally likely to take any value between 10 and 40, so

$$f(x) = \frac{1}{30} \qquad 10 \le x \le 40$$

(ii) The mean of X is

$$\frac{a+b}{2} = \frac{10+40}{2} = 25$$

The variance of X is

$$\frac{(b-a)^2}{12} = \frac{(40-10)^2}{12} = 75$$

As usual, the mean and variance are summary measures of the centre and spread of the distribution respectively. The graph of the pdf gives a useful way of thinking of the mean. Imagine that the pdf and the area under it has been cut out in wood. The point of the x axis under which you could place a pivot, to make a balanced see-saw, is the mean.

We can place the same interpretation on the variance as we did for discrete distributions in Chapter P2, Section 3; that is, when k is any positive number greater than 1:

> the probability that a random variable X lies within $k\sigma$ of its mean, μ, is at least
>
> $$1 - \frac{1}{k^2}$$

For example, suppose the average journey time by train from Norwich to Nottingham has a mean of 2.8 hours and a variance of 0.16 hours. The standard deviation is $\sqrt{0.16} = 0.4$, so we can instantly make the statement that the probability that the journey lasts between $2.8 - (2 \times 0.4)$ and $2.8 + (2 \times 0.4)$ hours; that is, $P(2 < X < 3.6)$, is at least

$$1 - \frac{1}{2^2} = 0.75$$

or that the probability that the journey lasts between $2.8 - (3 \times 0.4)$ and $2.8 + (3 \times 0.4)$ hours (that is, $P(1.6 < X < 4)$) is at least

$$1 - \frac{1}{3^2} = 0.8889$$

This will be true for any pdf, whatever the shape of the curve.

Whilst these statements may seem rather vague, they do give some feel for the likely spread of values for the random variable.

Continuous distributions

The pdf of a continuous random variable, X, is a function f(x) such that

(i)   its curve lies on or above the x axis
(ii) the area under the whole curve is 1
(iii) the area under the curve between a and b is P(a < X < b)

The uniform distribution

$$f(x) = \frac{1}{b - a} \qquad\qquad a \le x \le b$$

$$\mu = \frac{b + a}{2} \qquad\qquad \sigma^2 = \frac{(b - a)^2}{12}$$

1. Which of the following would you treat as continuous random variables?
    a. The number of goals scored in a football match by a particular team.
    b. The proportion of a cinema audience who smoke cigarettes.
    c. The number of washing machines sold in a day by a small shop.
    d. The number of washing machines sold in a day by a large retail firm.
    e. The amount owed by an individual to the Tax office, or owed by the Tax office to him/her at the end of a year.
    f. The *average* number of goals scored in a match by a particular football team during the whole season.

2. Where possible, for each of the random variables in question **1**, draw a possible probability density function (pdf).

3. An Anglia Railways train is due to arrive at 5.30 pm but in practice is equally likely to arrive at any time between *2 minutes early and 30 minutes late*. Let the time of arrival (expressed as minutes from due time) be X.
    Sketch the pdf, f(x), of the random variable X. Shade the areas on your graph corresponding to the following probabilities and calculate these.
    a. The probability that the train arrives before 5.40 pm.
    b. The probability that X is less than or equal to 10.
    c. The probability that the train is late, but less than 16 minutes late.

4. Figure 3.14 shows the pdf, f(x), of a continuous random variable X.
    a. What is the height of the pdf at x = 0?
    b. Shade the area corresponding to P(X > 1). Calculate this probability.

5. What are the mean and variance of the arrival time of the train in question **3**?

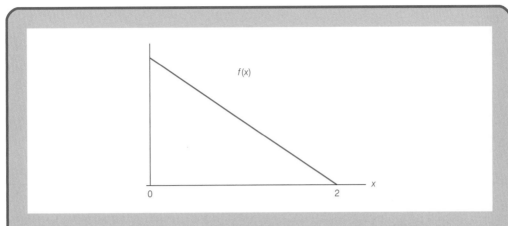

Figure 3.14

Solutions:

1. **a.** discrete, **b.** continuous, **c.** discrete, **d.** discrete, but we would model it using a pdf as there are a large number of possible values, **e.** continuous, **f.** continuous. Notice that although the number of goals in each match is discrete, the average is continuous.

2. **b.** The x axis must have a range between 0 and 1. We would expect a peak around the proportion of all cinema-goers who smoke. **d.** Again a peak at the average number sold, positive numbers on the x axis only. **e.** Both positive and negative amounts on the x axis. Presumably the pdf would tail off for very large positive and very large negative values. **f.** x from 0 to say 20?

3. This is a uniform distribution between -2 and 30 (minutes from due time): $f(x) = \frac{1}{32}$.
   a. The rectangle under $f(x) = \frac{1}{32}$ between -2 and 10 with an area of $\frac{12}{32}$.
   b. The answer is the same as **a.**
   c. The rectangle under $f(x)$ between 0 and 16 with an area of $\frac{16}{32}$.

4. **a.** The triangular area under the pdf must be equal to 1, so the height of the triangle is 1.
   b. Shade the area under $f(x)$ between 1 and 2. This is a triangle with base 1. Its height will be 0.5, as the ratio between the sides is the same as that of the big triangle, and so $P(1 < X < 2) = 0.25$.

5. The train time has a uniform distribution between -2 and 30 so $a = -2$ and $b = 30$ and using the formula for the mean and variance of a uniform distribution we have

$$\mu = \frac{a+b}{2} = \frac{-2+30}{2} = 14$$

and

$$\sigma^2 = \frac{(b-a)^2}{12} = \frac{(30+2)^2}{12} = 85.333$$

ASSESSMENT 1

1. Which of the following would you treat as continuous random variables? Explain your answers.
   a. The number of people who arrive for a particular charter flight.
   b. The number of mm of rain that falls on London on a particular day.
   c. The number of staff in a small office who are off sick on a particular day.
   d. The proportion of phone calls from a particular pay-phone on a particular day that take longer than two minutes.
   e. The duration of a phone call from a pay-phone.
   f. The number of telephone units on a telephone card that a particular call uses.

2. Draw a possible probability density function for the following random variables. State any assumptions you make.
   a. The percentage mark gained by a less able individual in an exam.
   b. The percentage mark gained by an able individual in an exam.
   c. The proportion of able students who pass the exam.
   d. The proportion of less able students who pass the exam.
   e. The time it takes you to travel to the university on a typical day.
   f. The percentage return over a month on a particular equity investment.

3. A random variable, Y, can take values between 0 and 0.5 and has the pdf $f(y) = 8y$.
   a. Calculate the probability that Y is larger than 0.25.
   b. Calculate the probability that Y is smaller than 0.1.
   c. Calculate the probability that Y lies between 0.1 and 0.25.

4. A financial analyst predicts that the return on Whizzco ordinary shares over the next 12-month period is equally likely to be any percentage between –2% and 4%. Assuming that the analyst is correct,
   a. Draw the probability density function of the return, X, and write down its formula, $f(x)$.
   b. Calculate the probability that the share has a positive return.
   c. Write down the mean and variance of the share's return.

2 The exponential distribution

This is another continuous distribution which arises often.

The exponential pdf

The graph in Figure 3.15 shows the pdf of an exponential random variable, X.

Notice that X cannot be negative, and that lower values are more likely than higher ones. The general form of the exponential pdf is

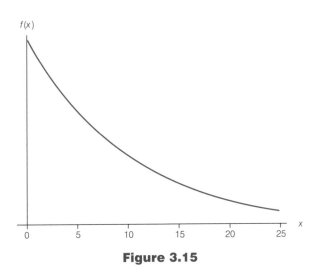

Figure 3.15

$$f(x) = \lambda e^{-\lambda x}$$

where λ (pronounced 'lambda') is a positive constant. For instance, $f(x) = 5e^{-5x}$ is the exponential pdf with $\lambda = 5$. As any number raised to the power of 0 is 1, the height of the curve at $x = 0$ is always λ.

When does it occur?

The exponential distribution has a special relationship with the Poisson distribution, so we will use the Poisson distribution to describe how it occurs.

Suppose a busy ticket office opens at 9am and customers arrive individually at random times. A possible pattern of arrivals during the first five minutes is shown on the diagram below. Each X represents the arrival of a customer.

```
 ├─X──────────┬───X──X───┬──────X────┬──────────┬──X──X──┬ · ·
 0  0.3       1  1.3 1.55 2     2.5   3          4  4.25 4.6  5   time
```

There are two ways in which we can look at the pattern of arrivals. **(i)** We can count the number of customers who arrive during each minute (1, 2, 1, 0 and 2 on the diagram above) or **(ii)** we can look at the times between successive arrivals or *inter-arrival* times (from the diagram 0.3, if we count the time up to the first arrival, 1.0, 0.25, 0.95, 1.75 and 0.35).

We have met **(i)** before. In Chapter P2, Section 5, we said that under certain conditions the number of times an event occurs in a time interval has a Poisson distribution. (The conditions are: **(i)** The event continues to occur at the same average rate; **(ii)** Events happen independently and individually, so the number of events occurring in any time interval is independent of the number of events that occur in any other *non-overlapping* time interval.) We will assume that these conditions hold for the ticket office and that the time interval of interest is a minute so that the number of customers who arrive during each minute-long period is a Poisson random variable.

The second, and new way of looking at the pattern of arrivals, **(ii)**, is to consider the *times between successive arrivals*. Because arrivals occur randomly, the time between them is a random variable, and further, as a time can take any non-negative value, the time between arrivals is a *continuous* random variable. Moreover, the following fact tells us that this continuous random variable has an exponential distribution.

When the number of times an event occurs in a time interval has a Poisson distribution with mean λ the number of these time intervals between successive occurrences has an exponential distribution with pdf, $f(x) = \lambda e^{-\lambda x}$.

So, there is a complementary relationship between the Poisson distribution and the exponential distribution. For instance, if the number of customers who arrive at the ticket office in a minute has a Poisson distribution with a mean of 1.25, the time in minutes between successive customers, X, is an exponential random variable with pdf $f(x) = 1.25e^{-1.25x}$. The relationship also works the other way round. That is, if the times between successive occurrences of an event have an exponential distribution the number of occurrences in unit time has a Poisson distribution.

At this point we should also say that there are other circumstances for which an exponential distribution may be appropriate. In particular, it is often used to model the length of time before a machine breaks down or, in queueing problems, the time it takes to serve a customer.

The graph in Figure 3.16 shows the exponential pdf when λ is 2, 4 and 10 respectively. Don't worry if you haven't sketched curves like this before, the key thing is to note that the pdf for $\lambda = 10$ is concentrated around smaller values of the random variable than the pdfs for $\lambda = 2$ or 4. This is to be expected, because when an average of 10 events happen in a unit time interval, the times between the events will tend to be smaller than when only 2 or 4 events happen in a unit time interval.

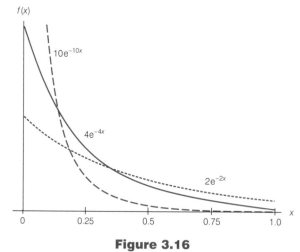

Figure 3.16

Check these

a. The number of customers entering a supermarket in a 1 minute interval has a Poisson distribution with a mean of 2.5. Write down the pdf of the time between the arrival of successive customers.

b. During a morning a lecturer makes herself available to students for advice. An average of 3 students arrive each hour. Suggest a probability distribution for the time between the arrival of students. What assumptions have you made?

c. The time in months between breakdowns of a photocopying machine is exponentially distributed with $\lambda = 0.5$. When a machine breaks down it is mended virtually instantaneously. What is the distribution of the number of breakdowns that occur in a month? How many breakdowns, on average, will occur during a month? How many breakdowns, on average, will occur in a year?

Solutions:

a. As the number of arrivals in a minute is Poisson mean 2.5, the time between arrivals will be exponential with parameter $\lambda = 2.5$, so the pdf will be $f(x) = 2.5e^{-2.5x}$.

b. If the number of students who arrive in an hour has a Poisson distribution with mean 3 the time between arrivals will be exponential with $\lambda = 3$. In order to assume that the number of students who arrive each hour is Poisson, we need to assume that conditions **(i)** and **(ii)** from the text hold.

c. If the time between events is exponential with $\lambda = 0.5$, the number of events in a time unit is Poisson with mean 0.5 so, on average, there will be 0.5 breakdowns a month. As the average rate is constant, during a year there will be an average of 6 breakdowns.

The mean and variance of the exponential distribution
We can deduce the mean of an exponential distribution from its relationship with the Poisson distribution.

Suppose that the number of customers arriving at a busy ticket office each minute has a Poisson distribution with mean 10. We know that this implies that the time between arrivals has an exponential distribution with $\lambda = 10$. However, because an average of 10 customers arrive each minute it also follows that the average time *between* arrivals must be 1/10 of a minute. (You may need to think about this, it is a question of logic rather than mathematics.)

We conclude that an exponential distribution with $\lambda = 10$, has mean 1/10. We could have applied the same logic to any mean number of arrivals, λ per minute. So, it follows that the mean of the exponential distribution with pdf $f(x) = \lambda e^{-\lambda x}$ is $1/\lambda$.

The variance of the exponential distribution with pdf $f(x) = \lambda e^{-\lambda x}$ can be shown (using more advanced maths) to be $\frac{1}{\lambda^2}$ so the standard deviation is the same as the mean.

Check these

The time in minutes, X, between the arrival of successive customers at a bank is exponentially distributed with a pdf of $f(x) = 0.4e^{-0.4x}$.

a. Write down the mean time between arrivals.

b. What is the mean number of customers who arrive in a minute?

Solution:

a. The mean is 1/0.4 = 2.5 minutes.

b. The number of customers who arrive in a minute is Poisson distributed with mean 0.4.

Check this

A manufacturer reports that the number of hours, X, for which their new design of CD player will work before requiring maintenance of any form has pdf $f(x) = 0.0008e^{-0.0008x}$. This information is considered too technical to be included in sales material, so they wish to report the mean and standard deviation only. What are they?

Solution:
This is an exponential pdf with $\lambda = 0.0008$. The mean and standard deviation of the distribution are both $\frac{1}{\lambda}$ so they are both $\frac{1}{0.0008} = 1250$.

Calculating exponential probabilities

Like all continuous random variables the probabilities associated with the exponential distribution can be found from the areas underneath the pdf. For instance, the probability $P(X < a)$ is the area under the pdf to the left of $x = a$ as shown in Figure 3.17.

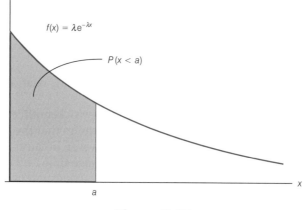

Figure 3.17

It is not immediately obvious how to calculate such an area as it isn't triangular or rectangular. However, there is a formula that will help.

The area under the pdf to the *left* of $x = a$, shown in Figure 3.17, is

$$1 - e^{-\lambda a}$$

It follows (as the area under the whole pdf is 1) that the area under the pdf to the *right* of a is $1 - (1 - e^{-\lambda a}) = e^{-\lambda a}$. That is, we have

$$P(X < a) = 1 - e^{-\lambda a} \text{ and } P(X > a) = e^{-\lambda a}$$

There is no need to learn both of these as one can be obtained from the other.

For example, when $f(x) = 0.25e^{-0.25x}$, $\lambda = 0.25$, so the probability that X is less than 3 is $P(X < 3) = 1 - e^{-0.25 \times 3} = 1 - e^{-0.75} = 0.527633$.

Check this

An investigation into waiting times at the casualty department of a regional hospital showed that at peak times patients arrive at an average rate of 0.9 per minute. What is the probability that a patient arrives less than 30 seconds after the previous one?

Solution:
Assuming that the number of customers who arrive each minute is a Poisson random variable, with mean 0.9, the time between arrivals, X, has an exponential distribution with $\lambda = 0.9$. We require $P(X < 0.5)$. Using the formula

$P(X < a) = 1 - e^{-\lambda a}$ gives $P(X < 0.5) = 1 - e^{-0.9 \times 0.5} = 0.362372$

Check this

The number of customers who join the 'less than 5 items' queue at a supermarket every minute has a Poisson distribution with mean 0.5. What is the probability that a customer arrives less than 1.5 minutes after the previous one?

Solution:
As the number of customers who arrive each minute is Poisson mean 0.5, the time between arrivals has an exponential distribution with $\lambda = 0.5$. The desired probability is $P(X < 1.5) = 1 - e^{-0.5 \times 1.5} = 1 - e^{-0.75} = 0.527633$.

Check this

The time between uses of a vending machine is modelled as an exponential distribution with $\lambda = 0.2$.
   What is the probability that there is a gap of more than 10 minutes between uses?

Solution:
A sketch of the pdf is given in Figure 3.18. We have indicated the desired probability, $P(X > 10)$, which is the area under the pdf curve to the right of $x = 10$.

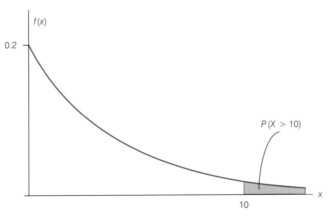

Figure 3.18

From $P(X > a) = e^{-\lambda a}$, $P(X > 10) = e^{-0.2 \times 10} = e^{-2} = 0.135335$. There is a 13.5% probability of a gap of more than 10 minutes between uses.

Check this

The number of squash bookings taken during an hour at a sports centre is a Poisson random variable with mean 2.1. Del works for 4 hours between breaks and is surprised that there are no bookings during this period. What is the probability that this happens?

Solution:
We require $P(X > 4)$ where X is the time between bookings. The number of bookings an hour averages 2.1 so $\lambda = 2.1$. We know that $P(X > 4) = e^{-2.1 \times 4} = e^{-8.4} = 0.0002249$. Del is understandably surprised.

Probabilities of the form $P(a < X < b)$ where both a and b are constants can be found by expressing them in terms of $P(X < a)$ and $P(X < b)$ or $P(X > a)$ and $P(X > b)$. This is easiest to see by shading the area corresponding to $P(a < X < b)$ on a graph of the pdf.

Check this

For the squash bookings example above (bookings are Poisson with mean 2.1), calculate the probability that the time between consecutive bookings is between 1 and 2 hours.

Solution:
The time between bookings is exponential with $\lambda = 2.1$. A rough sketch of the pdf (not to scale) is shown in Figure 3.19.

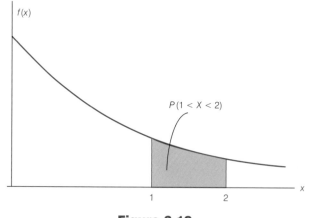

Figure 3.19

The required probability is the area under the pdf, between 1 and 2. Notice that this is the area under the curve to the right of 1, $P(X > 1)$, *less* the area under the curve to the right of 2, $P(X > 2)$. That is,

$$P(1 < X < 2) = P(X > 1) - P(X > 2)$$

From the formula $P(X > a) = e^{-\lambda a}$ we know that $P(X > 1) = e^{-2.1 \times 1} = e^{-2.1}$ and $P(X > 2) = e^{-2.1 \times 2} = e^{-4.2}$, so the desired probability is $= e^{-2.1} - e^{-4.2} = 0.107461$.

This way of subtracting one area from another to get a probability of the form $P(a < X < b)$ is useful for all continuous distributions, so it's worth spending some time on it now.

Check this

The time taken to serve a customer in an electronics shop is exponentially distributed with mean 5.6 minutes. What is the probability that it takes between 5 and 10 minutes to serve a customer?

Solution:
We require $P(5 < X < 10)$ where X has an exponential distribution with pdf

$$f(x) = \frac{1}{5.6}e^{-x/5.6}$$

So $P(X > a) = e^{-a/5.6}$

$P(5 < X < 10) = P(X > 5) - P(X > 10) = e^{-5/5.6} - e^{-10/5.6} = e^{-0.892857} - e^{-1.785714} = 0.241807$

Using a computer to calculate exponential probabilities

Most statistical software will calculate the *cumulative* exponential probabilities, $P(X < a)$, for you. In SPSS we select

Transform > Compute

and then use the **CDF.EXP** function.

In Excel we use the EXPONDIST function with arguments x, lambda, and, in a similar way to the binomial and Poisson functions, TRUE/FALSE to indicate a cumulative probability or not. However, beware that 'lambda' in Excel is the inverse of our λ; that is, it is the mean $(= 1/\lambda)$ of the desired exponential distribution.

The exponential distribution: summary

When the number of times an event occurs in a time interval has a Poisson distribution with mean λ, *the number of these time intervals between successive events*, X, has an exponential distribution with pdf

$$f(x) = \lambda e^{\lambda x}.$$

The mean and variance of X are

$$\mu = \frac{1}{\lambda} \quad \text{and} \quad \sigma^2 = \frac{1}{\lambda^2}$$

When a is a constant

$$P(X < a) = 1 - e^{-\lambda a}$$

and equivalently

$$P(X > a) = e^{-\lambda a}$$

1. The time (in minutes) it takes to find an error in a computer program has an exponential distribution with pdf $f(x) = 0.02e^{-0.02x}$

   a. Sketch this pdf.

   b. Calculate the probability that it takes more than an hour to find an error.

   c. What is the mean time it takes to find an error?

   d. What is the variance of the time it takes to find an error?

2. The time between vehicles arriving at a toll booth is exponentially distributed with mean 12 seconds. It takes 10 seconds for the driver to pay and for the barrier to lift. What proportion of drivers arrive less than 10 seconds after the previous car arrives?

3. The owner of SNIPS hair salon does not allow customers to make appointments but relies on customers walking in off the street. From past experience the number of customers who arrive each hour follows a Poisson distribution with an average of 4 customers per hour.

   (i) What is the distribution of the time between successive arrivals?

   (ii) What is the mean and standard deviation of the time between successive arrivals?

   (iii) If the owner has just seen one customer arrive, what is the probability that the next customer will arrive within 30 minutes?

   (iv) What is the probability that *no* customers arrive for a whole hour?

Solutions:

1. a. The usual exponential pdf, it starts from (0,0.02)

   b. $P(X > 60) = e^{-0.02 \times 60} = 0.301194$

   c. $\dfrac{1}{\lambda} = \dfrac{1}{0.02} = 50$ minutes

   d. $\dfrac{1}{\lambda^2} = \dfrac{1}{0.02^2} = 2500$ minutes

2. $P(X < 10) = 1 - e^{-10/12} = 0.565402$.

3. (i) Exponential with $\lambda = 4$, so $f(x) = 4e^{-4x}$. (ii) mean 0.25 hours, standard deviation 0.25. (iii) The information given was in hours, so we require $P(X < 0.5) = 1 - e^{-4/2} = 1 - e^{-2} = 0.864665$. (iv) $P(X > 1) = e^{-4 \times 1} = 0.018316$. Notice that this is the same as $P(0)$ for the Poisson distribution with mean 4.

1. The length of time a doctor spends with a patient has an exponential distribution with mean 10 minutes.

   a. Assuming that the doctor does not have any free time between patients how many patients, on average, does she see during an hour?

   b. What proportion of patients spend more than 15 minutes with the doctor?

2. An average of 0.3 serious road accidents occur on a dangerous by-pass in a year. What is the probability that two years pass without a serious road accident? What assumption did you make to answer this?

3. The number of telephone calls received each minute by the switchboard of a package holiday firm has a Poisson distribution with mean 3.2.

   a. What is the probability that the switchboard operator receives a call less than 10 seconds after the previous call?

   b. What is the probability that more than 30 seconds passes between calls?

   c. What is the average time between calls?

3 Introducing the normal distribution

The normal distribution is probably the most widely used and frequently occurring probability distribution. We will explain later why this is so. (By the way, 'normal' is the name of the distribution. It does not mean that other distributions are *ab*normal in any way!)

The pdf of a normal random variable, X, is 'bell-shaped' and symmetric about a value, μ ('mu'), as shown in Figure 3.20. The curve never actually touches the x axis, so any value of X is possible, although values of X a long way from μ are very unlikely.

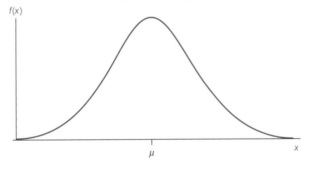

Figure 3.20 The pdf of a normal random variable.

The formula for the pdf of the normal distribution is

$$f(x) = \frac{1}{\sqrt{2\pi\sigma^2}} e^{-(x-\mu)^2/2\sigma^2}$$

We will not use this again so don't worry if it looks rather formidable, we just ask you to notice that it involves two constants, σ and μ (sigma and mu). There are a whole family of normal curves, each one specified by a particular pair of values for σ and μ.

Both μ and σ have a 'nice' interpretation. We have already said that the pdf is symmetric about μ, so it is no surprise that μ is the mean of the distribution. The other constant, σ^2, dictates how spread out and flat the 'bell-shape' is, and in fact σ^2 is the variance of the normal distribution. As an illustration Figure 3.21 shows the following normal pdfs:

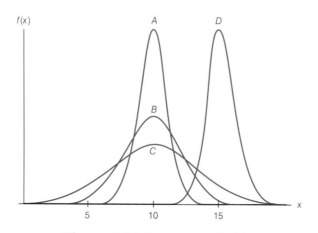

Figure 3.21 Some normal pdfs.

A	$\mu = 10, \sigma = 1$
B	$\mu = 10, \sigma = 2$
C	$\mu = 10, \sigma = 3$
D	$\mu = 15, \sigma = 1$

Pdfs A, B and C all have the mean 10, so they are all centred at $x = 10$. Of these three curves, C has the largest variance and so is the most 'spread out'. Curve B has a smaller variance and so is less spread out, and curve A has the smallest variance and so is the most 'squeezed in'. Curves A and D have the same variance, so they have exactly the same shape, but they have different means so they are centred at $x = 10$ and $x = 15$ respectively.

Some notation

As the normal distribution is entirely specified by its mean and variance a shorthand notation has been developed. $X \sim N(\mu, \sigma^2)$ means that the random variable X has a normal distribution with mean μ and variance σ^2. So, for instance, the curve shown in A above is the pdf of a $N(10,1)$ distribution, the curve in B is the pdf of a $N(10,4)$ distribution and so on.

The standard normal distribution

The normal distribution with mean $\mu = 0$ and variance $\sigma^2 = 1$, is called the *standard normal distribution*. The letter Z is usually used for a random variable that has this distribution. A graph of the standard normal pdf, $\phi(z)$, is shown in Figure 3.22. Notice that most of the area under the standard normal curve lies between -3 and $+3$.

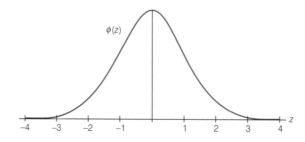

Figure 3.22 The pdf of the standard normal distribution.

When does the normal distribution arise?

Because the normal pdf peaks at the mean and 'tails off' towards the extremes, the normal distribution provides a good approximation for many naturally occurring random variables. However, the normal distribution occurs even more widely due to the following.

1. The total (and also the average) of a large number of random variables that have the same probability distribution approximately has a normal distribution. For instance, if the amount taken by a shop in a day has a particular (maybe unknown) probability distribution, the total of 100 days' takings is the sum of 100 identically distributed random variables and so it will (approximately) have a normal distribution.

   Many random variables are normal because of this. For example, the amount of rainfall that falls during a month is the total of the amounts of rainfall that have fallen each day or each hour of the month and so is likely to have a normal distribution. In the same way the average or total of a large sample will usually have a normal distribution. This will be important when we consider populations and samples in the *Statistics* part of this book.

2. The normal distribution provides approximate probabilities for the binomial distribution when n, the number of trials, is large. We consider this in Section 5 of this chapter.

Calculating probabilities: the standard normal distribution

The normal distribution is continuous and so its probabilities are calculated by obtaining the areas under the pdf curve.

For instance, suppose an individual's IQ score, X, has a normal distribution with mean $\mu = 100$ and standard deviation $\sigma = 15$. As the standard deviation is 15 we can write this $X \sim N(100, 15^2)$ or equivalently $X \sim N(100, 225)$. Figure 3.23 shows the areas under the pdf that correspond to $P(X < 85)$ and $P(115 < X < 120)$.

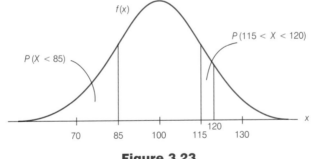

Figure 3.23

Unfortunately, there are no 'nice' formulae for calculating such areas so we have to look them up in tables of normal probabilities or use statistical software.

Using tables to calculate *standard* normal probabilities

We will start by evaluating probabilities for a *standard* normal random variable. This may not seem very useful, but in fact such probabilities form the basis of the calculation of *all* normal probabilities, as we shall see in the next section.

Standard normal probabilities of the form $P(Z < a)$ are listed in a table of *cumulative normal probabilities* like Table II at the end of this book (pp. 867–8). An outline of Table II is shown below.

Table II Cumulative standard normal probabilities $P(Z < a)$ where $Z \sim N(0,1)$.

a	0.00	0.01	0.02	0.03	0.04	0.05	0.06	0.07	0.08	0.09
−3.4										
−3.3										
−3.2										
−3.1										
⋮										
−1.5	0.0668	0.0655	0.0643	0.0630	0.0618	0.0606	0.0594	0.0582	0.0571	0.0559
−1.4	0.0808	0.0793	0.0778	0.0764	0.0749	0.0735	0.0721	0.0708	0.0694	0.0681
−1.3										
⋮										
0.0										
0.1										
0.2										
⋮										
1.6	0.9452	0.9463	0.9474	0.9484	0.9495	0.9505	0.9515	0.9525	0.9535	0.9545
⋮										
1.9	0.9713	0.9719	0.9726	0.9732	0.9738	0.9744	0.9750	0.9756	0.9761	0.9767
2.0	0.9772	0.9778	0.9783	0.9788	0.9793	0.9798	0.9803	0.9808	0.9812	0.9817
⋮										
3.3										
3.4										

For example, the probability that Z is less than −1.46 (that is $P(Z < -1.46)$) shown in Figure 3.24, can be found by looking at the row of the table labelled −1.4 and the column headed 0.06 and is 0.0721.

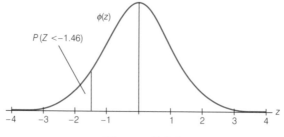

Figure 3.24

What is $P(Z < 1.96)$?

Solution:
Look on the 1.9 row and the 0.06 column of the outline table above to obtain 0.9750.

Now turn to Table II at the end of the book.

Calculate $P(Z < -0.52)$.

Solution:
Look on the –0.5 row and the 0.02 column, to obtain 0.3015.

Probabilities of the form $P(Z > a)$ or $P(a < Z < b)$ can be calculated by expressing them in terms of the cumulative probabilities $P(Z < a)$ given in Table II. It usually helps to draw a rough sketch of the standard normal pdf and mark the appropriate areas.

What is $P(Z > 2.05)$?

Solution:
A sketch is shown in Figure 3.25.

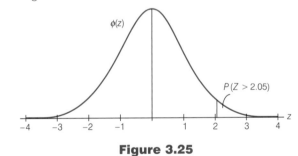

Figure 3.25

$P(Z > 2.05)$ is the area under the whole pdf (which is 1) *less* the area to the left of 2.05, i.e. it is $1 - P(Z < 2.05)$. From the outline of Table II, $P(Z < 2.05) = 0.9798$, so $P(Z > 2.05) = 0.0202$.

Calculate $P(Z > -1.52)$.

Solution:
We require $1 - P(Z < -1.52) = 1 - 0.0643 = 0.9357$.

Check this

Calculate $P(-1.96 < Z < 1.25)$.

Solution:
The required probability is shown in Figure 3.26.

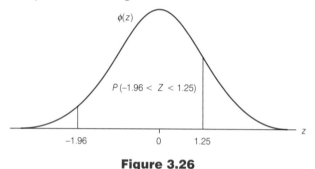

Figure 3.26

It is the area to the left of 1.25, $P(Z < 1.25)$ *less* the area to the left of -1.96, $P(Z < -1.96)$;
that is, $P(-1.96 < Z < 1.25) = P(Z < 1.25) - P(Z < -1.96) = 0.8944 - 0.0250 = 0.8694$ from
Table II.

Calculating percentage points

Sometimes we will know a cumulative probability but require the corresponding value of Z.
For instance, suppose we need to find the value a such that $P(Z < a) = 0.95$ as shown in
Figure 3.27.

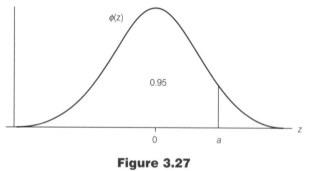

Figure 3.27

There are two ways to find a. First, we can use the table of cumulative normal
probabilities, Table II, *in reverse*. The body of the table contains $P(Z < a)$ so we need to find
0.95 in the body of the table and then look at the margins to see which value of a this
corresponds to. On inspection, 0.95 does not explicitly appear in the body of the table – the
entry for 1.64 is 0.9495 and the entry for 1.65 is 0.9505. It therefore seems a reasonable
guess to suppose that the value we seek lies midway between 1.64 and 1.65. We conclude
that $P(Z < 1.645) = 0.95$, although using the mid-point is an approximation.

The second way avoids this approximation and is the recommended method. Tables of *inverse normal probabilities* or *normal percentage points*, such as the one in Table III, give the value of *a* that corresponds to a particular cumulative probability, *p*. An extract from Table III is given below.

Percentage points of the standard normal distribution
The table gives values of a, where $P(Z < a) = p$

p	0.000	0.001	0.002	0.003	0.004	0.005	0.006	0.007	0.008	0.009
0.00		-3.0902	-2.8782	-2.7478	-2.6521	-2.5758	-2.5121	-2.4573	-2.4093	-2.3656
0.01	⋮	⋮	⋮	⋮	⋮	⋮	⋮	⋮	⋮	⋮
0.02										
0.03										
⋮	⋮	⋮	⋮	⋮	⋮	⋮	⋮	⋮	⋮	⋮
0.10	-1.2816	-1.2759	-1.2702	-1.2646	-1.2591	-1.2536	-1.2481	-1.2426	-1.2372	-1.2319
⋮	⋮	⋮	⋮	⋮	⋮	⋮	⋮	⋮	⋮	⋮
0.95	1.6449	1.6546	1.6646	1.6747	1.6849	1.6954	1.7060	1.7169	1.7279	1.7392
0.96	⋮	⋮	⋮	⋮	⋮	⋮	⋮	⋮	⋮	⋮
0.97										
0.98	⋮	⋮	⋮	⋮	⋮	⋮	⋮	⋮	⋮	⋮
0.99	2.3263	2.3656	2.4089	2.4573	2.5121	2.5758	2.6521	2.7478	2.8782	3.0902

To find *a* such that $P(Z < a) = 0.95$ using this table, we look in the row for 0.95, and, as the third decimal place of 0.95 is zero, the column corresponding to 0.000. This gives *a* = 1.6449, so we conclude that $P(Z < 1.6449) = 0.95$.

The value of a random variable that corresponds to a cumulative probability of *p* is called the 100*p*th *percentage point* or the 100*p*th *percentile*. So we have just found that the 95th percentage point (or 95th percentile) of the standard normal distribution is 1.6449. We will not use this terminology very much but you may well encounter it elsewhere.

Check this

Find *a* such that $P(Z < a) = 0.958$.

Solution:
From the *p* = 0.95 row of the extract from Table III, and the 0.008 column we obtain *a* = 1.7279.

Check this

The return on a particular ordinary share is known to have a standard normal distribution. What value is such that the probability that the return is smaller is 11%?

Solution:
We require *a* such that $P(Z < a) = 0.11$, shown in Figure 3.28.

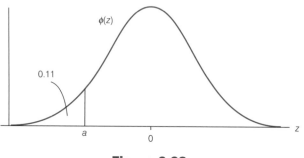

Figure 3.28

The entry at the intersection of the 0.11 row and the 0.000 column of Table III is –1.2265; that is, $P(Z < -1.2265) = 0.11$ and $a = -1.2265$. (We could also have used the cumulative probability table (Table II) in reverse and searched for 0.11 in the body of the table but this would have given the less accurate result that *a* is somewhere between –1.22 and –1.23.)

A dodge for calculating normal probabilities

There is a 'dodge' for calculating normal probabilities that is worth pointing out because it can save time.

As the standard normal distribution is symmetric about 0, the area under the pdf in the left-hand 'tail', $P(Z < -a)$, is the same as the area under the pdf in the right-hand tail, $P(Z > a)$, as shown in Figure 3.29.

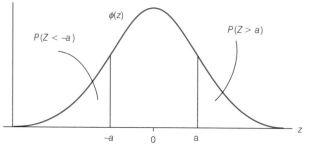

Figure 3.29

Check this

What is $P(Z > 1.3)$?

Solution:
This is the area under the normal curve to the *right* of 1.3 so we cannot look it up in Table II immediately; we would have to calculate $1 - P(Z < 1.3)$. However, it is quicker to say that $P(Z > 1.3) = P(Z < -1.3)$ which, from Table II, is 0.0968.

> ### Check this
>
> What is $P(Z > -0.2)$?
>
> **Solution:**
> $P(Z > -0.2)$ is equivalent to $P(Z < 0.2)$ as illustrated in Figure 3.30.
>
>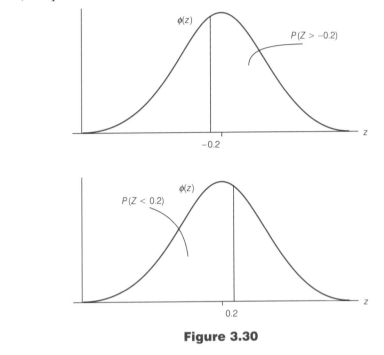
>
> **Figure 3.30**
>
> From Table II, $P(Z < 0.2) = 0.5793$.

> ### Check this
>
> The deviation in mm between the diameter of a manufactured pipe and the specified
> diameter can be positive or negative (or zero) and has a standard normal distribution. To
> be usable the diameter of a manufactured pipe must not differ from the specified diameter
> by more than 2mm. What is the probability of an *un*usable pipe?
>
> **Solution:**
> We need the total of areas A_1 (diameter too small) and A_2 (diameter too large) shown in
> Figure 3.31 (not to scale).
>   We could calculate each of these areas separately and then add them up. However, we
> know that $P(Z < -2)$ and $P(Z > 2)$ are the same, so we need only calculate one and then
> double the result. A_1, $P(Z < -2)$, is obtained directly from Table II and is 0.0228. So the
> total area in both 'tails' is $2 \times 0.0228 = 0.0456$. We conclude that just under 5% of the
> pipes are not usable.

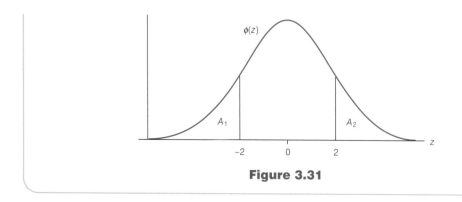

Figure 3.31

In the last example it would have been easier to talk about the probability that the *absolute value* of the deviation in the diameter of the pipe, Z is more than 2, written $P(|Z| > 2)$. The absolute value of a number is the amount by which the number differs from zero; that is, its value ignoring any minus sign. For instance, the absolute value of –3, written $|-3|$ is 3 and $|-5.2| = 5.2$ and so on. So $P(|Z| > 2)$ means the probability that Z differs from zero by more than 2, which points back to the combined areas in the tail to the left of –2 and the tail to the right of 2.

Check this

If Z is a standard normal random variable what is $P(|Z| > 1.5)$?

Solution:
This is the probability that Z differs from zero by more than 1.5 which is the combined area in both tails shown in Figure 3.32.

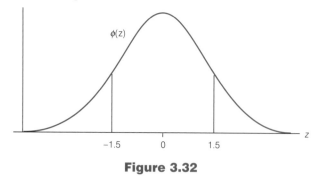

Figure 3.32

From Table II, $P(Z < -1.5) = 0.0668$ and so the area in both tails is $2 \times 0.0668 = 0.1336$.

1. *Z* is a standard normal random variable, i.e. *Z* ~ *N*(0,1). Draw a quick sketch showing the following probabilities and use tables to evaluate them.

   a. $P(Z \leq 0)$ **b.** $P(Z < 1.5)$ **c.** $P(Z < -0.34)$

   d. $P(Z < 0.34)$ **e.** $P(Z > 0.34)$ **f.** $P(Z > -0.21)$

2. *Z* is a *N*(0,1) random variable. Calculate the following probabilities. We find that drawing a rough sketch always helps!

   a. $P(1.4 < Z < 2)$

   b. $P(-0.51 < Z < 0.3)$

   c. $P(-0.2 < Z < 3.45)$

   d. $P(2.3 > Z > 1.5)$

3. *Z* is a standard normal random variable.

   a. Find a value *a* such that there is a $2\frac{1}{2}\%$ probability that *Z* is larger than *a*.

   b. Find the value *a* such that the probability of a smaller value is 0.01.

   c. Find *a* such that $P(Z < a) = 0.01$.

   d. Find *a* such that $P(Z > a)$ is 0.63.

4. Assuming that *Z* is a standard normal random variable, answer the following *without* using tables.

   a. If $P(Z > 1.35) = 0.0885$ what is $P(Z < -1.35)$?

   b. If $P(Z > 1.36) = 0.0869$ what is $P(Z > -1.36)$?

   c. If $P(Z > 1.9) = 0.0287$ what is $P(-1.9 < Z < 1.9)$?

   d. If $P(Z < -2.84) = 0.0023$ what is $P(|Z| > 2.84)$?

   e. Find two values a and b such that there is a 95% chance that Z lies between them, and 0 lies in the middle of them.

WORK CARD 3

Solutions:

1. **a.** *z* = 0 is the half-way point of a symmetric distribution so without tables you can say that $P(Z \leq 0) = 0.5$. **b.** $P(Z < 1.5) = 0.9332$. **c.** $P(Z < -0.34) = 0.3669$. **d.** $P(Z < 0.34) = 0.6331$. **e.** $P(Z > 0.34) = 1 - P(Z < 0.34) = 1 - 0.6331 = 0.3669$ or use $P(Z > 0.34) = P(Z < -0.34) = 0.3669$ from **c**. **f.** $P(Z > -0.21) = 1 - P(Z < -0.21) = 1 - 0.4168 = 0.5832$.

2. **a.** $P(1.4 < Z < 2) = P(Z < 2) - P(Z < 1.4) = 0.9772 - 0.9192 = 0.0580$.
   b. $P(-0.51 < Z < 0.3) = P(Z < 0.3) - P(Z < -0.51) = 0.6179 - 0.3050 = 0.3129$.
   c. $P(-0.2 < Z < 3.45) = P(Z < 3.45) - P(Z < -0.2) = 0.9997 - 0.4207 = 0.579$.
   d. $P(2.3 > Z > 1.5) = P(Z < 2.3) - P(Z < 1.5) = 0.9893 - 0.9332 = 0.0561$.

3. Use Table III (or, less accurately, look up the probability in the body of Table II).
   a. $P(Z < a) = 0.975$, so look up p = 0.975 in Table III to give a = 1.96.
   b. –2.3263. **c.** same as **b**. **d.** If $P(Z > a) = 0.63$ it follows that $P(Z < a) = 0.37$. Looking up p = 0.37 in Table III gives $a = -0.3319$.

4. **a.** $P(Z < -1.35)$ is identical to $P(Z > 1.35)$ so it too is 0.0885. **b.** A graph is recommended here. $P(Z > -1.36) = 1 - P(Z < -1.36)$, and $P(Z < -1.36)$ is the

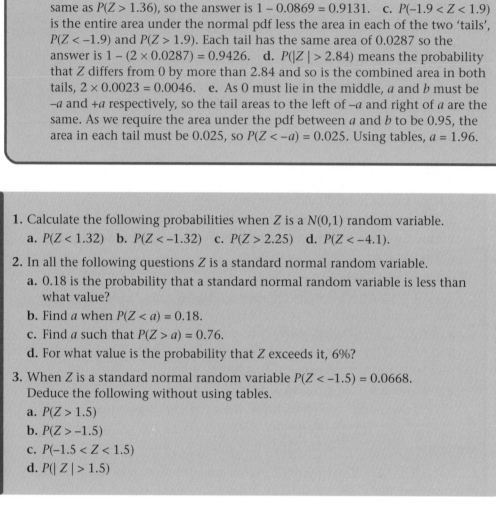

same as $P(Z > 1.36)$, so the answer is $1 - 0.0869 = 0.9131$.   **c.** $P(-1.9 < Z < 1.9)$ is the entire area under the normal pdf less the area in each of the two 'tails', $P(Z < -1.9)$ and $P(Z > 1.9)$. Each tail has the same area of 0.0287 so the answer is $1 - (2 \times 0.0287) = 0.9426$.   **d.** $P(|Z| > 2.84)$ means the probability that Z differs from 0 by more than 2.84 and so is the combined area in both tails, $2 \times 0.0023 = 0.0046$.   **e.** As 0 must lie in the middle, a and b must be $-a$ and $+a$ respectively, so the tail areas to the left of $-a$ and right of a are the same. As we require the area under the pdf between a and b to be 0.95, the area in each tail must be 0.025, so $P(Z < -a) = 0.025$. Using tables, $a = 1.96$.

1. Calculate the following probabilities when Z is a $N(0,1)$ random variable.

   a. $P(Z < 1.32)$ **b.** $P(Z < -1.32)$ **c.** $P(Z > 2.25)$ **d.** $P(Z < -4.1)$.

2. In all the following questions Z is a standard normal random variable.

   a. 0.18 is the probability that a standard normal random variable is less than what value?

   b. Find a when $P(Z < a) = 0.18$.

   c. Find a such that $P(Z > a) = 0.76$.

   d. For what value is the probability that Z exceeds it, 6%?

3. When Z is a standard normal random variable $P(Z < -1.5) = 0.0668$. Deduce the following without using tables.

   a. $P(Z > 1.5)$

   b. $P(Z > -1.5)$

   c. $P(-1.5 < Z < 1.5)$

   d. $P(|Z| > 1.5)$

4 Calculating normal probabilities

We will now see that *any* normal probability can be expressed in terms of a standard normal probability.

Standardising

Any normal random variable, X, that has mean μ and variance σ^2 can be *standardised* as follows:

   Take the variable X, and

(i) subtract its mean, μ, and then
(ii) divide by its standard deviation, σ.

We will call the result Z, so

$$Z = \frac{X - \mu}{\sigma}$$

For example, suppose, as earlier, that X is an individual's IQ score and that it has a normal distribution with mean $\mu = 100$ and standard deviation $\sigma = 15$, i.e. $X \sim N(100,15^2)$. To standardise an individual's IQ score, X, we subtract $\mu = 100$ and divide the result by $\sigma = 15$ to give

$$Z = \frac{X - 100}{15}$$

In this way, every value of X has a corresponding value of Z. For instance, when $X = 130$

$$Z = \frac{130 - 100}{15} = 2$$

and when $X = 90$

$$Z = \frac{90 - 100}{15} = -0.67$$

Notice that Z is the number of standard deviations that X lies from its mean. So, for the example above, an IQ of 130 is 2 standard deviations of 15 above the mean 100 and an IQ of 90 is 0.67 standard deviations of 15 below the mean.

Check this

The percentage monthly return on an ordinary share, X, has a normal distribution with mean 3 and variance 4. How would you calculate the standardised return?

In a particular month the return is $X = 6$. Standardise this and say how many standard deviations it is above or below the mean.

Solution:
To standardise we subtract the mean and divide by the standard deviation so the standardised return would be

$$Z = \frac{X - 3}{2}$$

When $X = 6$,

$$Z = \frac{6 - 3}{2} = 1.5$$

and $X = 6$ is 1.5 standard deviations above the mean.

The distribution of standardised normal random variables

The reason for standardising a normal random variable in this way is that:

a standardised normal random variable

$$Z = \frac{X - \mu}{\sigma}$$

has a standard normal distribution. That is,

$$Z = \frac{X - \mu}{\sigma} \sim N(0,1)$$

Another way of saying this is that the number of standard deviations that a normal random variable is away from its mean has a standard normal distribution. So if we take any normal random variable, subtract its mean and then divide by its standard deviation, the resulting random variable will have a standard normal distribution. We are going to use this fact to calculate (non-standard) normal probabilities.

Calculating probabilities

Consider the probability that an individual's IQ score is less than 85, $P(X < 85)$. The corresponding area under the normal pdf with mean $\mu = 100$ and standard deviation $\sigma = 15$ is shown in Figure 3.33.

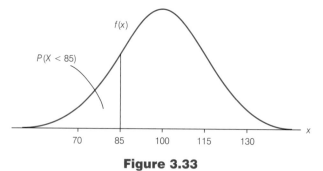

Figure 3.33

We cannot use normal tables directly because these give $N(0,1)$ probabilities. Instead, we will convert the statement $X < 85$ into an equivalent statement that involves the standardised score

$$Z = \frac{X - 100}{15}$$

because we know it has a standard normal distribution.

We start with

$$X < 85$$

To turn X into Z we must standardise the X, but to ensure that we preserve the meaning of the statement we must treat the other side of the inequality in exactly the same way. (Otherwise we will end up calculating the probability of another statement, not $X < 85$.) 'Standardising' both sides gives

$$\frac{X - 100}{15} < \frac{85 - 100}{15}$$

The left-hand side is now a standard normal random variable and so we can call it Z, and we have

$$Z < \frac{85 - 100}{15}$$

which is

$$Z < -1$$

So, we have established that the statement we started with, $X < 85$, is equivalent to $Z < -1$. This means that whenever an IQ score, X, is less than 85 the corresponding standardised score, Z, will be less than -1 and so the probability we are seeking, $P(X < 85)$, is the same as $P(Z < -1)$.

$P(Z < -1)$ is just a standard normal probability and so we can look it up in Table II in the usual way, which gives 0.1587. We conclude that $P(X < 85) = 0.1587$.

This process of rewriting a probability statement about X in terms of Z is not difficult if you are systematic and write down what you are doing at each stage. We would lay out the working we have just done for $P(X < 85)$ as follows.

Check this

X has a normal distribution with mean 100 and standard deviation 15. What is the probability that X is less than 85?

Solution:

$$P(X < 85) = P\left(\frac{X - 100}{15} < \frac{85 - 100}{15}\right) = P(Z < -1) = 0.1587 \text{ (from tables).}$$

Try the following.

Check this

Assuming that an individual's IQ score has a $N(100, 15^2)$ distribution, what is the probability that an individual's IQ score is more than 125?

Solution:
We require

$$P(X > 125) = P\left(\frac{X - 100}{15} > \frac{125 - 100}{15}\right) = P(Z > 1.67)$$

Table II gives $P(Z < 1.67) = 0.9525$, so we have $P(Z > 1.67) = 1 - P(Z < 1.67) = 1 - 0.9525 = 0.0475$.

Check this

For each of these write down the equivalent *standard* normal probability. (Don't bother to look up the probability in Table II – unless you are really keen!)

a. The IQ of a randomly chosen university student, X, is normally distributed with mean 115 and standard deviation 10. Consider the probability that a student has an IQ of over 150.

b. The number of people who visit an historic monument in a week is normally distributed with a mean of 10,500 and a standard deviation of 600. Consider the probability that fewer than 9000 people visit in a week.

c. The number of cheques processed by a bank each day is normally distributed with a mean of 30,100 and a standard deviation of 2450. Consider the probability that the bank processes more than 32,000 cheques in a day.

Solutions:

a. $P(X > 150) = P\left(\dfrac{X - 115}{10} > \dfrac{150 - 115}{10}\right) = P(Z > 3.5)$

b. $P(X < 9000) = P\left(\dfrac{X - 10{,}500}{600} < \dfrac{9000 - 10{,}500}{600}\right) = P(Z < -2.5)$

c. $P(X > 32{,}000) = P\left(\dfrac{X - 30{,}100}{2450} > \dfrac{32{,}000 - 30{,}100}{2450}\right) = P(Z > 0.78)$

Check this

A flight is *due* at Heathrow airport at 1800 hours. Its arrival time has a normal distribution with mean 1810 hours and standard deviation 10 minutes.

a. What is the probability that the flight arrives before its due time?

b. Passengers must check-in for a connecting flight by 1830 at the latest. What is the probability that passengers from the first flight arrive too late for the connecting flight? (Assume no travelling time from aircraft to check-in.)

Solution:
Let the time of arrival, in minutes past 1800, be X, so $X \sim N(10, 10^2)$.

a. We require

$$P(X < 0) = P\left(\dfrac{X - 10}{10} < \dfrac{0 - 10}{10}\right) = P(Z < -1) = 0.1587$$

b.

$$P(X > 30) = P\left(\dfrac{X - 10}{10} > \dfrac{30 - 10}{10}\right) = P(Z > 2) = 0.0228$$

Probabilities like $P(a < X < b)$ can be calculated in the same way. The only difference is that when X is standardised similar operations must be applied to both a and b. That is, $a < X < b$ becomes

$$\dfrac{a - \mu}{\sigma} < \dfrac{X - \mu}{\sigma} < \dfrac{b - \mu}{\sigma}$$

which is

$$\frac{a-\mu}{\sigma} < Z < \frac{b-\mu}{\sigma}$$

Check this

An individual's IQ score has a $N(100,15^2)$ distribution. What is the probability that an individual's IQ score is between 91 and 121?

Solution: We require $P(91 < X < 121)$. Standardising gives

$$P\left(\frac{91-100}{15} < \frac{X-100}{15} < \frac{121-100}{15}\right)$$

The middle term is a standardised normal random variable and so we have

$$P\left(\frac{-9}{15} < Z < \frac{21}{15}\right) = P(-0.6 < Z < 1.4) = 0.9192 - 0.2743 = 0.6449$$

Check this

For each of these write down the equivalent standard normal probability.

a. The length of metallic strips produced by a machine has mean 100cm and variance 2.25cm. Only strips with a weight between 98 and 103cm are acceptable. What proportion of strips will be acceptable? You may assume that the length of a strip has a normal distribution.

b. Scores in an exam are adjusted so that they have a normal distribution with an average mark of 56 and a standard deviation of 12. Students gaining between 40 and 70 are considered 'mainstream'. Consider the probability that a student gains a 'mainstream' score.

Solutions:

a. $X \sim N(100,2.25)$ so $P(98 < X < 103)$

$$= P\left(\frac{98-100}{1.5} < \frac{X-100}{1.5} < \frac{103-100}{1.5}\right) = P(-1.33 < Z < 2)$$

b. $X \sim N(56,12^2)$ so $P(40 < X < 70)$

$$= P\left(\frac{40-56}{12} < \frac{X-56}{12} < \frac{70-56}{12}\right) = P(-1.33 < Z < 1.17)$$

Calculating percentage points

Sometimes you will know a probability but want to calculate the corresponding value of X. For instance, you may need to find the value a, such that $P(X < a) = 0.95$. Again we can do this by changing the statement $X < a$ into an equivalent statement about Z by standardising X.

Check this

The random variable X is normally distributed with mean 20 and variance 16. What value of X is such that the probability that X is smaller is 35%?

Solution:
$X \sim N(20,16)$ and we require a such that $P(X < a) = 0.35$ as shown in Figure 3.34a.

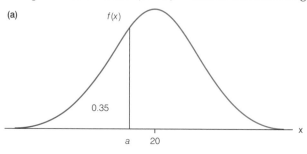

Figure 3.34a

We know $P(X < a) = 0.35$. Standardising this gives

$$P\left(\frac{X - 20}{4} < \frac{a - 20}{4}\right) = 0.35$$

$\frac{X-20}{4}$ is a standardised normal random variable, Z, so our problem becomes, find a such that

$$P\left(Z < \frac{a - 20}{4}\right) = 0.35$$

as shown in Figure 3.34b.

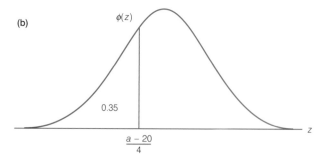

Figure 3.34b

When we look up 0.35 in Table III we obtain –0.3853; that is, $P(Z < -0.3853) = 0.35$. So, it follows that

$$\frac{a - 20}{4} = -0.3853$$

Solving this for a gives $a = (4 \times -0.3853) + 20 = 18.4588$.
   So the probability that X is less than 18.4588 is 35%.

According to a survey, salaries of dentists have an average of £48,000 with a standard deviation of £3500. If the salary of a dentist is normally distributed what salary is such that 20% of dentists have a higher salary?

Solution:
We require a, such that $P(X > a) = 0.2$. We will work in £1000s.
   $X \sim N(48, 3.5^2)$ so standardising $P(X > a) = 0.2$ gives

$$P\left(\frac{X - 48}{3.5} > \frac{a - 48}{3.5}\right) = 0.2$$

that is

$$P\left(Z > \frac{a - 48}{3.5}\right) = 0.2 \text{ as shown in Figure 3.35.}$$

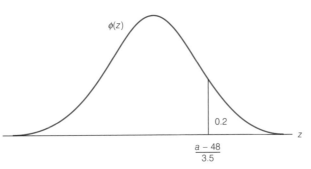

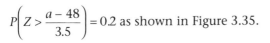

Figure 3.35

It follows that

$$P\left(Z < \frac{a - 48}{3.5}\right) = 0.8$$

and looking up 0.8 in Table III gives

$$P(Z < 0.8416) = 0.8$$

So

$$\frac{a - 48}{3.5} = 0.8416$$

and solving for a gives $a = 50.9456$.
   We conclude that 20% of dentists earn more than £50,946.

The amount a customer spends on a single visit to Rainsburys supermarkets has a normal distribution with mean £75 and standard deviation £21. Rainsburys wish to introduce a minimum amount for which credit cards may be used, which enables 80% of customers to pay by credit card. At what figure should this credit card minimum be set?

Solution:
We require a, such that

$P(X > a) = 0.8$, where $X \sim N(75,21^2)$

Standardising gives

$$P\left(\frac{X - 75}{21} > \frac{a - 75}{21}\right) = 0.8$$

which is

$$P\left(Z > \frac{a - 75}{21}\right) = 0.8$$

which is equivalent to

$$P\left(Z < \frac{a - 75}{21}\right) = 0.2$$

Using Table III gives $P(Z < -0.8416) = 0.2$, so we have

$$\frac{a - 75}{21} = -0.8416$$

Solving for a gives $a = (21 \times -0.8416) + 75 = £57.3264$.
  The credit card minimum should be set at £57.33.

Normal probabilities using software
Most statistical software can calculate cumulative normal probabilities $P(X < a)$ and percentage points (which some software call the *inverse cumulative probabilities*).
    Use SPSS's

Transform > Compute

command and then select the **CDF.NORMAL** function. You will need to specify the values for a, the mean and the standard deviation.

For instance, SPSS tells us that when $X \sim N(75,21^2)$, $P(X < 50) = 0.1169$, whereas by selecting the **IDF.NORMAL** function we find that the 20th percentage point of the same distribution is 57.3260.

This result differs slightly from our earlier manual calculation because the values in Table III are given to only 4 d.p., whereas SPSS's algorithm retains more decimal places in its calculations and so is more accurate.

In Excel you need the function NORMDIST to calculate normal and cumulative normal probabilities, and NORMINV to calculate the inverse cumulative probability.

WORK CARD 4

1. X is a normal random variable with mean $\mu = 5$ and variance $\sigma^2 = 4$.
   Calculate the following probabilities:
   a. $P(X > 5.7)$ **b.** $P(X < 3.4)$ **c.** $P(2.8 < X < 5.1)$
   d. $P(5.7 < X < 6.8)$

2. X is normally distributed with mean 10 and variance 9.
   Find a such that:
   a. the probability that X is less than a is 0.51
   b. $P(X > a) = 0.6$
   c. $P(X \geq a) = 0.05$
   d. $P(10 < X < a) = 0.05$

3. The yearly cost of dental claims for the employees of Notooth International is normally distributed with mean $\mu = £75$ and a standard deviation $\sigma = £25$.
   a. What proportion of employees can be expected to claim over £120 in a year?
   b. What yearly cost do 30% of employees claim less than?

4. Petrol consumption for all types of small car is normally distributed with $\mu = 30.5$ m.p.g. and $\sigma = 4.5$ m.p.g.
   A manufacturer wants to make a car that is more economical than 95% of small cars. What must be its m.p.g?

Solutions:

1. **a.** $P(X > 5.7) = P(Z > 0.35) = 0.3632$.   **b.** $P(X < 3.4) = P(Z < -0.8) = 0.2119$.
   c. $P(2.8 < X < 5.1) = P(-1.1 < Z < 0.05) = P(Z < 0.05) - P(Z < -1.1) = 0.5199 - 0.1357 = 0.3842$.   **d.** $P(5.7 < X < 6.8) = P(0.35 < Z < 0.9) = P(Z < 0.9) - P(Z < 0.35) = 0.8159 - 0.6368 = 0.1791$

2. Sketches will help you here.
   a. $P(X < a)$

   $$= P\left(\frac{X - 10}{3} < \frac{a - 10}{3}\right) = P\left(Z < \frac{a - 10}{3}\right) = 0.51$$

   Using tables $P(Z < 0.0251) = 0.51$, so

   $$\frac{a - 10}{3} = 0.0251 \text{ and } a = 10.0753$$

   b. $P(X > a) = 0.6$

   $$P\left(\frac{X - 10}{3} > \frac{a - 10}{3}\right) = P\left(Z > \frac{a - 10}{3}\right) = 0.6$$

   So $\dfrac{a - 10}{3} = -0.2533$ and $a = 9.2401$

   c. $P(X \geq a)$

$$= P\left(\frac{X-10}{3} \le \frac{a-10}{3}\right) = P\left(Z \le \frac{a-10}{3}\right) = 0.05$$

So $\dfrac{a-10}{3} = 1.6449$ and $a = 14.9347$

d. $P(10 < X < a)$

$$= P\left(\frac{10-10}{3} < \frac{X-10}{3} < \frac{a-10}{3}\right) = P\left(0 < Z < \frac{a-10}{3}\right)$$

$$= P\left(Z < \frac{a-10}{3}\right) - P(Z < 0) = 0.05$$

So $P\left(Z < \dfrac{a-10}{3}\right) - 0.5 = 0.05$ and $P\left(Z < \dfrac{a-10}{3}\right) = 0.55$

So $a - 10 = 0.1257$ and $a = 10.3771$

3. a. $P(X > 120) = P(Z > 1.8) = 0.0359$, so 3.59%.

   b. We require a, such that $P(X < a) = 0.3$, so

$$P\left(Z < \frac{a-75}{25}\right) = 0.3, \quad \frac{a-75}{25} = -0.5244 \text{ and } a = 61.89$$

   30% of employees claim less than £61.89.

4. We require a such that $P(X < a) = 0.95$, so

$$P\left(Z < \frac{a-30.5}{4.5}\right) = 0.95, \text{ so } \frac{a-30.5}{4.5} = 1.6449$$

   and $a = 37.90205$. 95% of small cars do less than 37.9 m.p.g.

---

1. X is a normal random variable with mean $\mu = -2$ and variance $\sigma^2 = 0.5$.
   Calculate the following:
   a. $P(X < -3.5)$
   b. $P(X > 0)$
   c. $P(-1.5 < X < -0.8)$

2. Calculate the following when $X \sim N(100, 64)$:
   a. $P(X > 120)$
   b. $P(X \le 99)$
   c. $P(90 < X < 100)$

3. X has a normal distribution with mean $\mu = 4$ and standard deviation $\sigma = 1.5$. Find
   a when $P(4 - a < X < 4 + a) = 0.8$.

4. The duration of a scheduled flight is normally distributed with a mean of 45 minutes and a standard deviation of 2 minutes.

   a. What is the probability that the flight takes less than 42 minutes?

   b. What is the probability that it takes between 40 and 50 minutes?

   c. What times do 5% of flights take longer than?

5. For a particular life insurance policy the lifetime of the policyholders follows a normal distribution with mean 72.2 years and standard deviation 4.4 years. One of the options of this policy is that the policyholder receives a payment on their 70th birthday and another payment every 5 years thereafter.

   a. What percentage of policyholders will receive at least one payment?

   b. What percentage will receive two or more?

5 The normal approximation to the binomial distribution

In this section we will see that binomial probabilities are difficult to calculate when the number of trials is large but that the normal distribution can provide a good approximation.

A reminder about the binomial distribution

From Chapter P2, Section 4, we know that the number of successes out of n independent, identical trials, each with a probability of success, p, is a binomial random variable, X, and that the probability of x successes is

$$P(x) = {}^nC_x \, p^x(1 - p)^{n-x}$$

where

$$^nC_x = \frac{n!}{x!(n - x)!}$$

Also, the mean of the binomial distribution is np and the variance is $np(1 - p)$.

Binomial probabilities are difficult when n is large!

When n is large, the calculation of $P(x)$ is rather cumbersome as it involves $n!$, $x!$ and $(n - x)!$ Calculation of probabilities like $P(X < a)$ or $P(X \le a)$ is even more awkward as it usually involves many individual binomial probabilities.

As an illustration, consider the following.

An airline deliberately overbooks flights because an average of 20% of the people who book don't arrive for the flight. (This is common practice as full-price passengers can use their tickets for a subsequent flight.) For a particular flight, 235 reservations have been made but only 200 seats are available.

What is the probability that more than 200 passengers arrive for the flight?

This is a binomial situation because we can regard each of the 235 passengers as an identical, independent trial (although this assumes, perhaps unrealistically, that the probability of the arrival or non-arrival of each passenger is unaffected by the arrival or non-arrival of the others) and the probability that each passenger arrives is 0.8. The number of passengers who arrive, X, is therefore a binomial random variable with $n = 235$ and $p = 0.8$. The mean of this binomial distribution is $np = 235 \times 0.8 = 188$ and the variance is $np(1 - p) = 235 \times 0.8 \times 0.2 = 37.6$.

We require

$$P(X > 200) = P(X = 201) + P(X = 202) + P(X = 203) + \ldots + P(X = 235)$$

The first of the probabilities on the right-hand side is

$$P(X = 201) = {}^{235}C_{201}\, 0.8^{201}\, 0.2^{34}$$

This expression is extremely 'nasty' to evaluate because it involves large factorials and high powers (try it and see!), yet to calculate $P(X > 200)$ we would need to evaluate another 34 probabilities of similar form! Not a pleasant prospect!

An approximation to the binomial distribution when n is large

Fortunately, when n is large it is possible to approximate binomial probabilities using a normal distribution.

We hinted at this in Chapter P2, Section 4, when we said that the graph of the binomial probabilities for $n = 200$ and $p = 0.15$ (repeated in Figure 3.36) forms a 'bell-shape'.

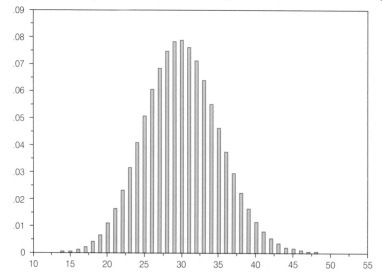

Figure 3.36 The binomial probability distribution when $n = 200$ and $p = 0.15$.

In the airline example the number of passengers who arrive has a binomial distribution with $n = 235$ and $p = 0.8$. The stepped outline on the graph in Figure 3.37 shows the probabilities of this distribution. The curve, on the other hand, is the pdf of the normal distribution with *the same mean and variance*. As you can see, the two shapes are very similar.

This is *not a coincidence*. In general, when n is large, the probabilities of a binomial distribution are approximately the same as the probabilities of a normal distribution *with the same mean and variance*. That is, with mean np and variance $np(1 - p)$.

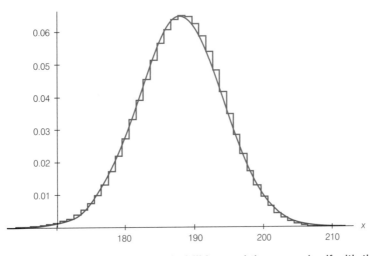

Figure 3.37 Binomial $n = 235$, $p = 0.8$ probabilities and the normal pdf with the same mean and variance.

However, the binomial distribution is a discrete distribution with probabilities $P(200)$, $P(201)$, $P(202)$ and so on, whereas the normal distribution is continuous, so we can only consider the probabilities of intervals like $P(199 < X < 200)$. To investigate which normal distribution probabilities approximate which binomial probabilities consider the close-up in Figure 3.38 of the graph in Figure 3.37 between $x = 198$ and $x = 204.5$.

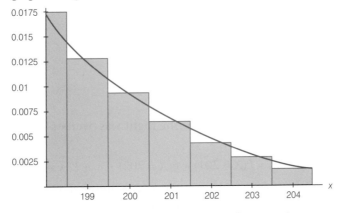

Figure 3.38 Close-up of part of Figure 3.37.

The area of the bar representing the binomial probability $P(X = 199)$ is almost the same as the area underneath the normal pdf between 198.5 and 199.5. In the same way, the area of the bar for $x = 200$ is almost the same as the area under the normal pdf between 199.5 and 200.5, and so on. A list of the (almost) equivalent binomial and normal probabilities on this graph is as follows.

Binomial (bars)	Normal approximation to binomial (area under curve)
$P(X = 199)$	$P(198.5 < X < 199.5)$
$P(X = 200)$	$P(199.5 < X < 200.5)$
$P(X = 201)$	$P(200.5 < X < 201.5)$
$P(X = 202)$	$P(201.5 < X < 202.5)$
$P(X = 203)$	$P(202.5 < X < 203.5)$
$P(X = 204)$	$P(203.5 < X < 204.5)$

Notice that the binomial probability $P(X = a)$ is approximated by the normal probability $P(a - 0.5 < X < a + 0.5)$.

So, for instance, the probability that exactly 200 passengers arrive for the flight described earlier, $P(X = 200)$, from the binomial distribution with $n = 235$ and $p = 0.8$, can be approximated by the normal probability $P(199.5 < X < 200.5)$ when the mean is $\mu = np = 188$ and the variance is $\sigma^2 = np(1 - p) = 37.6$. This normal probability can be calculated in the usual way as follows.

Check this

Calculate $P(199.5 < X < 200.5)$ when $X \sim N(188,37.6)$.

Solution:

$$P(199.5 < X < 200.5) = P\left(\frac{199.5 - 188}{\sqrt{37.6}} < \frac{X - 188}{\sqrt{37.6}} < \frac{200.5 - 188}{\sqrt{37.6}}\right)$$
$$= P(1.88 < Z < 2.04)$$
$$= P(Z < 2.04) - P(Z < 1.88)$$
$$= 0.9793 - 0.9699 = 0.0094$$

We originally required the probability that the flight was overbooked; that is, the binomial probability

$$P(X > 200) = P(X = 201) + P(X = 202) + \dots + P(X = 235)$$

This is the probability represented by all the bars of the binomial probability distribution to the right of and including $x = 201$. So the (almost) equivalent normal probability must include the near equivalent area to $P(X = 201)$ which is $P(200.5 < X < 201.5)$ and is therefore $P(X > 200.5)$, which is calculated below.

Check this

Calculate $P(X > 200.5)$ when $X \sim N(188,37.6)$.

Solution:

$$P(X > 200.5) = P\left(\frac{X - 188}{\sqrt{37.6}} > \frac{200.5 - 188}{\sqrt{37.6}}\right) = P(Z > 2.04) = 0.0207$$

So the probability that more than 200 passengers arrive for the flight is approximately 2.07%.

Some other (almost) equivalent probabilities are:

Binomial	Normal approximation to binomial
$P(X > 199)$	$P(X > 199.5)$
$P(X > 201)$	$P(X > 201.5)$
$P(X \geq 199)$	$P(X > 198.5)$
$P(X \geq 200)$	$P(X > 199.5)$

Check this

Calculate the probability that fewer than 180 passengers arrive for the flight.

Solution:
As earlier, the number of passengers arriving has a binomial $n = 235$ and $p = 0.8$ distribution with mean $np = 188$ and variance $np(1 - p) = 37.6$.

We require the binomial probability $P(X < 180)$. This is approximated by the $N(188,37.6)$ probability $P(X < 179.5)$ as we want to exclude the area under the curve that approximates the binomial probability $X = 180$. This is

$$P(X < 179.5) = P\left(\frac{X - 188}{\sqrt{37.6}} < \frac{179.5 - 188}{\sqrt{37.6}}\right) = P(Z < -1.39) = 0.0823$$

So the probability that fewer than 180 passengers arrive is about 8%.

We have not yet considered how large n needs to be for the approximation to be reasonably accurate. Various 'rules of thumb' have been put forward, but a reasonable rule is that *the approximation is good when both np and n(1 – p) are greater than or equal to 5*. So, before approximating a binomial probability in this way you should check that this condition is satisfied.

Check this

Of the students at my university, 40% live on campus. What is the probability that more than 100 out of a class of 200 students live on campus?

Solution:
X, the number of students in the class who live on campus, has a binomial distribution with $n = 200$ and $p = 0.4$. This distribution has mean $\mu = np = 80$ and variance $\sigma^2 = np(1 - p) = 48$. We require the (binomial) probability $P(X > 100)$, but as $np = 80$ and $n(1 - p) = 120$ are greater than or equal to 5, n is large enough for the normal probability $P(X > 100.5)$ to provide a good approximation.
   As $\mu = 80$ and $\sigma^2 = 48$,

$$P(X > 100.5) = P\left(\frac{X - 80}{\sqrt{48}} > \frac{100.5 - 80}{\sqrt{48}}\right) = P(Z > 2.96) = 0.0015$$

Check this

A statistician is marrying an accountant. The accountant calculates that they can afford to entertain no more than 100 guests at their wedding reception, and the hotel at which it is to be held will only cater for a minimum of 70 guests. The couple are going to send invitations to 120 people. The statistician estimates that the probability that each individual accepts the invitation is about 70%.

Using this model, estimate the probability that between 70 and 100 guests accept the invitation. Is 120 a good number of invitations to send?

Solution:
This is a binomial situation (assuming that each invitee's response is independent of the others), with $n = 120$ and $p = 0.7$. X is the number of individuals who accept the invitation. We require $P(70 \leq X \leq 100)$.

Using the normal approximation, (as $np = 84$ and $n(1 - p) = 36$ are both greater than or equal to 5), $\mu = np = 84$ and $\sigma^2 = np(1 - p) = 25.2$ and the approximating normal probability is $P(69.5 < X < 100.5)$. Standardising gives

$$P\left(\frac{69.5 - 84}{\sqrt{25.2}} < \frac{X - 84}{\sqrt{25.2}} < \frac{100.5 - 84}{\sqrt{25.2}}\right) = P(-2.89 < Z < 3.29) = 0.9995 - 0.0019 = 0.9976$$

120 seems a reasonable number of invitations to send as the probability that fewer than 70 or over 100 guests accept is only about 0.0024.

The normal approximation to the binomial distribution

When X has a binomial n, p distribution and n is large, its probabilities can be approximated by the probabilities of a normal distribution with the same mean $\mu = np$ and variance $\sigma^2 = np(1 - p)$ as follows:

Binomial np	Normal approximation
$P(X = a)$	$P(a - 0.5 < X < a + 0.5)$
$P(X \leq a)$	$P(X < a + 0.5)$
$P(X \geq a)$	$P(X > a - 0.5)$

The approximation is reasonable when $np \geq 5$ and $n(1 - p) \geq 5$.

WORK CARD 5

1. A random variable, X, comes from a binomial distribution with $n = 50$ and $p = 0.4$. What distribution does X follow approximately? Calculate the following probabilities approximately.

   a. The probability that X is less than or equal to 25.

   b. The probability that X is *equal* to 25.

2. 30% of computer analysts who are hired by Techtronics have programming experience.

   If a random sample of 35 analysts are selected what is the probability that fewer than 15 have had programming experience?

3. A telesales company promotes time-share deals by telephoning households at random during the evening. Historically, only 65% of heads of households are at home when called. A salesperson makes 50 calls in an evening.

   a. How many heads of household, on average, will the salesperson talk to during an evening?

   b. Their employer stipulates that each salesperson *must* speak to at least 20 heads of household in an evening, or lose the evening's pay. Calculate the (approximate) probability that a salesperson loses pay on a particular evening.

   c. What is the (approximate) probability that a salesperson interviews exactly 30 householders on a particular evening?

Solution:

1. As $np = 20$ and $n(1 - p) = 30$ are both greater than or equal to 5 we can approximate with the $N(20,12)$ distribution.

   a. We require the binomial probability $P(X \leq 25)$ which is approximated by the $N(20,12)$ probability $P(X < 25.5)$.

   $$P(X < 25.5) = P\left(Z < \frac{25.5 - 20}{\sqrt{12}}\right) = P(Z < 1.59) = 0.9441$$

   b. The binomial probability $P(X = 25)$ can be approximated using the $N(20,12)$ probability,

   $$P(24.5 < X < 25.5) = P\left(\frac{24.5 - 20}{\sqrt{12}} < Z < \frac{25.5 - 20}{\sqrt{12}}\right)$$
   $$= P(1.30 < Z < 1.59) = 0.9441 - 0.9032 = 0.0409$$

2. We require $P(X < 15)$ where X is binomial with $n = 35$, $p = 0.3$. As $np = 10.5$ and $n(1 - p) = 24.5$ this can be approximated using the $N(10.5, 7.35)$ probability $P(X < 14.5)$. This is

   $$P\left(Z < \frac{14.5 - 10.5}{\sqrt{7.35}}\right) = P(Z < 1.48) = 0.9306$$

3. a. X, the number of householders interviewed, is binomial with $n = 50$ and $p = 0.65$, so the mean $\mu = np = 32.5$.

b. We require $P(X \leq 19)$. As both np and $n(1 - p) = 17.5$, are greater than or equal to 5, we can approximate using the $N(32.5, 11.375)$ distribution.

$$P(X < 19.5) = P\left(Z < \frac{19.5 - 32.5}{\sqrt{11.375}}\right) = P(Z < -3.85)$$

which is too small to be included in Table II, and so is less than $P(Z < -3.4) = 0.0003$.

c. We require the normal probability

$$P(29.5 < X < 30.5) = P\left(\frac{29.5 - 32.5}{\sqrt{11.375}} < \frac{X - 32.5}{\sqrt{11.375}} < \frac{30.5 - 32.5}{\sqrt{11.375}}\right)$$

$$= P(-0.89 < Z < -0.59) = 0.2776 - 0.1867 = 0.0909$$

1. On my university's enrolment register 22% of students are 'mature'; that is, aged 21 or over at the start of their course.

   a. I take a random sample of 5 students from the enrolment register. What is the probability that exactly two students are 'mature'?

   b. I take a random sample of 100 students from the enrolment register. Calculate an approximate probability that *at least* 30 of these are mature.

2. A hotel has 50 double rooms. Historically, customers arrive for only 90% of reservations, so the hotel has a policy of taking bookings for 54 rooms.

   When the hotel has taken 54 bookings what is the probability that customers arrive for more than 50 bookings?

3. A production line cannot function on a particular day unless at least 90 out of its 100 workers are at work. Absentee rates for this class of work are approximately 5%. The line is overstaffed when 99 or more staff are present.

   a. What is the probability that the production line must shut down on a particular day?

   b. For what proportion of days is the line overstaffed?

Further reading: see p. xv

Anderson *et al.* (Statistics) contains more detail.

Mendenhall *et al.*

Newbold *et al.* takes a more mathematical approach than most 'business' texts and includes more advanced work on two random variables.

Probability formulae

A summary of the main Probability formulae

Measuring uncertainty

$$P(A \text{ AND } B) = P(A) + P(B) - P(A \text{ OR } B)$$

or equivalently

$$P(A \text{ OR } B) = P(A) + P(B) - P(A \text{ AND } B)$$

The conditional probability of event A given event B is

$$P(A \mid B) = \frac{P(A \text{ AND } B)}{P(B)}$$

It follows that

$$P(A \text{ AND } B) = P(A \mid B) \, P(B) = P(B \mid A) \, P(A)$$

Also,

$$P(A \text{ AND } B \text{ AND } C \text{ AND } D) = P(A) \, P(B \mid A) \, P(C \mid B \text{ AND } A) \, P(D \mid A \text{ AND } B \text{ AND } C)$$

Numerical outcomes

Mean $\mu = E(X) = \Sigma \, xP(x)$

Variance $\sigma^2 = E(X^2) - \mu^2 = \Sigma \, x^2 P(x) - \mu^2$

When $k > 1$, the probability that a random variable lies within $k\sigma$ of its mean, μ, is at least

$$1 - \frac{1}{k^2}$$

Distribution	$P(x)$	x	Mean	Variance
Binomial	$^{n}C_x \, p^x(1-p)^{n-x}$	$x = 0, 1, 2,..., n$	np	$np(1-p)$
Poisson	$\dfrac{\mu^x e^{-\mu}}{x!}$	$x = 0, 1, 2,...$	μ	μ

P3 **Continuous numerical outcomes**

Distribution	$f(x)$	x	Mean	Variance
Uniform	$\dfrac{1}{b-a}$	$a < x < b$	$\dfrac{b+a}{2}$	$\dfrac{(b-a)^2}{12}$
Exponential	$\lambda e^{-\lambda x}$	$x > 0$	$\dfrac{1}{\lambda}$	$\dfrac{1}{\lambda^2}$
Normal	$\dfrac{1}{\sqrt{2\pi\sigma^2}}e^{-(x-\mu)^2/2\sigma^2}$	$-\infty < x < \infty$	μ	σ^2

S   Statistics

- £28m was fed into fruit machines each day in Britain during 2001
Independent, July 2004

- An estimated 11,700,000 crimes were committed in year ended April 2004 compared with a peak of 19,300,000 in 1995
British Crime Survey

- The average student in England and Wales leaves higher education owing £12,069
BBC web site, July 2004

- The proportion of young people (18–20 years) applying for university places this autumn (Sept. 2004) is up 2.8% compared with a 6.1% rise in the age group
Independent, July 2004

- The survey, carried out, of course, by text message, also found that more than a third of the 16,300 respondents would prefer to decline invitations by text.
Independent, July 2004

We often read statements like these in newspapers or hear them on television. They are all examples of *statistics*. In everyday language a statistic just means a numerical fact but the subject or science of *Statistics* means much more. It splits into two broad areas: *descriptive statistics*, which you met in *Describing Data*, and *inferential* statistics, which forms the majority of the subject and which is our interest in this part of the book.

Descriptive Statistics covers the way a set of data is described using graphs and pictures or by calculating summary measures like the average.

Inferential Statistics is used whenever it is too expensive or impractical to collect all the data of interest, called the *population*, and only a *sample* of the data is available. It is the process by which information from the sample is used to *infer* information about the population.

Whilst we have complete knowledge of the sample of data, we do not usually know about the population exactly, and so any statements we make about the population will be uncertain and have to be expressed using probabilities. For this reason you will need to have covered *Probability* as well as *Describing Data* before you start this part of the book. Everything we said about using a computer in the introduction to *Describing Data* continues to apply.

S1
Estimation

I always find that statistics are hard to swallow and impossible to digest. The only one I can remember is that if all the people who go to sleep in church were laid end to end they would be a lot more comfortable.

Mrs Robert A Taft

Contexts

What is this chapter about?
This chapter explains how to select a sample of data and use it to make valid inferences about the wider set of data or *population* it came from.

Why is it useful?
Businesses and organisations frequently collect just a sample of the data of interest because it is too costly or impractical to obtain all the information, for instance, in surveys, product testing, quality control, auditing and market research.

Where does it fit in?
The subject of Statistics broadly divides into two parts: Descriptive Statistics, which we considered in Describing Data, is about summarising a set of data, whereas Inferential Statistics, which we consider in this part of the book, is concerned with using a sample of data to make wider inferences. Two key ideas underpin Inferential Statistics: estimation and testing. In this chapter we introduce estimation, and in the next chapter, testing.

What do I need to know?
You will need to cope with a few formulae and be able to rearrange some simple equations (Essential Maths), have a basic idea of probability and random variables, including the normal distribution (Probability) and be able to calculate sample means and variances (Describing Data).

Objectives

After your work on this chapter you should:

- understand the concept of a simple random sample and know how to select one;
- be able to estimate the population mean and variance;
- understand what a sampling distribution is;
- know about the sampling distribution of $\overline{X}$, the sample mean;
- know about the t distribution;
- be able to calculate and interpret confidence intervals for the mean, with and without a computer.

We gave you a taste of Statistics in *Describing Data*. However, as we said in the introduction, most of the techniques of Statistics are about using a sample of data to *infer* something about the larger set of data or population from which it came. In Chapters S1 and S2 we introduce you to the main ideas of *inferential Statistics*. To understand this work you will need to have covered the material in *Describing Data*, and *Probability*, in particular, the work on discrete and continuous random variables in Chapters P2 and P3.

1 Samples

Samples and populations

In *Describing Data* we saw how to describe a set of data, both by pictorial methods such as a histogram or bar chart, and by numerical summary with means, standard deviations, medians and so on. In practice, however, we do not usually have the luxury of knowing *all* the data of interest we only have the resources to obtain a randomly chosen sub-group or *sample* of measurements. This may be because it would be too expensive or time-consuming to collect all the data, or simply because complete collection is impossible.

In Statistics we refer to the wider set of data that is of interest as the *population* – whether we are talking about measurements on people, animals or things.

Consider the following examples.

TV companies usually require viewing figures the day after transmission. Special equipment can be installed in a home so that each member of the household presses a button every time they start or stop watching the television and the equipment logs who is watching which channel at what time. The information from all participating households is collected overnight via telephone lines and collated. In theory, every household in the country could be issued with this equipment, but it would be prohibitively expensive and not every household would cooperate. In practice, the equipment is issued to just a sample of households who are considered representative of the whole of the transmission area and the data from the sample are used to draw conclusions about the viewing habits.

Consider a company that manufactures batteries. The company needs to ensure that the average life of a battery is a particular number of hours. The only way of testing the life of a battery is to use it up and so it is only physically possible to test a sample of the goods.

Sometimes the population is infinite. For example, suppose we throw a die 5 times. We can regard these 5 throws as a sample of throws, from the infinite population of all the die throws ever made in the past, present or future. In the same way, a plant-geneticist who grows 20 pea plants with a view to studying their rate of growth is regarding these as a sample from the population of all the pea plants that could ever be grown. In these cases the sample is a few repetitions of a random variable and the population is an infinite number of repetitions of the same random variable.

Here are some more examples of populations and samples:

Population	Sample
● The electorate	● A political opinion poll
● All potential customers	● A market research survey
● All items produced by a production process	● A quality control sample
● All potential patients	● Patients chosen to test a new drug (a clinical trial)
● All ordinary shares on the stock market	● A stock market index like the FT-30 or Dow Jones

Our aim is to use the sample to make inferences about the population. Of course, when only a sample is available we can't make *exact* inferences about the population; there will always be some uncertainty. However, this uncertainty can be described precisely using probabilities – which is why we have already learnt about probability.

First, we will consider how to select a sample from a finite population.

Simple random sampling

The most straightforward way of selecting a sample is *simple random sampling*. A sample drawn in this way is called a *simple random sample* and is what most people will think of when they hear the word 'sample'.

The definition of a simple random sample is that *every possible sample of the same size must have an equal chance (probability) of being chosen.*

Suppose there are N units in the population and we wish to choose a sample of n of these. The number of ways in which this can be done is the same as the number of ways of selecting n objects out of N, which is the combination

$$^{N}C_n = \frac{N!}{n!(N-n)!}$$

(see Chapter P2, Section 4). As simple random sampling requires that the probability of selecting each of these is the same, the probability of choosing any one must be $1/^{N}C_n$.

Check this

Suppose there are only 5 units in a population, say A, B, C, D and E.

a. How many different samples of size 2 are possible?

b. List these to check your result.

c. When simple random sampling is used to select a sample of 2 from this population what is the probability of selecting a particular sample?

Solutions:

a. There are

$$^5C_2 = \frac{5!}{2!3!} = 10$$

different samples of size 2.

b. These are *AB, AC, AD, AE, BC, BD, BE, CD, CE* and *DE*.

c. Each possible sample must be equally likely and so have a probability of $\frac{1}{10}$ of being chosen.

Selecting a simple random sample

One way to select a simple random sample of 5 cards from a pack of cards would be to shuffle the pack thoroughly and then deal out 5 cards. In a similar way to select (a simple random sample of) 3 prize-winners in a draw we could put all the tickets in a 'hat' or 'bucket' and ask someone to select 3 of them. However, such mechanical means become impractical when the number of items in the population is large and so we need a more formal method of sample selection.

We illustrate using the following example.

A telephone company would like to know the proportion of yellow page subscribers who will renew for the next edition. They have a complete list of current subscribers – there are 10,200 in all, but it would be impractical and expensive to contact all of them and so they decide to telephone a sample of 50 subscribers.

To select a sample of 50 of the 10,200 subscribers at random the company must first think of the subscriber list as being numbered from 1 to 10,200. The problem of sample selection now becomes one of randomly selecting 50 integer numbers from 1 to 10,200 inclusive. This can be done using computer software or using tables of random numbers.

Selecting a simple random sample using a computer

Some computer software has a facility for randomly generating integer numbers within a specified range. SPSS, however, only allows you to generate *any* numbers within a range; that is, they can be fractional and will need to be rounded. If rounding is to produce integers between 1 and 10,200, the unrounded numbers need to be between 0.5 and 10,200.5 and so using

Transform > Compute

and then filling in

Target variable = **RND(RV.UNIFORM(0.5,10200.5))**

will do the trick.

Suppose the following random integers are generated:

807	6446	1094	3593	504	3625	8125	6640	3757	1347	9486
634	8776	3009	1880	2129	5919	4397	558	8343	6277	7245
2542	1029	6082	8880	2827	5955	2665	3315	3310	6211	9344
3676	105	2281	1377	9158	1195	6913	5558	7964	9083	2514
386	639	1	6105	2597	2653					

We would then form a sample from the 807th subscriber on the list, the 6446th, 1094th and so on.

We should note here that the random command described above may generate the same integer more than once so to get a sample of 50 *different* subscribers we should generate more than 50 integers and use the first 50 *different* ones.

Selecting a simple random sample *without* using a computer

When statistical software is not available a table of random numbers, like Table IV at the end of the book (p. 871), can be used to draw a sample. A few rows from a random number table are shown below.

07340	35237	80262	86251	71212	60487	94168	15901	65011
02048	33399	88485	97329	89258	49214	89019	24721	62072
59041	53531	37094	49462	91927	87603	96807	39820	48628
19094	90853	15216	10734	31918	05510	71413	83183	77748
82817	95485	04551	12531	68272	22939	09492	54673	09108

As you can see, a table of random numbers is just that – rows of digits, often grouped in fives for ease of reading. Although the table may include strings of digits like 99999 or 12345, which may not seem very 'random', the whole point is that the table was created by a procedure in which every digit, or sequence of digits, is equally likely to occur.

A table of random numbers can be used in any reasonable way to select a sample of integers within a certain range provided *each possible sample has an equal chance of selection*. For instance, to select 50 integers between 1 and 10,200 for the yellow pages subscribers example we would proceed as follows.

We pick an arbitrary starting point in the table and decide which way (column-wise or row-wise) we want to read the table. As we need integers of at most 10,200, which has 5 digits, we must consider the random digits in groups of 5. We then move systematically around the table, recording any 5-digit numbers that are between 1 and 10,200 but rejecting those which are 00000 or above 10,200 and any 5-digit numbers that have already been recorded. We continue in this way until we have 50 integers between 1 and 10,200.

For example, if we start at 33399 in the second row of the table above, and work row-wise, we will reject the 5-digit numbers 33399, 88485, 97329, ... and so on (because they are greater than 10,200) until we come to 05510 in the fourth row. The first subscriber in our sample would be number 5510. Continuing would give subscriber numbers 4551, 9492, 9108, ... and so on.

> ### Check this
>
> Suppose there are 520 items in a population, numbered from 1 to 520 inclusive. Use the random number table above to select a sample of 4 items.

Solutions:
As we require integers from 1 to 520 we must take the random digits in groups of 3. If we start at 35237 in the first row of the table and work down column-blocks we obtain 352, 373, 339 (reject 953), and 531.

Sampling from a column of the work area
Sometimes, the population of data may already be in a column of your work area. In this case a command like SPSS's

Data > Select Cases

will select a sample of values from a named column.

In Excel, the **Sampling** data analysis tool will select a sample from a named range of the worksheet.

Beware: bad sampling
When sampling, great care must be taken to make sure that the selected values are in no way biased or prejudiced.

In practice, biased samples occur because of badly planned or unthinking procedures and these can lead to false conclusions about the population.

Bad sampling procedures are common. How many times have you seen surveys in magazines asking readers about particular issues – often of a confidential nature – and inviting them to send in their replies. Only those with a particular interest in the subject and with time to spare are likely to respond. And we've all seen survey forms offering to enter respondents in a draw for a cash prize or a holiday. Surely, only those most in need will reply?

Check this

The following extracts are quoted from a British magazine and radio programme respectively – can you see what is wrong with the sampling procedures here? How could this have been avoided?

1. 'Do you feel intimidated or offended by people drinking in public places? Does the presence of people drinking make you avoid Bedford town centre?' These are some of the questions shoppers in Bedford town centre were asked to answer recently, as North Beds prepares to apply for a by-law to ban drinking alcohol in designated areas of the town.

2. 'There will be a traffic census at .... This will cause delays and drivers are advised to avoid the census point.'

Solution:

1. As the shoppers are already in Bedford town centre they are obviously not avoiding it, so the sample is biased towards people who are *not* intimidated by drinkers in these areas of the town. A well-constructed survey might question a sample of residents in the town – maybe chosen from the list of electors.

2. In the case of the traffic census, it is hardly representative of the normal level of traffic if radio announcements tell drivers to avoid the census point. The census results will therefore understate any congestion problems. Announcements about surveys at particular locations should not be leaked to the media.

WORK CARD 1

1. A television company is going to interview three members of a winning five-a-side football team. The captain democratically decides that the three members will be chosen at random. How many different samples could be drawn? The team comprises Nigel, Oliver, Peter, Quentin and Robin. List all possible samples.

2. A High Street bank has 32 branches in Eastern England, which can be numbered 1 to 32 inclusive. Head Office management wish to conduct a survey on staff morale in the branches. Select a sample of 10 banks using random number tables. How many different samples could be drawn?

3. Use a computer to draw a sample of size 50 of a random variable that is uniform over the interval 20 to 30. Plot the histogram. Does it resemble the uniform distribution?

Solutions:

1. $^5C_3 = 10$ different samples, *NOP, NOQ, NOR, NPQ, NPR, NQR, OPQ, OPR, OQR, PQR*.

2. Use random number tables to select two digits at a time, retain pairs 01 to 32 and reject 00 and 33 to 99. There are $^{32}C_{10}$ possible samples.

3. There should be *approximately* the same frequency in each (equal width) class of the histogram. The frequencies will (probably) not be exactly the same as the data is merely a sample.

ASSESSMENT 1

1. Select a random sample of 10 pages from this book. Describe your method.

2. A club has 40 members. In how many different ways can a committee of 10 people be chosen?

3. What is wrong with the following sampling procedures? How could you improve them?
   a. A sociologist is investigating the proportion of the population who are vegetarians. He decides to stand on the high street of a town and stop every 10th shopper who passes. There is a shoe-shop, a travel agent and a hamburger restaurant nearby.

b. To investigate how frequently residents of a town visit their doctor a sample of 50 households is selected at random. One person from each household is then selected at random for interviewing.

c. Conducting a survey into the family in 1994, the well-known researcher Shere Hite is reported to have sent out questionnaires in the UK to readers of two feminist magazines, Bradford University and a feminist organisation, 'Women Against Fundamentalism'. She received a 14% response from these groups.

4. Consider the Vizafizz market research survey from Describing Data DD2, Assessment 8. What wider population of individuals is the sample interviewed representative of? And what population do you think the drinks manufacturer is interested in? Discuss whether or not you think these populations coincide and point out any deficiencies in the choice of sample for the market research survey. Can you suggest any improvements?

2 Estimating from a sample

The whole point of sampling is to find out about the population from which the sample is drawn. However, a sample cannot tell us about the population *exactly* it can only *estimate* features of the population.

In this section we define the population mean and variance, explain how to estimate them from a sample and describe how to investigate how good these estimates are.

The distribution of the population

Consider randomly selecting a single value from a population. Before we select it, its value is unknown, so it is a random variable and has a probability distribution. This probability distribution is known as the *population distribution*.

Now consider selecting a second item from a population. When the population contains a large or infinite number of items, the value of the first item chosen will *not* affect the probabilities associated with the second. For instance, suppose 10% of people in the UK are over 180cm tall. If we choose one person from the UK population of, say, 58 million and find they are over 180cm tall, the proportion of people who are over 180cm tall out of the remaining 57 999 999 people will still be about 10%. The population is so large that the inclusion or exclusion of this individual will not affect its distribution. As a result, for all practical purposes, we can assume that each item in the sample, first, second, third and so on, has the same probability distribution and is independent of the others.

On the other hand, when the population is *not* large the probabilities associated with the value of any item in the sample will depend on what has been chosen previously. For example, if the population comprises a pack of cards and we are being dealt (a sample of) three cards the probability that the third card is an ace will depend on whether both, one or neither of the first two cards are aces. This dependence makes sampling complicated so *we will assume for our work on populations and samples that the population is large or infinite*, so that each item in the sample is independent of the others and has the same probability distribution, which is the population distribution.

Sometimes we will assume that the population distribution has a particular form, often a normal distribution.

The population mean and variance

It is usually too ambitious to estimate everything possible about the distribution of the population so we usually concentrate on estimating its mean and variance. As we did for probability distributions we will denote the population mean μ (pronounced 'mu') and the population variance σ^2 (pronounced 'sigma squared') respectively. So μ is the average value that an item selected from the population takes and σ^2 is the variance of the value it takes.[*]

Estimating the population mean and variance

As we have done before we will label the values in the sample $x_1, x_2, x_3, ..., x_n$. From *Describing Data* we know how to calculate the *sample* mean

$$\bar{x} = \frac{\Sigma x}{n}$$

and *sample* variance

$$s^2 = \frac{\Sigma x^2 - \frac{(\Sigma x)^2}{n}}{n - 1}$$

It seems natural to use these as estimates of the *population* mean and variance, μ and σ^2 respectively, and so we will do this.

Be careful here. Many people get confused between the *sample* and *population* means and variances. Remember that they are two different things:

> the **sample mean**, $\bar{x}$, is used to estimate the **population mean**, μ
>
> the **sample variance**, s^2, is used to estimate the **population variance**, σ^2

The sample mean, $\bar{x}$, and variance, s^2, can be calculated from a sample using the formulae given above, whereas the population mean and variance μ and σ^2 are usually unknown and so we want to estimate them.

As a refresher, try the following.

---

[*] It can be shown that when the population is finite and comprises $x_1, x_2, ..., x_N$, the population mean and variance are

$$\mu = \frac{\Sigma x}{N}$$

and

$$\sigma^2 = \frac{\Sigma (x - \mu)^2}{N}$$

respectively. However, as we do not have access to the whole population of data we cannot calculate them. Notice that these formulae are similar to those for the sample mean and variance (repeated in next sub-section) except that the population variance divides by N and not $n - 1$.

Check this

The percentage of glucose in a sample of 5 bars of toffee produced by a production process was as follows.

7.2 6.4 7.2 8.0 8.2

Use the sample to estimate the average percentage of glucose in the toffee and the variance of the percentage in each bar.

Solution:

$\Sigma x = 37.0, \ \Sigma x^2 = 275.88$

so

$$\bar{x} = \frac{37}{5} \quad \text{and} \quad s^2 = \frac{275.88 - \frac{37^2}{5}}{4} = 0.52$$

So an estimate of the mean percentage of glucose in the toffee is 7.4 and an estimate of the variance of the percentage of glucose in a bar is 0.52.

Sampling fluctuation

But how good are $\bar{x}$ and s^2 as estimators of the population mean and variance? Consider the following situation.

A bank is interested in the distribution of its account holders' uncleared credit balances as it is considering the introduction of a new charge structure. At present, the bank's computer system is such that it takes some time to establish the exact value of an account's uncleared balance and so it is impractical to obtain balances for all the account holders on any particular day. A graduate trainee is asked to take a random sample of 20 accounts and he obtains the following balances (£):

113	754	580	335	165	425	708	611	952	100	597	463	607
551	8	1100	517	456	597	118						

The mean of this sample is $\bar{x} = 487.85$ and its variance is $s^2 = 82481$, $s = 287.2$.

Due to a management error, a female colleague in another department is also asked to sample 20 account balances on the same day. She obtains the balances (£):

206	366	387	655	127	533	221	168	724	464	525
78	632	347	290	133	86	252	392	829		

which have mean $\bar{x} = 370.75$ and variance $s^2 = 49368$, $s = 222.2$.

Notice that the $\bar{x}$s and s^2s of the two samples, which we use as estimates of the population mean and variance, differ quite a bit although they are roughly of similar magnitude. In general, each sample that might be drawn will contain a different set of values and so will have a different sample mean $\bar{x}$ and sample variance s^2. In other words, $\bar{x}$ and the sample variance s^2 vary or fluctuate from sample to sample.

This fluctuation can be crucial. For instance, suppose an advertisement for a new model of car states that it does an average of 12 kilometres per litre at a speed of 80kph. A consumer car magazine obtains 5 such cars, test drives each of them for 200 kilometres at 80kph and obtains the following sample of consumptions:

11.2   12.1   12.1   10.9   11.7

The sample average of 11.6 is clearly lower than the advertisement's claim, so the question is, is the population mean really 12 and the lower sample mean due to sampling fluctuation or is the advertisement fraudulent?

We therefore need to investigate to what extent $\bar{x}$ and s^2 fluctuate. To investigate the nature of the fluctuation in $\bar{x}$ we could select a large number of samples of the same size from the population, calculate the mean of each sample and then draw a histogram of the sample means. The process is illustrated in Figure 1.1.

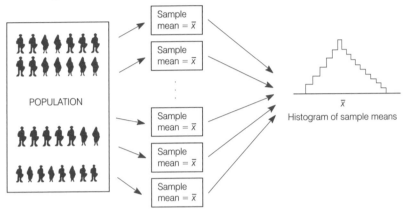

Figure 1.1

The histogram will give us some idea of the distribution of the $\bar{x}$s. Most statistical software has a facility that allows you to generate a sample of data from a population with a prescribed distribution so this can be done on a computer.

Check this

Suppose, for the car consumption example, that the kilometres per litre obtained from each test is normally distributed with mean $\mu = 12$, and variance $\sigma^2 = 1$; that is, the population mean and variance are 12 and 1 respectively. Use software to generate 1000 samples of size 5 from this distribution, calculate the mean of each sample and then plot a histogram of the sample means. Comment on the distribution of the sample means. Repeat the procedure for samples of size 10. Compare the distribution of the sample means for the two different sample sizes.

Solution:
We used SPSS as follows. The command

  Transform > Compute

was used to generate values of a normal random variable in specified column(s).

To do this we opened a worksheet with entries in 1000 rows of one column and then generated values in each of 5 columns of the worksheet using the numeric expression **RV.NORMAL (12,1)**. Each *row* of the data was then regarded as a sample. To calculate the mean of each row (sample) we used the **MEAN** function.

A histogram of the means of 1000 samples of size 5 from a $N(12,1)$ distribution is given in Figure 1.2.

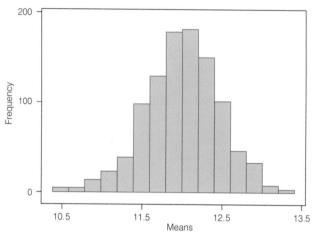

Figure 1.2 Means of samples of size 5.

Notice that the centre of the distribution is roughly at the population mean $\mu = 12$ and that the distribution is a bit like a normal distribution curve. The sample means range from a minimum of at least 10.4 to a maximum of at most 13.4. This tells us that even when the manufacturer's claim that $\mu = 12$ is true, a sample of size 5 could still have a mean as low as 10.4 or as high as 13.4.

When you do this your samples will contain different numbers so your histogram will have different frequencies, although it should have a similar shape.

Figure 1.3 shows a histogram of the means of 1000 samples of size 10 from a $N(12,1)$ distribution.

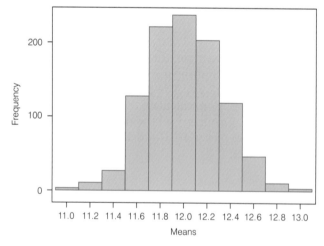

Figure 1.3 Means of samples of size 10.

Like Figure 1.2, this looks quite symmetric about 12 and has the 'bell-shape' of a normal distribution. The means range from about 10.9 to about 13.1 and seem to vary less than those of the samples of size 5 in Figure 1.2.

The experiment above establishes that the mean of a sample, $\bar{x}$, varies quite a bit from sample to sample. It appears that the means of larger samples vary less than those of smaller samples. Is this what you would expect intuitively?

Sampling distributions

Before a sample is selected its mean is unknown and so it is a random variable and as such has a probability distribution.

It is usual to use upper-case letters to denote random variables so we will use $\bar{X}$ for the sample mean when it is not yet known and so is a random variable, and $\bar{x}$ for the mean of a specific sample. (Readers can quite safely ignore this distinction – we include it only to please any statisticians who may be reading!) The probability distribution of $\bar{X}$ is sometimes called the *sampling distribution* of $\bar{X}$. It is of interest because it throws light on the reliability of the sample mean as an estimate of μ.

So, rather than drawing histograms of *a finite* number of sample means as we did in the **Check this** above, a more general and useful way of studying the variation in the sample mean is to consider the probability distribution of $\bar{X}$. Incidentally, the histograms would become more and more like the probability distribution as the number of sample means included increased.

In the next section we will see that there are some 'nice' results about the sampling distribution of $\bar{X}$ for large and infinite populations.

What about s^2?

We have already said that the sample variance, s^2, is used to estimate the population variance σ^2. Like $\bar{X}$, the sample variance, S^2, is a random variable and has a probability distribution that can also be called the sampling distribution of S^2.

As we did above, for $\bar{X}$, we could gain some idea of the sampling distribution of S^2 by generating a large number of samples, calculating the variance of each, and drawing a histogram of the sample variances.

WORK CARD 2

1. Some revision. The flight-times of 7 randomly selected flights from Stansted to Milan are (in minutes)

   98   112   119   111   98   95   120

   Estimate the variance and mean of all flight-times from Stansted to Milan.

2. Conduct your own experiment. Use a computer to generate a large number of samples of size 50 from an exponential distribution with mean 2. Plot a histogram of the sample means. Follow the same procedure for samples of size 10 from the same exponential distribution. How does the mean of the sample means relate to the mean of the exponential distribution that generated the samples? What do you notice about the distributions of the histograms?

   A manufacturer claims that the life of a battery has an exponential distribution with a mean of 2 hours. A consumer group tests a sample of 50 of these batteries and obtains a sample mean of 1.4. The manufacturer continues to maintain that the mean life is 2 and that this result is merely due to sampling fluctuation. What do you think?

Solutions:

1. $\Sigma x = 753$, $\Sigma x^2 = 81{,}659$, so $\bar{x} = 107.57$ and

    $$s^2 = \frac{81{,}659 - \frac{753^2}{7}}{6} = 109.62$$

2. The mean of the distribution of sample means will be approximately the same as the mean of the exponential distribution you have generated. The means of the samples of size 50 will be less spread out (have smaller variance) than the means of the samples of size 10. It is unlikely that any of your generated samples had a mean as small as 1.4, or below, which suggests that when the manufacturer's claim is true such a small value is improbable and so sheds considerable doubt on the manufacturer's claim.

1. Use a computer to investigate the sampling distribution of the mean of samples of size 15 from a uniform distribution. Compare your findings with those of samples of size 50 from the same distribution.

2. Conduct some research into the sentence length of quality (broadsheet) and tabloid newspapers.

    Use sampling methods to draw a sample of a reasonable size (at least 20 but ideally 50 or more) of sentences from a tabloid newspaper and record the number of words in each sentence. You will have to think about how to do this to avoid any bias. Do the same for a quality newspaper. Describe your sampling procedure. Using software display the distribution of each sample and estimate the mean and variance of the sentence lengths of tabloid and quality papers. Comment on your results.

    Techniques like these have been used by expert witnesses in court cases where authorship is in contention.

3 How good is an estimator?

We are using the sample mean, $\bar{x}$, to estimate the population mean μ. Recall that $\bar{X}$ is a random variable and so has a probability distribution, also called the sampling distribution.

In this section we give some 'nice' results about the sampling distribution of $\bar{X}$, which tell us how it relates to μ and so enable us to assess how good an estimator it is.

The mean of $\overline{X}$

Our first result is:

> ### 1. The expected value or mean of $\overline{X}$ is μ, the population mean.

This tells us that *in the long run* the sample mean, $\overline{X}$, averages out to be the population mean μ. This is a good thing – because it means that, 'on average', our estimator 'gets it right'. We say that $\overline{X}$ is an *unbiased* estimator of μ.

The variance of $\overline{X}$

As the average value of $\overline{X}$ is μ, we would like $\overline{X}$ to fluctuate as little as possible from μ, that is, we would like the variance of $\overline{X}$ to be as small as possible. Result 2 gives an expression for the variance of $\overline{X}$.

> ### 2. The variance of $\overline{X}$ is $\dfrac{\sigma^2}{n}$.

This says that the variance of the mean of a sample of size n is the population variance *divided by n*. This means that when n is larger the variance of $\overline{X}$ is smaller; that is, for larger samples $\overline{X}$ fluctuates less from the population mean and so is a more reliable estimator of μ. Is this what you would expect intuitively? (Yes, we think so!) The standard deviation of $\overline{X}$ is therefore $\sigma/\sqrt{n}$. Be warned that other texts and software often call this the *standard error* of $\overline{X}$ instead of the standard deviation of $\overline{X}$.

Remember that the expectation sign $E(\ )$ and $\mathrm{Var}(\ )$ can be used to denote the mean and variance of the expression in the brackets so we could write Results 1 and 2 succinctly as

1. $E(\overline{X}) = \mu$

2. $\mathrm{Var}(\overline{X}) = \dfrac{\sigma^2}{n}$

To illustrate the meaning of Results 1 and 2 we return to the car example in Section 2. Recall that the km driven per litre had a mean of $\mu = 12$ and variance $\sigma^2 = 1$. Result 1 tells us that for samples of any size the mean of the sampling distribution of $\overline{X}$ is $\mu = 12$. This explains why the histograms in Figures 1.2 and 1.3 both centre around 12.

Result 2 says that the sample mean has a variance of $\frac{1}{5}$ for samples of size 5, $\frac{1}{10}$ for samples size 10 and so on. This explains why the histogram in Figure 1.2 is more spread out than the histogram in Figure 1.3.

The type of distribution of $\overline{X}$

Our final two results apply in special circumstances only.

3. *When the population distribution is normal* (for any size of sample) the sampling distribution of $\bar{X}$ is normal.

This seems intuitively acceptable as it says that the mean of samples from a normally distributed population also has a normal distribution. It explains why the histograms in Figures 1.2 and 1.3 both look symmetric and roughly 'bell-shaped'.

4. *When the sample size n is large* (say 30 or more) the distribution of the sample mean, $\bar{X}$, is *approximately* normal. The approximation is better when *n* is larger.

Result **4** is more remarkable. It is saying that *whatever the distribution of the population*, the mean of a *large* sample has an (approximate) normal distribution. It is often called the Central Limit Theorem.

To understand this more we return to the credit balances at the bank from which the graduate trainees drew samples. A histogram of this population of 1002 account balances is shown in Figure 1.4. Notice that it is skewed to the right, so the population is *not* normally distributed. The mean of the whole population is 383.67, and the population variance is 77,975.

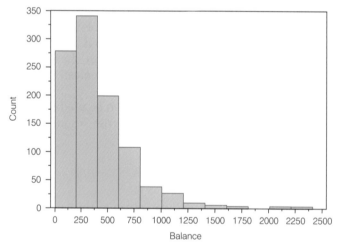

Figure 1.4 Histogram of the account balances data.

We drew 100 samples of size 5 from this population and a histogram of the sample means is shown in Figure 1.5. Notice that as these samples are small Result **4** does not apply and the distribution is still skewed. On the other hand, Figure 1.6 gives a histogram of the means of 100 samples of size 60. Now the sample size is large Result **4** applies and the sample means are approximately normally distributed.

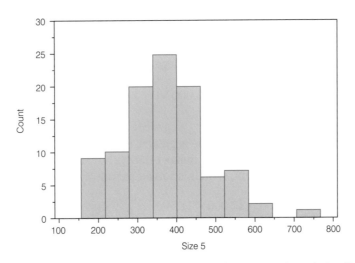

Figure 1.5 Histogram of the means of 100 samples of size 5.

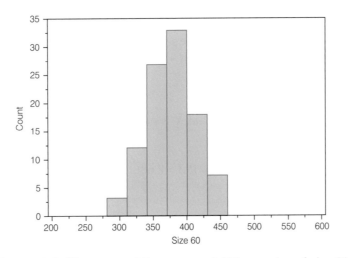

Figure 1.6 Histogram of the means of 100 samples of size 60.

Calculating probabilities about the sample mean

As the mean and variance of $\overline{X}$ are μ and σ^2/n (Results **1** and **2**), Results **3** and **4** state that the sample mean, $\overline{X}$, is

$$\textit{approximately } N\left(\mu, \frac{\sigma^2}{n}\right) \textit{ distributed for large samples and}$$

$$\textit{exactly } N\left(\mu, \frac{\sigma^2}{n}\right) \textit{ distributed for all samples from normal populations}$$

This enables us to calculate (at least approximately) probabilities about the mean of samples that are large and/or from a normal population.

Check this

The distribution of the starting salaries of college graduates in a given year had mean £11,500 and standard deviation £1000. What is the probability that a sample of 36 of these had an average salary of at least £12,000?

Solution:
We want $P(\overline{X} > 12{,}000)$. As the sample size is greater than 30, we know that $\overline{X}$ is approximately normally distributed with mean 11,500 and variance $\frac{1000^2}{36}$. We now have a typical normal probability problem, which is solved as follows.

$$P(\overline{X} > 12{,}000) = P\left(\frac{\overline{X} - 11{,}500}{\sqrt{1000^2/36}} > \frac{12{,}000 - 11{,}500}{\sqrt{1000^2/36}}\right) = P(Z > 3)$$

$$= 0.0013$$

Check this

Heights of European males are known to be normally distributed with mean 164cm and variance 15cm. What is the probability that a sample of 3 men has an average height of 170cm or more?

Solution:
As the population is normal we know that $\overline{X}$ is normally distributed with a mean of 164cm and a variance of $\frac{15}{3} = 5$. So

$$P(\overline{X} > 170) = P\left(\frac{\overline{X} - 164}{\sqrt{5}} > \frac{170 - 164}{\sqrt{5}}\right) = P(Z > 2.68)$$

$$= 0.0037$$

Quality control
The sampling distribution of the sample mean forms the basis of some quality control techniques.

Properties, like weight or size, of any goods produced by a repetitive production process may vary as time goes on. A production process is said to be 'in control' when all variation due to things that can be controlled – for instance, raw materials, efficiency of staff, temperature – has been eliminated leaving only the variation that is due to chance. When the process is in control a characteristic like weight or size is expected to have a steady mean μ and variance σ^2.

To test whether a process is in control, samples of size n are taken at regular time-intervals. When the process is in control the sample means should have mean μ and standard deviation $\sqrt{\sigma^2/n}$.

It is common practice to plot the sample characteristics against time on what is termed a *control chart*.

The control chart includes a horizontal line to indicate the process mean and two more horizontal lines called upper and lower control limits. It is assumed that when the process is in control the sample mean will almost always lie within these limits. If a sample mean occurs *outside* the control limits it is interpreted that the process is 'out of control' and investigation must ensue. The upper and lower control limits are usually taken as

$$\mu + 3\sqrt{\frac{\sigma^2}{n}} \quad \text{and} \quad \mu - 3\sqrt{\frac{\sigma^2}{n}}$$

as the values of a random variable are rarely more than three standard deviations from its mean.

Consider the following illustration.

When a pharmaceutical production process is in control the percentage of active ingredient in a tablet has mean $\mu = 32$ and variance $\sigma^2 = 14.4$. A sample of 10 tablets is taken from the process every minute. A control chart for the sample mean is shown in Figure 1.7. The upper and lower control limits are at

$$32 \pm 3\sqrt{\frac{14.4}{10}}$$

that is 28.4 and 35.6. Notice that for the first 19 or so minutes the sample mean lies within the control limits, but after that it exceeds the upper limit indicating that the process may be out of control.

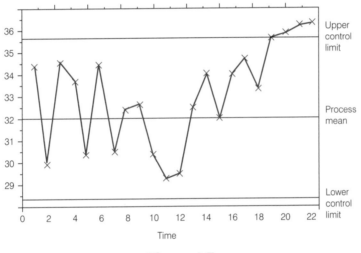

Figure 1.7

Statistical Quality Control is covered in more detail in *Business Modelling*, Chapter BM6.

Is S^2 a 'good' estimator?

All this section has been about the sample mean $\overline{X}$ but the same ideas apply to the sample variance S^2. The sample variance

$$s^2 = \frac{\Sigma x^2 - \frac{(\Sigma x)^2}{n}}{n - 1}$$

will vary from sample to sample, so it is a random variable and has a probability distribution.

It can be shown that

$$E(S^2) = \sigma^2$$

so, on average, the sample variance 'gets it right' and gives the population variance. (Incidentally, this is not true if the denominator of s^2 is n, which is why we use $n - 1$.) We say that s^2 is an *unbiased* estimator of σ^2.

The variance of S^2 is used less often and we suggest that you approach a more specialised statistics text if you require this. There are no 'nice' results on the shape of the distribution of S^2.

The key results of this section are:

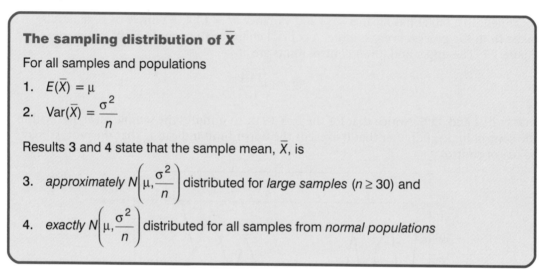

The sampling distribution of $\bar{X}$

For all samples and populations

1. $E(\bar{X}) = \mu$

2. $\text{Var}(\bar{X}) = \dfrac{\sigma^2}{n}$

Results 3 and 4 state that the sample mean, $\bar{X}$, is

3. *approximately* $N\left(\mu, \dfrac{\sigma^2}{n}\right)$ distributed for *large samples* ($n \geq 30$) and

4. *exactly* $N\left(\mu, \dfrac{\sigma^2}{n}\right)$ distributed for all samples from *normal populations*

WORK CARD 3

1. Assume that a population has mean $\mu = 30$ and standard deviation $\sigma = 5$ (variance 25). A sample of 20 items is to be taken. What will be the expected value, variance and standard error (= standard deviation) of the sample mean $\bar{X}$?

2. Suppose samples from the population in question **1** of sizes 30, 40 or 100 were taken. What happens to the variance and standard deviation of the sample mean as the sample size increases? Is this what you would expect? What probability distribution would you expect the mean of a large sample to have?

3. What probability distributions would you expect the means of the following samples to have? Or can't you tell?

   a. A sample of 100 of the final exam marks (%) of students taking a Mathematics degree at a large university. The average mark is 50% with a variance of 100%.

   b. A sample of the amount of 5 insurance claims made on a particular type of policy. Such claims are known to be normally distributed with mean $1000 and standard deviation $100.

c. A sample of 20 journey times on the London to Norwich train. From past studies journey times are known to be uniformly distributed between 110 and 130 minutes (variance is 33.33).

d. The duration of a sample of 20 bus journeys from the University to the city centre. Times are known to be normally distributed with mean 20 minutes and variance 9 minutes.

e. A sample of 100 journey times on the London to Norwich train, where journey times are known to be uniformly distributed between 110 and 130 minutes.

4. Bars of chocolate manufactured on a production line are known to have mean 50g and variance 100g. A sample of 64 bars is taken from the line every day. If the average weight is less than 46g the whole day's output is rejected. For what percentage of days is the whole output rejected?

5. A sample of 50 items is drawn from a population of manufactured products and the weight, X, of each item is recorded. Prior experience has shown that the weight has a probability distribution with $\mu = 6$ ounces and $\sigma = 2.5$ ounces.

   (i) Calculate the mean and variance of $\overline{X}$ the sample mean.

   (ii) What is the probability that the sample has a mean weight of more than 6.25 ounces?

   (iii) What is the probability that the sample has a mean weight of less than 5.5 ounces?

   (iv) How would the sampling distribution of $\overline{X}$ change if the sample size were increased to 100?

6. Use a computer to generate lots of samples of size 5 from a known probability distribution – say $N(2,1)$. For each sample calculate the sample variance. Draw a histogram of all the sample variances. What does the sampling distribution of the variance look like? What is the expected value of the sample variance?

Solutions:

1. $E(\overline{X}) = 30$, $\text{Var}(\overline{X}) = \frac{25}{20} = 1.25$
   So the standard deviation is $\sqrt{1.25} = 1.12$.

2. $\text{Var}(\overline{X}) = \frac{25}{30}, \frac{25}{40}, \frac{25}{100}$ respectively.

   The standard deviations will be the square roots of these. As the sample size increases the standard deviation gets smaller. Yes, we would expect the mean to be more reliable when the sample size is larger. When n is large $\overline{X}$ has a normal distribution with mean μ and variance σ^2/n.

3. **a.** Large sample so normal, mean 50 variance $\frac{100}{100}$.

   b. Small sample but population has normal distribution so $\overline{X}$ does as well. Mean is 1000, standard deviation is $\frac{100}{\sqrt{5}}$.

   c. Small sample and population not normal so we can't conclude anything about the distribution except that the mean will be 120 and the variance $\frac{33.33}{20}$.

d. Small sample but normally distributed so sample mean is normal, mean 20, variance $\frac{9}{20}$.

e. Same distribution as in **c** but now a large sample so the sample mean is normally distributed with mean 120 and variance $\frac{33.33}{100}$.

4. $\bar{X} \sim N\left(50, \frac{100}{64}\right)$ so

$$P(\bar{X} < 46) = P\left(Z < \frac{46 - 50}{\sqrt{100/64}}\right) = P(Z < -3.2) = 0.0007$$

so 0.07% of days.

5. (i) $E(\bar{X}) = 6$, $\text{Var}(\bar{X}) = \frac{2.5^2}{50}$

(ii) $P(\bar{X} > 6.25) = P\left(Z > \frac{6.25 - 6}{\sqrt{2.5^2/50}}\right) = P(Z > 0.71) = 0.2389$

(iii) $P(\bar{X} < 5.5) = P\left(Z > \frac{5.5 - 6}{\sqrt{2.5^2/50}}\right) = P(Z < -1.41) = 0.0793$

(iv) $\text{Var}(\bar{X})$ would now be $\frac{2.5^2}{100}$ and smaller than for a sample size of 50.

6. $E(S^2) = 1$. The histogram will be skewed to the right with a variance of about 0.5.

---

1. A sample of 5 items from a population with mean 0 and variance 9 is drawn. What is the expected value of the sample mean? What is the variance of the sample mean?

2. An individual considers investing £5,000 in each of 5 different stocks. The monthly rate of return, r, on each stock has mean $\mu = 10\%$ and standard deviation $\sigma = 4\%$. The investor's monthly return on the whole portfolio of 5 stocks is therefore $\bar{r} = \Sigma r/5$.

   (i) What is the variance of the investor's monthly return on the portfolio? This is a measure of the risk taken by the investor.

   (ii) Suppose the investor were to invest £5,000 in each of only *three* stocks, would her risk increase or decrease?

   (iii) Suppose she invested in 10 such stocks. What happens to the risk then?

3. Individual biscuits are normally distributed, have a mean weight of 20g and a standard deviation of 1.5g. They are sold in packets of 10 biscuits. The weight of the packaging is negligible. I buy a packet from my local supermarket. What is the probability that the mean weight of the biscuits I have bought is less than 19g?

4. The distribution of starting salaries of college graduates is known to be normal with mean £11,500 and variance £200,000.

   What is the probability that five graduates have an average salary of at least £12,000? Do we need to assume that the distribution of starting salaries is normal here?

5. Floppy disks are produced by a firm. The number of flaws, X, on a disk has the following probability distribution:

x	$P(x)$
0	0.75
1	0.15
2	0.10

   (i) Calculate the mean and standard deviation of the number of flaws per disk.

   (ii) Describe the distribution of the average number of flaws per disk in a sample of 400 disks. Calculate the mean and variance of this distribution.

   (iii) What is the probability that the mean number of flaws per disk in a batch of 400 is less than 0.3?

6. Use software to generate lots (the more the better) of samples of size 5 from any probability distribution for which you know the variance. Calculate the sample variance for each of these and draw a histogram of the sample variances. What is the expected value of the sample variance and does your histogram demonstrate this?

4 Interval estimates

So far we have used $\bar{x}$ to estimate μ and s^2 to estimate σ^2. However, it would be nice to be able to give an interval or range of values within which μ or σ^2 lay with a particular degree of precision. We will concentrate on finding an interval for the population mean μ. Remember, from Section 3, that

the sample mean, $\bar{X}$, is

$$\text{approximately } N\left(\mu, \frac{\sigma^2}{n}\right) \text{ distributed for } \textit{large samples } (n \geq 30)$$

and

$$\textit{exactly } N\left(\mu, \frac{\sigma^2}{n}\right) \text{ distributed for all samples from } \textit{normal populations}$$

We are going to use these results to construct an interval so what follows applies to *large samples and samples from normal populations only*. The table below shows the sort of data we are concerned with.

		Sample size	
		$n < 30$	$n \geq 30$
Population {	Non-normal	Can't do	OK
	Normal	OK	OK

For now, we will also make the artificial assumption that we know the variance of the population, σ^2.

Constructing an interval for the population mean

To construct an interval we reason as follows.

As $\overline{X}$ has an $N(\mu, \sigma^2/n)$ distribution we can standardise it (by subtracting its mean and dividing by its standard deviation – see Chapter P3, Section 4) to give a standard normal random variable

$$Z = \frac{\overline{X} - \mu}{\sqrt{\sigma^2/n}}$$

So, as Z has a $N(0,1)$ distribution, we can make the probability statement

$$P(-1.96 < Z < 1.96) = 0.95$$

illustrated in Figure 1.8.

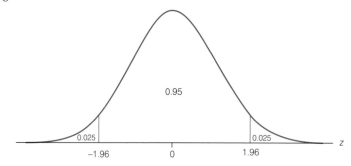

Figure 1.8

As

$$Z = \frac{\overline{X} - \mu}{\sqrt{\sigma^2/n}}$$

we can equivalently write

$$P\left(-1.96 < \frac{\overline{X} - \mu}{\sqrt{\sigma^2/n}} < 1.96\right) = 0.95$$

The inequality inside the brackets can be rearranged to any equivalent inequality and the probability that it holds will still be 0.95. As we want to find out something about μ we would like an inequality that has μ as the subject. It is not too difficult to show that an equivalent inequality to the one in brackets is

$$\overline{X} - 1.96\sqrt{\frac{\sigma^2}{n}} < \mu < \overline{X} + 1.96\sqrt{\frac{\sigma^2}{n}}$$

(We do the working in the **Check this** below.) So the probability that this is true is 0.95, that is,

$$P\left(\overline{X} - 1.96\sqrt{\frac{\sigma^2}{n}} < \mu < \overline{X} + 1.96\sqrt{\frac{\sigma^2}{n}}\right) = 0.95$$

This appears to be what we set out to find – an interval for μ with an associated probability. However, as we will see shortly, we need to be a bit careful about interpretation.

To see how we obtained the equivalent inequality above read on, otherwise hop to the next subsection.

Check this

Rearrange

$$-1.96 < \frac{\overline{X} - \mu}{\sqrt{\sigma^2/n}} < 1.96$$

so that μ is the subject.

Solution: To do this we must split the inequality into its two parts (see *Essential Maths*, Chapter EM3, Section 6) and deal with each part in turn.

Firstly, the left-hand side

$$-1.96 < \frac{\overline{X} - \mu}{\sqrt{\sigma^2/n}}$$

rearranges to

$$-1.96\sqrt{\frac{\sigma^2}{n}} < \overline{X} - \mu$$

and then

$$* \quad \mu < \overline{X} + 1.96\sqrt{\frac{\sigma^2}{n}}$$

In a similar manner, the right-hand side of the inequality

$$\frac{\overline{X} - \mu}{\sqrt{\sigma^2/n}} < 1.96$$

becomes

$$\bar{X} - \mu < 1.96\sqrt{\frac{\sigma^2}{n}}$$

and then

$$* \; \bar{X} - 1.96\sqrt{\frac{\sigma^2}{n}} < \mu$$

The two inequalities (asterisked) combine to give

$$\bar{X} - 1.96\sqrt{\frac{\sigma^2}{n}} < \mu < \bar{X} + 1.96\sqrt{\frac{\sigma^2}{n}}$$

as required.

Confidence limits and confidence intervals

We have established that

$$P\left(\bar{X} - 1.96\sqrt{\frac{\sigma^2}{n}} < \mu < \bar{X} + 1.96\sqrt{\frac{\sigma^2}{n}}\right) = 0.95$$

The interval, calculated for a particular sample

$$\bar{x} - 1.96\sqrt{\frac{\sigma^2}{n}} < \mu < \bar{x} + 1.96\sqrt{\frac{\sigma^2}{n}}$$

is called the *95% confidence interval for the population mean.* The values at each end of this interval:

$$\bar{x} - 1.96\sqrt{\frac{\sigma^2}{n}} \quad \text{and} \quad \bar{x} + 1.96\sqrt{\frac{\sigma^2}{n}}$$

are called the *95% confidence limits for the population mean.* You will often see these written more succinctly as

$$\bar{x} \pm 1.96\sqrt{\frac{\sigma^2}{n}}$$

Check this

A production process manufactures large chocolate chip cookies for sale individually at restaurant outlets. When the process is working satisfactorily the weights of individual cookies have a standard deviation of 2g. An inspection sample of 36 cookies gives an average weight of 98g. Calculate 95% confidence limits for the mean weight of cookies made by this process.

Solution:
The sample size is large so we *can* calculate confidence limits as described above. Substituting into

$$\bar{x} \pm 1.96\sqrt{\frac{\sigma^2}{n}} \quad \text{gives} \quad 98 \pm 1.96\sqrt{\frac{4}{36}}$$

and the confidence interval is from 97.35 to 98.65. We could write this as (97.35, 98.65).

Notice that the confidence interval

$$\bar{x} \pm 1.96\sqrt{\frac{\sigma^2}{n}}$$

will be narrower and so more helpful when the sample size n is larger, supporting intuition that larger samples are in some way 'better' than smaller ones.

Interpreting the confidence interval

We said earlier that we had to be a little careful in interpreting the confidence interval and we now explain why.

The probability that gave us the confidence limits was

$$P\left(\bar{X} - 1.96\sqrt{\frac{\sigma^2}{n}} < \mu < \bar{X} + 1.96\sqrt{\frac{\sigma^2}{n}}\right) = 0.95$$

Usually, a probability statement is something like $P(1 < X < 2)$, that is, it tells us the probability that a random variable (X here) lies between two fixed values (1 and 2). However, this probability statement is different because the quantity in the middle, μ, is *not* a random variable but a fixed quantity. It is the end points, the confidence limits, that are random because they involve $\bar{X}$, which differs from sample to sample. Consequently, this probability statement is saying that if we drew thousands of samples from a population and for each of them calculated the confidence limits

$$\bar{x} - 1.96\sqrt{\frac{\sigma^2}{n}} \quad \text{and} \quad \bar{x} + 1.96\sqrt{\frac{\sigma^2}{n}}$$

μ would lie between the pairs of confidence limits in about 95% of the samples.

As an illustration we generated 100 samples of size 50 from an exponential distribution with mean 5 (so the variance is 25). For each sample we calculated the confidence limits

$$\bar{x} - 1.96\sqrt{\frac{25}{50}} \quad \text{and} \quad \bar{x} + 1.96\sqrt{\frac{25}{50}}$$

We show the sample mean and the calculated limits for the first few and last few samples below.

Sample number	Sample mean	Confidence limits	
		Lower	Upper
1	4.77486	3.38893	6.16079
2	5.36204	3.97611	6.74797
3	6.60862	5.22269	7.99455
4	4.00339	2.61746	5.38932

		Confidence limits	
Sample number	Sample mean	Lower	Upper
5	6.10953	4.72360	7.49546
⋮	⋮	⋮	⋮
96	5.70366	4.31773	7.08959
97	4.09771	2.71178	5.48364
98	5.97336	4.58743	7.35929
99	4.74013	3.35420	6.12606
100	4.17951	2.79358	5.56544

Notice that the interval for Samples 1 and 2 *does* include the population mean, 5, but the interval for Sample 3 does *not* include 5. In fact, of the 100 samples 96 had confidence intervals that *did* contain the population mean and 4 had confidence intervals that did not. On average, we would expect 95 out of every 100 samples to give an interval that included the mean.

Another way of viewing confidence intervals is to suppose that you have to read a report that contains lots of 95% confidence intervals for the population means of lots of different quantities. On average, 95% of these intervals *will* contain the appropriate population mean, but 5% will not; that is, 95% confidence intervals are 'wrong' 5% of the time.

So, when we draw just one sample (as is usual) and calculate the confidence limits

$$\bar{x} - 1.96\sqrt{\frac{\sigma^2}{n}} \quad \text{and} \quad \bar{x} + 1.96\sqrt{\frac{\sigma^2}{n}}$$

there is a probability of 0.95 that these limits enclose the population mean. A succinct phrase which describes what a confidence interval is, which is sometimes useful, is:

> in 95% of samples an interval calculated in this way will include the population mean, μ.

Check this

From past analyses it is known that daily attendance at a swimming pool is normally distributed with variance 225. During a random sample of five days the following numbers of people used the pool each day:

220   196   210   186   222

Give a 95% confidence interval for the average number of people who use the pool in a day and explain what it means.

Solution:
The sample average is $\bar{x} = 206.8$. So the confidence limits are

$$206.8 \pm 1.96\sqrt{\frac{225}{5}} = 206.8 \pm 13.15$$

which we can write as (193.65, 219.95). So for 95% of samples an interval calculated in this way would include the mean number of people who use the pool in a day.

Confidence intervals for other percentages

Because we have used 95% confidence, in 5% of samples the population mean will *not* lie within the limits. Estimation error like this might be costly or dangerous (consider drug trials or emissions from a nuclear power station) in which case we need a confidence interval that includes the mean in 99%, 99.9% or even 99.999% samples.

Before we do this we introduce some new notation that will be useful.

We define $z_{0.005}$ to be the value such that $P(Z > z_{0.005}) = 0.005$ where Z is a standard normal random variable. That is, it is the value such that an area of 0.005 under the normal curve lies to the right of it as shown in Figure 1.9.

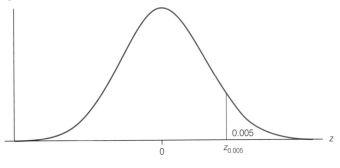

Figure 1.9

We can look up the value of $z_{0.005}$ in a table of normal percentage points like Table III. (See Chapter P3, Section 3.)

Check this

Find $z_{0.005}$ from a table of normal percentage points.

Solution:
$z_{0.005}$ is the value such that $P(Z > z_{0.005}) = 0.005$, so $P(Z < z_{0.005}) = 0.995$. Looking up $p = 0.995$ in Table III gives 2.5758, so $z_{0.005} = 2.5758$.

In general we will use the notation z_α to indicate the value that cuts off α in the right-hand tail of a standard normal distribution; that is, the value such that

$$P(Z > z_\alpha) = \alpha$$

> ### Check this
>
> Calculate:
>
> (i) $z_{0.01}$
>
> (ii) $z_{0.05}$
>
> **Solutions:**
>
> (i) $P(Z > z_{0.01}) = 0.01$, so $P(Z < z_{0.01}) = 0.99$ and we look up 0.99 in the table of percentage points (Table III) and obtain 2.3263.
>
> (ii) $P(Z > z_{0.05}) = 0.05$, so $P(Z < z_{0.05}) = 0.95$ so we look up 0.95 in the table of percentage points (Table III) and obtain 1.6449.

Returning to calculating confidence intervals for any percentage, recall that the 95% confidence interval is

$$\bar{x} \pm 1.96 \sqrt{\frac{\sigma^2}{n}}$$

Notice that this is

$$\bar{x} \pm z_{0.025} \sqrt{\frac{\sigma^2}{n}}$$

The general formula for a $(1 - \alpha)100\%$ confidence interval for the mean is

$$\bar{x} \pm z_{\alpha/2} \sqrt{\frac{\sigma^2}{n}}$$

For instance, to calculate the 99% confidence interval $(1 - \alpha)100 = 99$, so $\alpha = 0.01$, and we need $z_{0.005}$ so the 99% confidence interval for the mean is

$$\bar{x} \pm z_{0.005} \sqrt{\frac{\sigma^2}{n}}$$

which is

$$\bar{x} \pm 2.5758 \sqrt{\frac{\sigma^2}{n}}$$

In a similar way, the 96% confidence interval for the mean is

$$\bar{x} \pm z_{0.02} \sqrt{\frac{\sigma^2}{n}}$$

which is

$$\bar{x} \pm 2.0537 \sqrt{\frac{\sigma^2}{n}}$$

Check this

Write down a formula for the 90% confidence interval for the mean.

Solution:
$100(1 - \alpha) = 90$, so $\alpha = 0.1$, $\alpha/2$ is therefore 0.05 and the interval is

$$\bar{x} \pm z_{0.05}\sqrt{\frac{\sigma^2}{n}}$$

$z_{0.05}$ is the value such that 0.05 of the area under the standard normal curve lies to the right of it so we look up $p = 0.95$ in Table III, which gives 1.6449. The 90% confidence interval for the mean is therefore

$$\bar{x} \pm 1.6449\sqrt{\frac{\sigma^2}{n}}$$

Remember that this means that for 90% of samples, an interval calculated in this way will contain the population mean μ.

If you want to know why these confidence intervals are calculated like this, read on, otherwise proceed to the next **Check this**. The 95% confidence interval contains 1.96 because it was constructed from $P(-1.96 < Z < 1.96) = 0.95$. A confidence interval for any other percentage can be constructed in exactly the same way and so has the same form except that instead of 1.96, the number involved will be Q, such that

$$P(-Q < Z < Q) = \text{the appropriate percentage}$$

For example, a 99% confidence interval will contain the number Q such that $P(-Q < Z < Q) = 0.99$. If $P(-Q < Z < Q) = 0.99$ it follows that $P(Z > Q) = 0.005$ and so $Q = z_{0.005}$ as shown in Figure 1.10.

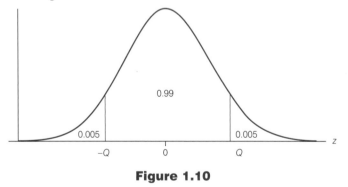

Figure 1.10

In general, the Q required for a $(1 - \alpha)100\%$ confidence interval is such that $P(Z > Q) = \alpha/2$ and so it is $z_{\alpha/2}$.

Now try a 98% confidence interval.

Check this

The percentage monthly return on a particular ordinary share is known to be normally distributed with standard deviation 0.5. A sample of returns from 10 randomly selected months gives a mean of $\bar{x} = 0.9\%$. Obtain a 98% confidence interval for the mean monthly return on this share.

   The formula is for a $100(1 - \alpha)\%$ interval and we require 98% so $\alpha = 0.02$, $\alpha/2 = 0.01$ and $z_{\alpha/2} = 2.3263$. The confidence interval is therefore

$$0.9 \pm 2.3263\sqrt{\frac{0.25}{10}} = 0.9 \pm 0.3678 \quad \text{or} \quad (0.53, \ 1.27)$$

In 98% of samples an interval calculated this way will include the population mean.
   As the confidence interval contains only positive values the investor can be fairly sure of a positive mean return.

The 95% confidence interval for the returns example above is

$$0.9 \pm 1.96\sqrt{\frac{0.25}{10}} = 0.9 \pm 0.31 \quad \text{or} \quad (0.59, \ 1.21)$$

Notice that the 98% confidence interval is wider than the 95% interval. A higher percentage confidence interval will always give a wider interval for a particular sample as shown in Figure 1.11. This makes sense because if a greater percentage of intervals are to include the population mean the interval must be less precise.

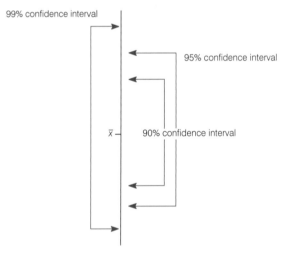

Figure 1.11

WORK CARD 4

1. In a telephone system the average duration of a sample of 60 calls is $\bar{x} = 4.26$ minutes. Previous history shows that the variance of all call durations is 1.21 minutes.

   Give 95% confidence limits for the mean length of calls on this system.

2. Calculate a 99% confidence interval for the mean length of a call on the telephone system in question. It should be wider than the 95% confidence interval. Write down carefully in words exactly what is meant by this interval.

3. A survey of 44 US companies who do business with Brazil were asked how many years they had been trading with Brazil. The sample mean was 10.455. Suppose that the population standard deviation is known to be $\sigma = 7.7$.

   (i) Construct a 90% confidence interval for the mean number of years that a company has been trading.

   (ii) Construct a 95% confidence interval for the mean number of years. Write down what the interval means in words.

   (iii) Which interval is wider?

Solutions:

1. $4.26 \pm 1.96\sqrt{\dfrac{1.21}{60}}$, i.e. (3.98, 4.54)

2. (3.89, 4.63). In 99% of samples an interval calculated in this way will include the population mean μ.

3. **(i)** $10.455 \pm 1.6449\sqrt{\dfrac{7.7^2}{44}}$, i.e. (8.55, 12.36)

   (ii) (8.18, 12.73). An interval calculated in this way will include the population mean for 95% of samples of this size.

   (iii) The 95% interval is wider. This is because the proportion of samples for which an interval calculated this way includes the population mean is larger (95%) so the interval must be less specific.

ASSESSMENT 4

1. When a 'gooing' machine is working properly, bars of Turkish delight have an average weight of 30g with a standard deviation of 1g.

   For quality control a sample of 50 bars is taken during the course of a day and the average weight, $\bar{x}$, is calculated. At the end of a particular day the sample average is 29.7. Calculate a 95% confidence interval for the mean weight of a bar on this day.

2. Calculate a 98% confidence interval for the mean weight of the bars described in question 1. Would you expect this interval to be wider or narrower than the interval calculated in question 1?

3. A regular daily flight is due to arrive at 1800 hours. Its arrival time has a normal distribution with mean 1810 hours and standard deviation 10 minutes.

A new air-traffic control system is installed but is criticised for causing delays in arrivals. To investigate this a sample of 20 flights gave a mean arrival time of 1812 hours. Give 95% confidence limits for the new mean arrival time.

5 Beware, variance unknown!

In Section 4 we constructed confidence intervals for the population mean. To do this we assumed that we knew the population variance σ^2. Whilst this may sometimes be reasonable – σ^2 may be known from past studies or because we are hypothesising that the sample comes from a particular population – in most situations *we do not know* σ^2. In this section we will see how to handle this, although again we will have to restrict ourselves to samples that are large or that are from a normally distributed population.

Introducing *t*

The confidence intervals in Section 4 were based on the fact that (for large samples approximately and normal populations exactly) $\overline{X}$ has a normal distribution with mean μ and variance σ^2/n so that

$$Z = \frac{\overline{X} - \mu}{\sqrt{\sigma^2/n}} \quad \text{has an } N(0,1) \text{ distribution}$$

Whilst this is still true we can't make use of this fact now because we don't know σ^2. However, we *can* use sample variance, S^2, instead of σ^2 in the expression for Z. We will now call this T, so

$$T = \frac{\overline{X} - \mu}{\sqrt{S^2/n}}$$

The snag here is that, whereas σ^2 was a fixed amount, S^2 is calculated from the sample, so it is a random variable. This means that T will fluctuate more from sample to sample than the corresponding Z, so it does *not* have a $N(0,1)$ distribution.

All is not lost, however, because when the population has a normal distribution

$$T = \frac{\overline{X} - \mu}{\sqrt{S^2/n}}$$

has a distribution called a *t distribution with n – 1 degrees of freedom (d.o.f.)*.

The *t* distributions

There is a whole family of *t* distribution curves and each is indexed by a number called the 'degrees of freedom'. The curves are very similar to standard normal distributions in that they are bell-shaped, symmetric and have zero mean but they are wider. As the number of degrees of freedom increases the *t* distribution gets narrower until for $n \geq 30$ the distribution is virtually the same as the standard normal distribution. We show *t* distribution curves for *n* = 3, *n* = 7 and the standard normal distribution in Figure 1.12. Notice that the pdfs of the *t* curves have much 'fatter' tails than the standard normal, so extreme values are more likely.

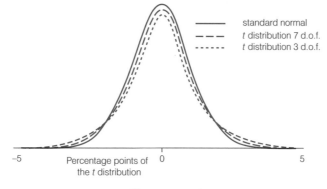

Figure 1.12

As with normal distribution probabilities, *t* probabilities are too complicated to work out on a calculator and so are given in tables. Table V (p. 872) is a table of the percentage points of the *t* distribution and an extract from it is shown below.

Table V
Percentage points of the *t* distribution
The table gives the value *a*, such that $P(T < a) = p$ where *T* is a random variable from a *t* distribution with *v* degrees of freedom

p	0.75	0.9	0.95	0.975	0.99	0.995	0.9995
v							
1	1.000	3.078	6.314	12.706	31.821	63.657	636.619
2	0.816	1.886	2.920	4.303	6.965	9.925	31.599
3	0.765	1.638	2.353	3.182	4.541	5.841	12.924
4	0.741	1.533	2.132	2.776	3.747	4.604	8.610
⋮	⋮	⋮	⋮	⋮	⋮	⋮	⋮
⋮	⋮	⋮	⋮	⋮	⋮	⋮	⋮
20	0.687	1.325	1.725	2.086	2.528	2.845	3.850
60	0.679	1.296	1.671	2.000	2.390	2.660	3.460
∞	0.674	1.282	1.645	1.960	2.326	2.576	3.291

Each row contains the percentage points of a *t* distribution with a particular number of degrees of freedom. For instance, for the *t* distribution with 4 degrees of freedom, $P(T < 2.776) = 0.975$. Notice that when the degrees of freedom are very large the percentage points (1.96, 1.645, etc. in the bottom row of the table above) are those of the standard normal distribution.

As a little practice in working with *t* probabilities use the extract above to find the following.

Check this

What value a from a t distribution with 20 d.o.f. is such that $P(T < a) = 0.90$? What value a from a t distribution with 4 d.o.f is such that $P(T > a) = 0.25$? Calculate the value, a, from a t distribution with 60 d.o.f. such that the probability of getting a larger value is 0.025?

Solutions:
$P(T < 1.325) = 0.90$, when the t distribution has 20 d.o.f.
$P(T > 0.741) = 0.25$ as $P(T < 0.741) = 0.75$ from the tables.
$P(T > 2.000) = 0.025$ so $a = 2.000$.

It will be useful to use the notation t_α in just the same way that we used z_α. That is, t_α is the value such that $P(T > t_\alpha) = \alpha$. So the area under the t curve to the right of t_α is α.

Check this

What are $t_{0.05}$ and $t_{0.01}$ for a t distribution with 12 d.o.f.?

Solution:
$t_{0.05}$ is the value such that $P(T > t_{0.05}) = 0.05$, so $P(T < t_{0.05}) = 0.95$. The row corresponding to 12 d.o.f and the column headed 0.95 in the t table (Table V) gives 1.782. So $t_{0.05} = 1.782$.
     In the same way $t_{0.01} = 2.681$.

Returning to confidence intervals
From Section 4, when we know the population variance, σ^2, the $100(1 - \alpha)\%$ confidence interval is

$$\bar{x} \pm z_{\alpha/2} \sqrt{\frac{\sigma^2}{n}}$$

This was constructed from the fact that

$$Z = \frac{\bar{X} - \mu}{\sqrt{\sigma^2/n}}$$

has a $N(0,1)$ distribution.
     When the variance, σ^2, is *not* known we can construct a confidence interval in much the same way but now it is based on the fact that

$$T = \frac{\bar{X} - \mu}{\sqrt{s^2/n}}$$

has a t distribution with $n - 1$ degrees of freedom.
     As a result, when we don't know the variance, σ^2, we need to make two changes to the confidence interval. First, we will have to use the sample variance, s^2, instead of σ^2. Second, we will have to use $t_{\alpha/2}$ with $n - 1$ d.o.f (where n is the size of the sample) instead of $z_{\alpha/2}$.
     The $100(1 - \alpha)\%$ confidence interval for the mean when σ^2 is unknown is therefore

$$\bar{x} \pm t_{\alpha/2} \sqrt{\frac{s^2}{n}}$$

For instance, the 98% confidence interval is given by

$$\bar{x} \pm t_{0.01} \sqrt{\frac{s^2}{n}}$$

To distinguish between confidence intervals for the mean for known variance and unknown variance it is sometimes useful to call them informally, 'z intervals' and 't intervals'.

Check this

A sample of 12 students from a large group obtain an average of 56.9% in an exam, and the sample variance is 25%. Give a 95% confidence interval for the mean exam mark for the whole group. You may assume that the exam marks have a normal distribution.

Solution:
The population variance is unknown so we must use a t interval. The formula is for a $100(1 - \alpha)\%$ interval and we require a 95% interval and so setting $100(1 - \alpha) = 95$ gives $\alpha = 0.05$ and the confidence interval is

$$\bar{x} \pm t_{0.025} \sqrt{\frac{s^2}{n}}$$

There are 12 in the sample so we require the t distribution with 11 d.o.f. $t_{0.025}$ is the value such that $P(T > t_{0.025}) = 0.025$, which for 11 d.o.f. is 2.201. The interval is therefore

$$56.9 \pm 2.201 \sqrt{\frac{25}{12}}$$

which is (53.72, 60.08). We conclude that in 95% of samples an interval calculated like this would include the population mean.

Check this

A JCB is rented out by a company. The duration in weeks of each rental is assumed to have a normal distribution. A random sample of the duration of 14 gives $\bar{x} = 2.1429$ and $s^2 = 1.6703$. Calculate a 99% confidence interval for the mean rental duration.

Solution:
The 99% interval is

$$\bar{x} \pm t_{0.005} \sqrt{\frac{s^2}{n}}$$

As the sample mean and variance have already been calculated the only problem is alighting on the correct t value. $t_{0.005}$ is the value such that $P(T > t_{0.005}) = 0.005$ or equivalently $P(T < t_{0.005}) = 0.995$. As the sample size is 14 we need the t distribution with 13 degrees of freedom. From t tables we obtain $t_{0.005} = 3.012$. The interval is therefore

$$2.1429 \pm 3.012 \sqrt{\frac{1.6703}{14}} \text{ or } (1.10, 3.18)$$

We conclude that in 99% of samples an interval calculated in this way will include the population mean.

Confidence intervals in practice

In practice you will not usually know the population variance, σ^2 suggesting that a t interval should be used, which requires the data to be normal. However, when the sample size is large the sample variance, s^2 will be a sufficiently good estimator of the population variance, σ^2 that we can just use s^2 in a z interval in place of σ^2. This has the advantage that, as we are using a z interval, we will *not* need the normality assumption.

Also, for large samples the t percentage points are very similar to the z percentage points, so it won't make much difference which type of interval you use.

We conclude that we can use z intervals or t intervals in the following circumstances.

$(1 - \alpha)$100% confidence intervals for the population mean

	Large sample $n \geq 30$	Small sample (normal population assumed)
Population variance σ^2 *Known*	$\bar{x} \pm z_{\alpha/2} \sqrt{\dfrac{\sigma^2}{n}}$	$\bar{x} \pm z_{\alpha/2} \sqrt{\dfrac{\sigma^2}{n}}$
Population variance σ^2 *Unknown*	$\bar{x} \pm z_{\alpha/2} \sqrt{\dfrac{s^2}{n}}$ or $\bar{x} \pm t_{\alpha/2} \sqrt{\dfrac{s^2}{n}}$	$\bar{x} \pm t_{\alpha/2} \sqrt{\dfrac{s^2}{n}}$

where $z_{\alpha/2}$ is the value such that $P(Z > z_{\alpha/2}) = \alpha/2$ and $t_{\alpha/2}$ is the value such that $P(T > t_{\alpha/2}) = \alpha/2$ when t has $n-1$ degrees of freedom.

Notice that the only time you *have* to use a t interval is for small samples when the population variance is unknown but that you must assume that the population is normal for these.

For large samples, where there is a choice you will probably want to use a z interval when you are doing the calculation by hand (to avoid using a t distribution table), whereas you will find that most computer software uses t intervals.

Confidence intervals using software

Statistical software will readily calculate confidence intervals for the mean. The sample is placed in a column of the worksheet.

SPSS calculates t intervals using

Analyze > Descriptive Statistics > Explore

You will have to enter the name of the column containing the sample.

The default confidence interval is 95% but this can be changed using the *Statistics* sub-dialog box.

A sample of 10 monthly returns is in the column named 'RETURNS' and is

0.8   1.7   0.5   0.6   0.8   0.8   0.8   0.7   1.3   1.0

SPSS's output for both 95% and 99% intervals is given below.

Descriptives

			Statistic	Std. Error
RETURNS	Mean		.9000	.11255
	95% Confidence Interval for Mean	Lower Bound	.6454	
		Upper Bound	1.1546	
	5% Trimmed Mean		.8778	
	Median		.8000	
	Variance		.127	
	Std. Deviation		.35590	
	Minimum		.50	
	Maximum		1.70	
	Range		1.20	
	Interquartile Range		.4000	
	Skewness		1.460	.687
	Kurtosis		2.068	1.334

Descriptives

			Statistic	Std. Error
RETURNS	Mean		.9000	.11255
	99% Confidence Interval for Mean	Lower Bound	.5342	
		Upper Bound	1.2658	
	5% Trimmed Mean		.8778	
	Median		.8000	
	Variance		.127	
	Std. Deviation		.35590	
	Minimum		.50	
	Maximum		1.70	
	Range		1.20	
	Interquartile Range		.4000	
	Skewness		1.460	.687
	Kurtosis		2.068	1.334

WORK CARD 5

1. Use Table V to calculate the following probabilities:

   $P(T < 1.476)$ when T has a t distribution with 5 d.o.f.

   $P(T > 0.686)$ when T has a t distribution with 21 d.o.f.

   $P(T > -2.764)$ when T has a t distribution with 10 d.o.f.

   $P(-2.764 < T < 2.764)$ when T has a t distribution with 10 d.o.f.

2. Calculate $t_{0.01}$ for a t distribution with 11 d.o.f. Calculate $t_{0.05}$ for a t distribution with 30 d.o.f. Compare this with $z_{0.05}$ and comment.

3. Computer operators at an insurance office are sent on a training course until they meet the required standard. The average number of days' training required by 15 operators is 53.87 with a standard deviation of 6.82. Give a 95% confidence interval for the mean number of days' training required by a computer operator. Assume that the distribution of the number of days' training is normal.

4. To assess the magnitude of recent rent rises in London an estate management agency randomly sampled and interviewed 32 residential building owners. The percentage rent rises over a year are given below.

1	5	0	4	2	2	3	0
0	-1	-5	4	6	-5	0	1
2.5	-2	3	1	3	1.2	1	0
2	2	-1	3	1	3	-2	1

   It may be useful to know that $\Sigma x = 35.7$ and $\Sigma x^2 = 227.69$.

   Calculate a 95% confidence interval for the average percentage rent rise and write down in words what it means. What assumption is necessary? Comment on whether or not you think rents have increased during this time.

5. A car rental company keeps records of the number of miles travelled during a one-day rental. For a sample of 110 rentals the mean was 85.5 and the standard deviation 19.3. Calculate the 90% confidence interval for the mean number of miles travelled in a day during a one-day rental.

Solutions:

1. 0.90   0.25   0.99   0.98

2. 2.718   1.697. This is quite close to the corresponding standard normal percentage point of 1.6449 because the number of d.o.f. is large.

3. The population variance is unknown and sample size is small so use a t interval. This is OK as we have been told to assume that the number of days' training has a normal distribution.

$$53.87 \pm 2.145 \sqrt{\frac{6.82^2}{15}}, \quad (50.09, 57.65)$$

4. Variance unknown but the sample size is large so we can just substitute s^2 instead of σ^2 in a z interval. No normality assumption is necessary as we have used z and the sample size is large. $s^2 = 6.0601$. This gives

$$1.1156 \pm 1.96\sqrt{\frac{6.0601}{32}}, \text{ i.e. } (0.26, 1.97)$$

As all the confidence interval is above zero, it seems likely that the average rent has increased. Only one sample in 20 would give an interval that does not include the population mean.

5. The variance is unknown but the sample size is large so we can approximate using a z interval.

$$85.5 \pm 1.6449\sqrt{\frac{19.3^2}{110}} \text{ gives } (82.47, 88.53)$$

ASSESSMENT 5

1. A sample of 10 taxi fares from the University to the centre of Norwich gave a mean of £3.80 and a sample standard deviation of 80p. Give a 95% confidence interval for the mean taxi fare. What assumptions are necessary?

2. The output voltage of power supplies manufactured by Clark products is believed to follow a normal distribution. Of primary concern to the company is the average output voltage of a particular power supply unit, believed to be 10 volts. 18 observations taken at random from this unit are shown below:

| 10.85 | 11.40 | 10.81 | 10.24 | 10.23 | 9.49 | 9.89 | 10.11 | 10.57 |
| 11.21 | 10.10 | 11.22 | 10.31 | 11.24 | 9.51 | 10.52 | 9.92 | 8.33 |

Use computer software to calculate 95% and 99% confidence intervals for the average output voltage for this power supply unit.
   Is the belief that $\mu = 10$ reasonable?

3. A machine tool is known to produce circular parts of a particular diameter with a precision equivalent to a variance of 0.2mm. A sample of 100 such parts is taken and gives a mean diameter of 50.2mm. Give a 99% confidence interval for the mean diameter of all such parts manufactured by this machine.

4. The following P/E ratios were obtained for a random sample of 8 stocks taken from the *Wall Street Journal*.

5   7   9   10   14   23   20   15

Calculate
   (i)   an estimator and
   (ii) a 95% confidence interval

for the mean P/E ratio on the New York stock exchange. State any assumptions that are necessary for your work.

5. Calculate a 95% and a 99% confidence interval for one (or more) of the following:
   (Collect the data from your fellow students and use a sample size of at least 8. State any assumptions that are necessary.)

ASSESSMENT 5 (CONTINUED)

(i)   The average hourly rate of pay students receive when doing work in the vacations.

(ii)   The average hourly rate of pay students receive when doing part-time work during term.

(iii)   The average amount of rent paid per week (including fuel bills) for private-sector student accommodation.

(iv)   Student weekly expenditure on transport – including bus and train fares, fuel, etc. but excluding fares home at the start and end of each teaching period.

6. Assuming that the data *are* representative of the wider population of potential customers use the data from the market research survey in *vizafizz* (see DD2, Assessment 8) to estimate the following and give appropriate 95% confidence intervals.

(i)   The average amount spent on drink in a week by a potential customer

(ii)   The average amount spent on drink in a week by males, and by females.

Do you need to make any assumptions for these confidence intervals to be valid?

7. The file *supermarket* contains records of supermarket check-out employees. In particular, the variable *blips* contains the average number of items processed using an electronic scanner (blips) per minute during a two-hour test period

(i)   Use a computer to calculate a 95% confidence interval for the mean number of items processed by an employee per minute.

(ii)   Now calculate a 90% confidence interval for the same mean.

(iii)   Which confidence interval is wider? Is this what you would expect intuitively? Why or why not?

Further reading: see p. xv

Further reading: see p. xv

Anderson *et al.* (Statistics) includes more detail, including how large a sample should be and the sampling distribution of a proportion.

Mendenhall *et al.*

Morris provides an alternative treatment and talks about types of sample other than the simple random sample.

Newbold *et al.* includes much more detail. It also considers alternative methods of choosing a sample: stratified and cluster sampling and how to determine sample size.

S2
Testing hypotheses

He uses statistics as a drunken man uses lamp-posts – for support rather than illumination.

Andrew Lang, 1844–1912, Scottish writer and poet

Contexts

What is this chapter about?
This chapter explains how to use a sample to test a theory about the larger set of data from which it is drawn.

Why is it useful?
The techniques in this chapter can be used to assess, for instance, whether a training course has improved performance, whether a new system has resulted in economies or whether an acceptable level of quality is being maintained.

An understanding of this chapter is essential for the remaining Statistics chapters and will help considerably with Chapters BM6, Controlling quality and BM7, Simulating reality.

Where does it fit in?
This chapter and the preceding chapter, S1 introduce the two ideas that underpin most of Inferential Statistics: estimation and testing. S1 introduced estimation and this chapter introduces hypothesis testing.

What do I need to know?
This chapter builds strongly on the previous one, S1 Estimation, so you will need to be happy with this and all its prerequisites, Essential Maths, Probability and Describing Data.

Objectives

After your work on this chapter you should:

- understand the concept of a statistical test;
- understand the ideas of the null and alternative hypotheses, significance levels and *p*-values;
- be able to perform a test of the mean, with and without a computer;
- understand the difference between one- and two-sided tests and the relationship of two-sided tests to confidence intervals;
- understand what a rejection region is and when it is useful.

1 Introduction to testing

In Chapter S1 we saw how to use a sample to estimate a population value like the mean or variance and how to produce a confidence interval for the population mean. Whilst this is often useful, we often only need to obtain a yes or no answer to a question about the population. For example:

- Does the population have a mean of 100?
- Is the production process still producing the same proportion of defective items?
- Has average performance improved?
- Is the male average better than the female average?

The technique of *statistical testing* or *hypothesis testing* endeavours to use a sample to answer questions like these and is the concern of this chapter.

As usual we can't expect to obtain *exact* answers about the population using a sample so we have to use probability to measure the uncertainty in our results. After performing a statistical test we hope to be able to make statements like, 'there is strong evidence that the population mean is 100' or 'there is little evidence that the male average is better than the female average'.

The idea of testing is one that people use instinctively in their everyday lives, so we will start with this.

The idea of testing

You probably conduct informal tests already without realising it. Consider the following scenario.

We have all met the middle-aged, usually right-wing character, who we will call Harold who mumbles on about the 'state of the world' and how 'it was different in my day'. At one of your meetings with Harold he makes the statement that, 'most students are left-wing extremists' (his main experience of students is from the 1970s). As a university student you feel that you have rather better first-hand knowledge of today's students than he has and, after a moment's thought, you reply 'but there are twenty students on my corridor and *none* of them is a left-wing extremist'. You feel that this is fairly strong evidence that 'most students' are *not* left-wing extremists and Harold's statement is wrong.

What you have done here is to regard the students on your corridor as a random sample of today's students. Your logic says that if Harold's statement is *assumed* to be correct and most of today's students are left-wing, the probability that none out of a sample of 20 students are left-wing must be very small. So either you have a 'fluke' (unlikely) sample or else Harold's statement is incorrect.

Another example. You are going to Sicily on holiday in March. Before you leave a friend tells you that Sicily has an average of 10 hours' sunshine a day during March. On the first three days of your holiday there are 7, 8 and 9 hours respectively. You consider that this is evidence that your friend is wrong.

Again you are using the first three days of your holiday as a sample. You have reasoned that if the average is 10 hours a day, the probability that a sample of 3 days has such a low average is small and so the assumption of an average of 10 hours sunshine is wrong.

In both cases your sample could be a fluke result – you might have chosen the most miserable period in March for years for your holiday and you might live on the most politically apathetic corridor of your university. So your 'test' results are not conclusive: they only give you evidence for or against a particular belief.

Here are some more 'intuitive' testing examples.

I suspect that Stephen, a new member of my French class, is very good at French. The teacher asks him three difficult questions at the start of the lesson and Stephen answers them all correctly. This supports my hypothesis that he speaks good French.

British train companies have a well-established reputation that their trains usually arrive late. A Singaporean student visiting Britain makes 3 train journeys of which 2 arrive late. The student concludes that this is strong evidence to support the train companies' reputation.

A colleague hands you the final draft of a report to proof-read telling you that 'There will only be a few mistakes'. On page one you count 5 typos and on page two there are 6. Without reading the document further you decide to hand it back to her for correction. Intuition tells you that if, as your colleague claims, the report was virtually error-free, the chance of so many mistakes in (a sample of) the first two pages would be small. You therefore reject your colleague's claim.

Check this

Can you think of an episode in the last couple of days in which you have intuitively conducted a test procedure?

If you're stuck – think of a conjecture you've made in the last few days – in conversation or to yourself, in thought. Now think of how you found evidence to support or reject the conjecture.

The structure of a test

All these examples have the following structure. The words in capitals are those most often used in testing.

1. A statement, claim or HYPOTHESIS about the population.
2. A TEST STATISTIC or value calculated from the sample.

3. Assuming that the hypothesis in **1** is true, the PROBABILITY (so far, assessed intuitively) of getting such an extreme value from the sample.
4. When the probability in **3** is small, the sample is *unlikely* to arise when the hypothesis is true so we REJECT the hypothesis. Alternatively, when the probability in **3** is large, then such a sample is quite likely to arise when the hypothesis is true, so there is no reason to reject the hypothesis.

Check this

Go through the five examples described in the text above and identify components **1**, **2**, **3** and **4** for each.

Solutions:

Left-wing students

1. The hypothesis is that most students are left-wing.
2. The test statistic is the number of students on my corridor who are left-wing.
3. Assuming that 'most students are left-wing' the probability of no left-wing students out of 20 is small.
4. The probability is small, so reject the hypothesis in **1**.

Sunshine in Sicily

1. I hypothesise that there is an average of 10 hours' sunshine in March in Sicily.
2. The test statistic is the average number of hours in the first 3 days of my holiday.
3. Assuming that the hypothesis in **1** is true the probability of such a low average in the first 3 days is small.
4. As the probability is small, reject the hypothesis in **1**.

Stephen's French

1. The hypothesis is that Stephen speaks good French.
2. The test statistic is the number of questions he answers correctly.
3. If Stephen is good at French the probability of answering three out of three difficult questions correctly is not small.
4. The probability is not small so I retain the hypothesis that Stephen is good at French.

Travelling on British trains

1. The more specific the hypothesis the better, so we adopt the hypothesis that British trains are is usually on time.
2. The number of train journeys out of 3 which arrive late.

3. Assuming that British trains are usually on time the probability that two or more trains (out of three) are late is small.

4. The probability is small so reject the hypothesis in **1**.

Proof-reading

1. The report has few errors.

2. The number of errors on the first two pages.

3. Assuming the report has few errors the probability of 11 or more errors on the first two pages.

4. The probability is small so reject the hypothesis.

Probability and testing

We hope that by now you have understood the *idea* behind testing. Briefly, we state a hypothesis, and then draw a sample. If, assuming the hypothesis is true, the sample result is unlikely, we reject the hypothesis.

To do statistical tests properly of course, we can't just assess the probability of the sample result intuitively, we need to calculate it exactly. You will be pleased to know, however, that you won't need any new knowledge of probability to do the tests in this book as the material in *Probability* is sufficient. This means that the most difficult thing about testing is working out *which* probability to calculate at step **3**. Once you have decided this you have merely set yourself a probability problem to solve, which is similar to those you've done before.

Try to follow the reasoning in the following examples. For each we enclose the probability calculations, which are merely revision, in { }.

For the moment we will take a probability of 0.05 as the threshold for supporting or rejecting the hypothesis. That is, if, when the hypothesis is true, the probability of such an extreme sample result is less than 0.05 we will reject the hypothesis and if it is greater we will retain it.

> ### Check this
>
> I claim that 10% of students are tee-total and do not drink alcohol; that is, 90% are drinkers. In a randomly chosen sample of 30 students *all* of them were drinkers. Does this support or lead me to reject my claim?
>
> **Solution:**
> My hypothesis is that 90% of students are drinkers. The test statistic is the number in the sample who are drinkers and so it is 30. I must therefore calculate the probability that as many as 30 of my sample are drinkers *assuming that 90% of students are drinkers*.
>
> {We calculate this as follows. The number of drinkers out of 30 is a binominal random variable so assuming $P(drinker) = 0.90$ the probability that 30 or more of a sample of 30 are drinkers is $P(30) = 0.90^{30} = 0.0424$.}
>
> So such an extreme sample result is unlikely (the probability is less than 5%) when the hypothesis is true. As the probability is small this provides evidence that I should reject the hypothesis. I conclude that more than 90% of students are drinkers.

Check this

Are academics slow learner drivers? It is known that 40% of all candidates pass their driving test first time. In a random sample of 10 academics who drive, only 2 passed first time. Does this give evidence that academics are poor driving test candidates?

Solution:
Our hypothesis is that academics are quite normal (well, as far as driving tests are concerned anyway) and that the probability of a first-time pass is 0.4. The test statistic is the number from the sample who passed first time, which is 2. We therefore require the probability of obtaining 2 or *fewer* first-time passes out of 10, when the probability of a first-time pass is 0.4. (Notice that we want the probability of such an extreme result.)

{This is a standard binomial distribution probability $P(X \leq 2)$ for which there are 10 trials and the probability of success is 0.4. So, $P(0) = 0.6^{10} = 0.006047$, $P(1) = 10 \times 0.6^9 \times 0.4 = 0.040311$ and $P(2) = {}^{10}C_2 \times 0.6^8 \times 0.4^2 = 0.120932$. So $P(X \leq 2) = 0.167290$.}

So approximately 17% of samples of this size from a population with a 'success' probability of 0.4 would contain 2 or fewer 'successes'. This sample result is quite likely to happen when the hypothesis is true and so there is no evidence to reject the hypothesis. We continue to believe that academics are 'normal' driving test candidates.

Check this

A mail order firm claims that 30% of orders will be delivered within 1 week of ordering, a further 50% within 1–2 weeks and 20% after 2 weeks. A competing company tests this claim by placing an order from three randomly selected parts of the country. Two of these deliveries take over 2 weeks and one takes 1–2 weeks. Does this support the mail order firm's claim?

The hypothesis is the mail order firm's claim. The test statistic is the result of the sample, that 2 deliveries took over 2 weeks and one took 1–2 weeks. The probability we need to calculate is the probability that the sample gives us this *or a more extreme* result, assuming that the hypothesis is true. (We must be careful *not* to find only the probability of one parcel taking 1–2 weeks and two taking over 2 weeks). The only more extreme result here is that all parcels take over 2 weeks, so we need P(2 take over 2 weeks and one takes 1–2 weeks) + P(all take more than 2 weeks) { $= 3 \times 0.2^2 \times 0.5 + 0.2^3 = 0.068$}.

So, if the firm's claim is true, 6.8% of samples would produce such extreme results. This probability is greater than the pre-chosen threshold of 0.05 and so we can retain the hypothesis although, as it is a 'borderline' case, we would perhaps be suspicious and perform another investigation.

The most commonly encountered test is one that tests a hypothesis about the mean of a population. We will consider examples like this in more detail later, but for now just try and follow the next example.

Check this

Do you remember the car consumption example from Chapter S1, Section 2? To recap, an advertisement for a new model of car states that it does an average of 12 kilometres per litre (kpl). To test this, a consumer car magazine obtains 5 such cars and obtains the following kpl for them.

  11.2   12.1   12.1   10.9   11.7

which has a mean of 11.6.
  Does this sample support the advertisement's claim? Assume that the kpl is normally distributed with variance 1.

Solution:
The hypothesis is the claim that the mean is 12 and we use the sample mean, $\bar{x}$, as the test statistic. We need the probability, assuming that the hypothesis is true, that we get such an extreme sample mean. That is, we require $P(\bar{X} < 11.6)$ when $\mu = 12$.
  {From Chapter S1, Section 3, we know that the mean of a sample from a normal population has an $N(\mu, \sigma^2/n)$ distribution where μ is the population mean, n is the sample size and σ^2 is the population variance. So in this case, assuming $\mu = 12$, $\bar{X}$ has a $N(12, \frac{1}{5})$ distribution. It follows that

$$P(\bar{X} < 11.6) = P\left(\frac{\bar{X} - 12}{\sqrt{\frac{1}{5}}} < \frac{11.6 - 12}{\sqrt{\frac{1}{5}}}\right)$$

$$= P(Z < -0.89) = 0.1867\}$$

So, when the population mean is 12 about 19% of samples will have a sample mean 11.6 or less. As this probability is greater than the threshold of 0.05 we retain the hypothesis and conclude that the sample provides no evidence that the advertiser's claim is false.

WORK CARD 1

1. As some practice in testing without getting bogged down in probability calculations write down the probability you would need to calculate to do each of the following tests, but do not calculate it.

    a. Electronic checkout operators at a supermarket are required to take an average of 2 seconds or less per item. From past studies the standard deviation of the time taken to process an item is known to be 0.2 seconds. During a test session a trainee processes 400 items in 840 seconds. Has she/he reached a satisfactory standard or not?

    b. Last season, gate receipts at a football ground averaged £55,000 with a standard deviation of £2000. At the first five matches this season gate receipts had an average of £53,000. Does this provide evidence that receipts have decreased or not?

    c. In a poll 44 out of the 100 people interviewed were in favour of capital punishment. Does this support the hypothesis that less than 50% of the population are in favour of capital punishment?

2. Try to work the following test all the way through. Look back and find a similar example in the text if you are stuck. The 'Cannabis Now' society newsletter states that 30% of students have taken (illegal) drugs at some time. A survey of

10 students finds that only one has ever taken these drugs. Test the publication's statement.

Solutions:

1. a. The hypothesis is that mean is 2, but sample mean is 2.1. We need the probability of getting a sample mean of 2.1 or more assuming that the population mean is 2. Use a standard deviation of 0.2 to calculate this.

    b. The hypothesis is that the mean is 55,000. We need the probability that the sample mean is 53,000 or less, assuming that the mean is 55,000. Take the standard deviation as 2000.

    c. The hypothesis is that 50% of the population are in favour of capital punishment. We require the probability of obtaining a sample result of 44 or fewer people out of 100 assuming that the probability of a person being in favour of capital punishment is 0.5.

2. We need the probability of there being 0 or 1 drug takers out of a sample of 10 assuming that the probability that an individual student has taken drugs is 0.3. This is a binomial situation so $P(0) = 0.7^{10} = 0.0282$ and $P(1) = {}^{10}C_1 \, 0.3 \, 0.7^9 = 0.1211$ so $P(0) + P(1) = 0.0282 + 0.1211 = 0.1493$ and 14.9% of samples would give such an extreme result when the hypothesis is true. This is not particularly small, when the newsletter's statement is true the sample result is quite likely so there is no evidence to reject the statement.

1. Describe the four components of a statistical test of the following, when appropriate data from a sample of students are available:

    a. The assertion that at least 20% of students at your university own cars.

    b. The statement that the mean age of students in your year is at most 18 years 6 months.

    c. The assertion that at least half of the students on your course hold a current full driving licence.

2. Try to work this test all the way through.
    I suspect that a colleague, who is responsible for appointments to my firm, may positively discriminate towards women. Last month he received an equal (large) number of applications from men and women for a job, and then selected 9 women and 1 man for interview. Does this provide evidence that he positively discriminates towards women?

2 **The structure of a test**

We have already covered most of the essential ideas of testing, albeit informally. In this section we elaborate on the four components of a test procedure and introduce some of the terminology that is used by textbooks and software.

1. The hypotheses

The statement or claim made about the population at the start of the test is called the *null hypothesis* and usually indicated by the symbol H_0 followed by a colon. For instance the null hypothesis that the population mean is 12 would be written

$$H_0 : \mu = 12.$$

At the start of the test we should also define another hypothesis, called the *alternative hypothesis*. This is the hypothesis that will be adopted if the test rejects H_0. It is written as H_1: For instance, the alternative hypothesis that the population mean is less than 12 is written $H_1 : \mu < 12$.

H_0 should be as specific as possible; for instance, $H_0 : \mu =$ 'something' instead of something vaguer like $H_0 : \mu <$ 'something', as we will have to calculate a probability assuming H_0 is true. H_1, on the other hand, will usually include an inequality sign.

Some null and alternative hypothesis pairs are

$H_0 : \mu = 100 \quad H_1 : \mu \neq 100$
(The population mean is or is not equal to 100)

$H_0 : \mu = 100 \quad H_1 : \mu < 100$
(The population mean is 100 or is less than 100)

$H_0 : p = 0.5 \quad H_1 : p \neq 0.5$
(The probability of a success, p, is or is not 0.5)

2. The test statistic

The value calculated from the sample that is used to perform the test is called the *test statistic*. It usually has a similar nature to the population value mentioned in the null hypothesis. For instance, if the null hypothesis is about the population mean, i.e.

$$H_0 : \mu = \text{'something'}$$

the test statistic might be $\overline{X}$ whereas if the null hypothesis is about the probability of a success in the population, p,

$$H_0 : p = \text{'something'}$$

the test statistic would be the number or proportion of successes in the sample.

3. The *p*-value

The probability that such an extreme test statistic occurs, *assuming that H_0 is true*, is called the *significance probability or p-value* and is usually denoted by the symbol p, i.e.

$$p = P(\text{such an extreme test statistic occurs})$$

when H_0 is true. Be careful not to confuse this p with the p we used above for the probability of a success in a binomial situation.

You will need to know the probability distribution of the test statistic when H_0 is true to calculate this.

4. The test result

When the *p*-value is *less than* a particular level, say 0.05, such an extreme sample result is unlikely to have occurred when the null hypothesis is true so we *reject H_0*.

When we reject H_0 in this way we *change* our default hypothesis from H_0 to H_1 and so we say that the test is *significant*.

When the *p*-value is *greater* than 0.05 samples such as this are quite likely to arise when H_0 is true so we conclude that there is *no* evidence to reject H_0 and we retain it. We say that the test result is *not significant* because it does *not* lead us to change our null hypothesis.

 Students often become confused about the reject/retain and significant/not significant terminology. Remember, when the test leads us to *change* our working hypothesis (reject H_0), it is *significant*.

The following example illustrates these four points.

Half the employees in a large accountancy firm have a degree. The manager of the Taxation department argues at a board meeting that she is disadvantaged in that less than half of the workers in her department have a degree. To check this the personnel officer selects a sample of 10 employees from the Taxation department and inspects their records. He finds that 3 of these have a degree. Does this give evidence to support the Taxation manager's claim?

1. The null hypothesis is H_0: $p = 0.5$, that half the workers in the Taxation department have a degree. The alternative hypothesis is H_1: $p < 0.5$, the manager's claim. Notice that we have made the null hypothesis, rather than the alternative hypothesis, an equality because we are going to have to calculate a probability assuming that H_0 is true so it needs to be as simple as possible.
2. The test statistic is the number of Taxation employees from the sample who have a degree and so is 3.
3. The *p*-value is the probability that the test statistic is so extreme, assuming that H_0 is true (that is, the probability that 3 or fewer (i.e. 3,2,1 or 0) employees from the sample of 10 have a degree), *assuming* that half the Taxation employees have a degree.

    The number of employees with a degree in a sample of 10 is a binomial random variable. When the null hypothesis is true the probability that an individual employee has a degree is 0.5 so

$$P(0) = 0.5^{10}, \quad P(1) = {}^{10}C_1\, 0.5^1\, 0.5^9, \quad P(2) = {}^{10}C_2\, 0.5^2\, 0.5^8, \quad P(3) = {}^{10}C_3\, 0.5^3\, 0.5^7$$

and the desired probability is the total of these:

$$p = P(X \le 3) = (1 + 10 + 45 + 120)\,0.5^{10} = 0.1719$$

4. As $p > 0.05$, the test is not significant, there is no evidence to reject H_0 and we can continue to assume that 50% of employees have a degree.

Significance levels

So far we have rejected H_0 when the *p*-value is less than 0.05 and retained H_0 when it is greater. However, the threshold value does not have to be 0.05, although it is usually set to 0.05 or 0.01. It is called the *significance level* of the test, so named because when the *p*-value is below the significance level the test is significant and when the *p*-value is greater than the significance level the test is *not* significant. The significance level is often given as a percentage.

In practice, the significance level must be decided *before the data is known* otherwise we might be tempted to 'cheat' when we look at the sample results and so bias the test towards retaining or rejecting H_0.

Errors and significance levels

We should emphasise that just because a test result says 'reject H_0' or 'retain H_0' this is by no means conclusive. We still don't know which hypothesis, H_0 or H_1, is really true and the test merely provides evidence to support one or the other.

In reality either H_0 or H_1 is true, and the test result can say 'reject H_0' or 'retain H_0' so there are 4 possibilities, which are shown on the diagram below.

		Reality	
		H_0 TRUE	H_1 TRUE
Test result	Retain H_0	OK	
	Reject H_0 (accept H_1)		OK

If H_0 is really true and the test says retain H_0, the test is correct, and if H_1 is really true and the test says reject H_0 the test is correct. These two possibilities are shown by OK above. The other two possibilities – retaining H_0 when H_1 is really true and rejecting H_0 when H_0 is really true – however, result in errors. Many books call these Type II and Type I errors as follows:

		Reality	
		H_0 TRUE	H_1 TRUE
Test result	Retain H_0	OK	Type II error
	Reject H_0 (accept H_1)	Type I error	OK

In an ideal world a 'good' test procedure would very rarely permit either type of error to happen; that is, the probability of a Type I error and the probability of a Type II error would both be small.

It so happens that *the probability of a Type I error is the same as the significance level.* (This is because the probability of rejecting H_0 when H_0 is true is the probability that p is less than the significance level when H_0 is true, which is the significance level itself.)

But, you might say, we choose the significance level of a test, so why don't we always set it as low as possible to reduce the probability of a Type I error? The answer is that we have not yet considered the Type II error. This is more difficult to quantify, but it can be shown that, as the probability of a Type I error *decreases*, the probability of a Type II error *increases* (and vice-versa). That is, the probability of one type of error offsets the probability of the other.

This is hard to illustrate for the general case, but the way in which the probabilities of Type I and Type II errors offset one another when testing for the population mean is shown in Figure 2.1. The curve on the left of Figure 2.1 shows the distribution of $\overline{X}$ when the null hypothesis $H_0: \mu = 1$ is true, whereas the one on the right shows the distribution of $\overline{X}$ assuming some other value for μ, say $H_1: \mu = 3$.

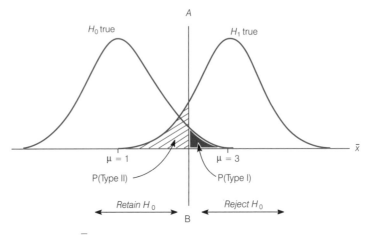

Figure 2.1 Distribution of $\bar{X}$, under H_0: $\mu = 1$, and H_1: $\mu = 3$, showing probabilities of type I and type II errors.

We reject H_0 for large values of $\bar{x}$ that give a p-value which is less than the significance level. So if a line AB is drawn so that the area under the H_0 distribution curve to the right of the line shown in black is equal to the significance level, all values of $\bar{x}$ to the right of this line result in rejecting H_0, (in Section 4 we will call these values the rejection region) and values to the left in retaining H_0. The probability of a Type I error is the same as the significance level and so is the black area but the probability of a Type II error is the probability of *not* rejecting H_0 when H_1 is true so this is the striped area under the H_1 curve to the left of the AB line.

Now consider what happens to the probability of a Type II error when the probability of a Type I error is reduced. To reduce the shaded area (which represents the probability of a Type I error) the AB line must move to the right. However, when the AB line moves in this way the shaded area that represents the probability of a Type II error is forced to increase.

The probability of a Type I error, P(reject H_0) when H_0 is true is controlled by the tester as it is the significance level and so we know that the probability of a 'reject H_0' test result being wrong is small as we have set it. However, the probability of a Type II error could still be very large, and as this is P(accept H_0) when H_1 is true, we must be aware that a test result of 'accept H_0' could well be an error, which is why we talk about 'not rejecting' or 'retaining' H_0 instead of 'accepting H_0'.

The structure of a test: a summary

The structure of a test

1. The hypotheses
Write down the null and alternative hypotheses, e.g.

H_0 : $\mu = $ 'something' and H_1: $\mu < $ 'something'

or

H_0: $p = 0.5$ and H_1: $p > 0.5$

Set the significance level to 0.05 or 0.01.

2. The test statistic
The sample mean $\bar{X}$, or the number or proportion of successes in the sample.

3. The p-value
The probability that such an extreme test statistic occurs, *assuming that H_0 is true*

$p = P$(such an extreme test statistic occurs) when H_0 is true

4. The test result
When p is smaller than the significance level such an extreme sample result is unlikely to have occurred when H_0 is true and so we *reject H_0*, the test result is **significant**.

When p is greater than the significance level the sample result is quite likely to have occurred when H_0 is true and so we retain H_0, the test result is **not significant**.

WORK CARD 2

1. Write down the null and alternative hypotheses in the following cases and for each say which probability you would calculate to obtain the p-value:

   a. During the last year the average quarterly charge on a private account held at a High Street bank was £25. The bank wishes to investigate whether the amount paid in charges has increased or not so they sample 50 accounts and obtain a mean charge of £25.50.

   b. A travel guide maintains that the average price of a set menu restaurant meal in France is 18 euros. A competing restaurant guide maintains that the average price is cheaper. A sample of 100 restaurants throughout France gave an average set menu price of 16 euros.

2. To test whether the mean retail price of a litre of unleaded fuel is 75p or whether it is higher, retail prices were collected from a sample of 20 service stations to give a mean of 75.2p. A significance level of 0.05 was agreed. Assuming that the prices are normally distributed, a test was performed which gave a p-value of 0.09.

   Write down the null and alternative hypotheses for this test. Is the test result significant or not? What conclusions can you draw?

3. At the outset of a similar test to that in question 2 it was decided that the significance level should be 0.01. What difference (if any) does this make to your conclusions?

4. Mustbe supermarkets claim that 40% of shoppers who go to out of town supermarkets regularly use Mustbe. A nationwide sample of 200 shoppers showed that 65 used Mustbe regularly. The probability of a proportion of 0.325 or less for a sample this size, when the population proportion is 0.4, is 0.002. Is this result significant at the 1% level or not? What conclusions can you draw?

5. The average duration of an appointment at a doctor's surgery is known to be 7 minutes, with a standard deviation of 2 minutes. A new doctor starts work at the surgery and appears to be taking a long time seeing patients. The surgery

manager takes a random sample of 3 surgery periods and calculates that the new doctor has seen 56 patients in a total of 7 hours. He intends to use a 5% significance level.

(i)   Write down the null and alternative hypotheses for this test.

(ii) What probability would you calculate to obtain a p-value? Suppose the p-value is 0.04.

(iii) Is the test significant or not? Write down the conclusions of the test.

(iv) Describe the two errors that might have occurred.

(v)   Write down the probability of one of the two types of errors.

(vi) Can you write down the probability of the second type of error?

Solution guidelines:

1. **a.** $H_0: \mu = 25$ $H_1: \mu > 25$. $P(\overline{X} > 25.5)$ when $\mu = 25$.
    b. $H_0: \mu = 18$ $H_1: \mu < 18$. $P(\overline{X} < 16)$ when $\mu = 18$.

2. $H_0: \mu = 75$ $H_1: \mu > 75$. As $p = 0.09 > 0.05$ the test is not significant, there is no evidence to reject H_0. There is no evidence that prices are above 75p per litre.

3. If the significance level is 0.01 the p-value is still greater, so we still cannot reject H_0. Our conclusions would be unchanged.

4. As $0.002 < 0.01$ the result is significant, we reject H_0, there is evidence that less than 40% of shoppers use Mustbe.

5. **(i)** $H_0: \mu = 7$ $H_1: \mu > 7$

    (ii) $P(\overline{X} \geq 7.5)$ when $\mu = 7$ and $\sigma = 2$. The sample mean has a normal distribution as the sample size is large.

    (iii) As $p < 0.05$ the test is significant. Reject H_0. There is evidence to suppose that the new doctor is taking longer than average with his patients.

    (iv) The Type I error is that the new doctor's mean appointment time is really 7 minutes, but the test decides that it is longer. Type II error is when the new doctor's mean appointment time is really greater than 7 minutes but the test decides that it is 7 minutes.

    (v)   The probability of Type I error is the same as the significance level 0.05.

    (vi) The probability of Type II error requires the exact probability distribution when H_1 is true but cannot be calculated for this example as $H_1: \mu \geq 7$ is not specific enough.

WORK CARD 2 (CONTINUED)

ASSESSMENT 2

1. Write down **(i)** the null and alternative hypotheses, **(ii)** the test statistic and **(iii)** which probability you would calculate for the p-value in the following situations:

   a. From past records 30% of a company's orders come from new customers. The firm has recently mounted a publicity campaign to attract new customers. To test the efficacy of this it agrees to take the next 20 orders as a sample.

b. When a carwash is working properly each wash takes a mean of 2 minutes 30 seconds and the duration is normally distributed. When it is faulty it takes longer on average. The proprietor tests the machine at the start of each week by running it 5 times.

2. One week the owner of the carwash in **1b.** obtains a mean duration of 2 minutes 45 seconds for his sample of 5 washes and calculates that when the machine is working properly the probability of obtaining such a small sample mean is $p = 0.17$. Is the test significant? Should he accept or reject the null hypothesis? Should he call in the engineer to repair the carwash machine?

3. At the end of each year the employees of a computing company are graded as not satisfactory, satisfactory or outstanding. Satisfactory and outstanding employees receive a bonus. The amount of bonus varies from employee to employee but is calculated so that the distribution of the bonus awarded to satisfactory employees is normally distributed with mean £1000 and standard deviation £100, whereas outstanding employees' bonuses are normally distributed with a mean of £2000 with a standard deviation of £500.

   I am interested in whether my husband, Paul, has been graded satisfactory or outstanding. He is characteristically stubborn and will not tell me, but I manage our domestic finances and his pay slip shows that he has been paid a bonus of £1200.

   (i)   Write down the null and alternative hypotheses that I wish to test.

   (ii)   Which probability do you need to calculate to obtain the p-value?

   (iii)   Perform the test at the 5% significance level. You will need to use normal distribution probabilities.

   (iv)   What do you conclude from the test?

   (v)   Write down the two sorts of error that could occur using such a test procedure.

3 Tests for the mean

We now consider tests about the population mean in more detail. To do these you will need to be fluent in calculating normal and t probabilities so if you're a bit rusty you should revise these now.

The hypotheses
We are concerned with testing the hypothesis that the population mean is a particular value, say μ_0. The null hypothesis is therefore

$$H_0: \mu = \mu_0$$

and the alternative hypothesis is

$$H_1: \mu > \mu_0 \quad \text{or} \quad H_1: \mu < \mu_0$$

For instance, for the car fuel consumption featured at the end of Section 1, the advertiser's claim that average consumption is 12 kpl is represented by $H_0: \mu = 12$ whereas the consumer group's suspicion that it is lower is given by $H_1: \mu < 12$.

A reminder of some distributions

Recall (from Chapter S1, Section 3) that the following result holds *exactly* when X is normally distributed and *approximately* when the sample size, n, is large,

$$\overline{X} \sim N\left(\mu, \frac{\sigma^2}{n}\right)$$

So, to calculate probabilities involving $\overline{X}$ we need to know the population variance, σ^2, and we standardise to give

$$Z = \frac{\overline{X} - \mu}{\sqrt{\sigma^2/n}} \sim N(0,1)$$

When σ^2 is unknown we can 'standardise' $\overline{X}$ using the sample variance s^2 instead, but now (provided X is normally distributed) the resulting random variable

$$T = \frac{\overline{X} - \mu}{\sqrt{s^2/n}}$$

has a t distribution with $n - 1$ degrees of freedom.

The test statistic

When the variance, σ^2, is known (assuming a large or normal sample), the test statistic is

$$z = \frac{\overline{x} - \mu_0}{\sqrt{\sigma^2/n}}$$

Notice that this is just the sample mean, $\overline{x}$, standardised using the hypothesised mean from H_0. When H_0 is true this comes from a $N(0,1)$ distribution.

For instance, continuing the car fuel consumption example, we have been told that the kpl (kilometres per litre) of a car is normally distributed with $\sigma^2 = 1$ and we are testing the null hypothesis $H_0: \mu = 12$. The mean of a sample of 5 cars is $\overline{x} = 11.6$. As the population variance is known the test statistic is

$$z = \frac{11.6 - 12}{\sqrt{\frac{1}{5}}} = -0.89$$

When $H_0: \mu = 12$ is true this comes from a standard normal distribution.

When the variance, σ^2, is not known (assuming that X is normally distributed) we standardise using s^2, so the test statistic is

$$t = \frac{\overline{x} - \mu}{\sqrt{s^2/n}}$$

When H_0 is true this comes from a t distribution with $n - 1$ degrees of freedom. For example, consider the following. Managers at a company wish to introduce a flexitime system whereby employees will be required to work 42 hours per week. Union representatives, however, argue that this will increase the amount of hours worked by staff. In a typical week 8 randomly chosen staff worked the following numbers of hours:

$$48 \quad 32 \quad 37 \quad 35 \quad 36 \quad 42 \quad 41 \quad 40$$

Test the union representatives' claim. You may assume that the hours worked by an employee are normally distributed. The sample mean is $\bar{x} = 38.875$ and the sample variance is $s^2 = 24.6964$.

The null and alternative hypotheses are $H_0: \mu = 42$ and $H_1: \mu < 42$. The population variance is *not* known, so the test statistic is

$$t = \frac{\bar{x} - \mu_0}{\sqrt{s^2/n}} = \frac{38.875 - 42}{\sqrt{\frac{24.6964}{8}}} = -1.78$$

When the null hypothesis is true, this comes from a t distribution with 7 degrees of freedom.

(In the car consumption example at the end of Section 1 we used $\bar{x}$ instead of z as the test statistic in order to keep things as intuitive as possible. This is only possible when σ^2 is known in which case it will give the same p-value as using z. In general, however, it is best to use z or t as the test statistic as described in this section because this will work both when σ^2 is known and when it is *not* known.)

The p-value

When the alternative hypothesis is $H_1: \mu < \mu_0$, *small* values of $\bar{x}$, and therefore of z or t, support H_1, and can be considered extreme so the p-value is the probability of such a small value of z or t occurring; that is,

$$p = P(Z < z) \quad \text{or} \quad p = P(T < t)$$

In a similar way, when the alternative hypothesis is $H_1: \mu > \mu_0$, large values of $\bar{x}$ and so of z or t are considered extreme, and therefore the p-value is the probability of such a large value of z or t; that is,

$$p = P(Z > z) \quad \text{or} \quad p = P(T > t)$$

For example, in the car fuel consumption test, the alternative hypothesis is $H_1: \mu < 12$ so $p = P(Z < -0.89)$ as shown in Figure 2.2.

Cumulative normal tables (Table II) give $p = P(Z < -0.89) = 0.1867$.

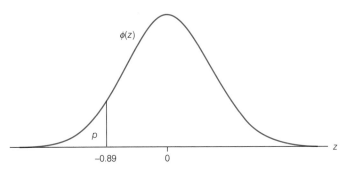

Figure 2.2

The test result

If the p-value exceeds the significance level of 5%, the test is not significant and we retain H_0. For the car consumption example $p = 0.1867$, which is greater than 5% so there is no evidence that the advertiser's claim is false.

Now a complete test for the mean when the population variance is known.

Check this

Each machinist in a shoe factory must produce an average of 50 or fewer defective parts each day. It is known that the variance of the number of defectives produced by a machinist in a day is 4. On a randomly chosen day, the 35 machinists produced an average of 51 defective parts. Is this evidence that the machinists are producing too many defective parts, on average?

Solution:

The null hypothesis is $H_0: \mu = 50$. The alternative is that the number of defectives is *more* than 50, so we have $H_1: \mu > 50$. The variance is known to be 4 so the test statistic is

$$z = \frac{51 - 50}{\sqrt{\frac{4}{35}}} = 2.96$$

When H_0 is true, this comes from a $N(0,1)$ distribution. Large values of z support H_1, so $p = P(Z > 2.96) = 0.0015$.

As $p < 0.05$ we reject H_0 in favour of H_1 and conclude that there *is* evidence that the machinists are producing too many defective parts.

And now we repeat and continue the flexitime example in which the population variance is *not* known, so the test statistic is

$$t = \frac{\bar{x} - \mu_0}{\sqrt{s^2/n}}$$

Check this

As before, managers at a company wish to introduce a flexitime system whereby employees will be required to work 42 hours per week. Union representatives, however, argue that this will increase the amount of hours worked by staff. In a typical week, 8 randomly chosen staff worked the following numbers of hours:

48   32   37   35   36   42   41   40

Test the union representatives' claim. You may assume that the number of hours worked by an employee is normally distributed.

The sample mean is $\bar{x} = 38.875$ and the sample variance is $s^2 = 24.6964$.

Solution:

We have already said that the null and alternative hypotheses are $H_0: \mu = 42$ and $H_1: \mu < 42$ and that test statistic is

$$t = \frac{\bar{x} - \mu_0}{\sqrt{s^2/n}} = \frac{38.875 - 42}{\sqrt{\frac{24.6964}{8}}} = -1.78$$

When the null hypothesis is true this comes from a t distribution with 7 degrees of freedom. The p-value is therefore $P(T < -1.78)$.

To find this probability we use t tables. The percentage points from Table V corresponding to 7 degrees of freedom are given below.

Table V
Percentage points of the t distribution
The table gives the value a, such that $P(T < a) = p$ where T is a random variable from a t distribution with v degrees of freedom

p	0.75	0.90	0.95	0.975	0.99	0.995	0.9995
v							
7	0.711	1.415	1.895	2.365	2.998	3.449	5.408

Notice that $P(T < -1.78)$ is not listed. This is not a problem, however, because, as we are doing a test, we only need to know whether the p-value is smaller or larger than the significance level of 0.05.

From the table, and the symmetry of the t distribution, we see that $0.05 < P(T < -1.78) < 0.10$, as shown in Figure 2.3.

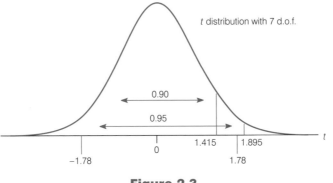

Figure 2.3

We conclude that as $p > 0.05$, the test is not significant although as $0.05 < p < 0.10$ the result is close to the borderline.

Check this

The weights (kg) of a sample of 10 cartons of chemical produced by a plant are

0.98 0.95 0.94 1.01 0.97 0.94 1.01 0.99 0.96 0.95

(The mean and variance of this sample are 0.97 and 0.000711 respectively.) The mean carton weight is supposed to be 1 kg, but the company suspects that the filling machine is underweighing. Test whether or not this is the case using a significance level of 0.05.

Solution:
The null hypothesis is $H_0: \mu = 1$ and the alternative hypothesis is $H_1: \mu < 1$. The test statistic is

$$t = \frac{0.97 - 1}{\sqrt{\dfrac{0.000711}{10}}} = -3.558$$

When H_0 is true, this comes from a t distribution with 9 d.o.f. As the alternative hypothesis contains a < sign, small weights are considered extreme and the p-value is

$$p = P(T < -3.558)$$

The t tables for 9 d.o.f. give $P(T < -3.250) = 0.005$ so $p < 0.05$ and we conclude that the test is significant and reject the null hypothesis. The sample gives evidence that the machine is underweighing.

Testing means in practice

It is natural to call the tests for the mean with test statistics z and t, z tests and t tests respectively (compare z intervals and t intervals).

As z and t tests are based on the same theory as z or t intervals, the choice of a z or t test is exactly the same as the choice of a z or t interval. Just as z intervals and t intervals give similar results and do not require the data to be normal for large samples (see S1, Section 5) so z tests and t tests can be used interchangeably for large samples and do not require the normality assumption. Again, you will probably do a z test when calculating by hand but a t test on a computer. A summary of when to use which type of test is given below. Notice again that you only *have to* use a t test when the sample size is small and the sample variance is unknown, but that you must assume that the data are normally distributed.

Testing the population mean

	Large sample ($n \geq 30$)	Small sample (normal population assumed)
Population variance σ^2 *known*	z	z
Population variance σ^2 *unknown* (so use s^2)	Either z or t	t

Check this

The percentage of alcohol in a low alcohol beer is permitted to have an average of at most 0.2%. A sample of 100 bottles taken from a batch has an average alcohol content of 0.22%. Is this batch OK or not? The variance of the percentage of alcohol in a bottle of this beer is not known but the variance of the sample is 0.006. Test using a 1% significance level.

We need to test $H_0: \mu = 0.2$ against $H_1: \mu > 0.2$. (Notice that the alternative hypothesis here is 'greater than' as we are interested in a violation of the regulations.) The test statistic is

$$z = \frac{0.22 - 0.2}{\sqrt{\dfrac{0.006}{100}}} = 2.58$$

As the alternative hypothesis is 'greater than', a high z suggests that we reject H_0 so the p-value is

$p = P(Z > 2.58) = 0.0049$

As $p < 0.01$ we reject H_0 in favour of H_1 and conclude that the sample does give evidence that this batch is faulty.

One- and Two-sided alternative hypotheses

So far, all the *alternative* hypotheses in our examples have been of the form $H_1: \mu < \mu_0$ or $H_1: \mu > \mu_0$. Sometimes, however, we may want an alternative hypothesis that just says 'is not equal to'; that is, $H_1: \mu \neq \mu_0$. Consider the following example.

A production line manufactures packets of potato crisps. When the line is working properly the packets have an average weight of 30g whereas when it is not working properly the mean weight deviates from this. The standard deviation of the weight of a packet is known to be 0.7g.

A sample of 50 packets is drawn and this has a mean weight of $\bar{x} = 29.83$g. Test, using a significance level of 5%, whether the production line is working properly or not.

Here the null hypothesis is $H_0: \mu = 30$ (that is, the machine is working properly), but the alternative hypothesis needs to be that the machine is *not* working properly; that is, $H_1: \mu \neq 30$ (mean is *not* equal to 30g).

We say that $H_1: \mu \neq 30$ is a *two-sided* hypothesis – because it includes values of μ on both sides of the value hypothesised in H_0.

As before, the variance is known so the test statistic is

$$z = \frac{\bar{x} - \mu_0}{\sqrt{\sigma^2/n}} = \frac{29.83 - 30}{\sqrt{\dfrac{0.7^2}{50}}} = -1.72$$

As usual, the p-value is the probability of such an extreme z; however, now, because the alternative hypothesis is $H_1: \mu \neq 30$, both large positive and large negative values of z can be considered extreme; that is, values that differ greatly from 0. The p-value is therefore the probability that Z differs from 0 by more than -1.72, and so is the total probability in *both* tails shown in Figure 2.4.

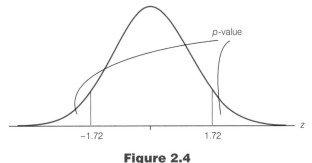

Figure 2.4

As the normal distribution is symmetric the area in each tail is the same and therefore

$$p = 2 \times P(Z < -1.72)$$
$$= 2 \times 0.0427 = 0.0854$$

Notice that we have calculated twice the probability that we would for a one-sided alternative hypothesis.

As $p > 0.05$ the test is not significant and there is no evidence to suppose that the machine is malfunctioning. However, if the test had been one-sided, the p-value would have been the area in one tail only (0.0427) and the test would have been significant.

As the p-value is spread between two 'tails' of the distribution, tests like this are also often called *two-tailed* tests.

If the test statistic is z, the area in the upper tail of the normal distribution is $P(Z < |z|)$ and so the p-value of a two-tailed test can be written succinctly as

$$p = 2P(Z > |z|) \text{ where } |z| \text{ means the absolute value of } z$$

Two-tailed tests can be performed in the same way when the test statistic is t. Again, the p-value is the area in both tails of the t distribution, so it is $2P(T > |t|)$.

Check this

Chloe is getting married and wishes to rent out her one-bedroom apartment. A property management advisor tells her that the average monthly rent for one-bedroom apartments in her area is £244. To test this, she approaches a property rental agency and selects 6 one-bedroom apartments at random from those available for rent. The monthly rentals of these are

  £320 £300 £220 £280 £230 £255

$s^2 = 1557.5$ and the sample mean is $\bar{x} = 267.5$. Do these substantiate the advisor's claim that the average rents are £244? You may assume that the rents are normally distributed.

Solution:
The null hypothesis is $H_0: \mu = 244$ and the alternative $H_1: \mu \neq 244$ so it is a two-sided test. The population variance is unknown so the test statistic is

$$t = \frac{\bar{x} - \mu_0}{\sqrt{s^2/n}} = \frac{267.5 - 244}{\sqrt{\frac{1557.5}{6}}} = 1.459$$

As the test is two-sided the p-value is the probability that T is as extremely different from 0 as this, so it is the area in both tails of the t distribution:

$$p = 2 \times P(T > 1.459)$$

From t tables (5 d.o.f.) $P(T > 1.476) = 0.1$ so $P(T > 1.459)$ is larger than 0.1 and the p-value is larger than 0.2. We conclude that the test is not significant (at a significance level of 5%) so there is no evidence to reject the property management advisor's claim that the mean rent is £244.

Confidence intervals and two-sided tests

There is a useful link between confidence intervals and two-sided tests. It is best explained by example.

When a null hypothesis, for instance $H_0: \mu = 5$, is retained at the 5% significance level, the hypothesised value of 5 lies within the 95% confidence interval for μ calculated from the same sample. The converse is also true – that if a value, for example 7, lies within the 95% confidence interval for μ, the corresponding hypothesis $H_0: \mu = 7$ will be retained in a test at the 5% significance level.

As further illustration, suppose a sample of size 40 has a mean of $\bar{x} = 5.2$ and that the population variance is known to be 2.5. The 95% confidence interval is

$$\bar{x} - 1.96\sqrt{\frac{2.5}{40}} < \mu < \bar{x} + 1.96\sqrt{\frac{2.5}{40}} \quad \text{or} \quad (4.71, 5.69)$$

Without any further calculation we can say that the sample would lead us to accept the null hypothesis $H_0\colon \mu =$ 'something', as long as the 'something' was between 4.71 and 5.69. So we would accept $H_0\colon \mu = 5$ but would have to reject $H_0\colon \mu = 6$.

Relationships like these apply to confidence intervals and two-sided tests at all significance levels. For example, when the null hypothesis is accepted at the 1% level, the hypothesised value will lie within 99% confidence limits and so on.

Check this

A 99% confidence interval for the mean contents of a batch of cans of paint is (1001, 1005) millilitres.

(i) Using the same sample would you retain or reject $H_0\colon \mu = 1000$ at the 1% level?

(ii) Would you reject $H_0\colon \mu = 1000$ at the 5% level?

(iii) Would you retain or reject $H_0\colon \mu = 1002$ at the 1% level?

Solution:

(i) As the hypothesised mean $H_0\colon \mu = 1000$ lies *outside* the 99% confidence interval, the test at a significance level of 1% would reject H_0, i.e. the *p*-value would be less than 1%.

(ii) If the *p*-value is less than 1% it is also less than 5% so we would reject at the 5% significance level as well.

(iii) The null hypothesis $H_0\colon \mu = 1002$ would be retained at a significance level of 1%, however, because 1002 lies within the 99% confidence interval.

Testing means using a computer

Testing is easy to do using statistical software. You just place the sample of data in a column and request which test you want. The danger of this ease is that the computer will also do inappropriate tests for you when requested. The user must therefore understand which tests are suitable in which circumstances and be able to interpret the output. Most statistical software includes a whole catalogue of tests, many beyond the scope of this book. However, all statistical tests have the same four-point structure that we have described.

In SPSS the command

Analyze > Compare Means > One-Sample T Test

tests for the mean, assuming that the population variance is unknown. The user has to supply the hypothesised value of μ.

We perform the following examples with SPSS but follow up with the manual calculations so that you can see what the software has done.

Check this

The price of a particular brand of soap at all outlets is known to be normally distributed with a mean of 50p. The following data gives the price in pence of this brand of soap at a sample of 10 late-night convenience stores.

45   59   58   49   55   41   66   75   39   48

Does the sample give evidence that convenience stores are charging a different mean price to other outlets?

Solution:
The null hypothesis is $H_0: \mu = 50$ and the alternative $H_1: \mu \neq 50$.
   The SPSS output is

One-Sample Statistics

	N	Mean	Std. Deviation	Std. Error Mean
SOAP	10	53.50	11.355	3.591

One-Sample Test

Test Value = 50

	t	df	Sig. (2-tailed)	Mean Difference	95% Confidence Interval of the Difference Lower	Upper
SOAP	.975	9	.355	3.50	–4.62	11.62

At a significance level of 0.05 this test result is *not* significant as $p = 0.355 > 0.05$, and we have no evidence to reject the hypothesis that the convenience stores are charging the same mean price as elsewhere.
   Notice that the p-value is called Sig. (2-tailed) in SPSS.
Without a computer, the sample variance is 128.9444, so

$$t = \frac{53.5 - 50}{\sqrt{128.944/10}} = 0.975$$

and

   $p = 2P(T > 0.975)$

   From Table V for the t distribution with 9 d.o.f., $P(T < 0.703) = 0.75$ and $P(T < 1.383) = 0.90$ so $P(T < 0.975)$ is between 0.75 and 0.90, $P(T > 0.975)$ is therefore between 0.25 and 0.10 and $0.20 < p < 0.50$, and our result is clearly *not* significant. We conclude that there is no evidence that the convenience stores are selling this soap at a different price.

   Note that SPSS performs a *two-sided* test. If a *one-sided* test is required we must divide the Sig.(2-tailed) probability by 2 as in the following example.

Check this

The age distribution at a college is known to be normally distributed with mean age 19.5 years. The ages of a sample of 7 students who have been offered college accommodation are given below. Test at the 1% level, the hypothesis that younger students are favoured.

17.9   18.2   19.1   20.3   17.8   17.4   17.8

Solution:
The null hypothesis is $H_0: \mu = 19.5$ which must be tested against $H_1: \mu < 19.5$, a one-sided alternative. We do not know the variance of the age of the students at this college and so we must use a t test. The SPSS output is as follows:

One-Sample Statistics

	N	Mean	Std. Deviation	Std. Error Mean
AGE	7	18.357	1.0081	.3810

One-Sample Test

Test Value = 19.5

	t	df	Sig. (2-tailed)	Mean Difference	95% Confidence Interval of the Difference Lower	Upper
AGE	−3.000	6	.024	−1.143	−2.075	−.211

The p value is $0.024/2 = 0.012$ and the result is *not* significant at the 1% level so technically there is no evidence to reject H_0, although the p-value is very much on the borderline. Further investigation might be a good idea.

Without a computer, the sample mean is 18.357 and the sample variance is 1.0162 so

$$t = \frac{18.357 - 19.5}{\sqrt{\frac{1.0162}{7}}} = -3.000$$

and we need to calculate

$$p = P(T < -3.000)$$

Using tables for t with 6 d.o.f. we cannot obtain this probability exactly but we can ascertain that it lies between 0.025 and 0.01.

TESTING for the mean

1.   The hypotheses
Write down the **null hypothesis** $H_0: \mu = \mu_0$
Write down the **alternative hypothesis**:

Is it one-sided? $H_1: \mu < \mu_0$ or $H_1: \mu > \mu_0$

or two-sided? $H_1: \mu \neq \mu_0$

Decide on the **significance level**

0.05 or 0.01 is usual

2.   **The test statistic**

	Large sample $n \geq 30$	Small sample (normal population assumed)
Population variance σ^2 *Known*	$z = \dfrac{\bar{x} - \mu_0}{\sqrt{\sigma^2/n}}$	$z = \dfrac{\bar{x} - \mu_0}{\sqrt{\sigma^2/n}}$
Population variance σ^2 *Unknown*	$z = \dfrac{\bar{x} - \mu_0}{\sqrt{s^2/n}}$ or $t = \dfrac{\bar{x} - \mu_0}{\sqrt{s^2/n}}$	$t = \dfrac{\bar{x} - \mu_0}{\sqrt{s^2/n}}$

When H_0 is true

z comes from a $N(0,1)$ distribution or

t comes from a t distribution with $n - 1$ degrees of freedom

3.   **The p-value**
When the alternative hypothesis is:

$H_1: \mu < \mu_0$, the p-value is $p = P(Z < z)$

$H_1: \mu > \mu_0$, the p-value is $p = P(Z > z)$

$H_1: \mu \neq \mu_0$, the p-value is $p = 2 \times P(Z > |z|)$
i.e. twice the area in the tail

The results for t are similar

4.   **The test result**
If p is smaller than the chosen significance level,

Reject H_0 and accept H_1, the test is **SIGNIFICANT**

If p is larger than the chosen significance level,

Retain H_0, the test is **NOT significant**

Write down the conclusion of your test in words. 'There is evidence that ...' 'There is no evidence that ...'

1. Management claim that the bonuses paid to workers at a plant average £1000. A random sample of 100 workers gives an average bonus of only £975. Bonuses are known to have a standard deviation of £100. Test the managements's claim against an alternative hypothesis of $H_1: \mu < 1000$ using a 1% significance level.

2. The manager of a hotel claims that the average guest bill for a weekend is £400. A local journalist, however, claims that prices have increased and that average bills are greater than £400. A sample of 40 bills gives a mean of £402. Previous records indicate that the variance of a bill is £400.

    (i)   Write down appropriate null and alternative hypotheses to test the manager's claim.

    (ii) Perform an appropriate test.

3. Legislation dictates that bottles of wine should contain an average volume of exactly 0.7 litre. A sample of 6 bottles from a wine importer gives a mean of 0.697 and a standard deviation of 0.01. Test whether the wine importer is underfilling bottles. State any assumptions that are necessary for the test.

4. Recent surveys have said that, on average, British people spend 24 hours a week watching television. A random sample of 84 people gave a mean of 23.5 hours and a sample variance of 5. Test whether or not British people spend an average of 24 hours a week watching television.

5. In 1990 a study estimated that the average value of US farmland was $778 per acre. A researcher believes that the value has increased since then and samples 23 farms across the country. The selling price of each farm (per acre) is given below:

750	800	680	910	845	790	1100	950	735	600
800	850	845	900	1150	1000	780	900	900	850
990	1200	850							

    Use a computer to perform an appropriate test.

6. We repeat **Work card 5** question 5 from Chapter S1.

    A car rental company keeps records of the number of miles travelled during a one-day rental. For a sample of 110 rentals, the mean was 85.5 and the standard deviation 19.3. You were asked to calculate a 90% confidence interval for the mean number of miles travelled in a day during a one-day rental. The answer was (82.47, 88.53).

    Quickly test the null hypothesis $H_0: \mu = 90$ against the alternative $H_1: \mu \neq 90$ at the 10 % significance level. What enables you to do this so quickly?

    Test the null hypothesis $H_0: \mu = 85$ against $H_1: \mu \neq 85$ at the 10% significance level. Can you test this null hypothesis at the 5% significance level without further calculations?

7. In a study of the efficiency of a lie-detector test, 1000 people were given the test. Of these 500 lied and 500 told the truth. The lie-detector said that 185 of those who were telling the truth were liars and that 120 of the liars told the truth.

Consider a single person, about to take a lie-detector test.

(i) Write down the null and alternative hypotheses for such a test.

(ii) Suppose the lie-detector says he is lying. Is this evidence that you should reject the null hypothesis or not?

(iii) Is the lie-detector test a good one or not? (Consider the probabilities of the two types of error that can occur.)

8. Recall that the file *supermarket* contains records of supermarket check-out employees and that the variable *blips* contains the average number of items processed per minute during a two-hour test period.

   The workers' union claims that the average number of items processed averages 10 per minute. Do the data support this claim?

   Head Office, however, state that the target of an average 10.5 items per minute is not being achieved. Do the data support their statement?

Solutions:

1. $H_1: \mu = 1000$ $H_1: \mu < 1000$. The population variance is known so the test statistic is

$$z = \frac{975 - 1000}{\sqrt{\frac{100^2}{100}}} = -2.5$$

$p = P(Z < -2.5) = 0.0062$ which is significant at 1% as $p < 0.01$. There is evidence that the average bonus is less than £1000.

2. **(i)** $H_0: \mu = 400$, $H_1: \mu > 400$.

   (ii) $z = \dfrac{402 - 400}{\sqrt{\frac{400}{40}}} = 0.63$

$p = P(Z > 0.63) = 0.2643$. As $p > 0.05$ the test is not significant and there is no evidence to suggest that the manager's claim is wrong.

3. $H_0: \mu = 0.7$, $H_1: \mu < 0.7$. The variance is unknown so we must use

$$t = \frac{0.697 - 0.7}{\sqrt{\frac{0.01^2}{6}}} = -0.735$$

$p = P(T < -0.735)$. t tables with 5 d.o.f. give $P(T < 1.476) = 0.90$ and $P(T < 0.727) = 0.75$, so by symmetry $0.10 < P(T < -0.735) < 0.25$ and the p-value is greater than 0.05. We conclude that the test is not significant. There is no evidence that bottles are being underfilled.

4. A two-tailed test. The sample size is large so we can use a z test. $p = 2P(Z < -2.05) = 2 \times 0.0202 = 0.0404$. This is not significant at the 1% level but it is significant at the 5% level. A borderline case. You should decide on the significance level *before* you perform the test.

5. Use a one-sided t test here. p-value is 0.0015 so the result is significant at 1%.

WORK CARD 3 (CONTINUED)

6. As 90 is outside the 90% confidence interval for μ, a test of H_0: $\mu = 90$ is significant (against a two-tailed alternative) at 10%. In a similar way, 85 is within the confidence interval so the test result is not significant – the p-value must be greater than 0.10. If the p-value is greater than 0.10, then it is also greater than 0.05 and the hypothesis will also not be significant at the 5% level.

7. **(i)** H_0: person tells truth. H_1: person lies.

   (ii) P(getting this result) when H_0 is true = P(detector says lying) when person is really telling truth

   $$= \frac{185}{500} = 0.37$$

   As this is greater than 0.05 the result is not significant so there is no reason to reject the null hypothesis.

   (iii) Two types of error can occur. Type I is that the lie-detector says the person is lying when they are really telling the truth and Type II is that the lie-detector says the person is telling the truth when the person is really lying. From **(ii)** P(Type I error) = $p = 0.05$ whereas P(Type II) = 120/500 = 0.24 which is rather high, suggesting that the lie-detector is not that good because there is a high probability of retaining H_0 when H_1 is really true.

8. A two-sided test is required to test the null hypothesis that the mean is 10 against the alternative that the mean is not 10. The mean number of blips for this sample is 9.93. Whilst this is below 10, the p-value is 0.821 so there is no evidence to reject the union's claim.

   Here we need to test Head Office's requirement that the mean is 10.5 against the one-sided alternative that the mean is less than 10.5 (presumably Head Office would be quite happy with a higher mean than 10.5). The p-value for the two-sided test is 0.074 so $p = 0.037$ for the one-sided test, which is significant at the 5% level. We conclude that the sample provides evidence that the target of 10.5 is not being reached.

ASSESSMENT 3

1. An electrical firm manufactures light bulbs that have a lifetime which is normally distributed with variance 1600. A sample of 30 such bulbs has an average life of 788. Test H_0: $\mu = 800$ against H_1: $\mu < 800$. Use a significance level of 0.04.

2. A production process gives components whose strengths are normally distributed with a mean of 40lbs and unknown variance. The process is modified and 12 components are selected at random giving strengths

   39.8   40.3   43.1   39.6   41.0   39.9   42.1   40.7   41.6   42.1   40.8   42.5

   Is there any evidence that the modified process gives stronger components? ($s^2 = 1.316591$ for this sample.)

3. Suppose in question 1 that the alternative hypothesis was H_1: $\mu \neq 800$. How would this affect the p-value? What is the conclusion of the test now?

4. 36 cans from a soft drink dispenser give an average content of 21.9 decilitres and a sample variance $s^2 = 1.42$. Could the manufacturers reasonably assert that the average contents of a can is 22.2 decilitres?

5. Last year the mean retail price of all hardcover books sold by a particular bookshop was $40 with a standard deviation of $15. This year's retail prices for 40 randomly selected sales are (to the nearest dollar):

   21 61 44 25 36 22 72 45 62 20 51 45 48
   48 52 22 51 38 39 26 81 45 51 37 46 42
   29 51 51 43 42 47 43 38 42 29 57 44 61 38

   Has the average price of hardcover books increased?

6. For the book example in question **5** suppose that the variance from last year was not known. Test whether retail prices have increased or not. (Use a computer.)

7. Write down a hypothesis about some aspect of a student's daily life that you would like to test. For instance, that students spend an average of £10 a week on drink, or an average of £20 a week on food, or that a student does 7.5 hours work a day or watches an average of 2 hours of television on a weekday. Write down an appropriate alternative hypothesis. Decide on the significance level you wish to use (5% or 1% is usual).

   Now collect a sample of data to test your null hypothesis. Accost your colleagues in as random a way as possible (so do not stand outside the sports hall and ask people how much sport they do, or outside the bar asking about expenditure on drink!). Ask as many students as is practical (at least 10). Using a computer, or otherwise, test your hypothesis and report your conclusions, stating any necessary assumptions about the distribution of the population.

8. Calculate 95% or 99% confidence limits for the population value you tested in question **7**. If you used a two-tailed test, describe how this interval relates to your test. If not, how would this interval relate to a two-sided version of your test?

9. Use a computer to generate 100 or more samples of size 10 from a normal distribution with mean 2 and variance 4. Pretend that you have been given these data and so you do not know the population variance or mean, although you may assume that the population is normal. For each sample test $H_0: \mu = 2$. On average, what proportion of samples would you expect to reject the null hypothesis? How many of your samples lead you to reject H_0?

4 **Rejection regions: another approach to testing**

There is an alternative to calculating the *p*-value of a test, which is called the *rejection region* or *critical region* method. As it is an alternative method, you could omit this section, but we include it as testing is often taught in this way.

The rejection region
When we do a statistical test, we use the sample to calculate the test statistic. This may be a *z* test or a *t* test as discussed in Section 3 or, when the situation is binomial, the number of successes in the sample. Some values of the test statistic will result in the null hypothesis being retained (because they give a *p*-value that is greater than the significance level) but the remainder will result in rejection of the null hypothesis.

The set of values of the test statistic that lead to rejection of the null hypothesis is called the *rejection region*.

Tests for the mean using rejection regions
Suppose we are testing $H_0: \mu = \mu_0$ against $H_1: \mu > \mu_0$ and that the population variance is known. Suppose also, that the significance level is α.

The test statistic is

$$z = \frac{\bar{x} - \mu_0}{\sqrt{\sigma^2/n}}$$

The *p*-value is $p = P(Z > z)$ which is the area in the right-hand tail of the standard normal distribution. We reject H_0 when the *p*-value is less than α. So all values of *z* that cut off an area less than α in the tail of the normal distribution are in the rejection region as shown in Figure 2.5.

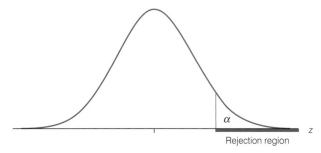

Figure 2.5

We previously used the notation z_α for the value such that $P(Z > z_\alpha) = \alpha$ so we conclude that when the alternative hypothesis is $H_1: \mu > \mu_0$, the rejection region is $z > z_\alpha$.

We illustrate by repeating the shoe machinist example, from Section 3.

> Check this
>
> Each machinist in a shoe factory must produce a mean of 50 or fewer defective parts each day. It is known that the variance of the number of defectives produced by a machinist in

a day is 4. On a randomly chosen day the 35 machinists produced an average of 51 defective parts.

Is this evidence that the machinists are producing too many defective parts on average? Use the rejection region method to test at a significance level of 5%.

Solution:
The null hypothesis is H_0: $\mu = 50$. The alternative is that the number of defectives is *more* than 50, so we have H_1: $\mu > 50$.

As the variance is known the test statistic is

$$z = \frac{\bar{x} - \mu}{\sqrt{\sigma^2/n}}$$

and as the alternative hypothesis includes a > sign the rejection region takes the form $z > z_{0.05}$ as described above. From normal percentage point tables (Table III) $z_{0.05} = 1.6449$ so the rejection region is $z > 1.6449$. That is, if the test statistic z is greater than 1.6449 we should reject the null hypothesis. Here

$$z = \frac{51 - 50}{\sqrt{\dfrac{4}{35}}} = 2.96$$

which is in the rejection region. We conclude that the null hypothesis should be rejected.

Now suppose that on another randomly chosen day the shoe machinists produce 50.5 defective parts. We can test the mean on this day almost instantly because we already know that the rejection region is $z > 1.6449$, and so all we need to do is to see whether or not the test statistic z lies in it. For the new sample

$$z = \frac{50.5 - 50}{\sqrt{\dfrac{4}{35}}} = 1.48$$

This is *not* in the rejection region and so we can retain the null hypothesis H_0: $\mu = 50$.

This is the main advantage of the rejection region method. Once the region is calculated it can be re-used for similar tests so that they can be done with very little extra work. This is especially useful for quality control when samples are taken from a production process at regular intervals.

Check this

After a training course on another randomly chosen day the 35 machinists in the shoe factory produced an average number of 50.2 defectives. Test whether the average number of defectives produced by a machinist in a day is more than 50.

Solution:
We already know that the rejection region is $z > 1.6449$. The test statistic is now

$$z = \frac{50.2 - 50}{\sqrt{\dfrac{4}{35}}} = 0.59$$

which is smaller than 1.6449 so we can retain the null hypothesis.

By similar reasoning, when the alternative hypothesis is $H_1: \mu <$ 'something', small values of z will lead us to reject the null hypothesis and so the rejection region takes the form $Z < -z_\alpha$.

Check this

We return to the car fuel consumption example again. Recall that the advertiser's claim was that the mean consumption is 12 whereas the consumer group suspect that it is smaller. The population is normally distributed with variance 1. A sample of 5 cars is taken that gives a mean of 11.6.

(i) What is the rejection region? Use a 5% significance level.

(ii) Use the rejection region to test the advertiser's claim.

Solution:

(i) The null hypothesis is $H_0: \mu = 12$. As the alternative hypothesis is $H_1: \mu < 12$ the rejection region is $z < -z_{0.05}$; that is, $z < -1.6449$.

(ii) The test statistic is

$$z = \frac{11.6 - 12}{\sqrt{\frac{1}{5}}} = -0.89$$

This does not lie in the rejection region so there is no evidence to reject the null hypothesis.

When the alternative hypothesis is two-sided, both large and small values of z lead us to reject the null hypothesis, so the rejection region comprises all values of z in the left- and right-hand tails of the standard normal distribution which have a total area of α, as shown in Figure 2.6.

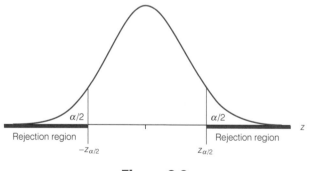

Figure 2.6

The rejection region for a two-sided test is therefore $z > z_{\alpha/2}$ *and* $z < -z_{\alpha/2}$ which can be written more succinctly as $|z| > z_{\alpha/2}$.

Again we use an example that we have done before.

Check this

A production line manufactures packets of potato crisps. When the line is working properly, the packets have an average weight of 30g. When it is not working properly, the mean weight deviates from this. The standard deviation of the weight of a packet is 0.7g. A sample of 50 packets has a mean weight of $\bar{x}$ = 29.83g. Test, at a significance level of 5%, whether the line is working properly or not.

Solution:
Here the null hypothesis is H_0: μ = 30 and the alternative hypothesis is H_1: $\mu \neq 30$ (mean is *not* equal to 30g).

As α = 0.05, and $\alpha/2$ = 0.025 the rejection region is $|z| > z_{0.025}$, which is $|z| > 1.96$. The test statistic is

$$z = \frac{\bar{x} - \mu_0}{\sqrt{\sigma^2/n}} = \frac{29.83 - 30}{\sqrt{\frac{0.7^2}{50}}} = -1.72$$

This does not lie in the rejection region so we retain the null hypothesis. There is no evidence that the machine is not working properly.

Check this

On another occasion the average of a sample of 50 packets of crisps is 30.31. Test whether the line is working correctly or not.

Solution:
We already know that the rejection region is $|z| > 1.96$. For this sample

$$z = \frac{\bar{x} - \mu_0}{\sqrt{\sigma^2/n}} = \frac{30.31 - 30}{\sqrt{\frac{0.7^2}{50}}} = 3.13$$

This is clearly within the rejection region and so we must reject the null hypothesis. There is evidence that the line is not working correctly.

The rejection region method works in just the same way when the population variance is *not* known, except that now the test statistic is

$$t = \frac{\bar{x} - \mu_0}{\sqrt{s^2/n}}$$

and we use the percentage points of the *t* distribution with $n - 1$ d.o.f.

Check this

Managers at a company wish to introduce a flexitime system whereby employees will be required to work 42 hours per week. Union representatives, however, argue that this will increase the amount of hours worked by staff. In a typical week, the hours worked by a sample of 8 randomly chosen staff had an average of 38.875 hours and a sample variance of 24.6964.

Test the union representatives' claim using the rejection region method and a 5% significance level.

Solution:
The null and alternative hypotheses are $H_0: \mu = 42$ and $H_1: \mu < 42$. As the population variance is unknown the test statistic is

$$t = \frac{\bar{x} - \mu_0}{\sqrt{s^2/n}}$$

As the alternative hypothesis is $H_1: \mu < 42$ (i.e. one-sided), the rejection region is $t < -t_{0.05}$. From t tables with 7 degrees of freedom (one less than the sample size), we find that $P(T < 1.895) = 0.95$ (i.e. $t_{0.05} = 1.895$), so the rejection region is $t < -1.895$. The test statistic is

$$t = \frac{38.875 - 42}{\sqrt{\frac{24.6964}{8}}} = -1.78$$

which is not in the rejection region and so there is no evidence to reject the null hypothesis.

A summary of the rejection regions for testing means is given below.

Rejection regions for testing $H_0: \mu = \mu_0$

	Test statistic	
	$z = \dfrac{\bar{x} - \mu}{\sqrt{\sigma^2/n}}$	$t = \dfrac{\bar{x} - \mu}{\sqrt{s^2/n}}$
Alternative hypothesis $H_1: \mu > \mu_0$	$z > z_\alpha$	$t > t_\alpha$
$H_1: \mu < \mu_0$	$z < -z_\alpha$	$t < -t_\alpha$
$H_1: \mu \neq \mu_0$	$|z| > z_{\alpha/2}$	$|t| > t_{\alpha/2}$

The advantages and disadvantages of using rejection regions

The main advantage of the rejection region method is that, once the rejection region has been calculated, it can be applied quickly to similar tests. In particular, the rejection regions for testing the mean take the forms shown in the summary above.

However, in this text, we have concentrated on the p-value approach to testing for the following reasons:

(i)   Computer software outputs a p-value for you.
(ii) The p-value tells you how near the result is to the 'border' between rejecting and retaining H_0, giving an idea of the weight of evidence for H_0, and not merely a retain/reject result.

(iii) We think that the idea is easier as a first approach to testing.
(iv) The rejection region for a test statistic, such as the number of successes in a sample, which has a discrete probability distribution, can be calculated only for a finite number of significance levels, which are not necessarily the usual ones like 0.01 or 0.05.

WORK CARD 4

1. Management claim that bonuses paid to workers in a plant average £1000 with a standard deviation of £100. A random sample of 100 workers gives an average bonus of only £975. Consider a test of the management's claim against an alternative hypothesis of $H_1 : \mu < 1000$. Use a 5% significance level.
   (i) What is the test statistic for this test?
   (ii) Write down the rejection region.
   (iii) Calculate the value of the test statistic. What is the result of the test?

2. The manager of a hotel claims that the average guest bill for a weekend is £400. A local journalist, however, claims that prices have increased and that average bills are greater than £400. A sample of 40 bills gives a mean of £402. Previous records indicate that $\sigma = 20$.
   (i) Write down the null and alternative hypotheses.
   (ii) Write down the rejection region. Use a significance level of 5%.
   (iii) Calculate the test statistic. What is the result of the test?
   (iv) Several months later the journalist takes another sample of bills from the same hotel and finds that the mean is £416. Test again whether the average bill has increased.

3. Recent surveys have said that, on average, British people spend 24 hours a week watching television. A random sample of 84 people gave a mean of 23.5 hours and a sample variance of 5.
   (i) Write down the null and alternative hypotheses which test whether or not British people spend an average of 24 hours a week watching television.
   (ii) What is the test statistic?
   (iii) Write down the rejection region of the test. Use a 5% significance level.
   (iv) Perform the remainder of the test and state your conclusions.

4. A production process produces metal bolts which must have an average weight of 80g. Every 20 minutes a sample of 20 bolts is drawn off the process and its mean and variance calculated. You may assume that the distribution of the weight of a bolt is normal.
   (i) How would you use a sample to test whether or not the average weight of a bolt was 80g at a particular time? Give the rejection region of the test.
   (ii) Suppose the first sample had a mean of 79g and a standard deviation of 4g. Perform your test and give your conclusions.
   (iii) The second, third and fourth samples had means of 79.6g, 82.7g and 78.2g respectively and standard deviations of 3.9g, 5.1g and 2.7g respectively. Test each of these samples and give your conclusions.

Solutions:

1. (i) $z = \dfrac{\bar{x} - \mu}{\sqrt{\sigma^2/n}}$

   (ii) $z < -z_{0.05}$, i.e. $z < -1.6449$.

   (iii) $z = -2.5$ which lies within the rejection region, so there is evidence that the average bonus is less than £1000.

2. (i) $H_0: \mu = 400$, $H_1: \mu > 400$.

   (ii) $z > z_{0.05}$, i.e. $z > 1.6449$.

   (iii) $z = \dfrac{\bar{x} - \mu_0}{\sqrt{\sigma^2/n}} = \dfrac{402 - 400}{\sqrt{\frac{20^2}{40}}} = 0.63$

   This is not within the rejection region so there is no evidence to reject the null hypothesis.

   (iv) Now

   $$z = \dfrac{416 - 400}{\sqrt{\frac{20^2}{40}}} = 5.06$$

   which is clearly in the rejection region so we must reject the null hypothesis. There is evidence that the average bill has increased.

3. (i) $H_0: \mu = 24$, $H_1: \mu \neq 24$.

   (ii) as the sample size is large the test statistic is

   $$z = \dfrac{\bar{x} - \mu_0}{\sqrt{s^2/n}}$$

   (iii) The rejection region is $|z| > z_{0.025}$, i.e. $|z| > 1.96$.

   (iv) $z = \dfrac{\bar{x} - \mu_0}{\sqrt{s^2/n}} = \dfrac{23.5 - 24}{\sqrt{\frac{5}{84}}} = -2.05$

   so $|z| = 2.05$ which exceeds 1.96 so z lies within the rejection region. There is evidence that British people do not watch an average of 24 hours television a week.

4. (i) Test $H_0: \mu = 80$ against $H_1: \mu \neq 80$. σ^2 is unknown and the sample size is small so the test statistic is

   $$t = \dfrac{\bar{x} - 80}{\sqrt{s^2/20}}$$

   The rejection region is $|t| > t_{0.025}$ where $t_{0.025} = 2.093$, i.e. $|t| > 2.093$ (19 d.o.f.).

   (ii) $t = \dfrac{79 - 80}{\sqrt{\frac{4^2}{20}}} = -1.118$

This is not within the rejection region so there is no evidence to suggest that the average weight of a bolt differs from 80g.

(iii) The ts for each of these are:

$$t = \frac{79.6 - 80}{\sqrt{\frac{3.9^2}{20}}} = -0.458, \quad t = \frac{82.7 - 80}{\sqrt{\frac{5.1^2}{20}}} = 2.368 \quad \text{and} \quad t = \frac{78.2 - 80}{\sqrt{\frac{2.7^2}{20}}} = -2.98$$

respectively, so the last two are in the rejection region giving some evidence that the production process is not producing the correct average weight at these times.

1. An electrical firm manufactures light bulbs that have a lifetime that is normally distributed with variance 1600. A sample of 30 such bulbs has an average life of 788. Test $H_0: \mu = 800$ against $H_1: \mu < 800$. Use a significance level of 0.04.

   (i) What is the rejection region?

   (ii) Perform the test.

2. A production process gives components whose strengths are normally distributed with mean 40lb and unknown variance. The process is modified and 12 components are selected at random giving strengths

   39.8   40.3   43.1   39.6   41.0   39.9   42.1   40.7   41.6   42.1   40.8   42.5

   Is there any evidence that the modified process gives stronger components? Use the rejection method. (The sample variance is 1.316591 and the sample mean is 41.125.)

   After further modification of the process, another sample of 12 components had a mean of 39.8 and standard deviation 1.1. Is there any evidence that this modification has produced an average weight that differs from 40lb? Use the rejection region method.

3. Suppose in question **1** that the alternative hypothesis was $H_1: \mu \neq 800$. How would this affect the rejection region? What is the conclusion of the test now?

4. Look at the data you collected for **Assessment 3**, question **7**. Find the rejection region for **(i)** a 5% significance level and **(ii)** a 1% significance level. Write down your null and alternative hypotheses again and use the rejection regions to test at the 5% and 1% significance levels. Check that the test results agree with those you obtained in **Assessment 3**.

Further reading: see p. xv

Anderson *et al.* (Statistics) not great for *p* values – it does rejection regions first.

Mendenhall *et al.*

S3
Correlation and regression

Un coup de dés jamais n'abolira le hazard. One throw of the dice will never abolish chance.

Stéphane Mallarmé

Contexts

What is this chapter about?
This chapter presents techniques for assessing the relationship, if any, between two variables and investigating whether some variables can be used to predict another.

Why is it useful?
The techniques of correlation and regression enable patterns or relationships in the data to be used as an aid to decision making. For instance, they might be used to investigate whether spending more on advertising increases sales revenue, whether age, mileage or engine size are related to the price of a second hand car or which factors affect job satisfaction at a multinational company.

Regression is also a way of investigating trends over time and so will be useful for forecasting in Chapter S4.

Where does it fit in?
The standard approach of Inferential Statistics is to assume that a particular mathematical relationship or *model* holds for the population and then use the sample to estimate it or test hypotheses about it. The linear regression model in this chapter is the simplest and most commonly used statistical model and so provides a useful introduction to this.

What do I need to know?
This chapter uses the concepts of estimation and hypothesis testing from S1 and S2, and of course, like these, requires the material in Essential Maths, Describing Data and Probability.

Objectives

At the end of this chapter you should be able to:

- calculate the sample correlation coefficient r;
- fit a least squares line to some data;
- calculate R^2, the coefficient of determination;
- estimate a simple linear regression using a calculator, test the slope coefficient and interpret the results;
- use a computer for simple linear regression;
- understand the multiple linear regression output generated by a computer.

Sometimes it seems natural to consider two or more random variables together. Some examples are:

- The monthly rate of inflation and the unemployment rate.
- The turnover of a business and its profit during the same period.
- The returns on two ordinary shares that are in the same stock market sector.
- Nationwide sales for three competing products.

We may be interested in whether the variables are related and if so, the nature of the relationship.

In this chapter we will see how a sample of values from two or more continuous random variables can be used to make inferences about the relationship between them.

1 Data that come in pairs

Paired data

We introduced the following data, which give the percentage returns on two shares for 9 consecutive months, in *Describing Data*.

Month	Share 1	Share 2
1	1.4	1.3
2	1.2	1.4
3	2.2	1.4
4	1.5	1.4
5	1.0	1.5
6	1.2	1.2
7	1.8	1.5
8	2.5	1.5
9	2.0	1.5

Here we have a sample of 9 *pairs* of data, (1.4, 1.3), (1.2, 1.4) and so on. The first item in each pair is a value of the random variable, X, the percentage return on Share 1 in a particular month and the second item in each pair is a value of the random variable, Y, which is the percentage return on Share 2 in the same month.

In general it will be helpful to label a sample of n paired values like this (x_1, y_1), (x_2, y_2) ... (x_n, y_n). So here, for example, $x_1 = 1.4$, $y_1 = 1.3$, ..., $x_9 = 2.0$ and $y_9 = 1.5$.

We want to use the sample to investigate the relationship (if any) between X and Y. In this case between the return on Share 1 and the return on Share 2 in a particular month. We start by displaying the data graphically.

Scatter plots

The most effective way to display paired data is to plot each pair as a coordinate point on a graph. This is called a *scatter* plot (see *Describing Data*, Chapter DD1, Section 3). In Figure 1.10 of Chapter DD1 we drew a scatter plot of the share return data and we repeat this in Figure 3.1.

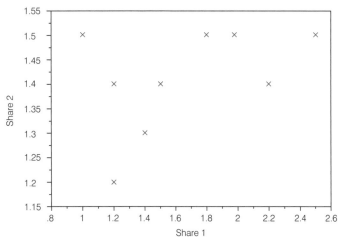

Figure 3.1 Scatter plot of the share return data.

From the plot it appears that when Share 1's return is large or small, Share 2's return is large or small as well.

Check this

The following data gives the total market value of 14 companies (in £million) and the number of stock exchange transactions in that company's shares occurring on a particular day. Draw a scatter plot. What does it suggest about the relationship between the market value of a company and the number of transactions in its shares?

Company	Market value	Number of transactions
1	6.5	380
2	5.2	200
3	0.4	15

Company	Market value	Number of transactions
4	1.7	50
5	1.9	40
6	2.4	40
7	3.2	41
8	4.7	18
9	10.1	210
10	12.5	190
11	13.1	200
12	5.5	55
13	2.5	38
14	1.5	20

Solution:
A scatter plot of the data is given in Figure 3.2.

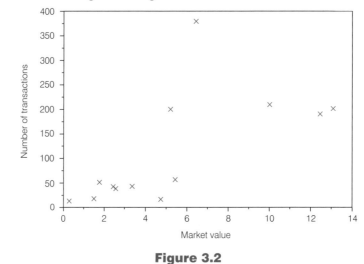

Figure 3.2

It suggests that as market value increases the number of transactions may also increase.

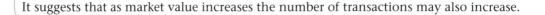

Drawing a scatter plot and assessing it by eye like this is a good first step in investigating the relationship between two random variables. However, it can be quite subjective as it is always possible to choose the scale and range of the axes to emphasise or underplay the strength of the relationship. (We discussed this in *Describing Data*). We therefore need a more objective measure of the strength of the relationship between the x_is and the y_is.

Introducing the sample correlation

The measure that is most widely used to gauge the strength of the relationship between the x_is and y_is is the *sample correlation*, which is usually represented by the symbol r.

The sample correlation is a measure of how closely the points on a scatter plot lie on a straight line. It always lies between +1 and –1 inclusive. If the points lie exactly on a straight line with a positive slope, $r = 1$, whereas if all the points lie exactly on a straight line with a negative slope, $r = -1$. The more the points scatter about the line the closer r is to 0. When $r = 0$ there is no linear relationship between the points although they might form some other pattern.

The graph in Figure 3.3(a) shows data that lies almost on a straight line with a positive slope, so the sample correlation is close to 1 whereas Figure 3.3(b) shows data that lies almost on a straight line with a negative slope so the sample correlation is close to –1 and Figure 3.3(c) shows data that does not have a linear pattern, so the sample correlation is close to 0.

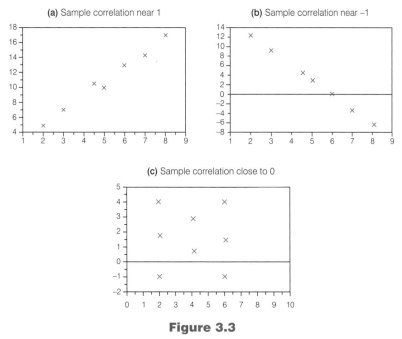

Figure 3.3

Calculating the sample correlation

Remember, the pairs of data points are (x_1, y_1), (x_2, y_2), ..., (x_n, y_n).

The sample correlation is calculated entirely from the sums Σx, Σx^2, Σy, Σy^2 and Σxy. We have used Σx and Σx^2 many times before (they are introduced in *Describing Data*) and Σy and Σy^2 are the corresponding quantities for the y_is; that is,

$$\Sigma y = y_1 + y_2 + \ldots + y_n \quad \text{and} \quad \Sigma y^2 = y_1^2 + y_2^2 + \ldots + y_n^2$$

so the only new quantity is Σxy which means the sum of each x multiplied by each y; that is,

$$\Sigma xy = x_1 y_1 + x_2 y_2 + x_3 y_3 + \ldots + x_n y_n$$

Check the following calculations for the market value and transactions data.

Check this

Calculate Σx, Σx^2, Σy, Σy^2 and Σxy when the x_is are the market values and the y_is are the number of stock exchange transactions.

Solutions:

$\Sigma x = 6.5 + 5.2 + \ldots + 1.5 = 71.2$

$\Sigma x^2 = 6.5^2 + 5.2^2 + \ldots + 1.5^2 = 582.66$

$\Sigma y = 380 + 200 + \ldots + 20 = 1497$

$\Sigma y^2 = 380^2 + 200^2 + \ldots + 20^2 = 317{,}399$

$\Sigma xy = (6.5 \times 380) + (5.2 \times 200) + \ldots + (1.5 \times 20) = 11{,}532.3$

To calculate the sample correlation we will use some intermediate quantities which will also be useful when we consider the least squares line in the next section. These are defined as

$$s_{xx} = \Sigma x^2 - \frac{(\Sigma x)^2}{n}, \quad s_{yy} = \Sigma y^2 - \frac{(\Sigma y)^2}{n} \quad \text{and} \quad s_{xy} = \Sigma xy - \frac{\Sigma x \Sigma y}{n}$$

pronounced, 's x x', 's y y' and 's x y'. Notice that s_{xx} is the numerator of the usual expression for the sample variance,

$$s^2 = \frac{\Sigma x^2 - \frac{(\Sigma x)^2}{n}}{n - 1}$$

and s_{yy} is the corresponding expression for the y_is. s_{xy} follows a similar pattern but uses both x and y.

Check this

Calculate s_{xx}, s_{yy} and s_{xy} for the market value and number of transactions data.

Solution:

$$s_{xx} = 582.66 - \frac{71.2^2}{14} = 220.5571$$

$$s_{yy} = 317{,}399 - \frac{1497^2}{14} = 157{,}326.9286$$

and

$$s_{xy} = 11{,}532.3 - \frac{71.2 \times 1497}{14} = 3918.9857$$

The sample correlation is

$$r = \frac{S_{xy}}{\sqrt{S_{xx}S_{yy}}}$$

where the positive square root is always taken in the denominator.

Check this

Calculate the sample correlation between the market value and the number of stock exchange transactions.

Solution:

$$r = \frac{3918.9857}{\sqrt{220.5571 \times 157{,}326.9286}} = 0.6653$$

So the sample correlation between the market value of a company and the number of transactions in its shares is 0.6653. We interpret this as follows.

(i)   It is not close to 0 so there is evidence of a linear relationship between the two variables.

(ii) It is positive so the 'slope' of the straight line is positive, that is, as market value increases so does the number of transactions.

(iii) It is not close to 1 or –1 and so the relationship is not a really strong one.

Check this

The following data shows the age in years, x, and the second-hand price ($\$100$), y, of a sample of 11 cars advertised in a local paper. What is the sample correlation between the age and the price?

You may make use of the fact that $\Sigma x = 58$, $\Sigma x^2 = 326$, $\Sigma xy = 3736$, $\Sigma y = 761$ and $\Sigma y^2 = 56785$.

x Age of car (years)	y Price ($100)
5	80
7	57
6	58
6	55
5	70
4	88
7	43
6	60
5	69
5	63
2	118

Solution:

$$S_{xx} = 326 - \frac{58^2}{11} = 20.1818$$

$$S_{yy} = 56{,}785 - \frac{761^2}{11} = 4137.6364$$

$$S_{xy} = 3736 - \frac{58 \times 761}{11} = -276.5455$$

So

$$r = \frac{-276.5455}{\sqrt{20.1818 \times 4137.6364}} = -0.9570$$

The sample correlation is very close to –1, indicating that there is a very strong linear relationship between the age of a car and its price. The minus sign indicates that as age increases, price decreases – which is what we would expect for second-hand cars.

To illustrate our earlier statement that the sample correlation is very much a measure of the *linear* relationship between the x_is and y_is and not just a measure of *any* relationship, consider the following (artificial) data.

x	y
4	29.00
3.2	26.76
7.1	25.59
3	26.00
8	21.00
10.2	2.96
4	29.00
3	26.00
1.6	18.44
2.3	22.71

These lie exactly on the quadratic curve $y = 10x - x^2 + 5$ and are shown on the scatter plot in Figure 3.4.

The sample correlation between the x_is and the y_is is –0.614531. (You could check this as an exercise.) So, although there is an exact relationship between the x_is, and the y_is, the sample correlation is not 1 or –1, or even near, because the sample correlation measures the strength of the *linear* relationship and not of *any* relationship.

Sample correlation using software

Most statistical software can calculate the sample correlation. Usually the x_is are entered in one column of the worksheet and the y_is in another and a single command produces the sample correlation.

The SPSS command is

Analyze > Correlate > Bivariate

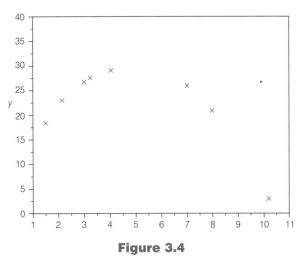

Figure 3.4

Alternatively, the CORREL() function in Excel can be used.

The sample correlation is

$$r = \frac{s_{xy}}{\sqrt{s_{xx} s_{yy}}}$$

where

$$s_{xx} = \Sigma x^2 - \frac{(\Sigma x)^2}{n}, \quad s_{yy} = \Sigma y^2 - \frac{(\Sigma y)^2}{n}$$

and

$$s_{xy} = \Sigma xy - \frac{\Sigma x \Sigma y}{n}$$

WORK CARD 1

1. For which of the following samples would a scatter plot be appropriate? Explain why or why not.

   (i) The ages of a class of students taking a French degree, and the ages of some of their contemporaries in a class of Business students.

   (ii) Demand for a supermarket chain's own brand of baked beans and the price of a can of these baked beans for 30 consecutive working days.

   (iii) The number of hours of work done in preparation for an exam by each student in a class of 30 Business students and the results of the exam for this class of students.

2. Calculate the sample correlation for the following samples without using a computer and comment.

Data A		Data B		Data C	
x	y	x	y	x	y
1	5	1	5	1	1
2	7	2	0	1	3
3	9	3	5	−1	1
4	11	4	0	−1	3

3. A company wishes to investigate whether the amount it spends on advertising prior to the launch of a new product is related to the sales volume of the product in the first month. Data from the last 8 product launches is shown below.

Product number	Advertising ($10,000)	Sales (1000 units)
1	50	157
2	25	152
3	21	69
4	65	218
5	30	134
6	40	173
7	25	81
8	40	113

Plot the data in a suitable manner and calculate the sample correlation. Comment briefly on the strength of the relationship. Confirm the sample correlation using computer software.

Solutions:

1. (i)   The data are two samples from two different groups of students, so they do not come in pairs and a scatter plot is inappropriate.

    (ii) The sample comprises the price and the demand for these baked beans on each of the 30 days so the data are paired and a scatter plot is useful.

    (iii) Yes, the data are paired so a scatter plot is useful. Each point will represent a student.

2. Data A. $\Sigma x = 10$, $\Sigma x^2 = 30$, $\Sigma y = 32$, $\Sigma y^2 = 276$, $\Sigma xy = 90$ so $s_{xx} = 5$, $s_{yy} = 20$ and $s_{xy} = 10$ and $r = 1$. There is a perfect linear relationship (with positive slope) between the x_is and the y_is. (You may have spotted this just by looking at the data and noticing that $y = 2x + 3$.)

Data B. $\Sigma x = 10$, $\Sigma x^2 = 30$, $\Sigma y = 10$, $\Sigma y^2 = 50$, $\Sigma xy = 20$ so $s_{xx} = 5$, $s_{yy} = 25$, $s_{xy} = -5$ and $r = -0.4472$. A not very strong negative correlation is indicated.

Data C. $\Sigma x = 0$, $\Sigma x^2 = 4$, $\Sigma y = 8$, $\Sigma y^2 = 20$, $\Sigma xy = 0$. $s_{xy} = 0$ so there is no need to calculate s_{xx} and s_{yy} as

$$r = \frac{s_{xy}}{\sqrt{s_{xx}s_{yy}}} = 0$$

These data have a sample correlation of 0.

3. A scatter plot of advertising (x) and sales (y) shows that the number of items sold tends to increase with the amount spent on advertising. $\Sigma x = 296$, $\Sigma y = 1097$, $\Sigma x^2 = 12,516$, $\Sigma y^2 = 167,253$ and $\Sigma xy = 44,754$, so $s_{xx} = 1564$, $s_{yy} = 16,826.875$ and $s_{xy} = 4165$. This gives

$$r = \frac{4165}{\sqrt{1564 \times 16,826.875}} = 0.8119$$

SPSS gives a sample correlation of 0.812.

1. The income in £100,000 (y) and number of patients in 100 (x) is recorded for a sample of 10 doctor's surgeries. Find the sample correlation given that $\Sigma x = 518$, $\Sigma y = 51$, $\Sigma x^2 = 27,100$, $\Sigma y^2 = 280.1$, $\Sigma xy = 2665$ and comment.

2. The following data gives (y) the number of months it took a sample of 10 school leavers to find employment and (x) the number of GCSE exam passes they each had. Calculate the sample correlation and comment.

Exam passes	Months
3	10
0	12
4	4
2	7
7	12
5	4
2	10
4	4

3. Would you expect the correlation of a sample of the following random variables to be close to –1, 1 or 0, positive or negative? Explain your answers.
   (i) The index of retail prices in the UK and a major UK stock market index at the end of a month.
   (ii) The age of the man and the age of a woman in a married couple.

(iii) The hours of study a student does for an exam and his/her exam result.

(iv) A person's income and the amount they spend on holidays.

(v) An accountancy graduate's degree result (as a percentage) and their starting salary in the accountancy profession.

(vi) The number of trains that arrive less than 5 minutes late at a major London station during a day and the number of passenger complaints at the station regarding travel that day.

4. Take a sample of at least 8 student couples. Ask each person their age in months and then plot the data in a suitable manner. Calculate the sample correlation between the age of the men and the age of the women. Is this what you would expect? Explain.

2 Fitting a straight line to the data

Whilst the sample correlation gives us a measure of the *strength* of the linear relationship between the x_is and the y_is we will now find the equation of the straight line that is most appropriate for the data.

The least squares line

One way of finding a straight line for the data would be to sketch one on a scatter plot by eye. We have done this for the market value and transactions data in Figure 3.5. Do you agree with the position of the line?

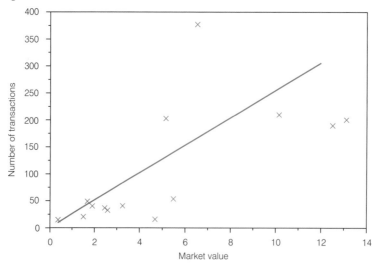

Figure 3.5

The position of a line drawn in this way depends very much on the drawer and so we really need a more objective way of finding the best straight line.

The most usual method of *fitting* a straight line to a set of data is called the *method of least squares*. Least squares looks at the *vertical* deviations of the points on the scatter plot from a line, shown by the dotted lines in Figure 3.6.

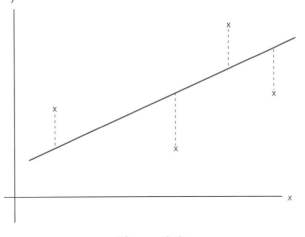

Figure 3.6

We will call these vertical deviations the *errors*. There will be n of them, one for each pair of data, which we will call $e_1, e_2, ..., e_n$. A 'good' line will have small errors and so one measure of the 'goodness' of a particular line is to calculate the sum of the *squared* values of the errors; that is

$$e_1^2 + e_2^2 + ... + e_n^2$$

The method of least squares gives us the straight line for which this quantity is smallest. If this straight line is $y = a + bx$, the formulae for a and b are

$$b = \frac{s_{xy}}{s_{xx}} \quad \text{and} \quad a = \frac{\Sigma y - b\Sigma x}{n}$$

where s_{xy} and s_{xx} are defined as earlier; that is,

$$s_{xx} = \Sigma x^2 - \frac{(\Sigma x)^2}{n}$$

and

$$s_{xy} = \Sigma xy - \frac{\Sigma x \Sigma y}{n}$$

These values of a and b are called the *least squares estimates* and the corresponding straight line is called the *least squares line*.

Check this

Calculate the least squares estimates for the market value and transactions data. Recall that there were 14 pairs of data, that $\Sigma x = 71.2$, $\Sigma y = 1497$, $s_{xx} = 220.5571$ and $s_{xy} = 3918.9857$.

Solution:

$$b = \frac{3918.9857}{220.5571} = 17.7686$$

and

$$a = \frac{1497 - 17.7686 \times 71.2}{14} = 16.5625$$

The least squares line is therefore $y = 16.5625 + 17.7686x$ as shown in Figure 3.7.

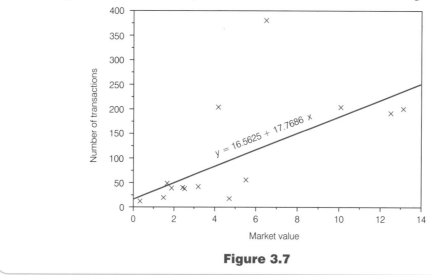

Figure 3.7

Prediction

Once the least squares line has been calculated it can be used to predict the value of y for a particular value of x. For instance, to predict the number of transactions that will occur when the market value is £10 million we merely insert $x = 10$ into the least squares line to give

$$y = 16.5625 + (17.7686 \times 10) = 194.2485$$

and the prediction is that 194.2485 transactions will take place in a day.

We do not expect such predictions to be exact because the sample data did not lie exactly on the least squares line. Also, whilst it is reasonable to assume that the least squares line gives a reasonable prediction for values of x of a similar magnitude to the data in the sample, we can't assume that the straight line 'continues forever'. For instance, it would be unreasonable to use the line above to predict the number of transactions for a company whose value is say, £100 million; that is, when $x = 100$.

Independent and dependent variables

When fitting the least squares line, the roles of the xs and the ys are *not* the same. This is because the criterion is to minimise the sum of the squared *vertical* deviations of the points from the line. (Had we attempted to minimise the sum of the squares of the *horizontal* deviations, the resulting straight line $x = a + by$ would *not* usually be equivalent.) In doing so we hope to find the best line to predict the value of y for a value of x. The Y random variable is often called the *dependent* (or response) variable and the X random variable the *independent* (or predictor or explanatory) variable.

Check this

The following data gives the annual sales figures (in \$10,000) of a successful company for the first 10 years since foundation.

Sales	Year
22	1
34	2
88	3
200	4
300	5
370	6
440	7
680	8
1000	9
1000	10
1100	11

Fit the least squares line that predicts sales from year. Use the line to predict sales for the years 12 and 13.

Solution:

Here the dependent variable is sales which we hope to explain using the independent variable year.

$\Sigma x = 66$, $\Sigma y = 5234$, $\Sigma x^2 = 506$, $\Sigma y^2 = 4{,}142{,}284$, $\Sigma xy = 44{,}494$. So $s_{xx} = 110$, $s_{yy} = 1{,}651{,}851.64$ and $s_{xy} = 13{,}090$, giving $b = 119$ exactly and $a = -238.1818$.

The predictions for years 12 and 13 are:

$y = -238.1818 + 119 \times 12 = 1189.82$ and $y = -238.1818 + 119 \times 13 = 1308.82$ respectively.

How good is the least squares line?

Whilst we know that the least squares line is the best straight line for the sample (in the sense that it is the line that gives the smallest sum of the squared errors) it may be that a straight line is wholly inappropriate for the data. We now introduce a measure called the *coefficient of determination* or just R^2, which indicates how suitable the least squares line is for the data.

Consider a scatter plot of points (x_1, y_1) and so on. For now, consider just the y_is. The sample variance of the y_is is

$$\frac{\Sigma(y - \bar{y})^2}{n - 1} = \frac{\Sigma y^2 - \frac{(\Sigma y)^2}{n}}{n - 1}$$

Notice that the numerator of this is

$$S_{yy} = \Sigma y^2 - \frac{(\Sigma y)^2}{n}$$

which is the total of the squared deviations of the y_is from their mean. We will call this numerator the *total sum of squares*, and use it as a measure of the total variation in the y_is. That is,

$$\text{Total sum of squares} = S_{yy} = \Sigma y^2 - \frac{(\Sigma y)^2}{n}$$

The total sum of squares can be split into two quantities called the *regression sum of squares* and the *error sum of squares* respectively; that is

$$\text{Total sum of squares} = \text{Regression sum of squares} + \text{Error sum of squares}$$

We have already met the *error sum of squares*. It is the sum of the squared vertical distances of the points on a scatter plot from the least squares line,

$$\text{Error sum of squares} = \Sigma e_i^2$$

and as such it is that part of the variation in the y_is that the least squares line does *not* explain.

The *regression sum of squares* is slightly less straightforward, but it represents that part of the variation in the y_is that the least squares line *does* explain or account for. We will explain it intuitively as follows.

Consider a single point (x_i, y_i). As shown in Figure 3.8 the height of the point y_i can be split into the part explained by the line, shown as 'height of line', and the remainder, which is the error, e_i, that we met before.

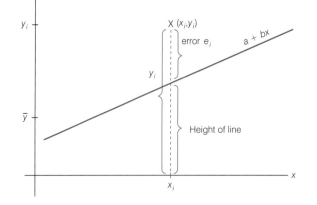

Figure 3.8

The *regression sum of squares* is an analogous quantity to the total sum of squares, but calculated for the explained part of the y_is; that is,

Regression sum of squares $= \Sigma(\text{Height of line} - \bar{y})^2$

As such it is a measure of the variation in the heights of the line.

When the least squares line is appropriate for the data, the errors will be small and the heights of the line large compared with the total sum of squares, and when it is *in*appropriate the errors will be larger and the heights of the line smaller. A sensible measure of the 'goodness' of the least squares line, called the *coefficient of determination* or R^2, is therefore

$$R^2 = \frac{\text{Regression sum of squares}}{\text{Total sum of squares}}$$

which is the proportion of the total sum of squares which is explained by the least squares line. As R^2 is a proportion it must lie between 0 and 1 and so it is often reported as a percentage. The nearer R^2 is to 1, the more closely the data lie to the least squares line whereas the smaller the value of R^2 the more widely the data are scattered around the line. An R^2 close to 1 indicates that the data almost lie on the least squares line, whereas a value close to 0 tells us that a straight line is not very useful for this data.

Calculating R^2

To calculate R^2 we need the regression sum of squares and the total sum of squares. We already know that

Total sum of squares $= s_{yy}$

and it can be shown mathematically that a formula for the regression sum of squares is

$$\text{Regression sum of squares} = \frac{s_{xy}^2}{s_{xx}}$$

So, as

$$R^2 = \frac{\text{Regression sum of squares}}{\text{Total sum of squares}}$$

it follows that

$$R^2 = \frac{s_{xy}^2}{s_{xx}s_{yy}}$$

Check this

Calculate the coefficient of determination, R^2, for the sales data. Recall that $s_{xx} = 110$, $s_{yy} = 1{,}651{,}851.64$ and $s_{xy} = 13{,}090$.

Solution:

$$R^2 = \frac{s_{xy}^2}{s_{xx}s_{yy}} = \frac{13{,}090^2}{110 \times 1{,}651{,}851.64} = 0.9430$$

This tells us that 0.9430 or 94.3% of the squared deviations of the y_is from the mean are accounted for by the least squares line. This is a very high proportion suggesting a very strong linear relationship between sales and year.

Calculating the error sum of squares
As

$$\text{Total sum of squares} = \text{Regression sum of squares} + \text{Error sum of squares}$$

and we have expressions for the total sum of squares and the regression sum of squares we can obtain the error sum of squares by subtraction; that is

$$\text{Error sum of squares} = s_{yy} - \frac{s_{xy}^2}{s_{xx}}$$

This will be useful later.

R^2 and the sample correlation
The very astute amongst you may have noticed that whereas

$$R^2 = \frac{s_{xy}^2}{s_{xx}s_{yy}}$$

the sample correlation between the x_is and the y_is is

$$r = \frac{s_{xy}}{\sqrt{s_{xx}s_{yy}}}$$

Yes, the sample correlation, r, is the square root of R^2. It takes a + or − sign depending on the sign of s_{xy}.

Check this

Calculate the error sum of squares and R^2 for the market value and transactions data. Recall that $s_{xx} = 220.5571$, $s_{yy} = 157{,}326.9286$ and $s_{xy} = 3918.9857$.

Solution:
The error sum of squares is

$$s_{yy} - \frac{s_{xy}^2}{s_{xx}} = 157{,}326.9286 - \frac{3918.9857^2}{220.5571} = 87{,}692.13$$

$$R^2 = \frac{s_{xy}^2}{s_{xx}s_{yy}} = \frac{3918.9857^2}{220.5571 \times 157{,}326.9286} = 0.4426$$

Least squares using a computer
Virtually all general-purpose statistical software will fit a least squares line to some data, and give the error, regression and total sums of squares and the R^2 value. However, it may also produce other output that you will not yet understand.

The SPSS command is

Analyze > Regression > Linear

The resulting dialog box will ask you to select the name of the column containing the Dependent variable (y) and the Independent variable (x). SPSS produced the following output. At present you will only understand the bold parts of the output.

Variables Entered/Removed (b)

Model	Variables Entered	Variables Removed	Method
1	MARKET (a)		Enter

a All requested variables entered
b Dependent Variable: TRANSACT

Model Summary

Model	R	R Square	Adjusted R Square	Std. Error of the Estimate
1	.665(a)	.443	.396	85.485

a Predictors: (Constant), MARKET

ANOVA (b)

Model		Sum of Squares	df	Mean Square	F	Sig.
1	Regression	69634.784	1	69634.784	9.529	.009 (a)
	Residual	87692.144	12	7307.679		
	Total	157326.929	13			

a Predictors: (Constant), MARKET
b Dependent Variable: TRANSACT

Coefficients (a)

Model		Unstandardized Coefficients		Standardized Coefficients	t	Sig.
		B	Std. Error	Beta		
1	(Constant)	16.563	37.134		.446	.664
	MARKET	17.769	5.756	.665	3.087	.009

a Dependent Variable: TRANSACT

The **regression** data analysis tool in Excel produces output in a slightly different, but broadly similar, form to SPSS.

A summary

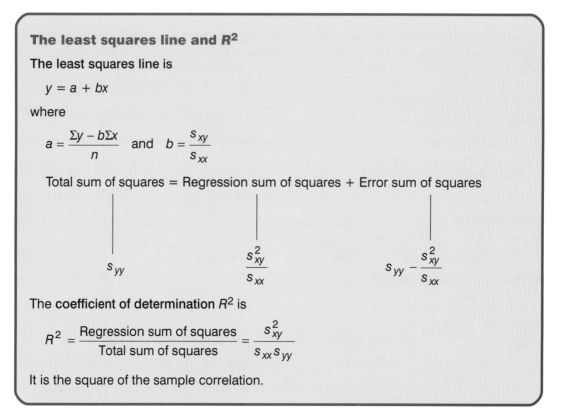

The least squares line and R^2

The least squares line is

$$y = a + bx$$

where

$$a = \frac{\Sigma y - b\Sigma x}{n} \quad \text{and} \quad b = \frac{S_{xy}}{S_{xx}}$$

Total sum of squares = Regression sum of squares + Error sum of squares

$$S_{yy} \qquad \frac{S_{xy}^2}{S_{xx}} \qquad S_{yy} - \frac{S_{xy}^2}{S_{xx}}$$

The **coefficient of determination** R^2 is

$$R^2 = \frac{\text{Regression sum of squares}}{\text{Total sum of squares}} = \frac{S_{xy}^2}{S_{xx}S_{yy}}$$

It is the square of the sample correlation.

WORK CARD 2

1. We repeat the data giving the age and price of a sample of second-hand cars advertised in a local paper.

x Age of car (years)	y Price ($100)
5	80
7	57
6	58
6	55
5	70
4	88
7	43
6	60
5	69
5	63
2	118

(i) Fit a straight line that expresses price in terms of the age of the car. We have already calculated $\Sigma xy = 3736$, $\Sigma x^2 = 326$, $\Sigma x = 58$, $\Sigma y^2 = 56{,}785$, $\Sigma y = 761$ and $s_{xx} = 20.1818$, $s_{yy} = 4137.6364$ and $s_{xy} = -276.5455$.

Is the line what you would expect?

(ii) Use the least squares line to predict the price of a 3-year-old and a 4-year-old car.

(iii) What does the slope of the line represent in terms of the price of a secondhand cars?

2. Calculate the error sum of squares and the coefficient of determination, R^2, for the data in question **1**. How does R^2 relate to the sample correlation $r = -0.9570$ calculated earlier?

3. The data giving the amount spent on advertising and the sales volume in the first month of 8 new products are repeated below from **Work card 1**, question **3**.

Product number	x Advertising ($10,000)	y Sales (1000 units)
1	50	157
2	25	152
3	21	69
4	65	218
5	30	134
6	40	173
7	25	81
8	40	113

We have already calculated the following quantities for this data, $\Sigma x = 296$, $\Sigma y = 1097$, $\Sigma x^2 = 12{,}516$, $\Sigma y^2 = 167{,}253$ and $\Sigma xy = 44{,}754$, $s_{xx} = 1564$, $s_{yy} = 16{,}826.875$ and $s_{xy} = 4165$.

Fit the least squares line that expresses sales in terms of advertising.

Predict the level of sales when $350,000 is spent on advertising.

4. Calculate the error sum of squares and the coefficient of determination for the data in question **3**.

5. Check your answers to questions **1–4** using statistical software. If your answers differ slightly from the computer's how do you explain this?

Solution:

1. (i) $b = \dfrac{s_{xy}}{s_{xx}} = -13.7027$ and $a = \dfrac{\Sigma y - b\Sigma x}{n} = 141.4324$

WORK CARD 2 (CONTINUED)

so the least squares line is $y = 141.4324 - 13.7027x$.

(ii) When $x = 3$, $y = 141.4324 - 13.7027 \times 3 = 100.32$ and when $x = 4y = 141.4324 - 13.7027 \times 4 = 86.62$.

(iii) For each additional year the prediction decreases by another 13.7027 so 13.7027 represents the estimated annual depreciation of a car.

2. The sum of squared errors

$$= s_{yy} - \frac{s_{xy}^2}{s_{xx}} = 4137.6364 - \frac{(-276.5455)^2}{20.1818} = 348.2116$$

$$R^2 = \frac{(-276.5455)^2}{20.1818 \times 4137.6364} = 0.9158 \text{ which is the square of } -0.9570.$$

3. $b = \dfrac{4165}{1564} = 2.6630$ and $a = \dfrac{1097 - 2.6630 \times 296}{8} = 38.5940$

Your results may differ slightly depending on the number of decimal places to which you rounded b. When $x = 35$, $y = 38.5940 + (2.6630 \times 35) = 131.799$.

4. Continuing from question 3, the error sum of squares is

$$s_{yy} - \frac{s_{xy}^2}{s_{xx}} = 16{,}826.875 - \frac{4165^2}{1564} = 5735.2989$$

$$R^2 = \frac{4165^2}{(1564 \times 16{,}826.875)} = 0.6592$$

5. You will get slightly different results depending on the number of places to which you rounded when you used your calculator.

1. The following data gives the total number of visitor days and lift capacity (skiers per hour) for 10 ski resorts during a period of normal snow conditions.

Resort	Lift capacity	Total visitor days
1	2,200	19,929
2	1,000	5,839
3	3,250	23,696
4	1,475	9,881
5	3,800	29,670
6	1,200	7,241
7	1,900	11,634
8	5,575	43,000

Resort	Lift capacity	Total visitor days
9	4,200	36,476
10	1,850	13,100

Fit a straight line to this data. Predict the number of visitor days when lift capacity is 3000.

Calculate R^2 and use this to obtain the sample correlation between the xs and the ys.

2. Using a calculator only, fit a least squares line to predict the age of the male given the age of the female from the boyfriend/girlfriend data you collected in **Assessment 1**, question **4**. If it is reasonable, use the line to predict the age of the male partner of **(i)** a girl aged 20 and **(ii)** a woman of 30.

Calculate the coefficient of determination. How does this relate to the sample correlation calculated earlier?

Confirm your results using a computer.

3 **The linear regression model**

A model for the relationship between X and Y

So far in this chapter we have

(i)   calculated the sample correlation as a measure of the strength of the linear relationship between a set of xs and ys.

(ii) found the straight line $y = a + bx$ that best explains the data (the least squares line) and calculated R^2 (the coefficient of determination), which is the proportion of the variation in the y_is explained by the line.

Both the above were calculated for one particular sample of data. For instance, the least squares line calculated for the sample of 14 companies on a particular day, explaining the number of transactions in their shares, y, in terms of their market value, x, was

$$y = 16.5625 + 17.7686x$$

However, we are not usually interested in the relationship between the xs and ys of a particular sample but in the general relationship between the random variables X and Y. For instance, for the market value and transactions data we would like to find a general way of explaining the number of transactions in a company's share in terms of the market value of the company that is valid for any company on any day.

In Statistics we usually investigate relationships between random variables by assuming a model of a particular form and then using a sample to estimate any constants that appear in it. In this section we develop a model, called the linear regression model, which is used to predict the value of Y for a particular value of X.

Introducing the linear regression model

As before we have two random variables X and Y. We will now suppose that the value of X is known and is x. The most straightforward model that might be used to predict Y is the linear equation

$$Y = \alpha + \beta x$$

where α and β (alpha and beta) are constants. However, as Y is a random variable it is unreasonable to suppose that this linear relationship holds exactly so we will extend the model so that this equation merely gives the *average value* of Y when $X = x$ and that the actual value of Y deviates from this by a random amount that has zero mean; that is,

$$Y = \alpha + \beta x + \text{random}$$

It is usual to represent the random amount using the symbol ε (epsilon) and to assume that its variance is σ^2. A complete specification of this model, called the *linear regression model*, is therefore

$$Y = \alpha + \beta x + \varepsilon$$

where $E(\varepsilon) = 0$ and $\text{Var}(\varepsilon) = \sigma^2$.

As it includes a random term it is a probabilistic or statistical model. The unknown constants in a probabilistic model, in this case, α, β and σ^2, are called the *parameters* of the model. We are going to assume that the linear regression model above holds for X and Y and then draw a sample of pairs of values of X and Y to *estimate* the parameters α, β and σ^2.

Estimating the model

It has been shown mathematically that the least squares estimators a and b are 'good' estimators of α and β so we will use these.

The only remaining parameter is σ^2, the variance of the random term. Again, mathematics can show that a 'good' estimate of this is given by

$$s^2 = \frac{\text{the error sum of squares}}{n - 2}$$

where, as usual, n is the number of pairs of data in the sample. So we have:

The **linear regression model** is

$$Y = \alpha + \beta x + \varepsilon \text{ where } E(\varepsilon) = 0 \text{ and } \text{Var}(\varepsilon) = \sigma^2$$

α and β are estimated by

$$a = \frac{\Sigma y - b\Sigma x}{n} \quad \text{and} \quad b = \frac{S_{xy}}{S_{xx}}$$

σ^2 is estimated by

$$s^2 = \frac{\text{the error sum of squares}}{n-2} = \frac{S_{yy} - \frac{S_{xy}^2}{S_{xx}}}{n-2}$$

There is often confusion between α, β and σ^2 and a, b and s^2. α, β, σ^2 are the constants or parameters of the model and as such we will never know their real values, whereas a, b and s^2 are calculated from the sample and are estimates. As a, b, and s^2 vary from sample to sample they are random variables. The situation is the same as $\bar{x}$ being an estimate of μ or the sample variance being an estimate of the population variance (also, confusingly, written σ^2 and s^2).

Check this

Estimate all the parameters of the linear regression model of the number of transactions on market value. Recall that there were 14 pairs of data and that the following quantities were calculated earlier: $s_{xx} = 220.5571$, $s_{yy} = 157{,}326.9286$, $s_{xy} = 3918.9857$, $\Sigma x = 71.2$, $\Sigma y = 1497$.

Solution:
The estimates of α and β are the least squares estimates calculated in Section 2:

$$b = \frac{3918.9857}{220.5571} = 17.7686 \quad \text{and} \quad a = \frac{1497 - (17.7686 \times 71.2)}{14} = 16.5625$$

so the estimated linear regression (= the least squares line) is $y = 16.5625 + 17.7686x$.
The estimate of σ^2 is

$$s^2 = \frac{s_{yy} - \frac{s_{xy}^2}{s_{xx}}}{n-2} = \frac{157{,}326.9286 - \frac{3918.9857^2}{220.5571}}{12} = \frac{87{,}692.1315}{12} = 7307.6776$$

Check this

We continue the analysis of the company sales data. Recall that data on company sales is available for a period of 11 consecutive years. Fit a linear regression model

$$Y = \alpha + \beta x + \varepsilon$$

to this data. Estimate $\sigma^2 = \text{Var}(\varepsilon)$.
We have already calculated the following: $\Sigma x = 66$, $\Sigma y = 5234$, $\Sigma x^2 = 506$, $\Sigma y^2 = 4{,}142{,}284$, $\Sigma xy = 44{,}494$. So $s_{xx} = 110$, $s_{yy} = 1{,}651{,}851.64$ and $s_{xy} = 13{,}090$, giving the least squares line $y = -238.1818 + 119x$.

Solution:
The estimated linear regression of sales on year is $Y = -238.1818 + 119x$, and the estimated variance of ε is

$$s^2 = \frac{1{,}651{,}851.64 - \frac{13{,}090^2}{110}}{9} = \frac{94{,}141.64}{9} = 10{,}460.1822$$

Interpretation and prediction

The linear regression model says that the average value of Y, when $X = x$, is $\alpha + \beta x$. It is therefore natural to use the least squares line $a + bx$ to predict the value of Y for a particular value of X.

Notice that when $X = x_0$ the average value of Y is

$$\alpha + \beta x_0$$

whereas when $X = x_0 + 1$ the average value of Y is

$$\alpha + \beta(x_0 + 1) = \alpha + \beta x_0 + \beta$$

So when X increases by 1, from x_0 to $x_0 + 1$, the average value of Y increases by β. (A negative value of β results in a decrease in the average value of Y.) β can therefore be interpreted as *the average change in Y for a unit increase in X*. The least squares estimate, b, is therefore an estimate of the average change in Y for a unit increase in X.

Check this

The estimated linear regression that expresses company sales, Y, in terms of the year, X, is $Y = -238.1818 + 119x$.
   Predict company sales in year 15 and estimate the average annual increase in sales.

Solution:
Predicted company sales are $-238.1818 + (119 \times 15) = 1546.82$.
   The model parameter β is the average increase in sales when year increases by 1. This is estimated by $b = 119$, so an estimate of the annual increase in sales is 119.

But do we really need X?

One of the main objectives of fitting a linear regression model is to predict the value of Y for a particular value of X. But is it worth all the trouble? Perhaps we could predict Y just as well *without* knowing the value of X? The advantage of using the linear regression model, and not just fitting a least squares line to a sample as discussed in Sections 1 and 2, is that we can test such things.

Consider the linear regression model

$$Y = \alpha + \beta x + \varepsilon$$

When $\beta = 0$ the second term on the right will be zero and the model will be

$$Y = \alpha + \varepsilon$$

Y does not depend on the value of X in any way, so X will *not* be useful for predicting Y.
   On the other hand, when $\beta \neq 0$ we have the usual model, so X *is* useful in predicting Y.
   This suggests that a way of finding out whether or not X is useful for predicting Y is to test the null hypothesis H_0: $\beta = 0$ against the alternative hypothesis H_1: $\beta \neq 0$.
   To do this test we will need to completely specify the probability structure of the linear regression model. We have already assumed that the random term in the model, ε, has zero mean and variance σ^2 but now *we make the additional assumption that ε has a normal distribution*, so that $\varepsilon \sim N(0,\sigma^2)$.
   We will describe the test using the four-point structure from Chapter S2.

1. Construct a null hypothesis and an alternative hypothesis. Set the significance level.

    Here we want $H_0: \beta = 0$ and $H_1: \beta \neq 0$ and we will choose a significance level of 0.05.

2. Calculate a value from the sample, called the test statistic.

    The test statistic used for this test is often called the *t ratio* and is

    $$t \text{ ratio} = \frac{b}{\sqrt{\dfrac{s^2}{s_{xx}}}}$$

    (The least squares estimate b, the estimate of σ^2, s^2 and s_{xx} are all calculated from the sample in the usual way). Notice that the t ratio is a scaled version of b, the sample estimate of β. In fact, s^2/s_{xx} is an estimate of the variance of b, so the t ratio is b scaled by its standard deviation.

    Recall that to perform a test we need to know the distribution of the test statistic when H_0 is true. The t ratio is used as a test statistic because it can be shown that when $H_0: \beta = 0$ is true, it comes from a t distribution with $n - 2$ degrees of freedom. (We encountered the t distribution originally in Chapter S1, Section 5. Recall that there are a whole series of t distribution curves, one corresponding to each number of 'degrees of freedom' and that they resemble the standard normal distribution but have fatter tails. We find t probabilities using a table like Table V.)

Check this

Recall that data on company sales (y) is available for a period of 11 consecutive years (x), and the least squares line is $y = -238.1818 + 119x$. Also, $s_{xx} = 110$ and $s^2 = 10{,}460.1822$.

(i)   Write down the fitted linear regression model.

(ii)   Write down the null and alternative hypotheses that can be used to test whether or not year is useful in predicting company sales.

(iii)   Calculate the t ratio that is used to test whether year is useful in predicting company sales.

(iv)   When the null hypothesis is true what distribution does this t ratio come from?

(v)   What additional assumption must be made for the t ratio to come from this distribution?

Solution:

(i)   The fitted linear regression is $Y = 238.1818 + 119x$, where the variance of ε is estimated by $s^2 = 10{,}460.1822$.

(ii)   The null and alternative hypotheses are $H_0: \beta = 0$ and $H_1: \beta \neq 0$.

(iii) $t \text{ ratio} = \dfrac{b}{\sqrt{\dfrac{s^2}{s_{xx}}}} = \dfrac{119}{\sqrt{\dfrac{10{,}460.1822}{110}}} = 12.20$

(iv)   When H_0 is true this comes from a t distribution with $n - 2 = 9$ degrees of freedom.

(v)   We must assume that the random terms of the model ε are normally distributed.

3. We calculate the probability of such an extreme test statistic, *assuming that H_0 is true*.
   As the alternative hypothesis is $H_1: \beta \neq 0$ and the t ratio is a scaled version of b both large and small values of the t ratio will support H_1 so the p-value is the probability of such a large or small t ratio; that is, $p = 2P(T > |\,t\text{ ratio }|)$. (The test is two-sided.)
4. If p is smaller than the significance level such an extreme sample result is unlikely to have occurred when H_0 is true and so we *reject H_0*. We say that the test result is significant. Otherwise we retain H_0 and the test result is *not* significant.
   When testing $H_0: \beta = 0$, a p-value less than the significance level leads us to accept $H_1: \beta \neq 0$ and conclude that we *do* need the X variable in the model; that is, *X is* useful in predicting Y. Otherwise we retain the null hypothesis $H_0: \beta = 0$ and conclude that X is *not* useful in predicting Y.

Check this

We have already calculated t ratio = 12.20 for the company sales data and said that under $H_0: \beta = 0$, this comes from a t distribution with 9 degrees of freedom.

(i)   Does this lead you to retain or accept the null hypothesis $H_0: \beta = 0$ at a significance level of 5%?

(ii)   Is year useful in predicting sales?

Solution:

(i)   The p-value is the probability of such an extreme value from the t distribution; that is, $p = 2P(T > 12.20)$ which is the probability in both tails in Figure 3.9 (not to scale).

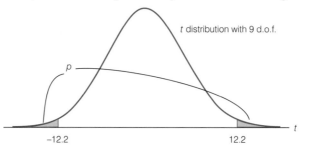

t distribution with 9 d.o.f.

−12.2   12.2

Figure 3.9

From Table V we see that for a t distribution with 9 degrees of freedom $P(T > 4.781) = 0.0005$. This means that the area in the left-hand tail in Figure 3.9 must be less than 0.0005. The total area in both tails must therefore be less than 2×0.0005, so $p < 0.001$. The exact probability is unimportant for testing as we only need to know whether it is above or below the significance level of 0.05.
   As $p < 0.05$ the observed t ratio is unlikely when H_0 is true, we therefore reject $H_0: \beta = 0$ and conclude that *X is* useful in predicting Y.

(ii)   Year is useful in predicting sales.

A summary of this testing procedure follows.

t ratios: Is X useful in predicting Y?

For the regression model $Y = \alpha + \beta x + \varepsilon$ where $\varepsilon \sim N(0, \sigma^2)$ we test

$H_0: \beta = 0$ X is *not* useful in predicting Y

against

$H_1: \beta \neq 0$ X *is* useful in predicting Y

The test statistic is

$$t \text{ ratio} = \frac{b}{\sqrt{\dfrac{s^2}{S_{xx}}}}$$

When H_0 is true this comes from a t distribution with $n - 2$ degrees of freedom.

The *p*-value is

$$p = 2P(T > |\, t \text{ ratio} \,|)$$

Check this

A linear regression model, $Y = \alpha + \beta x + \varepsilon$, was fitted to a sample of 25 supermarket employees in an attempt to explain the number of electronic blips per minute averaged by an employee on the checkout scanner in terms of the number of months they had worked there. The least squares estimates of α and β were $a = 5.2$ and $b = 0.012$.

The t ratio calculated from the sample to test the null hypothesis $H_0: \beta = 0$ against $H_1: \beta \neq 0$ was

$$t \text{ ratio} = \frac{b}{\sqrt{\dfrac{s^2}{S_{xx}}}} = 2.03$$

If the significance level of the test has been set at 5% what do you conclude?

Solution:
When $H_0: \beta = 0$ is true the t ratio comes from a t distribution with $n - 2 = 23$ degrees of freedom. The alternative hypothesis is two-sided so the *p*-value is $p = 2P(T > 2.03)$ where T has 23 d.o.f. Using t tables we see that $t_{0.025} = 2.069$ and $t_{0.05} = 1.714$ so $0.025 < P(T > 2.03) < 0.05$ and $0.05 < p < 0.10$. As $p > 0.05$ the test is not significant and there is no evidence to reject the null hypothesis. We conclude that the number of months of employment is not a useful predictor of electronic scanning speed.

Check this

We fitted a linear regression $Y = 16.5625 + 17.7686x$ to the market value and transactions data. Test whether the number of transactions in a company's shares can be predicted by the market value of the company.

The following quantities have already been calculated, $s_{xx} = 220.5571$, $s_{yy} = 157{,}326.9286$, $s_{xy} = 3918.9857$, and $s^2 = 7307.6776$ and there were 14 pairs of data.

Solution:
We need to test $H_0: \beta = 0$ against $H_1: \beta \neq 0$. The t ratio is

$$t \text{ ratio} = \frac{b}{\sqrt{\dfrac{s^2}{s_{xx}}}} = \frac{17.7686}{\sqrt{\dfrac{7307.6776}{220.5571}}} = 3.09$$

$p = 2P(T > 3.09)$ where T has 12 degrees of freedom. From Table V, $t_{0.005} = 3.055$ and $t_{0.0005} = 4.318$ so the p-value lies somewhere between 0.01 and 0.001 and we have a highly significant result – the sample gives strong evidence that market value is useful in predicting the number of transactions.

A word of warning
In the last example we concluded that the market value of a company is useful in predicting the number of transactions in the company's shares. From this it is tempting to infer that the size of a company's market value *causes* more transactions in its shares to occur. However, this need not be the case.

Just because a fitted regression model tells us that X is useful in predicting Y does *not* mean that X causes Y. As an example, consider sales of ice cream and sales of suntan lotion. In hot weather sales of ice cream increase and sales of suntan oil also increase, so ice cream sales may be a useful predictor of suntan oil sales. However, the act of buying an ice cream does not *cause* someone to buy some suntan oil. What is happening is that both ice cream sales and suntan lotion sales are directly influenced by a third factor, in this case, the weather.

In the UK in recent years there has been an increase in crime and an increase in the number of single-parent families. The two sets of figures are related in that they both show an upward trend. However, it has yet to be proven (by the sociologists, not the statisticians) that members of single-parent families are more likely to be criminals. The likelihood is that both increases are due to a third factor, the changing social structure of society.

So beware! Just because one variable is useful in *predicting* another does not mean that it *causes* the other.

Another word of warning
We should emphasise that the t ratio test is only valid if the assumption made at the start of this section is true, namely that the model is

$$Y = \alpha + \beta x + \varepsilon$$

where ε is normally distributed with mean 0 and variance σ^2.

Techniques are available, called 'diagnostic checking' or 'analysis of residuals', to test whether these assumptions are reasonable or not, but we refer the reader to Statistics textbooks with wider coverage (for instance, those suggested under 'Further reading' in the 'To the student ...' section at the front of this book).

The regression model using software
The regression facility in most statistical software calculates the t ratio and gives the corresponding p-value $p = 2P(T > |\, t \text{ ratio} \,|)$.

The quantity

$$\sqrt{\frac{s^2}{S_{xx}}}$$

that forms the denominator of the t ratio, is often given as well, in a column labelled, '**Std. Error**', **standard error**, or similar (because it is an estimated standard deviation of b) and s^2, the estimated variance of ε, or s, its square root is often given.

In SPSS, s is called the '**Std. Error of the Estimate**'.

It is also possible to test H_0: $\alpha = 0$ against H_1: $\alpha \neq 0$; that is, whether or not the constant term is useful in the model, so a t ratio for this test and an estimate of the standard deviation of a are also usually given.

Check this

The following SPSS output fits a linear regression model to the company sales data. Check that you understand what all the bold face means and how it is calculated.

Regression

Variables Entered/Removed (b)

Model	Variables Entered	Variables Removed	Method
1	YEAR (a)	.	Enter

a All requested variables entered
b Dependent Variable: SALES

Model Summary

Model	R	R Square	Adjusted R Square	Std. Error of the Estimate
1	.971(a)	.943	.937	102.275

a Predictors: (Constant), YEAR

ANOVA (b)

Model		Sum of Squares	df	Mean Square	F	Sig.
1	Regression	1557710.000	1	1557710.000	148.918	.000 (a)
	Residual	94141.636	9	10460.182		
	Total	1651851.636	10			

a Predictors: (Constant), YEAR
b Dependent Variable: SALES

Coefficients (a)

Model		Unstandardized Coefficients		Standardized Coefficients	t	Sig.
		B	Std. Error	Beta		
1	(Constant)	−238.182	66.138		−3.601	.006
	YEAR	119.000	9.752	.971	12.203	.000

a Dependent Variable: SALES

Solution:
The least squares estimates $a = -238.182$ and $b = 119.000$ are found in the 'Coefficients' box in the column headed 'B' and therefore a summary of the fitted model is:

SALES = −238.182 + 119.000 YEAR

The column headed **Std. Error** gives the denominators of the t ratios (which are the standard deviations of a and b).

The column headed '**t**' gives the t ratios for testing $H_0: \alpha = 0$ and $H_0: \beta = 0$ respectively, which is the '**B**' column divided by the '**Std. Error**' column. The '**Sig**' column gives the corresponding p-values, $p = 2P(T > |\ t$ ratio $|)$. For example, the p-value when testing $H_0: \beta = 0$ is $p = 2P(T > 12.203) = 0.000$. Note that it is not exactly 0 but zero to 3 decimal places. This is smaller than a significance level of, say, 5% and so leads us to reject $H_0: \beta = 0$ and conclude that year *is* useful in predicting sales.

In the '**Model Summary**' box, we see **Std. Error of the Estimate** = 102.275, which is the square root of s^2, the estimate of σ^2 and **R Square** = 0.943 is R^2, the coefficient of determination.

The table headed '**ANOVA**' shows the split of the total sum of squares (1,651,851.636) into the regression sum of squares (1,557,710.000) and the error sum of squares (94,141.636). The regression sum of squares divided by the total sum of squares gives the R^2 above.

A summary of all the results of this section is given below.

The linear regression model

The linear regression model is

$$Y = \alpha + \beta x + \varepsilon \text{ where } E(\varepsilon) = 0 \text{ and } \mathrm{Var}(\varepsilon) = \sigma^2$$

α and β are estimated by

$$a = \frac{\Sigma y - b\Sigma x}{n} \text{ and } b = \frac{S_{xy}}{S_{xx}}$$

and σ^2 is estimated by

$$s^2 = \frac{\text{the error sum of squares}}{n-2} = \frac{S_{yy} - \dfrac{S_{xy}^2}{S_{xx}}}{n-2}$$

where

$$s_{xx} = \Sigma x^2 - \frac{(\Sigma x)^2}{n}, \quad s_{yy} = \Sigma y^2 - \frac{(\Sigma y)^2}{n} \quad \text{and} \quad s_{xy} = \Sigma xy - \frac{\Sigma x \Sigma y}{n}$$

To test whether or not X is useful for predicting Y

$H_0: \beta = 0$ X is *not* useful in predicting Y

against

$H_1: \beta \neq 0$ X *is* useful in predicting Y

using

$$t \text{ ratio} = \frac{b}{\sqrt{\dfrac{s^2}{s_{xx}}}}$$

When H_0 is true this comes from a t distribution with $n - 2$ degrees of freedom so the p-value is

$$p = 2P(T > |t \text{ ratio}|)$$

WORK CARD 3

1. Consider the data in **Work card 2**, question **1**, on the prices, Y, and age, X, of a sample of 11 second-hand cars. We have already fitted the least squares line $y = 141.4324 - 13.7027x$ to this data and calculated $s_{xx} = 20.1818$, $s_{yy} = 4137.6364$ and $s_{xy} = -276.5455$.

   (i) Suggest a model that might be used to predict the price of a car from its age.

   (ii) Write down or calculate estimates of the parameters of this model.

   (iii) Predict the price of a 5-year-old car.

   (iv) Perform a test of whether age is useful in predicting the price of a second-hand car.

2. Some data giving the amount spent on advertising, x, and the sales volume, y, in the first month of 8 new products were given in **Work card 1**, question **3**.
   The fitted least squares line is $y = 38.5940 + 2.6630x$. You may also find it helpful to know that, as previously calculated, $s_{xx} = 1564$, $s_{yy} = 16,826.875$ and $s_{xy} = 4165$ and the sum of squared errors = 5735.2989.
   Write down estimates of the linear regression model. Test whether the amount spent on advertising is useful in predicting sales volume.

3. We have designed the following small data set so that you can work through the whole of the linear regression modelling procedure without using a computer.

Suppose that the xs are the number of staff working in a pub during an evening shift and y is the number of abusive customers encountered that evening for 5 consecutive Monday evenings.

x Number of staff	y Abusive customers
3	10
4	11
2	13
6	15
2	10

(i)   Fit a linear regression model that endeavours to explain the number of abusive customers in terms of the number of staff.

(ii) Use the model to predict the number of abusive customers when there are 5 staff working.

(iii) Calculate R^2, the coefficient of determination, for the data.

(iv) Test whether or not the number of staff is useful in predicting the number of abusive customers. What conclusion do you draw?

4.   The following data shows electricity sales figures in Great Britain over an 11-year period.

Sales	Year
140,374	1984
151,071	1985
156,931	1986
161,664	1987
173,925	1988
185,423	1989
193,907	1990
199,442	1991
206,370	1992
220,591	1993
213,888	1994

(i)   A scatter plot of the data is shown in Figure 3.10. Comment on it.

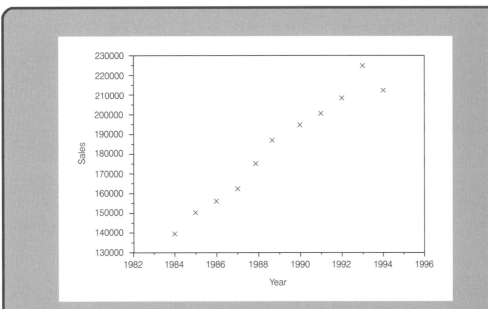

Figure 3.10

The following regression output was obtained using SPSS.

Model Summary

Model	R	R Square	Adjusted R Square	Std. Error of the Estimate
1	.989(a)	.978	.976	4231.284

a Predictors: (Constant), YEAR

ANOVA (b)

Model		Sum of Squares	df	Mean Square	F	Sig.
1	Regression	7192901318.409	1	7192901318.409	401.754	.000(a)
	Residual	161133875.227	9	17903763.914		
	Total	7354035193.636	10			

a Predictors: (Constant), YEAR
b Dependent Variable: SALES

Coefficients (a)

Model		Unstandardized Coefficients		Standardized Coefficients	t	Sig.
		B	Std. Error	Beta		
1	(Constant)	−15901723.500	802437.397		−19.817	.000
	YEAR	8086.409	403.437	.989	20.044	.000

a Dependent Variable: SALES

WORK CARD 3 (CONTINUED)

Use this output to answer the following questions.

(ii) Write down the fitted regression model. What assumption is usually made about the random term? Suggest an estimate for the variance of the random term.

(iii) What is meant by **R Square** on the output? Which other figures on the output is it calculated from and how?

(iv) From the output do you think that year is useful in predicting electricity sales? Explain your answer.

Solutions:

1. **(i)** The linear regression is $Y = \alpha + \beta x + \varepsilon$ where $Var(\varepsilon) = \sigma^2$.

   (ii) We have already calculated the estimates $b = -13.7027$ and $a = 141.4324$ but we need to estimate σ^2. We use

   $$s^2 = \frac{S_{yy} - \dfrac{s_{xy}^2}{S_{xx}}}{n-2} = \frac{4137.6364 - \dfrac{(-276.5455)^2}{20.1818}}{9} = 38.6902$$

   (iii) The predicted price when $x = 5$ is therefore $y = 141.4324 - 13.7027 \times 5 = 72.9189$.

   (iv) We have to test $H_0: \beta = 0$ against $H_1: \beta \neq 0$. The t ratio is

   $$t\text{ ratio} = \frac{b}{\sqrt{\dfrac{s^2}{S_{xx}}}} = \frac{-13.7027}{1.3846} = -9.90$$

   When H_0 is true the t ratio should come from a t distribution with $n - 2 = 9$ degrees of freedom. Using t tables we see that $t_{0.0005} = 4.781$ and so $p = 2P(T > | t \text{ ratio} |)$ is at most 0.001, the test is highly significant and we reject H_0. We conclude that age is useful in predicting the price of a second-hand car.

2. The estimated linear regression is merely the least squares line already calculated, $y = 38.5940 + 2.6630x$. In addition, we need to estimate σ^2 using

   $$s^2 = \frac{S_{yy} - \dfrac{s_{xy}^2}{S_{xx}}}{n-2}$$

   $$= \frac{\text{Sum of squared errors}}{8 - 2} = \frac{5735.2989}{6} = 955.8832$$

   To test whether advertising is useful in predicting sales volume we test $H_0: \beta = 0$ against $H_1: \beta \neq 0$. The test statistic is

   $$t\text{ ratio} = \frac{b}{\sqrt{\dfrac{s^2}{S_{xx}}}} = \frac{2.6630}{\sqrt{\dfrac{955.8832}{1564}}} = 3.4063$$

WORK CARD 3 (CONTINUED)

When the null hypothesis is true this comes from a t distribution with $n - 2 = 6$ degrees of freedom. From t tables we see that $t_{0.01} = 3.143$ and $t_{0.005} = 3.707$, so $p = 2P(T > |\,t\text{ ratio}\,|)$ is somewhere between 0.02 and 0.01 and the result is significant. We reject H_0 and conclude that yes, advertising is useful in predicting sales volume.

3. First of all we need all the sums. These are $\Sigma x = 17$, $\Sigma y = 59$, $\Sigma x^2 = 69$, $\Sigma y^2 = 715$, $\Sigma xy = 210$. From these we obtain

$$s_{xx} = 69 - \frac{17^2}{5} = 11.2, \quad s_{yy} = 18.8 \quad \text{and} \quad s_{xy} = 9.4$$

(i) $b = \dfrac{9.4}{11.2} = 0.8393$ and $a = \dfrac{59 - 0.8393 \times 17}{5} = 8.9464$

The estimated variance of the random term is

$$s^2 = \frac{s_{yy} - \dfrac{s_{xy}^2}{s_{xx}}}{n - 2} = \frac{18.8 - \dfrac{9.4^2}{11.2}}{3} = 3.6369$$

(ii) When $X = 5$ the predicted number of abusive customers is $y = 8.9464 + 0.8393 \times 5 = 13.1429$.

(iii) $R^2 = \dfrac{s_{xy}^2}{s_{xx}s_{yy}} = \dfrac{9.4^2}{11.2 \times 18.8} = 0.4196$

(iv) We must test $H_0: \beta = 0$ against $\beta \neq 0$. The test statistic is

$$t\text{ ratio} = \frac{b}{\sqrt{\dfrac{s^2}{s_{xx}}}} = \frac{0.8393}{\sqrt{\dfrac{3.6369}{11.2}}} = 1.4729$$

When $H_0: \beta = 0$ is true this comes from a t distribution with $n - 2 = 3$ degrees of freedom. The p-value is $p = 2P(T > 1.4729)$. From t tables $t_{0.25} = 0.765$ and $t_{0.10} = 1.638$, so p is between 0.2 and 0.5 and the test is not significant. We conclude that the number of staff is *not* useful in predicting the number of abusive customers.

4. (i) The scatter plot shows that the sample data very nearly lie on a straight line so there may be a linear relationship between year and electricity sales.

(ii) $Y = -15{,}901{,}723.500 + 8086.409x$. ε is assumed to be normally distributed with mean 0 and variance σ^2. σ^2 is estimated by s^2, the square root of which is given on the output as Std. Error of the Estimate, so $s^2 = 4231.284^2$.

(iii) **R Square** on the output is R^2, the coefficient of determination, which is the percentage of the variation in the ys that is explained by the model. It is calculated by dividing the regression sum of squares (7,192,901,318.409) by the total sum of squares (73,540,351,93.636).

WORK CARD 3 (CONTINUED)

(iv) The t ratio is 20.044, which, if the coefficient of year in the model is 0, comes from a t distribution with 9 degrees of freedom. The probability of such an extreme value is given by SPSS and to 3 d.p. is $p = 0.000$. As this is less than 5% it is significant so we reject the null hypothesis and conclude that year *is* useful in predicting electricity sales.

1. In **Assessment 1**, question **4**, you collected pairs of data which were the ages of male and female partners and in **Assessment 2**, question **2**, you fitted a least squares line to these data.

   Try to do the following without using a computer, and then confirm your answers using software.

   (i) Write down a linear regression model that expresses the age of the male in terms of the age of the female. Estimate all the parameters of this model.

   (ii) Perform a statistical test of whether the age of the female is useful in predicting the age of the male partner. Show your working and comment on your results.

2. Figures for the total supply of steel (10^6 tons) in the UK for a period of 29 consecutive years from 1946 are given below.

Year	Supply	Year	Supply
1 = 1946	14.36	16	23.42
2	14.56	17	21.90
3	16.11	18	24.40
4	17.19	19	28.75
5	17.72	20	28.34
6	17.66	21	26.57
7	18.77	22	26.50
8	19.09	23	29.04
9	19.80	24	30.01
10	21.91	25	30.62
11	22.89	26	27.62
12	23.33	27	28.28
13	20.97	28	30.87
14	21.26	29	28.62
15	25.99		

Using statistical software or otherwise:

(i) Estimate the linear regression of steel supply on year.

(ii) Is the model useful?

(iii) Would you use this model to predict the supply of steel in the year 2005?

3. Consider the following data which gives beer consumption (bulk barrels) and the number of infant deaths (thousands) for the years 1935–45.

Year	Beer consumption	Infant deaths
1935	60	23
1936	62	23
1937	61	25
1938	55	25
1939	53	26
1940	60	26
1941	63	29
1942	53	30
1943	52	30
1944	48	32
1945	49	33
1946	43	31

Using software or otherwise:

(i) Estimate the linear regression of infant deaths on year. (It will be easier to relabel the years 1, 2, 3, etc. The estimate of β will not be affected.) Is year useful in predicting infant deaths?

(ii) Estimate the linear regression of beer consumption on year. Is year useful in predicting beer consumption?

(iii) Now estimate the linear regression of infant deaths on beer consumption. Is beer consumption useful in predicting infant deaths?

(iv) Does your result in **(iii)** lead you to think that an increase in the consumption of beer causes infant deaths? Explain your answer.

4. The file *supermarket* contains data from 50 supermarket check-out employees, selected at random. In particular, the variable *blips* contains the average number of items processed per minute during a two-hour test period. The file also includes data on each employee's age and the number of months they have worked at the supermarket.

Use simple linear regression to assess whether the average number of blips can be predicted by

(i) age

(ii) number of months they have worked.

ASSESSMENT 3

4 Extending the linear regression model: the multiple linear regression model

Now we show how the linear regression model can be extended to include any number of independent variables.

The multiple regression model

The model we have considered so far,

$$Y = \alpha + \beta x + \varepsilon$$

is sometimes called the *simple* linear regression model, because it only involves one independent variable. However, frequently two or more independent random variables may be useful together to predict Y. For instance, the sales of a product may depend on the product's unit price, as well as the amount of advertising expenditure and the price of a competing product (three independent variables) or the number of fatal accidents during a time period may be predictable from the number of registered vehicles on the road and the price of petrol (two independent variables).

The simple linear regression model can be extended to include any number of independent X variables in which case it is called the *multiple linear regression model*.

Consider the following example.

On a small island state the government would like to be able to predict the number of mortgage loans issued by the state mortgage company (morts) from the amount of personal income in millions of local currency (income), the interest rate (interest) and the year.

A multiple linear regression model that may be suitable is

$$Y = \beta_0 + \beta_1 \text{income} + \beta_2 \text{interest} + \beta_3 \text{year} + \varepsilon$$

where ε is a random term which is assumed to have a normal distribution with mean 0 and variance σ^2, and β_0, β_1, β_2 and β_3 are the parameters of the model. That is, β_1 is the parameter that multiplies the amount of personal income, β_2 multiplies the interest rate and so on. Notice that this is a natural extension of the simple linear regression model.

To estimate the parameters of the model the government collects the following data over a 10-year period.

Morts	Income	Interest	Year
6,253	3.2	7.0	1
6,516	3.3	7.5	2
4,678	3.4	7.5	3
6,743	3.5	8.0	4
8,586	3.7	7.0	5
7,087	3.8	7.0	6
10,386	3.9	6.0	7
13,591	4.1	5.5	8
13,649	4.3	5.0	9
16,717	4.6	4.5	10

Notice that because there are three independent variables there are quadruples of data instead of pairs.

Estimating the parameters

The βs and σ^2 are unknown, so we need to estimate them from the sample. As we did for the simple linear regression model, to estimate the βs we choose the values (the least squares estimates) that give the minimum sum of the squared errors. There are formulae for these estimates, but they are tedious to calculate by hand and so we usually use a computer. **Note:** If the estimates of β_0, β_1, β_2 and β_3 are b_0, b_1, b_2 and b_3 respectively, the errors from fitting the model are $e = y - (b_0 + b_1 \text{income} + b_2 \text{interest} + b_3 \text{year})$ and the least squares estimates are the values of b_0, b_1, b_2 and b_3 that give the minimum value of Σe^2. σ^2 is estimated by

$$s^2 = \frac{\Sigma e^2}{n - k - 1}$$

where k is the number of independent variables, in this case $k = 3$.

Multiple linear regression output

Estimation of a multiple linear regression model is best done on a computer and in Excel and SPSS the commands are the same as those for simple linear regression (see Section 2).

The output below was generated by SPSS but most regression software produces something broadly similar.

Variables Entered/Removed (b)

Model	Variables Entered	Variables Removed	Method
1	YEAR, INTEREST, INCOME(a)	.	Enter

a All requested variables entered.
b Dependent Variable: MORTS

Model Summary

Model	R	R Square	Adjusted R Square	Std. Error of the Estimate
1	.972(a)	.944	.916	1154.865

a Predictors: (Constant), YEAR, INTEREST, INCOME

ANOVA (b)

Model		Sum of Squares	df	Mean Square	F	Sig.
1	Regression	135713208.880	3	45237736.293	33.919	.000(a)
	Residual	8002277.520	6	1333712.920		
	Total	143715486.400	9			

a Predictors: (Constant), YEAR, INTEREST, INCOME
b Dependent Variable: MORTS

Coefficients (a)

Model		Unstandardized Coefficients		Standardized Coefficients	t	Sig.
		B	Std. Error	Beta		
1	(Constant)	–3186.743	25478.477		–.125	.905
	INCOME	6772.230	6732.138	.770	1.006	.353
	INTEREST	–1683.706	885.741	–.497	–1.901	.106
	YEAR	–372.291	838.978	–.282	–.444	.673

a Dependent Variable: MORTS

Notice that this greatly resembles the simple linear regression output obtained earlier.

The fitted model and its interpretation

The least squares estimates are shown in the column headed B of the final table. From this we see that the estimate of β_0 is –3186.743, the estimate of β_1, the coefficient of income, is 6772.230 and so on. As usual we can use the fitted model for prediction. For instance, to predict the amount of mortgage loans when income is 4.0, interest rates are 7% in year 11 we would calculate

$$\text{MORTS} = -3186.743 + (6772.230 \times 4.0) - (1683.706 \times 7) - (372.291 \times 11) = 8021.034$$

However, we must be a little careful about how we interpret the model. The coefficient of each independent variable indicates the change in average mortgage loans *when all the other independent variables remain unchanged*. This italicised clause is important. For instance, the coefficient of income (6772.230) is positive. This means that *when the level of interest rates and the year are unchanged* a unit increase in income corresponds to an increase of 6772.230 in average mortgage loans. On the other hand, the coefficient of interest (–1683.706) is negative indicating that *when the level of income and the year are unchanged* a unit increase in interest rate produces, on average, a decrease of 1683.706 in mortgage loans. (Is this what you would expect?) Also, the coefficient of year is negative indicating that *when income and interest rates remain constant*, as time progresses the number of mortgage loans decreases.

Testing the independent variables

The column of the final table headed **Unstandardized Coefficients** and then **Std. Error** contains the estimated standard deviation of each of the least squares estimates. The **t** column is formed by dividing the **B** column by the **Std. Error** column.

Each *t* ratio tests whether a particular independent variable is useful in predicting the number of mortgage loans. For instance, consider the second independent variable, interest.

The full multiple linear regression model we are assuming is

$$Y = \beta_0 + \beta_1\text{income} + \beta_2\text{interest} + \beta_3 \text{ year} + \varepsilon$$

When $\beta_2 = 0$ the 3rd term on the right-hand side is 0 and the variable interest disappears from the model. So, to test whether or not interest can be omitted from this model we test

$$H_0: \beta_2 = 0 \text{ against } H_1: \beta_2 \neq 0$$

The test statistic is

$$t \text{ ratio} = \frac{b_2}{\text{Standard deviation of } b_2} = \frac{-1683.706}{885.741} = -1.901$$

When $H_0: \beta_2 = 0$ is true this comes from a t distribution with $n - k - 1$ degrees of freedom, where n is the number of data in the sample ($n = 10$ here) and k is the number of independent variables in the model ($k = 3$ here).

As usual the p-value is the probability of such an extremely large or small t ratio so $p = 2P(T > 1.901)$, which SPSS calculates as $p = 0.106$. As this p-value is greater than 5% our sample result is quite likely when the null hypothesis is true so there is not really any evidence to reject H_0, and we conclude that *when income and year are retained in the model* interest is not useful in predicting mortgage loans.

We can test each independent variable in a similar way. For our example, testing $H_0: \beta_1 = 0$ gives t ratio = 1.006, $p = 2P(T > 1.006) = 0.353$, so there is no reason to reject the null hypothesis, and we conclude that *when we retain interest and year in the model* income is not useful in predicting mortgage loans.

In the same way, testing $H_0: \beta_3 = 0$ gives a t ratio of -0.444 and $p = 2P(T > 0.444) = 0.673$ and we reach a similar conclusion; that is, *when we retain the other two variables*, year is not useful in predicting mortgage loans.

From this you may think that none of the independent variables are useful in predicting mortgage loans! So should we get rid of all of them and say that the whole model is useless? The answer is *no*. Remember that each variable is tested *in the presence of* the other variables, so each of these tests says that a variable can be omitted while the others remain so we can't eliminate all of the independent variables at once.

In this situation we would normally omit the variable that is 'least significant' in the sense that its t ratio is the least extreme (equivalently, its p-value is highest) and fit the model again. That is, as year has the least extreme t ratio, we would fit the model

$$Y = \beta_0 + \beta_1 \text{income} + \beta_2 \text{interest} + \varepsilon$$

Analysis of variance

Like the simple linear regression model the total sum of squares of the y_is splits into a quantity called the *regression sum of squares* and a quantity called the *error sum of squares*, although the formulae are different. (The column headed '**Sum of Squares**' in the table headed **ANOVA** gives this split.) R^2, which is the regression sum of squares divided by the total sum of squares, is shown in the table headed **Model Summary** and is 0.944 which is good as it is very near 1. σ^2 is estimated by

$$s^2 = \frac{\text{Error sum of squares}}{n - k - 1}$$

and the square root of this, s, is given.

The F test – an overall test of the model

The figure labelled **F** in the **ANOVA** table of the SPSS output is the test statistic for an overall test of the whole model. It tests the null hypothesis

$$H_0: \beta_1 = \beta_2 = \beta_3 = 0$$

against

$$H_1: \text{at least one of } \beta_1, \beta_2 \text{ and } \beta_3 \text{ is not zero}$$

Notice that when H_0 is true the model is just $Y = \alpha + \varepsilon$ so we can predict just as well without the independent variables. When H_1 is true a combination of one or more of the independent variables is useful in predicting Y.

The test statistic, F, is calculated from

$$F = \frac{\dfrac{\text{Regression sum of squares}}{k}}{\dfrac{\text{Error sum of squares}}{n-k-1}}$$

where, as before, n is the number of quadruples of data ($n = 10$ here) and k is the number of independent variables in the model ($k = 3$ here). For our sample, $F = 33.919$.

When H_0 is true the F calculated this way comes from a distribution called the F distribution but when H_1 is true it is likely to be larger. The p-value of the test is therefore the probability that an F random variable is larger than our sample F. For our example $p = P(F > 33.919)$.

We will not go into details about the F distribution here because SPSS calculates the probability for us and it appears in the **Sig.** column of the **ANOVA** table. For our example, $p = P(F > 33.919) = 0.000$ (to 3 d.p.). As this probability is very small it tells us that the value of F produced by our sample is extremely unlikely when H_0 is true so we can reject H_0 in favour of H_1. We conclude that some or all of the independent variables are useful in predicting Y; that is, the model *is* useful in predicting Y.

A warning

Like the t ratio test for the simple linear regression model, the t ratio tests and the F test are only valid for the multiple linear regression if the assumption that the random term, ε, is normally distributed with mean 0 and variance σ^2 is true. The reader is referred to further Statistics books for techniques, called 'diagnostic checking' or 'analysis of residuals' which test the data to see whether this is a reasonable assumption to make.

WORK CARD 4

1. In an investigation into the effect of ambulance crew size and bonus payment on productivity the following data were collected.

Crew size	Bonus (£)	Productivity
4	1900	42
4	2900	39
4	3100	48
4	3900	51
6	2100	49
6	3900	53
6	2900	61
6	3900	60

The following SPSS multiple regression output was obtained.

Model Summary

Model	R	R Square	Adjusted R Square	Std. Error of the Estimate
1	.837(a)	.701	.581	5.012

a Predictors: (Constant), BONUS, CREW

ANOVA (b)

Model		Sum of Squares	df	Mean Square	F	Sig.
1	Regression	294.292	2	147.146	5.859	.049(a)
	Residual	125.583	5	25.117		
	Total	419.875	7			

a Predictors: (Constant), BONUS, CREW
b Dependent Variable: PRODUCT

Coefficients (a)

Model		Unstandardized Coefficients		Standardized Coefficients	t	Sig.
		B	Std. Error	Beta		
1	(Constant)	14.121	10.799		1.308	.248
	CREW	4.896	1.797	.676	2.724	.042
	BONUS	.004	.002	.393	1.586	.174

a Dependent Variable: PRODUCT

(i) Write down the model that has been fitted to the data.

(ii) Use the model to predict productivity when crew size is 4 and the bonus is £3000.

(iii) Which independent variable, if any, may not be useful in predicting productivity? Explain your answer.

(iv) Is the model useful? Explain your answer.

(v) On the basis of the analysis above would you advise the analyst to fit another model to the data? If so, which model and why?

Solution:

(i) PRODUCT = 14.121 + 4.896CREW + 0.004BONUS.

(ii) PRODUCT = 14.121 + (4.896 × 4) + (0.004 × 3000) = 45.705.

(iii) Testing $H_0: \beta_1 = 0$ gives $p = 0.042$ which is significant so H_0 must be rejected and CREW is useful in predicting productivity. Testing $H_0: \beta_2 = 0$ gives $p = 0.174$ which is not significant so H_0 is retained and we conclude that BONUS may not be useful in predicting productivity.

(iv) F tests the hypothesis $H_0: \beta_1 = \beta_2 = 0$, i.e. that neither CREW nor BONUS are useful in predicting productivity. Here $F = 5.859$. The p-value is the probability

WC 4

of a larger F, $p = P(F > 5.859) = 0.049$ which is just significant (at 5%), so we conclude that the model is useful.

(v)   As BONUS is not useful in this model the next step would be to fit the model again but without the bonus variable, i.e. fit PRODUCT $= \beta_0 + \beta_1$CREW $+ \varepsilon$.

ASSESSMENT 4

1. Recall that *supermarket* contains data from a sample of 50 supermarket employees and that the variable *blips* contains the average number of items processed per minute during a two-hour test period. The file also contains data on each employee's age and the number of months they have worked at the supermarket. You are asked to investigate which factors are useful in predicting employee checkout speeds. In the first stage of your investigation you obtain the following multiple regression output from SPSS.

Model summary

Model	R	R Square	Adjusted R Square	Std. Error of the Estimate
1	.708 (a)	.501	.480	1.59438

a Predictors: (Constant), MONTHS, AGEYEARS

ANOVA (b)

Model		Sum of Squares	df	Mean Square	F	Sig.
1	Regression	120.151	2	60.076	23.633	.000 (a)
	Residual	119.476	47	2.542		
	Total	239.627	49			

a Predictors: (Constant), MONTHS, AGEYEARS
b Dependent Variable: BLIPS

Coefficients (a)

Model		Unstandardized Coefficients		Standardized Coefficients	t	Sig.
		B	Std. Error	Beta		
1	(Constant)	7.650	.686		11.145	.000
	AGEYEARS	2.E–02	.024	.084	.751	.456
	MONTHS	8.E–02	.013	.671	5.979	.000

a Dependent Variable: BLIPS

Use this output to answer the following.
(i)   What model has been fitted to the data?
(ii)   Is the model useful? Explain your answer.

ASSESSMENT 4 (CONTINUED)

(iii) Are both independent variables useful in predicting the average number of blips? Which one, if any, would you omit from the model? Explain your answer.

2. The data file *supermarket* also contains information on the employee's grade (0 = trainee, 1 = staff, 2 = supervisor) and the age they left full time education (16, 18 or 21).

Conduct one or more multiple linear regression analyses to investigate which factors among age, months, grade and education are the most useful predictors of the blip rate. Write a report explaining what you have done and why, and stating any conclusions you make.

A hint and cautionary note. Grade is 'different' from the other independent variables because it is a *categorical* variable. Although it takes the values 0, 1 or 2 (for trainee, staff or supervisor) these numbers merely serve to distinguish between the categories – a supervisor is not 'worth' twice as much as staff grade. We therefore need to take one category, say trainee, as a base or *reference* category and then construct a new variable to indicate whether or not the employee is staff or not, and another new variable to indicate whether the employee is a supervisor or not. *Supermarket* contains two such variables. Staff takes the value 1 if the employee is staff grade and 0 otherwise whereas supervr takes the value 1 if the employee is a supervisor and 0 otherwise. Variables like this are called *dummy* variables. When a dummy variable is included in a linear regression its coefficient is the *effect* on the predicted dependent variable due to the corresponding category. For instance, if the model includes the term

$$\beta \times \text{staff}$$

an additional $\beta \times 1$ (that is, β) will be added to the predicted dependent variable, blips when staff = 1 and an additional $\beta \times 0$, that is, nothing will be added when staff = 0.

Whilst the age the employee left education, 16, 18 or 21, does have some meaning, we don't really want to add a coefficient $\times 16$ to the model for the first category and the same coefficient $\times 18$ or $\times 21$ for the second and third, so the variable education is also categorical. Taking 16 as the reference category, we have created two dummy variables, educ18 and educ21, for the other two categories.

Dummy variables are included in the multiple linear regression model instead of the original categorical variable. To do this question you will therefore need to include the independent variables staff, supervr, educ18 and educ21 with ageyears and months.

3. Conduct your own mini-survey.

Ask a sample of 10–20 students how much they spend each week or month on a particular type of expenditure, e.g. food, beer, rent, clothes. At the same time collect data on two or more independent variables that might help to predict the level of expenditure on this item. For instance

(i) the student's age
(ii) their year of study

ASSESSMENT 4

(iii) the amount of grant, etc. they receive

Fit a multiple linear regression model to your data to predict expenditure from the independent variables. Test the usefulness of the model and the usefulness of each independent variable in the presence of the others. Comment on your results. If any of your variables are not significant, refit the model omitting just one of them and comment. Again, if any variables are not significant, omit one and refit the model. Continue until all the variables in the model are significant. This is your final model. Use it to predict expenditure for a particular set of values of the independent variables.

Further reading: see p. xv

Anderson *et al.* (Statistics) includes more detail, including more on using categorical variables in regression.

Newbold *et al.* includes much more, particularly on multiple regression and model building.

S4
Forecasting

A good accountant is someone who told you yesterday what the economists forecast for tomorrow.

Sir Miles Thomas

Contexts

What is this chapter about?
Data are frequently recorded at regular time intervals, for instance, daily stock market indices, the monthly rate of inflation or annual profit figures. In this chapter we show you how to display and model such data. We see how to detect trends and seasonal effects and use these to calculate seasonal indices and make forecasts.

Why is it useful?
Making forecasts allows organisations to make better decisions and to plan more efficiently. For instance, reliable forecasts enable a retail outlet to anticipate demand, hospitals to plan staffing levels and manufacturers to keep appropriate levels of inventory.

Where does it fit in?
There is a wide range of forecasting methods and most rely on statistical techniques, so forecasting can be regarded as a branch of statistics. However, it is sometimes included as a management science technique, such as those in the Business Modelling part of this book.

What do I need to know?
You will need the material in Describing Data and the previous Statistics chapters, S1, S2 and S3.

Objectives

After your work on this chapter you should be able to:

- display a time series and recognise whether it has a trend and/or a seasonal effect;
- calculate exponential forecasts and select an appropriate smoothing constant;
- assess how good forecasts are using mean squared or mean absolute error;
- isolate the trend using moving averages or regression;
- calculate seasonal indices using a multiplicative or additive model and seasonally adjust a series;
- make forecasts using an additive or multiplicative model.

Take any edition of a broadsheet newspaper, particularly the business section, and it is highly likely that it will contain at least one graph of a set of data that occurs at regular intervals of time. Examples of such data are the monthly rate of inflation, daily stock market indices and the number of new cars sold annually. Such sequences of data are called *time series*.

In this chapter we consider how to display time series, investigate whether or not they show any trend or seasonal pattern, and make use of this pattern, if any, to forecast future values of the series.

1 Displaying time series

Time series plots, trends and seasonal effects

The usual way to display a time series is with time on the horizontal axis of a graph and the data on the vertical axis. This is called a *time series plot*.

The graphs in Figures 4.1–4.5 show some typical time series plots.

The general level of the series in Figure 4.1 increases so we say that there is a *trend* in the series. Trends may be upwards (as here) or downwards.

The annual rainfall series in Figure 4.2 does not seem to have a trend – it fluctuates around a constant level.

The quarterly time series of UK primary fuel consumption in Figure 4.3 has a seasonal pattern – high in winter, low in summer – which is roughly repeated every year. We say that this series has a *seasonal effect*.

Figure 4.4 shows that jeans sales do *not* appear to exhibit a seasonal effect or a trend.

When the time series increases rapidly it is often easier to work with the log of the data. We talk about logs in Chapter MM1, but if you haven't met them before, the key point is that they systematically 'squash' the data to make the rate of increase less dramatic. Figure 4.5 shows the log (to base e) of the number of international airline passengers each month from January 1949 to December 1960. There is an obvious upward trend, and also a seasonal effect.

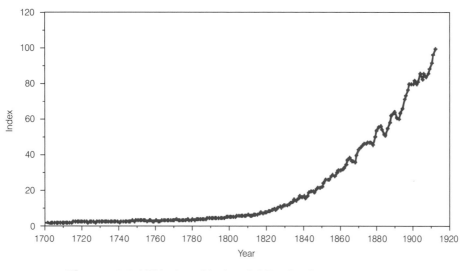

Figure 4.1 UK Index of Industrial Production, 1700–1920.

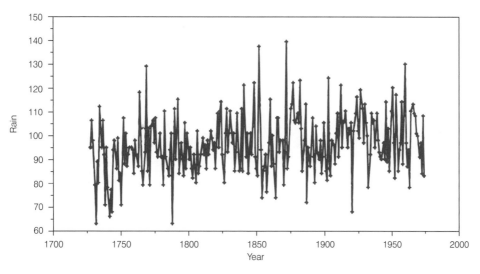

Figure 4.2 Annual rainfall.

Broadly speaking, a time series may have a trend or not, and may have a seasonal effect or not, as shown in Figure 4.6(a)–(d).

One of the main reasons for studying a time series is to make forecasts of future values of the series. Forecasting techniques are many and varied and the choice of method often depends on whether the series has a trend or seasonal effect or both.

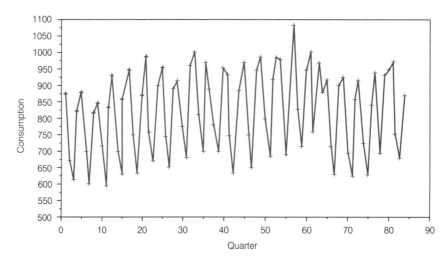

Figure 4.3 Quarterly UK primary fuel consumption.

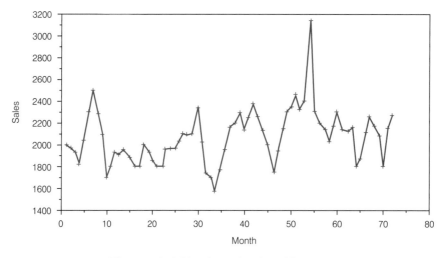

Figure 4.4 Number of pairs of jeans sold.

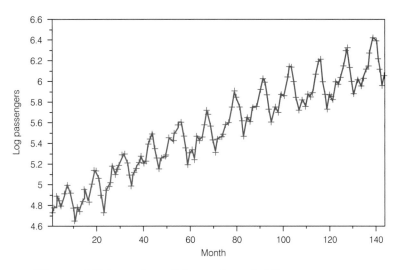

Figure 4.5 Log of monthly number of airline passengers.

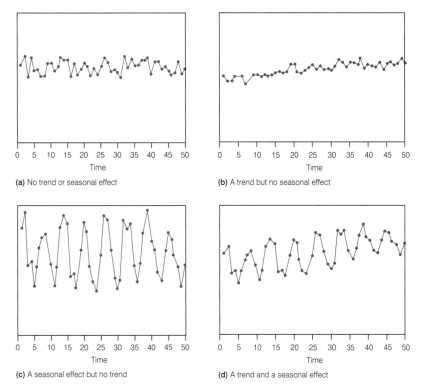

(a) No trend or seasonal effect

(b) A trend but no seasonal effect

(c) A seasonal effect but no trend

(d) A trend and a seasonal effect

Figure 4.6

1. Would you expect the following time series to have a trend or a seasonal effect, both, or neither? Explain your answers.

    (i)   Daily temperature over a 4-year period.

    (ii)   Monthly sales of ice-cream by a company over a 5-year period.

    (iii) Daily sales of beer in a bar over several weeks.

    (iv)   The number of private cars on the road in the UK on 31 December each year from 1930 to the present.

    (v)   A stock exchange index at close of business each day for 2 years.

Solution:

1. (i)   Seasonal, with 365 periods in the year, but no trend.

    (ii)   Seasonal and if the company has been steadily doing better or worse there could be an upward or downward trend.

    (iii) Sales would have a 7-day seasonal cycle each week.

    (iv)   A series with an upward trend but no seasonal effect.

    (v)   There might be a trend depending on the market history during the period, but there is not likely to be a seasonal effect.

1. Would you expect the following time series to have a trend and/or a seasonal effect – and if so, what are the seasons? Explain your answers briefly.

    (i)   Weekly sales of a well-established current affairs magazine.

    (ii)   The number of travellers on the London Underground each day for several weeks.

    (iii) Monthly unemployment figures.

    (iv)   The number of households in the UK that own a video recorder each month from 1983 to the present.

2. Find 2 graphs of time series in a newspaper and say whether each has a trend and/or a seasonal effect.

2 Introduction to forecasting

In this section we introduce forecasting via one of the most straightforward forecasting methods and then consider how different forecasting methods can be compared.

Notation

It will be useful to label the time series x_1, x_2, x_3, ..., x_n. This seems very much like what we did for a sample of data in *Describing Data* and *Statistics*. It is, but the crucial difference is that now, because the data have occurred through time, the sequence of the data matters, whereas it didn't before.

Exponential forecasting

This is one of the simplest methods of forecasting, but in its basic form it is only appropriate for series with *no trend or seasonal effect*. It is often used to predict the demand for a product in the next time period so that sufficient stock can be kept. (This is called demand forecasting.)

Suppose that it is currently time t and that demand for the product at this time is x_t. We would like to forecast the demand in the next time period; that is, we would like to predict x_{t+1}. We will call a forecast of x_{t+1}, made at time t, F_{t+1}.

Suppose further that the same situation held in the last time period so that at time $t-1$ we made a forecast of x_t, which we called F_t. Now that we have observed x_t we know that the error in this forecast is

$$e_t = x_t - F_t$$

An intuitive way of making the next forecast, F_{t+1}, would be to use the previous forecast, F_t, but to adjust it slightly to allow for the fact that it wasn't exactly right. We adjust it by adding on a proportion of the error. That is, we say

$$\text{Next forecast} = \text{Last forecast} + \text{A proportion of the last error}$$

that is,

$$F_{t+1} = F_t + \alpha(x_t - F_t)$$

where α (alpha) is a proportion so $0 \le \alpha \le 1$. We will discuss the value of α later but for now we will use $\alpha = 0.2$. Forecasts constructed in this way are called *exponential forecasts*.

Check this

It is currently the end of month 2. At the end of month 1 the manufacturer of an established brand of cat food forecasted that demand for the food during month 2 would be 67 (thousand tins) whereas the actual demand in month 2 was 76 (thousand tins). Calculate an exponential forecast of the demand in month 3, using $\alpha = 0.2$.

Solution:
The information we have been given is

$x_2 = 76$ and $F_2 = 67$

and we need to calculate F_3. The exponential forecasting formula given above gives $F_3 = F_2 + 0.2(x_2 - F_2)$; that is $F_3 = 67 + 0.2(76 - 67) = 68.8$. At the end of month 2 the exponential forecast of demand in month 3 is 68.8 (thousand tins).

As each month passes and the demand becomes known we can calculate the next forecast.

Check this

A month passes and it is now the end of month 3. The actual demand in month 3 turns out to be $x_3 = 83$. Calculate an exponential forecast of demand in month 4.

Solution:

$F_4 = F_3 + 0.2(x_3 - F_3) = 68.8 + 0.2(83 - 68.8) = 71.64.$

Table 4.1 Exponential forecasts of the cat food demand with $\alpha = 0.2$

Month	x_t	F_t	$e_t = x_t - F_t$
1	67		
2	76	67.00	9.00
3	83	68.80	14.20
4	78	**71.64**	6.36
5	68	72.91	−4.91
6	59	71.93	−12.93
7	69	69.34	−0.34
8	70	69.27	0.73
9	58	69.42	−11.42
10	69	67.14	1.86
11	75	67.51	7.49
12	69	69.01	−0.01
13	72	69.01	2.99
14	81	69.61	11.39
15	71	71.89	−0.89
16		71.71	

We can continue like this month by month. Table 4.1 shows the actual values and forecasts of cat food demand for 15 months. For simplicity and clarity of display, we have rounded each forecast to 2 d.p. before using it in subsequent calculations, although, in practice, we would usually round to more d.p.s. The values we have just used and calculated are shown in bold. The final column shows the error in making each forecast.

Notice that we started the calculations by using x_1 as the forecast of x_2; that is, by setting $F_2 = x_1$. The advantage of exponential forecasting is that the calculations are simple and so, if necessary, can be used to forecast the demand for many hundreds of different products without the need for complicated software.

Different values of α

So far we have arbitrarily used $\alpha = 0.2$ to calculate the exponential forecasts. α is called the *smoothing constant* and can take any value between 0 and 1. Let's look at how the choice of α affects the forecasts.

Recall that the exponential forecasts are calculated from

$$F_{t+1} = F_t + \alpha(x_t - F_t)$$

and that $x_t - F_t$ is the latest error.

When α is close to 0, only a small proportion of the latest error will be included in F_{t+1}, so the new forecast will not differ greatly from the previous forecast. Conversely, when α is close to 1, a large proportion of the latest error is included in F_{t+1}, so F_{t+1} is greatly influenced by the latest observed value, x_t. At the extremes, when $\alpha = 0$, $F_{t+1} = F_t$ and the forecasts are totally insensitive to any new data, and when $\alpha = 1$, $F_{t+1} = x_t$, so the latest observation is used as the forecast, without any regard to the earlier data in the series.

This means that it is more appropriate to use a small value of α (close to 0), when the original series is irregular and jagged as each new observation is not very helpful in forecasting ahead. Conversely, a large value of α (close to 1) is appropriate when the series is fairly smooth and the most helpful information comes from the current observation.

As an illustration, the graph in Figure 4.7 shows (i) the cat food data for 15 months, (ii) the forecast values for each month obtained using $\alpha = 0.2$ (as calculated earlier) and (iii) the forecast values for each month obtained in the same way but using $\alpha = 0.4$.

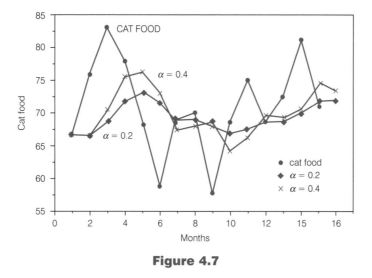

Figure 4.7

Notice that the forecasts obtained using $\alpha = 0.2$ produce a smoother version of the series than those calculated using $\alpha = 0.4$. This is because the $\alpha = 0.2$ series is less influenced by each observation as it happens. Notice also that both series of forecasts are smoother and less jagged than the original series. For this reason this technique is often called *exponential smoothing*.

Another way of choosing an appropriate value of α is to examine how well various values of α would have forecast the series in the past, but before we can do this we need a way of assessing how 'good' our forecasts are.

How good are the forecasts?

The error in each forecast is

$$e_t = x_t - F_t$$

We would expect a good forecasting procedure to result in small errors and a bad forecasting procedure to give large errors. It therefore seems sensible to use a criterion based on the errors, e_2, e_3, ..., e_n to compare different forecasting methods. Notice that there are only $n - 1$ errors because e_1 is not available as we have no forecast of x_1 at time 0.

Two criteria are most common:

● The *mean squared error*, or MSE, is the average of the *squares* of the errors, that is

$$\text{MSE} = \frac{\Sigma e_i^2}{n - 1}$$

● Whereas the *mean absolute error* is the average of the *absolute value* of the errors,

$$\text{MAE} = \frac{\Sigma |e_i|}{n - 1}$$

(Recall that $|e_i|$ means the absolute value of e_i, that, is the value ignoring the minus sign if there is one.)

For example, the MSE of the exponential forecasts of the cat food series (with $\alpha = 0.2$) given in Table 4.1 is

$$\text{MSE} = \frac{9^2 + 14.20^2 + 6.36^2 + (-4.91)^2 + ... + (-0.89)^2}{14} = \frac{844.47}{14} = 60.32$$

whereas the MAE is

$$\text{MAE} = \frac{9 + 14.20 + 6.36 + 4.91 + ... + 0.89}{14} = \frac{84.52}{14} = 6.04$$

Check this

A car hire company calculates the exponential forecast of the number of cars which will be required the following day for each of 11 consecutive days. A printout of their results is shown below, but unfortunately the printer mangled the paper and some of the entries are missing.

t	x_t	F_t	Absolute error	Squared error
1	110			
2	115	110.000	5.000	25.000
3	109	111.500	2.500	6.250
4	108			
5	106	109.925	3.925	15.406
6	111	108.748	2.252	5.074
7	107	109.423	2.423	5.872
8	112	108.696	3.304	10.915
9	114			
10	110	110.981	0.981	0.9627
11	111	110.687	0.313	0.0981
12		110.781		
			Total	95.7380

Because the computer calculates to more decimal places than are shown, the squared errors in the table are not necessarily exact squares of the absolute values. Use the printout to answer the following questions.

(i) What value of the smoothing constant, α, has been used?

(ii) Recalculate the forecasts for days 4 and 9. Predict the number of cars required on day 12.

(iii) Complete the absolute error and squared error columns (to 3 d.p.) and calculate the value of the MSE and MAE.

Solution:

(i) We know that $F_{t+1} = F_t + \alpha(x_t - F_t)$ so it follows that $F_3 = F_2 + \alpha(x_2 - F_2)$, so for this example $111.500 = 110 + \alpha(115 - 110)$. Solving for α gives $\alpha = 0.3$.

(ii) We require $F_4 = F_3 + 0.3(x_3 - F_3)$ so $F_4 = 111.50 + 0.3(109 - 111.50) = 110.750$. In the same way $F_9 = F_8 + 0.3(x_8 - F_8) = 108.696 + 0.3 \times (112 - 108.696) = 109.687$.

$$F_{12} = F_{11} + 0.3(x_{11} - F_{11}) = 110.687 + 0.3(111 - 110.687) = 110.781$$

(iii) The missing absolute errors are 2.75 and 4.313 and the missing squared errors are 7.5625 and 18.602. The total absolute error is therefore 27.761, so

$$\text{MAE} = \frac{27.761}{10} = 2.7761$$

whereas from the printout the total squared error is 95.7380 so MSE = 9.5738.

The choice of smoothing constant α

As we said above, criteria like MSE and MAE can be used to select the 'best' value of the smoothing constant α. The MSE (or the MAE) is calculated for several candidate values of α and the value which gives the smallest MSE (or MAE) is used to predict future values of the series.

Table 4.2 shows exponential forecasts of the cat-food data with the corresponding absolute and squared errors using smoothing constants $\alpha = 0.2$, $\alpha = 0.3$ and $\alpha = 0.4$.

The final row of Table 4.2 shows the totals of the absolute error and squared error columns. So (as already calculated) when $\alpha = 0.2$,

$$\text{MSE} = \frac{844.47}{14} = 60.32$$

when $\alpha = 0.3$,

$$\text{MSE} = \frac{856.07}{14} = 61.15$$

and when $\alpha = 0.4$,

$$\text{MSE} = \frac{863.75}{14} = 61.70$$

So, using the MSE criterion the smoothing constant $\alpha = 0.2$ has forecast best.

Table 4.2 Absolute and squared errors of exponential forecasts of the cat-food data.

x_t	F_t $\alpha = 0.2$	Absolute error	Squared error	F_t $\alpha = 0.3$	Absolute error	Squared error	F_t $\alpha = 0.4$	Absolute error	Squared error
67									
76	67.00	9.00	81.00	67.00	9.00	81.00	67.00	9.00	81.00
83	68.80	14.20	201.64	69.70	13.30	176.89	70.60	12.40	153.76
78	71.64	6.36	40.45	73.69	4.31	18.58	75.56	2.44	5.95
68	72.91	4.91	24.11	74.98	6.98	48.73	76.54	8.54	72.93
59	71.93	12.93	167.18	72.89	13.89	192.93	73.12	14.12	199.37
69	69.34	0.34	0.12	68.72	0.28	0.08	67.47	1.53	2.34
70	69.27	0.73	0.53	68.80	1.20	1.44	68.08	1.92	3.69
58	69.42	11.42	130.42	69.16	11.16	124.55	68.85	10.85	117.72
69	67.14	1.86	3.46	65.81	3.19	10.18	64.51	4.49	20.16
75	67.51	7.49	56.10	66.77	8.23	67.73	66.31	8.69	75.52
69	69.01	0.01	0.00	69.24	0.24	0.06	69.79	0.79	0.62
72	69.01	2.99	8.94	69.17	2.83	8.01	69.47	2.53	6.40
81	69.61	11.39	129.73	70.02	10.98	120.56	70.48	10.52	110.67
71	71.89	0.89	0.79	73.31	2.31	5.34	74.69	3.69	13.62
	71.71			72.62			73.21		
Total		84.52	844.47		87.90	856.07		91.51	863.75

The corresponding MAEs are

$$\frac{84.52}{14} = 6.04, \quad \frac{87.90}{14} = 6.28 \quad \text{and} \quad \frac{91.51}{14} = 6.54 \quad \text{respectively}$$

so the MAE criterion agrees with MSE, that $\alpha = 0.2$ produces the best forecasts on this set of data, although this need not always be the case.

On the whole, the MSE criterion is the most widely used for evaluating forecasts.

> **Check this**
>
> The following table shows the forecasts calculated for the car hire series using exponential forecasts with constants 0.1, 0.2 and 0.3 respectively, and calculations of the absolute error and squared error for each.
>
> **(i)** Fill in any gaps that occur.
>
> **(ii)** On the basis of this set of data, which of these smoothing constants would be best for forecasting future car requirements?

Day	x_t	F_t $\alpha = 0.1$	Abs error	Squared error	F_t $\alpha = 0.2$	Abs error	Squared error	F_t $\alpha = 0.3$	Abs error	Squared error
1	110									
2	115	110.000	5.000	25.000	110.000	5.000	25.000	110.000	5.000	25.000

Day	x_t	F_t $\alpha = 0.1$	Abs error	Squared error	F_t $\alpha = 0.2$	Abs error	Squared error	F_t $\alpha = 0.3$	Abs error	Squared error
3	109	110.500	1.500	2.250	111.000	2.000	4.000	111.500	2.500	6.250
4	108				110.600	2.600	6.760	110.750	2.750	7.563
5	106	110.115	4.115	16.933	110.080	4.080	16.646	109.925	3.925	15.406
6	111	109.704	1.296	1.681				108.748	2.253	5.074
7	107	109.833	2.833	8.027	109.611	2.611	6.818	109.423	2.423	5.872
8	112	109.550	2.450	6.003	109.089	2.911	8.474	108.696	3.304	10.915
9	114	109.795	4.205	17.683	109.671	4.329	18.739			
10	110	110.215	0.215	0.046	110.537	0.537	0.288	110.981	0.981	0.963
11	111	110.194	0.806	0.650	110.430	0.570	0.325	110.687	0.313	0.098
12		110.274			110.544			110.781		
		Total	2.477	8.380	Total	2.637	9.007	Total	2.776	9.574

Solution:

(i) Using $\alpha = 0.1$, $F_4 = 110.350$, so the absolute error is 2.350 and the squared error 5.523. Using $\alpha = 0.2$, $F_6 = 109.264$ so the absolute error is 1.736 and the squared error 3.014. When $\alpha = 0.3$, $F_9 = 109.687$ so the absolute error is 4.313 and the squared error is 18.602.

(ii) The MAEs and MSEs are found by dividing the total of the absolute error and the squared errors respectively by 10. So, of these three possible values of α, 0.1 has both the smallest MAE and the smallest MSE.

On the basis of this set of data it would seem most reasonable to use $\alpha = 0.1$ when making future forecasts.

Exponential forecasting on a computer
SPSS's

Analyze > Time Series > Exponential Smoothing

command calculates exponential forecasts but you will need to supply the smoothing constant using the **PARAMETERS** subdialog box. SPSS uses the average value of the series as the first forecast by default, but you can enter a different one in INITIAL VALUES, CUSTOM, STARTING although you will also have to set the TREND to 0. SPSS gives a quantity called SSE (sum of squared error) which is the numerator of our MSE. If you want it will calculate the SSE for several smoothing constants and choose the one that gives the smallest SSE and hence the smallest MSE.

The **exponential smoothing** data analysis tool in Excel will calculate exponential forecasts of a series in a named column or row. It asks you to supply the *damping factor*, by which it means $1 - \alpha$, so take care not to enter the smoothing constant, α, instead. The exponential forecasts are placed in a specified range in the same worksheet.

Exponential forecasting: Summary of formulae

Set $F_2 = x_1$ and then use

$$F_{t+1} = F_t + \alpha(x_t - F_t)$$

where $0 \leq \alpha \leq 1$

$$\text{MSE} = \frac{\sum e_i^2}{n-1} \qquad \text{MAE} = \frac{\sum |e_i|}{n-1}$$

1. Each day a video shop uses exponential forecasting with a smoothing constant of 0.4 to forecast the demand for videos the following day. An incomplete table of the calculations for four days is given below.

Day	Videos	Forecast
1	39	
2	28	$F_2 = 39$
3	42	$F_3 = ?$
4	45	$F_4 = ?$
		$F_5 = ?$

   Notice that they have started the forecasts by setting $F_2 = x_1$. Calculate F_3, F_4 and F_5.

2. In an exponential forecasting application to a time series of shipments of goods from inventory, the following results were obtained:

α	MSE	MAE
0.2	40	30
0.4	60	45
0.6	75	60
0.8	79	55

   (i) Based on MSE results, which of these values of α should lead to the most accurate forecasts?

   (ii) Based on MSE results should the forecaster investigate other values of the smoothing constant? Why?

   (iii) Answer (i) and (ii) with respect to the MAE criterion.

3. Column (1) of the following table shows the number of copies of *The Times* sold by a small newsagent on 15 consecutive days. Column (2) gives

exponential forecasts for $\alpha = 0.1$, and columns (3) and (4) for two further values of α.

Day	Sales x_t (1)	F_t for $\alpha = 0.1$ (2)	F_t (3)	F_t (4)
1	45			
2	47	45.00	45.00	45.00
3	49	?	45.60	46.00
4	51	45.58	46.62	47.50
5	38	46.12	47.93	49.25
6	45	45.31	44.95	43.63
7	47	45.28	44.97	44.32
8	52	45.45	45.58	45.66
9	48	46.11	47.51	48.83
10	46	46.30	47.66	48.42
11	49	46.27	47.16	47.21
12	39	46.54	47.71	48.11
13	42	45.79	45.10	43.56
14	47	45.41	44.17	42.78
15	49	?	45.02	44.89

(i) Fill the gaps for the forecasts when $\alpha = 0.1$.

(ii) Which values of the exponential smoothing constant have been used for the forecasts in columns (3) and (4)?

(iii) The total of the squared errors of the forecasts in column (2) is 256.32, and of the forecasts in column (3) is 294.39. Which of the three values of α gives the best forecasts when you use MSE as the criterion?

(iv) The MAEs of the forecasts in columns (3) and (4) are 50.82 and 54.18 respectively. Which value of α is favoured when MAE is used as the criterion?

Solutions:

1. $F_3 = F_2 + 0.4(x_2 - F_2) = 39 + 0.4(28 - 39) = 34.6$
   $F_4 = F_3 + 0.4(x_3 - F_3) = 34.6 + 0.4(42 - 34.6) = 37.56$
   $F_5 = F_4 + 0.4(x_4 - F_4) = 37.56 + 0.4(45 - 37.56) = 40.54.$

2. (i) $\alpha = 0.2$, because the MSE is smallest for this value.
   (ii) It would be worth trying even smaller values of α, as it has decreased with α.
   (iii) $\alpha = 0.2$ also seems best when MAE is the criterion, although this does not necessarily have to be the case.

3. (i) When $\alpha = 0.1$, $F_3 = 45.2$ and $F_{15} = 45.57$.

WORK CARD 2 (CONTINUED)

WORK CARD 2 (CONT.)

(ii)   Looking at F_3 in column (3). It must be true that $F_3 = F_2 + \alpha(x_2 - F_2)$. Substituting in the numbers we have, $45.60 = 45 + \alpha(47 - 45)$. Solving this for α gives $\alpha = 0.3$. In the same way, $\alpha = 0.5$ for the forecasts in column (4).

(iii) The sum of the squared errors of the forecasts in column (4) is 330.94, so $\alpha = 0.1$ has the smallest MSE.

(iv)   The sum of the absolute errors of the forecasts in column (2) is 49.19 so the forecasts in column (2), which were calculated using $\alpha = 0.1$, have the smallest MAE.

ASSESSMENT 2

1. The following table shows the exponential forecasts for a series in column (2) of monthly manufacturing inventories ($billions) for three different values of α.

Month (1)	x_t (2)	F_t $\alpha =$ (3)	$\alpha =$ (4)	$\alpha =$ (5)
1	145.5			
2	145.8	145.50	145.50	145.50
3	146.1	145.56	145.65	145.74
4	146.4	145.67	145.88	146.03
5	146.6	145.82	146.14	146.33
6	146.3	145.98	146.37	146.55
7	146.8	146.04	146.34	146.35
8	146.9	146.19	146.57	146.71
9	147.7	146.33	146.74	146.86
10	148.1	146.60	147.22	147.53
11	148.1			
12	147.5			
13				

(i)   Which values of α have been used to calculate these forecasts?

(ii)   Continue the forecasts for months 11, 12 and 13.

(iii) The MAE of the forecasts for months 2–12 for the first value of α is 0.78, of the second is 0.48 whereas the MSE of the forecasts for months 2–12, for the first value of α, is 0.76 and of the second is 0.28. Which of the three values of α gives the best forecasts using each criterion?

(iv)   Would you expect each criterion to choose the same value of α?

(v)   What does the favoured value of α suggest about the 'smoothness' of the original series?

2. Use a computer to calculate exponential forecasts for the car hire series featured in the previous **Check this** for a value of α other than 0.1, 0.2 or 0.3 that you think might produce a better MSE and/or MAE. Calculate the MSE and MAE of these forecasts and compare your value of α with 0.1, 0.2 and 0.3.

3 Coping with trend and seasonal effects

The exponential forecasting we described in Section 2 is only appropriate when there is no consistent upward or downward trend in the time series and when there is no seasonal effect.

In this section we consider series that have a seasonal effect and/or a trend.

Some models for time series

We have already denoted the time series $x_1, x_2, ..., x_n$ and have said that it may have a seasonal effect, a trend effect or both. A way in which we can formalise this is to say that the series is the *sum* of a trend component (which may be zero) and a seasonal component (which may be zero) and a random component which has no trend or seasonal pattern. That is, we say that the time series is generated by the *additive model*,

$$x_t = T_t + S_t + R_t$$

where T_t is the trend component, S_t is the seasonal component and R_t is the random component. Using this model the effect of the season at time t is to add S_t to the level of the series. That is, the series is raised or lowered by an amount which depends on the season.

An alternative model that may be appropriate is

$$x_t = T_t S_t R_t$$

Now the components are multiplied by each other so we call it a *multiplicative model*.

The multiplicative model says that the effect of a particular season is to *multiply* the level of the series by S_t. That is, the series is raised or lowered by a *proportion* which depends on the season. A multiplicative model is therefore appropriate when, as the trend decreases or increases, the seasonal effect decreases or increases in the same way. It is often used for sales data because if a steady increase in sales figures is observed over time, the differences between the seasons usually increase as well.

The time series plots in Figure 4.8 show two series with a similar trend, but (a) has an additive seasonal component and (b) has a multiplicative seasonal component. Notice that the seasonal 'shape' repeats for the additive model, but increases with the trend for the multiplicative model.

By breaking down the observed series x_t into its components S_t, T_t and R_t, we can seasonally adjust the data and make forecasts into the future.

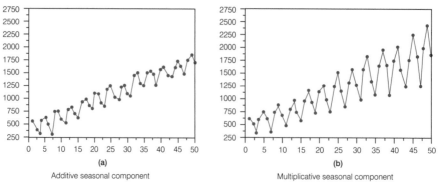

(a)
Additive seasonal component

(b)
Multiplicative seasonal component

Figure 4.8

Isolating the trend: centred moving averages

Centred moving averages give us a way of eliminating the seasonal component and so estimating the trend of a series. They also form the basis for many seasonal adjustment procedures.

We will explain using the following time series.

A small kitchen manufacturer obtains the following numbers of orders during each of 25 consecutive quarter years.

		Quarter			
		1	2	3	4
	1	24	20	17	21
	2	25	23	18	22
	3	27	23	22	22
Year	4	29	27	24	26
	5	31	29	23	28
	6	31	29	24	30
	7	33			

The plot of the data in Figure 4.9 shows that there is a seasonal effect as well as a trend.

First of all we create a new series, called the *moving average* series, from the original one. The first value of the new series will be the average of the first four items in the original series; that is,

$$\frac{x_1 + x_2 + x_3 + x_4}{4}$$

the second will be the average of the four values in the original series starting from the 2nd, that is

$$\frac{x_2 + x_3 + x_4 + x_5}{4}$$

the third will be

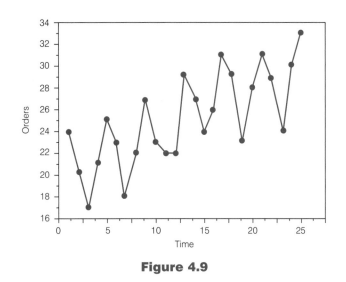

Figure 4.9

$$\frac{x_3 + x_4 + x_5 + x_6}{4}$$

and so on. For obvious reasons the new series is called a *four period* moving average.

It is easiest to perform these calculations when they are laid out in columns as shown below. Notice that we position each moving average at the average time of its constituents. For instance, as first item in the moving average series is

$$\frac{x_1 + x_2 + x_3 + x_4}{4}$$

we place it at time 2.5. As there are 25 values in the original series the final value in the moving average series is

$$\frac{x_{22} + x_{23} + x_{24} + x_{25}}{4}$$

which is positioned at time 23.5. In this way the moving average series will be 3 values shorter than the original series.

t	x_t	4 period moving average	t	x_t	4 period moving average
1	24		13	29	
					25.5
2	20		14	27	
		20.5			26.5
3	17		15	24	
		20.75			27
4	21		16	26	
		21.5			27.5
5	25		17	31	

t	x_t	4 period moving average	t	x_t	4 period moving average
		21.75			27.25
6	23		18	29	
		22			27.75
7	18		19	23	
		22.5			27.75
8	22		20	28	
		22.5			27.75
9	27		21	31	
		23.5			28
10	23		22	29	
		23.5			28.5
11	22		23	24	
		24			29
12	22		24	30	
		25			
			25	33	

At the moment the moving average series is at times 2.5, 3.5, 4.5, and so on which doesn't make much sense. We rectify this by calculating the average value of each pair of consecutive values in the moving average series and placing the result at the average of their times as shown in column 4 below. This is the *centred moving average* series.

t	x_t	4 period moving average	Centred moving average	t	x_t	4 period moving average	Centred moving average
1	24			13	29		25.25
						25.5	
2	20			14	27		26
		20.5				26.5	
3	17		20.625	15	24		26.75
		20.75				27	
4	21		21.125	16	26		27.25
		21.5				27.5	
5	25		21.625	17	31		27.375
		21.75				27.25	
6	23		21.875	18	29		27.5
		22				27.75	
7	18		22.25	19	23		27.75
		22.5				27.75	

t	x_t	4 period moving average	Centred moving average	t	x_t	4 period moving average	Centred moving average
8	22		22.5	20	28		27.75
		22.5				27.75	
9	27		23	21	31		27.875
		23.5				28	
10	23		23.5	22	29		28.25
		23.5				28.5	
11	22		23.75	23	24		28.75
		24				29	
12	22		24.5	24	30		
		25					
				25	33		

Notice that from our original series of 25 values, we have a centred moving average for time periods 3 to 23 inclusive.

Our hope is that as 4 consecutive values are included in the calculation of each centred moving average (one from each season), the series is now free from any seasonal pattern. The original and the centred moving average series of the kitchen data are shown on the graph in Figure 4.10 and we appear to have succeeded.

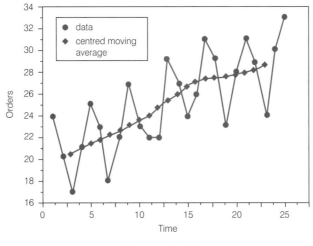

Figure 4.10

A by-product of this procedure (because we calculated averages) is that the random component of the series will have been smoothed out and so the centred moving average series gives us a clear idea of the trend.

We can apply this method to seasonal series with any number of seasons, say p seasons, by calculating the p-period moving averages. The kitchen data was quarterly and so we used $p = 4$. When p is even we will always have to 'centre' the series by calculating the average of consecutive moving average values so that the times correspond to those of the original series as we did for the kitchen data above, but when p is odd this will not be necessary.

Check this

A small example for you to try using a pocket calculator.

A satellite TV store has newly opened for business and is open just four days a week – Monday, Wednesday, Friday and Saturday. The number of satellite TV orders each day during the first 3 weeks of business is shown below.

WEEK 1				WEEK 2				WEEK 3			
M	W	F	S	M	W	F	S	M	W	F	S
3	5	7	8	3	6	9	10	4	7	11	13

Calculate the centred moving average series and comment on the trend.

Solution:
We need a 4 period moving average series.

Day											
1	2	3	4	5	6	7	8	9	10	11	12

Moving average

| | | 5.75 | 5.75 | 6 | 6.5 | 7 | 7.25 | 7.5 | 8 | 8.75 | |

Centred moving average

| | | | 5.75 | 5.875 | 6.25 | 6.75 | 7.125 | 7.375 | 7.75 | 8.375 | |

Moving averages on a computer

Using SPSS's

Transform > Create Time Series

function and then selecting **Centered moving average** from the function drop down list will calculate centred moving averages. The user must supply the variable to be averaged and the span (that is, the number of periods).

Excel's **moving average** data analysis tool calculates the moving average of a series.

Isolating the trend using regression

Another way to isolate the trend of a series, particularly if the trend seems to be linear, is to fit a straight line to the time series using regression. That is, we use the time series as the Y variable and time as the X variable and fit a linear regression model as described in Chapter S3.

The following least squares line (Figure 4.11) was fitted to the kitchen data

$$orders = 19.700000 + 0.416923\ time$$

Notice that the seasonal pattern makes the series vary around the line a lot. As a result the error sum of squares may be high, making the coefficient of determination, R^2, artificially low so that it understates the strength of the regression line. For this data $R^2 = 0.535$.

The estimated trend series therefore comprises the heights of the line; that is,

$$19.700000 + 0.416923\ time$$

corresponding to *time* = 1, $t = 2$, ..., $t = 25$. Notice that, unlike the centred moving average procedure, we do not 'lose' any data from each end of the series.

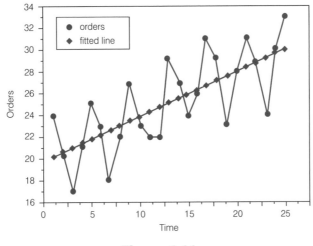

Figure 4.11

Seasonal indices

So far we have assumed that the model for the series is

$$x_t = T_t S_t R_t$$

or

$$x_t = T_t + S_t + R_t$$

These models allow the seasonal component, S_t, for the same season in different years to be different. For instance, for quarterly data S_1 does not have to be the same as S_5 or S_9 or S_{13}. It is often quite reasonable, however, to assume that the seasonal components are the same from year to year; that is, the effect of each season is the same through time. For instance, for quarterly data, $S_1 = S_5 = S_9 = ...$, $S_2 = S_6 = S_{10} = ...$ and so on. In this case, estimates of these seasonal components, S_t, are often called the *seasonal indices*. The seasonal indices measure the effect of each season and can be used to construct forecasts of the series.

We can obtain the seasonal indices using the estimated trend series (calculated via regression or the centred moving average series) considered above. The method we use varies slightly depending on whether we are assuming that an additive model or a multiplicative model is appropriate for the series. The difference is that we *divide* for the multiplicative model and *subtract* the same quantities for the additive model.

1. Calculating seasonal indices assuming the multiplicative model. The model is assumed to be

$$x_t = T_t S_t R_t$$

The estimated trend series we have just obtained is an estimate of T_t for each time period so if we divide the original data, x_t, by the corresponding values of the estimated trend series we should obtain an estimate of $S_t R_t$.

The following table shows these calculations for the kitchen data using the centred moving average as the estimated trend series. Check that you understand where all the entries come from.

t	x_t	Estimated trend series (centred MA)	$\dfrac{x_t}{\text{Estimated trend series}}$
1	24		
2	20		
3	17	20.625	0.8242
4	21	21.125	0.9941
5	25	21.625	1.1561
6	23	21.875	1.0514
7	18	22.25	0.8090
8	22	22.5	0.9778
9	27	23	1.1739
10	23	23.5	0.9787
11	22	23.75	0.9263
12	22	24.5	0.8980
13	29	25.25	1.1485
14	27	26	1.0385
15	24	26.75	0.8972
16	26	27.25	0.9541
17	31	27.375	1.1324
18	29	27.5	1.0545
19	23	27.75	0.8288
20	28	27.75	1.0090
21	31	27.875	1.1121
22	29	28.25	1.0265
23	24	28.75	0.8348
24	30		
25	33		

We estimate the index for a season by taking the average of the entries in the fourth column that are in that season. This is easiest to do by writing out the contents of the fourth column again with a row for each year and a column for each season as shown below.

Season			
1	2	3	4
		0.8242	0.9941
1.1561	1.0514	0.8090	0.9778
1.1739	0.9787	0.9263	0.8980
1.1485	1.0385	0.8972	0.9541
1.1324	1.0545	0.8288	1.0090
1.1121	1.0265	0.8348	
1.1446	1.0299	0.8534	0.9666	multiplicative seasonal index

So, the index for Season 1 is 1.1446, the index for Season 2 is 1.0299 and so on. This means that the data occurring in Season 1 is nearly 15% higher than it would be if there was no seasonal effect and Season 2 is about 3% higher than it would be if there was no seasonal effect.

Some texts will advise you to refine these multiplicative seasonal indices further by scaling them so that they average 1. For example, here the total of the four seasonal indices is 3.9945. We would like them to total 4, so if we multiply each index by $\frac{4}{3.9945}$ we will achieve this. The adjusted indices become

Season	1	2	3	4
Index	1.1462	1.0313	0.8546	0.9679

Check this

Calculate the seasonal indices for the satellite TV store series assuming that a multiplicative model is appropriate.

Day											
1	2	3	4	5	6	7	8	9	10	11	12
3	5	7	8	3	6	9	10	4	7	11	13

Centred MA: 5.75   5.875   6.25   6.75   7.125   7.375   7.75   8.375

$\frac{\text{Data}}{\text{MA}}$:   1.2174   1.3617   0.48   0.8889   1.2632   1.3559   0.5161   0.8358

Season			
1	2	3	4
		1.2174	1.3617
0.4800	0.8889	1.2632	1.3559
0.5161	0.8358		
0.4981	0.8624	1.2403	1.3588

multiplicative seasonal index

The total of the indices is 3.9596 so we can adjust the indices to total 4, by multiplying them by $\frac{4}{3.9596}$ to give 0.5032, 0.8712, 1.2530 and 1.3727.

---

2. Calculating seasonal indices for the additive model.

When the additive model is appropriate we proceed in exactly the same way except that we now subtract where we divided before.

We illustrate using the kitchen data again. Either the centred moving average series or the series obtained using regression methods can be taken as the estimated trend series. We will use the series obtained from the regression.

The model is additive so it assumes that

$$x_t = T_t + S_t + R_t$$

When we subtract the estimated trend series (an estimate of T_t) from the original data we obtain estimates of $S_t + R_t$ as shown in column (4) below.

t	x_t	Estimated trend series (from regression)	x_t – estimated trend
(1)	(2)	(3)	(4)
1	24	20.1169	3.8831
2	20	20.5338	–0.5338
3	17	20.9508	–3.9508
4	21	21.3677	–0.3677
5	25	21.7846	3.2154
6	23	22.2015	0.7985
7	18	22.6185	–4.6185
8	22	23.0354	–1.0354
9	27	23.4523	3.5477
10	23	23.8692	–0.8692
11	22	24.2862	–2.2862
12	22	24.7031	–2.7031
13	29	25.1200	3.8800
14	27	25.5369	1.4631
15	24	25.9538	–1.9538
16	26	26.3708	–0.3708
17	31	26.7877	4.2123
18	29	27.2046	1.7954
19	23	27.6215	–4.6215
20	28	28.0385	–0.0385
21	31	28.4554	2.5446
22	29	28.8723	0.1277
23	24	29.2892	–5.2892
24	30	29.7062	0.2938
25	33	30.1231	2.8769

So the series in column (4) are estimates of $S_t + R_t$. An estimate of the additive seasonal index can be found by finding the average of these for each season as shown below. In this way the effect of the random term R_t is averaged out.

Season			
1	2	3	4
3.8831	–0.5338	–3.9508	–0.3677
3.2154	0.7985	–4.6185	–1.0354
3.5477	–0.8692	–2.2862	–2.7031
3.8800	1.4631	–1.9538	–0.3708
4.2123	1.7954	–4.6215	–0.0385

Season			
1	2	3	4
2.5446	0.1277	−5.2892	0.2938
2.8769			
3.4514	0.4636	−3.7867	−0.7036

additive seasonal index

The result is a set of additive seasonal indices – one for each season.

Some texts adjust these so that they sum to 0. To do this they total the seasonal indices, giving −0.5753 here and divide by 4 to give −0.1438. Adding 0.1438 to each seasonal index will then produce a set of adjusted additive seasonal indices that total 0. For this example these are

Season	1	2	3	4
Index	3.5952	0.6074	−3.6429	−0.5598

Check this

Calculate seasonal indices for the satellite TV data assuming that an additive model is appropriate.

Solution:

Day

1	2	3	4	5	6	7	8	9	10	11	12
3	5	7	8	3	6	9	10	4	7	11	13

Centred MA 5.75 5.875 6.25 6.75 7.125 7.375 7.75 8.375

$\dfrac{\text{Data}}{\text{MA}}$ 1.25 2.125 −3.25 −0.75 1.875 2.625 −3.75 −1.375

Season			
1	2	3	4
		1.25	2.125
−3.25	−0.75	1.875	2.625
−3.75	−1.375		
−3.5	−1.0625	1.5625	2.375

additive seasonal index

We can adjust the indices to total 0 by adding $\frac{0.625}{4}$ to each one to give −3.3438, −0.9063, 1.7188, 2.5313.

Seasonally adjusting a series

Once the seasonal indices (multiplicative or additive) have been estimated as described above they can be used to produce a seasonally adjusted version of the original series.

When the multiplicative model $x_t = T_t S_t R_t$ is appropriate a seasonally adjusted series is obtained by *dividing* each item of the original series by the corresponding seasonal index as shown below for the kitchen data.

t	x_t	Seasonal index	Seasonally adjusted series
1	24	1.1462	20.9388
2	20	1.0313	19.3930
3	17	0.8546	19.8923
4	21	0.9679	21.6965
5	25	1.1462	21.8112
6	23	1.0313	22.3019
7	18	0.8546	21.0625
8	22	0.9679	22.7296
9	27	1.1462	23.5561
10	23	1.0313	22.3019
11	22	0.8546	25.7430
12	22	0.9679	22.7296
13	29	1.1462	25.3010
14	27	1.0313	26.1805
15	24	0.8546	28.0833
16	26	0.9679	26.8623
17	31	1.1462	27.0459
18	29	1.0313	28.1198
19	23	0.8546	26.9132
20	28	0.9679	28.9286
21	31	1.1462	27.0459
22	29	1.0313	28.1198
23	24	0.8546	28.0833
24	30	0.9679	30.9949
25	33	1.1462	28.7908

In a similar way, when the additive model $x_t = T_t + S_t + R_t$ has been assumed, the time series is seasonally adjusted by *subtracting* the appropriate seasonal index from each item in the series.

Many time series, particularly economic ones produced by government agencies, have strong seasonal components and are published in both raw (not adjusted) and seasonally adjusted forms. The method most widely used to seasonally adjust is the Census X – 11 method which is a refinement of using a centred moving average and assuming a multiplicative model in the method described here.

A summary of the work of this section follows.

Trend and seasonal effects

The **model** for a time series may be

Multiplicative $x_t = T_t S_t R_t$

or

Additive $x_t = T_t + S_t + R_t$

To estimate the trend
Either

calculate a centred moving average series

or

fit a linear regression model to the data

If it is reasonable to suppose that the seasonal component is the same in every year we can calculate the **seasonal indices**.

To calculate the seasonal indices when the model is multiplicative (additive):

(i) take the original series and divide by (subtract) the corresponding item of the series obtained above
(ii) calculate the average value of the series in (i) for each season
(iii) adjust the indices further so that they average 1 (total 0)

To seasonally adjust the original series take each item in the original series and divide by (or, for the additive model, subtract) the corresponding seasonal index.

WORK CARD 3

1. This relatively short time series has been devised so that the numerical calculations are not too onerous for you to do using a calculator. A British stately home has been open to the public for one day a year from 10am–4pm for the last three years. It is currently 12 noon on the fourth open day and the number of visitors in all the 2-hour periods so far are given below.

	Time period	Visitors
	10–12	1200
Year 1	12–2	1412
	2–4	1810
	10–12	1320
Year 2	12–2	1520
	2–4	2102

	Time period	Visitors
	10–12	1530
Year 3	12–2	1670
	2–4	2310
Year 4	10–12	1400

A graph of this time series is shown in Figure 4.12.

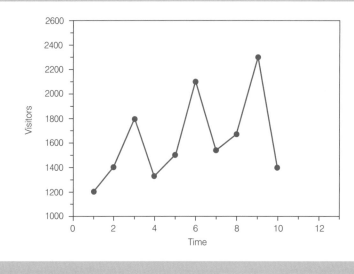

Figure 4.12

(i) From the graph, does the series appear to have a seasonal effect, a trend, neither or both? If there is a seasonal effect, how many seasons are there?

(ii) Is it clear from the graph whether an additive model or a multiplicative model is appropriate? If so, why?

(iii) Calculate a centred moving average series to eliminate the seasonal component.

(iv) Assuming a multiplicative model, use the centred moving average series to calculate the seasonal indices. How would you interpret the third seasonal index?

(v) Describe how would you use the seasonal indices to seasonally adjust the original series. Give the first three seasonally adjusted values.

2. The least squares line fitted to the data in question **1** is *visitors* = 1340.8 + 52.11*time*. The heights of the line are given below.

WORK CARD 3 (CONTINUED)

Time	Visitors	Regression
1	1200	1392.91
2	1412	1445.02
3	1810	1497.13
4	1320	1549.24
5	1520	1601.35
6	2102	1653.46
7	1530	1705.57
8	1670	1757.68
9	2310	1809.79
10	1400	1861.90

(i) Use the regression column to calculate seasonal indices assuming an additive model.

(ii) Describe how you would seasonally adjust the data.

Solutions:

1. (i) There appears to be both a seasonal effect (3 seasons) and a trend.

   (ii) The seasonal effect appears to increase with the trend suggesting that a multiplicative model is appropriate.

   (iii) and (iv) Calculations for the centred moving average and the data divided by the centred MA are given below.

Time	Visitors	Centred MA	Visitors/Centred MA
1	1200		
2	1412	1474.00	0.9579
3	1810	1514.00	1.1955
4	1320	1550.00	0.8516
5	1520	1647.33	0.9227
6	2102	1717.33	1.2240
7	1530	1767.33	0.8657
8	1670	1836.67	0.9093
9	2310	1793.33	1.2881
10	1400		

To calculate the seasonal indices we use

Season 1	Season 2	Season 3	
	0.9579	1.1955	
0.8516	0.9227	1.2240	
0.8657	0.9093	1.2881	
0.8587	0.9300	1.2359	multiplicative seasonal index

We could adjust these further so that they average 1. At present they total 3.0246, so if we multiply each index by $\frac{3}{3.0246}$ we will achieve this. The adjusted indices are 0.8517, 0.9224 and 1.2258. Visitors in the 2–4pm period are about 23% higher than if there was no 'seasonal' effect.

(v)   The seasonally adjusted values are found by dividing the original data by the appropriate seasonal indices, so the first three are

$$\frac{1200}{0.8517} = 1408.95, \quad \frac{1412}{0.9224} = 1530.79 \quad \text{and} \quad \frac{1810}{1.2258} = 1476.59$$

2.   (i)   The calculations are

Visitors	Estimated trend (from regression)	Additive seasonal index
1200	−192.91	−264.905
1412	−33.02	−67.350
1810	312.87	420.540
1320	−229.24	
1520	−81.35	
2102	448.54	
1530	−175.57	
1670	−87.68	
2310	500.21	
1400	−461.90	

We can adjust these indices so that they total 0. At present the total is 88.285, so subtracting 29.4283 from each will achieve this and give indices of −294.3333, −96.7783 and 391.1117.

(ii)   To seasonally adjust the series we would subtract the appropriate seasonal index from each data item.

1. The following data are UK primary fuel consumption (coal equivalent) for each quarter from 1980 quarter 1 to 1984 quarter 2 inclusive.

Year	1	2	3	4
1980	1001	759	969	871
1981	919	720	633	900
1982	927	704	630	857
1983	912	725	635	847
1984	938	692		

(i) Plot the data – is there any evidence of a trend?

(ii) A regression line of consumption on quarter was fitted using a computer package and the line $Y = 882.54 - 7.291x$ obtained. Use a computer to confirm this result. What is the value of R^2? Why is R^2 so low?

The following table shows the output from a spreadsheet that calculates seasonal indices for the fuel consumption series. Unfortunately, the printer is misbehaving and some of the column headings have not appeared.

(iii) Give suitable headings for all the columns.

(iv) Has a multiplicative or an additive model been assumed? Explain your answer.

(v) Calculate the first seasonal index.

(vi) Adjust the indices in an appropriate way.

(vii) Describe how you would seasonally adjust the original series, and demonstrate using the first three values.

(viii) Plot the deseasonalised series on the original time series plot of the original series and comment.

Time	Data			Index
1	1001	875.249	1.1437	
2	759	867.958	0.8745	0.8905
3	969	860.667	1.1259	0.8734
4	871	853.376	1.0207	1.0741
5	919	846.085	1.0862	
6	720	838.794	0.8584	
7	633	831.503	0.7613	
8	900	824.212	1.0920	
9	927	816.921	1.1347	
10	704	809.630	0.8695	
11	630	802.339	0.7852	
12	857	795.048	1.0779	

Time	Data		Index
13	912	787.757	1.1577
14	725	780.466	0.9289
15	635	773.175	0.8213
16	847	765.884	1.1059
17	938	758.593	1.2365
18	692	751.302	0.9211

2. A small project. Find a real seasonal time series of at least 3 seasonal cycles in published material or otherwise. (Government publications in your library are one possible source.)

(i)   Plot the series.

(ii)   Use a spreadsheet to calculate the seasonal indices using a method described in this chapter.

(iii) Seasonally adjust the series and plot the adjusted series on the same graph as the original series. Comment.

4 Forecasting series with a trend and seasonal effect

In Section 3 we decomposed the series into its trend and seasonal components. We will now assume that the same trend and seasonal behaviour continues into the future and use the decomposition to forecast the series.

Suppose that the additive model

$$x_t = T_t + S_t + R_t$$

is appropriate for the kitchen data. We can forecast future values of x_t by calculating forecasts of T_t, S_t and R_t and then adding them.

Future values of T_t are forecast using the linear regression line

$$orders = 19.700000 + 0.416923 \; time$$

which we have already fitted to the data.

S_t is estimated by the appropriate (additive) seasonal indices which we calculated as

Season	1	2	3	4
	3.5952	0.6074	−3.6429	−0.5598

The irregular component, R_t, is by its nature unpredictable, so the best forecast we can make of any R_t is zero.

We already know the number of orders for quarters 1 to 25 so we will calculate forecasts for periods 26, 27 and 28.

According to the model the number of orders at time 26 is

$$x_{26} = T_{26} + S_{26} + R_{26}$$

Our forecast of T_{26} is $19.700000 + (0.416923 \times 26) = 30.539998$ and (as the 26th quarter of the series is in the second quarter of the year) our forecast of S_{26} is 0.6074 so the forecast of x_{26} is

$$30.539998 + 0.6074 + 0 = 31.147398$$

In a similar way the forecasts of x_{27} and x_{28} are

$$19.700000 + (0.416923 \times 27) - 3.6429 + 0 = 27.3140$$

$$19.700000 + (0.416923 \times 28) - 0.5598 + 0 = 30.8140$$

These 3 forecasts are shown on a time series plot of the kitchen data in Figure 4.13.

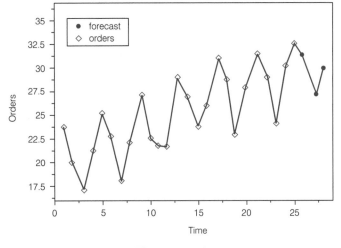

Figure 4.13

Forecasts can be made in a similar way when a multiplicative model is assumed but now the forecast trend and seasonal components must be multiplied together and the best forecast of the random component R_t is taken to be 1. That is

$$x_t = T_t S_t R_t$$

where T_t is calculated from the regression model fitted to the data, S_t is the appropriate multiplicative seasonal index and R_t is forecast as 1.

When a centred MA has been used to extract the trend from the data, instead of a regression line, there is no obvious way to obtain forecasts of T_t. However, the centred MA series can be plotted and then forecast by eye or a linear regression model can be fitted to the centred MA series.

1. The stately home visitors, data from **Work card 3**, question **1**, is repeated below.

	Time period	Visitors
	10–12	1200
Year 1	12–2	1412
	2–4	1810
	10–12	1320
Year 2	12–2	1520
	2–4	2102
	10–12	1530
Year 3	12–2	1670
	2–4	2310
Year 4	10–12	1400

In **Work card 3**, question **2**, the least squares line, *visitors* = 1340.8 + 52.11*time* was fitted to the data and, assuming an additive model, the seasonal indices were –294.333, –96.7783 and 391.1116.

(i) It is still the fourth day of opening and Lady Bracknell is in charge of afternoon teas in the tea tent. She would like a forecast of the number of visitors from 12 until 2 and from 2 until 4 today. Can you help?

Solution:

1. The additive model is $x_t = T_t + S_t + R_t$. The best forecast of T_t is 1340.8 + 52.11*time* and the best estimate of S_t is the appropriate seasonal index as given. So, to forecast periods 11 and 12 we use 1340.8 + 52.11 × 11 – 96.7783 = 1817.2317 and 1340.8 + 52.11 × 12 + 391.1117 = 2357.2317.

1. Continue the fuel consumption example from **Assessment 3**, question **1**. Use the seasonal indices and trend already found to forecast the series up to the end of 1985. Plot the forecasts. (For interest, the actual values of this series for these six quarters were 925, 946, 974, 746, 670 and 874.)

2. The number of passengers (in thousands) using a provincial airport each month are available for the last six and a half years (months 1 to 78). From this data the following least squares line has been calculated,

    passengers = 60.05 + 1.03*month*

    and, assuming a multiplicative model, the following seasonal indices have been obtained,

ASSESSMENT 4 (CONT.)

Season											
1	2	3	4	5	6	7	8	9	10	11	12
0.75	0.74	0.74	0.95	0.90	1.01	1.41	1.70	1.10	0.80	0.70	1.20

Calculate forecasts of the number of passengers who will use the airport during the next four months (months 79–82 inclusive).

3. Continue the project from **Assessment 3**, question **2**, by forecasting three or four periods into the future. Show and explain your working.

Further reading: see p. xv

Anderson *et al.* (Statistics) include a chapter on forecasting as does Newbold *et al.*

Hillier and Lieberman include a major chapter on forecasting.

Mendenhall *et al.*, where forecasting is also called time series.

Newbold *et al.* includes a class of models known as autoregressive moving average models.

S5
Comparing two populations

We are creatures of comparisons, because we are finite. We can only learn values or estimate truths by comparing them with others.

Frederick W. Faber, *Bethlehem*

Contexts

What is this chapter about?
In this chapter we use statistical techniques to compare two populations. For instance, to investigate the difference in average pay between males and females, to compare the petrol consumption of two brands of car or to assess the change in employees' performance after training.

Why is it useful?
There are numerous situations when competing processes, groups or time periods need to be compared and the results used to inform future decision making.

Where does it fit in?
The two main tools of Statistical Inference – estimation and testing – were used to make inferences about a single population in S1 and S2 and about the relationship between two variables in S3. In this chapter we apply estimation and testing to compare two populations.

What do I need to know?
You need to be very fluent with the ideas of estimation and testing in S1 and S2.

Objectives

After working on this chapter you should be able to:

- construct confidence intervals for and test the difference between two independent population means;
- understand when these techniques are appropriate and what assumptions need to be made about the populations;
- perform tests and construct confidence intervals for the difference in means when the data are paired.

The fundamental ideas of estimation and testing that you met in Chapters S1 and S2 underpin the whole of statistical inference. In those chapters we considered a single population only. We took a sample from it and used the sample to make inferences about the whole population. In this chapter we apply the same ideas to compare two populations of numerical data.

For instance, we might want to compare the exam marks of men with those of women, plants grown at a temperature of 10 degrees with those grown in a heated greenhouse or the daily returns on a particular ordinary share with the daily returns on another over the same time period.

We will concentrate our efforts on comparing the *means* of the two populations. The methods we use are only slight extensions of those in Chapters S1 and S2 and the notation we use parallels the notation in those chapters. It is therefore well worth taking time to understand Chapters S1 and S2 fully before tackling this chapter.

1 The difference between two means

Suppose we have two populations of numerical data and we want to compare the average of one population with the average of the second. As it is usually impractical, expensive, or impossible to collect all the data, we select a random sample of items from each population and use the samples to make inferences about the difference between the population means. In this way we have two samples of data to work with, one from each population.

For example, suppose an Internet service provider wishes to investigate the amount of time different types of clients spend on the Internet each day in order to target advertising appropriately. In particular, they would like to know whether young males (those under 25) use the Internet more than 'old' males (those aged 25 and over). Data on minutes of usage on a particular typical Saturday for a sample of 34 young males and a sample of 32 'old' males are shown below.

Young

25	25	45	20	25	20	35	75	0	0	0
25	65	75	45	0	70	125	150	80	75	15
20	15	65	55	45	45	50	35	60	95	70
45										

Old

0	25	125	5	45	0	35	0	15	55	40
0	35	30	40	20	45	190	60	170	0	0
35	0	15	85	55	25	40	10	15	20	

SPSS's **Analyze > Descriptive Statistics > Descriptives** command gives:

	N	Range	Minimum	Maximum	Mean		Std.
	Statistic	Statistic	Statistic	Statistic	Statistic	Std. Error	Statistic
YOUNG	34	150	0	150	46.91	5.95	34.685
OLD	32	190	0	190	38.59	8.16	46.180
Valid N (listwise)	32						

The mean of the sample of young males is 46.91 minutes and the mean of the sample of 'old' males is less, 38.59 minutes, so the difference between the sample means is 8.32 minutes. At first sight it appears that young males use the Internet more than 'old' males. However, our real interest is not in the sample means but in the difference between the two *population* means. If the samples were drawn again, from the same populations, the difference between the sample means would differ because, as with the mean of a sample and the sample variance, it is a random variable and varies from sample to sample. The difference in sample means of 8.32 could therefore be due to chance and not indicate a real difference in the mean Internet usage of young and old males. That is, it might arise even when young males and old males have the same average usage. As we did for the mean of a single population, we will construct confidence intervals for the difference in the population means and we will test whether it takes a particular value (usually zero) or not. To do this we will need some notation.

Notation for two populations and two samples

Just as we called the mean of a single population μ and its variance σ^2, we will now call the mean of the first population μ_1 and the variance of the first population σ_1^2. In the same way, the mean and variance of the second population will be μ_2 and σ_2^2 respectively. And, whereas in Chapters S1 and S2 the sample size was n and the sample mean was $\bar{x}$, we will now say that the sample from the first population has size n_1 and mean $\bar{x}_1$ and that the sample from the second population has size n_2 and mean $\bar{x}_2$.

The distribution of $\bar{X}_1 - \bar{X}_2$

For a single population we based the confidence intervals and tests for the mean, μ, on the following result about the sampling distribution of the sample mean, $\bar{X}$.

> **Result 1: The sampling distribution of $\overline{X}$**
>
> For large samples ($n \geq 30$) and samples from *normal populations* the sample mean, $\overline{X}$, has a $N(\mu, \sigma^2/n)$ distribution. (The result is approximate for large samples.)

It is saying that for large samples or normal populations we can take the sample mean, $\overline{X}$, as normally distributed with mean μ and variance σ^2/n.

We now want to know something about the *difference* between the two *population* means; that is, $\mu_1 - \mu_2$. We will construct confidence intervals and tests in exactly the same way as those for the mean but this time we will base them on the difference between the sample means, $\overline{x}_1 - \overline{x}_2$, instead of $\overline{x}$. The result on the sampling distribution of $\overline{X}_1 - \overline{X}_2$, on which we will base confidence intervals and tests, is given below. Notice that it parallels Result 1 exactly.

> **Result 2: The sampling distribution of $\overline{X}_1 - \overline{X}_2$**
>
> For large samples ($n_1, n_2 \geq 30$) and samples from *normal populations* the difference between the sample means, $\overline{X}_1 - \overline{X}_2$, has a
>
> $$N\left(\mu_1 - \mu_2, \frac{\sigma_1^2}{n_1} + \frac{\sigma_2^2}{n_2}\right)$$
>
> distribution. (The result is approximate for large samples.)

Result 2 is saying that provided we have large samples or normal populations we can take $\overline{X}_1 - \overline{X}_2$ as being normally distributed with mean and $\mu_1 - \mu_2$ and variance

$$\frac{\sigma_1^2}{n_1} + \frac{\sigma_2^2}{n_2}$$

Out of interest notice also that the expected value of the difference between the sample means, $\overline{X}_1 - \overline{X}_2$, is the difference between the population means, $\mu_1 - \mu_2$, so $\overline{X}_1 - \overline{X}_2$ is an unbiased estimator of $\mu_1 - \mu_2$.

As we are going to base confidence intervals and tests on Result 2 we will assume that the populations are normally distributed and/or we have large samples in all that follows.

Confidence intervals: variances known

As in the single sample case we will start by assuming that we know the variances of both populations, σ_1^2 and σ_2^2, and drop the assumption later. From Chapter S1 the 95% confidence interval for the population mean, μ, is

$$\overline{x} \pm 196\sqrt{\frac{\sigma^2}{n}}$$

where σ^2 is the variance of the population (assumed known) and n is the number of items in the sample. Notice from Result 1 that this has the form

$$\text{Estimator} \pm 1.96 \times \sqrt{\text{variance of estimator}}$$

In general, a 95% confidence interval based on any normally distributed unbiased estimator will have this form and so Result 2 implies that the 95% *confidence interval for the difference between two population means*, $\mu_1 - \mu_2$, is

$$\bar{x}_1 - \bar{x}_2 \pm 1.96\sqrt{\frac{\sigma_1^2}{n_1} + \frac{\sigma_2^2}{n_2}}$$

Check this

Before a training session for call centre employees a sample of 50 calls to the call centre had an average duration of 5 minutes, whereas after the training session a sample of 45 calls had an average duration of 4.5 minutes. The population variance is known to have been 1.5 minutes before the course and 2 minutes afterwards. Give a 95% confidence interval for the change in average call time.

Solution:
Both samples are large so it is reasonable to say that $\bar{X}_1 - \bar{X}_2$ is normally distributed and we can proceed. $\sigma_1^2 = 1.5$ and $\sigma_2^2 = 2$, and $\bar{x}_1 - \bar{x}_2 = 5 - 4.5 = 0.5$, so the confidence interval we require is

$$0.5 \pm 1.96\sqrt{\frac{1.5}{50} + \frac{2}{45}} \text{ or } (-0.0348, \ 1.0348)$$

An interval calculated this way would contain the difference in population means in 95% of samples. Notice that as the confidence interval includes zero, it allows the possibility that the course might *not* have resulted in a change in average call time.

Further, as a $100(1 - \alpha)\%$ confidence interval for a single population mean is

$$\bar{x} \pm z_{\alpha/2}\sqrt{\frac{\sigma^2}{n}}$$

a $100(1 - \alpha)\%$ confidence interval for the difference between two population means is

$$\bar{x}_1 - \bar{x}_2 \pm z_{\alpha/2}\sqrt{\frac{\sigma_1^2}{n_1} + \frac{\sigma_2^2}{n_2}}$$

where $z_{\alpha/2}$ is the percentage point of the normal distribution such that $P(Z > z_{\alpha/2}) = \alpha/2$.

Check this

Calculate a 99% confidence interval for the change in average call time.

Solution:
For the 99% interval $100(1 - \alpha) = 99$, so $\alpha = 0.01$ and we need $z_{0.005} = 2.5758$ instead of 1.96. The confidence interval is

$$0.5 \pm 2.5758 \sqrt{\frac{1.5}{50} + \frac{2}{45}} \text{ or } (-0.2028, 1.2028)$$

99% of intervals calculated in this way contain the difference between the population means.

In practice, we will not know the variances of the two populations when we don't even know their means so we need to adapt this procedure to cope with unknown population variances.

Confidence intervals: variances unknown

When the sample sizes are large ($n_1 \geq 30$ and $n_2 \geq 30$) the *sample* variances, s_1^2 and s_2^2, will be close to the population variances, so we can use them in the confidence interval instead of σ_1^2 and σ_2^2. The confidence interval for the difference in means becomes

$$\bar{x}_1 - \bar{x}_2 \pm z_{\alpha/2} \sqrt{\frac{s_1^2}{n_1} + \frac{s_2^2}{n_2}}$$

where s_1^2 is the variance of the first sample and s_2^2 is the variance of the second sample calculated in the usual way; that is,

$$s_1^2 = \frac{\Sigma x^2 - \frac{(\Sigma x)^2}{n_1}}{n_1 - 1}$$

summing over data in the first sample only and

$$s_2^2 = \frac{\Sigma x^2 - \frac{(\Sigma x)^2}{n_2}}{n_2 - 1}$$

summing over data in the second sample only.

Testing the difference between two means

Sometimes we are not interested in estimating the difference between two population means but we want to know whether they are the same or whether one is bigger than the other. For instance, if a pharmaceutical company develops a new version of a drug the key issue is whether or not it performs better than the old version.

From Chapter S2 we know that when we want a yes/no answer to a question about a population we use statistical testing and that all tests follow the same four-point structure: **1.** Hypotheses. **2.** Test statistic. **3.** *p*-value. **4.** Test result.

The test for the difference in two means has exactly the same structure and method as the test for a single mean; the only novelty is the choice of test statistic at Step 2.

The null hypothesis is that there is *no* difference between the population means; that is, $H_0: \mu_1 - \mu_2 = 0$. The alternative hypothesis can be that one mean is greater than the other (one-sided) (that is, $H_1: \mu_1 - \mu_2 > 0$ or $H_1: \mu_1 - \mu_2 < 0$) or it can be that there is a *difference* between the means (two-sided) (that is, $H_1: \mu_1 - \mu_2 \neq 0$).

As before, we start by assuming that we know the variances, σ_1^2 and σ_2^2, of both populations but relax the assumption later. We demonstrate the test using the call centre example.

Recall that before a training session a sample of 50 calls to the call centre had an average time of 5 minutes, whereas after the session a sample of 45 calls took an average time of 4.5 minutes. The population variance is known to have been 1.5 minutes before the training session and to be 2 minutes afterwards.

Suppose that the Call Centre company wants to test the hypothesis that the training session *decreases* average call time.

1. The hypotheses
The null hypothesis is that there is no change in average call time (that is, $H_0: \mu_1 - \mu_2 = 0$), whereas the alternative is that there is a decrease in average call time (that is, the first population mean is larger than the second, and so is $H_1: \mu_1 - \mu_2 > 0$). As usual we'll set the significance level to 0.05.

2. The test statistic
For tests of a single population mean the test statistic is

$$z = \frac{\bar{x} - \mu}{\sqrt{\dfrac{\sigma^2}{n}}}$$

where μ is the mean given in the null hypothesis. When H_0 is true, z is a standardised version of $\bar{x}$ so z comes from a standard normal distribution.

In the same way, the test statistic for testing the difference between *two* population means is

$$z = \frac{\bar{x}_1 - \bar{x}_2}{\sqrt{\dfrac{\sigma_1^2}{n_1} + \dfrac{\sigma_2^2}{n_2}}}$$

If you look back at Result **2** you will see that this is $\bar{x}_1 - \bar{x}_2$, standardised using its standard deviation

$$\sqrt{\frac{\sigma_1^2}{n_1} + \frac{\sigma_2^2}{n_2}}$$

and its mean when the null hypothesis is true, $\mu_1 - \mu_2 = 0$. So, when H_0 is true z comes from a standard normal distribution.

Check this

Calculate the test statistic, z, for the call centre example.

Solution:

$$z = \frac{5 - 4.5}{\sqrt{\dfrac{1.5}{50} + \dfrac{2}{45}}} = 1.83$$

3. The p-value
The *p*-value is the probability of getting such an extreme *z* as this when the null hypothesis is true so there is nothing new here.

> ## Check this
>
> Calculate the *p*-value for the call centre test.
>
> **Solution:**
> As the alternative hypothesis contains a 'greater than' sign, extreme means extremely large so $p = P(Z > 1.83) = 0.0336$.

4. The test result
As usual, if the *p*-value is smaller than the significance level the sample result is unlikely when the null hypothesis is true and we reject the null hypothesis in favour of the alternative hypothesis. If the *p*-value is greater than the significance level we retain the null hypothesis.

> ## Check this
>
> Is the test result for the call centre example significant or not?
>
> **Solution:**
> *p*-value = 0.0336 is less than the significance level of 0.05 so we reject the hypothesis that there is no decrease in average call time and adopt the alternative hypothesis, $H_1: \mu_1 - \mu_2 > 0$. We conclude that there *is* evidence of a decrease in average call time.

Try to hang on at all times to an intuitive interpretation of the *p*-value rather than just remembering 'small *p*-value means reject'. Here, the probability of getting such an extreme sample result when the population means are the same is only about 3% which is unlikely and so casts doubt on the hypothesis of equal means.

Two-sided alternative hypotheses
Suppose the alternative hypothesis for the call centre example had been two-sided; that is, that the training course made a *difference* to the average call time rather than just decreasing it. The only change to the test procedure would be at Step **3**, when calculating the *p*-value. As 'extreme' now means extremely large *or* extremely small and, as the normal distribution is symmetric, we have to double the probability we had before and the *p*-value will be $2 \times P(Z > 1.83) = 2 \times 0.0336 = 0.0672$. As this is more than 0.05 the result is no longer significant, and we retain the null hypothesis that there is no difference between the means although the *p*-value is very close to the borderline.

Confidence intervals and tests
The relationship between two-sided tests and confidence intervals that we mentioned in Chapter S2, Section 3, continues to hold and can be extremely useful. We repeat it here, in the context of the difference between two population means.

   Suppose that a 95% confidence interval for the difference between two means is reported as (–0.3, 1.3). This tells us that the null hypothesis, that the difference between two means is anything between –0.3 and 1.3, *would be retained* at the 5% level when tested against a two-sided alternative. We are usually interested in whether the difference between two population means is zero or not so, in particular, it tells us that the null hypothesis $H_0: \mu_1 - \mu_2 = 0$ would be retained when tested against the two-sided alternative, $H_0: \mu_1 - \mu_2 \neq 0$. A similar relationship holds between, say, 99% confidence intervals and tests at the 1% level or 90% confidence intervals and tests with a 10% significance level and so on. Because of this relationship, journals and reports frequently give the confidence interval *or* the *p*-value but not both.

Check this

The following 95% confidence intervals are reported for the mean difference in strength of two textiles. Which would reject, at the 5% level, the null hypothesis that the two textiles have the same strength when tested against the hypothesis that there is a difference?

a. (–10.9, 21.2)
b. (0.2, 21.2)
c. (–0.2, 0.56)

Solution:
a. and **c.** include zero so they would retain the null hypothesis of no difference, i.e. the *p*-value would be more than 0.05. **b.** does not include 0 and so would reject the hypothesis of no difference at the 5% significance level, i.e. the *p*-value would be less than 0.05.

Testing the difference between two means: variances unknown

In practice, of course, we usually don't know the population variances, so when the sample sizes are large ($n_1, n_2 \geq 30$), we use the sample variances, s_1^2 and s_2^2, in the test statistic instead and it is

$$z = \frac{\bar{x}_1 - \bar{x}_2}{\sqrt{\dfrac{s_1^2}{n_1} + \dfrac{s_2^2}{n_2}}}$$

As usual, when H_0 is true z comes from a standard normal distribution.

WORK CARD 1

1. The average hourly rate of pay for vacation work received by a sample of 40 Business students is £5.60, whereas the average received by a sample of 35 Maths students is £4.80. The sample standard deviation of the Business students' rate of pay was 1.8 and the sample standard deviation of the Maths students' rate of pay was 1.2. Construct a 99% confidence interval for the difference in means. State any assumptions that are necessary.

2. Using the data in question 1, test, at the 5% significance level, whether Business students on average earn more per hour than Maths students.

WORK CARD 1 (CONTINUED)

Solutions:

1. Here both sample sizes are large so we can use the sample variances in a z confidence interval. The interval is

$$5.6 - 4.8 \pm 2.5758 \sqrt{\frac{1.8^2}{40} + \frac{1.2^2}{35}}$$

This is 0.8 ± 0.90, or $(-0.1, 1.7)$.

2. We want to test $H_0: \mu_1 - \mu_2 = 0$ against $H_1: \mu_1 - \mu_2 > 0$. Both samples are large so the test statistic is

$$z = \frac{5.6 - 4.8}{\sqrt{\frac{1.8^2}{40} + \frac{1.2^2}{35}}} = 2.29$$

and the p-value is $P(Z > 2.29) = 0.011$, which is significant. There is evidence that Business students are paid more than Maths students.

ASSESSMENT 1

1. A study compares the salaries of Arts and Social Science graduates one year after graduation. A sample of 42 Arts graduates has an average salary of £13,560, with standard deviation £950, and a sample of 51 Social Science graduates has an average salary of £14,250 with standard deviation £1230. Does this provide evidence that the average salary of an Arts graduate one year after graduation differs from that of a Social Science graduate? Test at the 1% significance level.

2 Difference between two means: small samples

In the previous section we used the sample variances, s_1^2 and s_2^2, as approximations to the population variances, σ_1^2 and σ_2^2. When the sample size is small we can't do this because the sample variances will not be sufficiently good estimators of the population variances. Several methods are available, which make varying assumptions, but we will describe the most common method which is valid for *normal populations* only and which assumes that *both population variances are the same.*[*] It uses both samples to calculate a 'pooled' estimator of the common variance, σ^2, and then uses the pooled estimator in the usual formulae for the confidence interval and test statistic.

The pooled estimator of variance

We are now assuming that both populations have the same variance, σ^2. To estimate it we combine both samples to form the pooled estimator,

---

* This may or may not be a reasonable assumption. There are tests for the equality of two variances but these are beyond the scope of this book.

$$s_p^2 = \frac{(n_1 - 1)s_1^2 + (n_2 - 1)s_2^2}{n_1 + n_2 - 2}$$

The numerator doesn't look too attractive to calculate or remember but the following may help. The formula for the variance of a sample is

$$s^2 = \frac{\Sigma(x - \bar{x})^2}{n - 1}$$

so $s^2(n - 1) = \Sigma(x - \bar{x})^2$, the sum of the squared deviations of each item in the sample from the sample mean. This means that the numerator of s_p^2 is the sum of the squared deviations of every item in the first sample from the first sample's mean, plus the sum of the squared deviations of every item in the second sample from its mean. Consequently, s_p^2 is an estimator of the common variance which allows for the possibility that the two samples may come from populations with different means.

Testing the difference between two means for small samples

The test statistic is the same as usual but with both variance terms replaced by s_p^2; that is,

$$t = \frac{\bar{x}_1 - \bar{x}_2}{\sqrt{\frac{s_p^2}{n_1} + \frac{s_p^2}{n_2}}}$$

or equivalently

$$t = \frac{\bar{x}_1 - \bar{x}_2}{\sqrt{s_p^2\left(\frac{1}{n_1} + \frac{1}{n_2}\right)}}$$

Notice that we have called it t and not z. This is because using the pooled sample variance introduces more variability into the test statistic so that when the null hypothesis is true it comes from the t distribution with $n_1 + n_2 - 2$ degrees of freedom and not the standard normal distribution. A similar thing happened when we used the sample variance in the test for the single sample mean (Chapter S2, Section 5). As an aide-memoire notice that the degrees of freedom are the same as the denominator of s_p^2.

Remember, from Chapter S1, Section 5, that there are a whole family of t distribution curves, each indexed by a number 1, 2, 3, ... etc. which is called the number of degrees of freedom. The t curves are very similar in shape to the standard normal curve, but they have fatter tails. As the number of degrees of freedom increases, the t curve becomes more and more like the standard normal curve until, for 30 or more degrees of freedom, they are almost identical.

Try the following example.

Check this

The tensile strength of an aircraft part is a quality measure of interest. A sample of 8 parts manufactured with a traditional alloy has a mean tensile strength of 80 kg/mm^2 with a standard deviation of 15 kg/mm^2, whereas a sample of 10 parts manufactured with a new alloy has a mean tensile strength of 87 kg/mm^2 with a standard deviation of 14 kg/mm^2. Test at the 1% significance level whether the new alloy is stronger than the old one. State any assumptions you need to make to do the test.

Solution:
The sample sizes are small so we assume that tensile strength is normally distributed and that the variance is the same for both the traditional and new alloys.

1. The null hypothesis is $H_0: \mu_1 - \mu_2 = 0$. As the alternative hypothesis is that the mean tensile strength is *greater* for the new alloy, it is $H_1: \mu_1 - \mu_2 < 0$. The significance level is 0.01.

2. The test statistic is

$$t = \frac{\bar{x}_1 - \bar{x}_2}{\sqrt{s_p^2(\frac{1}{n_1} + \frac{1}{n_2})}}$$

where $\bar{x}_1 = 80$, $\bar{x}_2 = 87$, $n_1 = 8$ and $n_2 = 10$. When the null hypothesis is true this comes from a t distribution with $n_1 + n_2 - 2$ degrees of freedom.
As $s_1^2 = 15^2$ and $s_2^2 = 14^2$ the pooled estimator of the common variance is

$$s_p^2 = \frac{(n_1 - 1)s_1^2 + (n_2 - 1)s_2^2}{n_1 + n_2 - 2} = \frac{(7 \times 15^2) + (9 \times 14^2)}{8 + 10 - 2} = 208.69$$

and so the test statistic is

$$t = \frac{80 - 87}{\sqrt{208.69(\frac{1}{8} + \frac{1}{10})}} = -1.02$$

When the null hypothesis is true this comes from a t distribution with $8 + 10 - 2 = 16$ degrees of freedom.

3. The p-value is the probability of getting such an extreme t as this when the null hypothesis is true. As the alternative hypothesis includes a $<$ sign, this is

$$p = P(T < -1.02)$$

Software will calculate this probability exactly but if you are working with a calculator you need to use Table V, Percentage Points of the t Distribution, to get a range of the probability. The row for 16 degrees of freedom is

p	0.75	0.90	0.95	0.975	0.99	0.995	0.9995
16	0.690	1.337	1.746	2.120	2.583	2.921	4.015

Remember that this means that $P(T < 0.690) = 0.75$ and so on. Using the symmetry of the t distribution we can deduce that $0.10 < p\text{-value} < 0.25$.

4. As the p-value is greater than 0.01 we retain the null hypothesis and conclude that there is no evidence to suppose that the new alloy is stronger than the traditional one. In fact, as it is greater than 0.10 this sample result is quite likely to happen when the null hypothesis is true.

Confidence intervals for small samples
The $100(1 - \alpha)\%$ confidence interval for the difference in the population means for smaller samples is

$$\bar{x}_1 - \bar{x}_2 \pm t_{\alpha/2}\sqrt{s_p^2(\tfrac{1}{n_1} + \tfrac{1}{n_2})}$$

Notice that this has the same form as the confidence interval for large samples except that **(i)** it uses the pooled estimator of the common variance and **(ii)** it uses a percentage point of the t distribution instead of a percentage point of a standard normal distribution. These are the same changes that we made for the small sample t test above and the confidence interval makes the same assumptions that the populations are normal and have the same variance, and the number of degrees of freedom we use for the t distribution is again the number in the denominator of s_p^2; that is, $n_1 + n_2 - 2$.

Let's construct some confidence intervals for the aircraft part example.

Check this

Stating any assumptions that are necessary, give a 99% confidence interval and a 95% confidence interval for the change in tensile strength given by the new alloy. (**Reminder:** a sample of 8 traditional parts had a mean tensile strength of 80 kg/mm^2 and a standard deviation of 15 kg/mm^2, whereas a sample of 10 new parts had mean tensile strength of 87 kg/mm^2 and a standard deviation of 14 kg/mm^2.)

Solution:
We will continue to take the traditional alloy as the first population and the new alloy as the second and calculate confidence intervals for $\mu_1 - \mu_2$. However, note that a negative $\mu_1 - \mu_2$ indicates that the new alloy improves (increases) tensile strength. We already know that the pooled estimator of the population variances is $s_p^2 = 208.69$.

The t distribution we need is the one with $n_1 + n_2 - 2 = 8 + 10 - 2 = 16$ degrees of freedom. For the 99% confidence interval we need $t_{0.005}$ with 16 degrees of freedom, which is 2.921, so it is

$$80 - 87 \pm 2.921\sqrt{208.69\left(\frac{1}{8} + \frac{1}{10}\right)}$$

which is -7 ± 20.02 or $(-27.02, 13.02)$. This is wide partly because the samples are small but also because it is a 99% interval as opposed to a 95% interval.

In the same way the 95% interval uses $t_{0.025} = 2.120$ and is

$$80 - 87 \pm 2.120\sqrt{208.69\left(\frac{1}{8} + \frac{1}{10}\right)} \text{ or } (-21.53, 7.53)$$

1. 'New Car' magazine test drives each of two brands of new car five times. The fuel consumptions, kilometres per litre (kpl), for the two brands are

Brand	
A	B
10.9	12.1
11.1	11.8
13.0	11.6
10.4	10.5
11.2	11.9

   Calculate a 95% confidence interval for the Brand A mean less the Brand B mean, stating any assumptions that are necessary.

2. Test whether there is a difference between the average fuel consumption of the two brands of car in question **1**.

3. The price of a pint of a particular brand of lager in a randomly chosen selection of 5 Norwich pubs is given below in pence

   220, 230, 240, 225, 224 ($\bar{x}$ = 227.8, Σx^2 = 259,701)

   whereas the prices of a pint of the same brand of lager in a sample of 5 central London pubs are

   225, 230, 245, 252, 250 ($\bar{x}$ = 240.4, Σx^2 = 289,554)

   Does this small survey provide evidence that the average price of this brand of lager is higher in London than in Norwich? Calculate a 99% confidence interval for the difference in mean price.

Solutions:

1. Here, we only have small samples and we don't know the population variances so we will have to assume a common variance and assume normality. The sample means are 11.32 and 11.58 respectively and sample standard deviations 0.988 and 0.630, so the pooled estimate of the variance is

$$s_p^2 = \frac{(4 \times 0.988^2) + (4 \times 0.630^2)}{5 + 5 - 2} = 0.6865$$

   and the confidence interval using t with 8 degrees of freedom is

$$11.32 - 11.58 \pm 2.306 \sqrt{0.6865 \left(\frac{1}{5} + \frac{1}{5} \right)}$$

   i.e. (−1.47, 0.95). It is very vague, which isn't surprising because the sample sizes are small and the variances are unknown.

2. The test statistic is

WORK CARD 2

$$t = \frac{11.32 - 11.58}{\sqrt{0.6865(\frac{1}{5} + \frac{1}{5})}} = -0.50$$

There are 8 degrees of freedom so $P(T < -0.50) > 0.25$ and p-value > 0.5. There is no evidence to suggest that average petrol consumption for the two models differs. We could have deduced this from the confidence interval in **1**. As the 95% confidence interval included zero, the two-sided test of $\mu_1 - \mu_2 = 0$ will not be significant at the 5% level.

3. Here, we only have small samples and we don't know the population variances so we will have to assume a common variance and normality. The sample variances are 59.2 and 148.3 respectively, so the pooled estimate of the variance is

$$s_p^2 = \frac{(4 \times 59.2) + (4 \times 148.3)}{5 + 5 - 2} = 103.75$$

The test statistic is

$$t = \frac{227.8 - 240.4}{\sqrt{103.75(\frac{1}{5} + \frac{1}{5})}} = -1.9558$$

so p-value $= P(T < -1.9558)$ which for 8 degrees of freedom is between 0.025 and 0.05. At the 5% significance level there is evidence that London prices are higher than Norwich prices. The 99% confidence interval is

$$227.8 - 240.4 \pm 3.355\sqrt{103.75\left(\frac{1}{5} + \frac{1}{5}\right)}$$

i.e. $(-34.2, 9.0)$.

1. Collect a sample of hourly rates of vacation pay from two different sets of students. These might be male and female, Arts and Science students, or aged under or over 21.

    (i)   Construct an appropriate confidence interval for the difference in mean rates, assuming a common variance if necessary. What assumption(s) must you make about the populations from which the data are drawn and do these seem appropriate?

    (ii) Test the hypothesis that the mean rates of pay differ. Describe your test results carefully.

3 **Paired samples**

Sometimes (rarely) life gets easier. We will now see that some apparently two-sample situations can be reduced to just one sample.

Paired data

Sometimes there is something special about your data that means you won't need one of the two-sample tests in the previous sections. This 'something special' is that the data are *matched* or *paired*. By this we mean that the data were collected so that the first item in the first sample and the first item in the second are a natural pair in some way, as are the second items in the samples and so on. For instance, the first sample might be the blood pressure of patients before an operation and the second sample the blood pressure *of the same patients* after the operation. The idea is that any difference due to other factors, for instance, weight, age or state of health, for the blood pressure example is eliminated or controlled.

> ### Check this
>
> Which of the following samples are paired? Explain your answer.
>
> **a.** First sample: Number of hours of TV watched by 40 men.
> Second sample: Number of hours of TV watched by 40 women.
>
> **b.** First sample: Number of hours of TV watched in a week by 40 men.
> Second sample: Number of hours of TV watched in a week by the wives/partners of these men.
>
> **c.** First sample: Sales (£) of the book department of a store each month of a particular year.
> Second sample: Sales (£) of the stationery department each month of the same year.
>
> **d.** First sample: The keyboard speed of 38 employees before a training course.
> Second sample: The keyboard speed of the same 38 employees after the course.
>
> **e.** First sample: Salaries of 48 teachers at a private school.
> Second sample: Salaries of 48 teachers at a public school.
>
> **Solutions:**
>
> **a.** These are samples of any 40 men and any 40 women so there is no pairing.
>
> **b.** Now we have the same situation as **a.** but there is a pairing between the first of each sample, the second of each sample and so on.
>
> **c.** The pairing is now due to the months of the year. The first item in each sample will be the January figure, the second, February's and so on.
>
> **d.** The two samples are for the same set of employees so they are paired.
>
> **e.** Although the samples are the same size there is no pairing between the teachers in one sample and the teachers in the other. However, if we had chosen the samples so that the first teachers in each sample were of a similar age and taught the same subject, as were the second ones, and so on, the samples would be paired.

Notice that for paired samples the number of items in each sample must be the same. However, unpaired samples may or may not have the same number of items.

Testing and confidence intervals for paired samples

When the data are paired we calculate the differences between the pairs and work with these only. In this way we reduce the problem to a single-sample problem and use the single-sample confidence intervals and tests of Chapters S1 and S2. We will label the new, single-sample of differences, d_1, d_2, d_3, ..., d_n and call the sample mean of these $\bar{d}$. The null hypothesis is that the population mean of the differences, μ_d, is zero; that is, $H_0: \mu_d = 0$.

Check this

The table below shows the market valuations (£million) of 17 major companies before and after a rights issue. (The data are in *companies*.) The fourth column gives the differences (*Before* minus *After*) for each company. Test whether or not there is a difference in the mean market valuation of a company before and after a rights issue. State any assumptions you make.

Company	Before	After	Difference d
1	454	413	41
2	300	262	38
3	200	288	-88
4	125	151	-26
5	238	271	-33
6	430	391	39
7	780	823	-43
8	350	291	59
9	670	642	28
10	650	626	24
11	720	736	-16
12	420	453	-33
13	380	411	-31
14	310	315	-5
15	550	593	-43
16	127	155	-28
17	138	160	-22

Solution:
We work with the differences only. The null hypothesis is that the population mean of the difference is zero and the alternative hypothesis is that the mean difference is not zero; that is, $H_0: \mu_d = 0$ and $H_1: \mu_d \neq 0$. We need a one-sample test. The population variance is unknown so we will have to use the sample variance. Further, the sample size is small so we will have to assume normality and use t. The test statistic is therefore

$$t = \frac{\bar{d} - 0}{\sqrt{\dfrac{s_d^2}{n}}}$$

where s_d^2 is the sample variance of the differences.

From the sample of differences, we calculate $\Sigma d = -139$ and $\Sigma d^2 = 26{,}293$, so $\bar{d} = -8.1765$ and $s_d^2 = 1572.28$ and

$$t = \frac{-8.1765 - 0}{\sqrt{\dfrac{1572.28}{17}}} = -0.8502$$

When the null hypothesis is true this comes from a t distribution with $17 - 1 = 16$ degrees of freedom. As the alternative hypothesis is two-sided, the p-value is $2 \times P(T < -0.8502)$. Due to the symmetry of the t distribution $P(T < -0.8502) = P(T > 0.8502)$ which, from Table V, is between 0.10 and 0.25, so $0.20 < p\text{-value} < 0.50$. We conclude that the test is not significant; there is no evidence to suggest that market valuations change after a rights issue.

A glance at the market valuation data above confirms that high 'before' market valuations tend to be associated with high 'after' market values, which is hardly surprising. In other words, the market valuations before and after are *not* independent. The two-sample tests in the preceding sections assume that the two populations are independent and so are *not* appropriate here. By pairing data and working with the differences we hope to eliminate any effects on market valuation that apply to both numbers in a pair.

Confusion? Which test or interval?

There is often confusion about which test or confidence interval to use to compare two population means and people are frequently tempted to learn a catalogue of procedures by heart. However, we emphasise that if you invest time in understanding the underlying ideas, the choice of procedures and formulae will all seem easy and logical and enable you to interpret all manner of statistical tests in the future. We hope the algorithm below helps. Start from **1** until you find an appropriate procedure.

Comparing two population means

1. Are the two samples paired?
If so, calculate the differences and work with a single sample. To use the techniques in this book the population of differences will have to be normal and/or the sample will have to be large.

If the data are *not* paired, to use the tests in this book you will now need to assume that both populations are normally distributed and/or the sample sizes are both **large** and go to **2**.

2. Are the population variances σ_1^2 and σ_2^2 known?
If so use

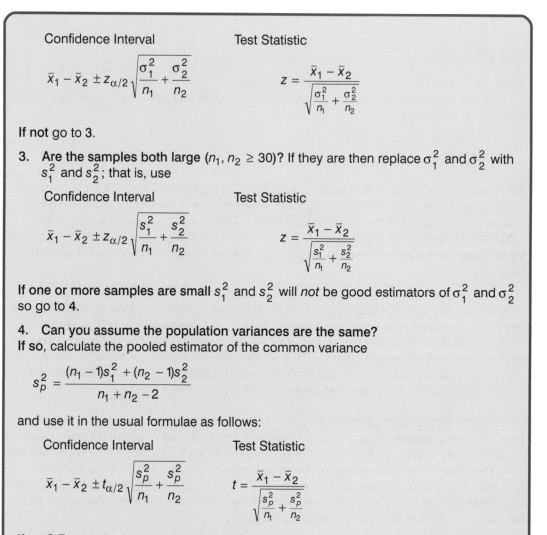

Confidence Interval   Test Statistic

$$\bar{x}_1 - \bar{x}_2 \pm z_{\alpha/2} \sqrt{\frac{\sigma_1^2}{n_1} + \frac{\sigma_2^2}{n_2}}$$

$$z = \frac{\bar{x}_1 - \bar{x}_2}{\sqrt{\frac{\sigma_1^2}{n_1} + \frac{\sigma_2^2}{n_2}}}$$

If not go to 3.

3. **Are the samples both large ($n_1, n_2 \geq 30$)?** If they are then replace σ_1^2 and σ_2^2 with s_1^2 and s_2^2; that is, use

Confidence Interval   Test Statistic

$$\bar{x}_1 - \bar{x}_2 \pm z_{\alpha/2} \sqrt{\frac{s_1^2}{n_1} + \frac{s_2^2}{n_2}}$$

$$z = \frac{\bar{x}_1 - \bar{x}_2}{\sqrt{\frac{s_1^2}{n_1} + \frac{s_2^2}{n_2}}}$$

If one or more samples are small s_1^2 and s_2^2 will *not* be good estimators of σ_1^2 and σ_2^2 so go to 4.

4. **Can you assume the population variances are the same?**
If so, calculate the pooled estimator of the common variance

$$s_p^2 = \frac{(n_1 - 1)s_1^2 + (n_2 - 1)s_2^2}{n_1 + n_2 - 2}$$

and use it in the usual formulae as follows:

Confidence Interval   Test Statistic

$$\bar{x}_1 - \bar{x}_2 \pm t_{\alpha/2} \sqrt{\frac{s_p^2}{n_1} + \frac{s_p^2}{n_2}}$$

$$t = \frac{\bar{x}_1 - \bar{x}_2}{\sqrt{\frac{s_p^2}{n_1} + \frac{s_p^2}{n_2}}}$$

If not? For small samples and unequal variances or small non-normal samples you will have to consult more advanced texts.

An alternative representation for *unpaired* samples (that is covering cases 2, 3 and 4 above) follows.

	Large samples ($n_1, n_2 \geq 30$)	Small samples (normal populations assumed)
Population variance σ^2 *Known*	use z, σ_1^2, σ_2^2	use z, σ_1^2, σ_2^2
Population variance σ^2 *Unknown*	use z, s_1^2, s_2^2 or t, s_1^2, s_2^2	assume equal variances and use t, s_p^2

In practice, a computer will usually use *t* when the variances are unknown, even for large samples, as in the one-sample case; hence the resemblance between this table and those for one-sample confidence intervals and testing at the end of Chapter S2, Section 3, and Chapter S1, Section 5.

Rejection regions

Many books use rejection regions instead of *p*-values (see Chapter S2, Section 4). We don't because

- you will usually use software to perform tests and this will give an exact *p*-value;
- the rejection region gives no indication of the strength of evidence for the null hypothesis, it only rejects or retains it.

Using a computer

In SPSS confidence intervals and tests for *paired samples* are calculated using

Analyze > Compare Means > Paired-Samples T Test

The samples must be in two columns of equal length. The default is a 95% confidence interval but an options sub-dialog box allows the user to change this. When the data are *not paired* the command is

Analyze > Compare Means > Independent-Samples T Test

The data should be placed in a single column but another column, the 'Grouping Variable column', contains, for instance, 1s and 2s to indicate which sample that observation belongs to.

In the dialog box you must assign the data variable and the grouping variable and define the values for the groups. You can also change the confidence level via the options sub-dialog box.

Output for a two-sided test and a 95% confidence interval for the Internet Service Provider data, from Section 1, is given below.

Group Statistics

	AGE	N	Mean	Std. Deviation	Std. Error Mean
USAGE	Young	34	46.91	34.685	5.948
	Old	32	38.59	46.180	8.164

Independent Samples Test

		Levene's Test for Equality of Variances		t-test for Equality of Means						
		F	Sig.	t	df	Sig. (2-tailed)	Mean Difference	Std. Error Difference	95% Confidence Interval of the Difference	
									Lower	Upper
USAGE	Equal variances assumed	.288	.593	.831	64	.409	8.32	10.015	−11.689	28.325
	Equal variances not assumed			.823	57.445	.414	8.32	10.101	−11.905	28.541

This output contains, in fact, three different tests. The columns under **t-test for Equality of Means** contain two *t* tests, one in each row. The first is the test we considered for small samples, which assumes that the variances of the two populations are equal and uses the pooled estimator of the variance, whereas the second is the one we used for large samples which allows the variances to be different. The output however also includes another test (in the two columns under **Levene's Test for Equality of Variances**) of whether the assumption of equal variances is reasonable.

In this example the test for equal variances gives, $p = 0.593$ (found under **Sig.**) indicating that there is no evidence to reject the hypothesis of equal variances and suggesting that it is quite reasonable to use the first **t** test, in the first row. The *p*-value of this test (in the column headed **Sig. (2-tailed)**) is 0.409, so there is no evidence that mean internet usage is different for young or old males. Notice that the *p*-value allowing unequal variances is 0.414 and so, for this example, the choice of test is not crucial although this is not always the case.

Confidence intervals for the difference in means appear in the final columns of output.

In Excel the statistical function **TTEST** outputs the *p*-value of a two-sided *t* test of the difference between two population means. Each sample must be in a separate array (single row or column). **TTEST** has an argument called 'tails', which should be 1 for a 1-tailed test or 2 for a 2-tailed test, and another called 'type', which should be a 1 for paired samples, 2 for the equal variance case and 3 for unequal variances. Again, it is up to the user to decide which test is appropriate. Confidence intervals must be programmed but the functions **TDIST** and **NORMDIST** will give the required percentage points of the *t* and standard normal distributions.

More confidence intervals and tests

Confidence intervals and tests can be constructed for any population measure using a suitable estimator from the sample. Although the method of construction is beyond the scope of this book there is no reason why you shouldn't be able to interpret any confidence interval or test you see reported.

For instance, every 95% confidence interval is such that it has a 95% chance of containing the population measure of interest.

The same holds for testing. The *p*-value is always the probability of obtaining such an extreme sample result assuming that the null hypothesis is true. If it is small (below the significance level) the sample result is unlikely when the null hypothesis holds and so we reject the null hypothesis.

All confidence intervals or tests are based on some assumptions; for instance, that the population is normally distributed or that the variance of two populations is the same. You should always be aware of these and consider their suitability for the data before you use the results of the confidence interval or test.

WORK CARD 3

1. The numbers of visitors to a stately home on five consecutive Saturdays are 353, 244, 367, 366 and 299 whereas the figures for the corresponding Sundays are 378, 255, 368, 401 and 305.

   (i)   Construct a confidence interval for the difference in means.

   (ii) Perform a test of whether the average Sunday figure is higher.

   (iii) Check your results using software.

WORK CARD 3 (CONTINUED)

2. Use a computer for this question. The US National Center for Health Statistics collects data on the daily intake of selected nutrients by race and income level. The data in the table below give the protein intakes in grams over a 24-hour period for independent random samples of 15 people with incomes below the poverty level and 10 people above it.

Daily protein intake	Below			Above	
	51.4	49.7	72.0	86.0	69.0
	76.7	65.8	55.0	59.7	80.2
	73.7	62.1	79.7	68.6	78.1
	66.2	75.8	65.4	98.6	69.8
	65.5	62.0	73.3	87.7	77.2

Do the data give evidence that there is a difference in mean protein intake between those with incomes above and below the poverty level?

Solutions:

1. This is paired data because the first items in the two samples are the Saturday and Sunday figures from the same weekend, as are the second items and so on.
   (i) The single-sample of differences (Sunday–Saturday) becomes 25, 11, 1, 35, 6 so $\bar{d} = 15.6$ and $s_{\bar{d}}^2 = 197.8$. The confidence interval uses t with 4 degrees of freedom so $t_{0.025} = 2.776$ and we have

   $$15.6 \pm 2.776\sqrt{\frac{197.8}{5}}$$

   which is 15.6 ± 17.46 or $(-1.86, 33.06)$.

   (ii) $t = \dfrac{\bar{d} - 0}{\sqrt{\dfrac{s_{\bar{d}}^2}{n}}} = 2.480$

   When the null hypothesis, $H_0: \mu_d = 0$, is true this comes from a t distribution with 4 degrees of freedom and p-value $= P(T > 2.480)$ is between 0.025 and 0.05 as the test is one-tailed. At the 5% significance level there *is* evidence to suggest that the Sunday figures are higher but at the 1% level there is not.

2. Assuming the population variances are equal and using the pooled variance estimate gives $t = -2.72$. $P(T < -2.72) = 0.0061$ (23 degrees of freedom). However, this is a two-tailed test so p-value $= 0.0122$ which is significant at the 5% level (but not at the 1% level). There is evidence to suggest a difference in average protein intake between people above and below the poverty level.

1. A double glazing company decides to pay some of its sales representatives by the hour instead of on commission. The sales (thousands of £) achieved during the sample period by 45 hourly paid and 40 commissioned representatives are given below and in the data file *doubleglazing*.

   Use a computer to test whether there is a difference between the mean sales figures of the two groups of representatives. Would it be wise to assume that the population variances are the same or not? Explain your answer.

Hourly		Commission	
54	61	74	72
62	59	64	62
57	51	56	68
69	65	63	52
53	68	79	70
65	54	63	61
59	69	59	67
60	60	65	52
44	59	81	61
58	56	74	82
63	54	71	59
59	70	71	77
60	71	71	56
44	65	60	49
45	64	81	87
66	55	75	84
70	60	71	88
59	61	60	
67	68	73	
55	59	65	
69	58	64	
72	64	86	
62		61	

2. Conduct a survey amongst a sample of male–female couples you know.
   (i) Use the data to give a 95% and 99% confidence interval for the average difference in their heights and comment.
   (ii) Now test the hypothesis that females are on average 2 inches (or 5 centimetres) shorter than their male other-halves. Describe your results fully.

   Some more two-population questions are included in **Assessment 3** of Chapter S6.

Further reading: see p. xv

Anderson *et al.* (Statistics) contains more detail as do Newbold *et al.* and Mendenhall *et al.*

S6
Categorical data

I ain't looking to block you up,
Shock or knock or lock you up,
*Analyse you, **categorise** you,*
Finalise you or advertise you.

Bob Dylan, 'All I really want to do' (1964)

Contexts

What is this chapter about?
This chapter considers estimation and testing for categorical data; that is, data that records a characteristic or quality, such as gender (male, female) or degree course (accountancy, business or economics).

It considers inferences about one characteristic and the relationship, if any, between two characteristics.

Why is it useful?
Categorical data arise frequently; for instance, whether a call to a call centre is answered within a minute or not, or whether the respondent in a market research survey is single, cohabiting, married, divorced or widowed.

Where does it fit in?
We have already said that the subject of Statistics can be divided into Descriptive Statistics and Inferential Statistics. In Describing Data we explained how data can be numerical or categorical and considered Descriptive Statistics for both types. In S3, S4 and S5 we applied estimation and testing, the fundamental ideas of Inferential Statistics (from S1 and S2), to numerical data. In this chapter we turn our attention to Inferential Statistics for categorical data.

What do I need to know?
You need to be very familiar with the ideas of estimation and testing presented in S1 and S2 and with the concept of categorical data from DD1, Pictures of data.

Objectives

By the end of your work on this chapter you should be able to:

● test and construct a confidence interval for a proportion;
● use the χ^2 test to test whether a sample of categorical data comes from a particular distribution;
● Perform a χ^2 test on a contingency table to test for independence.

Most of the data we have used so far have been *numerical* or *quantitative*; that is, they have taken numerical values. However, we saw in *Describing Data* that sometimes each data item is a characteristic or quality rather than a number in which case we say it is *categorical* or *qualitative*. For instance, the 20 answers to the question, 'Do you think we should reintroduce capital punishment?' shown below are categorical data.

Yes, No, Don't Know, Yes, Yes, No, No, No, Yes, Don't know, Don't know, Yes, Yes, No, Yes, No, No, No, No, Yes

Other examples of categorical data might be the gender (male or female) of voters, the brand of car (Ford, Rover, Honda etc.) that is driven, or the market sector (banking, pharmaceuticals, insurance etc.) of an ordinary share.

A list like the one above is long-winded and repetitive and no information is lost if we present the data as a table of *frequencies*. The frequencies of the replies to the capital punishment question are given below:

Category	Frequency
Yes	8
No	9
Don't know	3
Total	20

A set of data is usually a sample, drawn from a population. However, we are not usually interested in the frequencies in the sample for their own sake, but rather in the *proportions* of the *population* that fall into each category. We should point out that the proportion of the population in a category is exactly the same as the *probability* that a randomly chosen item from the population falls in that category. For instance, if 45% of the population is against capital punishment the probability that an individual from the population is against capital punishment is 0.45. As usual, a list of all the categories and their associated probabilities is called the *probability distribution*.

When there are only two categories we say the data are *binary*. Some examples of binary data are yes/no answers to a survey question, whether respondents are male or female and whether or not someone votes in an election. We start by considering binary data and then move on, in Sections 2 and 3, to more than two categories.

1 Proportions

Binary data has only two categories. We will call the proportion of the population in one of the two categories p. (The proportion in the other category is $1 - p$.) We would like to estimate p using a sample from the population.

A sensible estimator of p would seem to be the proportion of the *sample* who are in the category of interest, which we will call $\hat{p}$ ('p-hat'). (A 'hat' is often placed above a population measure to indicate an estimator of it.) This is comparable to using $\bar{x}$ to estimate μ, or s^2 to estimate σ^2.

For example, Middleton's Market Research would like to know the proportion of the UK adult population who saw a particular television advertisement. To estimate this they interview a sample of 400 randomly chosen adults and find that 80 of them saw the advert. An estimate of the proportion of the population who saw the advert, p, is therefore, $\hat{p} = 80/400 = 0.2$.

On its own $\hat{p}$ gives no indication of precision and so we would like to construct a confidence interval for the population proportion. We do this in a way analogous to constructing confidence intervals for the mean or the difference in means.

Confidence intervals for a proportion

Recall that a 95% confidence interval for the population mean, μ, is

$$\bar{x} \pm 1.96\sqrt{\frac{\sigma^2}{n}}$$

where σ^2 is the population variance and n is the sample size. We derived this from the fact that the sample mean, $\bar{X}$, has a

$$N\left(\mu, \frac{\sigma^2}{n}\right)$$

distribution (see Chapter S1). Notice that the confidence interval has the form

$$\text{estimator} \pm 1.96 \times \sqrt{\text{variance of estimator}}$$

It so happens that for large samples our estimator of p, $\hat{p}$, is approximately normally distributed[*] with mean p and variance $\frac{p(1-p)}{n}$. (To be a good approximation, the sample size n must be such that both $n\hat{p}$ and $n(1 - \hat{p})$ are greater than 5 so we should check this before performing any calculations.) Consequently, we can use normal probabilities to derive a confidence interval for p in much the same way as we did for μ and it will have the form above and therefore be

$$\hat{p} \pm 1.96\sqrt{\frac{p(1 - p)}{n}}$$

However, there is a problem. If you think about it, we can't calculate the quantity in the square root because we *don't* know the value of p. (If we did we wouldn't need to calculate a confidence interval to estimate it.) To get over this we use the sample proportion, $\hat{p}$, in place

---

[*] This follows from the binomial approximation to the normal distribution for large n in Chapter P3, Section 5.

of p in the formula although it does introduce a further approximation. An approximate 95% confidence interval for the population proportion, p, for large samples is therefore

$$\hat{p} \pm 1.96\sqrt{\frac{\hat{p}(1 - \hat{p})}{n}}$$

Remember, this means that in 95% of samples an interval calculated in this way will include the population proportion.

Check this

80 adults from the sample of 400 saw the television advertisement. Calculate an approximate 95% confidence interval for the proportion of the population who saw it.

Solution:
Here, $\hat{p} = 80/400 = 0.2$ and $n = 400$ so both $n\hat{p} = 80$ and $n(1 - \hat{p}) = 320$ are greater than 5 and we can continue. The 95% confidence interval is

$$0.2 \pm 1.96\sqrt{\frac{0.2 \times 0.8}{400}}$$

or (0.1608, 0.2392). Recall that this means that for 95% of samples an interval calculated in this way would contain the true population proportion.

Notice that if the sample size had been larger than 400, the number in the square root would have been smaller and the confidence interval would have been narrower and so more precise. This is exactly what we would intuitively expect from a larger sample.

The analogy with confidence intervals for the mean extends to confidence intervals for any percentage. Recall that a general expression for the $100(1 - \alpha)$% confidence interval for the population mean is

$$\bar{x} \pm z_{\alpha/2}\sqrt{\frac{\sigma^2}{n}}$$

($z_{\alpha/2}$ is the normal percentage point such that $P(Z > z_{\alpha/2}) = \alpha/2$; see Chapter S1, Section 4). In the same way a $100(1 - \alpha)$% confidence interval for the population proportion is

$$\hat{p} \pm z_{\alpha/2}\sqrt{\frac{\hat{p}(1 - \hat{p})}{n}}$$

Try this.

Check this

In a survey of 250 randomly chosen households in a town, 95 shop regularly at the local Mustbe supermarket. Construct an approximate 99% confidence interval for the proportion of households in the town who use the supermarket.

Solution:

$\hat{p} = 95/250 = 0.38$ and $n = 250$ so both $n\hat{p} = 95$ and $n(1 - \hat{p}) = 155$ are greater than 5 and we can continue. From the formula the confidence interval is

$$\hat{p} \pm z_{0.005}\sqrt{\frac{\hat{p}(1 - \hat{p})}{n}}$$

$z_{0.005}$ is the value from the standard normal distribution with a cumulative probability of 0.995; that is, $z_{0.005} = 2.5758$. The confidence interval is therefore

$$0.38 \pm 2.5758\sqrt{\frac{0.38 \times 0.62}{250}}$$

which is (0.3009, 0.4591). In 99% of samples an interval calculated in this way contains the population proportion, p.

Testing hypotheses about proportions

Returning to Middleton's Market Research, suppose now that the television channel which showed the advert claimed that it was seen by 25% of the adult population. Middleton's would like to know whether this claim is reasonable or not.

A naïve investigator might say that the sample invalidates the TV channel's claim because only 20% saw the advert. However, remember that a sample proportion varies from sample to sample and is only an estimate of the population proportion, so even when the population proportion is 25% it is possible that the sample proportion is only 20%. The question is whether the sample proportion is low because the population proportion is itself low or whether it is low because of sampling fluctuation.

To answer this sort of question properly we need to perform a statistical test of the TV channel's claim. It will follow the usual four-point structure; that is: **1.** The hypotheses; **2.** The test statistic; **3.** The p-value; and **4.** The test result (see Chapter S2, Section 2). In fact, you already have enough information to perform the test, but we'll work through it anyway. To avoid confusing the p-value with the population proportion, p, we will no longer use p as an abbreviation for p-value. (Some books use π for the population proportion to avoid this problem.) Throughout this chapter we will assume a significance level of $\alpha = 0.05$ unless otherwise stated.

We apply the four-point structure to test the TV channel's claim that $p = 0.25$ as follows:

1. The hypotheses are H_0: $p = 0.25$ (the TV channel's claim) and H_1: $p < 0.25$. (We do a one-sided test here because we are interested in whether the population proportion is 0.25 or whether the TV channel is over-stating and it is really smaller.)
2. The test statistic we use is the sample proportion, $\hat{p} = 80/400 = 0.2$.
3. The p-value. As usual, we want the probability of such an extreme sample result when the null hypothesis is true. Here, the alternative hypothesis is 'less than' so by extreme we mean smaller than and we need

$$p\text{-value} = P(\hat{p} < 0.2)$$

when H_0: $p = 0.25$ is true.

To evaluate this probability we need the probability distribution of $\hat{p}$. However, earlier in this section we said that for large samples the proportion in a sample, $\hat{p}$, is approximately normally distributed with mean p and variance $\frac{p(1-p)}{n}$ so we just have a normal probability to calculate, as follows:

$$p\text{-value} = P(\hat{p} < 0.2) = P\left(\frac{\hat{p} - p}{\sqrt{\frac{p(1-p)}{n}}} < \frac{0.2 - p}{\sqrt{\frac{p(1-p)}{n}}}\right)$$

When the null hypothesis is true $p = 0.25$ so this becomes

$$p\text{-value} = P\left(Z < \frac{0.2 - 0.25}{\sqrt{\frac{0.25(1-0.25)}{400}}}\right) = P(Z < -2.31) = 0.0104$$

4. The test result. The p-value of 0.0104 is less than the significance level of 0.05 which we set in **1.**, so we reject the null hypothesis in favour of the alternative hypothesis, H_1: $p < 0.25$. A sample result like this is very unlikely when the TV channel's claim is true, so we reject their claim.

Now try another example.

Check this

A sample of 200 workers from a very large company is taken on a particular day and 30 are found to be on sick leave. Test at a 5% significance level whether the proportion of the total workforce of the company who are on sick leave that day is 10% or whether it is higher.

Solution:
The hypotheses are H_0: $p = 0.10$ and H_1: $p > 0.10$ and $\hat{p} = 30/200 = 0.15$. The p-value is the probability that $\hat{p}$ is so large when H_0 is true; that is

$$p\text{-value} = P(\hat{p} > 0.15) = P\left(\frac{\hat{p} - 0.1}{\sqrt{\frac{0.1 \times 0.9}{200}}} > \frac{0.15 - 0.1}{\sqrt{\frac{0.1 \times 0.9}{200}}}\right)$$

$$= P(Z > 2.36) = 0.0091$$

The p-value is less than the 5% significance level so we reject the null hypothesis. The sample provides evidence that more than 10% of the workforce are on sick leave that day.

So far the alternative hypotheses have been one-sided, H_1: $p < 0.25$ and H_1: $p > 0.10$, but we could, of course, test a *two-sided* alternative hypothesis like H_1: $p \neq 0.25$ in much the same way. The only difference would be that at step **3.**, we would have to calculate the probability of such a small *or* such a large value of $\hat{p}$, so we would double the probability in one tail of the normal distribution.

Check this

Usually, 95% of the calls to a call centre last less than 5 minutes and the remaining 5% last longer. However, after staff attend a training course 16 out of a sample of 200 of their calls lasted longer than 5 minutes. Does this provide evidence (at the 5% significance level) that the training course has changed the proportion of calls that are shorter than 5 minutes?

Solution:
The hypotheses are H_0: $p = 0.95$ and H_1: $p \neq 0.95$ and $\hat{p} = 184/200 = 0.92$. As the alternative hypothesis is two-sided the p-value is the probability of such an extremely large or small sample proportion which is twice the probability of such a small proportion.

$$p\text{-value} = 2 \times P(\hat{p} < 0.92) = 2 \times P\left(\frac{\hat{p} - 0.95}{\sqrt{\frac{0.05 \times 0.95}{200}}} < \frac{0.92 - 0.95}{\sqrt{\frac{0.05 \times 0.95}{200}}} \right)$$

$$= 2 \times P(Z < -1.95) = 2 \times 0.0256 = 0.0512$$

As the p-value is greater than 0.05, strictly speaking it is not significant and there is no evidence to suggest that the proportion of calls has changed. However, the p-value is very borderline and we would probably investigate further. Notice that if the alternative hypothesis had been one-sided, the p-value would have been only 0.0256 and the test would have been significant.

Population proportions

The population proportion is p and the sample proportion is $\hat{p}$. Provided that $n\hat{p}$ and $n(1 - \hat{p})$ are greater than 5, an **approximate 95% confidence interval** for the population proportion is

$$\hat{p} \pm 1.96 \sqrt{\frac{\hat{p}(1 - \hat{p})}{n}}$$

and an **approximate $100(1 - \alpha)$% confidence interval** for the population proportion is

$$\hat{p} \pm z_{\alpha/2} \sqrt{\frac{\hat{p}(1 - \hat{p})}{n}}$$

The **test statistic** for a population proportion is $\hat{p}$ which is approximately normally distributed with mean p and variance

$$\frac{p(1 - p)}{n}.$$

WORK CARD 1

1. In a clinical trial 25 out of 40 patients who receive a new drug say that it improves their symptoms. Calculate a 95% confidence interval for the proportion of patients the drug will help in the future.

2. The hope is that 75% of patients will be helped by the new drug in question **1**. Test whether this is reasonable or whether it is optimistic.

3. Of the umbrellas produced by an umbrella factory, 8% are sub-standard and sold as seconds. After new equipment is installed 250 umbrellas are inspected

and 24 classified as sub-standard. Does this provide evidence that the new equipment has changed the proportion of sub-standard goods?

Solutions:

WORK CARD 1 (CONTINUED)

1. $n = 40$, $\hat{p} = 25/40 = 0.625$ and $z_{0.025} = 1.96$. np and $n(1 - p)$ are both greater than 5 so we can proceed. The confidence interval is

$$0.625 \pm 1.96\sqrt{\frac{0.625 \times 0.375}{40}} \text{ or } (0.4750, 0.7750)$$

So in 95% of samples an interval calculated in this way would contain the population proportion.

2. The null hypothesis is H_0: $p = 0.75$ and the alternative, H_1: $p < 0.75$. The test statistic is $\hat{p} = 25/40 = 0.625$ so

$$p\text{-value} = P(\hat{p} < 0.625) = P\left(\frac{\hat{p} - 0.75}{\sqrt{\frac{0.75 \times 0.25}{40}}} < \frac{0.625 - 0.75}{\sqrt{\frac{0.75 \times 0.25}{40}}}\right) = P(Z < -1.83) = 0.0336$$

There is evidence to reject the null hypothesis at the 5% level but not at the 1% level. The drug may be helping fewer than 75% of patients.

3. The question asks whether there has been a *change* in the proportion of substandard goods so we need a two-sided alternative hypothesis. The hypotheses are H_0: $p = 0.08$ and H_1: $p \neq 0.08$, the test statistic is $\hat{p} = 24/250 = 0.096$ and the p-value is the probability that such a large or small test statistic is observed. The probability of such a *large* test statistic is

$$P(\hat{p} > 0.096) = P\left(\frac{\hat{p} - 0.08}{\sqrt{\frac{0.08 \times 0.92}{250}}} > \frac{0.096 - 0.08}{\sqrt{\frac{0.08 \times 0.92}{250}}}\right) = P(Z > 0.93) = 0.1762$$

so the p-value is twice this, 0.3524. As it is above a 5% significance level, there is no evidence that there has been a change in the proportion of sub-standard goods.

ASSESSMENT 1

1. In an opinion poll 49 out of 100 voters said they would vote for the Labour party if a general election were held tomorrow. Assuming this sample is representative of the whole UK electorate, calculate a 90% confidence interval for the proportion of the UK electorate who would vote Labour in a general election.

2. Now suppose that the Labour party claim that they would obtain 60% of the vote if an election were held tomorrow. Does the sample described in question **1** support this claim or suggest that the true percentage might be lower?

3. Think of a question that you could ask colleagues and friends and which can only be answered by yes or no. For instance, 'Do you play sport?', 'Do you read a

newspaper every day?' or 'Do you speak a foreign language?'. Hazard a guess to the true proportion of 'yes' answers in the population and select a sample size on the basis of your guess. Now ask that number of people your question. Using the data from your survey:

(i) construct 95% and 99% confidence intervals for the proportion of 'yes' answers in the population;

(ii) test whether your original guess at the population proportion was reasonable or not. Present what you have done in a short written report.

2 **More than two categories**

In the last section we considered categorical data with two categories. We now move on to discussing categorical data with three or more categories.

Suppose there are c categories and that the probability that a randomly chosen item from the population falls in the first category is p_1, the probability that it falls in the second category is p_2 and so on. (Remember, these probabilities are just the same as the proportions of the population in each category.) Each item in the population must be in one category or another so the sum of the probabilities must be 1; that is, $p_1 + p_2 + ... + p_c = 1$. Collectively these probabilities form a *probability distribution*.

We would like to test a hypothesis about the ps. The usual four-point structure holds, so the only new material will be the choice of test statistic and its probability distribution.

Hypotheses about probabilities

A politician has stated that equal numbers of students live with their parents, in university residences, in rented accommodation and in their own homes. To investigate the truth of this a student newspaper randomly selects 200 university students and asks them where they are living. The survey results are as follows.

Where do you live?	Observed frequency
With parents	45
In university residences	50
Rented accommodation	93
Own home	12

Notice that we have now called the frequencies the *observed* frequencies. This is to distinguish them from some quantities called the *expected* frequencies, which we will introduce shortly.

The politician's statement is that the probability of each category is the same; that is,

$$p_1 = p_2 = p_3 = p_4 = 0.25$$

and this will be our null hypothesis.

The alternative hypothesis will be that the politician's statement is *not* true, that is, that *at least one* of p_1, p_2, p_3 and p_4 is *not* equal to 0.25.

The test statistic we use is usually called 'chi-squared' (pronounced 'ki squared') and denoted by the Greek letter χ^2. (It is always squared – we never talk about χ on its own.) To calculate it we are first going to need the expected frequencies.

Expected frequencies

If the null hypothesis is true we would expect, *on average*, a quarter of the sample of 200 students (that is, $200 \times 0.25 = 50$) to be in each category. We say that the *expected frequency* of each category is 50.

In general, the *expected frequency* of a category is the sample frequency we would expect, *on average*, when the null hypothesis is true. It is the sample size, n, multiplied by the appropriate p from the null hypothesis. The expected frequencies are therefore np_1, np_2, np_3 and so on.

Note that the observed frequencies are those in the sample and the expected frequencies are calculated from the probabilities.

Calculating the χ^2 test statistic

We will use O to denote the observed frequencies and E the expected frequencies and write them in a table as follows:

Where do you live?	O Observed frequency	E Expected frequency
With parents	45	50
In university residences	50	50
Rented accommodation	93	50
Own home	12	50

When the null hypothesis is true the observed frequencies and the expected frequencies will be similar so we would expect their differences, $O - E$, to be small. The test statistic is going to be a combined measure of the $(O - E)$s. However, if we just sum the $(O - E)$s a large positive one might cancel out a large negative one (in fact they total 0), so we can't just add them up. Also, it is the size of the $O - E$ relative to the Os and Es themselves which counts. We therefore *square* each $O - E$ to make it positive and then divide the result by E. That is, for each category we calculate

$$\frac{(O - E)^2}{E}$$

The χ^2 test statistic is the sum of these quantities over all categories,

$$\chi^2 = \sum \frac{(O - E)^2}{E}$$

When the null hypothesis is true we expect it to be small.

Check this

Calculate the χ^2 statistic for the accommodation data.

Solution:

We already know that the *O*s are 45, 50, 93 and 12 and the *E*s are 50, 50, 50, 50, so

$$\chi^2 = \frac{(45-50)^2}{50} + \frac{(50-50)^2}{50} + \frac{(93-50)^2}{50} + \frac{(12-50)^2}{50}$$

$$= \quad 0.50 \quad + \quad 0 \quad + \quad 36.98 \quad + \quad 28.88 \quad = 66.36$$

It is probably easier to do the calculations in columns as shown below, particularly when there are lots of categories.

Where do you live?	*O* Observed frequency	*E* Expected frequency	*O* − *E*	$\dfrac{(O-E)^2}{E}$
With parents	45	50	−5	0.50
In university residences	50	50	0	0
Rented accommodation	93	50	43	36.98
Own home	12	50	−38	28.88

$$\chi^2 = \sum \frac{(O-E)^2}{E}$$
$$= 66.36$$

The *p*-value

As usual, the *p*-value of the test will be the probability of getting such an extreme value of the test statistic when the null hypothesis is true. Here, large values of χ^2 support the alternative hypothesis, so by 'extreme' we mean extremely large and

$$p\text{-value} = P(\chi^2 > 66.36)$$

To calculate this probability we need to know something about the probability distribution of χ^2. (Yes, like $\bar{x}$, s^2 and $\hat{p}$ it is a function of the sample data and so is a random variable and, as such, has a probability distribution.) Fortunately, it is known that when the null hypothesis is true the χ^2 test statistic has *approximately* a distribution which is also called the χ^2 or chi-squared distribution.

The χ^2 distribution

Like the *t* distribution the χ^2 distribution is a continuous distribution and there are a whole family of curves, each one identified by an integer number called the degrees of freedom. (Out of interest, these curves are *not* symmetric like the normal or *t* distributions, but are skewed to the right, although they become more symmetric as the number of degrees of freedom increases.)

When the null hypothesis is true, the χ^2 test statistic comes approximately from a χ^2 distribution with *c* − 1 degrees of freedom, where *c* is the number of categories. However, the approximation is *not* good if any *expected* frequencies are small. A good rule of thumb is to insist that all the expected frequencies are at least 5. (If some are smaller, two or more categories can be merged into one, in which case their expected and observed frequencies are added and will be larger.)

As the *p*-value is the probability that a χ^2 random variable is *larger* than the test statistic we have calculated, we only need the probabilities in the upper-tail of the distribution and these are given in Table VI. The first few rows are shown below.

Table VI Percentage Points of the χ^2 Distribution.
The table gives the value *a* such that $P(\chi^2_v > a) = p$.

p	0.250	0.100	0.050	0.025	0.010	0.005	0.0005
v 1	1.323	2.706	3.841	5.024	6.635	7.879	12.116
2	2.773	4.605	5.991	7.378	9.210	10.597	15.202
3	4.108	6.251	7.815	9.348	11.345	12.838	17.730
4	5.385	7.779	9.488	11.143	13.277	14.860	19.997

Each row relates to the χ^2 distribution with a particular number of degrees of freedom (given by *v*). As the table heading says, the entries are the values for which the probability of a larger value is $p = 0.25$, $p = 0.10$ and so on. For instance, if we look at the 5th column of the table, the probability that a random variable from a χ^2 distribution with 3 degrees of freedom is greater than 11.345 is 0.01. We can write this as $P(\chi^2 > 11.345) = 0.01$. Software will give the probability exactly.

Check this

For the chi-squared distribution with 1 degree of freedom, what is $P(\chi^2 > 3.841)$?

Solution:
From the first row of the table, 0.05.

For the chi-squared distribution with 1 degree of freedom, what value, *a*, is such that $P(\chi^2 > a) = 0.005$?

Solution:
Find the entry in the 0.005 column of the table, 7.879.

Calculating the *p*-value
Returning to our example, recall that the *p*-value was $P(\chi^2 > 66.36)$. There are 4 categories so $c = 4$ and we need the χ^2 distribution with $c - 1 = 4 - 1 = 3$ degrees of freedom. We won't be able to find this probability exactly from the table but we can get a range within which it lies. From the table we have already found that $P(\chi^2 > 11.345) = 0.01$, but continuing along the row we see that $P(\chi^2 > 12.838) = 0.005$ and $P(\chi^2 > 17.730) = 0.0005$. $P(\chi^2 > 66.36)$ must be smaller than this so we can deduce that the *p*-value is *even smaller than* 0.0005.

Test conclusion
As the *p*-value is less than the significance level of 0.05 the test is significant and we reject the null hypothesis of equal probabilities. The observed frequencies are very unlikely to arise when the null hypothesis is true.

Standardised residuals

As the test is significant it might be interesting to look at the observed and expected frequencies again to get some idea of where the discrepancies lie. We repeat them below.

Where do you live?	O Observed frequency	E Expected frequency	$O - E$	$\dfrac{(O-E)^2}{E}$
With parents	45	50	−5	0.50
In university residences	50	50	0	0
Rented accommodation	93	50	43	36.98
Own home	12	50	−38	28.88

$$\chi^2 = \sum \frac{(O-E)^2}{E}$$
$$= 66.36$$

The final column shows the contribution of each category to the χ^2 statistic. The first and second categories have very small contributions (0.50 and 0), relative to those of the third and fourth categories (36.98 and 28.88), indicating that most of the deviation from the null hypothesis comes from these final two categories. However, these are always positive so it is more usual to use the square root of them to give the *standardised residuals*:

$$\frac{O - E}{\sqrt{E}}$$

These can be placed in a new column of the table as shown below.

Where do you live?	O Observed frequency	E Expected frequency	$O - E$	$\dfrac{(O-E)^2}{E}$	$\dfrac{O-E}{\sqrt{E}}$
With parents	45	50	−5	0.50	−0.707
In university residences	50	50	0	0	0
Rented accommodation	93	50	43	36.98	6.081
Own home	12	50	−38	28.88	−5.374

$$\chi^2 = 66.36$$

It can be shown that when the null hypothesis is true the standardised residuals have approximately a standard normal distribution. So, for instance, on average 95% of them will lie between −1.96 and 1.96. Also, their sign is the same as $O - E$ so they tell us whether the observed frequencies are above or below the expected ones. Here, the first two are small and between −1.96 and 1.96, whereas the third one is well outside this range (a standard normal variable of 6 is extremely unlikely) and positive, indicating that students are more likely to live in rented accommodation than the null hypothesis says. The fourth one is large and negative indicating that fewer students live in their own homes than suggested by the null hypothesis. We conclude that the deviation from the hypothesis of equal probabilities is due to more students living in rented accommodation and fewer living in their own homes.

Now try another example.

Check this

Every year Muscolino Tours give a questionnaire to a sample of customers returning from holiday in which they ask them to rate their holiday as excellent, very good, good, satisfactory or unsatisfactory. The results from this year's survey are shown below.

Rating	*This year* Observed frequency
Unsatisfactory	15
Satisfactory	10
Good	40
Very Good	50
Excellent	67
Total	182

Muscolino Tours pride themselves that traditionally only 5% of customers give an unsatisfactory rating, 10% satisfactory, 25% good, 30% very good and 30% excellent. Test whether these are reasonable probabilities for this year and, if appropriate, investigate where any differences lie.

Solution:
It is easiest to work this in a table as follows:

Rating	*O* Observed frequency	*E* Expected frequency	*O − E*	$\dfrac{(O-E)^2}{E}$	$\dfrac{O-E}{\sqrt{E}}$
Unsatisfactory	15	9.1	5.9	3.825	1.96
Satisfactory	10	18.2	−8.2	3.695	−1.92
Good	40	45.5	−5.5	0.665	−0.82
Very good	50	54.6	−4.6	0.388	−0.62
Excellent	67	54.6	12.4	2.816	1.68
				$\chi^2 = 11.389$	

There are 5 categories so we need the χ^2 distribution with $5 - 1 = 4$ degrees of freedom. The appropriate row of Table VI is shown below:

p	0.250	0.100	0.050	0.025	0.010	0.005	0.0005
4	5.385	7.779	9.488	11.143	13.277	14.860	19.997

$\chi^2 = 11.389$ lies between 11.143 and 13.277, so $P(\chi^2 > 11.389)$ lies between 0.025 and 0.010; that is, $0.01 < p$-value < 0.025, leading us to reject the null hypothesis at the 5% level of significance. We conclude that there *is* evidence that the probability distribution differs from the null hypothesis.

The standardised residuals are 1.96, –1.92, –0.82, –0.62 and 1.68. When the null hypothesis is true they should be approximately standard normal. The first is positive and right on the border at 1.96, suggesting that the proportion of unsatisfied customers may be higher than claimed by Muscolino, whereas the second standardised residual is close to the border at –1.92, suggesting that a smaller proportion of customers than hypothesised give a satisfactory rating.

Using a computer
You can perform a χ^2 test in Excel by placing the observed frequencies in one range and the expected frequencies in another. The **CHITEST** statistical function returns the p-value. For the Muscolino example it gives 0.02253002. SPSS does not perform the test directly but the cumulative probability of a χ^2 value can be calculated using

$$\textbf{Transform} > \textbf{Compute}$$

and choosing the **CDF.CHISQ** function.

Back to binary data?
In Section 1 we used the sample proportion, $\hat{p}$, to test a hypothesis about the population proportion p. For instance, for the TV advertisement data we tested the null hypothesis that 25% of the population had seen the advertisement against the alternative that fewer than 25% had. We obtained a z of –2.31 and a p-value of $P(Z < -2.31) = 0.0104$.

However, as binary data is just a special case of categorical data, an alternative test procedure would be to perform a chi-squared test on these data as follows.

Check this

Of 400 people in the survey, 80 have seen a particular TV advert. Test whether the proportion of the population who have seen it is 0.25 or not.

Solution:
The chi-squared calculations are shown in the table below. The expected frequencies are $400 \times 0.25 = 100$ and $400 \times 0.75 = 300$.

	O Observed frequency	E Expected frequency	$O - E$	$\dfrac{(O-E)^2}{E}$	$\dfrac{O-E}{\sqrt{E}}$
Yes	80	100	–20	4.000	–2
No	320	300	20	1.333	1.15
				$\chi^2 = 5.333$	

The p-value is $P(\chi^2 > 5.333)$ which, from Table VI, lies between 0.01 and 0.025 giving evidence that the proportion who watched the advertisement was *not* 0.25. If we use a computer we find that the exact p-value is 0.0208.

The χ^2 test we have just done is a two-sided test in the sense that it tests whether or not the population probabilities are 0.25 and 0.75. The test in Section 1, however, had a one-sided alternative hypothesis H_1: $p < 0.25$ but if it had been two-sided, H_1: $p \neq 0.25$, the p-value would have doubled to 0.0208, the p-value of the chi-squared test.

In fact, the χ^2 test is equivalent to a z test of a proportion with a two-sided alternative hypothesis. The p-values will be the same and, apart from rounding error, the χ^2 test statistic will always be the square of the z test statistic. (Here, 5.33 is approximately equal to 2.31^2.)

The z test has the advantage that we can use one-sided as well as two-sided alternatives, but the advantages of the χ^2 test are that it can cope with more than two categories and, as we shall see in the next section, it extends much more widely.

WORK CARD 2

1. A direct mail company claims that 15% of the letters it sends out result in enquiries but no sale, and 8% result in a sale. 500 letters were mailed: of these 87 resulted in enquiries only and 41 in sales. Test the company's claim.

2. The Cellar House pub sells five brands of beer. On a particular, typical, evening 17 customers drink Kingtown, 11 drink Four-Y, 15 drink Landlords, 9 drink Star and 13 drink Pelican. The landlord assumes this means that Kingtown is the most popular beer of the five. Is he right to do so? To obtain your answer test whether the five beers are equally popular.

Solutions:

1.

	O Observed frequency	E Expected frequency	$O-E$	$\dfrac{(O-E)^2}{E}$	$\dfrac{O-E}{\sqrt{E}}$
No response	372	385	−13	0.439	−0.663
Inquiry	87	75	12	1.92	1.386
Sale	41	40	1	0.025	0.158
				$\chi^2 = 2.384$	

The p-value is $P(\chi^2 > 2.384)$ and there are 3 categories so we need the χ^2 distribution with 2 degrees of freedom. From Table VI, $P(\chi^2 > 2.773) = 0.25$ so the p-value is greater than 0.25, the test is *not* significant and there is no evidence to reject the null hypothesis. As might be expected, the standardised residuals are all small.

2.

Beer	O Observed frequency	E Expected frequency	$O-E$	$\dfrac{(O-E)^2}{E}$	$\dfrac{O-E}{\sqrt{E}}$
Kingtown	17	13	4	1.231	1.110
Four-Y	11	13	−2	0.308	−0.555
Landlords	15	13	2	0.308	0.555

Beer	O Observed frequency	E Expected frequency	O − E	$\frac{(O-E)^2}{E}$	$\frac{O-E}{\sqrt{E}}$
Star	9	13	−4	1.231	−1.110
Pelican	13	13	0	0.000	0.000
				$\chi^2 = 3.078$	

The p-value is $P(\chi^2 > 3.078)$ and there are 4 degrees of freedom so from Table VI the p-value is at least 0.25. Although the Kingtown frequency is the highest such a result often happens by chance and there is no evidence here that the beers are not equally popular.

1. A national roadside breakdown company claims that it responds to 20% of breakdown calls within 20 minutes, 30% in 20–39 minutes, 30% in 40–59 minutes, 15% in 60–89 minutes and that it takes over 90 minutes in only 5% of call-outs. A consumer magazine conducts a survey of 80 call-outs and obtains the following frequencies.

< 20 minutes	20–39 minutes	40–59 minutes	60–89 minutes	90+ minutes
15	22	20	14	9

Use the sample data to test whether the breakdown company's claim is reasonable and comment.

2. Now use the test of a proportion from Section 1 to test whether the proportion of calls taking more than an hour is significantly greater than 20%. Compare your conclusion with that of question **1** and comment.

3. Collect your own data. Ask 20+ friends or acquaintances *one* of the following questions:
   (i) Which brand of beer (out of a list of 3 or 4) they prefer.
   (ii) Which supermarket chain (out of a list of 3 or 4) they shop at most.
   (iii) Which radio station (out of 3 or 4) they prefer to listen to.
   Now test the hypothesis that each of the alternative types of beer, supermarket or radio station are equally popular. Interpret your results carefully. Why did we ask you to list at most four? What would have happened if your interviewees had been given a larger number of choices?

3 Contingency tables

In the previous section we used the χ^2 test to test hypotheses about the probability distribution of a population. We are now going to see that the test is much more versatile because it can be used to compare the probability distributions of more than one population and that this is equivalent to a test of the *association* between two *categorical variables*.

Suppose we are interested in the probabilities that a graduate has a permanent job, temporary job, or is unemployed six months after graduation and we want to compare these probabilities for female graduates with those for male graduates.

The contingency table below shows the data from a sample of 310 such graduates.

	Permanent	Temporary	Unemployed	Total
Male	100	33	25	158
Female	90	40	22	152
Total	190	73	47	310

Hypotheses

Recall that we want to test whether the employment status probabilities for males are the same as those for females. The null hypothesis is therefore that the male probabilities are the same as the female probabilities, and the alternative hypothesis is that the male and female probabilities differ somehow.

We are going to use a χ^2 test again so we will need the observed frequencies and expected frequencies. The observed frequencies are those in the cells of the contingency table, but, as before, we need to calculate the expected frequencies.

Expected frequencies

We need an expected frequency for each cell of the contingency table. The rule for calculating the expected frequency, E, of a cell is

$$E = \frac{\text{row total} \times \text{column total}}{n}$$

where n is the total number in the sample.

For example, the expected frequency of the top-left-hand cell of the graduate employment table (male and permanent employment) is

$$E = \frac{158 \times 190}{310} = 96.84$$

The reason we calculate the expected frequencies in this way is as follows. If the probability distribution of employment status is the same for both males and females, a sensible estimator of the probability of permanent employment is the total number of graduates in permanent employment (the column total) divided by the sample size, n, that is, 190/310. The total number of males is the row total, 158. We would therefore expect, on average, $158 \times \frac{190}{310} = 96.84$ of the sample of 158 males to be in permanent employment, so this is the expected frequency.

Check this

What is the expected frequency of female and temporary employment?

Solution:

$$E = \frac{152 \times 73}{310} = 35.79$$

It is often convenient to write the expected frequencies in brackets after or below the observed frequencies as shown below.

	Permanent	Temporary	Unemployed	Total
Male	100 (96.84)	33 (37.21)	25 (23.95)	158
Female	90 (93.16)	40 (35.79)	22 (23.05)	152
Total	190	73	47	310

Calculating the expected frequencies in this way is the only novel part of the test, because we calculate

$$\chi^2 = \sum \frac{(O - E)^2}{E}$$

in exactly the same way as usual. The calculations are shown in the table below; check that you understand where they come from.

O Observed frequency	E Expected frequency	O – E	$\frac{(O-E)^2}{E}$
100	96.84	3.16	0.103
33	37.21	−4.21	0.476
25	23.95	1.05	0.046
90	93.16	−3.16	0.107
40	35.79	4.21	0.495
22	23.05	−1.05	0.048
			$\chi^2 = 1.275$

As usual, when the null hypothesis is true the value of χ^2 we have calculated comes from a χ^2 distribution but now the degrees of freedom are given by

(number of rows − 1) × (number of columns − 1)

So, for this example we need the χ^2 distribution with $(2 - 1)(3 - 1) = 1 \times 2 = 2$ degrees of freedom. Notice that the degrees of freedom are *not* one less than the total number of cells in the table.

The *p*-value is therefore $P(\chi^2 > 1.275)$, which, from Table VI (the row corresponding to $v = 2$), is greater than 0.25. We conclude that the test is not significant and we retain the null hypothesis that the probability distribution of employment status is the same for both men and women.

The χ^2 test and independence
In Chapter P1, Section 3 we said that two events are independent when knowledge of the outcome of one does *not* affect the probabilities of the other. In a similar way, we can say that two *random variables* are independent when knowledge of the value of one of them does *not* affect the probabilities of the other.

The null hypothesis we have just tested (and retained) is that knowledge of gender does *not* affect the probabilities associated with employment status so this is equivalent to saying that the two *categorical* variables, gender and employment status, are independent.

The χ^2 test applied to a contingency table is therefore not only a test of whether two or more populations have the same probability distribution, but is also a test of the *independence* of two categorical variables. It is sometimes called a test of *association* between the two variables.

Check this

The following table shows the numbers of unskilled, skilled and professional workers who have taken out medical insurance out of a randomly selected sample of 150 workers. Do the data give evidence that type of worker is independent of having medical insurance or not?

	Medical insurance	NO medical insurance	Total
Unskilled	5	45	50
Skilled	13	47	60
Professional	17	23	40
Total	35	115	150

Solution:
The expected frequencies are shown in brackets below:

	Medical insurance	NO medical insurance
Unskilled	5 (11.67)	45 (38.33)
Skilled	13 (14)	47 (46)
Professional	17 (9.33)	23 (30.67)

At a glance, the number of unskilled workers with medical insurance is considerably lower than the expected frequency and the number of professionals with medical insurance is much higher than expected.

We'll leave the calculations to you but the test statistic is $\chi^2 = 13.276$. (Your figure may be slightly different due to rounding.) If type of worker and medical insurance are independent this comes from a χ^2 distribution with $(3 - 1) \times (2 - 1) = 2$ degrees of freedom. From Table VI we see that the p-value is between 0.0005 and 0.005 and a computer calculates it as 0.001 to 3 decimal places.

We reject the hypothesis that professional status and medical insurance are independent at both the 5% and 1% significance levels.

Using a computer to test for independence

In SPSS use

Analyze > Descriptive Statistics > Crosstabs...

and enter the categorical variables under Row(s) and Column(s).

In the Statistics sub-dialog box tick Chi-square and in the Cells sub-dialog box tick Observed and Expected Counts and Standardized Residuals to produce the output for the gender and employment status data below.

Our previous calculations are slightly different due to rounding error when calculating by hand.

GENDER * EMPLOY Crosstabulation

			EMPLOY			Total
			permanent	temporary	unemployed	
GENDER	male	Count	100	33	25	158
		Expected Count	96.8	37.2	24.0	158.0
		Std. Residual	.3	−.7	.2	
	female	Count	90	40	22	152
		Expected Count	93.2	35.8	23.0	152.0
		Std. Residual	−.3	.7	−.2	
Total		Count	190	73	47	310
		Expected Count	190.0	73.0	47.0	310.0

Chi-Square Tests

	Value	df	Asymp. Sig. (2-sided)
Pearson Chi-Square	1.273 (a)	2	.529
Likelihood Ratio	1.274	2	.529
Linear-by-Linear Association	.104	1	.747
N of Valid Cases	310		

a 0 cells (.0%) have expected count less than 5. The minimum expected count is 23.05.

In Excel you must place the observed frequencies in one range and the expected frequencies (which you will have to program yourself) in another. The **CHITEST** statistical function calculates the *p*-value of the test but does *not* give you the χ^2 value or any standardised residuals.

1. Consider Muscolino tours again. The results from this year's and last year's questionnaires are shown below.

This year	
Rating	Observed frequency
Unsatisfactory	15
Satisfactory	10
Good	40
Very good	50
Excellent	67
Total	182

Last year	
Rating	Observed frequency
Unsatisfactory	13
Satisfactory	14
Good	35
Very good	55
Excellent	55
Total	172

Test whether there is a difference in the probabilities for the two years.
(i) Perform your calculations using a calculator.
(ii) Use a computer to check your answer.

2. A survey was conducted to obtain information on alcohol consumption. A random sample of 1772 adult males gave the following data.

Marital status	Teetotal	1–20 alcohol units a week	21 or more alcohol units a week	Total
Single	67	213	74	354
Married	411	633	129	1173
Widowed	85	51	7	143
Divorced	27	60	15	102
Total	590	957	225	1772

(i) Assuming that marital status and alcohol consumption are independent use a calculator to calculate the expected values of each cell. Comment briefly.
(ii) Test whether marital status and alcohol consumption are independent. State your conclusions clearly.

If it is appropriate, look at the standardised residuals to see where any discrepancies from the hypothesised probabilities lie.

3. Recall (from Describing Data 1, Assessment 5, question 1) that the file *sportscentre* contains data from a survey of 304 members of a university sports centre. It includes data on gender, status (staff, student or other), age (less than 22, 22–29, 30–49 or 50 and over), the number of visits in the last 3 months, whether the member used the pool during that period and whether they used the gym.
(i) Use this data to test whether use of the pool is independent of status.

WORK CARD 3

(ii)   Test whether the proportion of males and females using the pool are similar.

(iii) Investigate which *factors* (that is, gender, status, age group) are associated with gym usage.

Solutions:

1. (i)   It's probably best to lay out manual calculations in a table as we showed in the text. The χ^2 value is 2.281 which, when the null hypothesis is true, comes from a χ^2 distribution with $(2 - 1)(5 - 1) = 4$ degrees of freedom. From Table VI we see that the *p*-value is greater than 0.25 so there is no evidence of a significant difference between the probability distributions of the ratings of the two years.

    (ii) The SPSS output is

YEAR * RATING Crosstabulation

			RATING					Total
			Unsatisfactory	Satisfactory	Good	Very good	Excellent	
YEAR	This year	Count	15	10	40	50	67	182
		Expected Count	14.4	12.3	38.6	54.0	62.7	182.0
		Std. Residual	.2	–.7	.2	–.5	.5	
	Last year	Count	13	14	35	55	55	172
		Expected Count	13.6	11.7	36.4	51.0	59.3	172.0
		Std. Residual	–.2	.7	–.2	.6	–.6	
Total		Count	28	24	75	105	122	354
		Expected Count	28.0	24.0	75.0	105.0	122.0	354.0

Chi-Square Tests

	Value	df	Asymp. Sig. (2-sided)
Pearson Chi-Square	2.281 (a)	4	.684
Likelihood Ratio	2.284	4	.684
Linear-by-Linear Association	.247	1	.619
N of Valid Cases	354		

a 0 cells (.0%) have expected count less than 5. The minimum expected count is 11.66.

2. **(i)** The expected frequency of the top-left cell is $(354 \times 590)/1772 = 117.87$ and so on to give the following table of expected frequencies:

	Teetotal	1–20	21+
S	117.87	191.18	44.95
M	390.56	633.50	148.94
W	47.61	77.23	18.16
D	33.96	55.09	12.95

Comparing these with the observed frequencies we see that fewer single people and more widowed people are teetotal than would be expected if the probabilities of the alcohol consumption categories were the same for each marital status category.

(ii) $\chi^2 = 94.269$. There are $(3-1)(4-1) = 6$ degrees of freedom so the *p*-value is very small (0.000 to 3 decimal places). There is clear evidence that alcohol consumption and marital status are *not* independent. The standardised residuals are:

	Teetotal	1–20	21+
S	−4.69	1.58	4.33
M	1.03	−0.02	−1.63
W	5.42	−2.98	−2.62
D	−1.19	0.66	0.57

Fewer single people are teetotal and more are heavy drinkers than under the independence assumption. Further, more widowed people are teetotal and fewer are drinkers than by independence. This substantiates our intuitive impressions in **(i)**.

3. **(i)** SPSS gives

Crosstab

			pool user? no	pool user? yes	Total
staff	staff	Count	34	26	60
		Expected Count	28.8	31.2	60.0
		Std. Residual	1.0	−.9	
	student	Count	100	122	222
		Expected Count	106.6	115.4	222.0
		Std. Residual	−.6	.6	
	other	Count	12	10	22

(continues)

WORK CARD 3 (CONTINUED)

	Expected Count		10.6	11.4	22.0
	Std. Residual		.4	−.4	
Total	Count		146	158	304
	Expected Count		146.0	158.0	304.0

$\chi^2 = 2.96$, there are 2 degrees of freedom and the p-value is 0.228, so there is no evidence of any association between pool usage and status.

(ii)   Testing whether the proportions of males and females who use the pool are the same is equivalent to testing whether gender and pool usage are independent. $\chi^2 = 18.89$, there is only 1 degree of freedom and the p-value is 0.000 to 3 decimal places so there is strong evidence that the proportions differ. A table (produced by SPSS) of frequencies, expected frequencies and standardised residuals is shown below. The standardised residuals are large and negative for male pool users and large and positive for female pool users, suggesting that the proportion of females who use the pool is significantly higher than the proportion of males.

Crosstab

			pool user?		
			no	yes	Total
gender	male	Count	90	58	148
		Expected Count	71.1	76.9	148.0
		Std. Residual	2.2	−2.2	
	female	Count	56	100	156
		Expected Count	74.9	81.1	156.0
		Std. Residual	−2.2	2.1	
Total		Count	146	158	304
		Expected Count	146.0	158.0	304.0

(iii)   Testing gender and gym usage for independence gives $\chi^2 = 17.91$, 1 degree of freedom and $p = 0.000$, so there is strong evidence of an association. Testing status and gym gives $\chi^2 = 1.69$, 2 degrees of freedom and the p-value is 0.428, so there is no evidence of association. Finally, no association is found between age group and gym usage as $\chi^2 = 4.01$, there are 3 degrees of freedom and the p-value is 0.26. So the only factor that appears to be associated with gym usage is gender. On inspection we see that a higher proportion of males in the sample, 53%, use the gym, as opposed to 29% of females.

A big problem in statistics for students and practitioners alike is deciding *which* test is appropriate in which situation. So for practice we have included some questions that require material from both Chapter S5 and this chapter.

1. The number of accidents experienced by machinists in 3 departments of a factory during a one-year period are given below. Is there any evidence to suggest that the number of accidents differs from department to department? Notice that the data are in frequency form.

Department	Number of accidents	Frequency
Cutting	0	9
Cutting	1	15
Cutting	2 or more	10
Assembling	0	7
Assembling	1	13
Assembling	2 or more	8
Packaging	0	15
Packaging	1	7
Packaging	2 or more	6

2. A University careers centre is interested in whether starting salaries for male and female History graduates are similar. The starting salaries (£) for a sample of 8 men and 8 women who have recently graduated are given below. Test whether there is a significant difference between male and female salaries.

Male	Female
21,000	19,000
18,000	19,600
15,500	21,000
16,000	22,000
18,500	21,500
21,300	22,000
20,000	21,400
22,000	21,000

3. A market research company collects data in order to estimate the TV viewing habits of Americans; 20 married or cohabiting couples are selected at random. Their average weekly viewing times are as follows: M for man, W for woman.

ASSESSMENT 3

M	W	M	W	M	W	M	W	M	W
12	24	56	55	34	55	30	34	31	37
30	35	32	48	15	17	41	32	35	38
26	38	38	45	27	29	30	41	36	35
20	34	43	32	4	13	16	9	21	23

Does this sample give evidence that married or cohabiting women watch more television than their male partners?

4. Consider the number of attempts a driver required to pass their driving test, 1, 2, 3 etc. Investigate whether the number of attempts is independent of gender by collecting data from a sample of drivers. Remember to group categories if the expected frequencies are less than 5.

   Tabulate the data, describe your work and interpret your results.

5. Recall (from Describing Data 1, Assessment 5, question 1) that the file *sportscentre* contains data from a survey of 304 members of a university sports centre. It includes data on status (staff, student or other) and age (less than 22, 22–29, 30–49 or 50 and over).

   It is known that the proportions of students from the University in each age group are as follows.

Less than 22	60.5%
23–30	34.5%
31–49	3.5%
over 50	1.5%

Test whether the age distribution of student members of the sports centre is the same as the age distribution of students at the University.

6. Use the data from the Vizafizz market research survey in *vizafizz* (see DD2, Assessment 8) to investigate the following:

   (i)   Whether there is any association between the type of advertisement (type 1, type 2 or none) that the respondent saw and their gender.

   (ii)   Whether there is any association between which of these they saw and age group.

   (iii)   Whether there is any evidence of an association between the advertisement/picture that the respondent saw and whether they would drink Vizafizz.

   (iv)   Whether average estimated expenditure is similar for males and females.

   (v)   If whether or not the respondent would drink Vizafizz is associated with their gender or their age.

Using the results of your investigations in (i)–(v) write a brief report to the manufacturers of Vizafizz advising on their likely customer base and their TV advertising strategy, if any.

ASSESSMENT 3 (CONTINUED)

Further reading: see p. xv

Anderson *et al.* (Statistics) includes more detail, as does Newbold *et al.*

Mendenhall *et al.*

Statistics formulae

S1 Estimation

	Sample	Population
Mean	$\bar{x} = \dfrac{\Sigma x}{n}$	μ
Variance	$s^2 = \dfrac{\Sigma x^2 - \dfrac{(\Sigma x)^2}{n}}{n-1}$	σ^2

The sampling distribution of $\overline{X}$:

$$E(\overline{X}) = \mu \qquad \mathrm{Var}(\overline{X}) = \frac{\sigma^2}{n}$$

For large samples ($n \geq 30$), $\qquad \overline{X}$ is *approximately* $N\left(\mu, \dfrac{\sigma^2}{n}\right)$

For normal populations, $\qquad \overline{X}$ is *exactly* $N\left(\mu, \dfrac{\sigma^2}{n}\right)$

$(1 - \alpha)100\%$ confidence intervals for the population mean

	Large sample	Small sample (normal)
σ^2 known	$\bar{x} \pm z_{\alpha/2}\sqrt{\dfrac{\sigma^2}{n}}$	$\bar{x} \pm z_{\alpha/2}\sqrt{\dfrac{\sigma^2}{n}}$
σ^2 unknown	$\bar{x} \pm z_{\alpha/2}\sqrt{\dfrac{s^2}{n}}$	$\bar{x} \pm t_{\alpha/2}\sqrt{\dfrac{s^2}{n}}$
or	$\bar{x} \pm t_{\alpha/2}\sqrt{\dfrac{s^2}{n}}$	

where t has $n - 1$ degrees of freedom

S2 Testing hypotheses

Test statistic for the mean

	Large sample	Small sample (normal)
σ^2 known	$z = \dfrac{\bar{x} - \mu_0}{\sqrt{\dfrac{\sigma^2}{n}}}$	$z = \dfrac{\bar{x} - \mu_0}{\sqrt{\dfrac{\sigma^2}{n}}}$
σ^2 unknown	$z = \dfrac{\bar{x} - \mu_0}{\sqrt{\dfrac{s^2}{n}}}$	$t = \dfrac{\bar{x} - \mu_0}{\sqrt{\dfrac{s^2}{n}}}$
	or $\quad t = \dfrac{\bar{x} - \mu_0}{\sqrt{\dfrac{s^2}{n}}}$	

where t has $n - 1$ degrees of freedom

S3 Correlation and regression

Let

$$S_{xx} = \Sigma x^2 - \frac{(\Sigma x)^2}{n}, \quad S_{yy} = \Sigma y^2 - \frac{(\Sigma y)^2}{n} \quad \text{and} \quad S_{xy} = \Sigma xy - \frac{\Sigma x \Sigma y}{n}$$

Sample correlation coefficient $r = \dfrac{S_{xy}}{\sqrt{S_{xx} S_{yy}}}$

Total sum of squares = Regression sum of squares + Error sum of squares

$$S_{yy} \qquad = \qquad \frac{S_{xy}^2}{S_{xx}} \qquad + \qquad S_{yy} - \frac{S_{xy}^2}{S_{xx}}$$

Coefficient of determination $R^2 = \dfrac{\text{Regression sum of squares}}{\text{Total sum of squares}} = \dfrac{S_{xy}^2}{S_{xx} S_{yy}} = r^2.$

The linear regression model is

$$Y = \alpha + \beta x + \varepsilon \quad \text{where} \quad E(\varepsilon) = 0 \quad \text{and} \quad \text{Var}(\varepsilon) = \sigma^2$$

α and β are estimated by

$$a = \frac{\Sigma y - b\Sigma x}{n} \quad \text{and} \quad b = \frac{S_{xy}}{S_{xx}}$$

and σ^2 is estimated by

$$s^2 = \frac{\text{Error sum of squares}}{n - 2} = \frac{S_{yy} - \dfrac{S_{xy}^2}{S_{xx}}}{n - 2}$$

To test $H_0: \beta = 0$ against $H_1: \beta \neq 0$

$$t \text{ ratio} = \frac{b}{\sqrt{\dfrac{s^2}{S_{xx}}}}$$

S4 Forecasting
Exponential forecasting

$$F_2 = x_1$$

$$F_{t+1} = F_t + \alpha(x_t - F_t) \qquad \text{where } 0 \le \alpha \le 1$$

$$\text{MSE} = \frac{\Sigma e_i^2}{n-1} \qquad\qquad \text{MAE} = \frac{\Sigma |e_i|}{n-1}$$

S5 Comparing two populations
Normal populations or large samples only.

σ_1^2 and σ_2^2 known
Confidence interval for the difference between two population means

$$\overline{x}_1 - \overline{x}_2 \pm z_{\alpha/2}\sqrt{\frac{\sigma_1^2}{n_1} + \frac{\sigma_2^2}{n_2}}$$

Test for the difference between two population means

$$z = \frac{\overline{x}_1 - \overline{x}_2}{\sqrt{\dfrac{\sigma_1^2}{n_1} + \dfrac{\sigma_2^2}{n_2}}}$$

σ_1^2 and σ_2^2 UNKNOWN but large samples ($n_1, n_2 \ge 30$)
Use s_1^2 and s_2^2 in place of σ_1^2 and σ_2^2 in the above

σ_1^2 and σ_2^2 UNKNOWN but small samples
Assume the population variances are the same and use

$$s_p^2 = \frac{(n_1 - 1)s_1^2 + (n_2 - 1)s_2^2}{n_1 + n_2 - 2}$$

in place of σ_1^2 and σ_2^2 in the above

S6 Categorical data
An approximate $100(1 - \alpha)\%$ confidence interval for the population proportion is

$$\hat{p} \pm z_{\alpha/2}\sqrt{\frac{\hat{p}(1 - \hat{p})}{n}}$$

When the sample proportion is $\hat{p}$ and the population proportion is p, $\hat{p}$ is approximately normally distributed with mean p and variance

$$\frac{p(1 - p)}{n}$$

$$\chi^2 = \sum \frac{(O - E)^2}{E}$$

where the Os are the observed frequencies and the Es are the expected frequencies.

To test a probability distribution $E = n \times$ hypothesised probability

degrees of freedom = number of categories − 1.

To test for independence using a contingency table

$$E = \frac{\text{row total} \times \text{column total}}{n}$$

Degrees of freedom = (number of rows − 1) × (number of columns − 1)

BM BUSINESS MODELLING

In *Business Modelling* we introduce the most commonly used types of quantitative business model. Most attempt to assist the solution of a particular type of business problem, for instance:

- How can we make best use of our raw material and resources?

- What should our inventory (stock) control policy be?

- How should we best schedule a complex project?

- Which investment should we choose?

- How do we decide to accept or reject batches of output?

Each type of model is a representation of the real problem which is sufficiently simplified that we can use it to obtain some sort of solution. The art of modelling is to find a balance between reality and solvability. A complicated model may be realistic but too complicated to solve, whereas a simple model may be solvable but make simplifying assumptions about the real situation that are not appropriate and so give a misleading solution. Whilst some smaller models can be solved using a calculator, larger ones require a computer. By way of illustration, we have included examples of the use of current versions of Microsoft® Excel and the statistical software package SPSS, where appropriate, although other packages will offer similar facilities.

Most of *Business Modelling* can be tackled with the Maths background in *Essential Maths*. However, some knowledge of *Probability* and *Statistics* will be necessary to understand the final sections of Chapters BM6 and BM7, where indicated.

Chapter BM4, *Time and Money*, is slightly different in that it does not model a particular business problem but considers the changing value of money over time which has important repercussions for business decisions.

BM1
Linear programming models

'WHO are you?' he asked, for he had attended business college.

George Ade, *Chicago Record*, 16 March 1898

Contexts

What is this chapter about?
This chapter introduces linear programming, a way of calculating how to allocate limited resources like raw materials and labour to products or services to give the maximum possible profit or revenue. It explains how to set up a mathematical model of the situation and then solve it using a computer.

Why is it useful?
Linear programming is probably the most-used type of quantitative business model. It can be applied in any environment where finite resources must be allocated to competing activities or processes for maximum benefit; for instance, to select an investment portfolio of stocks to maximise return, to allocate a fixed budget between competing departments, or to allocate lorries to routes in a way that minimises the transportation costs incurred by a distribution company. It also forms the basis for solving some more specialised problems, the transportation, assignment and transhipment problems, and for a class of problems called integer programming problems.

Where does it fit in?
The subject in this part of the book, Business Modelling, is known more formally as Management Science or Operational Research, and linear programming is one of the key topics. In Management Science the business problem is usually represented using a mathematical model. A solution to the model is found and then used to inform decision-making. Whilst the maths is usually done on a computer, the skill of Management Science is in knowing which model to use, how to set it up for the computer and how to interpret and apply the results.

What do I need to know?
Fortunately, these days the maths required to solve most quantitative business models is usually done on a computer. However, to set up the business problem in a form that can be solved you will need the basic maths in Essential Maths. For linear programming the material in EM4 on modelling using straight lines is particularly important.

Objectives

By the end of your work on this chapter you should be able to:

● formulate a small linear programming problem and solve it using a graph;
● understand the limitations of linear programming;
● formulate a larger problem and use Excel to solve it;
● interpret the results from Excel, including the sensitivity analysis.

The function of most organisations is to transform the resources available to them, such as raw materials, components, machine time and labour, into products and/or services. To do this the organisation has to decide how much of each type of product or service to supply whilst staying within the bounds imposed by limits on these resources. Most organisations seek to do this in such a way as to make profit as large as possible or costs as small as possible. Linear programming is a way of modelling this type of management decision problem.

We should say here (before we lose half our readership) that linear programming has absolutely nothing to do with computer programming. It was given its name before 'programming' was associated with computers and 'programming', in this context, just means planning.

In general, linear programming can be applied to any environment where activities compete for the use of limited resources. For instance, a portfolio manager must decide how to allocate finite funds to several types of competing investment to maximise the return, or an agricultural planner allocates crops to a particular number of hectares and with a limited workforce. In a similar way, a chemical plant plans its production with limited raw materials in order to satisfy legislation about emissions and a logistics company plans which lorries to place on which routes to make all deliveries whilst ensuring that drivers work no longer than the legal number of hours.

Linear programming has two stages. First, the management-decision problem must be formulated as a linear programming model and then the model must be solved mathematically. When there are only two competing activities the mathematical solution can be found by drawing a graph but real problems are usually much larger and are solved using a computer.

In Section 1 we consider a small problem that can be solved graphically. Whilst this problem is too simplistic to represent a real-life problem it allows us to introduce the terminology and key ideas of linear programming. In Section 2 we consider the formulation of larger, more realistic, models and their computer solution.

1 A small linear programming problem

The chocolate manufacturer's problem
Consider the following problem.

A chocolate manufacturer produces two types of chocolate bar, Asteroids and Blackholes. Production of an Asteroid bar uses 10g of cocoa and 1 minute of machine time whereas a Blackhole bar requires 5g of cocoa and 4 minutes of machine time. Altogether 2000g of cocoa and 480 minutes of machine time are available each day. No other resources are required.

The manufacturer makes 10p profit from each Asteroid bar and 20p profit from each Blackhole bar.

How many Asteroid bars and how many Blackhole bars should the manufacturer produce each day in order to maximise profit?

Formulating the problem
To formulate the linear programming model the first thing to do is to define the *decision variables*. The chocolate manufacturer needs to decide the number of Asteroid bars and the number of Blackhole bars to produce so these are the decision variables for this problem. Let's define x as the number of Asteroid bars manufactured daily and y as the number of Blackhole bars.

A linear programming problem always has an expression to be maximised (or minimised) called the *objective function* and one or more *constraints* or restrictions. If we have defined the decision variables correctly we should be able to express the whole problem in terms of them.

In our example the quantity to be maximised is profit. As the manufacturer makes 10p profit from each Asteroid bar he will make $10x$ pence profit if he manufactures x of them. In the same way, Blackhole bars each make 20p profit so he will make $20y$ pence profit if he makes y bars. So if he manufactures x Asteroid bars and y Blackhole bars he will make $10x + 20y$ pence profit and the objective function, which we want to maximise, is

$$10x + 20y \quad \text{OBJECTIVE FUNCTION}$$

We want to find the values of x and y that make the objective function the highest. However, we can't make x and y, and hence the objective function, as large as we like because x and y are restricted or *constrained*; firstly, by the amount of cocoa that is available and secondly, by the amount of machine time.

An Asteroid bar uses 10g of cocoa and a Blackhole bar 5g, so the amount of cocoa required to produce x and y bars of each type is $10x + 5y$. Only 2000g of cocoa is available so the first constraint is

$$10x + 5y \leq 2000 \quad \text{COCOA CONSTRAINT}$$

Check this

What is the machine time constraint?

Solution:
1 minute of machine time is required for each Asteroid bar and 4 minutes for each Blackhole bar, so the total amount of machine time required to produce x and y bars of each type is $1x + 4y$ minutes. Only 480 minutes of machine time are available and so the second constraint is

$x + 4y \leq 480$ MACHINE TIME CONSTRAINT

As both decision variables represent physical quantities they must both be positive or zero and so there are two implicit *non-negativity constraints*

$$\left.\begin{array}{l} x \geq 0 \\ y \geq 0 \end{array}\right\} \text{ NON-NEGATIVITY CONSTRAINTS}$$

The complete linear programming problem is therefore

Maximise profit $= 10x + 20y$ OBJECTIVE FUNCTION

Subject to the constraints

$10x + 5y \leq 2000$ COCOA CONSTRAINT

$x + 4y \leq 480$ MACHINE TIME CONSTRAINT

$$\left.\begin{array}{l} x \geq 0 \\ y \geq 0 \end{array}\right\} \text{ NON-NEGATIVITY CONSTRAINTS}$$

Notice that the objective function is a linear function of x and y (each term is a number multiplied by x or y) and that the left-hand sides of the constraints are also linear functions of x and y. This is why these models are called linear programming models. Notice also that the right-hand side of the first two constraints is the amount of the corresponding resource that is available.

We have now completed the model formulation. All the information that we were originally given has now been 'translated' into the objective function and constraints. (It is usually worthwhile at this stage reading through the original problem description again to check that all the information has indeed been used.)

We are now ready to solve the linear programming problem.

Graphical solution of a linear programming problem

We are going to make use of the work on modelling using straight lines in *Essential Maths*, Chapter EM4, so if you are rusty a quick look at this chapter might be a good idea.

As we have only two decision variables, x and y, we can represent any pair of values of these as a point on a graph. As x and y cannot be negative we only need the positive parts of the axes as shown below.

However, each constraint of the linear programming model imposes a restriction on the values of x and y. We'll take the constraints of the chocolate manufacturer problem one at a time.

First consider the cocoa constraint, $10x + 5y \leq 2000$. We want to show all the points on the graph for which $10x + 5y \leq 2000$. The straight line $10x + 5y = 2000$ joins the points (200, 0) and (0, 400) as shown in Figure 1.1. All the x,y points on one side of this line satisfy the cocoa constraint because they are such that $10x + 5y < 2000$. All the points on the other side do *not* satisfy the cocoa constraint; that is, they are such that $10x + 5y > 2000$.

To find out which side of the line we want we pick any point on the graph and calculate whether it satisfies the cocoa constraint or not. For instance, if we pick $x = 0$ and $y = 0$ (to make the arithmetic easy), $10x + 5y = 10 \times 0 + 5 \times 0 = 0$ which *is* less than 2000 telling us that we want the points on the same side of the line as (0, 0). So, all the points on or below the straight line $10x + 5y = 2000$ satisfy the cocoa constraint $10x + 5y \leq 2000$ and are 'cocoa-feasible' as shown in Figure 1.1.

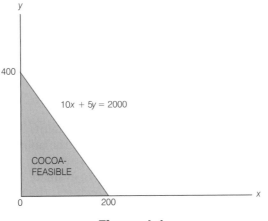

Figure 1.1

Now consider the machine time constraint, $x + 4y \leq 480$. The line $x + 4y = 480$ joins (480, 0) and (0, 120). The point (0, 0) is such that $x + 4y \leq 480$ and so all points on or below the line are 'machine-feasible' as shown in Figure 1.2.

Production levels must satisfy *both* constraints so we combine the last two graphs (Figures 1.1 and 1.2) to show the region of x,y points that are both cocoa-feasible *and* machine-feasible as in Figure 1.3. This region is called the *feasible region*. As you can see, the feasible region forms a quadrilateral (four-sided shape) whose corners are (0, 120), (0, 0), (200, 0) and the intersection of the two lines.

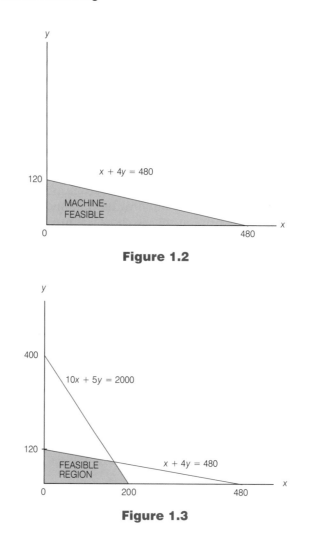

Figure 1.2

Figure 1.3

The only values of x and y that are allowed by the constraints are those in the feasible region. To solve our linear programming model we want the point x,y in the feasible region that gives the highest value of the objective function, $10x + 20y$.

An intuitive way of obtaining a solution would be to evaluate $10x + 20y$ for all the points in the feasible region and then pick the point for which it is the highest. However, there are a huge number of possible points in the feasible region and this would be extremely time-consuming (and tedious). Further, if x and y represented some other product, like types of petrol or chemicals which, unlike chocolate bars, did not have to be measured in whole numbers there would be an infinite number of points in the feasible region and this would be an *impossible* task. Fortunately, however, this need not be a problem as we have the following mathematical result.

> The maximum (and minimum) of the objective function lies at a corner point of the feasible region.

For our example this means that the maximum lies at one of the corner points of the quadrilateral; that is, at (0, 120), (0, 0), (200, 0) or the intersection of the two constraint lines. The intersection point is the solution of the following pair of linear equations:

$$10x + 5y = 2000$$
$$x + 4y = 480$$

We saw how to solve such pairs of linear equations in *Essential Maths*, Chapter EM4, Section 4, but try this for some revision.

Check this

Find the point where the lines $10x + 5y = 2000$ and $x + 4y = 480$ intersect.

Solution:
Multiplying the second equation by 10 gives

$10x + 5y = 2000$ and $10x + 40y = 4800$

Subtracting the first equation from the second gives

$0x + 35y = 2800$ so $y = 80$

Substituting this back into the first equation gives $10x + 400 = 2000$ so $x = 160$.
The intersection point is (160, 80).

So to find the maximum of the objective function (profit) we evaluate it at each of the corner points of the feasible region and compare. For instance, at (160, 80) the profit is $(10 \times 160) + (20 \times 80) = 3200$.

Check this

What is the profit at (0, 120)?

Solution:
It is $10 \times 0 + 20 \times 120$

The profit at each corner point of the feasible region is shown in Figure 1.4. The largest profit is 3200 at the point $x = 160$ and $y = 80$.
We conclude that the manufacturer must make 160 Asteroid bars and 80 Blackhole bars each day to obtain the maximum profit, which will be 3200 pence.

Optimising
So far we have found the maximum of the objective function and that the constraints represented ceilings on the amounts of resource available. Sometimes, however, we want to *min*imise a quantity – for instance costs, in which case the constraints will usually (but not always) give minimum requirements and so include a ≥ sign. Minimisations are solved graphically in much the same way as maximisations the only difference being that we want the corner point of the feasible region with the *minimum* value of the objective function.

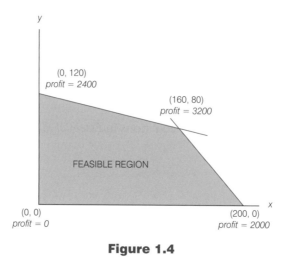

Figure 1.4

The general term for maximisations and minimisations is *optimisation* and we call the values of the decision variables at the maximum or minimum the *optimal solution*.

Types of solution

For the chocolate manufacturer problem just one corner point of the feasible region gave a maximum; that is, no corners of the feasible region 'tied' for the maximum value of the objective function. We call this a *unique optimal solution*. Whilst linear programming problems usually have unique solutions there are three other possibilities.

A linear programming model can have an infinite number of solutions. When there are two decision variables this happens when the same maximum or (minimum) value of the objective function occurs at two adjacent corner points of the feasible region. It can be shown mathematically that all the points on the line joining these corner points will also give the same value of the objective function so there are an infinite number of optimal solutions.

A linear programming model may be *infeasible* meaning that there are no values of the decision variables that satisfy all the constraints; that is, we have an impossible problem to solve.

Finally, the linear programming model might have an *unbounded* solution meaning that by changing the values of the decision variables we can make the objective function as large (for a maximisation) or small (for a minimisation) as we like. This usually happens because we have made a mistake in the model formulation, perhaps by missing out a crucial constraint or because we have entered the wrong numbers or functions into the computer.

Limitations of linear programming

The solution we obtained for the chocolate manufacturer's problem was a whole number of Asteroid bars and a whole number of Blackhole bars, which was fortunate because he can't make fractions of bars. In general, because the feasible region is a continuous area on the graph, the optimal solution of a linear programming problem can be fractional, which might not make sense. If we get a fractional solution an intuitive thing to do might be to round the solution to the nearest whole number. However, if you think about it, this rounding could take the point *outside* the feasible region. Also, even when the rounded values lie within the feasible region it can be shown that they do *not* necessarily give the optimal solution. When the decision variables take large values, the chances are that rounding won't make much difference and the rounded solution will be relatively close to the maximum (or minimum). However, when the decision variables are small, rounding can give a completely false solution that is nowhere near the maximum and a technique called *integer programming* should be used.

   Another limitation of the linear programming model is that the objective function and the constraints are all linear. By this we mean that every term is a number multiplied by a decision variable. In the production context this means that the amount of resource used to produce a unit and the amount of profit generated by a unit remain the same, regardless of the number of units produced. So, if production is doubled, the resources used will be doubled and the profit will be doubled and so on. This may not be appropriate for the real situation. For instance, higher production levels may reduce the manpower required per unit or increase the profit per unit.

WORK CARD 1

1. A small firm produces two types of wooden lampstands: rounded and angular. Both types require two hand-crafted processes: cutting and smoothing. Rounded lampstands require 1 hour of cutting and 3 hours of smoothing whereas angular lampstands require 2 hours of cutting but only 1 hour of smoothing. The firm has 400 man-hours of cutting available each week and 300 man-hours of smoothing. The firm calculates that they make £3 profit on each rounded lampstand and £4 profit on each angular lampstand.

   How many rounded and angular lampstands should they manufacturer each week in order to maximise profit?

2. A cookie factory makes two brands of biscuit. A batch of standard biscuits takes 20kg of flour and 2kg of butter, whereas a batch of deluxe biscuits requires 10kg of flour and 5kg of butter. The firm makes a profit of £2 on a batch of standard biscuits and a profit of £6 on a batch of deluxe biscuits.

   The company have at most 200kg of flour and 40kg of butter available each day.

   How many batches of standard and deluxe biscuits should the factory produce each day in order to maximise profit?

   Formulate this as a linear programming problem and solve the problem graphically.

3. Formulate the following problem as a linear programming model.

   A firm has 1000 man-hours available each week for manufacturing and can spend up to £700 a week on raw materials. They produce only 2 products: tankards and mugs. It takes 2 man-hours to manufacture a tankard and 1 man-hour to manufacture a mug and it costs £1 in raw materials to make either a tankard or a mug.

   The firm makes £2 profit on each tankard and £1.50 profit on each mug. Use a graph to find out how many of each product the firm should manufacture each week in order to maximise profit.

Solutions:

1. Let x and y be the number of rounded and angular lampstands respectively. The linear programming is to maximise $3x + 4y$ subject to $x + 2y \leq 400$ and $3x + y \leq 300$. To solve this draw the lines $x + 2y = 400$ and $3x + y = 300$ on a graph. Their point of intersection is (40, 180) so the feasible region is a quadrilateral with corners (0, 0), (0, 200), (100, 0) and (40, 180). The profit at each of these corner points is 0, 800, 300 and 840 respectively. The maximum profit will therefore be attained when $x = 40$ and $y = 180$.

2. Maximise $2x + 6y$ subject to $20x + 10y \leq 200$ and $2x + 5y \leq 40$. To solve graphically draw the lines $20x + 10y = 200$ and $2x + 5y = 40$ on a graph. The feasible region is given by the area enclosed by these lines and the x and y axes. The maximum of $2x + 6y$ lies at one of the corner points of the feasible region. The point of intersection of the two lines is (7.5, 5) and so the profit at this point is £45. The profit at (0, 0) is 0, at (10, 0) is £20 and at (0, 8) is £48. The company should therefore produce 8 batches of deluxe biscuits a day and abandon the manufacture of standard biscuits.

3. The formulation is maximise $2x + 1.5y$ subject to $2x + y \leq 1000$ and $x + y \leq 700$ where x is the number of tankards and y is the number of mugs manufactured in a week. To solve this graphically draw the lines $2x + y = 1000$ and $x + y = 700$ on a graph. The area enclosed by the axes and these lines is the feasible region. The values of x and y that maximise profit must lie at one of the corner points of this region; that is, at (500, 0), (0, 0), (0, 700) or the intersection of the two lines (300, 400). Evaluating the profit $2x + 1.5y$ at each of these points gives 1000, 0, 1050 and 1200 respectively. The maximum profit is therefore obtained when $x = 300$ and $y = 400$.

1. A firm wishes to spend at most £800 a week on raw materials and has at most 200 hours of machine time available a week. It takes half an hour of machine time to produce a silk tie and one hour to produce a wool scarf. The raw materials for a tie cost £5 and for a scarf cost £2. The firm only produces these two items. How many ties and scarves should the firm manufacture weekly to maximise profit when they obtain £2 profit for a tie and £3 for a scarf?

   a. Formulate the above as a linear programming problem.

   b. Solve the problem graphically.

   c. The company's wool scarves become very sought after when a pop idol is seen wearing one and so they are able to charge much more. Profit on a scarf increase to £8. What is the feasible region now? Has it changed? How many ties and scarves should now be produced each week?

2. This example is a little harder and should test whether you have really understood this section. The idea extends to portfolios when there are many hundreds of competing investments.

ASSESSMENT 1 (CONTINUED)

A fund manager has £10,000 to invest for a client to be divided into fixed interest, equities and property. For surety of return the client requires at least 50% to be placed in fixed interest and for liquidity that at most 30% be invested in property.

The projected return over the coming year is forecast to be 5% on the fixed interest investments, 7% on equities and 8% on property.

How should the £10,000 be split between the three types of investment in order to maximise the return over the coming year?

Hint: To formulate the linear programming problem use x as the amount invested in fixed interests, y as the amount invested in equities and then $10,000 - x - y$ will be the amount invested in property.

2 More complicated linear programming models

The graphical method will only work when there are two decision variables (one for each axis of the graph) so before we formulate a larger linear programming model let's see how we might solve it.

Using a computer to solve linear programmes

When linear programmes have more than two decision variables they are usually solved using a method called the *simplex method*. The simplex method is *iterative*, meaning that it performs similar calculations for each of a series of steps or iterations. In the simplex method each step identifies a corner point of the feasible region and the method moves from corner point to corner point gradually improving the value of the objective function until it finds the optimal solution. As each step requires a large number of small, repetitive, calculations the simplex method is usually carried out on a computer.

Linear programming models can have many hundreds of decision variables and hundreds of constraints, in which case specialist software is available. However, if you only have a small linear programming problem to solve you can use the **Solver** tool in Excel.

Solving linear programming problems using Excel

The **Solver** tool doesn't only solve linear programming models so its terminology differs slightly from the usual linear programming terminology. Before you use it you will have to set up the various parts of the model in cells of the worksheet as follows:

1. Choose the cells for the decision variables (say A1 and A2). Excel calls these cells the *adjustable cells*.
2. Type the objective function into a cell (say B1) as a formula in the decision variables; for instance, for the chocolate manufacturer problem enter =10*A1+20*A2. Excel calls this the *target cell*.
3. Choose the cells for the constraints (say C1 and C2). Type the *left*-hand side of each constraint (the part containing the decision variables) into one of these cells as a formula. For instance, for the chocolate manufacturer example enter =10*A1+5*A2 in C1 and =A1+4*A2 in C2.

Now you can use the **Solver** tool. The dialog box will ask you to enter the **Target Cell** (the objective function, B1), click maximum or minimum and enter the cells containing the decision variables (A1 and A2) where it says **By Changing Cells**. To input the constraints click **Add** and enter the cell where each constraint is, the sign in the constraint and a number for the right-hand side of the constraint. (So C1 ≤ 2000 and C2 ≤ 480 for our example.) You will also need to include the non-negativity constraints A1 ≥ 0 and A2 ≥ 0.

Now click **Options** and select **Assume Linear Model**. Return to the dialog box and click **Solve**.

The cells containing the decision variables will now contain the solution of the linear programming model. You can request any combination of three reports: the answer report, sensitivity report and the limits report.

Results from linear programming software

Output from the answer report of Excel's solver solution of the chocolate manufacturer's problem is shown below. Most of it is self-explanatory. The maximum value of the objective function, 3200, is shown first followed by the values of the decision variables at the solution.

Target Cell (Max)

Cell Name	Original Value	Final Value
B1	0	3200

Adjustable Cells

Cell Name	Original Value	Final Value
A1	0	160
A2	0	80

Constraints

Cell Name	Cell Value	Formula	Status	Slack
C1	2000	C1 <= 2000	Binding	0
C2	480	C2 <= 480	Binding	0
A1	160	A1 >= 0	Not Binding	160
A2	80	A2 >= 0	Not Binding	80

The final few lines classify each constraint as *binding* or *non-binding*, and give an amount of 'slack'. We say a constraint is binding when all of the corresponding resource is used up at the optimal solution. The amount of slack is the amount of the resource left over. For a binding constraint this will always be 0.

For example, the right-hand side of the first (cocoa) constraint tells us that 2000g of cocoa are available whereas the value of the left-hand side, $10x + 5y$ at the optimal solution, $x = 160$ and $y = 80$, is $(10 \times 160) + (5 \times 80) = 2000$ telling us that all 2000g are used up. We conclude that this constraint is *binding* and there is zero *slack*.

When some of a resource is left over we say the constraint is non-binding and the slack will be non-zero.

The final two lines do the same sort of thing for the non-negativity constraints and are not particularly useful to us.

Check this

Satisfy yourself that the second constraint (machine time) of the chocolate manufacturer example is indeed binding and has zero slack.

Solution:
The constraint is $x + 4y = 480$ so at the optimal solution $1 \times 160 + 4 \times 80 = 480$ units are used up. 480 units were available so there is no slack and the constraint is binding.

Formulating larger problems

Larger problems are formulated in the same way as two-variable ones. The key thing is to define the decision variables at the outset and, at the end of the formulation stage, make sure that you have expressed all the information in terms of these.

Try formulating the following linear programme yourself before you look at our formulation.

Check this

Hooper's Home Improvements manufacture 4 products: glass doors, windows, patio doors and solid doors. Each of these uses 5 square metres, 1 square metre, 9 square metres, and 12 square metres respectively of wood and 2, 3, 4 and 1 square metres respectively of glass. It takes 3 man-hours to build a glass door, 2 man-hours for a window, 5 for a patio door and 10 for a solid door. Altogether 1500 square metres of wood and 1000 square metres of glass are available each week and the 20 employees all work a 40-hour week.

Further, to satisfy orders Hooper's will have to make at least 40 glass doors, 130 windows and 30 patio doors, although because of diminishing popularity they have decided to make at most 10 solid doors.

Hooper's estimate the profit on a glass door to be £12, on a window to be £5, on a patio door £15 and on a solid door £10.

How many of each product should Hooper's make each week in order to maximise profit?

Solution:
Firstly, define the decision variables. These are the numbers of each product type that are made. Let x_1 be the number of glass doors, x_2 the number of windows, x_3 the number of patio doors and x_4 the number of solid doors. The objective function is

profit = $12x_1 + 5x_2 + 15x_3 + 10x_4$

and we want to maximise this.

The constraints are the restriction placed on the decision variables by the amount of wood, glass and man-hours available, the minimum levels to satisfy orders and the maximum amount of solid doors.

The amount of wood required is $5x_1 + x_2 + 9x_3 + 12x_4$ and we only have 1500 square metres so the wood constraint is

$5x_1 + x_2 + 9x_3 + 12x_4 \leq 1500$

In a similar way the glass constraint is

$2x_1 + 3x_2 + 4x_3 + x_4 \leq 1000$

As $20 \times 40 = 800$ man-hours are available the man-hours constraint is

$3x_1 + 2x_2 + 5x_3 + 10x_4 \leq 800$

The lower limits on the numbers of glass doors, windows and patio doors give the constraints

$x_1 \geq 40$

$x_2 \geq 130$

$x_3 \geq 30$

(Notice that although the problem is a maximisation these have a $\geq$ sign.)
And finally, the constraint due to the upper limit on solid doors is

$x_4 \leq 10$

At this point we read through the information again and check that we have made use of all of it. We have, so the complete linear programming model for this problem is

Maximise profit $= 12x_1 + 5x_2 + 15x_3 + 10x_4$

Subject to the constraints

$5x_1 + x_2 + 9x_3 + 12x_4 \leq 1500$	WOOD CONSTRAINT
$2x_1 + 3x_2 + 4x_3 + x_4 \leq 1000$	GLASS CONSTRAINT
$3x_1 + 2x_2 + 5x_3 + 10x_4 \leq 800$	MAN-HOURS CONSTRAINT
$x_1 \geq 40$	GLASS DOORS ORDER CONSTRAINT
$x_2 \geq 130$	WINDOWS ORDER CONSTRAINT
$x_3 \geq 30$	PATIO DOORS ORDER CONSTRAINT
$x_4 \leq 10$	SOLID DOORS CONSTRAINT

The non-negativity constraints are

$x_1 \geq 0$

$x_2 \geq 0$

$x_3 \geq 0$

$x_4 \geq 0$

but the first three are implied by the glass doors order constraint, windows order constraint and patio doors order constraint respectively and so we don't really need them.

There are four decision variables so we can't solve the problem graphically. However, the optimal solution is 130 glass doors, 130 windows, 30 patio doors and no solid doors as shown in the following Excel output. Notice that the man-hour constraint and the windows order and patio doors order constraints are binding. That is, all available man-hours are used and the minimum quantities of windows and patio doors are to be made.

Cell Name	Original Value	Final Value
B1	0	2660

Cell Name	Original Value	Final Value
A1	0	130
A2	0	130
A3	0	30
A4	0	0

Cell Name	Cell Value	Formula	Status	Slack
C1	1050	C1 <= 1500	Not Binding	450
C2	770	C2 <= 1000	Not Binding	230
C3	800	C3 <= 800	Binding	0
A1	130	C4 >= 40	Not Binding	90
A2	130	C5 >= 130	Binding	0
A3	30	C6 >= 30	Binding	0
A4	0	C7 <= 10	Not Binding	10
A4	0	A4 >= 0	Binding	0

Check this

From the Excel output above how much wood and glass are left over?

Solution:
The slacks for the wood and glass constraints are 450 and 230 so 450 square metres of wood and 230 square metres of glass are not used.

Constraint 4 has a slack of 90. However, the glass doors order constraint was a ≥ constraint so this doesn't mean that anything was left over. It means that the left-hand side of the constraint, at 130, is 90 units in excess of the minimum given on the right-hand side of the constraint.

Sensitivity analysis

Any model is only an approximation to reality and linear programming models are no exception. So the optimal solution to a linear programming model is only as good as the information that went into the model. *Sensitivity analysis* considers the effect on the optimal solution of changes in the model.

Excel's sensitivity report for the chocolate manufacturer problem is shown below but similar results will be produced by most linear programming software. The decision variables are in cells A1 and A2 and the constraints are in C1 and C2.

Adjustable Cells

Cell Name	Final Value	Reduced Cost	Objective Coefficient	Allowable Increase	Allowable Decrease
A1	160	0	10	30	5
A2	80	0	20	20	15

Constraints

Cell Name	Final Value	Shadow Price	Constraint R.H. Side	Allowable Increase	Allowable Decrease
C1	2000	0.571428571	2000	2800	1400
C2	480	4.285714286	480	1120	280

The first table concerns changes in the objective function; that is (for a maximisation), the amount of profit generated by a unit of a product. It tells us what might happen when *one* profit only is changed at a time.

The **Objective Coefficient** column shows the profits currently used in the model whereas the following two columns show by how much a single profit coefficient can increase or decrease without changing the optimal solution. For instance, profit on an Asteroid bar can decrease by 5 or increase by 30 and the optimal solution will still be (160, 80) provided the profit on a Blackhole bar does not change. Note that even when the optimal solution remains the same the optimal value of the objective function (the total profit) will have to be recalculated using the new profit figure. For example, if the profit on an Asteroid bar becomes 20, the optimal solution (160, 80) does not change but the objective function becomes $(20 \times 160) + (20 \times 80) = 4800$.

The second table of the sensitivity report concerns the amount of each resource that is available.

The **Constraint R.H. Side** column shows the current amounts of each resource available. The **Final Value** column shows the amount of the resources that are used in the optimal solution. (They are both used fully in this example.)

The **Shadow Price** column shows how much total profit will increase if one unit more of that resource becomes available and the amount available of the other resources remains the same. For instance, if we obtain an extra gram of cocoa profit will increase by 0.57 pence. In the same way, an extra minute of machine time will increase profit by 4.29 pence.

The shadow prices therefore give an upper limit on what we would be willing to pay to buy an extra unit of resource. If not all the resource is used at the optimal solution the constraint is non-binding, there is no benefit in obtaining an extra unit of it and the shadow price is zero.

However, shadow prices only work for small changes in the amount of resource. The **Allowable Increase** and **Allowable Decrease** columns show how much the amount of resource (the right-hand side of the constraint) can increase or decrease whilst this shadow price holds. For instance, available cocoa can increase by anything up to 2800g or decrease by anything up to 1400g and the total profit will increase or decrease by 0.57 pence for each additional or lesser gram of cocoa. For example, increasing the amount of cocoa available from 2000 to 2100 grams would increase profit by 57 pence. The shadow price, however, tells us nothing of the effect on the objective function of changes in amounts of resource outside this range. To find this we would have to change the right-hand side of the constraint and recalculate the solution.

A final report in Excel, the limits report, tells us by how much each decision variable can change without straying outside the feasible region; that is, violating one of the constraints.

WORK CARD 2

1. Ballester Electronics supplies each of four computer manufacturers with a particular chip which can be produced at any one of three of their factories. As the factories are in different areas it costs 93 pence to produce a chip at Factory 1, 105 pence at Factory 2 and 102 pence at Factory 3. The monthly production capacity at Factory 1 is 9000 chips, at Factory 2 is 10,000 chips and at factory 3 is 8000 chips. Sales forecasts project a monthly demand of 5100, 7200, 8000 and 5800 components for each of the computer manufacturers respectively.

   Ballester would like to find out how many microchips should be made at each factory to transport to each of the computer manufacturers. The transportation costs in pence per chip are shown below:

	Computer Manufacturer			
Factory	A	B	C	D
1	13	11	9	13
2	16	12	11	17
3	10	14	10	15

   Formulate an appropriate linear program.

2. Excel's sensitivity report for the Hooper's Home Improvements problem is shown below. Use it to answer the following questions, explaining your answers carefully. Incidentally, 1E+30 literally means 1×10^{30}, indicating that an indefinite increase/decrease is possible.

Adjustable Cells

Cell Name	Final Value	Reduced Cost	Objective Coefficient	Allowable Increase	Allowable Decrease
A1	130	0	12	1E+30	3
A2	130	−3	5	3	1E+30
A3	30	−5	15	5	1E+30
A4	0	−30	10	30	1E+30

Constraints

Cell Name	Final Value	Shadow Price	Constraint R.H. Side	Allowable Increase	Allowable Decrease
C1	1050	0	1500	1E+30	450
C2	770	0	1000	1E+30	230
C3	800	4	800	270	270

   (i) By how much can the profit on a solid door increase before the optimal solution changes?

(ii) What is the most Hooper's should be willing to pay staff for an hour's overtime?

(iii) And how many man-hours overtime should they be willing to pay at this rate before reconsidering?

(iv) Why is the shadow price of wood zero?

Solutions:

1. Each decision variable will be the amount that is manufactured at a particular factory for a particular manufacturer so there will be $3 \times 4 = 12$ in all. It is quite useful to use *two* subscripts to define them – one for the factory and one for the manufacturer. For instance, we use x_{1B} to indicate the number of chips made at Factory 1 for Manufacturer B. There are two types of cost: the production cost, which depends on factory only, and the transportation cost, which depends on both factory and manufacturer. A table showing the totals of these is given below.

	Manufacturer			
Factory	A	B	C	D
1	93 + 13 = 106	93 + 11 = 104	93 + 9 = 102	93 + 13 = 106
2	105 + 16 = 121	105 + 12 = 117	105 + 11 = 116	105 + 17 = 122
3	102 + 10 = 112	102 + 14 = 116	102 + 10 = 112	102 + 15 = 117

The formulation is

Minimise

$$106x_{1A} + 104x_{1B} + 102x_{1C} + 106x_{1D}$$
$$+ 121x_{2A} + 117x_{2B} + 116x_{2C} + 122x_{2D}$$
$$+ 112x_{3A} + 116x_{3B} + 112x_{3C} + 117x_{3D}$$

Subject to the constraints

$x_{1A} + x_{1B} + x_{1C} + x_{1D} \leq 9000$	CAPACITY FACTORY 1
$x_{2A} + x_{2B} + x_{2C} + x_{2D} \leq 10{,}000$	CAPACITY FACTORY 2
$x_{3A} + x_{3B} + x_{3C} + x_{3D} \leq 8000$	CAPACITY FACTORY 3
$x_{1A} + x_{2A} + x_{3A} \geq 5100$	DEMAND MANUFACTURER A
$x_{1B} + x_{2B} + x_{3B} \geq 7200$	DEMAND MANUFACTURER B
$x_{1C} + x_{2C} + x_{3AC} \geq 8000$	DEMAND MANUFACTURER C
$x_{1D} + x_{2D} + x_{3D} \geq 5800$	DEMAND MANUFACTURER D

$x_{1A} \geq 0, x_{1B} \geq 0, x_{1C} \geq 0, x_{1D} \geq 0$	
$x_{2A} \geq 0, x_{2B} \geq 0, x_{2C} \geq 0, x_{2D} \geq 0$	NON-NEGATIVITY CONSTRAINTS
$x_{3A} \geq 0, x_{3B} \geq 0, x_{3C} \geq 0, x_{3D} \geq 0$	

We could have used an equality sign for the demand constraints. However, the inequality will do just as well because, as the problem is a minimisation, there will be no benefit in over-supplying and demand will not be exceeded in the optimal solution.

WORK CARD 2

2. (i)   Profit on solid doors can increase by up to £30 i.e., to £40 before the optimal solution changes.

    (ii) The shadow price is £4 so overtime is only worthwhile to them if they can pay less than £4 an hour (unlikely).

    (iii) The shadow price remains at £4 for the next 270 man-hours.

    (iv) The shadow price of wood is zero because at the optimal solution not all the wood is used. If it had been beneficial to use more wood the optimal solution would have done so.

ASSESSMENT 2

1. Williamson's Dampers make five different types of damper. Each type must pass through two manufacturing processes and then be assembled by hand.

   The table below shows the number of minutes that each type of damper takes in each of the processes, the number of minutes of labour required to assemble a damper and the amount of profit a single damper brings.

Damper	A	B	C	D	E
Process 1	12	20	0	25	15
Process 2	10	8	16	0	0
Labour	20	19	21	18	22
Profit (pence)	55	60	35	40	20

Williamson's Dampers want to know how many dampers of each type they should manufacture in any week to maximise profit. 440 man-hours are available each week, 408 hours of Process 1 and 272 hours of Process 2.

   Formulate a linear programming model to solve this problem.

2. Use software to solve the model you have formulated in question 1 and answer the following.

   (i)   At the optimal solution which constraints are binding?

   (ii) If there are any non-binding constraints how much of which resource is left?

   (iii) Suppose the profit figure for Damper *E* was mis-typed and it really should have been 60 pence per unit. Will this affect the optimal solution? Reformulate the linear model and recalculate the solution if necessary. What if Damper *E* gives 65 pence profit per unit? Again, recalculate if necessary.

   (iv) Suppose extra machines can be hired for either Process 1 or Process 2. What can you say about how much Williamson's should pay for each extra minute of machine time?

3. Piff Fund Management has 4 investment alternatives for a 7-year planning horizon which are summarised in the following table along with their properties which are explained below.

Investment	Length of Investment	Estimated Annual Rate of Return	Risk Assessment	Growth Potential
Government Stock	3	5	1	0
Equity	5	7	3	10
Real Estate	7	10	5	15
Cash	0	2	1	0

The Length of Investment is the expected number of years required for the annual rate of return to be realised taking into account the possibility of reinvestment. The Estimated Annual Rate of Return is the percentage by which the investment is expected to grow if income is reinvested and the Risk Assessment is a subjective rating (1 is low risk, 5 is high) of the safety of the investment. Growth Potential is another subjective estimate of the potential increase in the capital value of the investment during the 7-year term.

Piff wishes to maximise the return on its portfolio of investments with the following restrictions:

The average length of the portfolio should be no more than 5 years.
The average risk assessment should be no more than 3.
The average growth potential should be at least 8.
To retain liquidity at least 10% of all funds should be retained as cash.

Formulate a linear programming model to calculate the proportions of total funds invested in the four alternatives that will maximise the average annual rate of return.

Hint: To make sure that the proportions sum to 1 you will have to include an equality constraint.
Use software to find the optimal solution.

Further reading: see p. xv

Further reading: see p. xv

Anderson *et al.* (Quantitative Methods) contains much more material on linear programming including some more involved applications. It also includes chapters on the related methods: integer linear programming and the transportation, assignment and transhipment problems.

Hillier and Lieberman includes the mathematical detail of how larger linear programming problems are solved using a method called the Simplex algorithm. It also includes the more advanced topics related to linear programming: the transportation and assignment problems, the transhipment problem and integer programming.

Hillier and Hillier or Winston give more advanced treatments, including the transportation and assignment problems.

BM2
Planning projects

No plan is worth a damn unless somebody makes it work.

William Feather, *Forbes* 120:186, 1977

Contexts

What is this chapter about?

Organisations frequently undertake projects that consist of many component parts that need to be completed by several departments and individuals. The parts are usually interrelated in the sense that some can't begin until others have finished. This chapter explains how all the component parts can be represented on a diagram and how this can be used to ascertain how long the project will take to complete, when each component must start and by how much time components can be delayed without delaying the project.

Why is it useful?

Some examples of such projects might be the development of a new product, the move to a new office, the construction of new buildings and roads or the design and installation of a new computer system. When a project involves many components and people its scheduling and control can't just be done on the back of an envelope, and a systematic approach is required. This chapter provides an introduction to some of the most widely used methods in industry, commerce and government.

Where does it fit in?

This chapter introduces the subject of Project Scheduling, which is a branch of Management Science or Operational Research. Originally, in the early years of Project Scheduling two key techniques were developed, the critical path method (CPM) and the program evaluation and review technique (PERT). Nowadays, however, the most useful features of both methods have been combined and you will see them referred to collectively as PERT/CPM.

What do I need to know?

You will need to be familiar with only the material in the Essential Maths chapters of this book.

Objectives

After your work on this chapter you should be able to:

- produce a precedence table for a project, and use it to draw a network;
- use the network to calculate earliest start times, latest finish times and floats and hence find the critical path;
- draw and interpret a Gantt chart.

In this chapter we describe a type of business model that helps plan the way a complex project is executed. By a project we mean a piece of work that has a clear start and finish and which is composed of any number of component parts or *activities*. Some examples are the construction of buildings and roads, computerising a system or the design and launch of a new product.

We would like to schedule the project to find out when each activity should start and finish and whether there is any flexibility in the timing.

Large projects may have many hundreds of activities and will be planned using specialist software. However, to understand the input and output you will need to know something about the underlying techniques. We describe these using a small project that we can work by hand.

1 Drawing a project planning network

Introducing the project

Brodders Software wants to move premises and the project manager for the move has identified the following activities and estimated their duration.

- A. Draw up the requirements study – 4 weeks
- B. Find suitable premises – 4 weeks
- C. Refurbish the building – 6 weeks
- D. Install cabling for the computer network – 2 weeks
- E. Move in the furniture – 1 week
- F. Install the computers – 2 weeks
- G. Print stationery with the new address – 2 weeks

However, the activities of a project can't be done in any order. For instance, Brodders can't refurbish the building before they have found suitable premises and they can't install the computers until the cabling is complete.

The precedence table

To define which activities must come before others we draw up a *precedence* or dependence table. This lists each activity with any activities that *immediately* precede it. The precedence table for the Brodders project is given below.

Activity		Preceding activities
A.	Requirements study	none
B.	Find suitable premises	A
C.	Refurbish building	B
D.	Install cabling	B
E.	Move in furniture	C
F.	Install computers	D, E
G.	Print stationery	B

Drawing the network

The next stage is to draw a *network* from the precedence table. This frequently involves a lot of trial and error so it is best to use a pencil and lots of scrap paper.

We start drawing a network on the left-hand side of the page with a single circle or *node* called the start node, which we'll label node **1**. From this we draw an arrow for every activity that has no preceding activities. For our (very simple) project only activity **A** has no preceding activities so we need only one arrow. At the end of this arrow we draw another node, which we'll call node **2**, to represent the completion of activity **A**. The result is shown in Figure 2.1.

Figure 2.1

We then draw an arrow out of node **2** for each activity that lists activity **A** as a preceding activity. Here there is only activity, **B**. Node **3** represents the completion of activity **B** as shown in Figure 2.2.

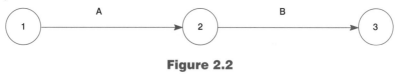

Figure 2.2

We continue in the same way. Activities **C**, **D** and **G** list **B** as a preceding activity so three arrows must leave node **3** as shown in Figure 2.3.

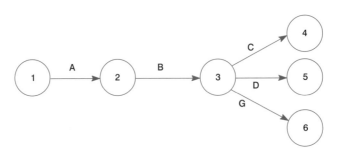

Figure 2.3

We continue until we have included all the activities in the network as shown in Figure 2.4.

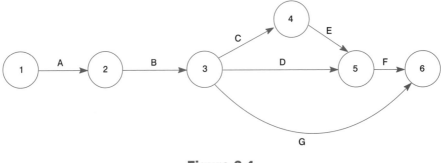

Figure 2.4

Notice that as both **D** and **E** precede **F** their arrows must end at the same node (node **5**). Also, just as we had a single start node we have a single final node (node **6**) representing completion of the entire project. It is also conventional to ensure that all arrows go from a lower numbered node to a higher numbered node.

There are two occasions when we might run into trouble drawing a network. Both require us to introduce an activity into the network called a *dummy activity*.

Logical dummies

To illustrate the need for a *logical dummy activity* suppose the precedence table for the Brodders project included an extra activity (**H**) of two weeks duration, which must be done after the cabling. The precedence table becomes

Activity		Preceding activities
A.	Requirements study	none
B.	Find suitable premises	A
C.	Refurbish building	B
D.	Install cabling	B
E.	Move in furniture	C
F.	Install computers	D, E
G.	Print stationery	B
H.	*Install telephones*	*D*

A logical dummy activity is required when an activity appears more than once in the preceding activity column but with different preceding activities. For instance, activity **D** appears on its own as a preceding activity of **H**, but with **E** as a preceding activity of **F**. The part of the network which shows **D** and **E** preceding **F** is shown in Figure 2.5.

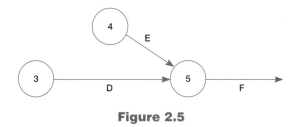

Figure 2.5

If we try to include activity **H** in Figure 2.5 we run into trouble. (Try it!) **D** precedes **H** but if we draw **H** going out of node **5** we imply that *both* **E** and **D** must happen before **H**, which is not true. The problem is that both **D** and **E** precede **F** but only **D** precedes **H**. To get round this we introduce a new node (which we'll label **3*** as it's an extra) at the end of **D** but before the end of **E**. If **H** is drawn going out of the new node it will have **D** but *not* **E** as a preceding activity, as required. This part of the network is shown in Figure 2.6.

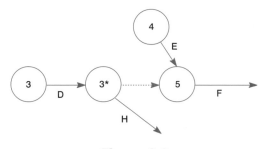

Figure 2.6

We have drawn a dotted arrow from node **3*** to node **5** to ensure the logic of the network. As it doesn't represent a real activity and takes zero time we say it represents a *dummy activity*.

Check this

Draw the complete Brodders network including activity **H**.

Solution:
You need to introduce node **3*** into Figure 2.5 and maybe space the nodes a little differently so that the arrows go from left to right.

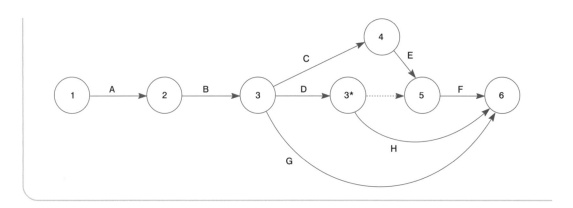

Uniqueness dummies

Computer software for network models frequently refers to the activities by their start and end nodes. For instance, **2–3** means the activity that starts at node **2** and finishes at node **3** (activity **B** above). This means that to identify each activity uniquely we can only allow one arrow between any two nodes.

However, a problem arises when two or more activities have exactly the same preceding activities and themselves precede the same other activities. For example, **C** and **D** in the precedence chart below both have the same preceding activities (**A** and **B**) and they both precede **E**.

Activity	Preceding activities
C	A B
D	A B
E	C D

If we try to draw this network both **C** and **D** connect nodes **2** and **3** as shown in Figure 2.7, so activity **2–3** could mean either **C** or **D** and is not uniquely defined.

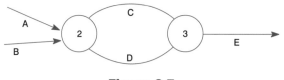

Figure 2.7

We alleviate this situation by introducing a new node, **2***, between nodes **2** and **3** which gives an 'alternative route' through the network for one of the activities. The arrow representing one of the activities can then go from node **2** to the new node and we can draw a dotted arrow from the new node to node **3** to represent a dummy activity as shown in Figure 2.8.

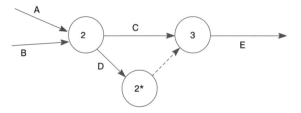

Figure 2.8

1. To buy a house in England the following activities must be completed:

Activity		Preceding activities
A.	Find the property	–
B.	Arrange the mortgage	–
C.	Legal work phase 1	A B
D.	Legal work phase 2	C
E.	Inform phone, gas and electricity companies	C
F.	Move furniture	D

Draw a project planning network for buying a house in England

2. Draw a network to represent the following project.

Activity	Preceding activities
A	–
B	A
C	A
D	–
E	B C
F	C D

Solutions:

1. You need an extra node between nodes **1** and **2** otherwise **A** and **B** will join the same two nodes. The network is

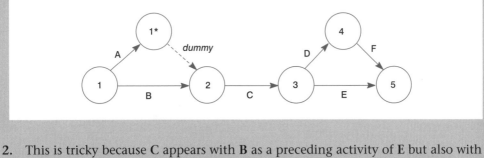

2. This is tricky because **C** appears with **B** as a preceding activity of **E** but also with **D** as a preceding activity of **F** so we will need an extra node after node **2**.

WORK CARD 1

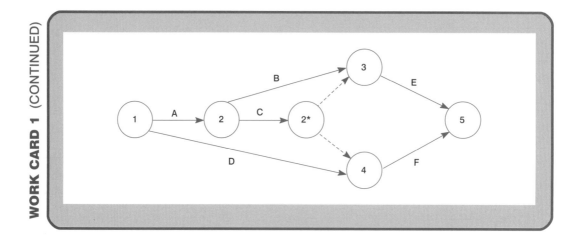

1. Creation Theatre are planning an open-air production somewhere in Nottinghamshire. They have already rehearsed but need to employ a professional actor to play the lead role. Here is a list of activities.

Activity		Preceding activities
A.	Find site	–
B.	Plan seating	A
C.	Appoint lead actor	A
D.	Start publicity	C
E.	Arrange ticket sales	A
F.	Set up sound system	B
G.	TV and radio interviews	C
H.	Set up lighting	C
I.	Dress rehearsal	F, H
J.	Final details	I

(i)   Draw a network for the project.

(ii) Now suppose that activity **G** of the Creation project in question **1** requires **D** as well as C as a preceding activity. What changes, if any, would you need to make to the network?

2. Think of a hypothetical or real project with at least 8 activities. (For example, planning a party with a group of friends, organising a wedding, arranging a group outing.) Describe the project and its activities, draw up a precedence table and construct a network. If there is no dummy variable describe an extra activity that would require you to introduce one and include it in the network.

2 **Scheduling activities**

In the original specification of the Brodders project we gave the estimated duration of each activity but we haven't used these yet. We want to use the network to find out when each activity must be started and/or finished and how tight the timing is for each.

We illustrate the method using the complete Brodders network (that is, including **H**). We repeat the complete network in Figure 2.9 but this time we include the duration of each activity.

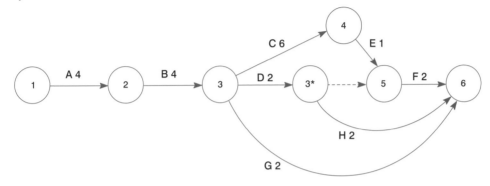

Figure 2.9 The complete Brodders network.

Earliest and latest event times

We are going to move through the network twice. The first time we are going to start at node **1** and work forwards calculating the earliest possible times at which each node can occur. The second time we are going to start at the finish node (node **6**) and work backwards calculating the latest possible time at which each node can occur.

First the forward pass. It is more complicated to explain than to do so we suggest you look at the appropriate nodes of Figure 2.9 as you read, and write the *earliest event times* above the nodes as we work them out.

Node **1** is the start node so we will say it happens at time 0 (write a 0 above node **1**). Node **2** follows on from activity **A**, which starts at time 0 and takes 4 weeks so the earliest event time for node **2** is 4 weeks. (Write a 4 above node **2**). Node **3** follows activity **B** which, from the 4 you've written above node **2**, starts at time 4 and takes 4 weeks so the earliest event time for node **3** is 8 weeks and we write an 8 above node **3**. In the same way **3*** follows activity **D** and so occurs 2 weeks later than node **3**, at 10 weeks, and node **4** occurs 6 weeks after node **3** at 14 weeks.

So far this has been simple because only one activity (arrow) has preceded each node. We now come on to node **5**. Figure 2.10 shows node **5** and the activities and nodes immediately

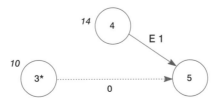

Figure 2.10 Nodes and activities immediately preceding node 5.

preceding it. Notice the italic earliest event times that we have just worked out above nodes **3*** and **4**.

Two activities, **E** and the *dummy*, lead into node **5** and they must *both* be completed before node **5** occurs. The earliest time at which **E** can be completed is the earliest event time for node **4** (the italic *14*) plus the duration of activity **E** (the bold *1*); that is, *14 + 1 = 15*. In the same way the earliest time at which the *dummy* activity can be completed is the earliest event time for node **3*** (the italic *10*) plus the duration of the *dummy* activity (the bold *0*); that is *10 + 0 = 10*. The earliest event time for node **5** is the *latest* of these two times (that is *15*), which we can now write on Figure 2.9, above node **5**.

In general, when a node has two or more preceding activities they must *all* finish before the node can occur so the earliest event time is the *maximum* of the times taken by the paths into the node.

Check this

What is the earliest event time for node **6**?

Solution:
Look at Figure 2.9 where you wrote in the earliest event times. Activities **F**, **G** and **H** immediately precede node **6**. Taking them one at a time:

F can be finished at time
earliest event time of node **5** (italic *15*) + duration of **F** (bold *2*) = *17*

G can be finished at
earliest event time of node **3** (italic *8*) + duration of **G** (bold *2*) = *10*

H can be finished at
earliest event time of node **3*** (italic *10*) + duration of **H** (bold *2*) = *12*

The earliest event time of node **6** is the greatest of these, *17*.

Figure 2.11 shows the network with all the earliest event times marked in italics.

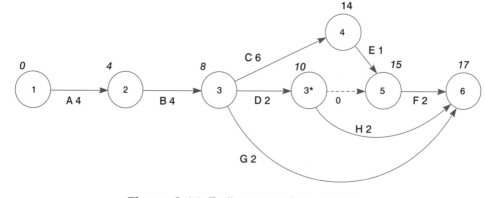

Figure 2.11 Earliest event times (italics).

Now for the *latest event times*. We find these in a similar way but we start at the end of the network, node **6**, and work backwards. For each node we want the latest time it can possibly happen for the project to be completed at time *17*.

The latest event time for node **6** is *17*, the overall duration of the project. We will write latest event times in italic *underneath* the nodes. We suggest you write them on Figure 2.11 as we go along.

Activity **F** follows node **5** and takes 2 weeks. To ensure completion by the latest event time of node **6** (*17*) activity **F** must be started by *17 – 2 = 15* weeks at the latest. In a similar way activity **E** follows node **4** and takes 1 week so the latest event time of node **4** is the latest event time of node **5** less 1 = *15 – 1 = 14*.

Both activity **H** and the *dummy* activity follow node **3*** as shown in Figure 2.12. Notice the latest event times in italic below nodes **5** and **6**.

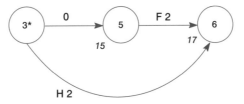

Figure 2.12 Node **3*** and the immediately following activities and nodes.

To ensure that node **5** occurs by its latest event time, (*15*), the *dummy* activity will have to start at time *15 – 0 = 15* at the latest. In a similar way, to ensure that node **6** occurs by its latest event time (*17*), activity **H** will have to start at the latest at time *17 – 2 = 15*. However, node **3*** represents the start of both these activities so at the latest it occurs at the *minimum* of these times. By coincidence here, they are both the same so the minimum is *15*.

In general, the latest event time for a node must allow all the immediately following activities to finish by the latest event time of their end nodes.

Now you try node **3**.

Check this

Calculate the latest event time for node **3**.

Solution:
3 activities, **C**, **D** and **G** immediately follow node **3**. Activity **C** must end by the latest event time of node **4** (*14*), activity **D** by the latest event time of node **3*** (*15*) and activity **G** by the latest event time of node **6** (*17*). The durations of **C**, **D** and **G** are 6, 2 and 2 weeks respectively. So **C** must start by time *14 – 6 = 8*, **D** by time *15 – 2 = 13* and **G** by time *17 – 2 = 15*. Node **3** must therefore occur by the earliest of these times; that is, week **8**.

We leave you to confirm that the latest event time for node **2** is *4* and for node **1** is *0*.

The network showing all earliest event times and latest event times above and below the nodes is shown in Figure 2.13.

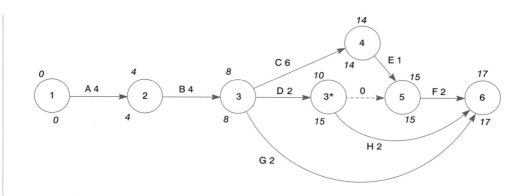

Figure 2.13 Network showing all the earliest and latest event times.

Calculating floats

We can now use the network to find out which activities are flexible in time and which aren't. For instance, look at activity D in Figure 2.13. It runs from node 3 to node 3*. The earliest start time for activity D is therefore the earliest event time of node 3 (*8 weeks*) and the latest finish time for activity D is the latest event time of node 3* (*15 weeks*). There are therefore *15 − 8 = 7* possible weeks in which to do activity D although it only has a duration of 2 weeks. We say that activity D has a *float* of 5 weeks. By this we mean that it could start up to 5 weeks later than the earliest event time preceding it or, equivalently, that its duration could be increased by 5 weeks without delaying the completion of the project. In general, the float of an activity is calculated as

$$\text{float} = \text{latest event time of following node}$$
$$- \text{earliest event time of preceding node}$$
$$- \text{duration of the activity}$$

Now consider activity E.

Check this

Calculate the float of activity E.

Solution:
The latest event time of node 5 is *15*, the earliest event time of node 4 is *14* and the duration of activity E is **1**, so

float = *15 − 14 − 1 = 0*

Activity E has a zero float which means that any delay in its start time or extension of its duration will increase the total duration of the project.

Any activity with a zero float is called a *critical* activity. Critical activities *must* start at the earliest start time of the preceding node and there is no flexibility in their duration.

Critical paths

The table below shows all the activities in the Brodders project, their earliest start times, latest finish times and floats.

Activity	Earliest start time	Latest finish time	Duration	Float
A	0	4	4	4 − 0 − 4 = 0
B	4	8	4	8 − 4 − 4 = 0
C	8	14	6	14 − 8 − 6 = 0
D	8	15	2	15 − 8 − 2 = 5
E	14	15	1	15 − 14 − 1 = 0
F	15	17	2	17 − 15 − 2 = 0
G	8	17	2	17 − 8 − 2 = 7
H	10	17	2	17 − 10 − 2 = 5

Notice that activities **A**, **B**, **C**, **E** and **F** are critical activities. They form a continuous path through the network called the *critical path*. The critical path is the longest route through the network from the start node to the final node. There may be more than one critical path.

Gantt charts

It is not always obvious from the network which activities should be happening at any particular time. A *Gantt chart* (named after its originator) has a row for each activity and a column for each time period and so shows the passage of time more clearly. By convention, the critical activities are shown at the top of the chart. The Gantt chart for the Brodders project is shown in Figure 2.14. Notice that the times at which the critical activities must happen are shown as solid areas. The times needed by non-critical activities are shown by a solid outline starting at their earliest start times whilst their floats appear as dotted outlines afterwards.

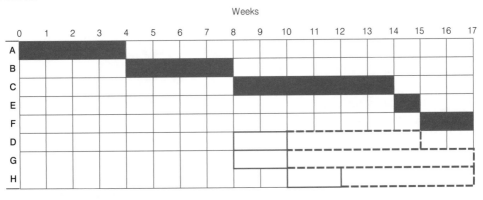

Figure 2.14 A Gantt chart for the Brodders project.

The Gantt chart enables us to see at a glance how many resources are required at any particular time. For instance, if each activity needs only one person, the chart for the Brodders project tells us that we need one person up to time 8, three people from time 8 to time 10, two between times 10 and 12 and just one from time 12 onwards. We can use the chart to adjust the timing of non-critical activities to spread the workload more evenly. Whilst we can move a non-critical activity to the right within the bounds of the dotted outline without delaying the project, we must remember that this may have knock-on effects for other activities because the original precedence table still holds. For instance, if activity **D** is moved a day later we have no choice but to postpone activity **H** by a day as well because it must follow **D**. As it happens, delaying both **D** and **H** by 2 days is a sensible thing to do because it means that no more than two people are required at any time.

Extensions

We have only had space to describe the basics of project planning using networks. Specialised computer software offers many extensions although the fundamental ideas remain the same.

For instance, we have assumed that the duration of each activity is known. In practice, of course, it is only an estimate and we need to consider the effects of changes in the duration of each activity. One way of doing this is to make three estimates of each activity's duration – a pessimistic one, a realistic one and an optimistic one, and then use this information (with some probability theory) to calculate the probability of completing the project by a particular date.

Sometimes it may be worth paying to reduce the duration of an activity; for instance, by paying overtime or hiring extra machines because it will reduce the total project duration and save money. This is called *crashing*. The time by which the duration of an activity can be reduced is known as the *crash time* and the costs of such a reduction are the *crash costs*. These can be compared to see which activities, if any, it would be most worthwhile to crash.

WORK CARD 2

1. Consider the buying a house project of **Work card 1**, question 1. The precedence table, along with the duration of each activity, is shown below.

Activity	Preceding activities	Duration (working days)
A. Find the property	–	10
B. Arrange the mortgage	–	5
C. Legal work phase 1	A B	20
D. Legal work phase 2	C	20
E. Inform phone, gas and electricity companies	C	5
F. Move furniture	D	1

   (i) Calculate the earliest and latest event times for each node.

   (ii) At what stage in the project would you expect to be able to inform the phone, gas and electricity companies? How long, at most, could you spend on this activity without delaying the project?

   (iii) Find the critical path(s).

2. Consider the following network. Find out which activities are critical and how much float the other activities have.

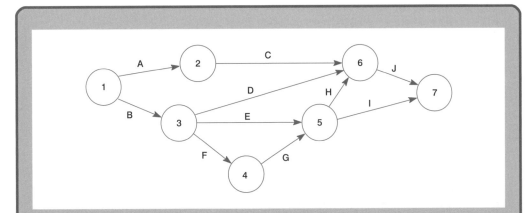

The activities and their estimated durations are shown below.

A 32   F 16
B 28   G 16
C 36   H 20
D 52   I 34
E 32   J 16

3. Draw a Gantt chart for the project in question 2. If each activity requires one team of workers, make suggestions for scheduling.

Solutions:

1. (i)   The earliest and latest event times for each node are

node	earliest	latest
1	0	0
1*	10	10
2	10	10
3	30	30
4	50	50
5	51	51

(ii)   Activity E goes from node 3 to node 5 so from the table above it can be started at time *30* at the earliest (earliest event time of node 3) and must finish by time *51* (latest event time of node 5). Its current duration is *5* but you could spend up to *21* days on it without delaying the project.

(iii) The floats for **A, B, C, D, E, F** are *10 – 0 – 10 = 0*; *10 – 0 – 5 = 5*; *30 – 10 – 20 = 0*; *50 – 30 – 20 = 0*; *51 – 30 – 5 = 16* and *51 – 50 – 1 = 0* respectively. So the critical path is **A, C, D** and **F**.

2. The earliest and latest event times are

node	earliest	latest
1	0	0
2	32	44
3	28	28
4	44	44
5	60	60
6	80	80
7	96	96

so the floats (latest event time of following node less earliest event time of preceding node – duration) are

A: $44 - 0 - 32 = 12$
B: $28 - 0 - 28 = 0$
C: $80 - 32 - 36 = 12$
D: $80 - 28 - 52 = 0$
E: $60 - 28 - 32 = 0$
F: $44 - 28 - 16 = 0$
G: $60 - 44 - 16 = 0$
H: $80 - 60 - 20 = 0$
I: $96 - 60 - 34 = 2$
J: $96 - 80 - 16 = 0$

The critical activities are therefore all those except **A**, **C** and **I**.

3.

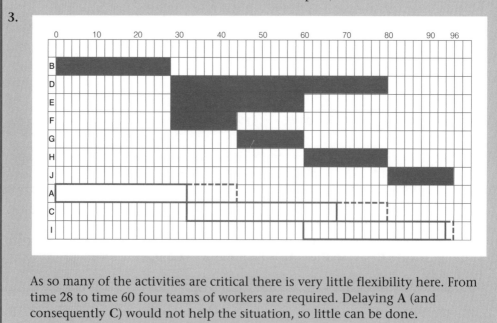

As so many of the activities are critical there is very little flexibility here. From time 28 to time 60 four teams of workers are required. Delaying A (and consequently C) would not help the situation, so little can be done.

ASSESSMENT 2

1. Return to the Creation Theatre project of **Assessment 1**, question **1**, and find the critical path(s). The precedence table is repeated below along with the duration of each activity.

Activity	Preceding activities	Duration (working days)
A. Find site	–	3
B. Plan seating	A	2
C. Appoint lead actor	A	6
D. Start publicity	C	2
E. Arrange ticket sales	A	3
F. Set up sound system	B	3
G. TV and radio interviews	C	5
H. Set up lighting	C	1
I. Dress rehearsal	F, H	1.5
J. Final details	I	2

2. Return to the network you drew for your own project in **Assessment 1**, question 2. Calculate the critical path and draw a Gantt chart for the project. Explain any repercussions for the timing of the various activities.

Further reading: see p. xv

Anderson *et al.* (Quantitative Methods) is an excellent source of further material, as are Hillier and Lieberman, and Hillier and Hillier.

Winston.

Morris provides an alternative exposition to ours.

BM3
Models for inventory control

Being good in business is the most fascinating kind of art.

Andy Warhol, *The Observer*, 1 May 1987

Contexts

What is this chapter about?

Inventory means goods or materials stored ready for sale or for a subsequent part of the manufacturing process. This chapter considers some basic models for the changing level of inventory over time and uses them to determine how and when inventory should be replenished at minimum cost.

Why is it useful?

Nearly all businesses and many organisations have the problem of deciding how much to store and when to replenish. On the one hand they need to store enough to satisfy demand and not lose trade or hold up the manufacturing process, but on the other hand, storing inventory ties up capital and incurs storage costs. For instance, a computer retailer must keep a sufficient supply of printer cartridges to supply customers or a chocolate factory must keep an adequate supply of wrappers for its product. Financial and service companies face similar decisions. For example, a water company must attempt to satisfy demand for water and a call centre must have enough staff to answer the phones at any time.

Where does it fit in?

Inventory modelling or Inventory control, like the subjects in the other chapters of this part of the book, is an area of Management Science or Operational Research. In this book we consider only inventory models that are deterministic; that is, which assume that demand for the item is known and constant. More advanced models allow demand to fluctuate and model it using probabilities.

What do I need to know?

You will need to be familiar with only the material in the Essential Maths chapters of this book.

Objectives

After your work on this chapter you should:

- understand what costs are incurred in keeping inventory;
- be able to formulate and solve a basic EOQ model;
- be able to adapt the model to allow for lead time and shortages;
- be able to use the variability coefficient to assess whether demand really is constant;
- know something of the ABC classification.

Most businesses have to store goods or materials ready for sale to the customer or for a subsequent part of the manufacturing process. Such stocks are called *inventory*. On the one hand the business must store enough to supply demand and not lose trade, yet on the other hand storing inventory incurs storage costs and ties up capital.

An *inventory control policy* is a set of rules, usually based on an *inventory model* of the inventory system, which suggests when and how many goods should be ordered to keep costs down and yet maintain customer goodwill.

Inventory models are also useful outside a business context. For instance, livestock for fattening, cash in the bank, water in reservoirs, blood in blood banks, and staff can all be regarded as inventory.

1 An inventory model

Inventory models
An inventory model represents the behaviour of an inventory system over time. It reflects the diminishing inventory as goods are sold and the increase in inventory as stores are replenished, in order to assess the various costs incurred for a particular inventory policy. Many variations are possible, depending on the assumptions made about the system. In particular, some assumptions must be made about the pattern of demand as this tells us the manner in which inventory is diminished.

The costs of keeping inventory
Four types of cost are incurred by keeping inventory: ordering costs, unit costs, holding costs and shortage costs.

When goods are purchased to store as inventory there will obviously be a charge per item or *unit cost* although this may be less for bulk orders. However, each order will also incur an *ordering* or *set-up* cost. This is a flat charge for delivery and administration or the cost of setting up a production run. The *holding cost* includes insurance costs and interest lost on the capital tied up in the goods as well as the cost of storage.

Finally, when an item is not available when required a *shortage cost* is incurred. This can be hard to quantify. It may be the additional cost of placing an order for immediate delivery, the cost of lost trade if the customer goes elsewhere or an intangible 'loss of goodwill' cost if the customer has to wait and becomes disgruntled.

The basic EOQ model

The basic Economic Order Quantity (EOQ) model is the very simplest (and so often the least realistic) model but it forms the basis of many others. It assumes that stock levels are gradually depleted at a constant rate; that is, demand occurs at a constant rate and that when stocks run out a fixed-size batch or 'lot' of new items is ordered and arrives instantaneously. Whilst the assumption of demand at a constant rate may be a good approximation to the real situation, the assumption of immediate delivery is obviously very unrealistic but we will live with it now and drop it later.

Figure 3.1 shows a single inventory cycle of the EOQ model. When stock levels reach zero a batch of items is received and is then used at a constant rate until stock levels return to zero again. (Since orders arrive immediately there is no point in ordering before stock levels reach zero as this would incur unnecessary holding costs.)

The only decision we have to make for the basic EOQ model is *how many* items to order in a batch. On the one hand, large batches are good because they last longer and we don't have to pay the order cost as often but on the other hand large batches give higher average inventory levels and so higher holding costs. Due to the simplified nature of the model, the total cost of inventory comes from just two sources: ordering cost and holding cost. The *economic order quantity* (EOQ) is the batch size that results in the lowest total of ordering and holding costs.

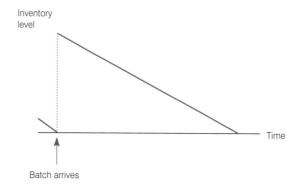

Figure 3.1 A single cycle of the basic EOQ model.

Before we can give the formula for the EOQ we need some notation. Let us suppose that demand for stock occurs at a constant rate of D per unit time and that the batch size is q (for quantity). We'll call the ordering cost K and the cost of holding a unit of stock for a unit of time, h.

Figure 3.2 shows several cycles of the basic EOQ model. Notice that because D units are used per unit time, it takes q/D time units to use up the batch of q items so each cycle lasts q/D time units.

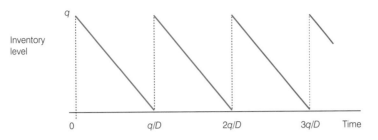

Figure 3.2 Inventory levels under the EOQ model.

The formula for the economic order quantity is

$$\text{EOQ} = \sqrt{\frac{2KD}{h}}$$

We'll explain where this comes from later but for now let's see how it is used.

Check this

A video manufacturer produces 8000 video recorders on a continuous production line every month. Each video requires a tape head unit and these are produced very quickly in batches. It costs £12,000 to set up the machinery to produce a batch and 30p a month to store and insure a tape head unit once made. How large should the batch size be to minimise total costs and how often will they have to set up a production run?

Solution:
Here $D = 8000$, $K = 12,000$ and $h = 0.3$. Using the formula

$$\text{EOQ} = \sqrt{\frac{2 \times 8000 \times 12,000}{0.3}} = 25,298.2$$

It doesn't make sense to talk about 0.2 of a tape head unit, so the batch size that minimises total costs would be 25,298. As only 8000 units are required each month, 25,298 units will last 25,298/8000 = 3.16 months so the manufacturer should produce a batch of tape head units every 3.16 months.

To get a feel for how the holding and set-up costs affect the EOQ try the following.

Check this

Now suppose the video manufacturer can arrange alternative storage for tape head units at only 20 pence per unit per month. How will this affect the EOQ and the frequency of production runs?

Solution:
Now $h = 0.20$ so the EOQ is

$$\sqrt{\frac{2 \times 8000 \times 12{,}000}{0.2}} = 30{,}984$$

As the storage cost is smaller, larger batches can be produced and a production run is needed less often, every 30,984/8000 = 3.87 months.

Now suppose that holding costs remain at 0.30 per unit per month but that the setup cost decreases to £10,000. What affect will this have on the EOQ and the frequency of production runs?

Solution:
Now $h = 0.30$ again but $K = 10{,}000$, making

$$\text{EOQ} = \sqrt{\frac{2 \times 8000 \times 10{,}000}{0.3}} = 23{,}094$$

which will last 23,094/8000 = 2.89 months. As set-up costs are cheaper it will pay to produce a batch more often.

Now you've had some practice with the EOQ we will make the following general observations. Recall that

$$\text{EOQ} = \sqrt{\frac{2KD}{h}}$$

First notice that as K increases the EOQ increases. This makes sense because if it is more costly to order, the company will place fewer orders and so, as demand occurs at a constant rate, the orders will have to be larger. Also, as h *increases* EOQ *decreases*. This also makes sense because if holding costs are greater we will want to keep lower levels of inventory and so order smaller amounts.

Also, notice that for a particular demand rate, D, the ratio of the ordering cost, K, to the holding cost, h, determines the EOQ. This means, for instance, that a set-up cost of 100 and a holding cost of 1 has the same EOQ as a set-up cost of 1000 and a holding cost of 10. It is also interesting that if, for example, demand is quadrupled, the EOQ will only double, because of the square root.

The basic EOQ model doesn't make any use of cost per unit because we are assuming that cost per unit is the same regardless of how much we order. Sometimes price reductions, known as *quantity discounts*, are given for ordering larger amounts and these can be built into more complicated versions of the EOQ model.

We finish this section by explaining where the EOQ formula came from. If you'd rather skip the maths rejoin us at the **Work card**, but otherwise read on.

The derivation of the economic order quantity
We have to consider the total of two types of cost: set-up cost and holding costs. The set-up cost is K for every inventory cycle. However, to make a fair comparison between different order quantities (and cycle lengths) we must compare costs *per time unit*. Have a look at Figure 3.2 again. The cycle length is q/D time units so the order cost incurred per time unit is K divided by this; that is, KD/q.

Calculation of holding cost is slightly more complicated. Because the stock level diminishes at a constant rate the average stock level during a complete cycle is half the batch, or $q/2$. As holding cost is h per item per time unit, this means that the average holding cost per time unit is $h \times q/2 = hq/2$.

The total of the set-up cost and the holding cost per time unit is therefore

$$\frac{KD}{q} + \frac{hq}{2}$$

If you don't know how to differentiate (see *More Maths*, Chapter MM3) you will have to believe us when we say that the value of q that gives the smallest total cost per time unit is

$$q = \sqrt{\frac{2KD}{h}}$$

However, if you know how to differentiate you can check the following calculation.

Check this

Find the value of q for which

$$\frac{KD}{q} + \frac{hq}{2}$$

is a minimum.

Solution:
To find the maximum or minimum of a function we differentiate and set the derivative equal to 0. Differentiating the expression above with respect to q gives

$$\frac{-KD}{q^2} + \frac{h}{2}$$

(you have to regard everything except q as a constant). Equating this derivative to 0 gives

$$\frac{-KD}{q^2} + \frac{h}{2} = 0$$

which we solve for q to give

$$q = \sqrt{\frac{2KD}{h}}$$

as required.

To be thorough we should also check that this value of q gives a minimum and not a maximum by finding the second derivative and checking that it is positive for this value of q (see *More Maths*, Chapter MM3).

1. Suppose that demand for a product occurs evenly at a rate of 20 units per week. Every time an order is placed a cost of $15 is incurred and it costs $0.20 per item a week to insure the goods and $0.10 per item per week to store the goods. How frequently should an order be placed and how many units should be ordered in a batch?

2. Matthews Motor Homes sell, on average, 5 'Harvey' models a week. The local supplier charges a flat rate of £1000 for each delivery regardless of size. Garaging costs for each motor home work out at £20 a week and insurance is £25 per motor home per week. Matthews prefer to place a regular, fixed-size order with the supplier and shortages are not allowed.
    How many 'Harveys' should Matthews order in a batch, and how often? What assumptions are implicit here?

Solutions:

1. $D = 20$, $K = 15$ and $h = 0.2 + 0.1 = 0.3$. So

$$\text{EOQ} = \sqrt{\frac{2 \times 20 \times 15}{0.3}} = 44.72$$

and the cycle length will be $44.72/20 = 2.24$ weeks. So an order of 45 units should be placed every $2\frac{1}{4}$ weeks.

2. $D = 5$, $K = 1000$, $h = 45$ so

$$\text{EOQ} = \sqrt{\frac{2 \times 1000 \times 5}{45}} = 14.91$$

So, to the nearest integer, they should order 15 motor homes every $14.91/5 = 3$ weeks. The model assumes that delivery is immediate and that demand occurs at a constant rate.

1. Loyal cabs use petrol at the rate of 8000 litres a month. Petrol is delivered in bulk at a cost of £250 and costs 65 pence per litre. It costs 1 pence per litre per month to store petrol.
    Assuming shortages are not allowed, determine how often and how much petrol to order.

2. The demand for a product is 500 units per week and the items are withdrawn uniformly from inventory. The items are ordered at a cost of $25 and it costs $0.05 to store a unit for a week.
    Assuming shortages are not allowed, calculate the order quantity and frequency of ordering.

2 **Making the model more realistic**

The basic EOQ model is a good start but several of the assumptions it makes are far from realistic, not least that deliveries arrive instantly and that shortages cannot occur. In this section we relax these assumptions.

Introducing lead time

In practice, goods cannot arrive instantly and there will be a *lead time*; that is, an order will take so many time units to arrive. We will build lead time into the EOQ model by assuming that it is always the same and is L time units.

Previously we waited until stock levels reached zero before reordering because the order arrived immediately. Now, we would still like the order to arrive when stock levels reach zero but to achieve this we will have to place the order exactly L time units earlier. During the lead time, L, $L \times D = LD$ units will be used so this means that we should order when the inventory level is down to LD. LD is called the *reorder level*.

A simple, non-automated, way of spotting when inventory gets down to the reorder level is to store stock in two places or *bins*. An amount equivalent to the reorder level is put aside in one bin and the remaining stock in the other bin. Stock is taken out of the remainder bin first. When it empties, the reorder level is left and it is time to place an order.

You should beware. If the reorder level is more than the batch size you will have to order more than one cycle ahead.

Check this

Recall, for the first video manufacturer example, 8000 tape head units are required a month and EOQ = 25,298. Suppose it takes one week, 0.25 of a month, to make a batch of tape head units. What is the reorder level?

Solution:
During 0.25 of a month 2000 tape head units will be used so the reorder level will be 2000.

Shortages allowed

So far we have conveniently ignored the possibility of running out of stock. This is called a *shortage* or *stock out* and is a very real possibility so we should build it into the model.

In general, allowing shortages enables the inventory cycle length to be increased, which saves set-up costs and holding costs but incurs shortage costs.

Shortage costs are often difficult to quantify and may take two general forms. The customer may go elsewhere in which case the penalty to the firm is the loss of revenue or profit from that sale. Alternatively, the customer may be willing to wait until the goods are available. This is called *backlogged demand* or *back ordering*. In this case the sale is not lost but the firm risks losing that customer's future trade and goodwill. We will model this last case.

The EOQ model with backlogged demand

We will regard backlogged demand as a negative inventory level. Suppose that the maximum stock level, which occurs at the start of a cycle, immediately after delivery of a batch, is M units. As the batch size is q this means that the inventory level immediately before delivery must have been $M - q$ units, a negative number. In other words, the shortage immediately before delivery was of $q - M$ units. Figure 3.3 shows the evolution of stock levels over time.

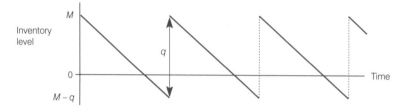

Figure 3.3 Inventory cycles for the EOQ model with backlogged demand.

We now introduce the shortage cost, s, which is the cost of being short of one item for one time unit.

We now have three types of cost: holding, set-up and shortage and we must decide on the values of q and M that make the total of these as small as possible. We'll consider the costs one at a time. The set-up cost is K per cycle as before.

To calculate the holding and shortage costs we have to break each cycle into two parts. Look again at Figure 3.3. In the first part of each cycle stock levels are positive and holding costs are incurred and in the second part of each cycle stock levels are negative and shortage costs are incurred.

The first part of each cycle lasts whilst the maximum stock level of M is used up; that is, for M/D time units. During this time the average stock level is $M/2$, so the holding cost *per cycle* is

$$h \times M/2 \times M/D = \frac{hM^2}{2D}$$

In a similar way, the maximum shortage is of $q - M$ units so the second part of each cycle lasts whilst this shortage is run-up; that is, for $(q - M)/D$ time units. During this time the average shortage is $(q - M)/2$, so the total shortage cost per cycle is

$$s \times \frac{q - M}{2} \times \frac{q - M}{D} = \frac{s(q - M)^2}{2D}$$

The total cost per cycle is therefore

$$K + \frac{hM^2}{2D} + \frac{s(q - M)^2}{2D}$$

However, to compare the costs for different values of q we must compare on a per time-unit basis because the cycle length depends on q. We therefore divide by the cycle length q/D to get the total cost per time unit,

$$\frac{KD}{q} + \frac{hM^2}{2q} + \frac{s(q - M)^2}{2q}$$

We want the values of q and M that make this expression as small as possible. This requires a technique called *partial differentiation*, which is beyond the scope of this book, but the solution is

$$M = \sqrt{\frac{2KD}{h}}\sqrt{\frac{s}{s+h}}, \quad q = \sqrt{\frac{2KD}{h}}\sqrt{\frac{s+h}{s}}$$

We will call this value of q EOQ* to distinguish it from the EOQ with no shortages allowed. Notice that EOQ* is the original EOQ adjusted by the factor

$$\sqrt{\frac{s+h}{s}}$$

which involves the shortage and holding cost, and M is EOQ multiplied by the inverse of this factor (one divided by it). As the shortage cost s gets bigger and bigger this factor gets closer and closer to 1 and so both EOQ* and M get closer to EOQ. This makes sense as it means that when shortages become prohibitively expensive the optimal order quantity reverts to the one that didn't allow shortages.

Try the following example.

Check this

For the video recorder example in Section 1, the set-up cost for a batch of tape heads was £12,000, demand for tape head units was 8000 a month and the holding cost was 30p per tape head unit a month. Now suppose that if we run out of tape head units we can continue to manufacture videos and install the tape heads later but that this will incur an inconvenience cost of £1.10 per tape head unit per month. Assume there no lead time.

What is the batch size, how often should goods be ordered, and what is the maximum stock level and maximum shortage?

Solution:
The batch size is

$$EOQ^* = 25{,}298\sqrt{\frac{1.4}{1.1}} = 28{,}540$$

Demand is 8000 per month so this will have to be ordered every 28,540/8000 = 3.6 months. The maximum stock level is

$$M = 25{,}298\sqrt{\frac{1.1}{1.4}} = 22{,}424$$

and maximum shortage is 28,540 – 22,424 = 6116.

More EOQ models

Although the EOQ models we have covered are simplifications of a real inventory system they are often found to be good approximations and their use is widespread. There are also many more variants of the EOQ model that relax more assumptions. For instance, they can allow for quantity discounts or let stock *arrive* at a constant rate. EOQ models have the advantage that the EOQ is simple to calculate and so can easily be calculated for many different product-lines.

But is demand really constant?

The key assumption of the EOQ model is that demand occurs at a constant rate. In practice this is often unrealistic and demand is often irregular or 'lumpy'. A way of assessing whether the assumption of constant demand is reasonable is to calculate something called the *variability coefficient*. This is calculated from the *sample mean* and *sample variance* of recent demand figures. We described how to calculate these quantities in *Describing Data*, Chapter DD2, but a brief explanation for those who are not familiar with them follows.

Suppose the demands in n typical time periods are x_1, x_2, x_3 and so on, so that the demand in the nth time period is x_n. The *sample mean* of these n demands is the average of these, which we call $\bar{x}$.

$$\bar{x} = \frac{x_1 + x_2 + x_3 + \ldots + x_n}{n}$$

The *sample variance* of these n demands is a measure of how varied or spread out the data are. Its formula is

$$s^2 = \frac{\Sigma x^2 - \frac{(\Sigma x)^2}{n}}{n - 1}$$

where Σx denotes the sum of all the xs, that is,

$$\Sigma x = x_1 + x_2 + \ldots + x_n$$

and Σx^2 denotes the sum of the x^2 terms,

$$\Sigma x^2 = x_1^2 + x_2^2 + x_3^2 + \ldots + x_n^2$$

The square root of the sample variance, s, is called the *sample standard deviation*.

The variability coefficient is

$$VC = \frac{s^2}{\bar{x}^2}$$

Notice that this is the square of the ratio of the sample standard deviation to the sample mean. If all the demands are similar the estimate of the sample standard deviation will be small compared to the sample mean and VC will be small. It has been suggested that the assumption of constant variance in the EOQ model is appropriate when $VC < 0.25$.

Other inventory models

Many inventory models have been developed, each making a different set of assumptions. Many drop the assumption of constant demand, using probability to allow demand in each time period to be unknown and random. Whilst the procedures we have considered monitor inventory levels through time and place an order of a fixed size when stock drops to a particular level, other models reorder at regular intervals but vary the size of the order. (When demand is constant these are equivalent.)

When no model seems suitable for a real system or a realistic model is too complicated to solve, a 'last resort' is to build a simulation model of the inventory system and experiment with this (see Chapter BM7).

Inventory control in practice

In practice, firms produce many different items and so it might seem a good idea to control inventory for each of them. However, although most stock-control systems are computerised they do cost something to run, and for low-value items the resultant savings may be too small to make stock control worthwhile. Studies have shown that, in practice, a small number of items account for the majority of the total inventory value and that it may be cost-effective to monitor inventory for these items only and to carry large stocks of low-value items. The ABC classification divides items into three categories for inventory control as follows.

A items. These are the expensive items. Typically, about 10% of items might be in this class but they would account for perhaps 70% of the value of the inventory. Inventory control for these items would be via an automatic system but stock levels would also be carefully monitored by management, and decisions made based on wider circumstances as well.

B items. These are the mid-value items. About 30% of items might be in this category accounting for about 20% of inventory value. Stock levels are monitored and controlled via an automatic system.

C items. Perhaps 60% of items but worth only 10% of the inventory. These might be left out of an automated system and large stocks kept.

The key formulae for the inventory models we have considered are listed in the box below.

Basic EOQ model

D is demand per unit time, K is ordering cost, h is holding cost per unit time.

$$EOQ = \sqrt{\frac{2KD}{h}}$$

EOQ model with backlogging

s is shortage cost per unit time, M is maximum inventory level.

$$M = \sqrt{\frac{2KD}{h}}\sqrt{\frac{s}{s+h}}, \quad EOQ^* = \sqrt{\frac{2KD}{h}}\sqrt{\frac{s+h}{s}}$$

The **variability coefficient** is

$$VC = \frac{s^2}{\bar{x}^2}$$

where

$$\bar{x} = \frac{x_1 + x_2 + x_3 + \ldots + x_n}{n} \quad \text{and} \quad s^2 = \frac{\Sigma x^2 - \frac{(\Sigma x)^2}{n}}{n-1}$$

1.   Return to the inventory problem in **Work card 1**, question **1**. Demand for a product occurs evenly at a rate of 20 units per week, the order cost is $15 and it costs $0.20 per item a week to insure the goods and $0.10 per item per week to store the goods. The EOQ was 44.72.

     (i)   Suppose orders take one week to arrive. How often would you order and how much would you order now? What would be the reorder level?

     (ii)   Now suppose that shortages are allowed and that they cost $1.50 per unit per week. How often would you order now and how much would you order? How much would the maximum shortage be?

2.   Continuing from **Work card 1**, question 2. Suppose, more realistically, that Matthews is the only stockist in the area and that their customers are willing to wait for a motor home if there isn't one in stock. In return, Matthews offer a discount of £50 for each week that a customer has to wait for a motor home. Initially suppose that orders arrive instantaneously.

     (i)   How many should they order in a batch?

     (ii)   What will be the maximum shortage?

     (iii)   At what stock level should they place an order?

     (iv)   If shortage costs increase to £70 per week per motor home, how many should they order in a batch? Does this make sense?

   Now suppose that the shortage cost is £50 as in **(i)**, **(ii)** and **(iii)** and that orders take two weeks to arrive. At what stock level should they place an order?

Solutions:

1.   **(i)**   The batch size and frequency of ordering will remain the same as **Work card 1**, question 1, but the orders must be placed when stock levels are $1 \times 20 = 20$.

     (ii) $s = 1.5$ and h is still 0.3. The optimal order quantity will be as before but multiplied by

$$\sqrt{\frac{s+h}{s}}, \text{ i.e. } 44.72\sqrt{\frac{1.5+0.3}{1.5}} = 48.99$$

     As demand is 20 they will need to order every $48.99/20 = 2.4$ weeks, and as the maximum order level is

$$M = 44.72\sqrt{\frac{1.5}{1.5+0.3}} = 40.82$$

     The maximum shortage will be $48.99 - 40.82 = 8.17$.

2.   **(i)**   Now we have a shortage cost of £50 per unit per week so

$$EOQ^* = 14.91\sqrt{\frac{s+h}{s}} = 14.91\sqrt{\frac{50+45}{50}} = 20.55$$

     (ii)   The maximum stock level will be

$$M = 14.91\sqrt{\frac{50}{50 + 45}} = 10.82$$

so the maximum shortage is 20.55 – 10.82 = 9.73 or around 10 motor homes.

(iii) As orders arrive instantaneously they should place an order when the maximum shortage is reached.

(iv) If shortage costs increase to £70 per motor home per week the order quantity reduces to

$$14.91\sqrt{\frac{70 + 45}{70}} = 19.11$$

This makes sense because higher shortage costs discourage shortages and so stock must be ordered more often and so in smaller batches.

As orders take 2 weeks to arrive, during which time there is demand for 10 motor homes, an order should be placed when stock levels are 10 higher than the maximum shortage; i.e. 9.74 – 10 = –0.26, so about zero motor homes remain in stock.

1 (i) In the Loyal cabs example, **Assessment 1**, question **1**, petrol is used at a rate of 8000 litres a month, costs 65 pence a litre and the delivery cost (regardless of quantity) is £250. Storage costs are 1 pence per litre per month. Now suppose that the supplier is not local and deliveries of petrol take 10 days or 1/3 of a month to arrive. At what level should Loyal place an order?

(ii) Suppose further that when petrol runs out, cab drivers go to their local service station and pay retail rates of 80p per litre. Is the EOQ model with backlogging appropriate in this case? If so, calculate the order quantity, but if not, explain why not.

2. (i) Continue **Assessment 1**, question **2**. If shortages are allowed, calculate the batch size for a shortage cost of $2, $3 and $4 per unit per week and comment.

(ii) If shortage costs are $2 per week, at what stock level would you place an order if delivery time is 2 weeks?

3. The following data are the weekly demands for the product in question **2** for a typical 12-week period.

497   501   520   540   490   490   520   530   540   520   515   520

Do these data support the assumptions of constant demand made by the EOQ model? Substantiate your answer.

Further reading: see p. xv

Anderson *et al.* consider these and other inventory control models including probabilistic models; that is, where the demand fluctuates and is modelled using probability.

Hillier and Lieberman consider much more advanced models, including those with fluctuating demand, as does Hillier and Hillier.

Winston includes probabilistic models.

BM4
Time and money

Money, it turned out, was exactly like sex, you thought of nothing else if you didn't have it and thought of other things if you did.

James Baldwin, US writer, *Nobody knows my name*

Contexts

What is this chapter about?
This chapter explains the basics of compound interest both for a single sum and for series of payments. It also considers how to assess the financial viability of a project from its costs and predicted income.

Why is it useful?
Even as a student you are probably besieged with financial literature – from advertisers trying to get you to borrow money, to your student loan information. When you begin work this bombardment will continue and expand as you consider buying cars and houses and saving for the future. As an individual therefore, an understanding of interest rates, returns and how payments and repayments are calculated is invaluable.

In businesses and organisations the choices can be even more complex. As well as coping with loans and finance they must decide how and when to make capital investments. A new piece of equipment will be expensive now but will generate additional income over the next ten years, so is it worth the investment? Alternatively, the new equipment could be leased – but would this be financially worthwhile? This chapter includes tools for assessing the financial viability of a project or business investment.

Where does it fit in?
This chapter is part of Financial Mathematics.

What do I need to know?
You will need to be fluent in the mathematics in Essential Maths. Some understanding of the material in MM1, Some special equations, will also be useful, although it is not essential.

Objectives

After your work on this chapter you should be able to:

● understand and calculate simple and compound interest;
● calculate the effective rate of interest;
● use discounting to calculate the present day value of future amounts;
● calculate the net present value (NPV) of a project;
● understand the concept of the internal rate of return (IRR) of a project;
● calculate the NPV and IRR using a computer;
● use geometric series to make calculations about series of equal payments;
● calculate the NPV and estimate the IRR of a series of payments;
● use a computer to make the above calculations for a series of payments.

Which would you rather have, £1000 now or £1000 in a year's time? Your answer to this question must surely be £1000 now. It is universally recognised that a sum of money now is more valuable than the same sum later, even if only because it can be invested now and earn some interest.

If you walk into a shop or bank you will see advertisements for a multitude of loan and investment possibilities. Similar choices face businesses and governments. In this chapter we explain how the amount of interest is calculated, how to calculate the present day worth of a future sum and how to assess whether or not an investment is worthwhile.

1 Calculating interest

Terminology
The amount of money invested or borrowed is called the *principal* and so it is usually denoted by the letter P. We will suppose that it is invested for n time periods. The amount of money that will be paid on the investment per time period is usually agreed to be a percentage, called the *interest rate*, of P. It is usual to express this as a decimal fraction, and call it r. For instance, an interest rate of 5% is written $r = 0.05$.

Simple interest
Suppose you place £200 in a bank's savings account at an interest rate of 10% and that at the end of every year the bank posts you a cheque for the interest. That is, the interest is *not* added to the account. *This is called simple interest.* The amount of interest you receive each year will be £200 × 0.1. So, for instance, after 8 years you will have received £200 × 0.1 × 8 = £160.

The amount of simple interest paid on an investment of P at an interest rate of r (expressed as a decimal) for n years is therefore

$$I = Prn$$

I invest £1000 for 5 years at a rate of 6% per year. If interest is paid to me directly at the end of each year, how much will I receive during a 5-year period?

Solution:

$I = 1000 \times 0.06 \times 5 = £300$

Compound interest

In practice, money paid in interest is usually reinvested so that it too can earn interest in the next time period. For instance, if you place £200 in a savings account at 10% per year interest, £20 interest will be paid at the end of the first year. If this is added onto the account, the balance will stand at £220 at the start of the second year. During the second year interest will then be earned on all of the £220 and so £220 × 0.1 = £22 will be paid. Interest calculated in this way is called *compound interest*.

Calculation of compound interest

Suppose you invest a principal of P at an interest rate of r (given as a decimal) per year. Consider what happens when interest is compounded.

At the end of year 1, the interest earned will be Pr, which will be added onto the original principal of P to give $P + Pr = P(1 + r)$. At the start of year 2 we start with $P(1 + r)$.

By the end of year two this too will become multiplied by $1 + r$ to give $P(1 + r)(1 + r) = P(1 + r)^2$.

In the same way, at the end of year 3 we will have $P(1 + r)^3$ and so on.

The general formula for the value at the end of the nth year of a principal of P, invested at an interest rate of r, is

$$S = P(1 + r)^n$$

For example, a sum of $1500 invested at an interest rate of 5% over 6 years would increase to

$$S = 1500(1.05)^6 = \$2010.14$$

£1000 is invested at an interest rate of 10%. What is the value of the investment at the end of year 7?

Solution:

$S = 1000(1.1)^7 = £1948.72$

Non-annual compounding: the effective rate of interest

Interest rates are usually quoted as a rate per year, called the *nominal* rate, but in practice interest may be paid monthly, quarterly or half-yearly rather than at the end of the year. (Another way of saying this is that interest is compounded monthly or quarterly, etc.) In this case, as the interest will be paid sooner, it can be reinvested earlier, making the actual or *effective* rate of interest larger.

For example, consider again an investment of £200 at a nominal annual rate of 10%, but suppose now that interest is compounded every half-year.

A nominal annual rate of 10% payable half-yearly means 5% every half year so at the end of the first half-year we will have

$$200(1.05)$$

and after the second half-year, i.e. the end of the first year, we will have

$$200(1.05)^2$$

If the effective rate of interest is i the value of £200 at the end of year 1 is

$$200(1 + i)$$

So to find the equivalent effective rate of interest we need to solve

$$200(1 + i) = 200(1 + 0.05)^2$$

for i. Dividing by 200 gives

$$1 + i = (1 + 0.05)^2$$

so $i = 0.1025$. Notice that this is slightly better than the quoted rate of 10%. This is because interest paid at the end of the first half-year can be reinvested at that time instead of at the year-end, so a little more money is made.

UK readers will notice that all advertisements for savings and loans quote something called the 'annual percentage rate'. This is the effective rate of interest and in the UK it is a legal requirement to display it in advertising.

Now we will find a general formula for the effective rate of interest.

Suppose an investment of P has a nominal rate of interest of r, which is payable x times a year. For instance, if interest is paid monthly, $x = 12$, if it is paid quarterly $x = 4$ and so on. Suppose as before that the effective rate of interest is i.

For a period of $\frac{1}{x}$th of a year, the interest rate is $\frac{r}{x}$, so at the end of the first period the principal, P, will become

$$P\left(1 + \frac{r}{x}\right)$$

At the end of the second period it will become

$$P\left(1 + \frac{r}{x}\right)^2$$

and at the end of the third period

$$P\left(1 + \frac{r}{x}\right)^3$$

and so on until at the end of year 1, x periods will have passed and the principal will become

$$P\left(1+\frac{r}{x}\right)^x$$

As the effective rate of interest is i, this must be equivalent to $P(1 + i)$, so to find the effective rate we must solve

$$P(1 + i) = P\left(1+\frac{r}{x}\right)^x$$

for i. To solve this we divide by P and subtract 1 so that the effective rate of interest when the nominal rate is r, payable x times a year, is

$$i = \left(1+\frac{r}{x}\right)^x - 1$$

Check this

Interest on a savings account is payable every half-year at a (nominal) rate of 6% per annum. What is the effective rate of interest?

Solution:
$r = 0.06$ and $x = 2$ because interest is payable twice yearly, so

$$i = \left(1+\frac{0.06}{2}\right)^2 - 1 = 0.0609$$

The effective rate of interest is 6.09%.

Check this

Now suppose that interest at a nominal rate of 6% is payable **(i)** quarterly and **(ii)** monthly. In each case calculate the equivalent effective interest rate.

Solution:

(i) $i = \left(1+\frac{0.06}{4}\right)^4 - 1 = 0.061364$

(ii) $i = \left(1+\frac{0.06}{12}\right)^{12} - 1 = 0.0616778$

We have just calculated the following effective rates for a nominal rate of interest of 6% payable:

yearly   0.06
half-yearly   0.0609
quarterly   0.061364
monthly   0.0616778

Notice that the effective rate increases as the interest is paid more frequently. This is because the interest can be reinvested sooner.

In theory we could increase the number of periods a year more and more and calculate the corresponding effective rates. We would find that the effective rate of interest gradually increases as the number of periods increases and becomes closer and closer to $e^r - 1$. If you haven't met e before it is a 'special' number with an infinite number of decimal places which starts as 2.71828.... Your calculator will have a button labelled e^x, which is used for calculations involving e. For example, when the nominal rate is 6% the effective rate of interest gradually increases towards $e^{0.06} - 1 = 0.061837$ (to 6 d.p.) as the number of periods increases.

Check this

The nominal rate of interest offered by a bank is 7%. Calculate the effective rate when it is compounded **(i)** quarterly **(ii)** monthly. What is the most that the effective rate can be, however frequently interest is compounded?

Solution:

(i) $i = 1.0175^4 - 1 = 0.071859$

(ii) $i = 1.00583333^{12} - 1 = 0.072290$

As the frequency increases the effective interest rate will approach $e^{0.07} - 1 = 0.072508$.

Non-annual compounding: the value of the investment

Recall that when interest is compounded annually the value of an investment of P at the end of n years is

$$S = P(1 + r)^n$$

We can also use this formula for interest that is compounded more frequently provided that we work entirely in payment periods, and not in years.

For instance, to find the value at the end of 6 years of £200 invested at a nominal rate of 12% payable half-yearly we must work entirely in half-year periods. There are a total of $6 \times 2 = 12$ half-yearly periods and each half-year pays $\frac{12}{2} = 6\%$ interest, so at the end of 6 years the value 2 of the investment will be

$$S = 200(1.06)^{12} = £402.44$$

Check this

A sum of $100 is invested at a nominal rate of 10% over 7 years. Calculate the sum that will accrue if interest is compounded twice a year.

Solution:
There are $7 \times 2 = 14$ payment periods and at each the interest is $\frac{10}{2} = 5\%$, so the sum accrued will be $S = 100(1.05)^{14} = \$197.99$.

Check this

Now suppose, as above, that a sum of $100 is invested at a nominal rate of 10% but that now interest is payable monthly. What is its value at the end of 7 years?

Solution:
There are $7 \times 12 = 84$ monthly periods and the interest rate for each is $\frac{10}{12} = 0.8333\%$. The sum that will accrue is therefore

$S = 100(1.008333)^{84} = \$200.79$

Finding P, r or n
The compound interest formula

$$S = P(1 + r)^n$$

contains four variables, S, P, r and n so if we know any three of them we can solve for the remaining one.

Check this

How much must I invest at a rate of 6% payable annually to obtain £5000 after 4 years?

Solution:
We have been told that $r = 0.06$, $S = 5000$ and $n = 4$ and we need to find P. As $S = P(1 + r)^n$ we need to solve

$5000 = P(1.06)^4$

for P. Rearranging gives

$P = \dfrac{5000}{1.06^4}$

so $P = £3960.47$.
   £3960.47 must be invested at 6% payable annually for four years to give £5000.

If you need to solve for the number of time periods of the investment, n, you will end up with an equation of the form $a = b^n$ to solve for n where a and b are numbers. If you know about logs you will be able to solve this (we cover them in *More Maths*, Chapter MM1) but if you don't you need to know that the solution to $a = b^n$ is

$$n = \frac{\log a}{\log b}$$

To calculate log the log of a number just enter the number in your calculator and press the **log** button; for instance, log 1.5 is 0.176091. Equivalently, the solution is

$$n = \frac{\ln a}{\ln b}$$

where **ln** indicates a different kind of log which you obtain by pressing the **ln** button on your calculator.

Check this

I have \$3600 and wish to invest it until it becomes at least \$6000. How many years will this take assuming that interest rates remain at 8% compounded annually?

Solution:
We know $P = 3600$, $S = 6000$ and $r = 0.08$ and we need to find n. Using the formula we need to solve

$6000 = 3600(1.08)^n$

for n.
Dividing both sides by 3600 gives

$\dfrac{6000}{3600} = 1.08^n$

so the solution is

$$n = \frac{\log 1.666667}{\log 1.08} = \frac{0.221849}{0.033424} = 6.64 \text{ years}$$

As interest is paid at the end of each year, at the end of year 6 the amount accrued will be less than \$6000. We must therefore wait for 7 years to have over \$6000.

Calculating interest

Simple interest

$I = Prn$

Compound interest

$S = P(1 + r)^n$

When the nominal rate of interest is r payable x times a year the **effective rate** is

$$i = \left(1 + \frac{r}{x}\right)^x - 1$$

As x increases the effective rate increases towards $e^r - 1$.

1. Calculate the value of the following investments:
   a. A sum of $400, invested at a rate of 5% at the end of 20 years.
   b. A sum of $3000 invested at a rate of 2% at the end of 5 years.
   c. An investment of $1000 invested at a rate of 9% at the end of 6 years.

2. You have a choice of two savings schemes. Scheme A offers 5% interest payable half-yearly and Scheme B offers 4.5% interest payable every 3 months. Which scheme do you prefer and why?

3. Three retail outlets stock the CD player you want but you need to borrow the money. Dock's offer you a credit scheme whereby interest is compounded monthly at a nominal rate of 14%, Chilly's offer you interest compounded quarterly at a nominal rate of 14.5% and Haley's offer you an effective rate of 14.75%. Which loan do you prefer and why? All have the same term (duration).

4. Determine the value after two years of £20,000 invested at a nominal rate of 8% per year when interest is compounded
   (i)   annually
   (ii) quarterly
   (iii) monthly

   Calculate the effective rate of interest in each case. Can you give an upper limit for this and if so what is it?

5. How much should be deposited now if we require £50,000 at the end of 15 years and the interest rate is 5% and payable
   (i)   annually?
   (ii) twice-yearly?

6. For how many years must I invest £20,000 if I want it to have a value of at least £50,000 and the interest rate is 6%, payable annually? How does your answer change if the interest is payable every six months?

Solutions:

1. a. $400 \times 1.05^{20} = \$1061.32$
   b. $3000 \times 1.02^5 = \$3312.24$
   c. $1000 \times 1.09^6 = \$1677.10$

WORK CARD 1

2. Scheme A has an effective rate of $1.025^2 - 1 = 0.050625$ (i.e. 5.0625%) whereas scheme B has an effective rate of $1.01125^4 - 1 = 0.04577$ (i.e. 4.577%). Scheme A is preferable as it has a higher effective rate.

3. Dock's give an effective rate of $1.0116667^{12} - 1 = 0.149342$ (i.e. 14.93%), Chilly's give a rate of $1.03625^4 - 1 = 0.153077$ (i.e. 15.3%), and the effective rate of Haley's is given as 14.75%. As you are paying the interest you want the effective rate to be small, so choose Haley's.

4. **(i)** $(£20,000)1.08^2 = £23,328$

    (ii)   There are 8 quarterly periods each paying 2% interest so $(£20,000)1.02^8 = £23,433.19$.

    (iii) $(£20,000)1.0066666^{24} = £23,457.76$

    The effective rates of interest are: **(i)** 8%; **(ii)** $i = 1.02^4 - 1 = 0.082432$; **(iii)** $1.0066666^{12} - 1 = 0.083000$.
    As the compounding frequency increases the effective rate will approach $e^{0.08} - 1 = 0.083287$.

5. **(i)**   We need to solve $50,000 = P1.05^{15}$ for P. This gives $P = £24,050.85$.

    (ii)   Now solve $50,000 = P1.025^{30}$, so $P = £23,837.13$.

6. We need to solve $20,000 \cdot 1.06^n = 50,000$ for n. Dividing by 20,000 and taking logs of both sides gives $n \log 1.06 = \log 2.5$, so

    $$n = \frac{\log 2.5}{\log 1.06} = 15.73 \text{ years}$$

    The number of years must be a whole number so we will not have over £50,000 until the end of year 16. When the interest is compounded every 6 months, the rate for each 6-month period is 3% and now n will be the number of 6-month periods of the investment, so we need to solve $20,000 \cdot 1.03^n = 50,000$ for n. This gives

    $$n = \frac{\log 2.5}{\log 1.03} = 30.9989$$

    6-month periods. So we must invest for 31 6-month periods (that is, 15 and a half years) to obtain £50,000.

1. Which would you prefer? (Do not calculate the values but explain your answer.)

    a. $1000 that has been invested for 2 years at 5% interest payable annually *or* $1000 that has been invested for 2 years at 5% interest payable every 6 months.

    b. $500 that has been invested for 3 years at 6% interest payable annually *or* $500 that has been invested for 3 years, where every 6 months 3% interest is added to the account.

2. a. Calculate the value at the end of the tenth year of £100 invested at an annual rate of interest of 12%.

b. Calculate the value at the end of the third year of $300 invested at an annual rate of 5%.

c. Calculate the value at the end of the fifth year of $500 invested at an annual rate of 12% compounded monthly. What is the effective annual rate in this case?

d. Calculate the value at the end of the fourth year of $500 invested at a nominal rate of 12% compounded quarterly. Calculate the effective annual rate.

e. What is the equivalent effective annual rate of an interest rate of 15% payable four times a year?

3. How much should I put in my savings account now if I want £5000 to buy a car in 2 years' time? Assume that the interest rate is 9% compounded monthly.

4. I currently have $3000, but require $5000 in 3 years' time. What rate of interest, payable annually, must I receive on the $3000 to make this possible? What is the equivalent rate payable monthly?

2 **Present values**

Present values

We have already seen that given the compound interest formula

$$S = P(1 + r)^n$$

we can calculate any one of the variables S, P, r and n, if we know the other three. In particular, this gives us a way of working out what value, P, must be invested in order to obtain a particular future sum, S. Rearranging the formula above gives

$$P = \frac{S}{(1+r)^n}$$

This process of working backwards from S to obtain P is called *discounting*, and in this context P is called the *present value* and r may be called the *discount rate* (instead of the interest rate).

Check this

Find the present value of £10,000 in 5 years' time if the discount rate is 12% payable annually.

Solution:
$S = 10,000$, $n = 5$ and $r = 0.12$ so

$$P = \frac{10,000}{1.12^5} = £5674.27$$

Present values give us the present-day worth of future amounts and so are a useful way of comparing different future sums of money.

Notice that the compound interest formula $S = P(1 + r)^n$ *multiplies* the principal by $(1 + r)^n$ to obtain the future sum S, whereas

$$P = \frac{S}{(1 + r)^n}$$

divides the future sum by the same expression, $(1 + r)^n$, to obtain the present value, P.

In Section 1 we saw that we can use the formula

$$S = P(1 + r)^n$$

when interest is compounded more frequently than once a year, provided that both n and r apply to the same compounding period. For instance, if £1000 is invested at 8% received half-yearly, the value after 3 years will be

$$S = 1000(1.04)^6 = £1265.32$$

because there are 6 half-yearly periods and the interest rate for a half-year is 4%.

In the same way the present value formula

$$P = \frac{S}{(1 + r)^n}$$

can also be used when interest is paid more frequently than once a year. For example, the present value of £3000 in 3 years' time at a discount rate of 8% payable half-yearly is

$$P = \frac{3000}{(1.04)^6} = £2370.94$$

Check this

Find the present value of £10,000 in 5 years' time if the discount rate is 12% compounded twice a year.

Solution:
There are $5 \times 2 = 10$ half-yearly time periods each paying 6% so the present value is

$$\frac{10{,}000}{1.06^{10}} = £5583.95$$

Check this

Find the present value of £10,000 in 5 years' time if the discount rate is 12% payable quarterly.

Solution:
There are $5 \times 4 = 20$ time periods and the discount rate is 3% for each so the present value is

$$\frac{10{,}000}{1.03^{20}} = £5536.76$$

Check this

Find the present value of £10,000 in 5 years' time if the discount rate is 12% payable monthly.

Solution:
There are 5×12 time periods, each paying an interest rate of 1% so the present value is

$$\frac{10,000}{1.01^{60}} = £5504.50$$

So the present values of £10,000 invested in 5 years' time at a discount rate of 12% paid at the following frequencies are

	Present value £
twice-yearly	5583.95
quarterly	5536.76
monthly	5504.50

Notice that the present value is smaller when interest is compounded more often. This is because the interest is received sooner so the sum has more chance to grow during the time of the investment and can be smaller to start off with.

Net present values

For most business projects, it is usual to have to outlay (invest) a sum at the start, and then expect to receive income from the project (revenue) at various times in the future. For example, suppose a company has the opportunity to buy a new machine now for £10,000. It intends to use the machine to manufacture a large order for which it will receive £7000 after 2 years and £5000 after 3 years.

A project like this can be assessed by assuming a discount rate and then calculating the present values of all the flows of money in and out. The total of the present values of money in (revenue), *less* the total of the present values of the money out (costs) is called the *net present value* (NPV). If the NPV is greater than 0 the project is regarded as profitable.

The table below calculates the net present value of the machine project assuming a discount rate of 5%.

End of year	(£)	Present value		(£)
0	−10,000			−10,000
2	+7000	$\dfrac{7000}{1.05^2}$	=	6349.21
3	+5000	$\dfrac{5000}{1.05^3}$	=	4319.19
		Net present value		£668.40

As the net present value (NPV) is positive we conclude that purchase of the new machine is worthwhile.

Check this

A property investment company has the opportunity to buy an office building now for £300,000. It will cost £100,000 to refurbish it, which will be payable at the end of year 1. The company expects to be able to lease it out for £500,000 in 3 years' time. What is the net present value of the project, assuming a discount rate of 6%?

Solution:
Constructing a table gives

End of year	(£)	Present value		(£)
0	−300,000			−300,000
1	−100,000	$\dfrac{-100,000}{1.06}$	=	−94,339.62
3	+500,000	$\dfrac{500,000}{1.06^3}$	=	419,809.64
		Net present value		£25,470.02

The project is profitable as the NPV is positive.

The internal rate of return

Consider again the company considering the purchase of a new machine. We calculated that when the discount rate is 5% the NPV is £668.40. If the discount rate were larger, the present value of future revenue would reduce, which, for this project, would reduce the NPV. For instance, the NPV assuming a discount rate of 7% is £195.56, as calculated below.

End of year	(£)	Present value		(£)
0	−10,000			−10,000
2	+7000	$\dfrac{7000}{1.07^2}$	=	6114.07
3	+5000	$\dfrac{5000}{1.07^3}$	=	4081.49
		Net present value		£195.56

Further calculations show that when the discount rate is 8% the NPV is −£29.47, when it is 9% the NPV is −£247.32 and when it is 10% the NPV is −£458.31. So the project breaks even; that is, the NPV is 0, at a discount rate of somewhere between 7% and 8%.

The discount rate at which a project has a net present value of zero is called the *internal rate of return* (IRR). We have seen that the project above has an IRR of between 7% and 8%. Suppose it is 7.8%. This tells us that the project is equivalent, to the investor, to an interest rate of 7.8% per year. So if the investor can invest her money elsewhere and obtain a higher rate than 7.8%, or needs to pay more than 7.8% to borrow money to finance the project, then the project is not worthwhile and should not be undertaken.

Sometimes (rarely) you will be able to calculate the IRR exactly as in the next example.

Check this

A financial group can make an investment of £340,000 now and receive £400,000 in two years' time. What is the internal rate of return?

Solution:
The NPV of this project is

$$NPV = -340{,}000 + \frac{400{,}000}{(1+i)^2}$$

where i is the discount rate. The IRR is the value of i that makes the NPV zero so it is the solution of

$$-340{,}000 + \frac{400{,}000}{(1+i)^2} = 0$$

We can solve this by adding 340,000 to both sides and then multiplying throughout by $(1 + i)^2$, to give

$$400{,}000 = 340{,}000(1 + i)^2$$

so

$$(1+i)^2 = \frac{400}{340}$$

and taking square roots gives $1 + i = 1.084652$.
   So the IRR is $i = 0.084652$.

In general, equating the NPV to 0 like this gives a nasty equation containing high powers of r, which will be difficult to solve without using equation-solving software.

Calculating NPV and IRR using a computer

Excel has functions to calculate both the net present value and the internal rate of return of a project. Whilst a computer will take some of the tedium out of the calculations it is very easy to enter arguments incorrectly and so you will still need a good understanding of the quantities being calculated to spot unlikely results. Be careful that you enter negative values for flows of money out and positive values for flows of money in, otherwise you will get some very strange results!

The **NPV** financial function calculates the net present value of a series of regular but unequal payments and receipts. Notice, however, that it considers only those at the *end* of time periods 1, 2, 3 etc. only, so any initial outlay will have to be subtracted from Excel's NPV to obtain the NPV of the whole project.

The **IRR** financial function gives the internal rate of return of a series of regular but unequal flows of money in a range of the worksheet. Beware, you must enter 0 explicitly in any time periods where no money flows in or out.

Check this

Use software to calculate the exact IRR for the company buying a new machine above, (initial outflow is £10,000 and there are inflows of £7000 and £5000 after 2 and 3 years respectively).

Solution:
Enter –10,000, 0, 7000, 5000 in a range of cells. The IRR function gives 0.07867.

Present values

The **present value** of a sum, S, in n periods' time when the discount rate is r per period is

$$P = \frac{S}{(1+r)^n}$$

The **net present value** of a project is the

Total present value of revenues – Total present value of costs

The discount rate at which

Net present value $= 0$

is the **internal rate of return**.

All the following can be worked with a calculator but you could check your results using a computer.

1. Determine the present value of $3000 in 3 years' time if the discount rate is 6%
   (i) compounded annually
   (ii) compounded six-monthly
   (iii) compounded quarterly

2. The present value of £11,000 in 10 years' time is £5000. What is the discount rate if interest is compounded (i) annually and (ii) monthly?

3. Project A requires an initial outlay of £100,000, but will return £40,000 at the end of each of years 2, 3 and 4 whereas project B requires an initial outlay of £140,000 but will return £40,000 at the end of years 1, 2, 3 and 4.
   (i) Calculate the NPV of each project if the discount rate is 6% compounded annually. On the basis of this which project would you invest in?
   (ii) Estimate the IRR for each of these projects. On the basis of the IRR which project would you prefer?

WORK CARD 2

4. A project has the following NPV at the following discount rates.

Discount rate (%)	NPV ($)
4	7600
5	5400
6	2400
7	−450
8	−2300

Estimate the IRR on the project. Suppose the money could be invested elsewhere at a rate of 8%; should the project be undertaken?

Solutions:

1. (i) $\dfrac{3000}{1.06^3} = £2518.86$

   (ii) $\dfrac{3000}{1.03^6} = £2512.45$

   (iii) $\dfrac{3000}{1.015^{12}} = £2509.16$

2. (i) Solve

   $$5000 = \dfrac{11{,}000}{(1+r)^{10}}$$

   for r. So

   $$(1+r)^{10} = \dfrac{11{,}000}{5000}$$

   Taking tenth roots gives $1 + r = 2.2^{1/10}$, so $1 + r = 1.08204$ and the discount rate is $r = 0.08204$.

   (ii) When interest is compounded monthly, we must solve

   $$5000 = \dfrac{11{,}000}{(1+r)^{120}}$$

   where r is now the rate for a 1-month period. Solving gives $r = 0.006592$, so the annual nominal rate would be 0.07910.

3. (i)

Year end	Project A (£)	Present value (£)	Project B (£)	Present value (£)
0	−100,000	−100,000	−140,000	−140,000
1			40,000	$\dfrac{40{,}000}{1.06} = 37{,}735.85$

WORK CARD 2 (CONTINUED)

Year end	Project A (£)	Present value (£)	Project B (£)	Present value (£)
2	40,000	$\dfrac{40,000}{1.06^2} = 35,599.86$	40,000	$\dfrac{40,000}{1.06^2} = 35,599.86$
3	40,000	$\dfrac{40,000}{1.06^3} = 33,584.77$	40,000	$\dfrac{40,000}{1.06^3} = 33,584.77$
4	40,000	$\dfrac{40,000}{1.06^4} = 31,683.75$	40,000	$\dfrac{40,000}{1.06^4} = 31,683.75$
		NPV 868.38		NPV −1395.77

The NPV of project B is negative whereas A's is positive so we would rather invest in project A.

(ii) As the NPV of project A at a discount rate of 6% is *just* positive, a slightly higher discount rate might make it *just* negative so we will try 6.5%. The NPV of A at 6.5% is –£526.74. The IRR therefore lies between 6% and 6.5%. In similar way, a discount rate slightly smaller than 6% may give a positive NPV for project B. The NPV at 5.5% is £206.00 so the IRR is between 5.5% and 6%. On the basis of the IRR project A looks better. As the IRR is a percentage, it doesn't take into account how much is being invested, so a project with a higher IRR than another may not have a higher NPV than the other.

4. The net present value is positive at 6% and negative at 7% so the IRR is between 6% and 7%. If the money can be invested elsewhere at 8% the project should not be undertaken.

ASSESSMENT 2

1. Calculate the present value of $5500 in 5 years' time when the discount rate is 9% and (i) payable annually, (ii) payable quarterly and (iii) payable monthly.

2. A man buys a new freezer and has the choice of making a single payment of £500 in 6 months' time or a single payment of £525 in 9 months' time. Assuming a discount rate of 12% nominal compounded monthly which should he choose?

3. You win a competition and have the choice of receiving $5000 now or $6250 in 18 months' time. Which would you prefer if the discount rate is 12% compounded quarterly?

4. Calculate the NPV of a project that requires an outlay of £20,000 now but should return £8000 at the end of year 2 and £14,000 at the end of year 4. Assume a discount rate of 3% compounded annually.

Estimate the IRR of this project.

5. Consider the following alternative investment projects:

Project	Initial (£) outlay	NPV (£)	IRR (%)
A	50,000	500	5.5
B	48,000	230	5.4
C	20,000	118	8.6

Why is the net present value of C lower than those of A and B and yet the IRR of C is higher than that of A and B?

If you had £50,000 to invest, but a savings account that pays 2% interest is also available which investment would you make and why?

3 Series of payments

Often, a series of equal payments is made at regular intervals. For instance, an individual who borrows a sum from his bank to buy a car usually repays in 24 or 36 monthly equal instalments. In this section we consider the sum accrued from a series of payments like this and also the present value of a series of such payments that are to be made.

Sums accrued

To start with we will keep things simple and consider annual payments only.

To save for retirement Matthew the actuary decides to place £1000 a year in an investment account at an interest rate of 5% (payable annually). He will make his first payment at the end of this year. What will be the value of his investment after 10 years?

We reason as follows.

The first payment will be made at the end of year 1, and so at the end of 10 years it will have been invested for 9 years and will have a value of

$$1000(1.05)^9$$

The next payment is made at the end of year 2, and so at the end of year 10 it will have been invested for 8 years will have a value of

$$1000(1.05)^8$$

It is easiest to work in a table.

End of year	Amount (£)	Value at the end of year 10
1	1000	1000 1.05^9
2	1000	1000 1.05^8
3	1000	1000 1.05^7
4	1000	1000 1.05^6
5	1000	1000 1.05^5
6	1000	1000 1.05^4
7	1000	1000 1.05^3
8	1000	1000 1.05^2
9	1000	1000 1.05
10	1000	1000

Notice the pattern.

At the end of year 10 the total value of all the payments will be the total of the third column. Reversing the order, this is

$$1000 + 1000\ 1.05 + 1000\ 1.05^2 + 1000\ 1.05^3$$
$$+ 1000\ 1.05^4 + 1000\ 1.05^5 + 1000\ 1.05^6 + 1000\ 1.05^7$$
$$+ 1000\ 1.05^8 + 1000\ 1.05^9$$

Notice that each term is 1.05 times the previous one. Such sums, where each term is a fixed multiple of the previous one are called *geometric series*. It would be possible to calculate this using a calculator as there are only 10 terms but longer series of payments would give a longer geometric series (consider 25 years of monthly payments, for instance – 300 terms) and calculating the sum would be extremely tedious. Fortunately, there is a mathematical formula for such sums that we will now introduce.

Geometric series

A sum of the form

$$a + aR + aR^2 + aR^3 + ... + aR^{n-1}$$

is called a *geometric series*. Notice that the first term is a, that there are n terms in all, and that each term is the previous one multiplied by R. R is often called the *geometric ratio*.

Check this

Which of the following are geometric series?

(i) $2 + 4 + 8 + 16 + 32$

(ii) $1 + 3 + 5 + 7 + 9 + 11$

(iii) $3 + 3x + 3x^2 + 3x^3$

(iv) $2b + 6b + 18b + 54b$

Solutions:

(i) is a geometric series with ratio 2, (ii) is not a geometric series as each term is the previous one plus 2, (iii) is a geometric series with ratio x and (iv) is a geometric series with ratio 3.

A quick way of calculating the value of the geometric series

$$a + aR + aR^2 + aR^3 + \ldots + aR^{n-1}$$

is given by the formula

$$a \cdot \frac{R^n - 1}{R - 1}$$

We will try a short series first, so that you can see that the formula works.

Check this

Use the formula for a geometric series to calculate

$3 + 6 + 12 + 24$

Solution:
The first term is 3, so $a = 3$. There are 4 terms, so $n = 4$. Each term is 2 times the previous one so $R = 2$. The sum is therefore

$$a \cdot \frac{R^n - 1}{R - 1} = 3 \cdot \frac{2^4 - 1}{2 - 1} = 3 \cdot \frac{15}{1} = 45$$

If you want to know why the formula works read on, otherwise rejoin us at the next **Check this** to try the formula on a longer series.

The sum of a geometric series is

$$S = a + aR + aR^2 + \ldots + aR^{n-1}$$

so R times this sum is

$$SR = aR + aR^2 + aR^3 + \ldots + aR^{n-1} + aR^n$$

Notice that many of the same terms appear in the expression for S and the expression for SR, so if we subtract the expression for S from the expression for SR we have

$$SR - S = aR + aR^2 + aR^3 + \ldots + aR^{n-1} + aR^n - (a + aR + aR^2 + \ldots + aR^{n-1})$$

$$= aR^n - a$$

That is,

$$SR - S = aR^n - a$$

We want an expression for S, so rearranging with S as the subject gives

$$S(R - 1) = aR^n - a$$

and then

$$S = a \cdot \frac{R^n - 1}{R - 1}$$

as given above.

Another example, in which the formula is used to sum a longer series follows.

Check this

Calculate

$$\frac{1}{2} + \frac{1}{2^2} + \frac{1}{2^3} + \dots + \frac{1}{2^{15}}$$

Here, $a = \frac{1}{2}$, $R = \frac{1}{2}$ and there are 15 terms so the sum is

$$\frac{1}{2} \frac{(\frac{1}{2})^{15} - 1}{\frac{1}{2} - 1} = 0.999969 \text{ (to 6 d.p.)}$$

Check this

Use the formula for a geometric series to calculate

$$1.2^3 + 1.2^5 + 1.2^7 + 1.2^9 + 1.2^{11} + 1.2^{13} + 1.2^{15} + 1.2^{17}$$

Here, the first term is 1.2^3 so $a = 1.2^3$ and there are 8 terms so $n = 8$. Each term is 1.2^2 times the previous one so $R = 1.2^2$. The sum is therefore

$$1.2^3 \frac{(1.2^2)^8 - 1}{1.2^2 - 1} = 1.2^3 \frac{1.2^{16} - 1}{1.2^2 - 1} = 68.681818 \text{ (to 6 d.p.)}$$

Sometimes it is useful to consider a geometric series that 'goes on forever'; that is, one that has an infinite number of terms, for instance

$$0.9 + 0.9^2 + 0.9^3 + 0.9^4 + \dots \text{ etc.}$$

When $-1 < R < 1$ each term gets smaller and smaller and it can be shown that the sum gets closer and closer to

$$\frac{a}{1 - R}$$

as the number of terms increases. We say that the series *converges* to

$$\frac{a}{1 - R}$$

However, if $R > 1$ or $R < -1$ the terms of the series get bigger and bigger and the sum gets larger and larger and we say the series does not converge. (When $R = 1$ or $R = -1$ the series does not converge either.)

Evaluate the following infinite geometric series $0.9 + 0.9^2 + 0.9^3 + \dots$ etc.

Solution:

$a = 0.9$, $R = 0.9$ so the sum is $\dfrac{a}{1-R} = \dfrac{0.9}{1-0.9} = 9$

Geometric series

A geometric series is a sum with n terms of the form

$a + aR + aR^2 + \dots + aR^{n-1}$

R is called the geometric ratio. The series can be evaluated as

$a \cdot \dfrac{R^n - 1}{R - 1}$

When there are an infinite number of terms

$a + aR + aR^2 + \dots = \dfrac{a}{1-R}$ provided $-1 < R < 1$

Back to savings schemes

We started this section with a savings plan whereby £1000 is placed in an account at the end of each year at an annual rate of 5%. We had established that the value of the investment at the end of year 10 is

$$1000 + 1000 \; 1.05 + 1000 \; 1.05^2 + 1000 \; 1.05^3 + 1000 \; 1.05^4$$
$$+ 1000 \; 1.05^5 + 1000 \; 1.05^6 + 1000 \; 1.05^7$$
$$+ 1000 \; 1.05^8 + 1000 \; 1.05^9$$

This is a geometric series with $a = 1000$, $n = 10$ and $R = 1.05$, so the sum is

$$a \cdot \frac{R^n - 1}{R - 1} = 1000 \; \frac{1.05^{10} - 1}{1.05 - 1} = £12{,}577.89$$

When the series of payments is made more frequently than annually, we can use geometric series to calculate the value provided that the interest is paid at the same frequency as the instalments.

Mark and Jane save £100 at the end of each month towards a new house. The annual (nominal) interest rate is 12% payable monthly. How much will have accrued after 2 years?

Solution:
As the annual nominal rate is 12%, 1% is payable every month. At the end of 2 years the first instalment, made at the end of month 1, will have been invested for 23 months and so will have a value of $100(1.01)^{23}$. The second instalment will have been invested for 22 months and so will have a value of $100(1.01)^{22}$ and so on, until the final instalment, made at the end of month 24, will be worth just £100. The total value of the investment at the end of year 2 will therefore be

$$100 + 100 \; 1.01 + 100 \; 1.01^2 + 100 \; 1.01^3 + \dots + 100 \; 1.01^{23}$$

which is a geometric series with $a = 100$, $R = 1.01$ and $n = 24$ and so is

$$a \cdot \frac{R^n - 1}{R - 1} = 100 \frac{1.01^{24} - 1}{1.01 - 1} = £2697.35$$

Check this

We save £500 at the end of every 6 months towards a new car, on which we earn 6% interest a year payable twice-yearly. How much will we have accumulated after 3 years?

Solution:
The value after 3 years will be

$$500 + 500 \; 1.03 + 500 \; 1.03^2 + 500 \; 1.03^3 + 500 \; 1.03^4 + 500 \; 1.03^5 = 500 \frac{1.03^6 - 1}{1.03 - 1} = £3234.20$$

Sometimes we want to know how many payments are necessary to accrue a particular sum. Try this.

Check this

If we save £500 every 6 months at a rate of 6% compounded half-yearly, how long will it take us to have at least £5000?

Solution:
This problem is presented 'backwards' in that now we have been given the value at the end of the investment period and we have to find the number of payments. Suppose the number of payments we must make is n.

n instalments will accumulate to

$$500 + 500 \; 1.03 + 500 \; 1.03^2 + 500 \; 1.03^3 + 500 \; 1.03^4 + \dots + 500 \; 1.03^{n-1}$$

There are n terms so the sum is

$$500 \frac{1.03^n - 1}{1.03 - 1}$$

which we know must be equal to 5000. n is therefore the solution to

$$500 \, \frac{1.03^n - 1}{1.03 - 1} = 5000$$

Rearranging gives

$$1.03^n = 1 + \frac{5000}{500} \, 0.03$$

and then

$$1.03^n = 1.3$$

At the end of Section 1 we said that the solution of the equation $a = b^n$ is

$$n = \frac{\log a}{\log b}$$

This tells us that

$$n = \frac{\log 1.3}{\log 1.03} = 8.876$$

and we need 9 instalments to have at least £5000.

The present value of a series of payments

Geometric series can also help us to evaluate the *present value* of a series of equal payments.

For example, suppose you win a prize in a competition. You are given the choice of receiving £5000 at the end of each year for 10 years, or a lump sum of £40,000 now. Which would you rather have? Assume a discount rate of 6%.

Consider the series of £5000s. The £5000 received at the end of year 1 has a present value of $\frac{5000}{1.06}$, the payment at the end of the second year a present value of $\frac{5000}{1.06^2}$ and so on. So the present value of the series of receipts is

$$\frac{5000}{1.06} + \frac{5000}{1.06^2} + \frac{5000}{1.06^3} + \frac{5000}{1.06^4} + \frac{5000}{1.06^5} + \frac{5000}{1.06^6} + \frac{5000}{1.06^7} + \frac{5000}{1.06^8} + \frac{5000}{1.06^9} + \frac{5000}{1.06^{10}}$$

This is a geometric series in which

$$a = \frac{5000}{1.06}, \quad R = \frac{1}{1.06}$$

and there are $n = 10$ terms. The usual formula gives

$$a \cdot \frac{R^n - 1}{R - 1} = \frac{5000}{1.06} \, \frac{(\frac{1}{1.06})^{10} - 1}{\frac{1}{1.06} - 1} = £36{,}800.44$$

On this basis, you would much prefer a sum of £40,000 now.

Loans repayable by instalments

When borrowing a sum of money, for instance to buy a house (a mortgage), it is usual to repay it by a series of regular equal instalments. The present value of the series of instalments will be the same as the amount borrowed.

Check this

Delia wishes to borrow a sum of money to buy a house. She wishes to repay exactly £300 a month for 25 years, starting at the end of the present month. How much can she borrow assuming an interest rate of 12% payable monthly?

Solution:
Altogether there will be $25 \times 12 = 300$ monthly repayments of £300. The interest rate is 1% per month. The present value of the repayments is therefore

$$\frac{300}{1.01} + \frac{300}{1.01^2} + \frac{300}{1.01^3} + \ldots + \frac{300}{1.01^{299}} + \frac{300}{1.01^{300}}$$

This is a geometric series with

$$a = \frac{300}{1.01}, \quad R = \frac{1}{1.01}$$

and $n = 300$ so the sum is

$$\frac{300}{1.01} \frac{(\frac{1}{1.01})^{300} - 1}{\frac{1}{1.01} - 1} = \text{£28,483.97}$$

Alternatively, the amount of the loan is fixed and the instalment is calculated from it.

Check this

Anne and Andy borrow £3000 over 3 years to buy a car. How much must they repay per month assuming an interest rate of 6% a year compounded monthly? The first repayment is at the end of month 1.

Solution:
Suppose the monthly instalment is X. The loan is to be repaid over 36 months at an interest rate of 0.5% a month, so the present value of the repayments is

$$\frac{X}{1.005} + \frac{X}{1.005^2} + \ldots + \frac{X}{1.005^{36}}$$

We require this to equal £3000, so X is the solution of

$$3000 = \frac{X}{1.005} + \frac{X}{1.005^2} + \ldots + \frac{X}{1.005^{36}}$$

The right-hand side is a geometric series, so

$$3000 = \frac{X}{1.005} \frac{(\frac{1}{1.005})^{36} - 1}{\frac{1}{1.005} - 1}$$

$$= 32.871016X$$

So $X = \text{£91.27}$. The monthly repayments must be £91.27.

Annuities

An annuity is the reverse of a loan. It is possible to go to a financial services company and pay a lump sum now, in exchange for a regular income (the annuity) over a particular period of time. This might be to pay for future school fees or a pension. The lump sum that must be paid for a particular annuity is, of course, the present value of that annuity.

Check this

How much should Stephen be charged now for an annual annuity of £1000, starting at the end of year 1, and continuing for 15 years in all, assuming that the discount rate is 10% payable annually?

Solution:

The present value is

$$\frac{1000}{1.1} + \frac{1000}{1.1^2} + \ldots + \frac{1000}{1.1^{15}}$$

which is a geometric series with

$$a = \frac{1000}{1.1}, \quad n = 15 \quad \text{and} \quad R = \frac{1}{1.1}$$

so it is

$$\frac{1000}{1.1} \frac{\left(\frac{1}{1.1}\right)^{15} - 1}{\frac{1}{1.1} - 1} = £7606.08$$

We can calculate the present values of annuities that are paid monthly or at some other frequency provided that the discount rate is compounded at the same frequency.

Check this

How much should Rob be charged now for a monthly annuity of £100, starting at the end of month 1 and continuing for 3 years, assuming a nominal annual interest rate of 6% payable monthly?

Solution:

The interest paid each month is 0.5% and there are 36 monthly periods. The present value is

$$\frac{100}{1.005} + \frac{100}{1.005^2} + \frac{100}{1.005^3} + \ldots + \frac{100}{1.005^{36}}$$

which is a geometric series and so is

$$\frac{100}{1.005} \frac{\left(\frac{1}{1.005}\right)^{36} - 1}{\frac{1}{1.005} - 1} = £3287.10$$

NPV and IRR for a series of payments

We can use geometric series to calculate the NPV and estimate the IRR for investment projects that include series of payments.

Recall that the NPV is just the total present value of a number of flows of money in and out (revenues and costs), whereas the IRR is the discount rate at which the net present value is 0.

Check this

A project requires an initial investment of £15,000. It will return an income of £2000 payable at the end of each year for the next 10 years.

(i) What is the NPV assuming a discount rate of 6%?

(ii) Estimate the IRR of the project.

Solution:

(i) The net present value of the costs and revenues is

$$-15,000 + \frac{2000}{1.06} + \frac{2000}{1.06^2} + \ldots + \frac{2000}{1.06^{10}}$$

The terms after the first form a 10-term geometric series with first term $\frac{2000}{1.06}$ and ratio $\frac{1}{1.06}$ so the NPV is

$$-15,000 + \frac{2000}{1.06} \frac{(\frac{1}{1.06})^{10} - 1}{\frac{1}{1.06} - 1} = -15,000 + 14{,}720.17 = -279.83$$

The NPV is negative so the project is not worthwhile.

(ii) The IRR is the discount rate at which the net present value is 0. A discount rate of 6% gave a NPV which was just negative. A slightly smaller discount rate will increase the present value of the income and maybe give a NPV which is positive. The NPV at a discount rate of 5% is

$$\text{NPV} = -15,000 + \frac{2000}{1.05} + \frac{2000}{1.05^2} + \ldots + \frac{2000}{1.05^{10}}$$

$$= -15,000 + \frac{2000}{1.05} \frac{(\frac{1}{1.05})^{10} - 1}{\frac{1}{1.05} - 1}$$

$$= -15,000 + 15{,}443.47 = £443.47$$

This is positive, so the NPV is 0 for a discount rate between 5% and 6%, so the IRR lies between 5% and 6%.

Using a computer for a series of payments

Excel has several financial functions for series of payments. They usually allow an initial payment at the start (argument **Pv**) and then a series of equal payments (**Pmt**) at regular intervals so if we only want the series of equal payments we must enter **Pv** = 0. Conversely, if we are only interested in a single payment, as in Section 1, we can set **Pv** equal to it and set **Pmt** = 0. The interest/discount rate is **Rate** and the number of time periods is **Nper**. As before, be very careful to enter flows out as negative and flows in as positive values.

- **FV** calculates the sum accrued from a series of regular payments made at the end of each time period.
- **NPER** gives the number of periods a regular payment must be made (negative) to obtain a particular sum accrued (**Fv**).
- **PMT** gives the amount of instalment necessary to repay a loan of **Pv** over a particular number of time periods at a particular rate.
- **PV** gives the present value of a series of equal payments (negative).
- **RATE** calculates the interest rate necessary for a given initial payment (negative) and a series of regular payments (also negative) to accrue to a particular future value (positive) after a given number of time periods.

Try these on a computer.

Check this

Use a computer to calculate the monthly repayment required for a loan of £2000 repayable over 4 years at an interest rate of 18% compounded monthly. The first repayment is at the end of month 1.

Solution:
Excel's **PMT** function with **Rate** = 0.015, **Nper** = 48 and **Pv** = 2000 gives a monthly repayment of £58.75.

Check this

Calculate the present value of a series of five annual end-year payments of £200 and an additional final payment of £2000 at the end of five years assuming a discount rate of 5%.

Solution:
Excel's **PV** function with **Rate** = 0.05, **Nper** = 5, **Pmt** = 200, **Fv** = 2000 gives £2432.95.

WORK CARD 3

1. Which of the following are geometric series?

   a. $0 + 2 + 4 + 6 + 8 + 10 + ... + 22$

   b. $1 + \dfrac{1}{2} + \dfrac{1}{3} + \dfrac{1}{4} + ... + \dfrac{1}{88}$

   c. $0.9 + 0.765 + 0.65025 + 0.5527125 + ...$ etc.

2. Evaluate the following:

   a. $1 + \dfrac{1}{3} + \dfrac{1}{3^2} + \dfrac{1}{3^3} + ... + \dfrac{1}{3^{12}}$

   b. $5 + 5\ 1.01 + 5\ 1.01^2 + 5\ 1.01^3 + ... + 5\ 1.01^{11}$

   c. $0.9 + 0.765 + 0.65025 + 0.5527125 + ...$

   d. Write down an expression for the following:

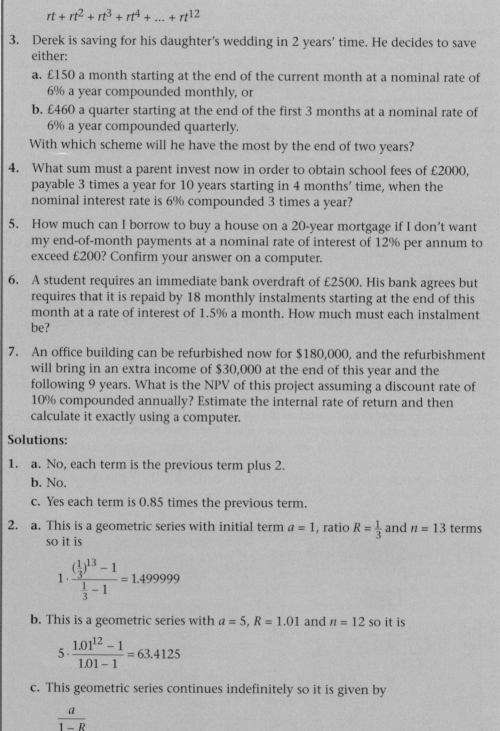

$$rt + rt^2 + rt^3 + rt^4 + \ldots + rt^{12}$$

3. Derek is saving for his daughter's wedding in 2 years' time. He decides to save either:

   a. £150 a month starting at the end of the current month at a nominal rate of 6% a year compounded monthly, or

   b. £460 a quarter starting at the end of the first 3 months at a nominal rate of 6% a year compounded quarterly.

   With which scheme will he have the most by the end of two years?

4. What sum must a parent invest now in order to obtain school fees of £2000, payable 3 times a year for 10 years starting in 4 months' time, when the nominal interest rate is 6% compounded 3 times a year?

5. How much can I borrow to buy a house on a 20-year mortgage if I don't want my end-of-month payments at a nominal rate of interest of 12% per annum to exceed £200? Confirm your answer on a computer.

6. A student requires an immediate bank overdraft of £2500. His bank agrees but requires that it is repaid by 18 monthly instalments starting at the end of this month at a rate of interest of 1.5% a month. How much must each instalment be?

7. An office building can be refurbished now for $180,000, and the refurbishment will bring in an extra income of $30,000 at the end of this year and the following 9 years. What is the NPV of this project assuming a discount rate of 10% compounded annually? Estimate the internal rate of return and then calculate it exactly using a computer.

Solutions:

1. **a.** No, each term is the previous term plus 2.

   b. No.

   c. Yes each term is 0.85 times the previous term.

2. **a.** This is a geometric series with initial term $a = 1$, ratio $R = \frac{1}{3}$ and $n = 13$ terms so it is

$$1 \cdot \frac{\left(\frac{1}{3}\right)^{13} - 1}{\frac{1}{3} - 1} = 1.499999$$

   b. This is a geometric series with $a = 5$, $R = 1.01$ and $n = 12$ so it is

$$5 \cdot \frac{1.01^{12} - 1}{1.01 - 1} = 63.4125$$

   c. This geometric series continues indefinitely so it is given by

$$\frac{a}{1 - R}$$

   where $a = 0.9$ and $R = 0.85$ so it is 6.

d. This is a geometric series with $a = rt$, $R = t$ and $n = 12$ terms so it is

$$rt\frac{t^{12}-1}{t-1}$$

3. **a.** The value at the end of 2 years is $150 \cdot 1.005^{23} + 150 \cdot 1.005^{22} + \ldots + 150 \cdot 1.005^{1}$ + 150 which is a geometric series of 24 terms, with $a = 150$ and $R = 1.005$ and so is

$$150\frac{1.005^{24}-1}{1.005-1} = £3814.79$$

b. This will accumulate to

$$460 \cdot 1.015^{7} + 460 \cdot 1.015^{6} + \ldots + 460 \cdot 1.015 + 460 = 460\frac{1.015^{8}-1}{1.015-1} = £3879.11$$

The quarterly scheme will be worth slightly more at the end of 2 years.

4. There are 30 payments of £2000, and each 4-month period has an interest rate of 2% so the present value is

$$\frac{2000}{1.02} + \frac{2000}{1.02^{2}} + \ldots + \frac{2000}{1.02^{30}} = \frac{2000}{1.02}\frac{(\frac{1}{1.02})^{30}-1}{\frac{1}{1.02}-1} = £44,792.91$$

5. The present value of the repayments is

$$\frac{200}{1.01} + \frac{200}{1.01^{2}} + \ldots + \frac{200}{1.01^{240}} = \frac{200}{1.01}\frac{(\frac{1}{1.01})^{240}-1}{\frac{1}{1.01}-1} = £18,163.88$$

6. Suppose each instalment is X. The present value of the repayments, discounted at 1.5% a month, must be equal to the loan of £2500, i.e.

$$\frac{X}{1.015} + \frac{X}{1.015^{2}} + \ldots + \frac{X}{1.015^{18}} = 2500$$

The left-hand side is a geometric series, so this becomes

$$\frac{X}{1.015}\frac{(\frac{1}{1.015})^{18}-1}{\frac{1}{1.015}-1} = 2500$$

and then $15.672560 X = 2500$, so $X = £159.51$.

7. $$NPV = -180,000 + \frac{30,000}{1.1} + \frac{30,000}{1.1^{2}} + \ldots + \frac{30,000}{1.1^{10}}$$

$$= -180,000 + \frac{30,000}{1.1}\frac{(\frac{1}{1.1})^{10}-1}{\frac{1}{1.1}-1} = \$4337.01$$

When the discount rate is increased slightly to 11% the NPV becomes −$3323.04, so the IRR is between 10% and 11%. Excel gives this as 10.558%.

WORK CARD 3 (CONTINUED)

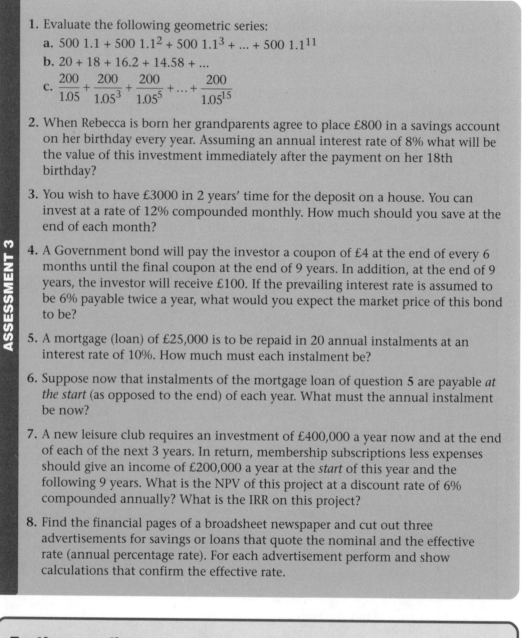

ASSESSMENT 3

1. Evaluate the following geometric series:
   a. $500 \cdot 1.1 + 500 \cdot 1.1^2 + 500 \cdot 1.1^3 + \ldots + 500 \cdot 1.1^{11}$
   b. $20 + 18 + 16.2 + 14.58 + \ldots$
   c. $\dfrac{200}{1.05} + \dfrac{200}{1.05^3} + \dfrac{200}{1.05^5} + \ldots + \dfrac{200}{1.05^{15}}$

2. When Rebecca is born her grandparents agree to place £800 in a savings account on her birthday every year. Assuming an annual interest rate of 8% what will be the value of this investment immediately after the payment on her 18th birthday?

3. You wish to have £3000 in 2 years' time for the deposit on a house. You can invest at a rate of 12% compounded monthly. How much should you save at the end of each month?

4. A Government bond will pay the investor a coupon of £4 at the end of every 6 months until the final coupon at the end of 9 years. In addition, at the end of 9 years, the investor will receive £100. If the prevailing interest rate is assumed to be 6% payable twice a year, what would you expect the market price of this bond to be?

5. A mortgage (loan) of £25,000 is to be repaid in 20 annual instalments at an interest rate of 10%. How much must each instalment be?

6. Suppose now that instalments of the mortgage loan of question 5 are payable *at the start* (as opposed to the end) of each year. What must the annual instalment be now?

7. A new leisure club requires an investment of £400,000 a year now and at the end of each of the next 3 years. In return, membership subscriptions less expenses should give an income of £200,000 a year at the *start* of this year and the following 9 years. What is the NPV of this project at a discount rate of 6% compounded annually? What is the IRR on this project?

8. Find the financial pages of a broadsheet newspaper and cut out three advertisements for savings or loans that quote the nominal and the effective rate (annual percentage rate). For each advertisement perform and show calculations that confirm the effective rate.

Further reading: see p. xv
Jacques provides a chapter on 'The Mathematics of Finance'.

Lawson, Hubbard and Pugh include a chapter.

BM5
Decision making

Ever notice that 'what the hell' is always the right decision?

Marilyn Monroe (1926–1962)

Contexts

What is this chapter about?
This chapter considers ways of summarising an organisational decision problem and hence determining which course of action is 'best', in some sense.

Why is it useful?
In organisations a decision can have several stages, and each choice at each stage can result in a different set of possible consequences. Also, a decision may involve multiple departments and individuals and so will need justifying across the organisation. With these levels of complexity a structured approach to decision making is required.

  This chapter provides an introduction to commonly used methods of summarising a decision problem and considers how you might go about deciding which course of action to take.

Where does it fit in?
The science of Decision Analysis is usually regarded as a branch of Management Science or Operational Research.

What do I need to know?
You will need to be familiar with the material in Essential Maths, and some knowledge of the first two chapters of Probability will be useful.

Objectives

After your work on this chapter you should be able to:

● construct a payoff table for a simple decision problem;
● understand the maximax, maximin, minimax regret and expected value criteria for solving decision problems;
● understand the concept of the expected value of an outcome;
● construct a decision tree and use it to select the optimal decision strategy

1 Introducing decision making

We are all faced with decisions in everyday life – some of greater importance than others. What shall I have for breakfast? Which university should I go to? Which route should I take to work this morning? Where should I go on holiday? Most of these personal decisions are made without a formal strategy but by drawing on our experience and intuition.

Business decisions tend to be more complex and involve many different factors. They often have major financial consequences and may need to be justified to senior staff and at board level. A more formal approach to decision making is therefore required. The science of *decision analysis*, which we introduce in this chapter, provides a structure for a decision problem and methods to help decision makers make 'better' decisions.

Any decision problem gives the decision maker a choice of at least two *courses of action*. In a perfect world the consequences of each course of action would be known exactly but in real life the consequences will depend on external events over which the decision maker has no control. In decision analysis we can allow for these uncertain events by assigning a probability to each possible outcome. To understand this chapter, it will therefore be helpful to have covered the material in the Probability section, in particular P1, *Measuring Uncertainty*.

A structure for the decision problem

A decision problem usually has the following four components:

1. An *objective*
2. The alternative *courses of action*
3. Events that are out of the decision maker's control which we will call *uncontrollable events*
4. A set of *payoffs* or *rewards*, one for each combination of course of action and uncontrollable event.

We explain these more fully below.

1. The objective

The objective is what we are trying to achieve. It could be to maximise profits, minimise costs, or maximise market share. Sometimes we may have a number of different, perhaps conflicting, objectives. For example, in choosing between different job opportunities we may wish to maximise salary, but we might also be concerned with job satisfaction, number of working hours, amount of time spent travelling to and from the workplace and so on. We will limit our attention to decisions with just one objective.

2. The alternative courses of action

Once we have decided on our objective, we must consider what alternative courses of action are open to us in order to achieve it. For example, a company introducing a new product to the marketplace may have to decide whether to build a large plant or a small plant. Or the same company may need to decide where to locate a new plant – in the north of England, the south of England, or Wales.

3. The uncontrollable events

Although all the courses of action are open to the decision maker, and he will be able to choose between them, the environment in which the decision problem occurs will usually be subject to external influences that are beyond the decision maker's control. We will call these *uncontrollable events*. For example, demand for a new product might be high, medium or low, or a competing brand may introduce a rival product, or not.

   The decision maker wants to make the 'best' decision, in spite of this uncertainty. In the earlier parts of this book we saw how uncertain events can be modelled using probability. It will therefore be useful to assign a probability to each uncontrollable event although we will not make use of these until Section 3 of this chapter. We can do this by looking at any data that is available from past occurrences of a similar situation, or make subjective estimates of the probabilities. For instance, if it has rained for 20% of the days in June in the last 10 years, then it is reasonable to say that the probability that it will rain on a particular June day is 0.2. The probabilities associated with all possible uncontrollable events must add up to 1.

4. The payoffs or rewards

The value of choosing a particular course of action and then having a particular uncontrollable event occur is called the *payoff* or *reward*. Payoffs may or may not take a monetary value. For instance, they might be profits, losses, revenues, reduction in pollution levels or costs. In practice they will not be known exactly but will need to be estimated using all the information available. A grid or table of all the payoffs for every combination of course of action and uncontrollable event is called a *payoff table*. We will consider these in the next section.

Check this

Identify the four components **1**, **2**, **3** and **4** in the following example.

   A waitress must decide whether to serve tables in the bar or the restaurant of her local pub on a particular evening. The landlady has agreed to pay her £20 for the evening if she works in the bar or £15 if she works in the restaurant on the basis that there are usually a few rowdy customers in the bar who are more difficult to please than those in the restaurant. The waitress estimates that about one evening in five is busy and results in high tips, whilst the other evenings are quiet and tips are low. High tips usually amount to £10 in the bar as opposed to £20 in the restaurant, whereas low tips are £5 in the bar and nothing at all in the restaurant. She has seen a new dress she wants to buy and so must earn as much as possible this evening.

Solution:

1. Her objective is to maximise her take-home pay.

2. The alternative courses of action are:
   (a) work in the bar
   (b) work in the restaurant

3. The uncontrollable events are whether the pub is busy or quiet.

4. The payoffs are the amounts she will take home if she works in the bar or in the restaurant.

The four components of a decision-making problem

1. **The objective**
What are you trying to achieve?

2. **The alternative courses of action**
The different courses of action that are open to you in order to achieve your objective.

3. **The uncontrollable events**
Events that might occur but which are outside your control.

4. **The payoffs or rewards**
The set of values, one resulting from each combination of course of action and uncontrollable event.

WORK CARD 1

1. For each of the following decision problems, determine the likely objective, the alternative courses of action, the uncontrollable events, and what the payoffs might be:

   (a) A retailer must decide whether to order a large quantity or a small quantity of a perishable item to sell in his convenience store. On any particular day there is a 40% chance that sales of this item will be high but there is a 60% chance that sales will be low.

   (b) At present I spend 60 minutes travelling to and from work each day and I am considering moving house to reduce this time to 5 minutes. However, my company is currently in the process of a reorganisation which could result in my place of work being moved closer to my present home. If this move goes ahead I would have a 10 minute journey if I remain at my current address, whereas I would have a 50 minute journey if I made the proposed house move.

Solution:

1. **(a)** The likely objective in this case is to maximise profit. The alternative courses of action are whether to order a large quantity or a small quantity of the perishable item. The uncontrollable events are the sales which could be high or low. The payoffs might be the profit achieved for each course of action under high or low sales.

   (b) The objective might be to minimise the time commuting to and from work or to minimise travelling costs. The alternative courses of action are whether to move house or not. The uncontrollable events are whether or not my place of work is changed. The payoffs might be the minutes travelling or the travelling costs associated with each course of action and uncontrollable event.

   Notice that we have not yet made use of the probabilities associated with the uncontrollable events.

1. Jane has just bought a new washing machine from a large electrical superstore. The appliance comes with a standard one year guarantee but the store manager wants to sell her an extended warranty for an additional two years at a cost of £55. Jane has done some research on this particular washing machine and believes there is a 5% chance the machine will break down during its second year in which case she would be charged £100 for repairs and there is a 15% chance that it will break down during its third year in which case she would be charged £180 for repairs.

   Determine the likely objective, the alternative courses of action, the uncontrollable events, and the payoffs of this decision problem.

2 Payoff tables

A payoff table is a useful way of representing simple decision problems, where there is just one decision and one set of uncontrollable events.

Consider the following example.

A company marketing a new product has found that sales have suddenly escalated and it is having difficulty coping with the increased demand. It can either invest £250,000 in improving equipment to enable this level of production to be sustained, or outsource production of this item. If production is kept in house the company will make a profit of £5 per item, whereas if production is outsourced profit per item will reduce to £2.

It is estimated that there is a 70% chance that demand will remain at 100,000 units for the coming year, a 20% chance that it will fall slightly to 75,000 units for the year and a 10% chance that current market conditions are a temporary 'blip' and demand will drop back to its former level of 10,000 units for the year.

It is anticipated that this product will only be saleable during the next 12 months, at the end of which time the new equipment will be worthless.

We can summarise this information by drawing a payoff table. Each row of the table corresponds to an alternative course of action open to the decision maker. In this case, the first row corresponds to making the new investment and the second row to outsourcing production as shown below.

ACTION (within our control)	New investment			
	Outsource			

The columns of the table represent the uncontrollable events, in this case the level of demand for the product as shown below.

			Uncontrollable events	
			DEMAND	(1000s of units)
		100	75	10
ACTION (within our control)	New investment			
	Outsource			

The body of the table contains the payoff resulting from each combination of course of action and uncontrollable event. For example, if the company makes the new investment and sales remain at 100,000 units then profit will be 100,000 × £5 = £500,000 less the cost of improving equipment, £250,000; that is £250,000. If it decides to outsource production of the new item and sales fall to 75,000 units then profit will be 75,000 × £2 = £150,000. The completed table is shown below.

PAYOFF in £000s

			Uncontrollable events	
			DEMAND	(1000s of units)
		100	75	10
ACTION (within our control)	New investment	250	125	−200
	Outsource	200	150	20

Notice that if sales drop to 10,000 units and the company makes the new investment they will make a loss of £200,000 (10,000 × £5 − £250,000).

Also notice that we have not yet included the probabilities in the payoff table.

WORK CARD 2

1. Prepare a payoff table for the waitress's decision problem from the last section, which is repeated below.

    A waitress must decide whether to serve tables in the bar or restaurant of her local pub on a particular evening. The landlady has agreed to pay her £20 for the evening if she works in the bar or £15 if she works in the restaurant on the basis that there are usually a few rowdy customers in the bar who are more difficult to please than in the restaurant. The waitress estimates that about one evening in five is busy and results in high tips, whilst the other evenings are quiet and tips are low. High tips in the bar usually amount to £10 as opposed to £20 in the restaurant whereas low tips in the bar are £5 and nothing at all in the restaurant. She has seen a new dress she wants to buy and so must earn as much as possible this evening.

2. A football club has 30 home matches during the season and in order to secure a substantial discount from its supplier would like to order a fixed batch size of meat pies for each match. Batches are available in multiples of 10 dozen and to comply with food hygiene standards must be consumed at the match for which they were ordered.

    The catering manager analyses sales of pies during the last season and produces the following table:

Pies sold per match (in dozens)	Percentage of matches
20	10
30	10
40	25
50	25
60	20
70	10

    Pies cost £3.60 per dozen and sell for £1.50 each.

    Prepare a payoff table to assist the catering manager in deciding how many dozen pies to order.

Solutions:

1. The courses of action open to the waitress are whether to work in the bar or the restaurant. The columns represent the uncontrollable events, i.e. the pub may be busy or quiet. The main body of the table contains the 'payoffs' she will receive in each case. For instance, if she works in the bar and the pub is busy she receives £20 from the landlady and £10 in tips, £30 in all.

Payoff in £s

		Uncontrollable events	
		Pub busy	Pub quiet
ACTION	Bar	30	25
	Restaurant	35	15

2. This time the rows represent the batch size ordered (since this is the decision we have to make) and the columns the number of pies sold (since these are the outcomes outside our control).

WORK CARD 2 (CONTINUED)

Profit in £s

		SALES					
		20	30	40	50	60	70
ORDER	20	288	288	288	288	288	288
	30	252	432	432	432	432	432
	40	216	396	576	576	576	576
	50	180	360	540	720	720	720
	60	144	324	504	684	864	864
	70	108	288	468	648	828	1008

The figures in the table represent the profit obtained for each combination of course of action and uncontrollable event. For instance, if the catering manager orders 40 dozen pies and sales are 30 dozen, profit is $360 \times £1.50 - 40 \times £3.60 = £396$. However, if he orders 40 dozen pies and potential sales are 50 dozen, he loses 10 dozen sales and so profit is $480 \times £1.50 - 40 \times £3.60 = £576$.

1. A newsstand operator stocks a weekly magazine called *COOL* aimed at the teen market. He must decide how many copies to order each week. Demand for the magazine has the following probabilities:

Weekly demand	Probability
10 copies	0.10
11 copies	0.15
12 copies	0.20
13 copies	0.25
14 copies	0.30

The magazine sells for £2.50 and costs the newsstand operator £1.50. Prepare a payoff table for each of the following circumstances.
(i)   The operator can return unsold copies for a full refund.
(ii) The operator cannot return any unsold copies.
(iii) The operator can return unsold copies but only receives a refund of £0.50 per copy.

3 Decision-making criteria

So far we have summarised the decision problem using a payoff table, but we have not yet considered how to make the decision!

In fact, there is no single way of choosing a 'best' course of action, and a variety of criteria can be used, according to the amount of risk we wish to take.

We will illustrate the use of some of these criteria using the company example from the last section. Recall that a company must decide whether to invest in improved equipment or whether to outsource production of a new product. The payoff table we constructed earlier is repeated below.

PAYOFF in £000s

		\multicolumn{3}{c}{Uncontrollable events}
		\multicolumn{2}{l}{DEMAND}	(1000s of units)
		100	75	10
ACTION	New investment	250	125	−200
(*within our control*)	Outsource	200	150	20

The maximax criterion

The maximax criterion simply says, for each course of action calculate the maximum possible payoff. Then pick the course of action that gives the maximum of these maximum payoffs (thus the name, maximax).

Check this

Use the maximax decision criterion to decide which course of action should be taken by the company.

Solution:
For new investment the maximum possible payoff is £250,000, whereas for outsourcing the maximum possible payoff is £200,000. The maximax criterion leads us to choose new investment.

By comparing the maximum payoffs for each course of action, maximax takes an optimist's view.

The maximin criterion

The maximin criterion, as a contrast, takes the pessimist's view. Instead of comparing the maximum payoff achievable by each course of action it compares the *minimum* payoffs. The course of action that gives rise to the greatest or *maximum* minimum payoff is selected. By comparing the minimum payoffs, the maximin solution is the least risky option.

Check this

Decide which course of action to follow using the maximin criterion.

Solution:
At worst, new investment results in a payoff of –£200,000 (i.e. a loss of £200,000), whereas outsourcing brings a payoff of at least £20,000. The highest of these is £20,000, so outsourcing is the maximin solution.

A number of approaches try to compromise between these two criteria. Two of these are mentioned below.

The minimax regret criterion

The minimax regret criterion uses the payoffs to calculate a set of *opportunity losses*; one for each combination of course of action and uncontrollable event.

The *opportunity loss* is the amount of payoff forgone by choosing this course of action rather than the one that results in the greatest payoff for this uncontrollable event.

For example, if demand is 100,000 units then by outsourcing the company incurs an opportunity loss of £50,000 since the payoff if they made a new investment would be £50,000 more. Similarly, if demand is 10,000 units then by investing in the new equipment they are forgoing a payoff of £20,000 and incurring instead a loss of £200,000, so the opportunity loss is £220,000.

A convenient way of displaying these values is by way of an opportunity loss table as shown below.

Opportunity loss in £000s

			Uncontrollable events	
			DEMAND	(1000s of units)
		100	75	10
ACTION (*within our control*)	New investment	0	25	–220
	Outsource	50	0	0

The minimax criterion is then applied to the opportunity loss table; that is, we choose the course of action that minimises the maximum opportunity loss.

For example, the maximum opportunity loss for new investment is £220,000 and for outsourcing is £50,000. The company should therefore outsource since this gives the smallest of these maximums.

The expected value criterion

So far we have not made use of the probability of each uncontrollable event. It would be desirable to incorporate these probabilities into the decision-making process. One way of doing this is to choose the course of action that has the highest *expected value*.

We explained the idea of expected values in Chapter P2, *Numerical Outcomes*, but we will review them briefly below. If you think you know how to calculate them anyway go straight to the next **Check this**.

The expected value of a reward or gain is the long-run average value it would assume if the situation that produces it were repeated a large number of times. To calculate it we multiply each value the reward can take by its probability and then add them all up. For instance, suppose in a game I can win £10 with a probability of 0.4 or win £5 with probability 0.6. The expected value of my win is

$$£10 \times 0.4 + £4 \times 0.6 = £6.40$$

That is, if I played the game many, many times my average win would be £6.40 per game. (How good or bad this is would depend on how much I had paid to play the game. If the game fee were £7 it would be a bad deal for me but if it were £6 it would be good.)

Check this

Parking charges at a small out of town car park are as follows:

Up to two hours	£1
From two to four hours	£2
From four to eight hours	£5
Over eight hours	£8

A survey carried out by the town council reports that the length of stay of cars at this car park has the following probabilities.

Up to two hours	0.60
From two to four hours	0.20
From four to eight hours	0.15
Over eight hours	0.05

Calculate the expected value of the charge per car.

Solution:
Just multiply each charge by its probability and then add them up, that is

$$£1 \times 0.6 + £2 \times 0.2 + £5 \times 0.15 + £8 \times 0.05 = £2.15$$

On average, the charge per car is £2.15.

Now try calculating the expected values of each course of action from a payoff table. We will use the payoff table produced in the last section.

Check this

Recall that a company must decide whether to invest in improved equipment or whether to outsource production. The payoff table is repeated below. Calculate the expected value of each of these actions and hence decide which it should take. Notice that the probability of each uncontrollable event appears in brackets at the top of each column.

PAYOFF in £000s

		DEMAND	(1000s of units)	
		Uncontrollable events		
		100 (0.7)	75 (0.2)	10 (0.1)
ACTION *(within our control)*	New investment	250	125	−200
	Outsource	200	150	20

Solution:

New investment will give a payoff of £250,000 with a probability of 0.7, or £125,000 with a probability of 0.2 or –£200,000 with a probability of 0.1. The expected value if the company makes new investment is therefore

Expected value (new investment)
= 0.7 × £250,000 + 0.2 × £125,000 + 0.1 × –£200,000 = £180,000

In a similar way the expected value if the company chooses to outsource is

Expected value (outsource)
= 0.7 × £200,000 + 0.2 × £150,000 + 0.1 × £20,000 = £172,000

The 'best' decision, on an expected value basis, is therefore to invest in improved equipment, as the expected value is higher.

As a general rule it is quite useful, especially when there are several courses of action, to append another column to the payoff table for the expected values as shown below.

PAYOFF in £000s

		DEMAND	(1000s of units)		Expected value
		Uncontrollable events			
		100 (0.7)	75 (0.2)	10 (0.1)	
ACTION *(within our control)*	New investment	250	125	−200	180
	Outsource	200	150	20	172

At this point we should point out that because expected value is a long-run average its usefulness in determining the best course of action can be limited. It is more suited to situations that are repeated many times.

For example, a sandwich bar has to decide on the number of packs of sandwiches to order each day. Daily demand varies and any packs unsold at the end of the day are worthless. In this situation it is not unreasonable to calculate the expected values of ordering different batch sizes and to select the one that gives rise to the highest expected return, since even if they 'get it wrong' some days they will 'get it right' on others and over the course of many days these under/over provisions will be 'evened out'.

However, if we are considering a one-off business decision, such as whether to build a large plant or a small plant at a new site on the outskirts of a large city, then there is no opportunity for the 'evening out' process to take place over a number of repetitions of the same situation.

For example, suppose there is a 60% chance that a large plant will give rise to a profit of £2 million and a 40% chance it will lead to a loss of £250,000, whereas there is a 50% chance a small plant will result in a profit of £1 million and a 50% chance it will result in a profit of £100,000.

Whilst the expected value of building the large plant (£1.1 million) is greater than that of building the small plant (£550,000), if the company builds the large plant it risks losing £250,000, which it may not be prepared to do. Expected values do not take this into account.

This being said, the expected value method of choosing which course of action to take is widely used in practice. Many large organisations make large numbers of decisions and are able to sustain losses on some projects which represent only a small part of their overall operations.

WORK CARD 3

1. I roll a standard six-sided die. If the uppermost face is an even number I win £5, if it lands with 5 on the uppermost face I win £2, otherwise I lose £10.
    What is the expected value of my gain?

2. My son's school is organising a raffle. It has sold 200 tickets at 50p each. The first ticket drawn from a hat will win £50. I have bought 5 tickets.
    What is my expected gain?

3. If I don't put any money in the parking meter when I park, there is a one in twenty chance the traffic warden will give me a ticket and I will have to pay £60. The cost of parking is £2.50. On an expected values basis should I risk not paying?

4. Use the four criteria discussed in this section to decide whether the waitress referred to in sections 1 and 2 of this chapter should work in the bar or the restaurant. The payoff table is repeated below, but now includes the probabilities of the uncontrollable events.

Payoff in £s

		Uncontrollable events	
		Pub busy (0.2)	Pub quiet (0.8)
ACTION	Bar	30	25
	Restaurant	35	15

5. For **Work card 2**, question 2, use all four criteria to determine which batch size the football club should use. The payoff table is repeated below, but now includes the probabilities of the uncontrollable events.

Profit in £s

		SALES					
		20 (0.10)	30 (0.10)	40 (0.25)	50 (0.25)	60 (0.20)	70 (0.10)
	20	288	288	288	288	288	288
	30	252	432	432	432	432	432
ORDER	40	216	396	576	576	576	576
	50	180	360	540	720	720	720
	60	144	324	504	684	864	864
	70	108	288	468	648	828	1008

Solutions:

1. $P(\text{even number}) = 0.5$, $P(\text{die lands } 5) = \frac{1}{6}$. Expected gain $= 0.5 \times £5 + \frac{1}{6} \times £2 - \frac{2}{6} \times £10 = 0.50$, i.e. an expected loss of 50p per game.

2. $P(\text{win}) = 5/200$, $P(\text{lose}) = 195/200$. Expected gain $= 5/200 \times £50 - 195/200 \times £0 = £1.25$. Since I have paid £2.50 for my tickets then my expected loss is £1.25 (£1.25 − £2.50).

3. Expected cost (not paying) $= 1/20 \times £60 = £3$. Therefore it is not worth risking not paying.

4.

Payoff in £s

		Uncontrollable events		
		Pub busy (0.2)	Pub quiet (0.8)	Expected value
ACTION	Bar	30	25	26
	Restaurant	35	15	19

Using the maximax criterion she should work in the restaurant as this potentially gives rise to the greatest payoff (£35).

Using the maximin criterion she should work in the bar as the least payoff she would receive is £25.

Using the minimax regret criterion we would produce the following opportunity loss table:

	Pub busy	Pub quiet
Bar	£5	£0
Restaurant	£0	£10

The option that minimises the maximum opportunity loss is working in the bar.

Using expected values she should work in the bar as this option gives rise to the greatest expected value.

5.

Profit in £s

			SALES					
		20 (0.10)	30 (0.10)	40 (0.25)	50 (0.25)	60 (0.20)	70 (0.10)	EV
	20	288	288	288	288	288	288	288
	30	252	432	432	432	432	432	414
ORDER	40	216	396	576	576	576	576	522
	50	180	360	540	720	720	720	585
	60	144	324	504	684	864	864	603
	70	108	288	468	648	828	1008	585

Using the maximax criterion, 70 dozen pies should be ordered.
Using the maximin criterion, 20 dozen pies should be ordered.
The opportunity loss table is shown below.

		SALES					
		20 (0.10)	30 (0.10)	40 (0.25)	50 (0.25)	60 (0.20)	70 (0.10)
	20	0	144	288	432	576	720
	30	36	0	144	288	432	576
ORDER	40	72	36	0	144	288	432
	50	108	72	36	0	144	288
	60	144	108	72	36	0	144
	70	180	144	108	72	36	0

An order of 60 pies gives the smallest maximum opportunity loss of £144. Therefore 60 dozen pies should be ordered.
Using expected values, 60 dozen pies should be ordered.

ASSESSMENT 3

1. A motor insurance company calculates that in a given year each policyholder will make a minor claim of $1000 with a probability of 0.1 and a major claim of $10,000 with a probability of 0.01.
   The company has set the annual premium at $250.
   What is the expected profit per policy holder for the insurance company?

2. I pay £5 to play a game where I toss a coin and roll a standard six-sided die.

ASSESSMENT 3 (CONTINUED)

If the coin lands heads and I roll a six, I win £10.

If the coin lands heads and I roll a number other than six, I win £4.

What is the expected value of my gain?

3. Use each of the four decision criteria in this section to decide how many copies of *COOL* magazine should be ordered by the newsstand operator in **Assessment 2**, question 1. You have already calculated the payoff tables under each of three different sets of circumstances. Now assume that unsold copies can be returned for a full refund.

For convenience the question is repeated below.

A newsstand operator stocks a weekly magazine called *COOL* aimed at the teen market. He must decide how many copies to order each week. Demand for the magazine has the following probabilities:

Weekly demand	Probability
10 copies	0.10
11 copies	0.15
12 copies	0.20
13 copies	0.25
14 copies	0.30

The magazine sells for £2.50 and costs the newsstand operator £1.50.

4 Decision trees

As we have already said, payoff tables are useful when we have just one decision to make and one set of uncontrollable events. When one decision and one set of uncontrollable circumstances leads to other decisions and/or other sets of uncontrollable events an invaluable way of viewing the problem clearly and helping the decision maker to make his decision is to draw a *decision tree*.

The process of preparing a decision tree can be quite complicated and is best illustrated by way of an example.

Introducing Dylan's Kitchenware

Dylan's Kitchenware has designed a revolutionary toaster which staggers the timing of the toast so that the second slice pops up 5 minutes after the first, enabling the proud owner to butter and eat the first slice before the second is produced and ensuring that both slices can be eaten piping hot.

Dylan thinks that there is a 60% probability that a rival company will soon be entering the same market with a very similar product and must decide whether to launch his product immediately, whether to consult an industrial espionage agent to gather more information about the existence of a rival company or whether to sell his design.

Dylan accepts that new products of this kind generally have a 60% chance of success.

If no rival enters the market and the toaster is a success then Dylan can expect to receive £100,000, but if the toaster does not become popular then he expects to break even.

If, however, a rival does enter the market then there will be price competition and he will receive £40,000 if the product is successful, but will lose £10,000 if it is not.

If Dylan sells his design he can expect to receive £35,000.

The industrial espionage agent has quoted a fixed fee of £2,000. In the past, similar investigations by this agent have indicated that a rival will enter the market 50% of the time. If the agent says a rival is going to enter the market there is a 10% chance of him being wrong and a 90% chance of him being right, whereas if he says that a rival is not going to enter the market there is a 30% chance of him being wrong and a 70% chance of him being right.

What should Dylan do?

Drawing the decision tree

The key to drawing a decision tree is to work from left to right, starting at the present and moving towards future events and decisions.

A decision tree is made up of junction points, called *nodes,* and *branches* which connect the nodes. The junction points are either squares or circles. A square node represents a decision and branches representing the alternative courses of action will come out of it. A circle or uncertainty node represents a set of uncontrollable events. The branches coming out of it represent alternative outcomes that occur according to chance and which are outside the decision maker's control.

We start by drawing a square node on the left-hand side of the page to represent the first decision we have to make. From this we draw branches for each alternative course of action; in our example, one will represent launching the product immediately, one consulting the industrial espionage agent and one selling the design.

The result is shown in Figure 5.1.

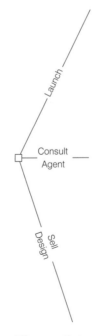

Figure 5.1

If we decide to launch the product immediately we need make no more decisions, but there are two sets of uncontrollable events to consider. The first is whether or not a rival enters the market and the second is whether or not the product is successful. Both of these are outside our control and therefore will follow an uncertainty node (a circle).

To represent the rival/no rival events we draw a circle with two branches out of it: one representing the outcome 'rival' and one representing the outcome 'no rival'. Next we draw circles at the end of each of these branches followed by a further two branches in each case, representing 'success' and 'no success'. The result is shown in Figure 5.2.

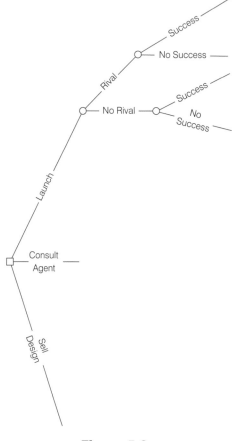

Figure 5.2

Now we consider the part of the tree emanating from the 'Consult Agent' course of action. The first set of uncontrollable events to consider is whether the agent says 'yes, a rival company is going to enter the market' or 'no, a rival company is not going to enter the market'. Again, these outcomes are outside our control and will therefore follow an uncertainty node, as shown in Figure 5.3.

At the end of the branches 'Agent says "yes"' and 'Agent says "no"' we have drawn a square node. This is because at this point we have to make another decision in the light of this new information. We must now decide whether it is better to launch the product or sell the design.

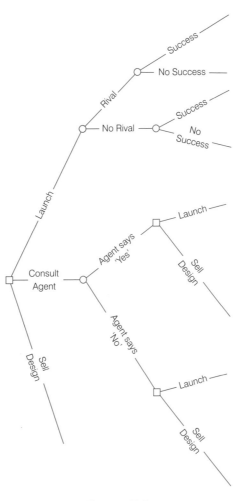

Figure 5.3

If we decide to launch the product at this point we must again consider the two sets of uncontrollable events mentioned earlier; that is, whether or not a rival does enter the market and whether or not the product is successful.

This completes all branches of the decision tree, as shown in Figure 5.4. Notice that the 'sell design' branch has no further branches as there are no subsequent actions or events.

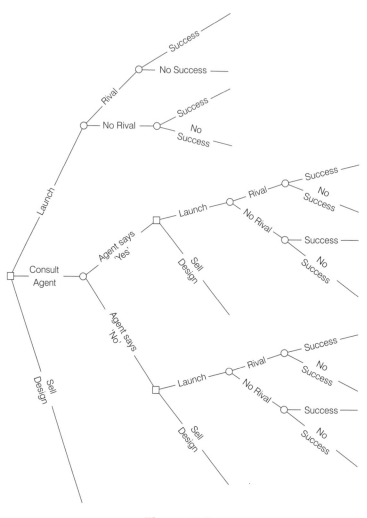

Figure 5.4

Each route through the tree from left to right represents one possible combination of decisions and uncontrollable events and as such has a payoff attached to it.

It will be convenient to allocate each route a number so that we can refer to it easily, as shown in Figure 5.5.

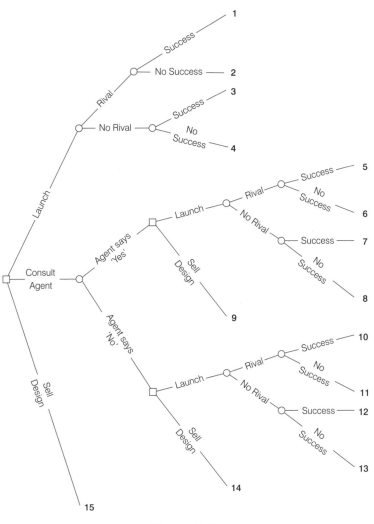

Figure 5.5

The payoffs associated with each route can be calculated using the information given at the start of this example.

Check these

What is the payoff for route **6: consult industrial espionage agent – agent says 'yes' – launch product – rival enters market – product is not successful**?

What is the payoff for route **14: consult industrial espionage agent – agent says 'no' – sell design**?

Solutions:
Route 6: If a rival enters the market and the product is not successful, we lose £10,000. Since we also have to pay £2,000 for the services of the agent then the total payoff of this option is a loss of £12,000. This is shown in italics in Figure 5.6.

Route **14**: If we sell the design having employed the services of an agent then we will receive £35,000, but will have incurred costs of £2,000, leaving us a net gain of £33,000 as shown in italics in Figure 5.6.

All payoffs are included in Figure 5.6.

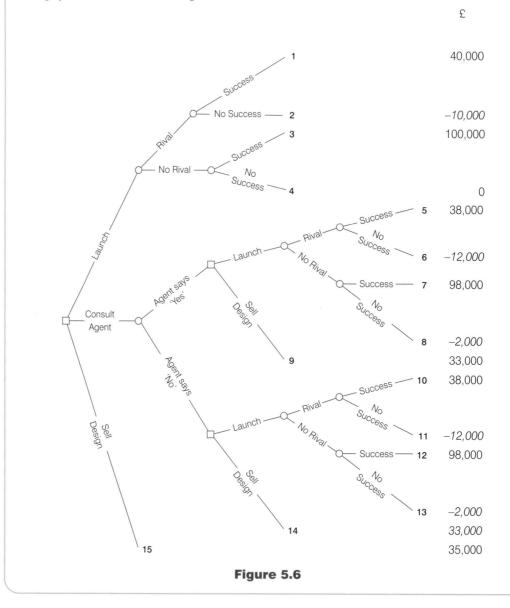

£

1	40,000
2	−10,000
3	100,000
4	0
5	38,000
6	−12,000
7	98,000
8	−2,000
9	33,000
10	38,000
11	−12,000
12	98,000
13	−2,000
14	33,000
15	35,000

Figure 5.6

To complete the decision tree, each branch representing an uncontrollable event must be marked with the probability of it occurring assuming that all decisions and uncontrollable events leading up to that branch have already happened. The probabilities are given in the initial description of this problem at the start of this section.

First consider route **1**. The first branches representing uncontrollable events relate to the 'rival'/'no rival' outcomes and the probabilities associated with each of these outcomes can be marked on the tree. The probability that a rival company will enter the market assuming that the product has been launched immediately is 0.6. This value is therefore entered on the tree between the two circles on route **1** as shown in italics in Figure 5.7.

£

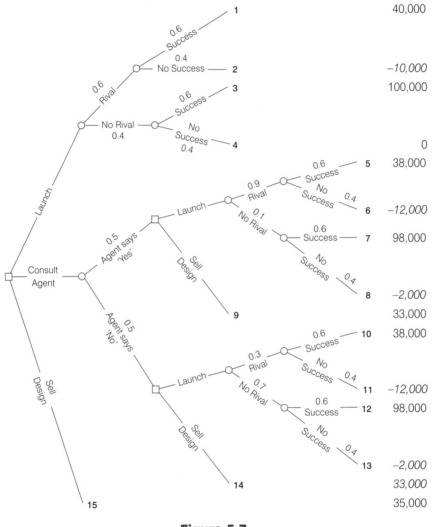

Figure 5.7

Now try the following.

Check these

What is the probability that a rival company enters the market assuming that the industrial espionage agent has said it will? (This probability is marked on the tree between the last two circles on routes **5** and **6**.)

What is the probability that a rival company will enter the market if the industrial espionage agent has said it will not? (This probability is marked on the tree between the last two circles on routes **10** and **11**.)

Solutions:
The probability of a rival entering the market given that the agent says it will is 0.9, whereas the probability of a rival entering the market if the agent has said it will not is 0.3. (These probabilities are entered on the branches representing **consult espionage agent – agent says 'yes' – rival enters market** and **consult espionage agent – agent says 'no' – rival enters market** respectively, as shown in Figure 5.7.)
   Figure 5.7 includes all such probabilities.

The tree now summarises all available information about the decision problem. We now need to calculate the 'best' course of action to take and will use expected values for this.

Calculating expected values

As each circle node represents a set of uncontrollable events we can calculate an expected value for it by summing the alternative payoffs that could be obtained from that point multiplied by their respective probabilities.
   For ease of reference the circles have been identified on the tree in Figure 5.8 as **A**, **B**, **C**, **D**, **E**, **F**, **G**, **H**, **I** and **J** and the three square nodes or decision points have also been identified as **DP1**, **DP2** and **DP3**.
   We start with the rightmost circles on each route.
   For example, the rightmost circle on route **1** is node **A** and we can calculate the expected value for this node as follows.
   There is a 0.6 probability of obtaining a payoff of £40,000 and a 0.4 probability of obtaining a payoff of –£10,000.
   Therefore,

$$\text{Expected value at node } \mathbf{A} = 0.6 \times £40,000 + 0.4 \times -£10,000 = £20,000$$

Check these

What are the expected values at nodes **B**, **C**, **D**, **E** and **F**?

Solutions:
   Expected value at node **B** is $0.6 \times £100,000 + 0.4 \times £0 = £60,000$

   Expected value at node **C** is $0.6 \times £38,000 + 0.4 \times -£12,000 = £18,000$

   Expected value at node **D** is $0.6 \times £98,000 + 0.4 \times -£2,000 = £58,000$

   Expected value at node **E** is $0.6 \times £38,000 + 0.4 \times -£12,000 = £18,000$

   Expected value at node **F** is $0.6 \times £98,000 + 0.4 \times -£2,000 = £58,000$

Once we have calculated the expected values at these nodes we move back through the tree (from right to left) to the preceding node in each case and calculate the expected value there, using previously calculated expected values.

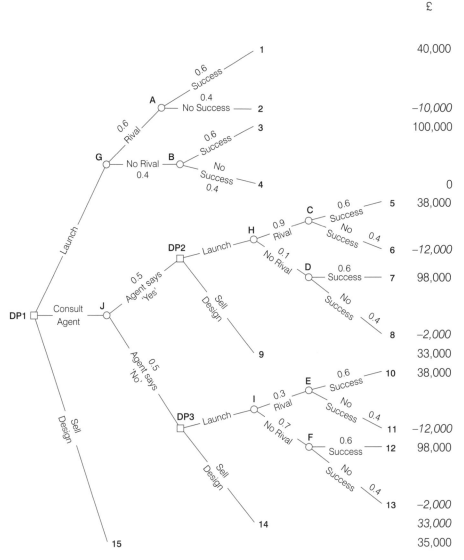

Figure 5.8

Check these

What are the expected values at nodes **G**, **H** and **I**?

Solutions:

Expected value at node **G** is 0.6 × (Expected value at node **A**) + 0.4 × (Expected value at node **B**) = 0.6 × £20,000 + 0.4 × £60,000 = £36,000

Expected value at node **H** is 0.9 × (Expected value at node **C**) + 0.1 × (Expected value at node **D**) = 0.9 × £18,000 + 0.1 × £58,000 = £22,000

Expected value at node **I** is 0.3 × (Expected value at node **E**) + 0.7 × (Expected value at node **F**) = 0.3 × 18,000 + 0.7 × £58,000 = £46,000

We continue this process until we reach the leftmost circle node on each route through the tree.

The only complication to this process is when we arrive at a square node or a decision point. At this point we must make a decision as to which course of action to take, so we choose the branch that gives the greatest expected value. Since we are working backwards through the tree the first decision points we reach will be decision points 2 and 3.

At decision point 2 (**DP2** in Figure 5.8) the agent has told us that a rival company will soon be entering the market, and we have calculated that if we launch the product our expected gain is £22,000 (the expected value at node **H**) and if we sell the design our expected gain is £33,000. Therefore, at this decision point, we would choose the option that gives rise to the greatest expected value; that is, we would sell the design.

Check this

What course of action should we take at decision point 3?

Solution:
At decision point 3 (**DP3** in Figure 5.8) the agent has told us that a rival company will not enter the market, and we have calculated that if we launch the product our expected gain is £46,000 (the expected value at node **I**) and if we sell the design our expected gain is £33,000. Hence at this decision point we would choose to launch the new product.

Finally, we will arrive at node **J** and can calculate the expected value at this point taking into account the decisions we have already made at decision points 2 and 3.

Since there is a 0.5 probability of the agent telling us that a rival will enter the market, in which case we would decide to sell the design, and a 0.5 probability of the agent telling us that a rival will not enter the market, in which case we would launch the product,

$$\text{Expected value at node } \mathbf{J} = 0.5 \times £33,000 + 0.5 \times £46,000 = £39,500$$

We are now ready to make the initial important decision at decision point 1 on the tree diagram (**DP1** in Figure 5.8). To do this we consider the three initial courses of action open to us together with their respective expected values and select the most favourable option.

If we launch the product, our expected value is £36,000 (expected value at node **G**); if we consult the agent, our expected value is £39,500 (expected value at node **J**); and if we sell the design then our expected value is £35,000 (the payoff for travelling along this route through the tree). Therefore our decision should be to consult the espionage agent. If he says a rival company is about to enter the market then we would sell the design and if he says a rival will not enter the market we would launch the new product.

We have seen how we can use a decision tree to represent a decision problem involving a sequence of decisions and a number of sets of uncontrollable events and how we can use it to choose between alternative courses of action.

As in all business modelling, we should not forget that our model of the decision problem is based upon a set of assumptions and therefore the solution should not be regarded as a definitive answer. However, decision trees are an important tool commonly used in the workplace to summarise, present and help solve complex business decision problems.

1. A company has to choose between three projects.
    Project A has a 50% chance of producing a return of £10,000, a 30% chance of producing a return of £5,000 and a 20% chance of producing a return of £2,000.
    Project B has a 70% chance of a £15,000 return, a 20% chance of an £8,000 return and a 10% chance of a zero return.
    Project C has a 15% chance of a £20,000 return, a 60% chance of a £12,000 return and a 25% chance of making a loss of £5,000.
    Draw a decision tree and hence decide which project the company should choose.

2. Given the following decision tree, answer the questions below.

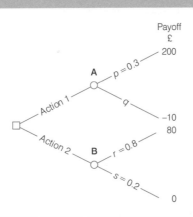

    a. What is probability q?
    b. What is the expected value at A?
    c. What is the expected value at B?
    d. What decision would you make?
    e. How would p and q have to change in order for you to change your mind?

3. I must decide whether to buy a cheap unbranded iron for £12 or a well-known make for £19. There is no guarantee with the cheap model, so if it breaks down during the first year I will simply have to buy another at the same price. My friend Tracy has used these irons for many years and thinks that about one in five of them breaks down during the first year. The more expensive iron is, however, guaranteed so that if it breaks during the first year, the manufacturer will replace it free of charge. The manufacturer claims that this is only likely to happen in about one in every 50 cases.

Draw a decision tree and hence decide which iron I should buy in order to minimise costs in the first year.

4. You are considering the purchase of some new computerised machinery for your factory, and have to decide between buying it immediately or waiting a few months, since the price of the equipment has been falling steadily over the past year. You have been advised that, if you wait for 6 months, there is a 60% chance that the price will fall to £12,000; otherwise it will remain steady at £16,000.

    If you buy now, the £16,000 cost can be reduced by the £2,000 saving that you expect will result from the increased efficiency due to the new machine being operative over the 6-month period.

    a. Assuming that your objective is to minimise expected costs, draw a decision tree to determine what course of action you should take.

    b. The estimate that there is a 60% chance that the price will fall is only approximate. By how much must this probability decrease before you would consider changing your mind?

5. I own a Wedgwood vase and need to decide whether to sell it now or keep it for another year in the hope that it will appreciate in value. If I sell it now I will receive £40, but my father is an antique dealer and he thinks there is a 65% chance that it will increase in value over the coming year; if this is the case, I will be able to sell it for £75 in a year's time. If it does not increase in value I will still be able to sell it at the current market value. However, I am very clumsy and there is a 20% chance that I will knock the vase over and break it during the next year. Draw a decision tree to represent this situation and hence decide whether or not I should sell the vase.

Solutions:

1.

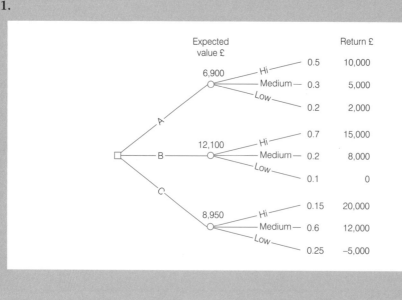

Expected value(Project A) = £6,900

Expected value(Project B) = £12,100

Expected value(Project C) = £8,950

Therefore choose Project B

2. **(i)**   Probability $q = 0.7$

   (ii)   Expected value at A = $0.3 \times 200 - 0.7 \times 10 = £53$

   (iii)   Expected value at B = $0.8 \times 80 + 0.2 \times 0 = £64$

   (iv)   Choose decision 2 since it gives rise to the greatest expected value.

   (v)   In order for you to change your mind, $200p - 10(1 - p) \geq 64$. Hence, $210p - 10 \geq 64$ or $p \geq 74/210 = 0.3524$. To two decimal places any value of p greater than or equal to 0.36 will do.

3.

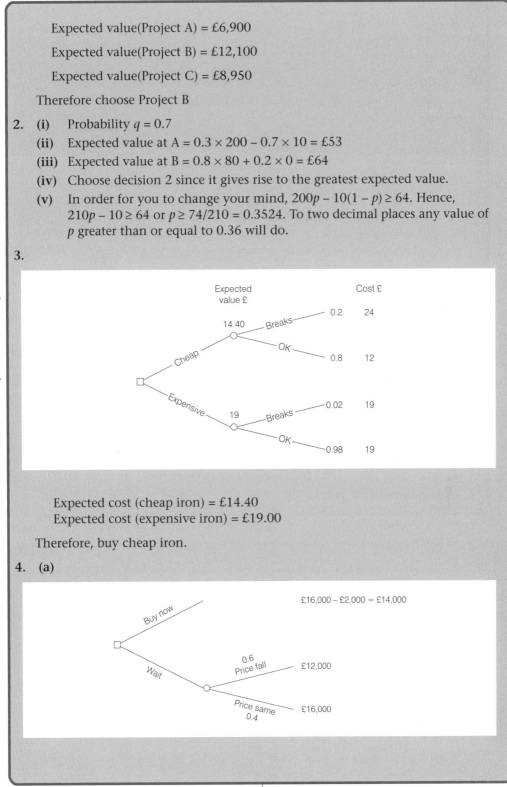

Expected cost (cheap iron) = £14.40
Expected cost (expensive iron) = £19.00

Therefore, buy cheap iron.

4. **(a)**

Expected cost is £14,000 if you buy now and $0.6 \times £12,000 + 0.4 \times £16,000 =$ £13,600 if you wait. You should wait as this option gives rise to the lower expected cost.

(b) $12,000x + 16,000(1 - x) = 14,000$. If we solve this for x we find that $x = 0.5$ and therefore the probability would have to fall to 0.5 before we would consider changing our minds.

5.

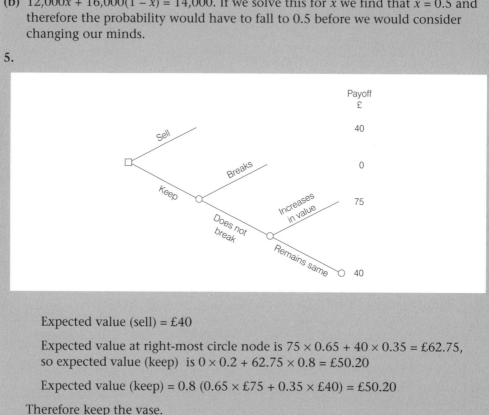

Expected value (sell) = £40

Expected value at right-most circle node is $75 \times 0.65 + 40 \times 0.35 = £62.75$, so expected value (keep) is $0 \times 0.2 + 62.75 \times 0.8 = £50.20$

Expected value (keep) = $0.8 (0.65 \times £75 + 0.35 \times £40) = £50.20$

Therefore keep the vase.

1. Strollers potato snacks company is considering an advertising campaign to increase sales of its 'spicy curls' line. The snacks are sold in 200g packets and the company makes a profit of 50p per packet.

If no advertising is carried out, the sales director is convinced that annual sales of the snacks will be 100,000.

If he decides to carry out the advertising campaign he can either opt for a small local campaign at a cost of £10,000 p.a. or a large national one at a cost of £100,000 p.a.

Projected sales under the two campaigns are likely to follow the probability distributions below:

Projected sales (Units per year)	Small campaign	Large campaign
100,000	0.3	0.1
200,000	0.4	0.2
300,000	0.1	0.2
400,000	0.1	0.2
500,000	0.1	0.3

Draw a decision tree to decide which campaign (if any) the sales director should adopt.

The sales director is now informed that the profit figure per packet he was given is not accurate. What profit figure should lead him to change his mind in favour of the other campaign? What profit figure should lead him to decide that neither campaign is worthwhile?

2. Rannoch Electronics is considering the production of a new component with a five-year product lifetime.

In order to produce this item it would need to build a new plant. The production manager at Rannoch must decide whether to build a large plant at an estimated cost of £1,000,000 or a small plant at an estimated cost of £600,000. The company has already carried out some preliminary research and believes there is a 65% chance that demand for the new component will be high and a 35% chance that demand will be low.

If demand is high, annual cash flows will be £400,000 a year for each of the next five years if the large plant is built or £150,000 a year if the small plant is built.

If demand is low, corresponding annual cash flows will be £50,000 a year if the small plant is built or a loss of £50,000 a year if the large plant is built.

The production manager has a third option available, which is to delay his decision while further research is carried out. If the results of this research are favourable then there is a 90% chance of high demand for the product and a 10% chance of low demand, whereas if the results are adverse there is a 40% chance of high demand and a 60% chance demand will be low. If the production manager decides to carry out this additional research then he will forfeit one year's sales, although cash flows will otherwise be the same as if he had built the small or large plant immediately.

If the results of the additional research are adverse, the manager has the option of shelving the project.

Draw a decision tree to help the production manager decide which course of action is best assuming that there is a 50% chance that the research will lead to favourable results and a 50% chance it will lead to adverse results.

ASSESSMENT 4 (CONTINUED)

BM6
Controlling quality

Work was like a stick. It had two ends. When you worked for the knowing you gave them quality, when you worked for the fool you simply gave him eye-wash.

Alexander Solzhenitsyn (Russian novelist), *One day in the life of Ivan Denisovich* (1962)

Contexts

What is this chapter about?
This chapter introduces Statistical Quality Control, a collection of techniques for monitoring and controlling quality with a view to reducing the proportion of defective goods and services.

Why is it useful?
Manufacturing processes have used quality control techniques for a long time and service industries are beginning to use them, so they can be applied in most organisations.

Where does it fit in?
Quality Management is an all-encompassing philosophy that can be applied throughout an organisation to reduce defective and sub-standard performance. In recent years it has expanded greatly as a subject and may be known by different names elsewhere. The part of the subject used to measure, monitor and control quality, and which is the concern of this chapter, can be called Statistical Quality Control. Most of the techniques of statistical quality control are based on well-known statistical tools and so it is usually regarded as a branch of Statistics.

What do I need to know?
This chapter assumes only that you are familiar with Essential Maths although some optional, fuller explanations require the Probability and Statistics parts of this book.

Objectives

At the end of your work on this chapter you should be able to:

● plot and interpret a control chart for the mean;
● construct and interpret an *R*-chart using the sample ranges;
● construct and interpret a *p*-chart using the proportion of satisfactory items;
● understand the effects of sample size and frequency of sampling on a control chart.

When a customer buys a product or service they have an expectation that it will meet their requirements. These requirements are what we mean by *quality*. A huge amount of effort can be spent detecting poor quality and correcting it but *Quality Management* is about trying to minimise the numbers of defective and sub-standard goods in the first place. Until recently it was applied largely in manufacturing environments but now it is also used in service-related activities.

Statistical quality control is a collection of methods for measuring, monitoring, controlling and improving quality. It is largely done 'on line' in the sense that it is done whilst observing the production process. Some methods are well known, like scatter plots and histograms (see *Describing Data*, Chapter DD1) but some are unique to quality control.

Although statistical methods play a major role in Quality Management, it is an all-encompassing philosophy that must be applied continuously at every stage in the production process and at every level of the organisation. In the last few decades it has been a rapidly-evolving area, subject to numerous, sometimes conflicting, schools of thought, buzzwords and acronyms. So, beware, the same methods may be called different things in different places and some seemingly complicated names can be a cover for quite basic procedures.

You should be able to understand the main ideas in this chapter with no background in probability or statistics. However, some fuller explanations which *do* rely on the probability and statistics chapters of this book are given in some clearly indicated subsections.

1 Control charts for the mean

Being in control

Typically, when a good or service is produced we would like it to be of a standard quality. That is, for particular machine settings or raw materials we would like the product to have particular, predictable, measurements or characteristics. For instance, we would like it to have a particular weight, capacity or strength.

However, we live in a random world and we cannot expect such measurements to be *exactly* the same for every item. In practice, they will be subject to some random variation, often called *noise*, which is the sum of many small unavoidable causes.

When the only source of variation in the quality measurement is due to noise we say that the process is *in control*. However, from time-to-time extra variation is introduced due to what are known as *special causes* or *assignable causes*. These might be defective materials, operator fatigue or machine error. In this case we say that the process is *out of control*.

The aim of *statistical process control* is to monitor the variation in the quality measurements to detect when the process shifts to an out-of-control state. The most powerful statistical process control tool is the *control chart*.

Control charts

Betournay's Pharmaceuticals manufacture tablets. The amount of active ingredient in a tablet is important and when the process is in control it is known that this has an average or *mean* of 32mg. As discussed above, it would be unreasonable to expect *every* tablet to contain exactly this amount, it will vary slightly from tablet to tablet.

To monitor the process, a sample of 10 tablets is taken from the process every minute, the amount of active ingredient in each tablet is measured and the average of the 10 measurements, the sample mean, is calculated.

A control chart for this situation is shown in Figure 6.1. Notice that it is merely a plot of the sample means or averages against time. However, notice also that there are three horizontal lines. The *centre line* represents the average or mean of the process when it is in control. When the process is in control the sample means will vary randomly around this. The other two lines are the *upper control limit* and the *lower control limit*. We will see how they are calculated in due course but their positions are chosen specially so that when the process is in control *most* of the sample means lie between them. A sample mean outside the control limits suggests that the process might be out of control, although we can never be certain, as it might just be a fluke result. In Figure 6.1 the sample means lie within the upper and lower control limits for the first 19 or so time periods, but after that they exceed the upper control limit suggesting that the process may be out of control.

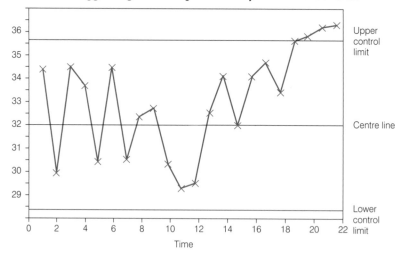

Figure 6.1 A typical control chart.

In general, if the points on the control chart behave in any non-random or systematic way there is cause for concern, even if they are all inside the control limits. For instance, 10 consecutive points above the centre line might suggest that the process is out of control even if they were all below the upper control limit.

Whilst a person can look at a control chart and spot non-random patterns by eye, control charts are usually generated automatically and the control system must be given a set of rules to tell it what constitutes a 'pattern'.

Patterns on control charts

We want to find patterns on the control chart which suggest that the process is out of control. When the process is in control any pattern, however extreme, is possible so we can never be absolutely certain whether the process is in control or not. However, some patterns will be so unlikely when the process is in control that we can take them as indications of an out-of-control state. For instance, a *run up* of length 8 (that is, 8 consecutive points which steadily increase in magnitude) is extremely unlikely when the system is in control and can be taken as an indication of an out-of-control state. In general, a *run* is any sequence of points of the same type. For instance, it might be a sequence of decreasing points or a sequence of points above or below the centre line. Other patterns that might suggest that the process is out of control are a cyclic pattern in the points, which might be due to operator fatigue or overheating of machinery, or alternating points.

Calculating the control limits

To explain how the control limits are calculated we need some notation. We will use the Greek letter μ (pronounced 'mu') to denote the mean or average of the process when it is in control. This is a familiar idea to those who have read Chapter P2, *Numerical Outcomes*. The centre line on the control chart is therefore

$$\text{Centre line} = \mu$$

We will also need the concept of the *variance* of a random quantity. Again, those who have studied Chapter P2 will be familiar with this idea. The variance of a random quantity is a measure of how much it fluctuates or varies. It is usually given by the symbol σ^2, called 'sigma squared'. The square root of this is called the *standard deviation* and is represented by the Greek letter σ, 'sigma'. (Those who have read *Describing Data*, Chapter DD2, will have heard the terms *sample* variance and *sample* standard deviation before. The concept is similar here, the difference being that these are measures of the spread of a particular sample, whereas σ^2 and σ are measurements of the spread of all the possible values that might ever occur.)

The upper and lower control limits of a control chart such as the one in Figure 6.1 are given by

$$\text{Upper control limit (UCL)} = \mu + 3\frac{\sigma}{\sqrt{n}}$$

$$\text{Lower control limit (LCL)} = \mu - 3\frac{\sigma}{\sqrt{n}}$$

where σ is the standard deviation of the process characteristic of interest and n is the number of items in each sample. For example, for the Betournay's Pharmaceuticals example in Figure 6.1 suppose that the variance of the amount of active ingredient in a tablet is known to be $\sigma^2 = 14.4$ so the standard deviation is $\sigma = 3.79$. As the sample size is $n = 10$, the upper and lower control limits are

$$\text{Upper control limit} = 32 + 3\frac{3.79}{\sqrt{10}} = 35.6$$

$$\text{Lower control limit} = 32 - 3\frac{3.79}{\sqrt{10}} = 28.4$$

Returning to the general formulae, notice that the upper and lower control limits are the same distance, $3\sigma/\sqrt{n}$, from the centre line. Notice also that if the standard deviation were larger, the upper and lower control limits would be further from the centre line. This means that when normal variation of the process is high, the sample means can deviate more from the centre line without suggesting that the process is out of control. Also, if the sample size, n, is larger, the control limits will be nearer the centre line and so less variation in the sample means is allowable before an out-of-control state is indicated.

2-sigma and 3-sigma control limits

The control limits above are called *3-sigma* control limits. It can be shown that under certain circumstances* *when the process is in control* the probability that a sample mean lies outside the 3-sigma control limits is 0.0027. (We explain this in the next subsection for those who know about probability and statistical testing.) This means that *when the process is in control* 0.27% (that is, an average of 1 in every 370 sample means) lies outside the control limits and gives a 'false alarm'.

Sometimes, a '2' is used in place of the '3' in the control limits in which case they are called *2-sigma* control limits. Under the same assumptions as above*, the probability that a sample mean lies outside the 2-sigma limits when the process is in control is 0.046. That is, an average of 4.6% or about 1 in 20 of the sample means lies outside the control limits when the process is in control. So, whilst 2-sigma limits are narrower, and therefore more sensitive to changes in the mean level of the process than 3-sigma limits, they give a false alarm more often. We will work with '3-sigma' control limits unless we say otherwise.

Connection with statistical testing

Those of you who know about statistical testing (Chapter S2) may well have realised that something very familiar is going on here. (If you don't know about testing then go on to the next subsection.)

Each time we take a sample we are really doing a statistical test. For Betournay's Pharmaceuticals the null hypothesis is that the process is in control; that is, $H_0: \mu = 32$ and the alternative hypothesis is that it is not; that is, $H_1: \mu \neq 32$. The test statistic is the mean of the sample, $\bar{x}$. As the alternative hypothesis is two-sided, very large and very small values of $\bar{x}$ (that is, those outside the control limits) lead us to reject the null hypothesis.

The significance level of the test is the probability that we reject $H_0: \mu = 32$ when it is really true and so is the probability, when the process is in control, that $\bar{X}$ lies outside the control limits.

However, we know that (when the population is normal or the sample size is large) $\bar{X}$ has a normal distribution with mean μ and variance σ^2/n (Chapter S1, Section 3). The 3-sigma control limits are

$$\mu - 3\frac{\sigma}{\sqrt{n}} \text{ and } \mu + 3\frac{\sigma}{\sqrt{n}}$$

so the probability, when the null hypothesis is true, that a sample mean lies outside these is the probability that a normal random variable lies more than 3 standard deviations from its

---

* The measurement must be *normally* distributed (see *Statistics*, Chapter S 1) or the samples must be large.

mean; that is, 0.0027 (Chapter P3, Section 4). So, using 3-sigma control limits is approximately equivalent to testing the mean at a 0.27% significance level.

In a similar way the probability, when the null hypothesis is true, of exceeding the 2-sigma control limits is the probability that a normal random variable lies more than 2 standard deviations from its mean, which is approximately 0.046. Using 2-sigma control limits is therefore approximately equivalent to testing the mean at a 5% significance level each time we take a sample.

Estimating the process mean and variance

Whilst the process may have a long history, and it may be reasonable to assume that the process mean and variance are known, this is rarely the case and they will usually have to be *estimated*. To do this we take a large number of *preliminary samples* when the process is thought to be in control. The mean of *all* the preliminary sample means, which is often written $\bar{\bar{x}}$ and called 'x double-bar', is used to estimate the process mean, μ.

Estimates of the process variance, σ^2, are often based on the average of the ranges of the preliminary samples. By range we mean the largest measurement less the smallest measurement of each sample. '3-sigma' control limits for the sample mean are then given by

$$\text{Upper control limit (UCL)} = \bar{\bar{x}} + A_2 \bar{R}$$

$$\text{Lower control limit (LCL)} = \bar{\bar{x}} - A_2 \bar{R}$$

where $\bar{R}$ is the average of the sample ranges. A_2 is a particular number that depends on how many items there are in the sample and which we look up in a table. It represents the relationship between the variance of the process and the range of a sample of this size. Table 6.1 shows A_2 and two other numbers that we will use shortly.

Table 6.1 Factors for calculating control charts.

Sample size	A_2	D_3	D_4
2	1.880	0	3.267
3	1.023	0	2.575
4	0.729	0	2.282
5	0.577	0	2.115
6	0.483	0	2.004
7	0.419	0.076	1.924
8	0.373	0.136	1.864
9	0.337	0.184	1.816
10	0.308	0.223	1.777
15	0.223	0.348	1.652
20	0.180	0.414	1.586
25	0.153	0.459	1.541

If any points in the preliminary samples suggest that the process is out of control then any assignable causes should be investigated and, if necessary, these points eliminated from calculations for the control limits. That is, we must be sure that the preliminary samples on which we are basing our estimates are taken when the process is in control.

Check this

The following table shows the average percentage of fat in samples of 7 pots of chocolate dessert and the range of each sample. (Percentages were measured to an integer number.) Taking these as preliminary samples, calculate upper and lower control limits for the average fat content.

Sample	Sample mean	Range
1	22.5	9
2	21.2	10
3	25.0	11
4	24.2	12
5	26.1	13
6	27.2	14
7	24.1	13
8	23.8	15
9	22.7	16
10	25.3	12
11	27.4	11
12	26.2	10
13	24.3	13
14	22.6	12

Solution:
The average of the sample means is $\bar{\bar{x}} = 24.47$, and the average range is $\bar{R} = 12.21$. Using these as estimates on which to base the control chart, the upper and lower control limits are $24.47 + 0.419 \times 12.21 = 29.59$ and $24.47 - 0.419 \times 12.21 = 19.35$. All points lie within these limits and there are no obvious long runs, so the process appears to be in control.

Using software
In SPSS

Graphs > Control

enables you to draw a control chart. The data from the samples are placed in a single column and another column is used to indicate the sample number.

More specialised software for process control, however, allows the user to select from a set of 'tests' or rules for spotting patterns, often called, 'tests for special causes'. Examples of such tests might be, *one point more than 3 sigmas from center line* or *nine points in a row on same side of center line* and so on.

Check this

Interpret the following control chart and output for the mean amount of active ingredient in samples of 10 tablets.

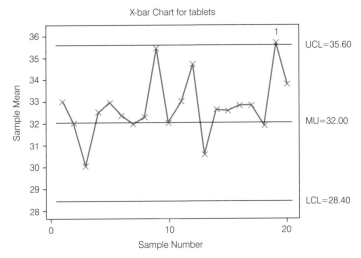

X-bar Chart for tablets

TEST 1. One point more than 3.0 sigmas from center line.
Test Failed at points: 19

Solution:
The only indication that the process may be out of control is at point 19 where the observation is above the upper control limit.

WORK CARD 1

1. The weight, in grams, of samples of 3 cheesecakes baked by Barbara's Cheesecake factory and taken every hour are shown below, along with their averages and ranges. Assuming that the mean weight of a cheesecake when a process is in control is 250g and the standard deviation is 5g, construct a control chart for the mean and comment.
    The data are in *cheesecake*.

Sample no.	Cheesecake samples			Average	Max	Min	Range
1	258	258.37	253.73	256.70	258.37	253.73	4.64
2	259.4	255	258.35	257.58	259.4	255	4.4
3	253.37	253.59	243.75	250.24	253.59	243.75	9.84
4	246.97	264.9	249.01	253.63	264.9	246.97	17.93
5	245.86	245.96	256.05	249.29	256.05	245.86	10.19
6	261.3	258.59	261.56	260.48	261.56	258.59	2.97
7	252.62	255.5	252.37	253.50	255.5	252.37	3.13

WORK CARD 1 (CONTINUED)

Sample no.	Cheesecake samples			Average	Max	Min	Range
8	269.02	251.6	229.26	249.96	269.02	229.26	39.76
9	260.36	260.82	243.75	254.98	260.82	243.75	17.07
10	242.87	237.66	254.91	245.15	254.91	237.66	17.25
11	254.82	264.23	242.53	253.86	264.23	242.53	21.7
12	244.49	251.25	249.72	248.49	251.25	244.49	6.76
13	244.42	259.32	256.14	253.29	259.32	244.42	14.9
14	254.45	255.14	251.93	253.84	255.14	251.93	3.21
15	253	242.17	244.27	246.48	253	242.17	10.83
16	259.04	250.92	248.41	252.79	259.04	248.41	10.63
17	257.21	253.07	255.59	255.29	257.21	253.07	4.14
18	244.9	247.62	248.86	247.13	248.86	244.9	3.96
19	253.16	251.17	254.58	252.97	254.58	251.17	3.41
20	241.68	247.78	253.15	247.54	253.15	241.68	11.47

2. Now suppose that the mean and standard deviation of the process in question **1** above are *not* known. Using all the samples in **1** as preliminary samples, calculate upper and lower control limits. Do the data suggest that the process is out of control during the preliminary period?

Solutions:

1. Using the known standard deviation, the upper and lower control limits are

$$250 + 3\sqrt{\frac{25}{3}} = 258.7 \quad \text{and} \quad 250 - 3\sqrt{\frac{25}{3}} = 241.3$$

The 6th sample mean is outside these limits. The first and second sample means are both outside the 2-sigma limits (255.77 and 244.22).

2. The average of the averages is 252.16 and the average range is 10.91. Using these as estimates on which to base the control chart, the upper and lower control limits are 252.16 + 1.023 × 10.91 = 263.3 and 252.16 − 1.023 × 10.91 = 241.0. All points lie within these limits and there are no obvious long runs so the process appears to be in control.

ASSESSMENT 1

1. A new type of battery is designed to have an average lifetime of 64 hours with standard deviation 5 hours. 30 samples of four such batteries are taken from a process to estimate the control limits and then a further 20 samples are taken. The data are shown below and are in *battery*.

Sample	Lifetime			
1	53	59	53	59
2	58	62	63	59
3	61	61	61	67
4	50	49	55	59
5	61	55	53	66
6	58	64	55	61
7	57	60	56	55
8	65	61	62	71
9	58	59	56	56
10	64	61	56	61
11	63	64	61	61
12	63	55	64	65
13	61	63	61	59
14	60	58	60	66
15	65	59	55	67
16	63	50	59	54
17	58	55	50	70
18	54	61	56	70
19	58	65	59	60
20	55	66	64	55
21	57	57	59	62
22	61	59	66	57
23	53	51	57	58
24	68	56	57	69
25	54	54	55	62
26	56	69	57	63
27	61	64	63	62
28	63	64	62	60
29	62	64	67	57
30	64	56	54	61
31	56	62	55	59
32	67	57	63	60
33	65	49	55	54
34	63	57	63	49
35	61	68	60	66
36	66	64	59	62

Sample	Lifetime			
37	59	59	65	59
38	58	55	56	68
39	61	65	60	51
40	65	57	61	63
41	57	56	63	54
42	54	64	63	51
43	47	57	55	65
44	67	58	67	60
45	53	60	66	58
46	69	61	57	67
47	65	51	59	59
48	55	60	64	58
49	69	51	61	56
50	60	55	62	69

(i) Without using software, calculate upper and lower control limits assuming that the desired mean and standard deviation hold. Calculate the means of the first 10 samples and comment.

(ii) Using software, use the first 30 samples of data to calculate the control limits and construct a control chart for the sample means. Perform any tests that are available in your software, report the results and comment.

2 *R*-charts and *p*-charts

Controlling the range

Even if the mean of a process is in control, the quality measurement may *vary* more than it should in an in-control state. To monitor the variation in the process we draw an *R*-chart using the *ranges* of the samples. The control limits are constructed from $\bar{R}$, the average of the sample ranges, as follows.

$$\text{Upper control limit} = D_4\bar{R}$$

$$\text{Lower control limit} = D_3\bar{R}$$

where D_3 and D_4 depend on the size of the sample and are taken from Table 6.1. The centre line is

$$\text{Centre line} = \bar{R}$$

Small sample ranges are good news because they indicate very little variation in the quality measurement. However, we calculate lower control limits for the range because ranges below the lower control limit suggest an improvement in the process variation which it may be useful to know about. For small samples D_3 is zero and so the lower control limit is 0 anyway.

Check this

We repeat below the ranges of the 14 samples of 7 pots of chocolate dessert from the last section. Construct an R-chart.

Sample	Range	Sample	Range
1	9	8	15
2	10	9	16
3	11	10	12
4	12	11	11
5	13	12	10
6	14	13	13
7	13	14	12

Solution:
The average of these ranges is $\bar{R}$ = 12.21. As each sample has size 7 we need 0.076 and 1.924 from Table 6.1. The lower and upper control limits are therefore 0.076 × 12.21 = 0.93 and 1.924 × 12.21 = 23.49 respectively. An R-chart follows. The control limits are slightly different due to rounding in the manual calculations.

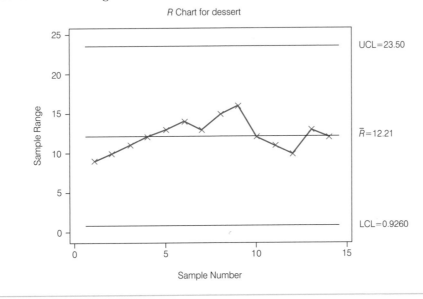

If the process is out of control in the sense that there is too much variability, the control limits for the mean will be misleading, so it is usual to construct an R-chart before a chart for the mean.

Attribute control charts

The quality characteristic of interest is not always a numerical measurement. Sometimes, the product or service has, or does not have, a particular feature or *attribute*. In particular, we are usually interested in whether it is satisfactory or defective. In this case the *proportion* of items in the sample that possess the attribute is recorded on the control chart instead of the sample mean. A control chart produced in this way is called a *p*-chart.

Suppose that when the process is in control the proportion of items with the characteristic of interest is known and is *p*. The 3-sigma upper and lower control limits for a proportion are

$$\text{Upper control limit} = p + 3\sqrt{\frac{p(1-p)}{n}}$$

$$\text{Lower control limit} = p - 3\sqrt{\frac{p(1-p)}{n}}$$

and the centre line is

$$\text{Centre line} = p$$

The upper and lower control limits are valid for large values of n only. If you know about normal distributions (Chapter P3), the control limits are calculated in this way because, for large samples, the proportion in the sample with a particular characteristic has, approximately, a normal distribution with mean p and variance $\frac{p(1-p)}{n}$. The control limits are, therefore, 3 standard deviations away from p in the same way as they are for control charts for the mean.

Check this

When a process is in control the proportion of satisfactory items is 90%. Samples of 80 items are taken every 10 minutes and the proportion of items in each sample which are satisfactory is observed. Calculate the upper and lower control limits for the proportion of satisfactory items.

Solution:

There are 80 items in each sample and the in-control proportion is $p = 0.9$ so the limits are

$$0.9 + 3\sqrt{\frac{0.9(1-0.9)}{80}} = 1.0006 \quad \text{and} \quad 0.9 - 3\sqrt{\frac{0.9(1-0.9)}{80}} = 0.7994$$

Check this

A *p*-chart is shown below along with some test results. Does the process appear to be in control? Comment.

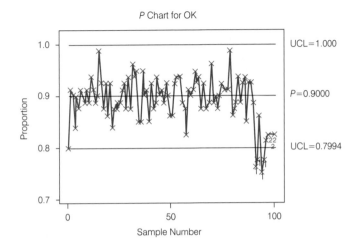

P Chart for OK

TEST 1. One point more than 3.0 sigmas from center line.
Test Failed at points: 91 92 94 95
TEST 2. Nine points in a row on same side of center line.
Test Failed at points: 98 99 100

Solution:
Four points after the 90th time-period are below the lower control limit and all the points from the 90th onwards are below the centre line. The chart suggests that the process is going out of control and producing a smaller proportion of satisfactory goods towards the end of the sample period.

In practice, like *R*-charts and mean charts, the proportion of satisfactory items when the process is in control will not be known and so we use the average proportion of a set of preliminary samples instead of *p* in the above.

Designing a control chart
We have already discussed the choice of control limits for a control chart but designing a control chart also requires that we choose the sample size and the frequency of sampling. We would like to detect an out-of-control state as soon as possible, so in an ideal world large samples, which are more sensitive to changes in the process, would be taken very frequently.

In the past, when control charts were plotted by hand, there were physical limits to the frequency at which samples could be taken, but now they are produced by automatic sensing equipment and computers the frequency can be increased. However, there are usually still some limitations on the total amount of sampling effort that can be used. The issue is therefore one of obtaining a balance between sample size and frequency of sampling.

It is sometimes useful to look at the *average run length* (ARL) of the control chart. This is the average number of time periods that must be sampled before the control limits are exceeded. We have already seen, for the '3-sigma' chart, that when the process is in control an average of 1/0.0027 = 370 points would have to be plotted between out-of-control signals; that is, the ARL when the process is in control is 370. As this is a false alarm we would like the ARL to be large. In a similar way, it is possible to work out the *out-of-control*

ARL which is the number of samples needed to give an out-of-control warning when the process has shifted by a particular amount. As this is desirable we would like it to be small. Increasing the sample size will decrease the out-of-control ARL enabling shifts in the process to be detected sooner. Tables of ARLs for process shifts of particular magnitudes and sample sizes are available.

Other tools for statistical process control

We have only been able to give you an introduction to statistical process control. There are many extensions for different types of data. For instance, what do you do if there is only one observation in each sample (you haven't got a sample range to use). Further, control charts are only one tool of statistical process control, although perhaps the most-used.

WORK CARD 2

1. Returning to Barbara's cheesecake factory from **Work card 1**, recall that samples of 3 cheesecakes are taken every hour. Construct an *R*-chart and comment.

2. The following data are 40 samples of size 5 taken from a surgical-tool manufacturing process. They give the diameter in mm of a hole in the tool. The first 20 samples are to be used to estimate the control limits. Use software to produce a control chart for the sample mean and an *R*-chart and comment. The data are in *holes*.

Sample	Diameter (mm)				
1	3.40	3.36	3.07	3.07	3.58
2	3.30	3.14	3.04	2.98	3.09
3	3.10	2.92	3.37	3.26	3.12
4	3.12	2.98	2.88	2.97	3.29
5	3.23	3.32	3.23	2.85	3.29
6	3.43	3.32	3.35	3.53	3.28
7	3.28	3.27	2.98	3.22	2.99
8	3.35	2.93	3.11	3.01	3.24
9	2.99	2.99	3.20	3.30	3.13
10	3.07	3.40	3.02	3.06	3.27
11	2.95	3.12	2.99	3.45	3.11
12	3.08	3.00	3.45	2.95	3.23
13	3.15	3.35	3.12	3.05	3.00
14	3.37	3.24	3.25	2.87	2.94
15	3.44	3.25	3.09	3.38	2.86
16	2.98	3.56	3.27	2.84	3.46
17	3.28	3.35	3.26	3.24	3.44
18	3.02	3.29	3.14	2.98	2.94
19	2.91	2.92	3.19	3.27	3.39
20	2.97	3.26	2.80	3.33	3.09

Sample	Diameter (mm)				
21	2.86	2.95	3.02	3.48	3.27
22	3.15	3.31	3.07	3.15	3.15
23	3.30	2.84	2.89	3.11	3.19
24	3.28	3.67	3.08	3.04	3.20
25	3.45	3.65	3.19	3.43	3.39
26	3.23	3.09	3.31	3.03	3.52
27	3.40	3.29	3.30	3.05	3.00
28	3.37	3.15	3.60	3.02	3.21
29	3.13	3.54	3.06	3.42	2.70
30	3.06	3.29	3.00	2.78	3.11
31	3.21	3.42	3.36	3.39	3.00
32	3.11	3.23	2.94	3.26	3.89
33	3.39	3.33	3.05	2.93	3.49
34	3.58	3.06	3.23	3.20	2.54
35	3.04	3.46	3.40	2.85	2.87
36	3.13	3.08	3.11	3.19	3.14
37	3.30	3.34	3.66	3.67	3.31
38	3.60	3.81	3.72	3.24	3.50
39	3.56	3.46	3.70	3.82	3.72
40	3.50	3.40	4.10	3.90	3.70

3. It is desirable that telephone calls to a call centre are answered within 20 seconds. Each day a sample of 100 calls is taken and the number of calls that are answered within 20 seconds is recorded. The results for 20 days are shown below. The data are in *call centre*.

Day	Calls	Day	Calls
1	82	11	78
2	86	12	75
3	84	13	77
4	86	14	82
5	83	15	81
6	90	16	79
7	90	17	83
8	85	18	87
9	82	19	85
10	80	20	87

(i)   Calculate upper and lower control limits assuming that 85% of calls are answered within 20 seconds when the process is in control.

(ii)   Now calculate the control limits from the data.

(iii) Construct both control charts and comment.

Solutions:

1. The mean range of the samples is 10.91. Multiplying by $D_4 = 2.575$ and $D_3 = 0$ gives 28.09 and 0 for the upper and lower limits respectively. The R-chart is shown below. Point 8 is very extreme and should perhaps be looked at carefully.

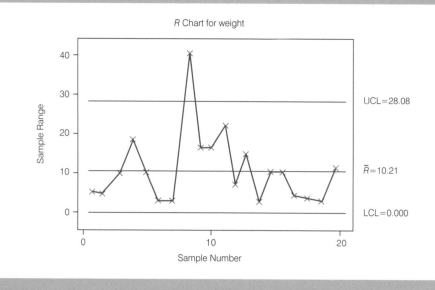

2. The average of the means of the first 20 samples is 3.165 and using the range to estimate the control limits gives upper and lower limits of 3.412 and 2.919 respectively. There is clearly a problem for the later samples. Some test output is shown below.

```
TEST 1. One point more than 3.00 sigmas from center line.
Test Failed at points: 25 37 38 39 40

TEST 3. Six points in a row all increasing or all decreasing.
Test Failed at points: 40

TEST 5. 2 out of 3 points in a row more than 2 sigmas from center line (on
one side of CL).
Test Failed at points: 38 39 40

TEST 6. 4 out of 5 points in a row more than 1 sigma from center line (on
one side of CL).
Test Failed at points: 40
```

The R-chart looks better. The average range is 0.4265 and control limits are 0.9018 and 0. Two samples between the 30th and 40th slightly exceed these 3-sigma limits.

3. **(i)** As $p = 0.85$ the upper and lower control limits are

$$0.85 + 3\sqrt{\frac{0.85(1-0.85)}{100}} = 0.957 \quad \text{and} \quad 0.85 - 3\sqrt{\frac{0.85(1-0.85)}{100}} = 0.743$$

Plotting the sample proportions on a chart shows no points out of this range. However, nine consecutive points lie below the centre line up to point 17 which may be cause for concern. There may have been a problem that was rectified later.

(ii) When the first ten samples are used to estimate the control limits the estimate of p is extremely close to 0.85 and so the control limits are much the same as in **(i)**. A similar warning occurs.

1. **(i)** Using software use the first 30 samples of the battery lifetime data in **Assessment 1** to calculate control limits for the range. Comment on the results.

   (ii) Now use estimates taken from all 50 samples to produce control charts for the sample mean and range. Comment.

2. The number of students who attend, out of 75 who are registered, is recorded for every lecture of a 30-lecture course. The data are given below (row-wise) and are in attendance.

54	48	49	48	53
50	51	55	53	59
48	56	56	51	56
59	49	50	54	54
45	49	41	53	40
48	52	45	47	35

   (i) Calculate the upper and lower control limits for a p-chart when it is acknowledged that the proportion of students who usually attend is 70%.

   (ii) Calculate the upper and lower control limits for a p-chart using the data from the first 15 lectures. How do they compare with those in **(i)**?

   (iii) Construct a p-chart for the whole data set using the control limits you calculated in **(ii)** and comment.

Further reading: see p. xv

Montgomery and Runger is a useful further source on quality control, as is Anderson *et al.* (Statistics).

Newbold *et al.* include slightly more detail than we do and use the software Minitab.

BM7
Simulating reality

The camera makes everyone a tourist in other people's reality, and eventually in one's own.

Susan Sontag, *New York Review of Books* (1974)

Contexts

What is this chapter about?
In this chapter we consider how to simulate the way a real-life system works over time.

Why is it useful?
Simulating a system allows us to experiment to assess the likely consequences of various changes without causing disruption to the real system. For example, a simulation of a distribution company could be used to investigate whether changes in route allocations or shift patterns resulted in reduced costs or speedier deliveries.

Simulation is the most-used Management Science tool after linear programming. This is mainly because there is no, 'set' form of model and so it can be used when none of the other Management Science models is appropriate.

Where does it fit in?
Simulation is usually regarded as an area of Management Science or Operational Research. It draws heavily on Probability to model uncertain happenings, and on Statistics to analyse the results of the simulation.

What do I need to know?
Sections 1 and 2 of this chapter require Essential Maths. A knowledge of Probability will help greatly for section 3 but is essential for section 4.

Objectives

After your work on this chapter you should:

- be able to use a table to run a simple simulation;
- be able to generate some random inputs using random number tables or a computer;
- understand next-event and fixed-increment time advance mechanisms;
- understand what a transient period is;
- recognise when a binomial, Poisson, uniform, normal or exponential distribution is appropriate for a simulation and generate sequences of random inputs from these distributions;
- know something about the single server queue, its limitations and why queuing problems tend to be simulated.

Simulation is the technique of *imitating* the way a real-life *system* changes over time. By system we mean one or more components or *entities* which interact with each other. For instance, if the system of interest is an airport the entities might be the runway, arriving and departing aircraft, service vehicles, air-traffic controllers, ground staff and so on. Other systems might be a computer network, hospital, supermarket, manufacturing plant or, for weather simulations, our atmosphere.

In this chapter we introduce the idea of simulation and see how the behaviour of the entities can be modelled. The final section, Section 4, requires some knowledge of probability distributions.

1 Why simulate?

Simulation allows us to consider the effects of changes to a system without actually changing it. It is used when experimenting with the real system would be too disruptive, costly or dangerous, or would take a ridiculous length of time.

For example, suppose that some specialist wards of a hospital are nearly always full and patients have to be turned away, whereas other specialist wards often have empty beds. The hospital management would like to change the types of care offered by the various wards to spread utilisation more evenly and so allow more patients to be treated. There are several possible ways of making the changes but they all require disruptive movement of equipment and transfer of staff at considerable expense.

A simulation would model the arrival of patients, their allocation to appropriate wards and the duration of their stay and so demonstrate the likely pattern of usage for each set of changes. It could then be used to 'experiment', in a way that would not be possible with the real system, to find successful ways of controlling utilisation.

The business models we have considered so far have had two main limitations:

- First, so that a solution can be found, they have had to take a particular mathematical form. This often means that the models have had to make restrictive assumptions that may not be appropriate for the real system. For instance, linear programming models are made up of linear equations and the basic EOQ model assumes that demand is constant.
- Second, the linear programming, inventory and network models we have considered are all *deterministic*, meaning that they assume that there is no uncertainty in the system. More advanced models of these types allow random quantities to be modelled using probability; that is, they are *stochastic* but there are usually particular 'patterns', called probability distributions, which the probabilities must take to ensure a solution exists.

Simulation models overcome both these problems because they can be as flexible as you want them to be. First, any logical relation or relationship between the entities can be modelled, and second, any probability distribution can be represented. The downside of this flexibility is that simulation models do not have a solution as such. They are executed or *run* through time recording the state of the system as it changes. Each time a stochastic simulation is run it produces one picture or *realisation* of how the real system could evolve over time. When it is run again, different random quantities, albeit with similar characteristics as before, will be generated and used and another, slightly different, realisation will be produced. In this way, a simulation is like an experiment. During each run statistics are collected that measure the performance of the system. To obtain a representative sample of performance measures we repeat the experiment; that is, run the simulation a number of times and/or for a long time period.

All but the very simplest simulation models need to be programmed and run on a computer. More complicated simulations will have to be written using specialist computer software but simpler ones can be programmed using a spreadsheet. In this chapter we illustrate the main ideas of simulation using some simple examples that can be calculated by hand.

2 A simple simulation

Introducing the car-wash

Geoff's Car-Wash currently offers only one sort of car-wash but Geoff is considering the purchase of a new machine that would offer three types: Quick, which takes 3 minutes; Super, which takes 4 minutes, and the Superwax which takes 9 minutes. However, Geoff is concerned that customers may have to queue too long for the new car-wash and/or that it may be under- or over-utilised. He would therefore like to know something about the average time a customer would have to wait and the proportion of time the new car-wash would be busy. We are therefore going to develop a simulation of the new car-wash to estimate these quantities and help him make his purchase decision.

Random inputs

To simulate the operation of the new car-wash we need to generate the times at which customers arrive and the type of car-wash chosen by each customer. These times and choices must be typical of the times and choices that would happen in the real system and we will see how to obtain them in due course. For now, however, we will assume that we already have a sequence of numbers that are typical of the times in minutes between customers arriving, the *inter-arrival* times and that this starts

$$2, 1, 4, 5, 0, 1, 10, \ldots$$

and another sequence of the numbers 3, 4 and 9 which represents the duration of car-washes:

$$3, 3, 4, 9, 3, 4, 3, \ldots$$

These two sequences of numbers will determine what happens for the whole of the simulation. We call them the random *inputs* to the simulation.

We are going to present the simulation in a table, one row for each customer. The first column will identify the customer and the following two columns will contain the random inputs as shown below. We will add more columns shortly.

Geoff's Car-Wash

Customer number	Inputs	
	Inter-arrival time	Wash time
1	2	3
2	1	3
3	4	4
4	5	9
5	0	3
6	1	4
7	10	3

Event times

Remember, we are interested in how long customers would have to wait for the new car-wash and the proportion of time it would be busy.

To calculate how long each customer has to wait we need to know the time they arrive and the time they enter the car-wash (immediate if the wash is empty). And to know for how long the machine is busy or idle we need to know the time each car-wash starts and ends. These times, called *event times*, can be deduced from the random inputs. We are going to place the event times in the next few columns of the table.

Outputs

Once we know the event times we can use them to calculate the time each customer has to wait (*Waiting time*) and the time the machine is busy (*Busy time*). These are the *outputs* or *responses* of the simulation because they are the measurements we are interested in and we will show them in the final columns of the table.

The full form of the table is shown below. Whilst this is a manual simulation, computer software might also represent the simulation in this way. So far only the random inputs have been entered but we will see shortly that all the other columns can be calculated from the random input columns.

Geoff's Car-Wash

	Inputs		Event times			Outputs	
Customer number	Inter-arrival time	Wash time	Arrival time	Wash start	Wash end	Waiting time	Busy time
1	2	3					
2	1	3					
3	4	4					
4	5	9					
5	0	3					
6	1	4					
7	10	3					

Starting the simulation

We'll start the simulation by assuming that it starts at time 0 and that the car-wash is empty at that time. These are the *initial conditions*. We then build it up one row (or customer) at a time.

First the event times for customer 1. The first *Inter-arrival time* is 2, so customer 1 arrives at time 2 and we enter a 2 in the first row of the *Arrival time* column. The car-wash is empty so customer 1 drives in immediately and the first *Wash start* is also at time 2. From the *Wash time* input customer 1 chooses the 3-minute wash so his *Wash end* is at time 2 + 3 = 5.

And now the output columns. As customer 1's *Arrival time* is 2 and his *Wash start* time is also 2, his *Waiting time* is 2 – 2 = 0 minutes. Further, the machine was in use for 3 minutes with customer 1 and so *Busy time* = 3.

All the table entries for customer 1 are shown below. Check that you can see where they have come from.

	Inputs		Event times			Outputs	
Customer number	Inter-arrival time	Wash time	Arrival time	Wash start	Wash end	Waiting time	Busy time
1	2	3	2	2	5	0	3

Check this

Continue the simulation for the second customer. (The second *Inter-arrival time* is 1 and the second *Wash time* is 3.)

Solution:

Customer 2 arrives 1 minute after customer 3, at time 3. Customer 1 does not leave the wash until time 5 so customer 2 has to wait until time 5 to start. He takes 3 minutes so finishes at time 8 having run-up 2 minutes of *Waiting time* and having kept the car-wash busy for 3 minutes.

	Inputs		Event times			Outputs	
Customer number	Inter-arrival time	Wash time	Arrival time	Wash start	Wash end	Waiting time	Busy time
1	2	3	2	2	5	0	3
2	1	3	3	5	8	2	3

We continue in this vein and complete the table for a further five customers.

Check this

Complete the simulation table for the first 7 customers.

Solution:

Car-wash simulation for 7 customers

	Inputs		Event times			Outputs	
Customer number	Inter-arrival time	Wash time	Arrival time	Wash start	Wash end	Waiting time	Busy time
1	2	3	2	2	5	0	3
2	1	3	3	5	8	2	3
3	4	4	7	8	12	1	4
4	5	9	12	12	21	0	9
5	0	3	12	21	24	9	3
6	1	4	13	24	28	11	4
7	10	3	23	28	31	5	3
					Total	28	29

Summary statistics

When the simulation is complete we calculate summary statistics from the outputs. Here, the total *Waiting time* for the 7 customers is 28 minutes so the average *Waiting time* is 4 minutes and the car-wash is busy for 29 minutes out of 31 minutes, 94% of the time. Our initial impression, from this short simulation, is that that although the machine is going to be well-used, customers will have to wait several minutes on average. However, we have only simulated 7 customers so the average *Waiting time* we have calculated is based on a sample of size 7 and as such is *not* likely to be a good estimate of the average *Waiting time* of the new car-wash. To get a better estimate we would need to simulate the car-wash for many more customers.

To run the simulation for longer periods it would be sensible to program a spreadsheet. *Arrival time* is the previous customer's *Arrival time* plus the current customer's *Inter-arrival time*; *Wash start* is the maximum of the *Arrival time* of the current customer and the *Wash end* time of the previous customer; *Wash end* time is *Wash start* plus *Wash time*; *Waiting time* is *Wash start* minus *Arrival time* and *Busy time* is equal to the *Wash time*.

1. A newsagent works alone in his shop and it always takes him one minute to serve a customer. Simulate the newsagent's shop for a 30-minute interval using the following customer inter-arrival times (minutes)

    1, 0, 2, 1, 2, 0, 4, 1, 0, 0, 0, 2, 2, 2, 2, 1, 1, 2, 2, 5

    Estimate the proportion of time the newsagent is busy serving customers and the average number of minutes a customer has to wait.

Solution:

1. A suitable table for the simulation starting at time 0 with no customers in the shop might be:

	Inputs		Event times		Output	
Customer number	Inter-arrival time	Arrival time	Service start	Service end	Server busy	Waiting time
1	1	1	1	2	1	0
2	0	1	2	3	1	1
3	2	3	3	4	1	0
4	1	4	4	5	1	0
5	2	6	6	7	1	0
6	0	6	7	8	1	1
etc.						
					Total	

The total of the *Server busy* column divided by 30 estimates the proportion of time the newsagent is busy and the total of the *Waiting time* column divided by the number of customers estimates the average number of minutes a customer has to wait.

1. Think of a system that is familiar to you. For instance, you might consider the kitchen you share with other students or the car park at your university. Decide which entities of the system you wish to model and which statistics you want to measure. For instance, for the kitchen example the entities might be the hobs, oven and the microwave and the students coming in to use them, and you might be interested in the proportion of time the hobs, microwave and oven are used.

    Devise column headings for a table for a simulation of this system. State which columns would contain inputs and write down, using words or symbols, how the event-times columns and output columns would be derived from these.

    Now write down an arbitrary (but vaguely realistic) sequence of numbers for each input and calculate the first few lines of the simulation. (We will see how to obtain sequences of random inputs more sensibly in the next section.) Use a spreadsheet if you wish.

3 Generating random inputs

In Section 2 we saw how to build a simple simulation model but we didn't tell you how to obtain the two sequences of random inputs. In this section we see how to generate random sequences to represent different types of input. For the later parts of this section some knowledge of probability (Chapters P2 and P3) would be an advantage but is not essential.

The random inputs to a simulation should reflect the uncertainty in the real system as closely as possible. That is, we would like to generate the sequences of numbers so that they are typical of those which might occur in the real system.

For instance, for Geoff's Car-Wash in Section 1 we said that the new car-wash offered three durations of wash: 3 minutes, 4 minutes and 9 minutes. Suppose that a similar car-wash at a comparable location has been observed over a long period and that 60% of customers choose the 3-minute car-wash, 30% the 4-minute car-wash and the remaining 10% chose the 9-minute car-wash. We would like the simulation to choose the *Wash time* for each customer with the same probabilities; that is, we would like the *Wash time* to be 3 minutes with a probability of 0.6, 4 minutes with probability 0.3 and 9 minutes with a probability of 0.1. In statistical parlance we would like to generate a *discrete random variable*, X, with the following *probability distribution*. (See *Probability*, Chapter P2).

x	$P(x)$
3	0.6
4	0.3
9	0.1

We should also assume something else about the sequence of *Wash times*. The choice of *Wash time* for any customer should not be influenced in any way by the *Wash time* chosen by any previous (or later) customers. In statistical language we require that the *Wash times* are *statistically independent*.

We will see shortly that numbers can be generated with particular probabilities using a spreadsheet or statistical software like SPSS. However, in the absence of such things, if you only need to generate a few numbers you can use a table of *random numbers*.

Tables of random numbers
If you have read Chapter S1 (*Estimation*) you will already know about tables of random numbers, but we explain them again here. A few rows from a random number table (Table IV) are shown below.

```
07340  35237  80262  86251  71212  60487  94168  15901  65011
02048  33399  88485  97329  89258  49214  89019  24721  62072
59041  53531  37094  49462  91927  87603  96807  39820  48628
19094  90853  15216  10734  31918  05510  71413  83183  77748
82817  95485  04551  12531  68272  22939  09492  54673  09108
```

As you can see, a table of random numbers is just that – rows of digits, often grouped in blocks for ease of reading. Although the table might include strings of digits like 99999 or 12345 which may not seem very 'random', the whole point is that it was created by a procedure in which every digit has an equal chance of being any digit from 0 to 9 regardless of what precedes it. So, for instance, even if we already have a sequence like 9999 the next digit still has a one in ten chance of being a 9. This means that if we pick an arbitrary starting place in Table IV and take individual digits, or pairs of digits (or threes or fours ... and so on), each possible digit (0 to 9), pair (00, 01, ..., 99), (or three or four ... and, so on), is equally likely to occur.

Generating discrete random variables

For the car-wash example we want to generate a *Wash time* of 3 with a probability of 0.6, 4 with a probability of 0.3, and 9 with a probability of 0.1. For this we can use single digits from the random number table. We are going to *assign* each random digit from 0 to 9 inclusive to one of the possible *Wash times* (3, 4 or 9) as follows:

Random digit	Wash time
0	3
1	3
2	3
3	3
4	3
5	3
6	4
7	4
8	4
9	9

Notice that six of the 10 random digits have been assigned to a *Wash time* of 3, three of the 10 random digits have been assigned to a *Wash time* of 4 and just one to a *Wash time* of 9. In this way, if we pick a digit at random from Table IV there is a 6/10 = 60% chance it will give a 3-minute *Wash time*, a 3/10 = 30% chance it will give a 4-minute *Wash time* and a 1/10 = 10% chance it will give a *Wash time* of 9 minutes, as required.

To generate a sequence of *Wash times* with the desired probability we start at an arbitrary place in Table IV and write down the *Wash times* implied by the random digits we find. For instance, if we start from the second batch of random digits in the third row of the table above and move right we have random digits 535313709449462 ... which we assign to *Wash times* 3, 3, 3, 3, 3, 3, 4, 3, 9, 3, 3, 9, 3, 4, 3 respectively.

The probabilities we require will not always be convenient multiples of 10%. Try the following example.

> ### Check this
>
> Generate a sequence of ten numbers representing the weekly demand for an aircraft part when past data indicates that there is a 3% chance that demand will be for 4 parts, 13% for 3 parts, 19% for 2 parts, 32% for 1 part and 33% for no parts.
>
> **Solution:**
> As the probabilities are expressed as percentages and not tens of percentages we will have to take *pairs* of random digits from the table. Any way of assigning pairs of random digits

to demands for parts is acceptable provided that 3 out of the 100 possible pairs are assigned a demand of 4, 13 pairs a demand of 3, 19 pairs a demand of 2, 32 a demand of 1 and 33 a zero demand. We assign the pairs from 00 to 99 as follows:

Random digits	Demand
00–02	4
03–15	3
16–34	2
35–66	1
67–99	0

Taking the final column block of random numbers from the extract above in pairs we have 65, 01, 16, 20, 72, 48, 62, 87, 77, 48 which give 1, 4, 2, 2, 0, 1, 1, 0, 0, and 1 units of demand respectively.

Generating random numbers using a computer

In practice it is much easier to use a spreadsheet or statistical software to generate discrete random variables.

In Excel you must place the possible values in a column and the associated probabilities in the corresponding rows of the column immediately to the right. You then need the **random number generation** data analysis tool. In the dialog box request a **discrete distribution** and supply the location of the values and their probabilities, called the **value and probability input range**. You will also be asked for the **output range**, that is the row and column range where you wish the generated numbers to be placed.

A histogram of 50 demands generated this way is shown in Figure 7.1.

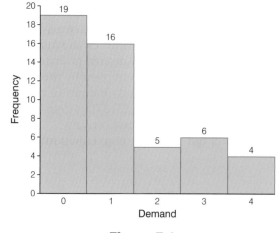

Figure 7.1

It is important to realise that these 50 simulated numbers are a *sample* of all possible aircraft part demands. So, for instance, the proportion of 0s in the sample will not necessarily be the same as the desired probability of 0.33, although we would expect it to be vaguely similar (it is 19/50 = 0.38). Roughly speaking, the larger the number of values simulated, the closer we expect the proportions in the data to be to the desired probabilities.

Time mechanisms for simulations

For the car-wash simulation we took one customer at a time, a row of the table for each customer. This is called a *next-event time-advance* mechanism. An alternative, which may be more appropriate for some simulations, is the *fixed-increment time-advance* method. With this method we look at the system at regular time-points. At each time-point we check which events have happened since the last time-point. The following is an example of a fixed-increment time-advance simulation.

Check this

Daily demand at an outlet that sells video recorders over a typical 100-day period is as follows:

Daily demand	Observed frequency
0	10
1	10
2	15
3	20
4	20
5	15
6	10
	100

The outlet obtains video recorders directly from the manufacturer. These are ordered in batches of 15 and a cost of £20 per batch is payable on ordering. The Manager of the outlet reckons that, on average, half the orders arrive at the start of the day, 5 working days after placing the order, and the others arrive at the start of the day, 2 days after ordering. He also calculates that each video recorder in stock contributes an extra £1 per day to insurance costs and estimates that storage space and maintenance amount to another £0.50 per day, per video recorder.

The shop is in a busy retail area and if there isn't a video recorder in stock customers go elsewhere and trade is lost. The manager assesses that each customer turned away amounts to £12 in lost profit.

The manager wants to choose between two alternative policies:

(i) Order a batch of 15 video recorders weekly, or

(ii) Wait until stocks fall below a particular level (chosen sensibly) and then order enough batches to 'top up' stocks to at least this level.

Design a simulation for each policy and run each through enough days to illustrate the method. State the initial conditions of the model.

Solution:
As stock level is assessed daily, it would seem sensible to use a fixed-time-increment of a day for this simulation. The random inputs will be daily demand and, for each delivery, how many days it takes to arrive. The outputs will be the balance of stock at the end of

each day, and the carrying cost (£1.50 per day per video recorder), ordering cost (£20) and cost of lost sales (£12 each). These are all shown in the table below.

Demand must be generated with the following probability distribution:

x	P(x)
0	0.1
1	0.1
2	0.15
3	0.2
4	0.2
5	0.15
6	0.10

We will assign random digits 00–09 to 0 demand, digits 10–19 to demand of 1, 20–34 to 2 and so on. We take the final row of random digits given earlier in this section which is repeated below.

82817   95485   04551   12531   68272   22939   09492   54673   09108

This gives demands of 5, 5, 5, 3, 5, 0 and so on.

For each delivery there is a 50% chance it arrives after 5 working days and a 50% chance it arrives after 2 days, so we assign the digits 0–4 to 5 days and 5–9 to 2 days. Using the sequence of random digits 2782842 ... gives delivery times of 5, 2, 2, 5, 2, 5, 5 and so on.

The table below shows the results of the simulation over 15 days under policy (ii), placing an order when stock levels fall below 10. We assume that we have 15 video recorders in stock at the end of day 0.

End day	Demand	Delivery?	Balance	Carrying cost	Place order?	Delivery time	Ordering cost	Lost-sales cost	Total cost
0	–	–	15	22.5	–		–	–	22.5
1	5	–	10	15	–		–	–	15
2	5	–	5	7.5	yes	5	20	–	27.5
3	5	–	0	0	–	–	–	–	0
4	3	–	0	0	–	–	–	36	36
5	5	–	0	0	–	–	–	60	60
6	0	–	0	0	–	–	–	–	0
7	4	+15	11	16.5	–	–	–	–	16.5
8	1	–	10	15	–	–	–	–	15
9	2	–	8	12	yes	2	20	–	32
10	2	–	6	9	–	–	–	–	9
11	4	+15	17	25.5	–	–	–	–	25.5
12	2	–	15	22.5	–	–	–	–	22.5
13	2	–	13	19.5	–	–	–	–	19.5

End day	Demand	Delivery?	Balance	Carrying cost	Place order?	Delivery time	Ordering cost	Lost-sales cost	Total cost
14	2	–	11	16.5	–	–	–	–	16.5
15	3	–	8	12	yes	2	20	–	32
								Total	349.5

Notice that at the end of day 2 stocks drop below 10, an order is placed, delivery time is 5 days and the order arrives at the start of day 7. In the meantime, stocks run out on day 3, and so on day 4 three customers are turned away and on day 5 a further 5 customers with consequent lost-sales cost.

Now consider policy (i) – place a weekly order of 15 regardless of stock levels. The following table shows the results of the simulation. Notice that we have used the same demand and delivery-time inputs as the policy (ii) simulation in order to compare like with like. We start with the same initial balance of 15 and place an order on day 0 and every 5th day after.

End day	Demand	Delivery?	Balance	Carrying cost	Place order?	Delivery time	Ordering cost	Lost-sales cost	Total cost
0	–	–	15	22.5	yes	5	20	–	42.5
1	5	–	10	15	–	–	–	–	15
2	5	–	5	7.5	–	–	–	–	7.5
3	5	–	0	0	–	–	–	–	0
4	3	–	0	0	–	–	–	36	36
5	5	+15	10	15	yes	2	20	–	35
6	0	–	10	15	–	–	–	–	15
7	4	+15	21	31.5	–	–	–	–	31.5
8	1	–	20	30	–	–	–	–	30
9	2	–	18	27	–	–	–	–	27
10	2	–	16	24	yes	2	20	–	44
11	4	–	12	18	–	–	–	–	18
12	2	+15	25	37.5	–	–	–	–	37.5
13	2	–	23	34.5	–	–	–	–	34.5
14	2	–	21	31.5	–	–	–	–	31.5
15	3	–	18	27	yes	5	20	–	47
								Total	452

Under this ordering policy we are only out of stock once on day 4 but the delivery on day 12 arrives when stock was not particularly low, resulting in higher carrying costs. As a result, the total cost is considerably higher than the total cost of policy (ii). Of course, in practice, we would run both simulations many times or for much longer before drawing any conclusions.

Initial conditions: a warning

In general, we should be very aware of the effect of the initial conditions of the simulation. Starting the video recorder simulation with a stock level lower or higher than 15 might greatly affect the first few time periods (you could try and see). For instance, if we were to start the simulation with zero stock the first few days would incur high lost-sales costs. This initial period is called the *transient period* or *warm-up period*. If the simulation is run for a sufficient length of time the effects of the warm-up period will be small. However, to eliminate bias due to the choice of initial conditions it is quite usual to let the simulation run for a while before recording the output.

WORK CARD 3

1. Go back to our simulation of Geoff's Car-Wash from Section 2. Suppose that it is now estimated that 50% of customers choose a 3-minute wash, 33% a 4-minute wash and the remaining 17%, the 9-minute wash. Use tables or a computer to generate a sequence of *Wash times* and use it to recalculate the simulation of 7 customers in Section 2.

2. The number of seconds it takes an emergency-call centre to respond to a telephone call has the following probability distribution.

x	P(x)
1	0.1
2	0.15
3	0.25
4	0.25
5	0.15
6	0.1

    (i) Describe how you would use random number tables to generate a sequence of response times and demonstrate it by generating 10 such times.

    (ii) Now use a computer to generate 100 such times. Plot a histogram (like Figure 7.1) of the times. How many of the response times would you expect to be in the 1-second category, 2-second category and so on, and how many actually are? Comment.

3. Describe, in your own words, what is meant by the transient period of a simulation and how one should treat it.

    Solution guidelines:

    1. If you do this using a table of random numbers, you will have to take the random digits in pairs. 00–49 could be assigned to 3 minutes, 50–82 to 4 minutes and 83–99 to 9 minutes.

WC 3 (CONTINUED)

2. (i)   One way would be to assign 00–09 to 1, 10–24 to 2, 25–49 to 3 and so on.
    (ii) When you generate 100 such times you would expect, on average, a tenth of them (that is, 10) to be in the 1-second category, 0.15 of them (that is, 15) to be in the 2-second category and so on. However, the 100 randomly generated numbers are a sample of all possible times and so these frequencies will not occur exactly and your histogram will almost certainly differ slightly from the values you expect.

3. See the subsection on initial conditions but use your own words.

ASSESSMENT 3

1. Take the simulation you planned in **Assessment 2**. Decide on a finite number of possibilities for each of the inputs and assign probabilities to each possibility. (We will use more realistic assumptions later.) Generate a stream of random numbers and 10 or more lines of the simulation. Calculate the summary statistics and comment.

2. Describe, in your own words, two ways in which time can be treated in a simulation.

4 Simulating from other probability distributions

To understand this section you really need to know about probability distributions (Chapters P2 and P3) although we have included some revision.

In the previous section we learnt how to generate discrete random variables like the car-wash *Wash times* or *demand* for video recorders when there are only a finite number of possible values, each with a particular probability. However, not all types of input to a simulation can have their uncertainty characterised in this way. For instance, the *times* between cars arriving at the car-wash need not be integer and can take any value from 0 upwards, so an infinite number of values are possible. (We call this a *continuous random variable*.)

To make the simulation a good representation of the real system we want the generated input sequences to be as typical as possible of the real inputs and so we need a repertoire of probability distributions that can be used to model the inputs. The probability distributions that occur most frequently are the *binomial* and *Poisson* distributions (Chapter P2) and the *uniform*, *normal* and *exponential* distributions (Chapter P3). Most statistical software includes routines that generate random variables from these and other distributions.

Which probability distribution?

Whilst it's easy to use a computer to obtain sequences of values from a particular probability distribution, it is not so easy to decide *which* probability distribution is appropriate in the first place. Frequently, the *nature* of the input will give some indication of the type of distribution, but choosing an appropriate probability distribution is not an exact science. Ideally, some data from the real system should be collected and a histogram (see *Describing Data*, Chapter DD1) drawn to see what shape the distribution has. A variant on the chi-squared goodness of fit test (Chapter S6) could be performed on the data to test whether a particular distribution is reasonable or not.

A brief review of the main probability distributions and the circumstances in which they occur follows.

When every integer (whole number) in a range is equally likely we say the random variable has a *discrete uniform* distribution. For instance, if every integer between 100 and 200 inclusive is equally likely, each has a probability of 1/101 of occurring. A discrete uniform distribution would be appropriate for generating the winning ticket numbers in a lottery when the tickets are numbered consecutively.

If there are a fixed number, usually called n, identical 'trials' and each trial can be a success or a failure with a probability, p, of success then the number of trials out of the n that are a success has a *binomial* probability distribution (see Chapter P2, Section 4). The trials must be independent, meaning that the outcome of one must not affect the probability of the outcome of any of the others. Examples are the number of individual customers out of ten entering a shop who buy something, the number of girls in families of five children or the number of students out of a class of 40 who turn up each week for the lecture. When n is large, the normal distribution (see below) with mean np and variance $np(1 - p)$ is a good approximation to the binomial distribution. For this we usually define n 'large' as np and $n(1 - p)$ both greater than or equal to 5.

A *Poisson* random variable (Chapter P2, Section 5) can take positive integer or zero values only and is usually appropriate for the number of occurrences in a time interval of a particular, fairly rare, event. For instance, the number of air crashes over British airspace in a month or the number of individuals joining a queue during a (short) time interval. When the mean of a Poisson distribution is 5 or more the normal distribution with the same mean and with variance equal to the mean is a good approximation to the Poisson distribution. Also, if the number of events that occur in a unit time-period has a Poisson distribution with mean μ, the time between these events has an exponential distribution (see below) with mean $1/\mu$ (see Chapter P2, Section 2).

The *uniform* distribution is the simplest. Every value within a range is equally likely (Chapter P3, Section 1). The values generated by the **RAND()** function in Excel are uniform on the range between 0 and 1.

The *normal* distribution (Chapter P3, Section 3) may be suitable when the histogram is roughly bell-shaped and symmetrical. Further, if an input can be viewed as the sum or average of a large number of smaller, similar, items then it may have a normal distribution. For instance, daily rainfall is the sum of the rainfall over each minute of a day, monthly sales figures are totals of the sales figures for individual days of the month and so on. The normal distribution also occurs frequently as it is an approximation to the Poisson and binomial distributions when the mean and n respectively are large as described above.

The *exponential* distribution (see Chapter P3, Section 2) may be suitable if the histogram is skewed to the right; small values are more likely to occur than larger ones. It is often appropriate for modelling the time between random events, or the length of time an activity takes. If the time between two events has an exponential distribution with mean λ, the *number* of such events that occur in any unit of time has a Poisson distribution with mean $1/\lambda$.

Check this

Which probability distributions might you expect the following random variables to have and why?

(i)   The time between telephone calls to a call centre.

(ii)   The number of mortgages issued by the local branch of a bank in a week if they issue an average of 30 a year (ignore seasonal fluctuations).

(iii)   The actual number (not the average) of the mortgages in **(ii)** issued in a year.

(iv)   The number of customers who return a purchase for a refund to a shop out of 8 customers assuming that on average 10% of customers return goods.

(v)   The number of customers who return a purchase for a refund to the shop in **(iv)** out of 100 customers.

Solution:

(i)   Exponential because the number of calls received in a small unit of time is likely to be Poisson distributed making the times between calls exponential.

(ii)   The number issued in a particular week has an average of about 30/52, i.e. it is small so issuing a mortgage is a rare event which might be modelled by a Poisson distribution with mean 30/52.

(iii)   Normal mean 30 as this can be regarded as the sum of mortgages issued in each of the 52 weeks.

(iv)   Here we have a binomial situation with $n = 8$ independent trials assuming customers do not make and return purchases in groups, and a success probability of $p = 0.10$.

(v)   Binomial $n = 100$, $p = 0.1$ but this time np and $n(1 - p)$ are both greater than 5 so we could use a normal distribution mean 10 and variance 9.

Using a computer

Statistical software and spreadsheets can easily generate sequences of data from these distributions.

For instance, in SPSS

Transform > Compute

and the **RV.NORMAL** function will generate a normal probability distribution. In general, the user will be asked where the generated data is to be placed and will have to supply the mean for the exponential and Poisson distributions, n and p for the binomial and the mean and variance for the normal distribution.

In Excel the **random number generator** data analysis tool allows you to generate numbers from a normal, Poisson, uniform or binomial distribution and place them in a particular area of the worksheet. You will have to specify the mean for the Poisson distribution (Excel calls it λ (lambda)), mean and standard deviation for the normal distribution and n and p for the binomial.

The values generated by Excel's **RAND()** function are uniform (0,1). An advantage of the **RAND()** function is that every time the worksheet is recalculated a new set of random numbers appear making it easy to rerun the simulation. (Alternatively, pressing F9 will recalculate them.)

If you are familiar with logs (*More Maths*, Chapter MM1) you can generate exponential random numbers in Excel using **RAND()** as above, taking the natural log (ln) of it, putting a minus sign in front and multiplying by the mean of the exponential distribution required; that is, entering the formula = –2*ln(RAND()) for exponential mean 2 and so on.

Putting this all together

We are now ready to insert more realistic inter-arrival times into the car-wash simulation. Times between events are often modelled by the exponential distribution so we will assume that inter-arrival times are exponentially distributed with mean 4. We can generate these with Excel or SPSS as described above.

Seven such times (as generated by Excel) are

  1.29824062 2.81150749 7.19853211 6.28930402 1.5658657 0.68205789 2.16609417

For the car-wash simulation, below, we have rounded them to one decimal place. The *Wash times* remain the same as before. This time, the first 7 customers take over 36 minutes. When customer 7 arrives customer 5 is still waiting so a queue builds up.

	Inputs		Event times			Outputs	
Customer number	Inter-arrival time	Wash time	Arrival time	Wash start	Wash end	Waiting time	Busy time
1	1.3	3	1.3	1.3	4.3	0	3
2	2.8	3	4.1	4.3	7.3	0.2	3
3	7.2	4	11.3	11.3	15.3	0	4
4	6.3	9	17.6	17.6	26.6	0	9
5	1.6	3	19.2	26.6	29.6	7.4	3
6	0.7	4	19.9	29.6	33.6	9.7	4
7	2.2	3	22.1	33.6	36.6	11.5	3
					Total	28.8	29

Any degree of complexity can be built into a simulation. For instance, it might be realistic to say that if there are more than, say, 3 cars waiting at the car-wash any newly arriving customers decide to wash their cars another time and go away. This could be built into the simulation model if we wanted.

Simulation and queues

Many problems where simulation is helpful are *queueing* problems in the general sense that some entities in the system may have to wait for a service to become available even if they do not physically stand in line. For example, queues may be jobs waiting to be processed by a computer, patients on a waiting list for an operation or telephone calls waiting to be answered.

Businesses and organisations usually need to find a balance between spending more money to control queues by employing extra staff and/or facilities, and losing customers or making them dissatisfied by keeping them waiting.

Queuing structures are many and varied. There may be a single server or multiple servers, who may have similar characteristics or not. Customers (we'll call waiting entities customers even if they are not people) can arrive singly, in groups of fixed- or variable-size, and may form a single queue or separate queues at multiple service points. Customers may be served in order of arrival or may be prioritised in some way. Sometimes, customers can go away if the queue length appears too long.

When some fairly specific assumptions are made about the structure of the queuing system and the probability distributions of inter-arrival and service times, it is sometimes possible to solve a queuing model mathematically. An advantage of this is that an exact solution can be found, but the disadvantages are that the model isn't flexible and the assumptions may not be realistic. We give you one, simple, example to illustrate the idea – it is called the *single-server* queue. Our notation is taken directly from *queuing theory*.

The single-server queue

The structure of this queue is the simplest possible. There is a single server and customers arrive individually and are served on a 'first come, first served' basis.

We assume that the times between arrivals have an exponential distribution with parameter λ, mean $1/\lambda$. Notice that this implies that the number of customers who arrive in a time period is Poisson distributed with mean λ. We call λ the *arrival rate*.

We also assume that service times have an exponential distribution. This time the parameter is μ and so the mean is $1/\mu$. If the server served continuously they would serve an average of μ customers an hour, so we call μ the *service rate*.

If the arrival rate is greater than the service rate the queue will get longer and longer so we usually assume that $\lambda < \mu$.

The restrictive assumptions we have made, that the inter-arrival and service times are exponential, are such that some of the characteristics of the queue can be calculated mathematically. We will not go into their derivation here but some results follow.

---

1. The probability that the server is busy $= \dfrac{\lambda}{\mu}$

Notice that this is the same as the probability that an arriving customer has to queue, and is the ratio of the arrival rate to the service rate.

---

2. The average (= mean) number of customers in the queue (excluding the person being served) is

    $$\frac{\lambda^2}{\mu(\mu - 1)}$$

3. The average time a customer spends in the system (including the time they are being served) is

    $$\frac{1}{\mu - \lambda}$$

Check this

Customers arrive at a bar at an average rate of 0.2 per minute. Val, the bar-person, takes an average of 2.5 minutes to serve each customer. Stating any assumptions you make, answer the following.

(i) For what proportion of time is Val busy serving customers?

(ii) On average, how long will it take a customer to wait and be served?

(iii) On average, how many customers will be waiting to be served at any one time?

Solution:
To find a solution to this queuing problem we are going to have to make the restrictive assumption that both inter-arrival times and service times follow an exponential distribution. We have been given the mean service time, 2.5, so the service rate is $\mu = 1/2.5 = 0.4$ per minute. The arrival rate is 0.2 a minute so $\lambda = 0.2$.

(i) The probability that Val is busy serving a customer is $0.2/0.4 = 0.5$, that is, 50% of the time.

(ii) It will take $1/(0.4 - 0.2) = 5$ minutes, on average, for a customer to wait and be served.

(iii) The average queue-length will be $\frac{0.2^2}{0.4(0.4-0.2)} = 0.5$ customers.

In practice, the assumptions of a mathematical queueing model are usually too restrictive to make the model useful and so simulation is used to allow the model to be more realistic.

WORK CARD 4

1. Which distribution would you use to model the following and why?
   (i) The operational time before a photocopier breaks down.
   (ii) The number of employees in a department of 20 people who are off sick on any one day.
   (iii) Out of a large number of machines in an office, the number that break down on any one day.

2. Generate 50 or more random variables from the exponential distribution with mean 5. Plot a histogram of these and comment.

3. Make the newsagent simulation (**Work cards 1 and 2**, question 1) more realistic. Suppose now that the inter-arrival times of customers are exponential with mean 1.5 minutes and that service time is exponential with mean 1 minute. Perform a simulation and estimate the proportion of time for which the newsagent is occupied. Now, using queuing theory, calculate what you would expect this proportion to be, on average.
   Do you think the assumption of an exponential distribution for the service times and inter-arrival times seems reasonable? Comment.

WORK CARD 4 (CONTINUED)

Solutions:

1. **(i)** Exponential because it is used to model times between random events.

    (ii) Binomial if we assume that there are 20 people (trials) and each has the same probability of being off sick on a day. This assumes that the probability of any one person being off sick is not affected by whether any of the others are off sick or not, and so does not allow for contagious diseases or epidemics.

    (iii) This is the number of rare events that occur on any day and so is best modelled by a Poisson distribution.

2. The histogram will have broadly the same shape as the exponential distribution, that is, skewed to the right or positively skewed.

3. This is a single-server queue. The mean inter-arrival time is 3/2 minutes so $\lambda = 2/3$ and the mean service time is 1 minute, so $\mu = 1/1 = 1$. Using the queuing theory results in this chapter, the proportion of time the server is busy is $\lambda/\mu = (2/3)/1 = 2/3$ of the time. You would expect the results of the simulation to be of a similar magnitude but they are only based on a sample.

    The exponential inter-arrival times will only be reasonable if customers arrive in ones and not in groups. If the time taken to serve a customer is similar for every customer (for instance, if it is just a question of taking some money) then an exponential distribution would not be appropriate. However, if a variety of tasks are involved, of different lengths, then the exponential distribution may be appropriate.

ASSESSMENT 4

1. Go back to the simulation you did in **Assessments 1 and 2**. Decide on sensible probability distribution(s) for the random inputs and generate a sequence of numbers for each of them. Re-run your simulation with these numbers. Comment on the results of your simulation.

2. Return to the newsagent's shop simulation from **Work card 4**, above. A new bus-stop is to be located outside the newsagents, and consequently he will be much busier. He anticipates that some customers will still arrive independently and have the same inter-arrival distribution as before but as well as this he estimates that 3 customers will arrive every 5 minutes because of the bus. The newsagent is considering taking on an assistant but the assistant is likely to have an average service time of only 1.5 minutes.

    Devise a simulation of the newsagents with the new custom from the bus-stop both with and without the new assistant. Is the new assistant a good idea? Explain and comment.

Further reading: see p. xv

Anderson *et al.* include a chapter on simulation. They also have a complete chapter on queuing models (waiting line models) which we have only mentioned in passing.

Hillier and Lieberman, and Hillier and Hillier both include chapters on simulation and queuing models.

Statistical tables*

*Reproduced by kind permission of G. J. Janacek

Table I: Cumulative Binomial Probabilities $P(X \le a)$

Example: $P(X \le 4) = 0.6331$ when X is a binomial random variable with $n = 10$, $p = 0.4$

$n = 5$

$a \backslash p$	0.10	0.15	0.20	0.25	0.30	0.35	0.40	0.45	0.50
0	0.5905	0.4437	0.3277	0.2373	0.1681	0.1160	0.0778	0.0503	0.0313
1	0.9185	0.8352	0.7373	0.6328	0.5282	0.4284	0.3370	0.2562	0.1875
2	0.9914	0.9734	0.9421	0.8965	0.8369	0.7648	0.6826	0.5931	0.5000
3	0.9995	0.9978	0.9933	0.9844	0.9692	0.9460	0.9130	0.8688	0.8125
4	1.0000	0.9999	0.9997	0.9990	0.9976	0.9947	0.9898	0.9815	0.9688
5	1.0000	1.0000	1.0000	1.0000	1.0000	1.0000	1.0000	1.0000	1.0000

$n = 6$

$a \backslash p$	0.10	0.15	0.20	0.25	0.30	0.35	0.40	0.45	0.50
0	0.5314	0.3771	0.2621	0.1780	0.1176	0.0754	0.0467	0.0277	0.0156
1	0.8857	0.7765	0.6554	0.5339	0.4202	0.3191	0.2333	0.1636	0.1094
2	0.9841	0.9527	0.9011	0.8306	0.7443	0.6471	0.5443	0.4415	0.3438
3	0.9987	0.9941	0.9830	0.9624	0.9295	0.8826	0.8208	0.7447	0.6563
4	0.9999	0.9996	0.9984	0.9954	0.9891	0.9777	0.9590	0.9308	0.8906
5	1.0000	1.0000	0.9999	0.9998	0.9993	0.9982	0.9959	0.9917	0.9844
6	1.0000	1.0000	1.0000	1.0000	1.0000	1.0000	1.0000	1.0000	1.0000

$n = 7$

$a \backslash p$	0.10	0.15	0.20	0.25	0.30	0.35	0.40	0.45	0.50
0	0.4783	0.3206	0.2097	0.1335	0.0824	0.0490	0.0280	0.0152	0.0078
1	0.8503	0.7166	0.5767	0.4449	0.3294	0.2338	0.1586	0.1024	0.0625
2	0.9743	0.9262	0.8520	0.7564	0.6471	0.5323	0.4199	0.3164	0.2266
3	0.9973	0.9879	0.9667	0.9294	0.8740	0.8002	0.7102	0.6083	0.5000
4	0.9998	0.9988	0.9953	0.9871	0.9712	0.9444	0.9037	0.8471	0.7734
5	1.0000	0.9999	0.9996	0.9987	0.9962	0.9910	0.9812	0.9643	0.9375
6	1.0000	1.0000	1.0000	0.9999	0.9998	0.9994	0.9984	0.9963	0.9922
7	1.0000	1.0000	1.0000	1.0000	1.0000	1.0000	1.0000	1.0000	1.0000

$n = 8$

$a \backslash p$	0.10	0.15	0.20	0.25	0.30	0.35	0.40	0.45	0.50
0	0.4305	0.2725	0.1678	0.1001	0.0576	0.0319	0.0168	0.0084	0.0039
1	0.8131	0.6572	0.5033	0.3671	0.2553	0.1691	0.1064	0.0632	0.0352
2	0.9619	0.8948	0.7969	0.6785	0.5518	0.4278	0.3154	0.2201	0.1445
3	0.9950	0.9786	0.9437	0.8862	0.8059	0.7064	0.5941	0.4770	0.3633
4	0.9996	0.9971	0.9896	0.9727	0.9420	0.8939	0.8263	0.7396	0.6367
5	1.0000	0.9998	0.9988	0.9958	0.9887	0.9747	0.9502	0.9115	0.8555
6	1.0000	1.0000	0.9999	0.9996	0.9987	0.9964	0.9915	0.9819	0.9648
7	1.0000	1.0000	1.0000	1.0000	0.9999	0.9998	0.9993	0.9983	0.9961
8	1.0000	1.0000	1.0000	1.0000	1.0000	1.0000	1.0000	1.0000	1.0000

$n = 9$

$a \backslash p$	0.10	0.15	0.20	0.25	0.30	0.35	0.40	0.45	0.50
0	0.3874	0.2316	0.1342	0.0751	0.0404	0.0207	0.0101	0.0046	0.0020
1	0.7748	0.5995	0.4362	0.3003	0.1960	0.1211	0.0705	0.0385	0.0195
2	0.9470	0.8591	0.7382	0.6007	0.4628	0.3373	0.2318	0.1495	0.0898
3	0.9917	0.9661	0.9144	0.8343	0.7297	0.6089	0.4826	0.3614	0.2539
4	0.9991	0.9944	0.9804	0.9511	0.9012	0.8283	0.7334	0.6214	0.5000
5	0.9999	0.9994	0.9969	0.9900	0.9747	0.9464	0.9006	0.8342	0.7461
6	1.0000	1.0000	0.9997	0.9987	0.9957	0.9888	0.9750	0.9502	0.9102
7	1.0000	1.0000	1.0000	0.9999	0.9996	0.9986	0.9962	0.9909	0.9805
8	1.0000	1.0000	1.0000	1.0000	1.0000	0.9999	0.9997	0.9992	0.9980
9	1.0000	1.0000	1.0000	1.0000	1.0000	1.0000	1.0000	1.0000	1.0000

$n = 10$

$a \backslash p$	0.10	0.15	0.20	0.25	0.30	0.35	0.40	0.45	0.50
0	0.3487	0.1969	0.1074	0.0563	0.0282	0.0135	0.0060	0.0025	0.0010
1	0.7361	0.5443	0.3758	0.2440	0.1493	0.0860	0.0464	0.0233	0.0107
2	0.9298	0.8202	0.6778	0.5256	0.3828	0.2616	0.1673	0.0996	0.0547
3	0.9872	0.9500	0.8791	0.7759	0.6496	0.5138	0.3823	0.2660	0.1719
4	0.9984	0.9901	0.9672	0.9219	0.8497	0.7515	0.6331	0.5044	0.3770
5	0.9999	0.9986	0.9936	0.9803	0.9527	0.9051	0.8338	0.7384	0.6230
6	1.0000	0.9999	0.9991	0.9965	0.9894	0.9740	0.9452	0.8980	0.8281
7	1.0000	1.0000	0.9999	0.9996	0.9984	0.9952	0.9877	0.9726	0.9453
8	1.0000	1.0000	1.0000	1.0000	0.9999	0.9995	0.9983	0.9955	0.9893
9	1.0000	1.0000	1.0000	1.0000	1.0000	1.0000	0.9999	0.9997	0.9990
10	1.0000	1.0000	1.0000	1.0000	1.0000	1.0000	1.0000	1.0000	1.0000

$n = 11$

$a \backslash p$	0.10	0.15	0.20	0.25	0.30	0.35	0.40	0.45	0.50
0	0.3138	0.1673	0.0859	0.0422	0.0198	0.0088	0.0036	0.0014	0.0005
1	0.6974	0.4922	0.3221	0.1971	0.1130	0.0606	0.0302	0.0139	0.0059
2	0.9104	0.7788	0.6174	0.4552	0.3127	0.2001	0.1189	0.0652	0.0327
3	0.9815	0.9306	0.8389	0.7133	0.5696	0.4256	0.2963	0.1911	0.1133
4	0.9972	0.9841	0.9496	0.8854	0.7897	0.6683	0.5328	0.3971	0.2744
5	0.9997	0.9973	0.9883	0.9657	0.9218	0.8513	0.7535	0.6331	0.5000
6	1.0000	0.9997	0.9980	0.9924	0.9784	0.9499	0.9006	0.8262	0.7256
7	1.0000	1.0000	0.9998	0.9988	0.9957	0.9878	0.9707	0.9390	0.8867
8	1.0000	1.0000	1.0000	0.9999	0.9994	0.9980	0.9941	0.9852	0.9673
9	1.0000	1.0000	1.0000	1.0000	1.0000	0.9998	0.9993	0.9978	0.9941
10	1.0000	1.0000	1.0000	1.0000	1.0000	1.0000	1.0000	0.9998	0.9995
11	1.0000	1.0000	1.0000	1.0000	1.0000	1.0000	1.0000	1.0000	1.0000

$n = 12$

$a\backslash p$	0.10	0.15	0.20	0.25	0.30	0.35	0.40	0.45	0.50
0	0.2824	0.1422	0.0687	0.0317	0.0138	0.0057	0.0022	0.0008	0.0002
1	0.6590	0.4435	0.2749	0.1584	0.0850	0.0424	0.0196	0.0083	0.0032
2	0.8891	0.7358	0.5583	0.3907	0.2528	0.1513	0.0834	0.0421	0.0193
3	0.9744	0.9078	0.7946	0.6488	0.4925	0.3467	0.2253	0.1345	0.0730
4	0.9957	0.9761	0.9274	0.8424	0.7237	0.5833	0.4382	0.3044	0.1938
5	0.9995	0.9954	0.9806	0.9456	0.8822	0.7873	0.6652	0.5269	0.3872
6	0.9999	0.9993	0.9961	0.9857	0.9614	0.9154	0.8418	0.7393	0.6128
7	1.0000	0.9999	0.9994	0.9972	0.9905	0.9745	0.9427	0.8883	0.8062
8	1.0000	1.0000	0.9999	0.9996	0.9983	0.9944	0.9847	0.9644	0.9270
9	1.0000	1.0000	1.0000	1.0000	0.9998	0.9992	0.9972	0.9921	0.9807
10	1.0000	1.0000	1.0000	1.0000	1.0000	0.9999	0.9997	0.9989	0.9968
11	1.0000	1.0000	1.0000	1.0000	1.0000	1.0000	1.0000	0.9999	0.9998
12	1.0000	1.0000	1.0000	1.0000	1.0000	1.0000	1.0000	1.0000	1.0000

$n = 13$

$a\backslash p$	0.10	0.15	0.20	0.25	0.30	0.35	0.40	0.45	0.50
0	0.2542	0.1209	0.0550	0.0238	0.0097	0.0037	0.0013	0.0004	0.0001
1	0.6213	0.3983	0.2336	0.1267	0.0637	0.0296	0.0126	0.0049	0.0017
2	0.8661	0.6920	0.5017	0.3326	0.2025	0.1132	0.0579	0.0269	0.0112
3	0.9658	0.8820	0.7473	0.5843	0.4206	0.2783	0.1686	0.0929	0.0461
4	0.9935	0.9658	0.9009	0.7940	0.6543	0.5005	0.3530	0.2279	0.1334
5	0.9991	0.9925	0.9700	0.9198	0.8346	0.7159	0.5744	0.4268	0.2905
6	0.9999	0.9987	0.9930	0.9757	0.9376	0.8705	0.7712	0.6437	0.5000
7	1.0000	0.9998	0.9988	0.9944	0.9818	0.9538	0.9023	0.8212	0.7095
8	1.0000	1.0000	0.9998	0.9990	0.9960	0.9874	0.9679	0.9302	0.8666
9	1.0000	1.0000	1.0000	0.9999	0.9993	0.9975	0.9922	0.9797	0.9539
10	1.0000	1.0000	1.0000	1.0000	0.9999	0.9997	0.9987	0.9959	0.9888
11	1.0000	1.0000	1.0000	1.0000	1.0000	1.0000	0.9999	0.9995	0.9983
12	1.0000	1.0000	1.0000	1.0000	1.0000	1.0000	1.0000	1.0000	0.9999
13	1.0000	1.0000	1.0000	1.0000	1.0000	1.0000	1.0000	1.0000	1.0000

$n = 14$

$a\backslash p$	0.10	0.15	0.20	0.25	0.30	0.35	0.40	0.45	0.50
0	0.2288	0.1028	0.0440	0.0178	0.0068	0.0024	0.0008	0.0002	0.0001
1	0.5846	0.3567	0.1979	0.1010	0.0475	0.0205	0.0081	0.0029	0.0009
2	0.8416	0.6479	0.4481	0.2811	0.1608	0.0839	0.0398	0.0170	0.0065
3	0.9559	0.8535	0.6982	0.5213	0.3552	0.2205	0.1243	0.0632	0.0287
4	0.9908	0.9533	0.8702	0.7415	0.5842	0.4227	0.2793	0.1672	0.0898
5	0.9985	0.9885	0.9561	0.8883	0.7805	0.6405	0.4859	0.3373	0.2120
6	0.9998	0.9978	0.9884	0.9617	0.9067	0.8164	0.6925	0.5461	0.3953
7	1.0000	0.9997	0.9976	0.9897	0.9685	0.9247	0.8499	0.7414	0.6047
8	1.0000	1.0000	0.9996	0.9978	0.9917	0.9757	0.9417	0.8811	0.7880
9	1.0000	1.0000	1.0000	0.9997	0.9983	0.9940	0.9825	0.9574	0.9102
10	1.0000	1.0000	1.0000	1.0000	0.9998	0.9989	0.9961	0.9886	0.9713
11	1.0000	1.0000	1.0000	1.0000	1.0000	0.9999	0.9994	0.9978	0.9935
12	1.0000	1.0000	1.0000	1.0000	1.0000	1.0000	0.9999	0.9997	0.9991
13	1.0000	1.0000	1.0000	1.0000	1.0000	1.0000	1.0000	1.0000	0.9999
14	1.0000	1.0000	1.0000	1.0000	1.0000	1.0000	1.0000	1.0000	1.0000

n = 15

a*p*	0.10	0.15	0.20	0.25	0.30	0.35	0.40	0.45	0.50
0	0.2059	0.0874	0.0352	0.0134	0.0047	0.0016	0.0005	0.0001	0.0000
1	0.5490	0.3186	0.1671	0.0802	0.0353	0.0142	0.0052	0.0017	0.0005
2	0.8159	0.6042	0.3980	0.2361	0.1268	0.0617	0.0271	0.0107	0.0037
3	0.9444	0.8227	0.6482	0.4613	0.2969	0.1727	0.0905	0.0424	0.0176
4	0.9873	0.9383	0.8358	0.6865	0.5155	0.3519	0.2173	0.1204	0.0592
5	0.9978	0.9832	0.9389	0.8516	0.7216	0.5643	0.4032	0.2608	0.1509
6	0.9997	0.9964	0.9819	0.9434	0.8689	0.7548	0.6098	0.4522	0.3036
7	1.0000	0.9994	0.9958	0.9827	0.9500	0.8868	0.7869	0.6535	0.5000
8	1.0000	0.9999	0.9992	0.9958	0.9848	0.9578	0.9050	0.8182	0.6964
9	1.0000	1.0000	0.9999	0.9992	0.9963	0.9876	0.9662	0.9231	0.8491
10	1.0000	1.0000	1.0000	0.9999	0.9993	0.9972	0.9907	0.9745	0.9408
11	1.0000	1.0000	1.0000	1.0000	0.9999	0.9995	0.9981	0.9937	0.9824
12	1.0000	1.0000	1.0000	1.0000	1.0000	0.9999	0.9997	0.9989	0.9963
13	1.0000	1.0000	1.0000	1.0000	1.0000	1.0000	1.0000	0.9999	0.9995
14	1.0000	1.0000	1.0000	1.0000	1.0000	1.0000	1.0000	1.0000	1.0000

n = 16

a*p*	0.10	0.15	0.20	0.25	0.30	0.35	0.40	0.45	0.50
0	0.1853	0.0743	0.0281	0.0100	0.0033	0.0010	0.0003	0.0001	0.0000
1	0.5147	0.2839	0.1407	0.0635	0.0261	0.0098	0.0033	0.0010	0.0003
2	0.7892	0.5614	0.3518	0.1971	0.0994	0.0451	0.0183	0.0066	0.0021
3	0.9316	0.7899	0.5981	0.4050	0.2459	0.1339	0.0651	0.0281	0.0106
4	0.9830	0.9209	0.7982	0.6302	0.4499	0.2892	0.1666	0.0853	0.0384
5	0.9967	0.9765	0.9183	0.8103	0.6598	0.4900	0.3288	0.1976	0.1051
6	0.9995	0.9944	0.9733	0.9204	0.8247	0.6881	0.5272	0.3660	0.2272
7	0.9999	0.9989	0.9930	0.9729	0.9256	0.8406	0.7161	0.5629	0.4018
8	1.0000	0.9998	0.9985	0.9925	0.9743	0.9329	0.8577	0.7441	0.5982
9	1.0000	1.0000	0.9998	0.9984	0.9929	0.9771	0.9417	0.8759	0.7728
10	1.0000	1.0000	1.0000	0.9997	0.9984	0.9938	0.9809	0.9514	0.8949
11	1.0000	1.0000	1.0000	1.0000	0.9997	0.9987	0.9951	0.9851	0.9616
12	1.0000	1.0000	1.0000	1.0000	1.0000	0.9998	0.9991	0.9965	0.9894
13	1.0000	1.0000	1.0000	1.0000	1.0000	1.0000	0.9999	0.9994	0.9979
14	1.0000	1.0000	1.0000	1.0000	1.0000	1.0000	1.0000	0.9999	0.9997
15	1.0000	1.0000	1.0000	1.0000	1.0000	1.0000	1.0000	1.0000	1.0000

n = 17

a*p*	0.10	0.15	0.20	0.25	0.30	0.35	0.40	0.45	0.50
0	0.1668	0.0631	0.0225	0.0075	0.0023	0.0007	0.0002	0.0000	0.0000
1	0.4818	0.2525	0.1182	0.0501	0.0193	0.0067	0.0021	0.0006	0.0001
2	0.7618	0.5198	0.3096	0.1637	0.0774	0.0327	0.0123	0.0041	0.0012
3	0.9174	0.7556	0.5489	0.3530	0.2019	0.1028	0.0464	0.0184	0.0064
4	0.9779	0.9013	0.7582	0.5739	0.3887	0.2348	0.1260	0.0596	0.0245
5	0.9953	0.9681	0.8943	0.7653	0.5968	0.4197	0.2639	0.1471	0.0717
6	0.9992	0.9917	0.9623	0.8929	0.7752	0.6188	0.4478	0.2902	0.1662
7	0.9999	0.9983	0.9891	0.9598	0.8954	0.7872	0.6405	0.4743	0.3145
8	1.0000	0.9997	0.9974	0.9876	0.9597	0.9006	0.8011	0.6626	0.5000
9	1.0000	1.0000	0.9995	0.9969	0.9873	0.9617	0.9081	0.8166	0.6855
10	1.0000	1.0000	0.9999	0.9994	0.9968	0.9880	0.9652	0.9174	0.8338
11	1.0000	1.0000	1.0000	0.9999	0.9993	0.9970	0.9894	0.9699	0.9283
12	1.0000	1.0000	1.0000	1.0000	0.9999	0.9994	0.9975	0.9914	0.9755
13	1.0000	1.0000	1.0000	1.0000	1.0000	0.9999	0.9995	0.9981	0.9936
14	1.0000	1.0000	1.0000	1.0000	1.0000	1.0000	0.9999	0.9997	0.9988
15	1.0000	1.0000	1.0000	1.0000	1.0000	1.0000	1.0000	1.0000	0.9999
16	1.0000	1.0000	1.0000	1.0000	1.0000	1.0000	1.0000	1.0000	1.0000

$n = 18$

$a\backslash p$	0.10	0.15	0.20	0.25	0.30	0.35	0.40	0.45	0.50
0	0.1501	0.0536	0.0180	0.0056	0.0016	0.0004	0.0001	0.0000	0.0000
1	0.4503	0.2241	0.0991	0.0395	0.0142	0.0046	0.0013	0.0003	0.0001
2	0.7338	0.4797	0.2713	0.1353	0.0600	0.0236	0.0082	0.0025	0.0007
3	0.9018	0.7202	0.5010	0.3057	0.1646	0.0783	0.0328	0.0120	0.0038
4	0.9718	0.8794	0.7164	0.5187	0.3327	0.1886	0.0942	0.0411	0.0154
5	0.9936	0.9581	0.8671	0.7175	0.5344	0.3550	0.2088	0.1077	0.0481
6	0.9988	0.9882	0.9487	0.8610	0.7217	0.5491	0.3743	0.2258	0.1189
7	0.9998	0.9973	0.9837	0.9431	0.8593	0.7283	0.5634	0.3915	0.2403
8	1.0000	0.9995	0.9957	0.9807	0.9404	0.8609	0.7368	0.5778	0.4073
9	1.0000	0.9999	0.9991	0.9946	0.9790	0.9403	0.8653	0.7473	0.5927
10	1.0000	1.0000	0.9998	0.9988	0.9939	0.9788	0.9424	0.8720	0.7597
11	1.0000	1.0000	1.0000	0.9998	0.9986	0.9938	0.9797	0.9463	0.8811
12	1.0000	1.0000	1.0000	1.0000	0.9997	0.9986	0.9942	0.9817	0.9519
13	1.0000	1.0000	1.0000	1.0000	1.0000	0.9997	0.9987	0.9951	0.9846
14	1.0000	1.0000	1.0000	1.0000	1.0000	1.0000	0.9998	0.9990	0.9962
15	1.0000	1.0000	1.0000	1.0000	1.0000	1.0000	1.0000	0.9999	0.9993
16	1.0000	1.0000	1.0000	1.0000	1.0000	1.0000	1.0000	1.0000	0.9999
17	1.0000	1.0000	1.0000	1.0000	1.0000	1.0000	1.0000	1.0000	1.0000

$n = 19$

$a\backslash p$	0.10	0.15	0.20	0.25	0.30	0.35	0.40	0.45	0.50
0	0.1351	0.0456	0.0144	0.0042	0.0011	0.0003	0.0001	0.0000	0.0000
1	0.4203	0.1985	0.0829	0.0310	0.0104	0.0031	0.0008	0.0002	0.0000
2	0.7054	0.4413	0.2369	0.1113	0.0462	0.0170	0.0055	0.0015	0.0004
3	0.8850	0.6841	0.4551	0.2631	0.1332	0.0591	0.0230	0.0077	0.0022
4	0.9648	0.8556	0.6733	0.4654	0.2822	0.1500	0.0696	0.0280	0.0096
5	0.9914	0.9463	0.8369	0.6678	0.4739	0.2968	0.1629	0.0777	0.0318
6	0.9983	0.9837	0.9324	0.8251	0.6655	0.4812	0.3081	0.1727	0.0835
7	0.9997	0.9959	0.9767	0.9225	0.8180	0.6656	0.4878	0.3169	0.1796
8	1.0000	0.9992	0.9933	0.9713	0.9161	0.8145	0.6675	0.4940	0.3238
9	1.0000	0.9999	0.9984	0.9911	0.9674	0.9125	0.8139	0.6710	0.5000
10	1.0000	1.0000	0.9997	0.9977	0.9895	0.9653	0.9115	0.8159	0.6762
11	1.0000	1.0000	1.0000	0.9995	0.9972	0.9886	0.9648	0.9129	0.8204
12	1.0000	1.0000	1.0000	0.9999	0.9994	0.9969	0.9884	0.9658	0.9165
13	1.0000	1.0000	1.0000	1.0000	0.9999	0.9993	0.9969	0.9891	0.9682
14	1.0000	1.0000	1.0000	1.0000	1.0000	0.9999	0.9994	0.9972	0.9904
15	1.0000	1.0000	1.0000	1.0000	1.0000	1.0000	0.9999	0.9995	0.9978
16	1.0000	1.0000	1.0000	1.0000	1.0000	1.0000	1.0000	0.9999	0.9996
17	1.0000	1.0000	1.0000	1.0000	1.0000	1.0000	1.0000	1.0000	1.0000

Table II: Cumulative Standard Normal Probabilities
$P(Z < a)$ where $Z \sim N(0,1)$

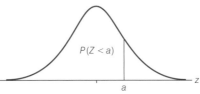

Example: $P(Z < -1.92) = 0.0274$

a	0.00	0.01	0.02	0.03	0.04	0.05	0.06	0.07	0.08	0.09
−3.4	0.0003	0.0003	0.0003	0.0003	0.0003	0.0003	0.0003	0.0003	0.0003	0.0002
−3.3	0.0005	0.0005	0.0005	0.0004	0.0004	0.0004	0.0004	0.0004	0.0004	0.0003
−3.2	0.0007	0.0007	0.0006	0.0006	0.0006	0.0006	0.0006	0.0005	0.0005	0.0005
−3.1	0.0010	0.0009	0.0009	0.0009	0.0008	0.0008	0.0008	0.0008	0.0007	0.0007
−3.0	0.0013	0.0013	0.0013	0.0012	0.0012	0.0011	0.0011	0.0011	0.0010	0.0010
−2.9	0.0019	0.0018	0.0018	0.0017	0.0016	0.0016	0.0015	0.0015	0.0014	0.0014
−2.8	0.0026	0.0025	0.0024	0.0023	0.0023	0.0022	0.0021	0.0021	0.0020	0.0019
−2.7	0.0035	0.0034	0.0033	0.0032	0.0031	0.0030	0.0029	0.0028	0.0027	0.0026
−2.6	0.0047	0.0045	0.0044	0.0043	0.0041	0.0040	0.0039	0.0038	0.0037	0.0036
−2.5	0.0062	0.0060	0.0059	0.0057	0.0055	0.0054	0.0052	0.0051	0.0049	0.0048
−2.4	0.0082	0.0080	0.0078	0.0075	0.0073	0.0071	0.0069	0.0068	0.0066	0.0064
−2.3	0.0107	0.0104	0.0102	0.0099	0.0096	0.0094	0.0091	0.0089	0.0087	0.0084
−2.2	0.0139	0.0136	0.0132	0.0129	0.0125	0.0122	0.0119	0.0116	0.0113	0.0110
−2.1	0.0179	0.0174	0.0170	0.0166	0.0162	0.0158	0.0154	0.0150	0.0146	0.0143
−2.0	0.0228	0.0222	0.0217	0.0212	0.0207	0.0202	0.0197	0.0192	0.0188	0.0183
−1.9	0.0287	0.0281	0.0274	0.0268	0.0262	0.0256	0.0250	0.0244	0.0239	0.0233
−1.8	0.0359	0.0351	0.0344	0.0336	0.0329	0.0322	0.0314	0.0307	0.0301	0.0294
−1.7	0.0446	0.0436	0.0427	0.0418	0.0409	0.0401	0.0392	0.0384	0.0375	0.0367
−1.6	0.0548	0.0537	0.0526	0.0516	0.0505	0.0495	0.0485	0.0475	0.0465	0.0455
−1.5	0.0668	0.0655	0.0643	0.0630	0.0618	0.0606	0.0594	0.0582	0.0571	0.0559
−1.4	0.0808	0.0793	0.0778	0.0764	0.0749	0.0735	0.0721	0.0708	0.0694	0.0681
−1.3	0.0968	0.0951	0.0934	0.0918	0.0901	0.0885	0.0869	0.0853	0.0838	0.0823
−1.2	0.1151	0.1131	0.1112	0.1093	0.1075	0.1056	0.1038	0.1020	0.1003	0.0985
−1.1	0.1357	0.1335	0.1314	0.1292	0.1271	0.1251	0.1230	0.1210	0.1190	0.1170
−1.0	0.1587	0.1562	0.1539	0.1515	0.1492	0.1469	0.1446	0.1423	0.1401	0.1379
−0.9	0.1841	0.1814	0.1788	0.1762	0.1736	0.1711	0.1685	0.1660	0.1635	0.1611
−0.8	0.2119	0.2090	0.2061	0.2033	0.2005	0.1977	0.1949	0.1922	0.1894	0.1867
−0.7	0.2420	0.2389	0.2358	0.2327	0.2296	0.2266	0.2236	0.2206	0.2177	0.2148
−0.6	0.2743	0.2709	0.2676	0.2643	0.2611	0.2578	0.2546	0.2514	0.2483	0.2451
−0.5	0.3085	0.3050	0.3015	0.2981	0.2946	0.2912	0.2877	0.2843	0.2810	0.2776
−0.4	0.3446	0.3409	0.3372	0.3336	0.3300	0.3264	0.3228	0.3192	0.3156	0.3121
−0.3	0.3821	0.3783	0.3745	0.3707	0.3669	0.3632	0.3594	0.3557	0.3520	0.3483
−0.2	0.4207	0.4168	0.4129	0.4090	0.4052	0.4013	0.3974	0.3936	0.3897	0.3859
−0.1	0.4602	0.4562	0.4522	0.4483	0.4443	0.4404	0.4364	0.4325	0.4286	0.4247
0.0	0.5000	0.4960	0.4920	0.4880	0.4840	0.4801	0.4761	0.4721	0.4681	0.4641
z	0.00	0.01	0.02	0.03	0.04	0.05	0.06	0.07	0.08	0.09

Table II: Cumulative Standard Normal Probabilities
$P(Z < a)$ where $Z \sim N(0,1)$

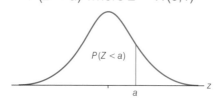

$P(Z < a)$

Example: $P(Z < -1.92) = 0.0274$

a	0.00	0.01	0.02	0.03	0.04	0.05	0.06	0.07	0.08	0.09
0.0	0.5000	0.5040	0.5080	0.5120	0.5160	0.5199	0.5239	0.5279	0.5319	0.5359
0.1	0.5398	0.5438	0.5478	0.5517	0.5557	0.5596	0.5636	0.5675	0.5714	0.5753
0.2	0.5793	0.5832	0.5871	0.5910	0.5948	0.5987	0.6026	0.6064	0.6103	0.6141
0.3	0.6179	0.6217	0.6255	0.6293	0.6331	0.6368	0.6406	0.6443	0.6480	0.6517
0.4	0.6554	0.6591	0.6628	0.6664	0.6700	0.6736	0.6772	0.6808	0.6844	0.6879
0.5	0.6915	0.6950	0.6985	0.7019	0.7054	0.7088	0.7123	0.7157	0.7190	0.7224
0.6	0.7257	0.7291	0.7324	0.7357	0.7389	0.7422	0.7454	0.7486	0.7517	0.7549
0.7	0.7580	0.7611	0.7642	0.7673	0.7703	0.7734	0.7764	0.7794	0.7823	0.7852
0.8	0.7881	0.7910	0.7939	0.7967	0.7995	0.8023	0.8051	0.8078	0.8106	0.8133
0.9	0.8159	0.8186	0.8212	0.8238	0.8264	0.8289	0.8315	0.8340	0.8365	0.8389
1.0	0.8413	0.8438	0.8461	0.8485	0.8508	0.8531	0.8554	0.8577	0.8599	0.8621
1.1	0.8643	0.8665	0.8686	0.8708	0.8729	0.8749	0.8770	0.8790	0.8810	0.8830
1.2	0.8849	0.8869	0.8888	0.8907	0.8925	0.8944	0.8962	0.8980	0.8997	0.9015
1.3	0.9032	0.9049	0.9066	0.9082	0.9099	0.9115	0.9131	0.9147	0.9162	0.9177
1.4	0.9192	0.9207	0.9222	0.9236	0.9251	0.9265	0.9279	0.9292	0.9306	0.9319
1.5	0.9332	0.9345	0.9357	0.9370	0.9382	0.9394	0.9406	0.9418	0.9429	0.9441
1.6	0.9452	0.9463	0.9474	0.9484	0.9495	0.9505	0.9515	0.9525	0.9535	0.9545
1.7	0.9554	0.9564	0.9573	0.9582	0.9591	0.9599	0.9608	0.9616	0.9625	0.9633
1.8	0.9641	0.9649	0.9656	0.9664	0.9671	0.9678	0.9686	0.9693	0.9699	0.9706
1.9	0.9713	0.9719	0.9726	0.9732	0.9738	0.9744	0.9750	0.9756	0.9761	0.9767
2.0	0.9772	0.9778	0.9783	0.9788	0.9793	0.9798	0.9803	0.9808	0.9812	0.9817
2.1	0.9821	0.9826	0.9830	0.9834	0.9838	0.9842	0.9846	0.9850	0.9854	0.9857
2.2	0.9861	0.9864	0.9868	0.9871	0.9875	0.9878	0.9881	0.9884	0.9887	0.9890
2.3	0.9893	0.9896	0.9898	0.9901	0.9904	0.9906	0.9909	0.9911	0.9913	0.9916
2.4	0.9918	0.9920	0.9922	0.9925	0.9927	0.9929	0.9931	0.9932	0.9934	0.9936
2.5	0.9938	0.9940	0.9941	0.9943	0.9945	0.9946	0.9948	0.9949	0.9951	0.9952
2.6	0.9953	0.9955	0.9956	0.9957	0.9959	0.9960	0.9961	0.9962	0.9963	0.9964
2.7	0.9965	0.9966	0.9967	0.9968	0.9969	0.9970	0.9971	0.9972	0.9973	0.9974
2.8	0.9974	0.9975	0.9976	0.9977	0.9977	0.9978	0.9979	0.9979	0.9980	0.9981
2.9	0.9981	0.9982	0.9982	0.9983	0.9984	0.9984	0.9985	0.9985	0.9986	0.9986
3.0	0.9987	0.9987	0.9987	0.9988	0.9988	0.9989	0.9989	0.9989	0.9990	0.9990
3.1	0.9990	0.9991	0.9991	0.9991	0.9992	0.9992	0.9992	0.9992	0.9993	0.9993
3.2	0.9993	0.9993	0.9994	0.9994	0.9994	0.9994	0.9994	0.9995	0.9995	0.9995
3.3	0.9995	0.9995	0.9995	0.9996	0.9996	0.9996	0.9996	0.9996	0.9996	0.9997
3.4	0.9997	0.9997	0.9997	0.9997	0.9997	0.9997	0.9997	0.9997	0.9997	0.9998
z	0.00	0.01	0.02	0.03	0.04	0.05	0.06	0.07	0.08	0.09

Table III: Percentage Points of the Standard Normal Distribution
The table gives values of a where P(Z < a) = p

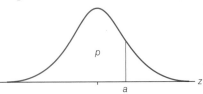

Example: find a such that P(Z < a) = 0.05; solution: a = –1.6449

p	0.000	0.001	0.002	0.003	0.004	0.005	0.006	0.007	0.008	0.009
0.00	–∞	–3.0902	–2.8782	–2.7478	–2.6521	–2.5758	–2.5121	–2.4573	–2.4093	–2.3656
0.01	–2.3263	–2.2904	–2.2571	–2.2262	–2.1973	–2.1701	–2.1444	–2.1201	–2.0969	–2.0749
0.02	–2.0537	–2.0335	–2.0141	–1.9954	–1.9774	–1.9600	–1.9431	–1.9268	–1.9110	–1.8957
0.03	–1.8808	–1.8663	–1.8522	–1.8384	–1.8250	–1.8119	–1.7991	–1.7866	–1.7744	–1.7624
0.04	–1.7507	–1.7392	–1.7279	–1.7169	–1.7060	–1.6954	–1.6849	–1.6747	–1.6646	–1.6546
0.05	–1.6449	–1.6352	–1.6258	–1.6164	–1.6072	–1.5982	–1.5893	–1.5805	–1.5718	–1.5632
0.06	–1.5548	–1.5464	–1.5382	–1.5301	–1.5220	–1.5141	–1.5063	–1.4985	–1.4909	–1.4833
0.07	–1.4758	–1.4684	–1.4611	–1.4538	–1.4466	–1.4395	–1.4325	–1.4255	–1.4187	–1.4118
0.08	–1.4051	–1.3984	–1.3917	–1.3852	–1.3787	–1.3722	–1.3658	–1.3595	–1.3532	–1.3469
0.09	–1.3408	–1.3346	–1.3285	–1.3225	–1.3165	–1.3106	–1.3047	–1.2988	–1.2930	–1.2873
0.10	–1.2816	–1.2759	–1.2702	–1.2646	–1.2591	–1.2536	–1.2481	–1.2426	–1.2372	–1.2319
0.11	–1.2265	–1.2212	–1.2160	–1.2107	–1.2055	–1.2004	–1.1952	–1.1901	–1.1850	–1.1800
0.12	–1.1750	–1.1700	–1.1650	–1.1601	–1.1552	–1.1503	–1.1455	–1.1407	–1.1359	–1.1311
0.13	–1.1264	–1.1217	–1.1170	–1.1123	–1.1077	–1.1031	–1.0985	–1.0939	–1.0893	–1.0848
0.14	–1.0803	–1.0758	–1.0714	–1.0669	–1.0625	–1.0581	–1.0537	–1.0494	–1.0450	–1.0407
0.15	–1.0364	–1.0322	–1.0279	–1.0237	–1.0194	–1.0152	–1.0110	–1.0069	–1.0027	–0.9986
0.16	–0.9945	–0.9904	–0.9863	–0.9822	–0.9782	–0.9741	–0.9701	–0.9661	–0.9621	–0.9581
0.17	–0.9542	–0.9502	–0.9463	–0.9424	–0.9385	–0.9346	–0.9307	–0.9269	–0.9230	–0.9192
0.18	–0.9154	–0.9116	–0.9078	–0.9040	–0.9002	–0.8965	–0.8927	–0.8890	–0.8853	–0.8816
0.19	–0.8779	–0.8742	–0.8705	–0.8669	–0.8633	–0.8596	–0.8560	–0.8524	–0.8488	–0.8452
0.20	–0.8416	–0.8381	–0.8345	–0.8310	–0.8274	–0.8239	–0.8204	–0.8169	–0.8134	–0.8099
0.21	–0.8064	–0.8030	–0.7995	–0.7961	–0.7926	–0.7892	–0.7858	–0.7824	–0.7790	–0.7756
0.22	–0.7722	–0.7688	–0.7655	–0.7621	–0.7588	–0.7554	–0.7521	–0.7488	–0.7454	–0.7421
0.23	–0.7388	–0.7356	–0.7323	–0.7290	–0.7257	–0.7225	–0.7192	–0.7160	–0.7128	–0.7095
0.24	–0.7063	–0.7031	–0.6999	–0.6967	–0.6935	–0.6903	–0.6871	–0.6840	–0.6808	–0.6776
0.25	–0.6745	–0.6713	–0.6682	–0.6651	–0.6620	–0.6588	–0.6557	–0.6526	–0.6495	–0.6464
0.26	–0.6433	–0.6403	–0.6372	–0.6341	–0.6311	–0.6280	–0.6250	–0.6219	–0.6189	–0.6158
0.27	–0.6128	–0.6098	–0.6068	–0.6038	–0.6008	–0.5978	–0.5948	–0.5918	–0.5888	–0.5858
0.28	–0.5828	–0.5799	–0.5769	–0.5740	–0.5710	–0.5681	–0.5651	–0.5622	–0.5592	–0.5563
0.29	–0.5534	–0.5505	–0.5476	–0.5446	–0.5417	–0.5388	–0.5359	–0.5330	–0.5302	–0.5273
0.30	–0.5244	–0.5215	–0.5187	–0.5158	–0.5129	–0.5101	–0.5072	–0.5044	–0.5015	–0.4987
0.31	–0.4959	–0.4930	–0.4902	–0.4874	–0.4845	–0.4817	–0.4789	–0.4761	–0.4733	–0.4705
0.32	–0.4677	–0.4649	–0.4621	–0.4593	–0.4565	–0.4538	–0.4510	–0.4482	–0.4454	–0.4427
0.33	–0.4399	–0.4372	–0.4344	–0.4316	–0.4289	–0.4261	–0.4234	–0.4207	–0.4179	–0.4152
0.34	–0.4125	–0.4097	–0.4070	–0.4043	–0.4016	–0.3989	–0.3961	–0.3934	–0.3907	–0.3880
0.35	–0.3853	–0.3826	–0.3799	–0.3772	–0.3745	–0.3719	–0.3692	–0.3665	–0.3638	–0.3611
0.36	–0.3585	–0.3558	–0.3531	–0.3505	–0.3478	–0.3451	–0.3425	–0.3398	–0.3372	–0.3345
0.37	–0.3319	–0.3292	–0.3266	–0.3239	–0.3213	–0.3186	–0.3160	–0.3134	–0.3107	–0.3081
0.38	–0.3055	–0.3029	–0.3002	–0.2976	–0.2950	–0.2924	–0.2898	–0.2871	–0.2845	–0.2819
0.39	–0.2793	–0.2767	–0.2741	–0.2715	–0.2689	–0.2663	–0.2637	–0.2611	–0.2585	–0.2559
0.40	–0.2533	–0.2508	–0.2482	–0.2456	–0.2430	–0.2404	–0.2378	–0.2353	–0.2327	–0.2301
0.41	–0.2275	–0.2250	–0.2224	–0.2198	–0.2173	–0.2147	–0.2121	–0.2096	–0.2070	–0.2045
0.42	–0.2019	–0.1993	–0.1968	–0.1942	–0.1917	–0.1891	–0.1866	–0.1840	–0.1815	–0.1789
0.43	–0.1764	–0.1738	–0.1713	–0.1687	–0.1662	–0.1637	–0.1611	–0.1586	–0.1560	–0.1535
0.44	–0.1510	–0.1484	–0.1459	–0.1434	–0.1408	–0.1383	–0.1358	–0.1332	–0.1307	–0.1282
0.45	–0.1257	–0.1231	–0.1206	–0.1181	–0.1156	–0.1130	–0.1105	–0.1080	–0.1055	–0.1030
0.46	–0.1004	–0.0979	–0.0954	–0.0929	–0.0904	–0.0878	–0.0853	–0.0828	–0.0803	–0.0778
0.47	–0.0753	–0.0728	–0.0702	–0.0677	–0.0652	–0.0627	–0.0602	–0.0577	–0.0552	–0.0527
0.48	–0.0502	–0.0476	–0.0451	–0.0426	–0.0401	–0.0376	–0.0351	–0.0326	–0.0301	–0.0276
0.49	–0.0251	–0.0226	–0.0201	–0.0175	–0.0150	–0.0125	–0.0100	–0.0075	–0.0050	–0.0025
p	0.000	0.001	0.002	0.003	0.004	0.005	0.006	0.007	0.008	0.009

Table III: Percentage Points of the Standard Normal Distribution
The table gives values of a where $P(Z < a) = p$

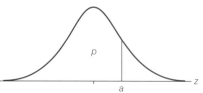

Example: find a such that $P(Z < a) = 0.05$; solution: $a = -1.6449$

p	0.000	0.001	0.002	0.003	0.004	0.005	0.006	0.007	0.008	0.009
0.50	0.0000	0.0025	0.0050	0.0075	0.0100	0.0125	0.0150	0.0175	0.0201	0.0226
0.51	0.0251	0.0276	0.0301	0.0326	0.0351	0.0376	0.0401	0.0426	0.0451	0.0476
0.52	0.0502	0.0527	0.0552	0.0577	0.0602	0.0627	0.0652	0.0677	0.0702	0.0728
0.53	0.0753	0.0778	0.0803	0.0828	0.0853	0.0878	0.0904	0.0929	0.0954	0.0979
0.54	0.1004	0.1030	0.1055	0.1080	0.1105	0.1130	0.1156	0.1181	0.1206	0.1231
0.55	0.1257	0.1282	0.1307	0.1332	0.1358	0.1383	0.1408	0.1434	0.1459	0.1484
0.56	0.1510	0.1535	0.1560	0.1586	0.1611	0.1637	0.1662	0.1687	0.1713	0.1738
0.57	0.1764	0.1789	0.1815	0.1840	0.1866	0.1891	0.1917	0.1942	0.1968	0.1993
0.58	0.2019	0.2045	0.2070	0.2096	0.2121	0.2147	0.2173	0.2198	0.2224	0.2250
0.59	0.2275	0.2301	0.2327	0.2353	0.2378	0.2404	0.2430	0.2456	0.2482	0.2508
0.60	0.2533	0.2559	0.2585	0.2611	0.2637	0.2663	0.2689	0.2715	0.2741	0.2767
0.61	0.2793	0.2819	0.2845	0.2871	0.2898	0.2924	0.2950	0.2976	0.3002	0.3029
0.62	0.3055	0.3081	0.3107	0.3134	0.3160	0.3186	0.3213	0.3239	0.3266	0.3292
0.63	0.3319	0.3345	0.3372	0.3398	0.3425	0.3451	0.3478	0.3505	0.3531	0.3558
0.64	0.3585	0.3611	0.3638	0.3665	0.3692	0.3719	0.3745	0.3772	0.3799	0.3826
0.65	0.3853	0.3880	0.3907	0.3934	0.3961	0.3989	0.4016	0.4043	0.4070	0.4097
0.66	0.4125	0.4152	0.4179	0.4207	0.4234	0.4261	0.4289	0.4316	0.4344	0.4372
0.67	0.4399	0.4427	0.4454	0.4482	0.4510	0.4538	0.4565	0.4593	0.4621	0.4649
0.68	0.4677	0.4705	0.4733	0.4761	0.4789	0.4817	0.4845	0.4874	0.4902	0.4930
0.69	0.4959	0.4987	0.5015	0.5044	0.5072	0.5101	0.5129	0.5158	0.5187	0.5215
0.70	0.5244	0.5273	0.5302	0.5330	0.5359	0.5388	0.5417	0.5446	0.5476	0.5505
0.71	0.5534	0.5563	0.5592	0.5622	0.5651	0.5681	0.5710	0.5740	0.5769	0.5799
0.72	0.5828	0.5858	0.5888	0.5918	0.5948	0.5978	0.6008	0.6038	0.6068	0.6098
0.73	0.6128	0.6158	0.6189	0.6219	0.6250	0.6280	0.6311	0.6341	0.6372	0.6403
0.74	0.6433	0.6464	0.6495	0.6526	0.6557	0.6588	0.6620	0.6651	0.6682	0.6713
0.75	0.6745	0.6776	0.6808	0.6840	0.6871	0.6903	0.6935	0.6967	0.6999	0.7031
0.76	0.7063	0.7095	0.7128	0.7160	0.7192	0.7225	0.7257	0.7290	0.7323	0.7356
0.77	0.7388	0.7421	0.7454	0.7488	0.7521	0.7554	0.7588	0.7621	0.7655	0.7688
0.78	0.7722	0.7756	0.7790	0.7824	0.7858	0.7892	0.7926	0.7961	0.7995	0.8030
0.79	0.8064	0.8099	0.8134	0.8169	0.8204	0.8239	0.8274	0.8310	0.8345	0.8381
0.80	0.8416	0.8452	0.8488	0.8524	0.8560	0.8596	0.8633	0.8669	0.8705	0.8742
0.81	0.8779	0.8816	0.8853	0.8890	0.8927	0.8965	0.9002	0.9040	0.9078	0.9116
0.82	0.9154	0.9192	0.9230	0.9269	0.9307	0.9346	0.9385	0.9424	0.9463	0.9502
0.83	0.9542	0.9581	0.9621	0.9661	0.9701	0.9741	0.9782	0.9822	0.9863	0.9904
0.84	0.9945	0.9986	1.0027	1.0069	1.0110	1.0152	1.0194	1.0237	1.0279	1.0322
0.85	1.0364	1.0407	1.0450	1.0494	1.0537	1.0581	1.0625	1.0669	1.0714	1.0758
0.86	1.0803	1.0848	1.0893	1.0939	1.0985	1.1031	1.1077	1.1123	1.1170	1.1217
0.87	1.1264	1.1311	1.1359	1.1407	1.1455	1.1503	1.1552	1.1601	1.1650	1.1700
0.88	1.1750	1.1800	1.1850	1.1901	1.1952	1.2004	1.2055	1.2107	1.2160	1.2212
0.89	1.2265	1.2319	1.2372	1.2426	1.2481	1.2536	1.2591	1.2646	1.2702	1.2759
0.90	1.2816	1.2873	1.2930	1.2988	1.3047	1.3106	1.3165	1.3225	1.3285	1.3346
0.91	1.3408	1.3469	1.3532	1.3595	1.3658	1.3722	1.3787	1.3852	1.3917	1.3984
0.92	1.4051	1.4118	1.4187	1.4255	1.4325	1.4395	1.4466	1.4538	1.4611	1.4684
0.93	1.4758	1.4833	1.4909	1.4985	1.5063	1.5141	1.5220	1.5301	1.5382	1.5464
0.94	1.5548	1.5632	1.5718	1.5805	1.5893	1.5982	1.6072	1.6164	1.6258	1.6352
0.95	1.6449	1.6546	1.6646	1.6747	1.6849	1.6954	1.7060	1.7169	1.7279	1.7392
0.96	1.7507	1.7624	1.7744	1.7866	1.7991	1.8119	1.8250	1.8384	1.8522	1.8663
0.97	1.8808	1.8957	1.9110	1.9268	1.9431	1.9600	1.9774	1.9954	2.0141	2.0335
0.98	2.0537	2.0749	2.0969	2.1201	2.1444	2.1701	2.1973	2.2262	2.2571	2.2904
0.99	2.3263	2.3656	2.4089	2.4573	2.5121	2.5758	2.6521	2.7478	2.8782	3.0902
p	0.000	0.001	0.002	0.003	0.004	0.005	0.006	0.007	0.008	0.009

Table IV: Random Digits

12880	39481	06719	67889	24177	18615	88755	72544	93802	58151
26820	49041	93121	95991	31169	16611	52030	65875	23226	39246
66779	26615	80802	21830	25534	74512	75988	00219	82246	56990
37207	48270	78543	87410	16506	99199	92167	04675	13795	37759
74605	61368	81168	20333	21479	50641	91707	30808	94056	84188
46712	95941	93071	43028	48125	19946	81238	66300	27209	74507
53722	18053	06335	11473	40195	56495	93174	05056	79334	42141
86114	45679	98061	36244	51931	95687	12406	83263	94012	73639
67772	90277	07583	89648	07633	60643	89637	89734	16930	40209
57548	19290	62738	12883	57848	87408	44982	91135	95644	01200
26276	59332	26216	86763	49716	88089	50438	11110	44016	83192
66404	53203	96214	00709	19574	42047	78308	94007	38079	94567
62797	22541	49794	52353	64738	69385	61473	29120	11364	39414
98466	31486	17698	50166	82828	29069	02337	23852	91925	62126
27906	69732	25269	65624	41969	65308	21254	79295	83127	18489
51665	45021	12910	46268	96228	94785	67658	41164	17771	94679
04996	00183	77927	72863	41688	81582	31484	30254	45654	98456
51327	47253	60249	52125	81916	34508	47819	51022	58582	27113
60753	19609	40683	65708	73833	90581	25402	49749	32423	53498
04432	75920	88683	47557	67072	30067	90355	45227	35217	78525
83561	95916	03440	92334	28345	29035	13309	11497	35872	24941
46213	41158	40623	46633	51153	81169	85428	15987	05911	59229
12523	12900	89242	54927	05867	04408	14906	64293	19107	51579
22907	45835	98845	94912	48343	03111	80528	53821	67864	74362
05897	64294	74026	23175	51320	24866	92382	10329	95177	00930
59296	92383	21849	62789	12137	30955	19625	48944	47514	12568
44361	77117	03349	49138	48075	81060	85438	05885	29832	04355
40014	71537	36099	33749	87906	85903	68194	93508	57702	71619
29898	98373	76707	31606	82430	80283	01316	72944	91645	50953
91363	67070	21979	87718	95629	27988	11723	80561	62014	48630
24352	08673	09717	74545	52049	82870	36260	42230	23797	48479
50237	13262	71172	43316	96448	34916	66253	21641	50831	65330
48163	46784	81546	96119	11193	73893	18853	59299	87122	02441
84685	47433	79679	90214	05611	12224	91988	29030	36286	06598
67132	82119	87984	95821	03362	54700	62041	65781	07806	36368
49596	27300	42321	74669	40202	01101	91326	46030	46799	42549
74365	89107	44609	75610	31342	08919	13005	73187	59236	03644
76498	09120	20286	24130	25063	66525	65539	87647	42930	93994
26514	82508	14281	98182	84929	04443	72889	16046	61083	50276
95570	01252	67735	87393	69840	05371	27658	86971	10388	75443
14921	52039	34501	35423	43449	00685	88410	77442	01189	04506
62463	83721	60729	88138	40996	94151	78095	08267	93146	69092
12697	78211	74804	58968	27766	64839	80714	24397	45898	20428
80666	14592	26762	89786	51531	17685	81886	41071	91767	12044
62027	45650	40274	97316	77431	16589	53236	53905	48708	31411
48006	37604	35718	55943	95509	60687	71535	08377	86638	62185
77186	90530	05797	14540	52108	30843	67760	14874	30867	73790
51258	97221	84790	93495	18693	56038	84299	05404	86018	03517
41227	34710	79716	41146	67735	10798	90091	22852	81275	55162
25157	73527	88038	00948	16030	17142	95983	15331	84862	32656

Table V: Percentage Points of the t Distribution
The table gives the value a, such that P(T < a) = p where T is a random variable from a t distribution with v degrees of freedom (d.o.f.)

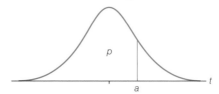

Example: P(T < 2.093) = 0.975 where T has 19 d.o.f.

p v	0.75	0.90	0.95	0.975	0.99	0.995	0.9995
1	1.000	3.078	6.314	12.706	31.821	63.657	636.619
2	0.816	1.886	2.920	4.303	6.965	9.925	31.599
3	0.765	1.638	2.353	3.182	4.541	5.841	12.924
4	0.741	1.533	2.132	2.776	3.747	4.604	8.610
5	0.727	1.476	2.015	2.571	3.365	4.032	6.869
6	0.718	1.440	1.943	2.447	3.143	3.707	5.959
7	0.711	1.415	1.895	2.365	2.998	3.499	5.408
8	0.706	1.397	1.860	2.306	2.896	3.355	5.041
9	0.703	1.383	1.833	2.262	2.821	3.250	4.781
10	0.700	1.372	1.812	2.228	2.764	3.169	4.587
11	0.697	1.363	1.796	2.201	2.718	3.106	4.437
12	0.695	1.356	1.782	2.179	2.681	3.055	4.318
13	0.694	1.350	1.771	2.160	2.650	3.012	4.221
14	0.692	1.345	1.761	2.145	2.624	2.977	4.140
15	0.691	1.341	1.753	2.131	2.602	2.947	4.073
16	0.690	1.337	1.746	2.120	2.583	2.921	4.015
17	0.689	1.333	1.740	2.110	2.567	2.898	3.965
18	0.688	1.330	1.734	2.101	2.552	2.878	3.922
19	0.688	1.328	1.729	2.093	2.539	2.861	3.883
20	0.687	1.325	1.725	2.086	2.528	2.845	3.850
21	0.686	1.323	1.721	2.080	2.518	2.831	3.819
22	0.686	1.321	1.717	2.074	2.508	2.819	3.792
23	0.685	1.319	1.714	2.069	2.500	2.807	3.768
24	0.685	1.318	1.711	2.064	2.492	2.797	3.745
25	0.684	1.316	1.708	2.060	2.485	2.787	3.725
26	0.684	1.315	1.706	2.056	2.479	2.779	3.707
27	0.684	1.314	1.703	2.052	2.473	2.771	3.690
28	0.683	1.313	1.701	2.048	2.467	2.763	3.674
29	0.683	1.311	1.699	2.045	2.462	2.756	3.659
30	0.683	1.310	1.697	2.042	2.457	2.750	3.646
40	0.681	1.303	1.684	2.021	2.423	2.704	3.551
50	0.679	1.299	1.676	2.009	2.403	2.678	3.496
60	0.679	1.296	1.671	2.000	2.390	2.660	3.460
70	0.678	1.294	1.667	1.994	2.381	2.648	3.435
80	0.678	1.292	1.664	1.990	2.374	2.639	3.416
90	0.677	1.291	1.662	1.987	2.368	2.632	3.402
100	0.677	1.290	1.660	1.984	2.364	2.626	3.390
120	0.677	1.289	1.658	1.980	2.358	2.617	3.373
∞	0.674	1.282	1.645	1.960	2.326	2.576	3.291

Table VI: Percentage Points of the χ^2 Distribution
The table gives the value a such that $P(\chi_v^2 > a) = p$

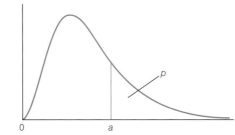

Example: $P(\chi^2 > 7.815) = 0.05$ where χ^2 has 3 d.o.f.

p	0.250	0.100	0.050	0.025	0.010	0.005	0.0005
v 1	1.323	2.706	3.841	5.024	6.635	7.879	12.116
2	2.773	4.605	5.991	7.378	9.210	10.597	15.202
3	4.108	6.251	7.815	9.348	11.345	12.838	17.730
4	5.385	7.779	9.488	11.143	13.277	14.860	19.997
5	6.626	9.236	11.070	12.833	15.086	16.750	22.105
6	7.841	10.645	12.592	14.449	16.812	18.548	24.103
7	9.037	12.017	14.067	16.013	18.475	20.278	26.018
8	10.219	13.362	15.507	17.535	20.090	21.955	27.868
9	11.389	14.684	16.919	19.023	21.666	23.589	29.666
10	12.549	15.987	18.307	20.483	23.209	25.188	31.420
11	13.701	17.275	19.675	21.920	24.725	26.757	33.137
12	14.845	18.549	21.026	23.337	26.217	28.300	34.821
13	15.984	19.812	22.362	24.736	27.688	29.819	36.478
14	17.117	21.064	23.685	26.119	29.141	31.319	38.109
15	18.245	22.307	24.996	27.488	30.578	32.801	39.719
16	19.369	23.542	26.296	28.845	32.000	34.267	41.308
17	20.489	24.769	27.587	30.191	33.409	35.718	42.879
18	21.605	25.989	28.869	31.526	34.805	37.156	44.434
19	22.718	27.204	30.144	32.852	36.191	38.582	45.973
20	23.828	28.412	31.410	34.170	37.566	39.997	47.498
21	24.935	29.615	32.671	35.479	38.932	41.401	49.011
22	26.039	30.813	33.924	36.781	40.289	42.796	50.511
23	27.141	32.007	35.172	38.076	41.638	44.181	52.000
24	28.241	33.196	36.415	39.364	42.980	45.559	53.479
25	29.339	34.382	37.652	40.646	44.314	46.928	54.947
26	30.435	35.563	38.885	41.923	45.642	48.290	56.407
27	31.528	36.741	40.113	43.195	46.963	49.645	57.858
28	32.620	37.916	41.337	44.461	48.278	50.993	59.300
29	33.711	39.087	42.557	45.722	49.588	52.336	60.735
30	34.800	40.256	43.773	46.979	50.892	53.672	62.162
31	35.887	41.422	44.985	48.232	52.191	55.003	63.582
32	36.973	42.585	46.194	49.480	53.486	56.328	64.995
33	38.058	43.745	47.400	50.725	54.776	57.648	66.403
34	39.141	44.903	48.602	51.966	56.061	58.964	67.803
35	40.223	46.059	49.802	53.203	57.342	60.275	69.199
36	41.304	47.212	50.998	54.437	58.619	61.581	70.588
37	42.383	48.363	52.192	55.668	59.892	62.883	71.972
38	43.462	49.513	53.384	56.896	61.162	64.181	73.351
39	44.539	50.660	54.572	58.120	62.428	65.476	74.725
40	45.616	51.805	55.758	59.342	63.691	66.766	76.095
45	50.985	57.505	61.656	65.410	69.957	73.166	82.876
50	56.334	63.167	67.505	71.420	76.154	79.490	89.561
60	66.981	74.397	79.082	83.298	88.379	91.952	102.695
70	77.577	85.527	90.531	95.023	100.425	104.215	115.478
80	88.130	96.578	101.879	106.629	112.329	116.321	128.261
90	98.650	107.565	113.145	118.136	124.116	128.299	140.782

Index

μ *see* mu
χ^2 *see* chi-squared distribution
Σ *see* sigma

A AND B event   344–9
A OR B event   344–9
ABC classification   753
absolute value   458
accrued interest   172–3
activity   726
   float   736
   preceding   730
addition of fractions   40–6, 54
additive model   627, 633,
   635–9
aggregate indices   316–318
alternative hypothesis   533–45
   contingency table   689
   linear regression model
      588–9
   one- and two-sided   545–6
   and rejection regions
      556–60
   testing for mean   549
AND events   344–9
AND probabilities   360–7
annual percentage rate   760
annuities   783
   discount rates   783
   present values   783
arrival rate   857
assignable causes, quality
   control   822
association, test of   689
averages, *see also* expected value
   run length   833

back ordering *see* backlogged
   demands
backlogged demands   749–51,
   753
bar charts   271–4
base   2 logarithms 169
base   10 logarithms 169
base *e* logarithms   229–33
base periods   315
base values   314–15
base-weighted index   317
bases, logarithms   162–71
batch size   744–5, 749
binary data   673

and categorical data   686–7
binding constraints   716, 717
binomial distribution   398–415
   cumulative probabilities
      405–6
   mean   408–9
   normal approximation to
      471–6
   plots   409–11
   probabilities   399–406
   probabilities, using a
      computer   408
   simulation   853–4
   summary   411–12
   tables of probabilities   406–8,
      862–6
   variance   408–9
   when *n* is large   471–8
brackets
   expanding   57–64
   introduction   11–12
   layers of   12
   multiplying out   57–64
   products of   61–4
break-even analysis   199–201
budget constraints, linear
   equations   147
business modelling   703–860

calculators   14–19
   decimal places   16–17
   estimates   15–16
   ln key   165
   log key   165
   logarithms   165, 166
   operations, order of   14–15
   powers   88
   rounding   16–17
   scientific notation   17–18
   significant figures   16–17
   to calculate variance   306
calculus *see* differentiation
cancelling fractions   34–40
car-wash, simulation   841–4
categorical data   217, 672–98
   binary data   686–7
chi-squared test   681–98
   formulae   702
   p-value   686
   population proportion
      674–80

cells, spreadsheets   24–5
centre line
   control chart   822–34
   p-chart   832
   R-chart   831
centred moving averages   628,
   630–2
Chebysheff's result
   for data set   301–2
   for random variable   394
chi-squared distribution
   682–3, 873
chi-squared test   681–2
   and independence   691–2
   software   686, 692
classes   257
   frequency   319
   width   261–5, 318–20
co-ordinates, straight lines
   134–5
coefficient of determination
   578–80
coefficients   136
   of least squares line   577–82
   in linear equations   136–45
   in quadratic functions
      195–6
columns, spreadsheets   24
combinations   399–402
combining events, probability
   344–52
common denominator   42–6
common factors   38
comparing population means
   649–65
comparing two populations
   649–70
complementary events,
   probability   338–40
compound interest   759–65
   curve   212–13
   non-annual   760–5
   summary   764–5
computers   255, 263–75
computer software *see* Excel,
   SPSS statistical software
conditional probabilities
   352–60
   calculating   353–5
   dependent events   356–7,
      364–5

independent events 356–60, 364–5
terminal node 369
on a Venn diagram 353–4
confidence interval for proportion 674–6
confidence intervals for difference between two means 651–3, 659–60, 664–5
computer, on a 667–8
confidence intervals for the mean 505–24
on a computer 520–1
interpretation 509–10
large samples 520
summary 520
and two-sided tests 546–7
variance known 505–16
variance unknown 516–21
confidence limits 508–9
constants 22
quadratic functions 194
constraints, linear programming 707–13, 715–20
contingency tables 281–2, 689
categorical data 689–702
chi-squared test statistic 689–92
expected frequencies 689–92
observed frequencies 689–92
continuous compounding curve 213
continuous distributions 438
continuous random variables 377–8
expected value 436
exponential 440–1
probability distributions for 428–30
uniform 434–6
variance 436
control charts
2-sigma 824
3-sigma 824
attributes 832–3
centre line 822–33
control limits 822–33
designing 833–4
for mean 820–37
for proportion 832
P-charts 830–3
R-charts 830–1
software 826–7
and testing 824
for variance 823, 832
control limits 822–34
2-sigma 824–5

3-sigma 824–6, 832, 833
calculating 823–4
controlling quality 820–37
convergence, geometric series 778
correlation 277, 563–610
coefficient 566–71
sample 566–71
costs, inventory system 744–53
courses of action, alternative 790–2, 794
crashing, project planning 738
critical activities, project planning 736–8
critical paths, project planning 737–8
crossing points, quadratic curve 195
cube roots, powers 86–7
cumulative binomial probabilities 405–8
tables 862–6
cumulative normal probabilities 451–2
cumulative standard normal probabilities, tables 867–8
current-weighted price index 316
curve sketching 217–18
curved graphs 148–9
curves
common functions 203–7
compound interest 213
continuous compounding 213
gradient of 221–8
inflexion point 248–50
maxima/minima 246–52
production 213–14
quadratic functions 192–208
sales 215
tangent of 222–4
turning/stationary points 242–53

data
binary 673–4, 686–7
categorical 271–4, 674, 686–7
describing 256–326
distribution of 257
grouped in classes 318–22
numerical 271, 673
misrepresentation of 286–9
paired 277–85, 563–84, 663–5
pictures of 256–66
qualitative 271

quantitative 271, 673
sequential 271, 278
summarising 291–326
data set see data
decimal places, calculator 16
decision analysis 790
decision making 789–819
courses of action 790
criteria 797–803
objective 790–2
decision trees 804–18
branches 805
drawing 805–12
nodes 805
decision variables, linear programming 707–8, 711–20
demand
Economic Order Quantity 744–53
elasticity of 237–9
inelastic 239
denominator 35
density functions 427–38
dependent events 356, 364–5
joint probability of 363
dependent variables, regression 577
derivatives 225–54
interpretation 234–40
notation 226–7
second 245–52
see also differentiation
describing data 256–326
descriptive statistics 481–2
deterministic models 841
differentiation 221, 225–54
of a difference 230–1, 233
and gradients 225–6
of a logarithm 229–30, 232
of a multiple 231–2
notation 226–7
summary 232–3
of a sum 230–1, 233
discount rate 767–72
discrete random variables 377–9, 427–8
probability distribution 430
discrete uniform distribution 854
distributions see also probability distributions
of a set of data 257
of a population 490–1
sampling distributions 495
skewed 295–6
division
by zero 8, 106

of fractions 46, 50–3
of powers 75–7
dummy
  activity 728–35
  logical 728–9
  uniqueness 730

earliest event times 733–6
Economic Order Quantity
    (EOQ) 744–55
  backlogged demand/back
    ordering 749–51, 753
  batch size 744, 749
  demand 744–52
  formula 745, 751
  lead time 749
  reorder level 749
  shortages/stock out 749
  variability coefficient 752–3
effective interest rate 760–5
elasticity of demand 237–9
EOQ *see* Economic Order
    Quantity
equations
  equivalent 101–4
  formulation of 94, 97–8,
    108–11
  guessing solutions 97–101
  linear 135–8, 147–56
  for problem solving 93–132
  rearranging 111–14
  solution of 97–100, 108–11
  straight lines 133–7, 143–4,
    151
  subject of 112–15
  substitution 95–6, 111,
    118–20
  transposing 112–14
equivalent fractions 34–40
error sum of squares, in
    regression 577–82
errors
  forecasting 619–26
  in hypothesis testing 534–7
  Type I error 535–7
  Type II error 535–7
estimates *see also* estimation
  rough 15–16
estimation 483–524, 699
  of difference between two
    means 651–3, 659–60,
    664–5
  of linear regression model
    586–7
  of multiple linear regression
    model 603
  of population mean and
    variance 491–2

of process mean and variance
    825–6
of trend 632, 633–7
event times
  project planning 733–6
  simulation 842–4, 849, 856
events
  A AND B 344–9
  A OR B 344–9
  combining 344–52
  complementary 338–40
  dependent 356, 363–5
  independent 356–65
  mutually exclusive 348–9,
    357
  Poisson distribution 415–17
Excel software 255
  bar charts 274
  basic statistics 311
  binomial probability 408
  chi-squared test statistic 692
  comparing population mean
    668
  exponential forecasting 623
  exponential probability 447
  frequency distribution 265
  generating probability
    distributions 855–6
  generating random numbers
    848
  histogram 265
  internal rate of return 771–2
  least squares line 581
  linear programming 715–17,
    718–20
  linear regression model
    592–4
  moving averages 632
  net present values 771–2
  normal probability 468
  payments, series of 784–5
  pie charts 274
  Poisson probability 421
  sample correlation 571
  sampling 488
  scatter plots 278
  time series plots 278
expanding brackets 57–64
expectation *see* expected value
expected frequencies
  categorical data 680–8
  contingency tables 689–92
expected value 384–7
  compared with $\bar{x}$ 387
  of a continuous distribution
    436–8
  of difference between means
    650–1

of a function of X 388–9
  as long run average 384–5
  of sample mean 496–7
  of X^2 387–8
expected value criterion
    798–801, 812–14
exponential distribution
    440–8
  mean 443
  and Poisson distribution
    441–2
  probabilities 444–7
  probabilities using a
    computer 447
  simulation 854
  variance 443
exponential smoothing 619

F test 606
factorial 401
factorising 64–9
  benefits of 65
  quadratic equations, to solve
    179
  quadratic expressions 66–9
factors 64
  common 38
feasible regions, linear
    programming 710–15, 720
final nodes, project planning
    728
fixed order quantity 117
fixed-increment time-advance
    mechanisms 849
floats, project planning 736
forecasting
  additive model 644–5
  errors 619–23
  estimating trends 633–4,
    635–6, 639
  exponential 617–24
  four period moving average
    628–31
  mean absolute error 619–26,
    633–5, 641–2, 646
  mean squared error 619–26
  moving average 628–33
  multiplicative model 645
  notation 616–17
  seasonal effects 627–44
  seasonal indices 633–7, 639
  seasonally adjusting series
    637–8
  smoothing constant 618–19,
    622–3
  trend and seasonal effects
    627–44
formulae 21

categorical data 701–2
combination 399–400, 403–5
compound interest 759, 763
correlation 700
Economic Order Quantity 745, 751
expected value 385
forecasting 701
linear regression model 586
normal distribution 449
Poisson distribution 417
present values 767, 772
probability summary 479–80
quadratic equations 176–9, 183
quadratic functions 175
regression 700–1
sample correlation 571
sample mean 306
statistics summary 699–702
testing hypotheses 700
variance 306
formulating
    equations 94, 97–8, 108–10
    inequalities 123–9
    linear programming models 707–8, 717–20
four period moving averages 628–31
fractional powers 85–90
fractions 34–56
    addition of 40–5, 54
    cancelling 38–9, 48–50, 52
    common denominator 42–5
    division of 46, 50–3
    equivalent 34–40
    lowest common denominator of 42–5
    lowest terms 37–40
    multiplication of 46–51, 52, 54
    operations, order of 54
    quotients 35
    reciprocals 51
    simplest terms 37–40
    subtraction of 40–5, 54
frequencies 258, 272, 319
    on a computer 263–4
    expected 681
    observed 680
    relative 258
frequency distribution 265
functions 189–91
    curved L-shaped 206
    demand 241
    expected value of 388–9

inverse 165–6
    linear 134–7, 191
    marginal product of labour 236–7
    marginal revenue 235–6
    maxima/minima of 221
    non-linear 189, 196–223
    objective 707–13, 715, 720–1
    turning/stationary points 250
    see also quadratic functions

Gantt charts 737–8
geometric ratios 776, 779
geometric series
    present values 781–2
    sums accrued 776–9
global maxima/minima 242–5
gradient
    of a curve 221–8
    and derivatives 226
    and differentiation 227
    negative 143
    positive 143
    of straight line 141–44
    and tangents 223–4
graph sketching 134–8
    functions 192–224
    quadratic functions 196–9
    straight lines 137–9
grouped data 318–24

histograms 257–65
    class width 261–3
    number of classes 263
    and probability density functions 430–2
    and relative frequencies 257–65, 271–5
    skewed distributions 260, 265, 269, 295–7
    software 263–5
    symmetric distributions 260, 295–7
holding costs 744–7, 750–1
hypotheses 527–8, 533
hypothesis testing see testing

imaginary solution to equation 177
independence, test of 691–2
independent events 356
    joint probabilities for 361–5
    and mutually exclusive events 357
independent variables, regression 577

index numbers 314–17
indices
    aggregate 316–17
    constructing 314–15
    powers 70–91
inelastic demand 239
inequalities 123–32
    applications of 124–5
    rearranging 125–8, 171–2
    signs 123
inferential statistics 481–3
inflexion point 248–50
initial conditions, simulation 843
inputs, simulation 841–47
instalments, loan repayment 781–2
integer programming 713
inter-arrival times 842–4, 856
inter-quartile range 309–10
intercepts, with y axis 140–1, 144
interest rates
    annual percentage rate 760
    discounting 767
    internal rate of return 770–2
    net present value 769–72
    nominal 760
    present value 767–74
    principal 758
internal rate of return (IRR) 770–2
    for series of payments 784
    software 771–2
interpolation 309
interval estimates 505–15
    see also confidence intervals
inventory control 742–56
    ABC classification 753
    batch size 749
    costs 744–53
    holding costs 744–7, 750–1
    lead time 749
    ordering costs 744–7
    set-up costs 744–7, 750
    shortage costs 744, 749–51
    unit costs 744–53
    see also Economic Order Quantity
inverse functions 165–6
inverse normal probabilities 455
IRR see internal rate of return
isolating trends
    centred moving average 628, 630–2
    regression 632–3
iterative method 715

joint probability   344
  calculating   360–7
  of dependent events   363–4
  for independent events   361–4

Laspeyre price index   316
latest event times   733–7
lead times, Economic Order
    Quantity   749
leaf units   267–70
least squares line   574–582
  coefficient of determination
      577–82
  dependent variable   577
  error sum of squares   577–82
  errors   575
  estimates   575
  fitting   575
  prediction   576
  regression sum of squares
      577–82
  software   580–1
  summary   582
  total sum of squares   577–82
linear functions   135–6
linear equations
  budget constraint   147
  coefficients   136–9, 147–8
  modelling   146–9
  pairs of   150–7, 711
  simultaneous   150–1, 156
  solving pairs of   151–4, 156
  and straight lines   135–7,
      151–3
  supply and demand models
      146
  types of solution   154–6
linear programming models
  binding constraint   716, 718
  constraints   707–13, 716–23
  decision variables   707–8,
      712–20
  feasible region   709–15, 720
  graphical solution of   708–11
  iterative method   715–16
  limitations of   712–13
  non-binding constraint   716,
      718
  non-negativity constraint
      708, 718
  objective function   707–8,
      710–12, 715, 720
  optimal solution   711–12,
      715, 719–20
  optimisation   711–12
  problem formulation   707–8,
      717–19
  sensitivity analysis   719–20

simplex method   715
simultaneous equations   711
  software   715–16, 718–19
  unbounded solution   712
  unique optimal solution   712
linear regression model
    585–606
  assumptions   585–6
  and correlation   580
  estimating   586–7
  F test   605–6
  interpretation   588
  multiple   602–6
  prediction   588
  simple   585–601
  software   592–4, 603–6
  summary   594–5
  testing   589–92
  for trends   632–3
ln key   165
loan repayments   781–2
local maxima/minima   242–5
log key   165
logarithms   161–74, 182–3
  bases   162–71
  on calculator   165, 166
  differentiation of   229–30,
      232
  evaluating   163–4, 166
  inequalities   171–2
  inverse function   165–6
  manipulation of   164–5, 167
  and powers   165–6
  solving equations   168–72
logical dummy activities,
    project planning   728–9
logs see logarithms
lower control limits
  control chart   822–33
  p-chart   832–3
  R-chart   830–1
lower quartiles   309–10
lowest common denominator
    42–5
lowest terms, fractions   37–40

MAE see mean absolute errors
manipulating logarithms   164–7
marginal functions   234–7
marginal product of labour
    function   236–7
marginal revenue function
    235
market equilibrium   156–7
matched data see paired data
maxima
  global   242–4
  local   242–4

second derivatives   245–6
maximax criterion   797
maximin criterion   797–8
maximising   242–53
mean
  on a computer   311
  of data in classes   320–1
  of population   491
  of random variable   385–7
  of sample   492
  of a set of data   293
  see also expected value
mean absolute error (MAE)
    578–9, 619–26, 633–5, 646
mean squared error (MSE)
    619–26
median   293–8, 320
minima
  global   242–4
  local   242–4
  second derivatives   245–6
minimax regret criterion   798
minimising   242–53
MINITAB statistical software
    255
minus numbers see negative
    numbers
mode
  of data   295–6, 298, 320
  spreadsheets   24–5
moving average   638–31
  centred   628–32
  forecasting   629–32
  software   632–3
MSE see mean squared error
mu (μ)   385
  and sample mean   387
multiple linear regression
    602–6
  assumptions   602
  interpretation   604
  test statistic   606
multiples, differentiation of
    231–3
multiplication
  brackets   57–64
  by zero   106
  fractions   46–50, 51–2, 55
  powers   72–4, 77
multiplicative model   627,
    633–5, 639, 645
mutually exclusive events
    348–9, 357
  Venn diagram   349

negative
  gradient   143
  powers   72, 77

negative numbers
   addition   4–6
   division   7–8
   multiplication   6–7
   sign conventions   7
   subtraction   4–6
net present value (NPV)
   769–72
   of series of payments   784
   software   771–2
networks, project planning
   727–41
next-event time-advance
   mechanisms, simulation
   849
nodes
   project planning   727–41
   tree diagram   368–9
nominal rates of interest   759–60
non-annual compound interest
   effective rate   759–62
   investment value   762–4
non-binding constraints
   716–18
non-convergence, geometric
   series   778
non-critical activities   737–8
non-linear functions   189,
   197–223
non-negativity constraints
   708, 718
normal distribution   449–71
   approximation to binomial
      distribution   471–6
   formula   449
   mean   450
   notation   449–50
   probabilities   451–68
      using a computer   468
   simulation   853–4
   standardising   460–1
   standard normal   450–60
   tables   452, 869–70
   variance   449–50
NPV see net present values
null hypothesis   533–7
   contingency tables   689–92
   linear regression model   589
   and rejection regions   555–60
   testing for mean   539–40,
      654
   testing for proportions   676,
      680
numerator   35
numerical data   271

objective function   707, 711,
   716

observed frequencies
   categorical data   680–8
   contingency table   689–92
one-sided alternative hypothesis
   545–6
operations, order of   10–15, 54
opportunity loss   798
optimal solution   712–13, 715,
   720
optimisation, linear
   programming   712–13
OR events   344–9
ordering costs   743–7
outputs, simulation   842–4,
   856

p-charts   830–3
   centre line   832
   lower control limit   832–3
   software   833–4
   upper control limit   832–3
p-values   533–4
Paasche index   316
paired data   277–8, 281–5,
   564–601
   displaying   277–8
paired samples   663–70
   confidence interval   664–5
   testing   663–5, 667
pairs of linear equations
   150–7
parameters, linear regression
   model   586, 603
patterns, control charts   823
payments, series of   775–88
   internal rate of return   784
   present value of   781–4
   software   784–5
payoffs   790–2, 794, 809
payoff tables   793–6, 800
pdfs see probability density
   functions
percentage points
   chi-squared distribution
      683, 873
   normal distribution   465–8
   standard normal distribution
      454–5, 869–70
   t distribution   517–18, 872
percentages   55–7
   for confidence interval
      511–14
   reporting   282–3
pictorial representations
   257–66, 319–20
pie charts   274
   software   274
planning projects   726–41

plots
   scatter   277–8, 565
   time series   612–16
Poisson distribution
   approximation to binomial
      418
   and exponential distribution
      441–2
   mean   421
   probabilities   417
   on a computer   421
   rare events   415–16
   simulation   854
   summary   421
   variance   421
pooled variance estimator
   657–8
population   292
   distribution   490–1
   mean   491
   proportion   673–4
   variance   491
population mean   491, 497
   confidence interval   505–24
   testing   539–62
population proportion   673–4
   confidence interval   674–6
   testing   676–8
population variance   491, 502
positive
   gradient   143
   numbers   4, 6
powers   70–91
   applications   74, 88–9
   on a calculator   88
   cube roots   86
   division of   75–6
   fractional   85–91
   indices   161–2
   multiplication of   72–4, 77
   negative   72, 77
   of a power   74–5, 77
   of products   80–5
   of quotients   80–5
   square roots   86
precedence table   727–30
predictions
   least squares line   576
   linear regression model   588
preliminary samples   825
present values   767–9, 772
   annuity   783
   of series of payments   775–6,
      781–4
price elasticity   237–9
principal   758
probability
   of AND event   344–9

complementary events
338–40
cumulative   405–6
inverse normal   455
of OR event   344–9
subjective   332–3
and testing   529–31
probability density functions
(pdfs)   427–56
for discrete random variables
430
drawing   432–4
exponential distribution
440–1
and histograms   430–2
normal distribution   449–6,
453
uniform distribution   434–6
probability distributions
378–9, 673
binomial   380, 398–415
chi-squared   683
of continuous random
variables   428
and distributions of data
381
exponential   440–7
normal   449–71
Poisson   380, 415–21
simulation   846, 853–5
uniform   434
process mean   822–6
process variance   823–6
production
costs   146–7
curves   213–14
products
of brackets   61–3
of powers   80–5
project planning   725–41
activity   726
activity float   736
crashing   738
critical activity   736–8
critical path   737–8
dummy activity   728–30
event times   733–7
floats   736
Gantt chart   737–8
logical dummy activity
728–9
networks   727–41
node   727–41
non-critical activities
737–8
precedence table   727–30
scheduling activities   733–8
uniqueness dummies   730

proportions   672–8
confidence interval   674–5
testing   676–8

quadratic curves   192–208
quadratic equations   161,
174–87
definition   174–5
factorising   179
imaginary solutions   177
no solution   177
real solution   177
solving   176–86
quadratic expressions   66–9
quadratic functions   192
break-even analysis   199–201
plotting   194–9
sketching   194–9
qualitative data   271
quality control   500–1, 820–37
assignable causes   822
average run lengths   833–4
p-chart   830, 832–4
process mean   825–7
process variance   825–7
R-chart   830–4
and statistical testing   824–5
quality management   821
quantitative data   271
quantity discounts   746
quartiles   309–10, 320
queues, simulation   856–7
assumptions   856–8
single-server   856–7
queuing problems   856–7
queuing theory   856–7
quotients   12
powers of   80–4

R^2 see coefficient of determination
R-charts
centre line   830
lower control limits   830–2
upper control limits   830–2
random inputs, simulation
842–4
generating   846–8
random number tables   487,
846–8, 871
random variables   375–88
Chebysheff's result   394
continuous   377–8
discrete   377–8, 427–8
expectation of   384–91
expected value of   385–91
mean of   385–9
and probability distributions
379–84, 430

standard deviation of   392,
395
variance of   391–8
range, data sets   299
rates of change   221–54
rearranging equations   111–14
inequalities   125–8, 171
logarithms   171–2
reciprocals   50
regression see linear regression
regression sum of squares
578–82
rejection regions   555–60,
667
advantages   559–60
and p-values   555
testing for mean   555–60
relative frequencies data sets
257–65, 271–4
relative frequency approach
331, 353
reorder level, Economic Order
Quantity   749
repaying loans   781–2
residuals, standardised   684
analysis of   592
rewards   790–2
roots, powers   86–7
rounding numbers   16–17

2-sigma control limits   824
3-sigma control limits   824–6,
832–4
sample correlation, r 566–71
on a computer   570–1
and R^2 580–2
summary   571
sample mean, $\bar{x}$ 293, 295–6,
491
distribution of   497–8
mean   497
variance   497
samples   292, 484–5
selecting   486–9
simple random   485–6
sample variance, s^2 298–306,
491
distribution   502
sampling
bad   488–9
distribution   495
fluctuation   492–3
selecting a simple random
sample   486–8
scatter plots   277–8, 565–6
software   278
scheduling projects   725–41
scientific notation   17–18

seasonal effects 612–13, 627–44
seasonal indices 633–9
seasonal adjustment 637–8
second derivatives 245–52
    evaluation 245–6
    maxima/minima 246–7
    notation 245
sensitivity analysis 719–20
service rate 857
set-up cost 743–7, 750
shortage cost 743, 749–51
sigma (Σ) 304–6
signs
    inequalities 123–4
    negative numbers 6–8
    symbols 27–8
significance level
    hypothesis testing 534–7
    quality control 824–5
significance probabilities see p-values
significant figures 16–17
simple interest 758–9, 764–5
simple random sampling 485–90
simplest terms 37–40
simplex method 715
simplifying expressions 33–91
simulation 839–59
    event times 842–4, 849, 856
    generating random inputs 846–53
    initial conditions 843
    inter-arrival times 842–3, 856
    next-event time mechanism 849
    outputs 842–4, 856
    probability distributions 853–8
    and queuing problems 857
    random inputs 841–2
    single-server queue 857
    summary statistics 844–5
    time mechanisms 849–51
    transient period 852
    warmup period 852
simultaneous linear equations 150, 156, 711
single variable graphs 191
single-server queues 857
skewed
    binomial distributions 409–10
    histograms 260, 265, 269, 295–7
slack, linear programming 716–19

slope, straight line 141–4
smoothing constants 618–23
software see Excel; SPSS statistical software
solving equations 98–111
    guessing 97
    guidelines 104
    pairs of linear equations 151–6
    quadratic 176–86, 195–6
    unknown powers 168–72
spread, data sets 298–304
spreadsheets
    cells 24–5
    columns 24
    modes 24
    rows 24
    symbolic expression 24
    values mode 24
    to calculate variance 306
SPSS statistical software
    binomial distribution 408
    bar charts 273–4
    categorical data 273–4
    chi-squared tests 686, 692
    confidence intervals 520–1, 667
    contingency tables 284
    control charts 826
    descriptive statistics 311, 650
    exponential probabilities 447
    exponential smoothing 623
    histograms 264–5
    least squares lines 581
    linear regression 593–4
    moving averages 632
    multiple linear regression 603–6
    normal probabilities 468
    paired samples 667
    pie charts 274
    Poisson distribution 421
    random numbers 486–7, 855
    sample correlation 570–1
    sampling 488
    scatter plots 277–8
    stem and leaf diagrams 269
    time series plots 278
    normal random variable 493
    testing means 547–9
    t intervals 520–1
square roots 86
standard deviation for control charts 823–4, 832
    of sample 300

of random variable 392, 395
standard error 497
standard normal distribution 450–60
    percentage points 869–70
    probability density function 453–4
    tables 452–4, 867–8
standardised residuals 684
start nodes 727
stationary points
    classification of 246–7, 248–50
    curve sketching 247–8
    finding 242–53
statistical process control 820–837
statistical tables
    cumulative binomial probability 862–6
    cumulative standard normal probability 867–8
    percentage points chi-squared distribution 873
    percentage points standard normal distribution 869–70
    percentage points t distribution 872
    random numbers 871
statistical testing see testing
statistics 481–702
    descriptive 481
    formulae 699–702
    inferential 481–4
stem and leaf diagrams 267–71
stem units 267–70
stochastic simulation 841
stock exchange index 316
stock levels, evolution of 750
stock out 749
straight lines
    equation 134–7, 143–4, 151
    fitting to data 574–82
    functions 133–7
    gradient 141–4
    graphs of 134–5, 139
    linear equations 135–7, 151
    sketching 137–8
    slope of 141–4
subjective probabilities 332–3
subject of equation 112–16
substitution
    equations 95–7, 111
    expressions 118–22
    symbols 21–2
subtraction of fractions 40–6, 54

summarising data 291–326
summary statistics simulation
    844–5
summation sign *see* sigma
sum accrued 775–80
sums, differentiation of 230–1,
    233
supply and demand models
    linear equations 146
    quadratic equations 176
symbolic expressions,
        spreadsheets 24
symbols 20–1
    addition 27–9
    collecting like terms 28–9
    division 28
    equivalent expressions 30–1
    fractions 38–9
    multiplication conventions
        28–30
    negative 27–8
    subtraction 27–9
symmetric distribution 260,
    295–8
symmetry
    binomial distribution
        409–10
    quadratic curves 193–201,
        204

t distribution 516–19
t intervals 516–21
t ratios, linear regression
    589–92
tables *see* statistical tables
tangents
    to curve 223–4
    and gradients 223–4
terminal nodes 368–9
testing 525–62, 668
    chi-squared test 681, 686–7
    on a computer 547, 667–8

difference between means
    649, 653–8, 664–8
    the idea of 526–7
    in linear regression 588–91,
        604–6
    for mean 541–7
    for proportion 676–8
    structure of a test 527–8,
        533–7
test statistic 533, 540–1
time series 612
    models 627–8
    plots 612–15
total sum of squares 578–82
transient period 852
transposing equations 111–14
tree diagrams
    construction 368
    nodes 368–9
trends 612–16, 627–44
    isolation of 627, 630–3
turning points *see* stationary
    points
two-sided alternative hypothesis
    545–6, 655
two-sided tests 546–7, 655
two-tailed tests 546–7
Type I error, hypothesis testing
    535–7
Type II error, hypothesis testing
    535–7

U-shaped functions 194–8,
    204
unbounded solution, linear
    programming 712
uncontrollable events 790–2,
    794, 807–8
uniform distribution 434–6,
    854
    simulation 854

unique optimal solutions
    712–13
uniqueness dummies 730
unit cost, inventory control
    744–53
upper control limits
    control chart 822–33
    p-chart 832–3
    R-chart 830–2
upper quartiles 309–10

variability coefficient, inventory
    control 752–3
variables 22
    dependent 577
    independent 577
    see also random variables
variance
    calculating 306
    and Chebysheff 394
    of a continuous distribution
        436–8
    of a random variable 391–4
    of S^2 501–2
    of a sample 298–300, 304–6
    of sample mean 496–7
    of a set of data 298–300,
        304–6
Venn diagrams 337–8
    A AND B 345, 347
    A OR B 346–7
    conditional probability
        353–5
    mutually exclusive events
        349

warmup period, simulation
    852
width, class 261–5, 318–20

z intervals 505–16